GUIDE TO
LITERARY AGENTS
2016

includes a one-year online subscription to **Guide to Literary Agents** on

Where & How to Sell What You Write

THE ULTIMATE MARKET RESEARCH TOOL FOR WRITERS

To register your *Guide to Literary Agents 2016* book and **start your one-year online subscription to listings related to literary agents**, scratch off the block below to reveal your activation code, then go to www.WritersMarket.com. Find the box that says "Purchased a Deluxe Edition?" then click on "Activate Your Account" and enter the activation code. It's that easy!

UPDATED MARKET LISTINGS FOR YOUR INTEREST AREA
EASY-TO-USE SEARCHABLE DATABASE • RECORD-KEEPING TOOLS
PROFESSIONAL TIPS & ADVICE • INDUSTRY NEWS

Your purchase of *Guide to Literary Agents* gives you access to updated listings related to literary agents (valid through 12/31/16). For just $9.99, you can upgrade your subscription and get access to listings from all of our best-selling Market Books. Visit **www.WritersMarket.com** for more information.

WritersMarket.com
Where & How to Sell What You Write

25th ANNUAL EDITION

GUIDE TO LITERARY AGENTS

2016

Chuck Sambuchino, Editor

WRITER'S DIGEST
BOOKS

WritersDigest.com
Cincinnati, Ohio

Guide to Literary Agents 2016. Copyright © 2015 F+W: A Content & E-Commerce Company. Published by Writer's Digest Books, an imprint of F+W, 10151 Carver Road, Suite 200, Blue Ash, Ohio 45242. Printed and bound in the United States of America.

Publisher: Phil Sexton

Writer's Market website: www.writersmarket.com
Writer's Digest website: www.writersdigest.com

Distributed in Canada by Fraser Direct
100 Armstrong Avenue
Georgetown, Ontario, Canada L7G 5S4
Tel: (905) 877-4411

Distributed in the U.K. and Europe by F+W: A Content & E-Commerce Company
Brunel House, Newton Abbot, Devon, TQ12 4PU, England
Tel: (+44) 1626-323200, Fax: (+44) 1626-323319
E-mail: postmaster@davidandcharles.co.uk

Distributed in Australia by Capricorn Link
P.O. Box 704, Windsor, NSW 2756 Australia
Tel: (02) 4577-3555

Library of Congress Catalog Number 31-20772
ISSN: 0084-2729
ISBN-13: 978-1-59963-940-6
ISBN-10: 1-59963-940-8

Attention Booksellers: This is an annual directory of F+W: A Content & E-Commerce Company. Return deadline for this edition is December 31, 2016.

Edited by: Chuck Sambuchino
Designed by: Alexis Brown
Production coordinated by: Debbie Thomas

CONTENTS

FROM THE EDITOR 01

HOW TO USE GUIDE TO LITERARY AGENTS 02

GETTING STARTED

WHAT AN AGENT DOES 06

ASSESSING CREDIBILITY 11

CONTACTING AGENTS

CRAFTING A QUERY
by Kara Gebhart Uhl 16

QUERY LETTER FAQS
by Chuck Sambuchino 27

HOW TO WRITE A SYNOPSIS
by Chuck Sambuchino 33

NONFICTION BOOK PROPOSALS
by Chuck Sambuchino 36

PERSPECTIVES

AGENTS EVALUATE FIRST PAGES
by Paul S. Levine, Marisa Corvisiero, Adriann Ranta and Patricia Nelson 42

CREATE GREAT CHARACTERS
by Elizabeth Sims 54

9 WAYS TO A NONFICTION BOOK DEAL
by Susan Shapiro 60

HOW NOT TO START YOUR BOOK
by Chuck Sambuchino 64

CREATE YOUR WRITER PLATFORM
by Chuck Sambuchino 69

DEBUT AUTHORS TELL ALL
by Chuck Sambuchino 75

GLA SUCCESS STORIES 90

RESOURCES

NEW AGENT SPOTLIGHTS
by Chuck Sambuchino...96

GLOSSARY OF INDUSTRY TERMS 99

MARKETS

LITERARY AGENTS...*108*

CONFERENCES *264*

INDEXES

LITERARY AGENT SPECIALTIES INDEX....................................... *303*

AGENT NAME INDEX...*325*

FROM THE EDITOR

The same month that this edition of *GLA* is released (September 2015), I will also see my next humor book hit store shelves, as well. (It's a parody survival guide called *When Clowns Attack,* because let's be honest—clowns are freaky.) I mention this good news because the first person I thank in the book's acknowledgments section is, in fact, my agent. This is because she believed in the project from the beginning and helped me every step of the way. Even now, seven years into our partnership, she is still my advocate and right hand.

The story of my most recent book is just another reminder of how valuable a good literary agent can be to any writer seeking a traditional book deal. And if you, too, want to find a helpful and enthusiastic advocate, you've come to the right place. Welcome to the 25th edition of the *Guide to Literary Agents*. And as *GLA* reaches this quarter-century milestone, rest assured we have plenty of great instruction in these pages to help you get published: spotlights on new agents actively building their lists, query letter examples, synopsis writing tips, lists of writers' conferences, and more. All in all, we've compiled individual info on more than 1,000 agents in this edition.

Please stay in touch with me through my blog—guidetoliteraryagents.com/blog—or on Twitter (@chucksambuchino) and continue to pass along feedback and success stories. Until we next meet, good luck on your writing journey. (And don't forget to access your free webinar download at www.writersmarket.com/gla16-webinar.)

Chuck Sambuchino
Editor, *Guide to Literary Agents / Children's Writer's & Illustrator's Market*
Author, *Get a Literary Agent* (2015); *Create Your Writer Platform* (2012)

HOW TO USE GUIDE TO LITERARY AGENTS

Searching for a literary agent can be overwhelming, whether you've just finished your first book or you have several publishing credits on your résumé. More than likely, you're eager to start pursuing agents and anxious to see your name on the spine of a book. But before you go directly to the listings of agencies in this book, take time to familiarize yourself with the way agents work and how you should approach them. By doing so, you will be more prepared for your search, and ultimately save yourself effort and unnecessary grief.

Read the articles

This book begins with feature articles that explain how to prepare for representation, offer strategies for contacting agents, and provide perspectives on the author/agent relationship. The articles are organized into three sections appropriate for each stage of the search process: **Getting Started** and **Contacting Agents**. You may want to start by reading through each article, and then refer back to relevant articles during each stage of your search.

Because there are many ways to make that initial contact with an agent, we've also provided a section called **Perspectives**. These personal accounts from agents and published authors offer information and inspiration for any writer hoping to find representation.

Decide what you're looking for

A literary agent will present your work directly to editors or producers. It's the agent's job to get her client's work published or sold, and to negotiate a fair contract. In the **Literary Agents** section, we list each agent's contact information and explain what type of work the agency represents as well as how to submit your work for consideration.

For face-to-face contact, many writers prefer to meet agents at **Conferences**. By doing so, writers can assess an agent's personality, attend workshops and have the chance to get more feedback on their work than they get by mailing submissions and waiting for a response. The conferences section lists conferences agents and/or editors attend. In many cases, private consultations are available, and agents attend with the hope of finding new clients to represent.

1. **WHY DO YOU INCLUDE AGENTS WHO ARE NOT SEEKING NEW CLIENTS?** Some agents ask that their listings indicate they are currently closed to new clients. We include them so writers know the agents exist and know not to contact them at this time.

2. **WHY DO YOU EXCLUDE FEE-CHARGING AGENTS?** We have received a number of complaints in the past regarding fees, and therefore have chosen to list only those agents who do not charge reading fees.

3. **WHY ARE SOME AGENTS NOT LISTED?** Some agents may not have responded to our requests for information. We have taken others out of the book after receiving serious complaints about them.

4. **DO I NEED MORE THAN ONE AGENT IF I WRITE IN DIFFERENT GENRES?** It depends. If you have written in one genre and want to switch to a new style of writing, ask your agent if she is willing to represent you in your new endeavor. Most agents will continue to represent clients no matter what genre they choose to write. Occasionally, an agent may feel she has no knowledge of a certain genre and will recommend an appropriate agent to her client. Regardless, you should always talk to your agent about any potential career move.

5. **WHY DON'T YOU LIST MORE FOREIGN AGENTS?** Most American agents have relationships with foreign co-agents in other countries. It is more common for an American agent to work with a co-agent to sell a client's book abroad than for a writer to work directly with a foreign agent. We do list agents in the United Kingdom, Australia, Canada and other countries who sell to publishers both internationally and in the United States. If you decide to query a foreign agent, make sure they represent American writers (if you're American). Some may request to only receive submissions from Canadians, for example, or UK residents.

6. **DO AGENTS EVER CONTACT A SELF-PUBLISHED WRITER?** If a self-published author attracts the attention of the media or if his book sells extremely well, an agent might approach the author in hopes of representing him.

7. **WHY WON'T THE AGENT I QUERIED RETURN MY MATERIAL?** An agent may not answer your query or return your manuscript for several reasons. Perhaps you did not include a self-addressed, stamped envelope (SASE). Many agents will discard a submission without a SASE. Or, the agent may have moved. To avoid using expired addresses, use the most current edition of *Guide to Literary Agents* or access the information online at WritersMarket.com. Another possibility is that the agent is swamped with submissions. An agent can be overwhelmed with queries, especially if the agent recently has spoken at a conference or has been featured in an article or book. Also, some agents specify in their listings that they never return materials of any kind.

Utilize the extras

Aside from the articles and listings, this book offers a section of **Resources**. If you come across a term with which you aren't familiar, check out the Resources section for a quick explanation. Also, note the gray tabs along the edge of each page. The tabs block off each section so they are easier to flip to as you conduct your search.

Finally—and perhaps most importantly—are the **Indexes** in the back of the book. These can serve as an incredibly helpful way to start your search because they categorize the listings according to different criteria. For example, you can look for literary agents according to their specialties (fiction/nonfiction genres).

Listings in *Guide to Literary Agents* are compiled from detailed questionnaires, phone interviews, and information provided by agents. The industry is volatile, and agencies change frequently. We rely on our readers for information on their dealings with agents, as well as changes in policies or fees that differ from what has been reported to the editor of this book. Write to us (Guide to Literary Agents, F+W Media, 10151 Carver Road, Suite 200, Cincinnati, OH 45242) or e-mail us (literaryagent@fwmedia.com) if you have new information, questions, or problems dealing with the agencies listed.

Listings are published free of charge and are not advertisements. Although the information is as accurate as possible, the listings are not endorsed or guaranteed by the editor or publisher of *Guide to Literary Agents*. If you feel you have not been treated fairly by an agent or representative listed in *Guide to Literary Agents*, we advise you to take the following steps:

- First try to contact the agency. Sometimes one letter or e-mail can clear up the matter. Politely relate your concern.
- Document all your correspondence with the agency. When you write to us with a complaint, provide the name of your manuscript, the date of your first contact with the agency and the nature of your subsequent correspondence.
- We will keep your letter on file and attempt to contact the agency. The number, frequency and severity of complaints will be considered when we decide whether or not to delete an agency's listing from the next edition.
- *Guide to Literary Agents* reserves the right to exclude any agency for any reason.

WHAT AN AGENT DOES

The scoop on day-to-day responsibilities.

A writer's job is to write. A literary agent's job is to find publishers for her clients' books. Because publishing houses receive more and more unsolicited manuscripts each year, securing an agent is becoming increasingly necessary. But finding an eager and reputable agent can be a difficult task. Even the most patient writer can become frustrated or disillusioned. As a writer seeking agent representation, you should prepare yourself before starting your search. Learn when to approach agents, as well as what to expect from an author/agent relationship. Beyond selling manuscripts, an agent must keep track of the ever-changing industry, writers' royalty statements, fluctuating market trends—and the list goes on.

So, once again, you face the question: Do I need an agent? The answer, much more often than not, is yes.

WHAT CAN AN AGENT DO FOR YOU?

For starters, today's competitive marketplace can be difficult to break into, especially for unpublished writers. Many larger publishing houses will only look at manuscripts from agents—and rightfully so, as they would be inundated with unsatisfactory writing if they did not. In fact, approximately 80 percent of books published by the five major houses are acquired through agents.

But an agent's job isn't just getting your book through a publisher's door. The following describes the various jobs agents do for their clients, many of which would be difficult for a writer to do without outside help.

BEFORE YOU SUBMIT YOUR FICTION BOOK:

1. Finish your novel manuscript or short-story collection. An agent can do nothing for fiction without a finished product. Never query with an incomplete novel.
2. Revise your manuscript. Seek critiques from other writers or an independent editor to ensure your work is as polished as possible.
3. Proofread. Don't ruin a potential relationship with an agent by submitting work that contains typos or poor grammar.
4. Publish short stories or novel excerpts in literary journals, which will prove to prospective agents that editors see quality in your writing.
5. Research to find the agents of writers whose works you admire or are similar to yours.
6. Use the Internet and resources like *Guide to Literary Agents* to construct a list of agents who are open to new writers and looking for your category of fiction. (Jump to the listings sections of this book to start now.)
7. Rank your list according to the agents most suitable for you and your work.
8. Write your novel synopsis.
9. Write your query letter. As an agent's first impression of you, this brief letter should be polished and to the point.
10. Educate yourself about the business of agents so you will be prepared to act on any offer. This guide is a great place to start.

AGENTS KNOW EDITORS' TASTES AND NEEDS

An agent possesses information on a complex web of publishing houses and a multitude of editors to ensure her clients' manuscripts are placed in the right hands. This knowledge is gathered through relationships she cultivates with acquisitions editors—the people who decide which books to present to their publisher for possible publication. Through her industry connections, an agent becomes aware of the specializations of publishing houses and their imprints, knowing that one publisher wants only contemporary romances while another is interested solely in nonfic-

tion books about the military. By networking with editors, an agent also learns more specialized information—which editor is looking for a crafty Agatha Christie–style mystery for the fall catalog, for example.

AGENTS TRACK CHANGES IN PUBLISHING

Being attentive to constant market changes and shifting trends is another major requirement of an agent. An agent understands what it may mean for clients when publisher A merges with publisher B and when an editor from house C moves to house D. Or what it means when readers—and therefore editors—are no longer interested in Westerns, but can't get their hands on enough suspense novels.

AGENTS GET YOUR WORK READ FASTER

Although it may seem like an extra step to send your work to an agent instead of directly to a publishing house, the truth is an agent can prevent you from wasting months sending manuscripts that end up in the wrong place or buried in someone's slush pile. Editors rely on agents to save them time, as well. With little time to sift through the hundreds of unsolicited submissions arriving weekly in the mail, an editor is naturally going to prefer a work that has already been approved by a qualified reader (i.e., the agent) who knows the editor's preferences. For this reason, many of the larger publishers accept agented submissions only.

AGENTS UNDERSTAND CONTRACTS

When publishers write contracts, they are primarily interested in their own bottom line rather than the best interests of the author. Writers unfamiliar with contractual language may find themselves bound to a publisher with whom they no longer want to work. Or, they may find themselves tied to a publisher that prevents them from getting royalties on their first book until subsequent books are written. Agents use their experiences and knowledge to negotiate a contract that benefits the writer while still respecting the publisher's needs. After all, more money for the author will almost al-

ways mean more money for the agent—another reason they're on your side.

AGENTS NEGOTIATE—AND EXPLOIT—SUBSIDIARY RIGHTS

Beyond publication, a savvy agent keeps in mind other opportunities for your manuscript. If your agent believes your book also will be successful as an audio book, a Book-of-the-Month-Club selection or even a blockbuster movie, she will take these options into consideration when shopping your manuscript. These additional opportunities for writers are called subsidiary rights. Part of an agent's job is to keep track of the strengths and weaknesses of different publishers' subsidiary rights offices to determine the deposition of these rights regarding your work. After contracts are negotiated, agents will seek additional moneymaking opportunities for the rights they kept for their clients.

AGENTS GET ESCALATORS

An escalator is a bonus an agent can negotiate as part of the book contract. It is commonly given when a book appears on a bestseller list or if a client appears on a popular television show. For example, a publisher might give a writer a $30,000 bonus if he is picked for a book club. Both the agent and the editor know such media attention will sell more books, and the agent negotiates an escalator to ensure the writer benefits from this increase in sales.

AGENTS TRACK PAYMENTS

Because an agent receives payment only when the publisher pays the writer, it's in the agent's best interest to make sure the writer is paid on schedule. Some publishing houses are notorious for late payments. Having an agent distances you from any conflict regarding payment and allows you to spend time writing instead of making phone calls.

AGENTS ARE ADVOCATES

Besides standing up for your right to be paid on time, agents can ensure your book gets a better cover design, more attention from the publisher's marketing department, or other benefits you may not know to ask for during the publishing process. An agent also can provide advice during each step of the way, as well as guidance about your long-term writing career.

ARE YOU READY FOR AN AGENT?

Now that you know what an agent is capable of, ask yourself if you and your work are at a stage where you need an agent. Look at the to-do lists for fiction and nonfiction writers in this article, and judge how prepared you are for contacting an agent. Have you spent enough time researching or polishing your manuscript? Does your nonfiction book proposal include everything it should? Is your novel completely finished? Sending an agent an incomplete project not only wastes your time, but also may turn off the agent in the process. Is the work thoroughly re-

vised? If you've finished your project, set it aside for a few weeks, then examine it again with fresh eyes. Give your novel or proposal to critique group partners ("beta readers") for feedback. Join up with writing peers in your community or online.

Moreover, your work may not be appropriate for an agent. Most agents do not represent poetry, magazine articles, short stories, or material suitable for academic or small presses; the agent's commission does not justify spending time submitting these types of works. Those agents who do take on such material generally represent authors on larger projects first, and then adopt the smaller items as a favor to the client.

If you believe your work is ready to be placed with an agent, make sure you're personally ready to be represented. In other words, consider the direction in which your writing career is headed. Besides skillful writers, agencies want clients with the ability to produce more than one book. Most agents say they're looking to represent careers, not books.

WHEN DON'T YOU NEED AN AGENT?

Although there are many reasons to work with an agent, some authors can benefit from submitting their own work directly to book publishers. For example, if your project focuses on a very specific area, you may want to work with a small or specialized press. These houses usually are open to receiving material directly from writers. Small presses often can give more attention to writers than large houses can, providing editorial help, marketing expertise, and other advice. Academic books or specialized nonfiction books (such as a book about the history of Rhode Island) are good bets for unagented writers.

Beware, though, as you will now be responsible for reviewing and negotiating all parts of your contract and payment. If you choose this path, it's wise to use a lawyer or entertainment attorney to review all contracts. Lawyers who specialize in intellectual property can help writers with contract negotiations. Instead of earning a commission on resulting book sales, lawyers are paid for their time only.

And, of course, some people prefer working independently instead of relying on others. If you're one of these people, it's probably better to submit your own work instead of constantly butting heads with an agent. Let's say you manage to sign with one of the few literary agents who represent short-story collections. If the collection gets shopped around to publishers for several months and no one bites, your agent may suggest retooling the work into a novel or novella(s). Agents suggest changes—some bigger than others—and not all writers think their work is malleable. It's all a matter of what you're writing and how you feel about it.

BEFORE YOU SUBMIT YOUR NONFICTION BOOK:

1. Formulate a concrete idea for your book. Sketch a brief outline, making sure you'll have enough material for a book-length manuscript.
2. Research works on similar topics to understand the competition and determine how your book is unique.
3. Write sample chapters. This will help you estimate how much time you'll need to complete the work, and determine whether or not your writing will need editorial help. You will also need to include 1–4 sample chapters in the proposal itself.
4. Publish completed chapters in journals and/or magazines. This validates your work to agents and provides writing samples for later in the process.
5. Polish your nonfiction book proposal so you can refer to it while drafting a query letter—and you'll be prepared when agents contact you.
6. Brainstorm three to four subject categories that best describe your material.
7. Use the Internet and resources like *Guide to Literary Agents* to construct a list of agents who are open to new writers and looking for your category of nonfiction.
8. Rank your list. Research agent websites and narrow your list further, according to your preferences.
9. Write your query. Give an agent an excellent first impression by professionally and succinctly describing your premise and your experience.
10. Educate yourself about the business of agents so you can act on any offer.

ASSESSING CREDIBILITY

Check out agents before you query.

Many people wouldn't buy a used car without at least checking the odometer, and savvy shoppers would consult the blue books, take a test drive and even ask for a mechanic's opinion. Much like the savvy car shopper, you want to obtain the best possible agent for your writing, so you should do some research on the business of agents before sending out query letters. Understanding how agents operate will help you find an agent appropriate for your work, as well as alert you about the types of agents to avoid.

Many writers take for granted that any agent who expresses interest in their work is trustworthy. They'll sign a contract before asking any questions and simply hope everything will turn out all right. We often receive complaints from writers regarding agents *after* they have lost money or have work bound by contract to an ineffective agent. If writers put the same amount of effort into researching agents as they did writing their manuscripts, they would save themselves unnecessary grief.

The best way to educate yourself is to read all you can about agents and other authors. Organizations such as the Association of Authors' Representatives (AAR; aaronline.org), the National Writers Union (NWU; nwu.org), American Society of Journalists and Authors (ASJA; asja.org) and Poets & Writers, Inc. (pw.org), all have informational material on finding and working with an agent.

The magazine *Publishers Weekly* (publishersweekly.com) covers publishing news affecting agents and others in the publishing industry. The Publishers Lunch newsletter (publishersmarketplace.com) comes free via e-mail every workday and offers news on agents and editors, job postings, recent book sales and more.

Even the Internet has a wide range of sites where you can learn basic information about preparing for your initial contact, as well as specific details on individual agents. You can also find online forums and listservs, which keep authors connected and allow them to share experiences they've had with different editors and agents. Keep in mind, however, that not everything printed on the Web is fact; you may come across the site of a writer who is bitter because an agent rejected his manuscript. Your best bet is to use the Internet to supplement your other research.

Once you've established what your resources are, it's time to see which agents meet your criteria. Below are some of the key items to pay attention to when researching agents.

LEVEL OF EXPERIENCE

Through your research, you will discover the need to be wary of some agents. Anybody can go to the neighborhood copy center and order business cards that say "literary agent," but that title doesn't mean she can sell your book. She may lack the proper connections with others in the publishing industry, and an agent's reputation with editors can be a major strength or weakness.

Agents who have been in the business awhile have a large number of contacts and carry the most clout with editors. They know the ins and outs of the industry and are often able to take more calculated risks. However, veteran agents can be too busy to take on new clients or might not have the time to help develop an author. Newer agents, on the other hand, may be hungrier, as well as more open to unpublished writers. They probably have a smaller client list and are able to invest the extra effort to make your book a success.

If it's a new agent without a track record, be aware that you're taking more of a risk signing with her than with a more established agent. However, even a new agent should not be new to publishing. Many agents were editors before they were agents, or they worked at an agency as an assistant. This experience is crucial for making contacts in the publishing industry, and learning about rights and contracts. The majority of listings in this book explain how long the agent has been in business, as well as what she did before becoming an agent. You could also ask the agent to name a few editors off the top of her head who she thinks may be interested in your work and why they sprang to mind. Has she sold to them before? Do they publish books in your genre?

If an agent has no contacts in the business, she has no more clout than you do. Without publishing prowess, she's just an expensive mailing service. Anyone can make photocopies, slide them into an envelope and address them to "Editor." Unfortunately, without a contact name and a familiar return address on the envelope, or a phone call from a trusted colleague letting an editor know a wonderful submission is on its way, your work will land in the slush pile with all the other submissions that don't have representation. You can do your own mailings with higher priority than such an agent could.

PAST SALES

Agents should be willing to discuss their recent sales with you: how many, what type of books and to what publishers. Keep in mind, though, that some agents consider this information confidential. If an agent does give you a list of recent sales, you can call the publishers' contracts department to ensure the sale was actually made by that agent. While it's true that even top agents are not able to sell every book they represent, an inexperienced agent who proposes too many inappropriate submissions will quickly lose her standing with editors.

You can also find out details of recent sales on your own. Nearly all of the listings in this book offer the titles and authors of books with which the agent has worked. Some of them also note to which publishing house the book was sold. Again, you can call the publisher and affirm the sale. If you don't have the publisher's information, simply go to your local library or bookstore to see if they carry the book. Consider checking to see if it's available on websites like Amazon.com, too. You may want to be wary of the agent if her books are nowhere to be found or are only available through the publisher's website. Distribution is a crucial component to getting published, and you want to make sure the agent has worked with competent publishers.

TYPES OF FEES

Becoming knowledgeable about the different types of fees agents may charge is vital to conducting effective research. Most agents make their living from the commissions they receive after selling their clients' books, and these are the agents we've listed. Be sure to ask about any expenses you don't understand so you have a clear grasp of what you're paying for. Described here are some types of fees you may encounter in your research.

Office fees

Occasionally, an agent will charge for the cost of photocopies, postage and long-distance phone calls made on your behalf. This is acceptable, so long as she keeps an itemized account of the expenses and you've agreed on a ceiling cost. The agent should only ask for office expenses after agreeing to represent the writer. These expenses should be discussed up front, and the writer should receive a statement accounting for them. This money is sometimes returned to the author upon sale of the manuscript. Be wary if there is an upfront fee amounting to hundreds of dollars, which is excessive.

Reading fees

Agencies that charge reading fees often do so to cover the cost of additional readers or the time spent reading that could have been spent selling. Agents also claim that charging reading fees cuts down on the number of submissions they receive. This practice can save the agent time and may allow her to consider each manuscript more extensively. Whether such promises are kept depends upon the honesty of the agency. You may pay a fee and never receive a response from the agent, or you may pay someone who never submits your manuscript to publishers.

Officially, the Association of Authors' Representatives' (AAR) Canon of Ethics prohibits members from directly or indirectly charging a reading fee, and the Writers Guild of America (WGA) does not allow WGA signatory agencies to charge a reading fee to WGA members, as stated in the WGA's Artists' Manager Basic Agreement. A signatory may charge you a fee if you are not a member, but most signatory agencies do not charge a reading fee as an across-the-board policy.

WARNING SIGNS! BEWARE OF . . .

- Excessive typos or poor grammar in an agent's correspondence.

- A form letter accepting you as a client and praising generic things about your book that could apply to any book. A good agent doesn't take on a new client very often, so when she does, it's a special occasion that warrants a personal note or phone call.

- Unprofessional contracts that ask you for money up front, contain clauses you haven't discussed, or are covered with amateur clip-art or silly borders.

- Rudeness when you inquire about any points you're unsure of. Don't employ any business partner who doesn't treat you with respect.

- Pressure, by way of threats, bullying, or bribes. A good agent is not desperate to represent more clients. She invites worthy authors but leaves the final decision up to them.

- Promises of publication. No agent can guarantee you a sale. Not even the top agents sell everything they choose to represent. They can only send your work to the most appropriate places, have it read with priority, and negotiate you a better contract if a sale does happen.

- A print-on-demand book contract or any contract offering you no advance. You can sell your own book to an e-publisher any time you wish without an agent's help. An agent should pursue traditional publishing routes with respectable advances.

- Reading fees from $25–$500 or more. The fee is usually nonrefundable, but sometimes agents agree to refund the money if they take on a writer as a client, or if they sell the writer's manuscript. Keep in mind, however, that payment of a reading fee does not ensure representation.

- No literary agents who charge reading fees are listed in this book. It's too risky of an option for writers, plus non-fee-charging agents have a stronger incentive to sell your work. After all, they don't make a dime until they make a sale. If you find that a literary agent listed in this book charges a reading fee, please contact the editor at literaryagent@fwmedia.com

Critique fees

Sometimes a manuscript will interest an agent, but the agent will point out areas requiring further development and offer to critique it for an additional fee. Like reading fees, payment of a critique fee does not ensure representation. When deciding if you will benefit from having someone critique your manuscript, keep in mind that the quality and quantity of comments varies from agent to agent. The critique's usefulness will depend on the agent's knowledge of the market. Also be aware that agents who spend a significant portion of their time commenting on manuscripts will have less time to actively market work they already represent.

In other cases, the agent may suggest an editor who understands your subject matter or genre, and has some experience getting manuscripts into shape. Occasionally, if your story is exceptional, or your ideas and credentials are marketable but your writing needs help, you will work with a ghostwriter or co-author who will share a percentage of your commission, or work with you at an agreed-upon cost per hour.

An agent may refer you to editors she knows, or you may choose an editor in your area. Many editors do freelance work and would be happy to help you with your writing project. Of course, before entering into an agreement, make sure you know what you'll be getting for your money. Ask the editor for writing samples, references or critiques he's done in the past. Make sure you feel comfortable working with him before you give him your business.

An honest agent will not make any money for referring you to an editor. We strongly advise writers not to use critiquing services offered through an agency. Instead, try hiring a freelance editor or joining a writer's group until your work is ready to be submitted to agents who don't charge fees.

CRAFTING A QUERY

How to write a great letter that gets agents' attention.

by Kara Gebhart Uhl

So you've written a book. And now you want an agent. If you're new to publishing, you probably assume that the next step is to send your finished, fabulous book out to agents, right? Wrong. Agents don't want your finished, fabulous book. In fact, they probably don't even want *part* of your finished, fabulous book—at least, not yet. First, they want your query.

A query is a short, professional way of introducing yourself to an agent. If you're frustrated by the idea of this step, imagine yourself at a cocktail party. Upon meeting someone new, you don't greet them with a boisterous hug and kiss and, in three minutes, reveal your entire life story including the fact that you were late to the party because of some gastrointestinal problems. Rather, you extend your hand. You state your name. You comment on the hors d'oeuvres, the weather, the lovely shade of someone's dress. Perhaps, after this introduction, the person you're talking to politely excuses himself. Or, perhaps, you become best of friends. It's basic etiquette, formality, professionalism—it's simply how it's done.

Agents receive hundreds of submissions every month. Often they read these submissions on their own time—evenings, weekends, on their lunch break. Given the number of writers submitting, and the number of agents reading, it would simply be impossible for agents to ask for and read entire book manuscripts off the bat. Instead, a query is a quick way for you to, first and foremost, pitch your book. But it's also a way to pitch yourself. If an agent is intrigued by your query, she may ask for a partial (say, the first three chapters of your manuscript). Or she may ask for the entire thing.

As troublesome as it may first seem, try not to be frustrated by this process. Because, honestly, a query is a really great way to help speed up what is already a monumentally slow-paced industry. Have you ever seen pictures of slush piles—those piles of unread queries on many well-known agents' desks? Imagine the size of those slush piles if they held full manuscripts instead of one-page query letters. Thinking of it this way, query letters begin to make more sense.

Here we share with you the basics of a query, including its three parts and a detailed list of dos and don'ts.

PART I: THE INTRODUCTION

Whether you're submitting a 100-word picture book or a 90,000-word novel, you must be able to sum up the most basic aspects of it in one sentence. Agents are busy. And they constantly receive submissions for types of work they don't represent. So upfront they need to know that, after reading your first paragraph, the rest of your query is going to be worth their time.

An opening sentence designed to "hook" an agent is fine—if it's good and if it works. But this is the time to tune your right brain down and your left brain up—agents desire professionalism and queries that are short and to-the-point. Remember the cocktail party and always err on the side of formality. Tell the agent, in as few words as possible, what you've written, including the title, genre, and length.

In the intro, you also must try to connect with the agent. Simply sending 100 identical query letters out to "Dear Agent" won't get you published. Instead, your letter should be addressed not only to a specific agency but a specific agent within that agency. (And double, triple, quadruple check that the agent's name is spelled correctly.) In addition, you need to let the agent know why you chose her specifically. A good author-agent relationship is like a good marriage. It's important that both sides invest the time to find a good fit that meets their needs. So how do you connect with an agent you don't know personally? Research.

1. Make a connection based on an author or book the agent already represents.

Most agencies have websites that list who and what they represent. Research those sites. Find a book similar to yours and explain that, because such-and-such book has a similar theme or tone or whatever, you think your book would be a great fit. In addition, many agents will list specific genres/categories they're looking for, either on their websites or in interviews. If your book is a match, state that.

2. Make a connection based on an interview you read.

Search agents' names online and read any and all interviews they've participated in. Perhaps they mentioned a love for X and your book is all about X. Perhaps they mentioned that they're looking for Y and your book is all about Y. Mention the specific interview. Prove that you've invested as much time researching them as they're about to spend researching you.

3. Make a connection based on a conference you both attended.

Was the agent you're querying the keynote speaker at a writing conference you were recently at? If so, mention it, and comment on an aspect of his speech you liked. Even better, did you meet the agent in person? Mention it, and if there's something you can say to jog her memory about the meeting, say it. Better yet, did the agent specifically ask you to send your manuscript? Mention it.

Finally, if you're being referred to a particular agent by an author that agent already represents—that's your opening sentence. That referral is guaranteed to get your query placed at the top of the stack.

PART II: THE PITCH

Here's where you really get to sell your book—but in only three to 10 sentenc-es. Consider a book's jacket flap and its role in convincing readers to plunk down $24.95 to buy what's in between those flaps. Like a jacket flap, you need to hook an agent in the confines of very limited space. What makes your story interesting and unique? Is your story about a woman going through a mid-life crisis? Fine, but there are hundreds of stories about women going through mid-life crises. Is your story about a woman who, because of a mid-life crisis, leaves her life and family behind to spend three months in India? Again, fine, but this story, too, already exists—in many forms. Is your story about a woman who, because of a mid-life crisis, leaves her life and family behind to spend three months in India, falls in love with someone new while there and starts a new life—and family? And then has to deal with everything she left behind upon her return? *Now* you have a hook.

Practice your pitch. Read it out loud, not only to family and friends, but to people willing to give you honest, intelligent criticism. If you belong to a writing group, workshop your pitch. Share it with members of an online writing forum. Know anyone in the publishing industry? Share it with them. Many writers spend years writing their books. We're not talking about querying magazines here; we're talking about querying an agent who could become a lifelong partner. Spend time on your pitch. Perfect it. Turn it into jacket-flap material so detailed, exciting and clear that it would be near impossible to read your pitch and not want to read more. Use active verbs. Write your pitch, put it aside for a week, then look at it again. Don't send a query simply because you finished a book. Send a query because you finished your pitch and are ready to take the next steps.

PART III: THE BIO

If you write fiction for adults or children, unless you're a household name or you've recently been a guest on some very big TV or radio shows, an agent is much more interested in your pitch than in who you are. If you write nonfiction, who you are—more specifically, your platform and publicity—is much more important. Regardless, these are key elements that must be present in every bio:

1. Publishing credits

If you're submitting fiction, focus on your fiction credits—previously published works and short stories. That said, if you're submitting fiction and all your previously published work is nonfiction—articles, essays, etc.—that's still fine and good to mention. Don't be overly long about it. Mention your publications in bigger magazines or well-known literary journals. If you've never had anything published, don't say you lack official credits. Simply skip this altogether and thank the agent for his time.

2. Contests and awards

If you've won many, focus on the most impressive ones and those that most directly relate to your work. Don't mention contests you entered and weren't named in. Also, feel free to leave titles and years out of it. If you took first place at the Delaware Writers Conference for your fiction manuscript, that's good enough. Mentioning details isn't necessary.

3. MFAs

If you've earned or are working toward a Master of Fine Arts in writing, say so and state the program. Don't mention English degrees or online writing courses.

4. Large, recognized writing organizations

Agents don't want to hear about your book club and the fact that there's always great food, or the small critique group you meet with once a week. And they really don't want to hear about the online writing forum you belong to. But if you're a member of something like the Romance Writers of America (RWA), the Mystery Writers of America (MWA), the Society of Children's Book Writers and Illustrators (SCBWI), the Society of Professional Journalists (SPJ), the American Medical Writers, etc., say so. This shows you're serious about what you do and you're involved in groups that can aid with publicity and networking.

5. Platform and publicity

If you write nonfiction, who you are and how you're going to help sell the book once it's published becomes very important. Why are you the best person to write it and what do you have now—public speaking engagements, an active website or blog, substantial cred in your industry—that will help you sell this book?

Finally, be cordial. Thank the agent for taking the time to read your query and consider your manuscript. Ask if you may send more, in the format she desires (partial, full, etc.).

Think of the time you spent writing your book. Unfortunately, you can't send your book to an agent for a first impression. Your query *is* that first impression. Give it the time it deserves. Keep it professional. Keep it formal. Let it be a firm handshake—not a sloppy kiss. Let it be a first meeting that evolves into a lifelong relationship—not a rejection slip. But expect those slips. Just like you don't become best friends with everyone you meet at a cocktail party, you can't expect every agent you pitch to sign you. Be patient. Keep pitching. And in the meantime, start writing that next book.

DOS AND DON'TS FOR QUERYING AGENTS

DO:

- Keep the tone professional.

- Query a specific agent at a specific agency.

- Proofread. Double-check the spelling of the agency and the agent's name.

- Keep the query concise, limiting the overall length to one page (single space, 12-point type in a commonly used font).

- Focus on the plot, not your bio, when pitching fiction.

- Pitch agents who represent the type of material you write.

- Check an agency's submission guidelines to see how to query—for example, via e-mail or mail—and whether or not to include a SASE.

- Keep pitching, despite rejections.

DON'T:

- Include personal info not directly related to the book. For example, stating that you're a parent to three children doesn't make you more qualified than someone else to write a children's book.

- Say how long it took you to write your manuscript. Some bestselling books took 10 years to write—others, six weeks. An agent doesn't care how long it took—an agent only cares if it's good. Same thing goes with drafts—an agent doesn't care how many drafts it took you to reach the final product.

- Mention that this is your first novel or, worse, the first thing you've ever written aside from grocery lists. If you have no other publishing credits, don't advertise that fact. Don't mention it at all.

- State that your book has been edited by peers or professionals. Agents expect manuscripts to be edited, no matter how the editing was done.

- Bring up screenplays or film adaptations—you're querying an agent about publishing a book, not making a movie.

- Mention any previous rejections.

- State that the story is copyrighted with the U.S. Copyright Office or that you own all rights. Of course you own all rights. You wrote it.

- Rave about how much your family and friends loved it. What matters is that the agent loves it.

- Send flowers or anything else except a self-addressed stamped envelope (and only if the SASE is required), if sending through snail mail.

- Follow up with a phone call. After the appropriate time has passed (many agencies say how long it will take to receive a response), follow up in the manner you queried— via e-mail or mail.

KARA GEBHART UHL, formerly a managing editor at *Writer's Digest* magazine, now freelance writes and edits in Fort Thomas, Ky. She also blogs about parenting at pleiadesbee.com. Her essays have appeared on The Huffington Post, *The New York Times*' Motherlode and *TIME: Healthland*. Her parenting essay, "Apologies to the Parents I Judged Four Years Ago" was named one of *TIME*'s "Top 10 Opinions of 2012."

① SAMPLE QUERY 1: LITERARY FICTION
Agent's Comments: Jeff Kleinman (Folio Literary Management)

From: Garth Stein
To: Jeff Kleinman
Subject: Query: "The Art of Racing in the Rain" ①

Dear Mr. Kleinman:

② Saturday night I was participating in a fundraiser for the King County Library System out here in the Pacific Northwest, and I met your client Layne Maheu. He spoke very highly of you and suggested that I contact you.

③ I am a Seattle writer with two published novels. I have recently completed my third novel, *The Art of Racing in the Rain*, and I find myself in a difficult situation: My new book is narrated by a dog, and my current agent ④ told me that he cannot (or will not) sell it for that very reason. Thus, I am seeking new representation.

⑤ *The Art of Racing in the Rain* is the story of Denny Swift, a race car driver who faces profound obstacles in his life, and ultimately overcomes them by applying the same techniques that have made him successful on the track. His story is narrated by his "philosopher dog," Enzo, who, having a nearly human soul (and an obsession with opposable thumbs), believes he will return as a man in his next lifetime.

⑥ My last novel, *How Evan Broke His Head and Other Secrets*, won a 2006 Pacific Northwest Booksellers Association Book Award, and since the award ceremony a year ago, I have given many readings, workshops and lectures promoting the book. When time has permitted, I've read the first chapter from *The Art of Racing in the Rain*. Audience members have been universally enthusiastic and vocal in their response, and the first question asked is always: "When can I buy the book about the dog?" Also very positive.

⑦ I'm inserting, below, a short synopsis of *The Art of Racing in the Rain*, and my biography. Please let me know if the novel interests you; I would be happy to send you the manuscript.

Sincerely,
Garth Stein

① Putting the word "Query" and the title of the book on the subject line of an e-mail often keeps your e-mail from falling into the spam folder. ② One of the best ways of starting out correspondence is figuring out your connection to the agent. ③ The author has some kind of track record. Who's the publisher, though? Were these both self-published novels, or were there reputable publishers involved? (I'll read on, and hope I find out.) ④ This seems promising, but also know this kind of approach can backfire, because we agents tend to be like sheep—what one doesn't like, the rest of us are wary of, too (or, conversely, what one likes, we all like). But in this case getting in the "two published novels" early is definitely helpful. ⑤ The third paragraph is the key pitch paragraph and Garth gives a great description of the book—he sums it up, gives us a feel for what we're going to get. This is the most important part of your letter. ⑥ Obviously it's nice to see the author's winning awards. Also good: The author's not afraid of promoting the book. ⑦ The end is simple and easy—it doesn't speak of desperation, or doubt, or anything other than polite willingness to help.

② SAMPLE QUERY 2: YOUNG ADULT
Agent's Comments: Ted Malawer (Upstart Crow Literary)

Dear Mr. Malawer:

I would like you to represent my 65,000-word contemporary teen novel *My Big Nose & Other Natural Disasters.*

① Seventeen-year-old Jory Michaels wakes up on the first day of summer vacation with her same old big nose, no passion in her life (in the creative sense of the word), and all signs still pointing to her dying a virgin. Plus, her mother is busy roasting a chicken for Day #6 of the Dinner For Breakfast Diet.

② In spite of her driving record (it was an accident!), Jory gets a job delivering flowers and cakes to Reno's casinos and wedding chapels. She also comes up with a new summer goal: saving for a life-altering nose job. She and her new nose will attract a fabulous boyfriend. Nothing like the shameless flirt Tyler Briggs, or Tom who's always nice but never calls. Maybe she'll find someone kind of like Gideon at the Jewel Café, except better looking and not quite so different. Jory survives various summer disasters like doing yoga after sampling Mom's Cabbage Soup Diet, Enforced Mother Bonding With Crazy Nose Obsessed Daughter Night, and discovering Tyler's big secret. But will she learn to accept herself and maybe even find her passion, in the creative (AND romantic!) sense of the word?

③ I have written for *APPLESEEDS, Confetti, Hopscotch, Story Friends, Wee Ones Magazine,* the *Deseret News, Children's Playmate* and Blooming Tree Press' *Summer Shorts* anthology. I won the Utah Arts Council prize for *Not-A-Dr. Logan's Divorce Book.* My novels *Jungle Crossing* and *Going Native!* each won first prize in the League of Utah Writers contest. I currently serve as an SCBWI Regional Advisor.

④ I submitted *My Big Nose & Other Natural Disasters* to Krista Marino at Delacorte because she requested it during our critique at the summer SCBWI conference (no response yet).

Thank you for your time and attention. I look forward to hearing from you.

Sincerely,
Sydney Salter Husseman

① With hundreds and hundreds of queries each month, it's tough to stand out. Sydney, however, did just that. First, she has a great title that totally made me laugh. Second, she sets up her main character's dilemma in a succinct and interesting way. In one simple paragraph, I have a great idea of who Jory is and what her life is about—the interesting tidbits about her mother help show the novel's sense of humor, too. ② Sydney's largest paragraph sets up the plot and the conflict, and introduces some exciting potential love interests and misadventures that I was excited to read about. Again, Sydney really shows off her fantastic sense of humor, and she leaves me hanging with a question that I needed an answer to. ③ She has writing experience and has completed other manuscripts that were prize-worthy. Her SCBWI involvement—while not a necessity—shows me that she has an understanding of and an interest in the children's publishing world. ④ The fact that an editor requested the manuscript is always a good sign. That I knew Krista personally and highly valued her opinion was, as Sydney's main character Jory would say, "The icing on the cake."

③ SAMPLE QUERY 3: NONFICTION (SELF-HELP)
Agent's Comments: Michelle Wolfson (Wolfson Literary Agency)

Dear Ms. Wolfson:

❶ Have you ever wanted to know the best day of the week to buy groceries or go out to dinner? Have you ever wondered about the best time of day to send an e-mail or ask for a raise? What about the best time of day to schedule a surgery or a haircut? What's the best day of the week to avoid lines at the Louvre? What's the best day of the month to make an offer on a house? What's the best time of day to ask someone out on a date? ❷

My book, *Buy Ketchup in May and Fly at Noon: A Guide to the Best Time to Buy This, Do That, and Go There*, has the answers to these questions and hundreds more.

❸ As a long-time print journalist, I've been privy to readership surveys that show people can't get enough of newspaper and magazine stories about the best time to buy or do things. This book puts several hundreds of questions and answers in one place—a succinct, large-print reference book that readers will feel like they need to own. Why? Because it will save them time and money, and it will give them valuable information about issues related to health, education, travel, the workplace and more. In short, it will make them smarter, so they can make better decisions. ❹

Best of all, the information in this book is relevant to anyone, whether they live in Virginia or the Virgin Islands, Portland, Oregon, or Portland, Maine. In fact, much of the book will find an audience in Europe and Australia.

❺ I've worked as a journalist since 1984. In 1999, the Virginia Press Association created an award for the best news writing portfolio in the state—the closest thing Virginia had to a reporter-of-the-year award. I won it that year and then again in 2000. During the summer of 2007, I left newspapering to pursue book projects and long-form journalism.

❻ I saw your name on a list of top literary agents for self-help books, and I read on your website that you're interested in books that offer practical advice. *Buy Ketchup in May and Fly at Noon* offers plenty of that. Please let me know if you'd like to read my proposal.

Sincerely,
Mark Di Vincenzo

❶ I tend to prefer it when authors jump right into the heart of their book, the exception being if we've met at a conference or have some other personal connection. Mark chose clever questions for the opening of the query. All of those questions are, in fact, relevant to my life—with groceries, dinner, e-mail and a raise—and yet I don't have a definitive answer to them. ❷ He gets a little more offbeat and unusual with questions regarding surgery, the Louvre, buying a house and dating. This shows a quirkier side to the book and also the range of topics it is going to cover, so I know right away there is going to be a mix of useful and quirky information on a broad range of topics. ❸ By starting with "As a long-time print journalist," Mark immediately establishes his credibility for writing on this topic. ❹ This helps show that there is a market for this book, and establishes the need for such a book. ❺ Mark's bio paragraph offers a lot of good information. ❻ It's nice when I feel like an author has sought me out specifically and thinks we would be a good fit.

④ SAMPLE QUERY 4: WOMEN'S FICTION
Agent's Comments: Elisabeth Weed (Weed Literary)

Dear Ms. Weed:

① Natalie Miller had a plan. She had a goddamn plan. Top of her class at Dartmouth. Even better at Yale Law. Youngest aide ever to the powerful Senator Claire Dupris. Higher, faster, stronger. This? Was all part of the plan. True, she was so busy ascending the political ladder that she rarely had time to sniff around her mediocre relationship with Ned, who fit the three Bs to the max: basic, blond and boring, and she definitely didn't have time to mourn her mangled relationship with Jake, her budding rock star ex-boyfriend.

The lump in her right breast that Ned discovers during brain-numbingly bland morning sex? That? Was most definitely not part of the plan. And Stage IIIA breast cancer? Never once had Natalie jotted this down on her to-do list for conquering the world. When her (tiny-penised) boyfriend has the audacity to dump her on the day after her diagnosis, Natalie's entire world dissolves into a tornado of upheaval, and she's left with nothing but her diary to her ex-boyfriends, her mornings lingering over "The Price is Right," her burnt-out stubs of pot that carry her past the chemo pain, and finally, the weight of her life choices—the ones in which she might drown if she doesn't find a buoy.

② *The Department of Lost and Found* is a story of hope, of resolve, of digging deeper than you thought possible until you find the strength not to crumble, and ultimately, of making your own luck, even when you've been dealt an unsteady hand.

③ I'm a freelance writer and have contributed to, among others, *American Baby, American Way, Arthritis Today, Bride's, Cooking Light, Fitness, Glamour, InStyle Weddings, Men's Edge, Men's Fitness, Men's Health, Parenting, Parents, Prevention, Redbook, Self, Shape, Sly, Stuff, USA Weekend, Weight Watchers, Woman's Day, Women's Health*, and ivillage.com, msn.com and women.com. I also ghostwrote *The Knot Book of Wedding Flowers*.

If you are interested, I'd love to send you the completed manuscript. Thanks so much! Looking forward to speaking with you soon.

Allison Winn Scotch

① The opening sentence reads like great jacket copy, and I immediately know who our protagonist is and what the conflict for her will be. (And it's funny, without being silly.) **②** The third paragraph tells me where this book will land: upmarket women's fiction. (A great place to be these days!) **③** This paragraph highlights impressive credentials. While being able to write nonfiction does not necessarily translate over to fiction, it shows me that she is someone worth paying more attention to. And her magazine contacts will help when it comes time to promote the book.

⑤ SAMPLE QUERY 5: MAINSTREAM/COMEDIC FICTION
Agent's Comments: Michelle Brower (Folio Literary Management)

Dear Michelle Brower:

① "I spent two days in a cage at the SPCA until my parents finally came to pick me up. The stigma of bringing your undead son home to live with you can wreak havoc on your social status, so I can't exactly blame my parents for not rushing out to claim me. But one more day and I would have been donated to a research facility."

Andy Warner is a zombie.

After reanimating from a car accident that killed his wife, Andy is resented by his parents, abandoned by his friends, and vilified by society. Seeking comfort and camaraderie in Undead Anonymous, a support group for zombies, Andy finds kindred souls in Rita, a recent suicide who has a taste for consuming formaldehyde in cosmetic products, and Jerry, a 21-year-old car crash victim with an artistic flair for Renaissance pornography.

② With the help of his new friends and a rogue zombie named Ray, Andy embarks on a journey of personal freedom and self-discovery that will take him from his own casket to the SPCA to a media-driven, class-action lawsuit for the civil rights of all zombies. And along the way, he'll even devour a few Breathers.

Breathers is a contemporary dark comedy about life, or undeath, through the eyes of an ordinary zombie. In addition to *Breathers*, I've written three other novels and more than four dozen short stories—a dozen of which have appeared in small press publications. Currently, I'm working on my fifth novel, also a dark comedy, about fate.

Enclosed is a two-page synopsis and the first chapter of *Breathers*, with additional sample chapters or the entire manuscript available upon request. I appreciate your time and interest in considering my query and I look forward to your response.

Sincerely,
Scott G. Browne

① What really draws me to this query is the fact that it has exactly what I'm looking for in my commercial fiction—story and style. Scott includes a brief quote from the book that manages to capture his sense of humor as an author and his uniquely relatable main character (hard to do with someone who's recently reanimated). I think this is a great example of how query letters can break the rules and still stand out in the slush pile. I normally don't like quotes as the first line, because I don't have a context for them, but this quote both sets up the main concept of the book *and* gives me a sense of the character's voice. This method won't necessarily work for most fiction, but it absolutely is successful here. **②** The letter quickly conveys that this is an unusual book about zombies, and being a fan of zombie literature, I'm aware that it seems to be taking things in a new direction. I also appreciate how Scott conveys the main conflict of his plot and his supporting cast of characters—we know there is an issue for Andy beyond coming back to life as a zombie, and that provides momentum for the story.

QUERY LETTER FAQS

Here are answers to 19 of the most tricky and confusing query questions around.

....

by Chuck Sambuchino

Readers and aspiring writers often find querying literary agents to be intimidating and terrifying. Here are some important questions and answers to consider as you craft your query letter.

When contacting agents, the query process isn't as simple as, "Just keep e-mailing until something good happens." There are ins, outs, strange situations, unclear scenarios, and plenty of what-have-you's that block the road to signing with a rep. In short, there are plenty of murky waters out there in the realm of submissions. Luckily, writers have plenty of questions to ask. Here are some of the most interesting (and important) questions and answers regarding protocol during the query process.

When should you query? When is your project ready?

There is no definitive answer, but here's what I suggest. Get other eyes on the material—"beta readers"—people who can give you feedback that is both honest and helpful. These beta readers (usually members of a critique group)

will give you feedback. You do not want major concerns, such as, "It starts too slow" or "This character is not likeable." Address these problems through revisions. After rewriting, give it to more beta readers. If they come back with no major concerns, the book is ready, or at least very close.

How should you start your query? Should you begin with a paragraph from the book?

I would not include a paragraph from the book nor would I write the letter in the "voice" of one your characters—those are gimmicks. If you choose, you can just jump right into the pitch—there's nothing wrong with that. But what I recommend is laying out the details of your book in one easy sentence: "I have a completed 78,000-word thriller titled *Dead Cat Bounce*." I suggest this because jumping into a pitch can be jarring and confusing. Think about it. If you started reading an e-mail and the first sentence was simply "Billy has a problem," you don't know if Billy is an adult or a child, or if he is being held captive by terrorists versus being nervous because his turtle is missing. In other words, the agent doesn't know whether to laugh or be worried. He's confused. And when an agent gets confused, he may just stop reading.

Can you query multiple agents at the same agency?

Generally, no. A rejection from one literary agent usually means a rejection from the entire agency. If you query one agent and she thinks the work isn't right for her but still has promise, she will pass it on to fellow agents in the office who can review it themselves.

Should you mention that the query is a simultaneous submission?

You certainly can, but you don't have to. If you say it's exclusive, they'll understand no other eyes are on the material. If you say nothing, they will assume multiple agents must be considering it right now. However, some literary agents will specifically request in their guidelines to be informed if it's a simultaneous submission.

Even if an agent doesn't request it, should you include a few sample pages with your query letter?

This is up to you. When including sample pages, though, remember to paste the pages below the query letter. Do not attach them in a document. Also, do not include much— perhaps 1–5 pages. Most people ask-

ing this question probably have more faith in their opening pages than in their query. That's understandable, but keep in mind that while including sample pages may help with an occasional agent who checks out your writing, it doesn't solve the major problem of your query being substandard. Keep working on the query until you have faith in it, regardless of whether you sneak in unsolicited pages or not.

Can your query be more than one page long?

The rise of e-queries removed the dreaded page break, so now it's easy to have your query go over one page. This does not necessarily mean it's a wise move. Going a few sentences over one page is likely harmless, but you don't need a query that trends long. Lengthy letters are a sign of a rambling pitch, which will probably get you rejected. Edit and trim your pitch down as need be. Find beta readers or a freelance query editor to give you ideas and notes. Remember that a succinct letter is preferred, and oftentimes more effective. An exception to this, however, is querying for nonfiction books. Nonfiction queries have to be heavy on author platform, and those notes (with proper names of publications and organizations and websites, etc.) can get long. Feel free to go several sentences over one page if you have to list out platform and marketing notes, as long as the pitch itself is not the item making your letter too long.

How do you follow up with an agent who hasn't responded to your submission?

This is a complicated question, and I'll try to address its many parts.

First, check the agency website for updates and their latest formal guidelines. They might have gone on leave, or they might have switched agencies. They may also have submission guidelines that state how they only respond to submissions if interested. So keep in mind there might be a very good reason as to why you shouldn't follow up or rather why you shouldn't follow up right now.

However, let's say an agent responds to submissions "within three months" and it's been three and a half months with no reply. A few weeks have passed since the "deadline," so now it's time to nicely follow up. All you do is paste your original query into a new e-mail and send it to the agent with a note above the query that says, "Dear [agent], I sent my query below to you [length of time] ago and haven't heard anything. I'm afraid my original note got lost in a spam filter, so I am pasting it below in the hopes that you are still reviewing queries and open to new clients. Thank you for considering my submission. Sincerely, [name]." That's it. Be polite and simply resubmit. If an agent makes it sound like he does indeed respond to submissions but doesn't have

a time frame for his reply, I say follow up after three months.

But before you send that follow up, make sure you are not to blame for getting no reply. Perhaps your previous e-mail had an attachment when the agent warned, "No attachments." Perhaps your previous e-mail did not put "Query" in the subject line even though the agent requested just that. Or perhaps your previous e-mail misspelled the agent's e-mail address and the query truly got lost in cyberspace. In other words, double-check everything. If you send that follow up and the agent still doesn't reply, it's probably time to move on.

Can you re-query an agent after she rejects you?

You can, though I'd say you have about a 50/50 shot of getting your work read. Some agents seem to be more than open to reviewing a query letter if it's undergone serious editing. Other agents, meanwhile, believe that a no is a no—period. In other words, you really don't know, so you might as well just query away and hope for the best.

How many query rejections would necessitate a major overhaul of the query?

Submit no more than 10 queries to start. If only 0–1 respond with requests for more, then you've got a problem. Go back to the drawing board and overhaul the query before the next wave of 6–10 submissions. Doing this ensures that you can try to identify where you're going wrong in your submission.

Should you mention that you've self-published books in the past?

In my opinion, you don't have to. If you self-published a few e-books that went nowhere, you don't have to list every one and their disappointing sales numbers. The release of those books should not affect your new novel that you're submitting to agents. However, if your self-published projects experienced healthy sales (3,000-plus print books, 10,000-plus e-books), mention it. Only talk about your self-published projects if they will help your case. Otherwise, just leave them out of the conversation and focus on the new project at hand.

Should you mention your age in a query? Do agents have a bias against older writers and teenagers?

I'm not sure any good can come from mentioning your age in a query. Usually the people who ask this question are either younger than 20 or older than 70. Some literary agents may be hesitant to sign older writers because reps are looking for career clients, not simply individuals with one memoir/book to sell. If you're older, write multiple books to convince an agent that you have several projects in you, and do not mention your age in the query to be safe.

Should you mention in the query that your work is copyrighted and/or has had book editing?

No. All work is copyrighted the moment you write it down in any medium, so saying something that is obvious only comes off as amateurish. On the same note, all work should be edited, so saying that the work is edited (even by a professional editor) also comes off as amateurish.

Is it better to send a query over snail mail or e-mail?

If you have a choice, do not send a snail mail query. They're more of a hassle to physically produce, and they cost money to send. Ninety percent (or more) of queries are sent over e-mail for two very good reasons. E-mail is quicker, in terms of sending submissions and agents' response time, and it's free. Keep in mind that almost all agents have personal, detailed submission guidelines in which they say exactly what they want to receive in a submission and how they want to receive it. So you will almost always not have a choice in how to send materials. Send the agent what they asked for, exactly how they asked for it.

What happens when you're writing a book that doesn't easily fall into one specific genre? How do you handle that problem in a query letter?

Know that you have to bite the bullet and call it *something*. Even if you end up calling it a "middle grade adventure with supernatural elements," then you're at least calling it something. Writers really get into a pickle when they start their pitches with an intro such as, "It's a sci-fi western humorous fantastical suspense romance, set in steampunk Britain … with erotic werewolf transvestite protagonists." Fundamentally, it must be something, so pick its core genre and just call it that—otherwise your query might not even get read. I'm not a huge fan of writers comparing their work to other projects (saying, "It's X meets Z"— that type of thing), but said strategy— comparing your book to others in the marketplace—is most useful for those authors who have a hard time describing the plot and tone of their tale.

If you're writing a memoir, do you pitch it like a fiction book (complete the whole manuscript) or like a nonfiction book (a complete book proposal with a few sample chapters)?

I'd say 80 percent of agents review memoir like they would a novel. If interested, they ask for the full book and consider it mostly by how well it's written. I have met several agents, however, who want to see a nonfiction book proposal—either with some sample chapters, or sometimes in addition to the whole book. So to answer the question, you can choose to write only the manuscript, and go from there. Or you can choose to complete a proposal, as well, so you have as many weapons as possible as you move forward. (In my opinion, a writer who has both a complete memoir manuscript and nonfiction book proposal seems like a professional who is ahead of the curve and wise to platform matters—and, naturally, people in publishing are often attracted to writers who are ahead of the curve and/ or can help sell more books.)

If you're pitching a novel, should the topics of marketing and writer platform be addressed in the query?

Concerning query letters for novels, the pitch is what's paramount, and any mention of marketing or platform is just gravy. If you have some promotional credentials, these skills will definitely be beneficial in selling more books when your title is released. But a decent platform will not get a mediocre novel published. Feel free to list worthwhile, impressive notes about your platform and marketing skills, but don't let them cloud your writing. Remember, the three most crucial elements to a novel selling are *the writing, the writing, the writing.*

Do you need to query conservative agents for a conservative book? A liberal agent for a liberal book?

I asked a few agents this question and some said they were willing to take on any political slant if the book was well written and the author had a great writer platform. A few agents, on the other hand, said they needed to be on the same page politically with the author for a political/religious book, and would only take on books they agreed with. Bottom line: Some will be open-minded; some won't. Look for reps who have taken on books similar to yours, and feel free to query other agents, too. The worst any agent can say is no.

If you're writing a series, does an agent want you to say that in the query?

The old mentality for this was no, you should not discuss a series in the query, and instead just pitch one book and let any discussion naturally progress to the topic of more books, if the agent so inquires. However, I've overheard more and more literary agents say that they do want to know if your book is the potential start of the series. So, the correct answer, it appears, depends on who you ask. In circumstances like these, I recommend crafting an answer to cover all bases: "This book could either be a standalone project or the start of a series." When worded like this, you disclose the series potential, but don't make it sound like you're saying, "I want a 5-book deal or NOTHING." You'll sound like an easy-to-work-with writing professional and leave all options open.

Can you query an agent for a short story collection?

I'd say 95 percent of agents do not accept short story collection queries. The reason? Collections just don't sell well. If you have a collection of short stories, you can do one of three things:

1) Repurpose some or all of the stories into a novel, which is much easier to sell. 2) Write a new book—a novel—and sell that first to establish a reader base. That way, you can have a base that will purchase your next project—the collection—ensuring the publisher makes money on your short stories.

3) Query the few agents who do take collections and hope for the best. If you choose this third route, I suggest you get some of the stories published to help the project gain some momentum. A platform and/or media contacts would help your case, as well.

CHUCK SAMBUCHINO (chucksambuchino.com, @chucksambuchino) edits the *Guide to Literary Agents* (guidetoliteraryagents.com/blog) as well as the *Children's Writer's & Illustrator's Market*. His pop humor books include *How to Survive a Garden Gnome Attack* (film rights optioned by Sony) and *When Clowns Attack: A Survival Guide* (Sept. 2015, Ten Speed Press). Chuck's other writing guides include *Formatting & Submitting Your Manuscript (3rd. Ed.)*, *Create Your Writer Platform*, and *Get a Literary Agent*. Besides that, he is a husband, guitarist, father, dog owner, and cookie addict.

HOW TO WRITE A SYNOPSIS

6 tips to compose your novel summary.

by Chuck Sambuchino

I've never met a single person who liked writing a synopsis. Seriously—not one. But still, synopses are a necessary part of the submission process (until some brave publishing pro outlaws them), so I wanted to share tips and guidelines regarding how to compose one.

A synopsis is a *summary* of your book. Literary agents and editors may ask to see one if you're writing an adult novel, a memoir, or a kids novel (young adult, middle grade). The purpose of a synopsis request is for the agent or editor to evaluate what happens in the three acts of your story and decide if the characters, plot and conflict warrant a complete read of your manuscript. And if you haven't guessed yet, these summaries can be pretty tough to write.

SYNOPSIS GUIDELINES

Here are some guidelines that will help you understand the basics of synopsis writing, no matter what your novel or memoir is about:

1. Reveal everything major that happens in your book, including the ending. Heck, revealing the story's ending is a synopsis's defining unique characteristic. You shouldn't find a story's ending in a query or in-person pitch, but it does leak out in a synopsis. On this note, know that a synopsis is designed to explain *everything major* that happens, not to tease—so avoid language such as "Krista walks around a corner into a big surprise." Don't say "surprise," but rather just tell us what happens. This touches upon a bigger point. The No. 1 failure of a synopsis is that it confuses the reader. Have no language in your page that is vague and undefined that could lead to multiple interpretations. One of the fundamental purposes of a synopsis is to show your book's narrative arc, and that the story possesses staple elements, such as rising action, the three-act structure, and a satisfying ending.

2. Make your synopsis one page, single-spaced. There is always some disagreement on length. This stems from the fact that synopses used to trend longer (four, six, or even eight pages!). But over the last five years, agents have requested shorter and shorter synopses—with most agents finally settling on 1-2 pages, total. If you write yours as one page, single-spaced, it's the same length as two pages, double-spaced—and either are acceptable. There will be the occasional agent who requests something strange, such as a "five-page synopsis on beige paper that smells of cinnamon!" But trust me, if you turn in a solid one-page work, you'll be just fine across the board. In my opinion, it's the gold standard.

3. Take more care and time if you're writing genre fiction. Synopses are especially difficult to compose if you're writing character-driven (i.e., literary) fiction, because there may not be a whole lot of plot in the book. Agents and editors understand this, and put little (or no) weight into a synopsis for literary or character-driven stories. However, if you're writing genre fiction—specifically categories like romance, fantasy, thriller, mystery, horror, or science fiction—agents will quickly want to look over your characters and plot points to make sure your book has a clear beginning, middle and end, as well as some unique aspects they haven't seen before in a story. So if you're getting ready to submit a genre story, don't blow through your synopsis; it's important.

4. Feel free to be dry, but don't step out of the narrative. When you write your prose (and even the pitch in your query letter),

there is importance in using style and voice in the writing. A synopsis, thankfully, not only can be dry, but probably *should* be dry. The synopsis has to explain everything that happens in a very small amount of space. So if you find yourself using short sentences like "John shoots Bill and then sits down to contemplate suicide," don't worry. This is normal. Lean, clean language is great. Use active verbs and always strive for clarity. And lastly, do not step out of the narrative. Agents do not want to read things such as "And at the climax of the story," "In a rousing scene," or "In a flashback."

5. Capitalize character names when characters are introduced. Whenever a new character is introduced, make sure to CAPITALIZE them in the first mention and then use normal text throughout. This helps a literary agent immediately recognize each important name. On this subject, avoid naming too many characters, and try to set a limit of five, with no more than six total. I know this may sound tough, but it's doable. It forces you to excise smaller characters and subplots from your summary—actually strengthening your novel synopsis along the way. Sometimes writers fall in love with a minor character or joke or setting, and insist on squeezing in mentions of these elements into the synopsis, even though they are not a piece of the larger plot. These mistakes will water down your summary, and also cause the synopsis to be more than one page.

6. Use third person, present tense. The exception of this is memoir. While you can write your memoir synopsis in third person, it's probably a better idea to write it in first person. "Feeling stifled: I enlist in the Army that very day."

Every agent has a different opinion of the synopsis. Some agents openly state in interviews that they're well aware of how difficult a synopsis is to write, and they put little consideration into them. But we must presume that most or all of the agents who do not openly speak out against synopses put some weight into them, and that's why it's important for you to treat this step with care.

A poor synopsis will confuse the reader, and during the pitching process, confusion = death. A poor synopsis will also reveal big problems in your story, such as strange plot points, how ridiculous acts of God get the main character out of tight situations, or how your romance actually ends in a divorce (a major category no-no).

CHUCK SAMBUCHINO (chucksambuchino.com, @chucksambuchino) edits the *Guide to Literary Agents* (guidetoliteraryagents.com/blog) as well as the *Children's Writer's & Illustrator's Market*. His pop humor books include *How to Survive a Garden Gnome Attack* (film rights optioned by Sony) and *When Clowns Attack: A Survival Guide* (Sept. 2015, Ten Speed Press). Chuck's other writing guides include *Formatting & Submitting Your Manuscript (3rd. Ed.)*, *Create Your Writer Platform*, and *Get a Literary Agent*. Besides that, he is a husband, guitarist, father, dog owner, and cookie addict.

NONFICTION BOOK PROPOSALS

Pitch your nonfiction with confidence.

by Chuck Sambuchino

A *book proposal* is a business plan that explains all the details of a nonfiction book. Since your project is not complete during the pitching stages, the proposal acts as a blueprint and diagram for what the finished product will look like, as well as exactly how you will promote it when the product is in the marketplace.

Better yet, think about it like this: If you wanted to open a new restaurant and needed a bank loan, you would have to make a case to the bank as to why your business will succeed and generate revenue. A book proposal acts in much the same way. You must prove to a publisher that your book idea is a proven means to generate revenue—showing that customers will buy your worthwhile and unique product, and you have the means to draw in prospective customers.

"There are several factors that can help a book proposal's ultimate prospects: great writing, great platform, or great information, and ideally all three," says Ted Weinstein, founder of Ted Weinstein Literary. "For narrative works, the writing should be gorgeous, not just functional. For practical works, the information should be insightful, comprehensive, and preferably new. And for any work of nonfiction, of course, the author's platform is enormously important."

If you're writing a work of fiction (novel, screenplay, picture book) or memoir, the first all-important step is to simply *finish* the work, because agents and editors will consider it for publication based primarily on how good the writing is. On the other hand, when you have a nonfiction project of any kind, you do *not* need to finish the book to sell it. In fact, even if you're feeling ambitious and knock out the entire text, finishing the book will not help you sell it because all an editor really needs to see are several sample chapters that adequately portray what the rest of the book will be like.

THE STRUCTURE OF A BOOK PROPOSAL

A book proposal is made up of several key sections that flesh out the book, its markets, and information about the author. All

"Concerning how to write a compelling nonfiction book proposal: 1) Spill the beans. Don't try to tantalize and hold back the juice. 2) No BS! We agents learn to see right through BS, or we fail rapidly. 3) Get published small. Local papers, literary journals, websites, anything. The more credits you have, the better. And list them all (although not to the point of absurdity) in your query. Why does everyone want to pole-vault from being an unpublished author to having a big book contract? It makes no sense. You have to learn to drive before they'll let you pilot the Space Shuttle."

- Gary Heidt (Signature Literary)

of these important sections seek to answer one of the three main questions that every proposal must answer:

1. What is the book, and why is it timely and unique?
2. What is its place in the market?
3. Why are you the best person to write and market it?

Every book proposal has several sections that allow the author to explain more about their book. Though you can sometimes vary the order of the sections, here are the major elements (and suggested order) that should be addressed before you pitch a nonfiction book to a literary agent.

TITLE PAGE. Keep it simple. Put your title and subtitle in the middle, centered—and put your personal contact information at the bottom right.

TABLE OF CONTENTS (WITH PAGE NUMBERS). A nonfiction book proposal has several sections, and can run many pages, so this is where you explain everything the agent can find in the proposal, in case they want to jump around immediately to peruse different sections at different times.

OVERVIEW. This section gets its name because it's designed to be an overview of the entire proposal to come. It's something of a "greatest hits" of the proposal, where you discuss the concept and content, the evidence of need for this new resource in the market, and your platform. Overviews typically run 1–3 double-spaced pages, and immediately make the case as to why this book is worthwhile for consideration and timely for readers *now*. Another way to think about this section is by imagining as it as an extended query letter, because it serves the same purpose. If an agent likes your overview, they will review the rest of the document to delve deeper into both you and your ideas. The overview is arguably the most important part of the proposal. "Your overview is the sizzle in your nonfiction book proposal," says agent Michael Larsen of Larsen/Pomada Literary Agents. "If it doesn't sell you and your book, agents and editors won't check the bones (the outline of your book) or try the steak (your sample chapter)."

FORMAT. This section explains how the book will be formatted. Remember that your finished, completed product does not physically exist, and all nonfiction books look different from one another in terms of appearance. So spell out exactly what it will look like. What is the physical size of the book? What is your estimated word count when everything is said and done? How long after the contract is signed will you be able to submit the finished product? Will there be sidebars, boxed quotes, or interactive elements? Will there be photos, illustrations, or other art? (If so, who will be responsible for collecting this art?)

SPINOFFS (OPTIONAL). Some nonfiction projects lend themselves to things like sequels, spinoffs, subsidiary rights possibilities, and more. For example, when I pitched my political humor book for dog lovers, *Red Dog / Blue Dog*, this is the section where I mentioned the possibility of a tear-off calendar if the book succeeded, as well as a possible sequel, *Red Cat / Blue Cat*. Unlike other sections of a proposal, this one is optional, as some ideas will *not* lend to more variations.

CHAPTER LIST. While you will only be turning over a few completed, polished chapters, agents still want to know exactly what will

be in the rest of the book. So list out all your chapter concepts, with a paragraph or so on the content of each. This section is important, as it shows that, although the book is not complete, the author has a very clear path forward in terms of the exact content that will fill all the pages.

SAMPLE CHAPTERS. Although you do not have to finish the book before pitching nonfiction, you do have to complete 2–4 book chapters as an appropriate sample. The goal is to write chapters that you believe give a great representation as to what the book is about. Typical sample chapters include the book's first chapter, and 1–3 more from different sections of the book. Your goal is to make these chapters represent what the final product will be like in both appearance and content. So if the book is going to be funny, your sample chapters better be humorous. If the book will be infused with art and illustrations, gather what images you can to insert in the pages. The sample chapters are the one place in a proposal where the author can step out of "business mode" and into "writer mode"—focusing on things like voice, humor, style, and more.

TARGET AUDIENCES. You've probably heard before that "a book for everyone is a book for no one," so target your work to small, core, focused audience groups. This section is your chance to prove an *evidence of need*. Or, as agent Mollie Glick of Foundry Literary + Media says, "You want an original idea—but not too original."

For example, when I was listing audiences for my book, *How to Survive a Garden*

"Know your market. This is a business, and the more time and effort you expend in studying and understanding the demands of your [niche], the more likely you'll meet with success."

- Gina Panettieri (Talcott Notch Literary Services)

Gnome Attack, they were 1) garden gnome enthusiasts, 2) gardeners, 3) survival guide parody lovers, and 4) humor book lovers. Note how I resisted the urge to say "Everyone everywhere loves a laugh, so I basically see the entire human population snatching this bad boy up at bookstores."

When I was pitching a book on historical theaters around the country, my audiences were 1) theater lovers, 2) historical preservationists in the regions where featured theaters are located, 3) nostalgia lovers, and 4) architecture buffs and enthusiasts. Again, the audiences were concise and focused. I proved I had done my research and honed in on the exact pockets of people who would pay money for what I was proposing.

And once you identify these audiences, you must *quantify* them. If you want to write a book about the history of the arcade game Donkey Kong, a logical target audience would be "Individuals who currently play Donkey Kong"—but you must quantify the audience, because an agent has no idea if that audience size is 1,000 or 500,000. So tell them what it really is—and explain how you came to find that true number. You can find these quantifying numbers by seeing where such audiences get their news. For example,

if donkeykongnews.com has a newsletter reach of 12,000 individuals, that is a proven number you can use. If the official Donkey Kong Twitter account has 134,000 followers, that will help you, as well. If *Classic Games Magazine* has a circulation of 52,000, that number can help you, too. "Use round, accurate numbers in your proposal," says Larsen. "If a number isn't round, qualify it by writing nearly, almost or more than (not over). Be ready to provide sources for statistics if asked."

COMPARATIVE TITLES. This is where you list any and all books that are similar to yours in the marketplace. What you're aiming for is showing that many books that have similarities to your title exist and have healthy sales, but no one book accomplishes everything yours will do. If you can show that, you've made an argument that your book is unique (and therefore worthwhile), and also that people have shown a history of buying such a book (and therefore the book is even more worthwhile). You're essentially trying to say "Books exist on Subject A and books exist on Subject B, but no book exists on Subject AB, which is exactly what my book, [*Title*], will do."

You can find comparative titles by searching through the appropriate bookshelf in Barnes & Noble or any local book-store, as well as by scouring Amazon. Once you have your list, it's your time to write them all down—laying out details such as the publisher, title, year, and any signs of solid sales (such as awards or a good Amazon sales ranking). After you explain a book's specifics, you should quickly say why your book is different from it. At the same time, don't trash competing books. Because your book shares some similarity to it, you don't want your own work to come under fire.

MARKETING / WRITER PLATFORM. This massively important section details all the many avenues you have in place to market the work to the audiences you've already identified. This section will list out your social media channels, contacts in the media, personal marketing abilities, public speaking engagements, and much more. This section is of the utmost importance, as an agent needs to be assured you can currently market your book to thousands of pos-sible buyers, if not more. Otherwise, the agent may stop reading the proposal. "Develop a significant following before you go out with your nonfiction book. If you build it, publishers will come," says agent Jeffery McGraw of The August Agency. "How visible are you to the world? That's what determines your level of platform. Someone with real platform is the 'go to' person in their area of expertise. If you don't make yourself known to the world as the expert in your field, then how will [members of the media] know to reach out to you? Get out there. Make as many connections as you possibly can."

AUTHOR BIO / CREDENTIALS. Now is your chance to explain what makes you qualified to write the content in this book. Tell the agent things such as your degrees, memberships, endorsements, and more. Anything that qualifies you to write this book but is not technically considered "platform" should go in this section.

AN AGENT EXPLAINS 3 COMMON BOOK PROPOSAL PROBLEMS

1. Lack of a story arc. Many failed nonfiction proposals are mere surveys of a subject. The books that sell have strong characters who are engaged in some project that eventually is resolved. Don't do a book about slime mold. Do a book about the Slime Mold Guy who solved the mystery of slime mold.

2. Skimpiness. I like big fat proposals. Writers worry too much about how much reading editors have to do and they self-defeatingly try to keep proposals short. Busy editors are not the problem. A great proposal will hook a reader within a few pages and keep that reader spellbound until the last page no matter how long. Short, skimpy proposals often quit before they can get me, or an editor, truly immersed and engaged. You aren't just informing us about your book; you are recruiting us into joining you on what is going to be a long and expensive expedition. If crazy, fire-eyed Christopher Columbus wants me to join him on his trip to the "Here Be Monsters" part of the ocean, I'd like to inspect his ships very, very carefully before I set sail. Editors are scared to buy books because they are so often wrong. Thoroughness builds confidence.

3. Extrapolation. Many proposals say, in effect, "I don't know all that much about this subject, but give me a six-figure contract and I will go and find out everything there is to know." I understand the problem writers face: How are they supposed to master a subject until after they've done the travels, interviews, and research? Nevertheless, unless you are already an established writer, you can't simply promise to master your subject. Book contracts go to those who have already mastered a subject. If you haven't mastered your subject but you really think you deserve a book contract, try to get a magazine assignment so that you can do at least some of the necessary research, funded by the magazine. But if you're just winging it, I probably can't help you unless you have a superb platform.

Sidebar courtesy of literary agent Russell Galen (Scovil Galen Ghosh Literary Agency).

CHUCK SAMBUCHINO (chucksambuchino.com, @chucksambuchino) edits the *Guide to Literary Agents* (guidetoliteraryagents.com/blog) as well as the *Children's Writer's & Illustrator's Market*. His pop humor books include *How to Survive a Garden Gnome Attack* (film rights optioned by Sony) and *When Clowns Attack: A Survival Guide* (Sept. 2015, Ten Speed Press). Chuck's other writing guides include *Formatting & Submitting Your Manuscript (3rd. Ed.)*, *Create Your Writer Platform*, and *Get a Literary Agent*. Besides that, he is a husband, guitarist, father, dog owner, and cookie addict.

AGENTS EVALUATE FIRST PAGES

Hear agents' thoughts and notes in real time.

by Paul S. Levine, Marisa Corvisiero, Adriann Ranta, and Patricia Nelson

Writing a compelling first page is very difficult. It's a balancing act of action, description, and dialogue, and somehow—no matter what it is you're writing about—you've got to make it interesting and employ a unique voice. Because a reader wants to get pulled in on Page 1, that means agents & editors put a lot of stock into that important first page, as well. And when we writers get a rejection, we all wonder: *Where did I go wrong? At what point did the agent give up?*

So to help you understand exactly what goes through an agent's mind, we've asked four literary agents to participate in a "First Pages Read" so you can see exactly when an agent stops considering your submission and why. In this article you will find 10 real, unpublished first pages of manuscripts. (The pages are anonymous, and the writers have given their consent for this article. Only the genres are mentioned on each submission.) The agents explain exactly when they would stop reading the page (and thus issue a rejection) and why. So pay attention to where and why the agents

stopped—or *didn't* stop—and the advice they had to share. But before we begin, meet the four participating literary agents:

Paul S. Levine is the founder of Paul S. Levine Literary Agency. He is based in Southern California. As an entertainment lawyer, Levine has written the legal contracts for several books adapted as movies-for-television. With more than a quarter of a century of experience in the entertainment and book industries, he is able to act as both literary agent and publishing attorney for his clients. Wherever you see the number ❶ in the following pages, that is the point in the page where Levine stopped reading.

Marisa Corvisiero is the founder of Corvisiero Literary. She is based in the New York area. During the few years prior to starting her own agency, Corvisiero worked with the L. Perkins Agency, while also serving as a literary consultant and an attorney practicing law in New York City. Wherever you see the number **2** in the following pages, that is the point in the page where Corvisiero stopped reading.

Adriann Ranta is a literary agent with Wolf Literary Services. She is based in the New York area, and represents *New York Times* bestselling and award-winning authors, journalists, illustrators, and graphic novelists, as well as actors, stuntwomen, makeup artists, and many other pioneering creative thinkers and leaders in their fields. Wherever you see the number **3** in the following pages, that is the point in the page where Ranta stopped reading.

Patricia Nelson is a literary agent with Marsal Lyon Literary Agency and is based in Southern California. Before joining the agency, she interned at The Angela Rinaldi Literary Agency and in the children's division at Running Press. Patricia represents adult, young adult, and middle grade fiction, and is actively looking to build her list. Wherever you see the number **4** in the following pages, that is the point in the page where Nelson stopped reading.

An article like this shows agents' specific reasons for why they reject a submission. It also shows the extremely subjective nature of the business. After all, one agent could review a scene and say "Too much description" while another reads the same text and is entranced by the same description. Such subjective contradiction is nothing new, and just goes to show you that, when submitting fiction, memoir, or narrative nonfiction, you should steadily cast a wide net and contact many agents, because you never know which rep will be the one that completely falls in love with your storytelling, plot, and voice.

Also: It's very important to note that just because an agent says no to one of the following submissions does not mean that the writer in question has a poor book or is a poor writer. All it means is simply that the book does not start in the right place, and the submission doesn't pull the agent in with story conflict or writing skill.

So let's get started, and you can get a rare, valuable glimpse into how multiple agents quickly review and dissect your writing on Page 1. Remember that the numbers you see in each page's text represent the *exact point* where the literary agent would stop reading and issue a rejection. If agents' numbers appear at the *bottom* of the Page 1 text, that means that agent read the entire first page.

1. COZY MYSTERY

"This is not a good sign," Aryn Flynn muttered as she locked her apartment door. Normally, autumn in Germany is glorious—golden, sharp, and clear. But today, a blanket of dull gray pressed down, sucking all the color out of the last autumn leaves. As she unlocked her Peugeot convertible ❶, a gust of wind made a grab for the sophomore essays she'd spent three hours grading last night. She snatched them just in time and slammed the car door. Jamming the papers back into her wicker basket, she implored the gods through clenched teeth, "Please, please, just let me get through this day."

The faculty parking lot was nearly empty at this hour, and a steady drizzle pattered onto the front courtyard of Römerberg American High School. Aryn checked her reflection in the rear-view mirror. Her curly hair was already beginning to frizz from the damp weather; soon it would be a springy copper halo, despite the expensive "smoothing serum" she'd applied to tame it. She wrinkled her upturned nose, the feature that made her look younger than her thirty-seven years.

"Great," she muttered, "just the look I want today—Little Orphan Annie."

There's no such thing as tenure for a new teacher. Everything depends upon clearing that first hurdle: the principal's performance evaluation. She's completely at his mercy, and if anything goes wrong, she may as well kiss her job good-bye. Today Aryn would face her first official classroom observation by Dirk Barnard, affectionately known as "Dirk the Jerk" by his staff ❹. Aryn had set her alarm an hour early in order to be guaranteed a chance to photocopy today's poetry lesson. This job on an overseas Air Force base had been a lifesaver, and this morning's class had to be perfect. Going back home was not an option. ❷ ❸

1. **LEVINE**: Just tell the story by showing, not telling.

2. **CORVISERO**: There was enough detail and an interesting tone here to keep me reading until the end of the page, but I admit that, as of now, the only hook is the tension about "Dirk the Jerk," and whether he is a possible love interest or suspect. I detected no hint of a mystery coming on, so if one isn't introduced soon, I would not continue reading.

3. **RANTA**: I read to the bottom of the first page but wouldn't read more. The setting is unique, and I liked the details (Peugeot), but nothing has happened in this first page except a woman getting out of her car. I want more detail (where in Germany?) and less characters talking to themselves, which feels like a limp substitute for action or dialogue.

4. **NELSON**: This started out strong. Where this author goes astray, though, is this last paragraph, which abruptly shifts from a great "showing" voice to all "telling." I'm getting a big block of backstory/context, when I would rather be shown Aryn's anxiety and her contentious relationship with her boss as the story unfolds.

2. NARRATIVE NONFICTION

Early Thursday morning, January 3, 1856, miners and townspeople left their warm homes in the tree-covered foothills surrounding Placerville, California, and now stood huddled in the frosty cold outside the town's post office—waiting ❶. They were anxious to see John A. Thompson. He was the only one who had volunteered to deliver mail ninety miles across the mountain wilderness of the Sierra Nevada buried in snow.

A murmur rose as the crowd parted to let the twenty-eight-year-old Norwegian pass. On his shoulder, he carried two thin boards, called snowskates (skis), and a six-foot-long pole. A board, brimmed hat pulled tight to his head hid his blonde hair.

Some thought him "demented." Others seeing how he was dressed may have wondered how he'd survive. He wore a short, wool coat known as a Mackinaw jacket. Two pockets were stuffed with salty, dried beef and crackers. Another held a small box of matches—his only camping gear ❹.

John carried no blankets. He didn't want the burden of extra bulk. He'd blackened his face with charcoal to protect his blue eyes from the sun's glare. At his waist, a leather holster held a revolver in case he met wolves, his only fear.

Postmaster A.W. Thatcher welcomed John, then lifted a sack filled with mail and helped him strap it to his back. It weighed sixty pounds, as much as six, ten-pound sacks of potatoes. John shouldered his snowskates and pole. ❷ He walked through the crowd and turned east onto Main Street then strode up the muddy street pass shops in wooden buildings toward the snow above town. He was eager to begin this new adventure. ❸

> 1. **LEVINE:** Way too much information in one sentence.
>
> 2. **CORVISIERO:** I thought that the narrative was disorganized in the middle of the page. We are told that people thought him "demented" because of how he is dressed, and immediately after that statement we are told about the contents of his pockets, which no one would know about. The answer comes in the next paragraph when the author tells us that he does not carry a blanket. I felt that the lack of proper sequential logic impedes proper flow of the text and may detach the readers.
>
> 3. **RANTA:** I'd continue reading, but the first page raises some red flags, mainly grammatical ones. There are a number of improper commas and typos, which add to a jilted feel from the sentences themselves. Just on a fundamental level, I didn't understand if John was coming or going. The content, however, is really interesting, and I love the detail.
>
> 4. **NELSON:** Like many submissions, this one has issues with "telling." John is observed only from the outside, by the townspeople, so we know how it *looks* to deliver mail on skis but not how it *feels*, making it hard for the reader to find an access point into the scene.

3. SCIENCE FICTION

The spacecraft plunges at full speed toward the center ❶ of the time portal ❸, a circular structure eight miles wide in the orbit of Venus. The control station in orbit around the portal activates the sequence of events preceding the time leap. All systems are go. ❷

The center of the ring is targeted by a two-second salvo from the lasers mounted around the asteroid belt. Such a concentration of rays produces, at a minuscule point, a temperature one septillion times that of the surface of the sun. A multiple particle accelerator, embedded in the giant loop, speeds up two trains of four particles to almost the speed of light. Linear cannons in the last stage hurl the particles against the furnace. In a synchronized sequence, the particles crash into each other, emanating a massive amount of energy. Space is cleaved. ❹

A mini black hole appears in the geometric center of the circle. An unstable temporal vortex opens a split-second before the arrival of the ship. The event overshadows the brightness of Venus for two seconds and is discernible to the naked eye in the skies of Jupiter. It is a blaze more powerful than the largest supernova ever observed from Earth.

The high-energy collisions generate enough density to sustain the event a little longer. Peripheral lasers around the portal then inject the energy required to control the opening of the vortex. This is the gateway to another dimension. The spacecraft goes in and gets out in one continuous movement. To an external observer it's as if the vehicle kicked against the portal and instantly reversed course. The forward tip surfaces the vortex as the rear end dives in.

1. **LEVINE**: This is just a personal preference, but I find present tense off-putting here.

2. **CORVISIERO**: The author is telling us what we are seeing instead of describing it. There is nothing interesting, eloquent, or creative here. Also, we aren't even told which particles are being crashed against each other to cause the massive explosion that would cause the black hole. The science is inaccurate. Even if it is fiction, it needs to be plausible and well researched.

3. **RANTA**: Brilliant detail is the heart of successful science fiction, and very general terms like "full speed" and "time portal" makes the very first sentence feel generic and boring. How can the reader be interested if they can't picture the craft or its journey? How will your science fiction be different from the thousands of others?

4. **NELSON**: This opening has a problem that I see quite often in science fiction submissions that cross my desk—it's so detailed and dense with world-building that it's hard to find an access point into the story. In general, being intrigued by a character is what makes me want to read more, and there's no character here at all.

4. PARANORMAL ROMANCE

"I'm drowning," I struggled to shout. "Jeffrey, I'm drowning."

Fortunately Ella recorded the words I spoke in my past life regression, because I didn't recall anything. What I heard on the tape must have been the words I remembered before my birth in this life. She had quickly brought me out of the trance. **❶**

* * *

Michael had traveled over 50 years through time to find the woman he loved. And I wasn't sure if the woman he had sought was me—or someone else.

What mattered was he had become my Michael. I peacefully looked at him each morning, asleep in my large bed, now our bed, and experienced a sense of amazement that he was here with me in my time and my place. He was not in his world—or that in between space where we had first met. **❹**

As handsome as I had thought he'd be when I first sensed his presence, those many months ago, he was not a physical being then. **❸** That happened later. But I didn't care. It was not his sensitive, good looks **❷** that made me love him.

It was an absolute knowledge that we belonged together regardless of how absurd our finding each other might be. And it was an instant acceptance that his love for me was one that had lasted through eternity. I couldn't explain that feeling, nor could I explain how he had travelled in time.

---

1. **LEVINE**: I'm confused. I can't figure out who's who or what's what.

2. **CORVISIERO**: Good looks aren't sensitive. This is a cliché description that doesn't make literal sense. I found it strange that the author would start with Ella pulling the MC out of a trance about her birth. The first paragraph is like a short prologue that makes no sense. The next paragraph jumps to something completely unrelated. This sort of technique is distracting, and it threatens to diminish the reader's ability to connect with the story.

3. **RANTA**: I have no idea what's going on. I'm disoriented and confused. Michael appears to be a time-traveler who's been reunited with the main character, but the sentence construction is confusing as well, which compounds the clarity issue. "What I heard on the tape must have been the words I remembered before my birth in this life" was a sentence I had to spend some time unpacking, which isn't an auspicious start.

4. **NELSON**: This sounds like it's headed towards a unique and potentially interesting premise, but unfortunately, it falls victim to one of the deadly flaws of opening pages—it confuses me to the point of giving up. There's a *lot* happening in these first 150 words: drowning, trances, time travel, a romance, some sort of alternate "between space." It's great to create a sense of mystery to encourage the reader to continue, but in short, I'm lost.

5. MAINSTREAM FICTION

Nora clutched her mother's book as she surveyed ❶ the Abbey Church of Fontevraud. The white stone, thick arches, and black, scaly roof sat like a squat mushroom on the bright green lawn of the medieval abbey. The façade was plain, unadorned like its later gothic descendants would be, but the whitewashed beauty reached into her imagination and turned up the corners of her mouth.

She absentmindedly rubbed the folded down page where her mother had written *July 28th, Fontevraud*. And here was Nora, visiting this historic abbey the same day that her mother had visited, five years earlier. Nora loved that coincidence.

But she didn't love the way she'd been feeling ever since her class arrived in the Loire Valley. A throbbing headache had intensified over the days leading up to the abbey visit. She rubbed her forehead, her eyes closed against the afternoon sun. Maybe she had just built up the trip too much in her mind, putting too much pressure on herself as usual. Releasing the clip that held up her thick hair eased the tension, and she sighed as the tangled waves fell to her shoulders.

"Are you okay?" Nora's roommate, Maddie, pulled her earbuds off to scrutinize her.

Nora wrinkled her nose. "I still have a headache."

"I would milk that headache for every nap I could," said Maddie. "God forbid you miss another church tour." She waved her arms in an exaggerated flourish, smiling at Nora's mock outrage.

"Just another church tour?" Nora held up her book, *The Life of Eleanor of Aquitaine,* and pointed at the cover. "It's where *she* was buried." ❷ ❸ ❹

---

1. **LEVINE**: "Surveyed" is too pretentious, unless she's actually a surveyor.

2. **CORVISIERO**: I was rewarded with an explanation to some of the questions I had by reading to the end of the page. I think that this has potential, but it needs editing. Some of the expressions and syntax used need to be tweaked for clarity and effect.

3. **RANTA**: I love this first page and would definitely read more. Great detail, clean sentences, interesting introduction to themes to come. My only note is you don't pull earbuds "off," you pull them "out"—but hardly a rejectable offense!

4. **NELSON**: This first page really worked for me! I have a sense of place and atmosphere without the setting being belabored too much. I get some clues as to the kind of person Nora is, and with the last line, I have a hint of where the plot is headed and enough questions to keep me reading. I'm intrigued to find out more, which is exactly what a good first page should do.

6. MEMOIR

My first true love was not with a boyfriend, but with a French bulldog named Grizzly. He is stuffed inside a black doggy duffle bag ❶, and climbs on top of his siblings, squirming and worming his way to the pinnacle of a puppy pile. It looks like a moving pyramid of pigs snorting their way out to freedom. My breeder Sarah grabs Grizzly by the nape of the neck with one hand as if she is snatching up Chow Mein noodles with chopsticks, and plops him on our plate—her living room floor. French bulldog puppies sell out faster than the latest iPhone, and I know I have to act fast. Sara had sent me photos a week prior to our visit of the entire litter before my boyfriend Jeff and I arrived at her house. The four Frenchie puppies came in an assortment of colors and various breeder-designated superhero names: ❹

- Cream-colored Storm,
- A fawn named Elektra
- Black and Tan brindled Zorro
- Black and White pied Batman

His brother and sisters were all adorable, but they didn't quite tug at my heartstrings the way Zorro did, with those seductive, take-me-home bulging blue eyes. In one of his photos, Zorro sat stoically in front of Sara's fireplace with a big belly hanging down to his hind legs. I was instantly enamored. Now I just had to get Jeff to fall in love the way I was smitten with him. His stiff body language on the car ride up to Sara's showed his clear hesitation. ❸ I could tell he didn't want to share in the expense or the responsibility of a dog. Our relationship had always been about freedom. Any one of us could walk out at a moment's notice because we didn't own anything together. ❷

1. **LEVINE**: You don't need "with" in the first line. Also, why is this in present tense?

2. **CORVISIERO**: The writing here is solid. It held my attention to the end even though I was starting to question why I should be reading a story about someone loving their dog more than their boyfriend. In other words, I didn't get the hook. Toward the end of the page, the author began delivering the needed details about her relationship with Jeff and how they had gotten to this point. So I would have continued to read more.

3. **RANTA**: The writing is capable, and who doesn't love a puppy pile, but what's the unique, universal angle? Why will a general readership care about Grizzly? I'm not convinced the author is looking beyond her own love for him.

4. **NELSON**: This author has started with a great first sentence and has what seems like a fun story idea and strong voice. A concern, though, is that the author switches back and forth between past and present tense several times in this first paragraph, which makes me confused about when exactly the events described are happening.

7. MEMOIR

The first time I saw the old woman I was crouched on my hunkers, hidden deep in the tall, uncut late winter grass hay. My brother Danny and two of his buddies stood at the creek's edge twenty feet from where I peered, unseen, from between the grass stalks. They had their pants flies unzipped and were concentrating on who could pee with the most accuracy, using a large maple leaf floating in an eddy pool against the far bank for target practice. They took turns, laughing and gesturing with glee, rating each other's attempts on a scale from one to ten. Eventually the boys ran out of ammunition, zipped up their pants and resorted to throwing rocks.

I was concentrating so hard on watching the contest without making a sound that I missed the rustle of approaching footsteps. When the hand touched my shoulder I startled and fell plop on my behind wounding my dignity (if I had had any) worse than my fanny. I let out a screech and scrambled to my feet. Danny's head shot round as if on a swivel. He spotted my blue shorts and striped Tee shirt bright against the soft golds and tans of standing hay, his brows beetling together in an ominous scowl as he recognized me.

"You was spyin' on us, wasn't you, Leah! Oh boy—are you gonna get it!" Danny shook his fist in my direction ❸, his face glowing crimson as he realized what he and his buddies had been doing. The boys turned as a unit and splashed down the creek, muttering among themselves and plotting retribution.

"I did not mean to startle thee, girl. Are thee all right?" queried a pleasant voice behind me. I rose to my feet and rotated to put a face to the voice—a wrinkled, tanned gnome face, back lit and featureless. *The oldest person I have ever seen crouches before me, offering a steadying hand. I flinch from her and bolt a few feet backward. She stands up, brushing dust and grass stems from her long, black skirt. The gnome-face splits apart with a wide grin.* ❷ ❹

1. Levine did not review this page.

2. **CORVISIERO**: I read the entire page because I found the situation interesting. I think it is a strong way to begin the story. That said, the last few sentences shouldn't be in italics.

3. **RANTA**: This has some pleasant scene-setting, but the writing doesn't feel especially strong. Phrases like "wounding my dignity (if I had had any)" and "I let out a screech" and "shook his fist" are a bit hackneyed and didn't make me feel like this book will be offering anything especially fresh or memorable.

4. **NELSON**: My first red flag went up with the dialogue, which struck me as a little tinny, but more importantly, at this point in the page, I started to feel a bit lost as to what kind of story this was. I'm not clear why some of the page is in italics, and I'm also confused by the two speakers with two different dialects—what time period does this take place in? This is a case where I think the author needs to ease me into the story a little more slowly.

8. MIDDLE GRADE

The Kawishiwi River ran fast in July.

"Hey, Scooter, come here. I have a treat for you." Even though Pete was four years older than me, he had to hang with me on family vacations. "You're almost eleven. You can handle this," he said.

Mom butted in. "Be careful. You know Sam's not as experienced as you are." She was always worried about something, especially about me. When she wanted to embarrass me, she told everyone she named me Sam because it conjured up someone sweet and gentle.

Pete lifted the fiberglass canoe so it wouldn't scrape over the granite shelf where we'd stashed it for the night. He flipped it over and slipped it into the water so sweet that it barely made a sound.

I shoved the life jacket to the middle of the canoe and climbed into the bow so Pete could steer from the stern.

Once we were away from shore, Pete whispered, "We're going to shoot the spillway."

I swallowed, maybe gulped was more like it. I didn't want to disappoint him, but I couldn't keep from saying it: ❸ "No, Pete, Mom will kill us."

He just laughed.

Even if Mom didn't kill us, the spillway might. The water gushed over an old dam and dropped practically six feet to where it churned around the rocks at the bottom.

"What about the rocks?" I asked. ❶ ❷

1. **LEVINE**: I liked this and read the entire page. It made me want to keep reading—I want to know what happens.

2. **CORVISIERO**: I read the entire page. This author is setting up the plot quite nicely. I would keep reading. My only concern thus far is that, at times, the voice sounds a bit like an adult telling a story of something that happened when he was a child. If writing in the first-person point of view, the voice needs to sound legitimate to the age group being represented.

3. **RANTA**: Great opening line, but the writing starts to fall apart with heavy-handed dialogue tags ("Mom butted in," "Pete whispered") and lost me with too much telling, not showing: "She was always worried about something, especially me" and "I didn't want to disappoint him." This story has a great setting and interesting character dynamics, and the dread is already building, but the writer needs to get out of the way.

4. Nelson did not review this page.

9. URBAN FANTASY / MAGICAL REALISM

In the dark crept something darker, but I dismissed it as merely shadows. A swaying branch perhaps, or a deer tensing until I finished stuffing the can with garbage. Something abnormal never crossed my mind, not even with my scalp prickling and my heart pounding. After all, excitement in this town meant the first gunshot of open season, and battered morels sizzling in oil. Muggings were rare here, murder nonexistent. Crimes occurred behind closed doors, and often by a man who swore he loved you.

I started back up the walkway but froze mid-step when I entered the porch light's glow. It flickered, then dimmed, and I didn't feel the security I normally did. I felt *exposed*, as if the light was an agent of the shadows, highlighting my position for all the night to see. Behind me, wind chimes dinged in the gnarled oak tree. Woodsmoke drifted on the breeze. I released a shaky breath but the cloud of mist didn't leave my lips; it fled with my body-heat, as if the night was a singing siren, her music luring my warmth away. Dread seeped into my marrow ❸. Unseen eyes bore into the back of my skull. I rubbed my arms and summoned the courage to glance over my shoulder. The sky was clouded, the darkness beyond the oak tree expanding into infinity. The world seemed empty. Hollow. If I listened closely I might have heard the shadows echo. But still, it was only blackness. ❹

❶ *Stop being a goose, Miriam. The night is just playing tricks with your imagination*, I told myself, unaware the dark would soon make me tremble more than any nightmare. But right then, in a nowhere town in rural Appalachia, shivering on a cement walkway in flannel pajamas and fuzzy penguin slippers on a cloudy, winter night, I did not believe in magic or mystical creatures. ❷

1. **LEVINE**: This paragraph should open the story, so we know the narrator is female.

2. **CORVISIERO**: This is a great start to a suspenseful urban fantasy. I read the entire page without pause and was captivated. I have only one criticism: The author has a tendency to overdo drama. The reader needs to have the opportunity to draw some conclusions and shouldn't be underestimated by repetitive details said in different words.

3. **RANTA**: There are some lovely turns of phrase here, but these opening sentences are a bit too thick with description, which finally reached purple with "dread seeped into my marrow." There are only so many ways an author can convey unease before the reader is ready for some action.

4. **NELSON**: This first page has a lot going for it—the writing here is strong, with some nice voice. But I would stop reading at this point because this set-up feels very familiar. To be honest, many of the submissions that I pass on are actually fairly well written, but the market is tough and "fairly well-written" isn't enough. The story has to feel fresh and different as well. Starting with a common opening makes it less likely that a submission will stand out enough from the crowd to get me intrigued.

10. YOUNG ADULT

"Dad I know, but if I wear clothes they might see me."

"I don't think you've thought this through? You can't be sure when you'll become visible again and if you're on the way to school or…" ❸

"I *can* tell when it's going to stop, so then I could run for cover."

Dad looked at me and shook his head. "Bob, you just have to trust my judgment on this. Don't let that happen. Don't walk around without clothes. This is not a suggestion. This is something serious. Do not do this. Do you understand?"

I knew he was right but I was still thinking of all the fun I could have being invisible and being where no one could see me, even if it was a little cold sometimes, and now I realize it might be dangerous and I gotta work at making some clothes invisible too. ❶

One of the worst things about being smart is that grown-ups expect you to act different than the other kids. More grown up or something, and that's hard ❹. When they made me take a test in school and they found out my IQ, Mom was really happy but Dad said to not let it go to my head, "Smart kids are only as smart as the things they accomplish." He always has a saying for everything and I sort of understood what he meant this time, but I'm a kid and what can I accomplish? Well, I got a clue this summer. That's when I realized that knowing things can really be fun. ❷

1. **LEVINE**: Too long and convoluted—I don't understand what's happening. After this, the next paragraph has way too much exposition.

2. **CORVISIERO**: I love this interesting concept, so I read the entire page, but I believe that most agents would stop reading at the second narrative paragraph. I had to slow down to try to understand all the details that were cramped into it. This story is categorized as a young adult story, but the voice of the protagonist sounds more middle grade.

3. **RANTA**: I'm not invested in these characters to find their dialogue interesting yet, and for a book titled "The Invisible Boy," this feels a bit on the nose. These opening lines make me think the book is missing the nuance and subtlety that'd make it an interesting read. It also sounds very young for a young adult audience.

4. **NELSON**: This page definitely has a strong voice, which is great—but the problem here is that the sample is labeled young adult, and the voice feels too young for that category. This protagonist reads as somewhere in the 8-10 years old range to me, whereas YA protagonists are generally 14 years old and up. If this sample was labeled middle grade, I might have a completely different reaction to it, because I would be going in with different expectations.

CREATE GREAT CHARACTERS

15 ideas on how to bring characters to life.

....

by Elizabeth Sims

If you've ever finished reading a piece of fiction and thought, *I'm going to miss those people*, you've experienced true identification with the characters. This is one of the hallmarks of great fiction, and it doesn't happen by chance. (Please post a review wherever you hang out online.)

In creating compelling characters, the best authors work purposefully, and they don't waste time—or words. Whether working in short form or long, they know how to sketch characters quickly and accurately, then add dimension in nimble strokes as they go. Difficult? It doesn't have to be. The hacks that follow can help you swiftly establish a character in a short story, and they also can make for economy and originality in longer fiction, particularly in your opening chapters, when it's crucial to draw readers in and make them care about your people right away.

1. TURN UP THE CONTRAST

As a university student, I learned how to make photographs using film, chemicals, paper, and time. When I was stumped as to how to improve a photograph, I would fiddle with the variables that affected contrast, knowing that sharper contrast often resulted in a more arresting picture.

It stands to reason: When something is viewed in contrast to another thing, it becomes keener, more vivid. In fiction, you can use countless aspects of character to differentiate and enhance: Holmes and Watson (temperament), Scrooge and Cratchit (morality), Romeo and Juliet (loyalty), HAL 9000 and Dave (humanity).

Here's how the romantic Watson sums up Holmes' heart: "He never spoke of the softer passions, save with a gibe and a sneer." Sir Arthur Conan Doyle took care to make the two men as different as possible, while uniting them through intellectual friendship.

Take risks! How about pairing a 6-year-old genius with her demented grandpa? An Army drill instructor with a sleazy Mafia hood?

2. HOLD THEM HOSTAGE

Even small contrasts can be dramatic when amplified by *context*. In his well-loved Victorian novel *Tom Brown's School Days,* Thomas Hughes created characters who existed at their boys' school within a narrow range of age, race, privilege, values—and yet what a binful of personalities! In the pressure of a microcosm from which there is no escape, minor differences loom larger: a few inches of height, a few years of age, a propensity to follow, a propensity to lead, a weakness for pleasure, a disinclination toward responsibility.

Prompt your characters into memorable action by forcing them into close proximity. Think beyond a literal hostage situation (which itself can be a great choice): perhaps a pair of truck drivers who must share a sleeper cab on a long-haul trip, or a bartender who's being stalked by a regular customer.

3. DO SOME COSTUME DESIGN

While rewatching *The Birds* recently, I noticed that once Tippi Hedren gets to Bodega Bay, the character wears the same gorgeous green Edith Head suit through the rest of the movie (because she's stuck there without luggage). It reminded me of another

Alfred Hitchcock classic, *North by Northwest,* wherein man-on-the-run Cary Grant remains in one exquisite gray suit.

A characterizing outfit is a great visual, you might think, *but how could that work on the page?* Consider Holden Caulfield's red hunting hat. There's symbolism there (alienation, perhaps; searching—or hunting), and after a point, mere mention of it plucks a little thread of emotion in the attentive reader.

In my latest novel, *Left Field,* one of my characters is the catcher on a women's slow-pitch softball team. To highlight her insecurity, I portrayed her as always wearing unnecessarily extreme safety gear: mask, chest protector, etc.

START WITH A NAME

In her bestselling Hunger Games trilogy, Suzanne Collins uses names to help distinguish many different characters while adding subtle meaning. For instance, Thresh is from the agricultural district. Cato (an homage to the Roman military figure and statesman Cato the Elder?) is a highly skilled warrior and leader.

If that seems too overt, try this: Instead of focusing on a character's primary identification, brainstorm a secondary trait that's hidden at first. A woman with a secret might be called Pearl, an alcoholic might be nicknamed Tip, and so forth. Be sparing with allegorical names—they can get tiresome in quantity, but their selective use can enrich your readers' experience.

5. SEND TRAITS TO WAR

William Shakespeare is terrific to study for character development in all grades of coarse and fine. He gives Macbeth, for instance, enough strength of character to be ruthlessly ambitious, but he also bestows him with a guilty conscience. Macbeth can't figure out how to have both a clean life and a triumphant one, so he blows everything and ends up annihilated.

Matching up contradictory traits within one character is story gold. To hit on something quickly, zero in on your character's key positive trait—valor, ingenuity, compassion—then write a short scene that reveals a fleck of the exact opposite. The warm, generous music teacher finds herself intensely envious of her star pupil, to the point of fantasizing about … sabotage at the upcoming recital?

6. SCAR TENDER FLESH

Everybody carries scars, both physical and psychological. Give one or two to your characters. The way a character deals with past pain can be deeply revealing: Is he a stoic? Or a wuss who will do anything to avoid more discomfort? A scar can represent a price paid for wisdom, or it can fuel a vengeful life.

It's easy to drop a scar into a character's life. In Flannery O'Connor's famously chilling short story "A Good Man Is Hard to Find," the Misfit clearly carries psychological scars having to do with whatever led him to murder his own father, and presumably more scars from his sub-sequent imprison-ment. Captain Ahab's leg, missing down the gullet of the eponymous Moby Dick, fuels his monomaniacal—and doomed—drive to destroy the beast.

7. PUT IN A ROCK, THEN ADD A HARD PLACE.

The impossible choice serves as a lightning quick reveal of a character's true self. Usually we see this technique at the heart of a dramatic novel—William Styron's *Sophie's Choice*, for instance.

But the impossible choice can be used in a smaller, quicker way any time: The alcoholic nun must choose between a drink today and the confessional tomorrow; the little boy must choose which best friend to give his extra candy bar to; the army sentry must decide in a split second whether to shoot the apparently confused pregnant woman, who might be rushing forward with a bomb under her blouse instead of an unborn baby.

8. TAKE THEM TO THE BANK.

Another brushstroke you can use to paint a character's true colors is the handling of money. In Thomas Wolfe's *You Can't Go Home Again*, the minor character of Nebraska Crane is introduced early. In the famous train scene, he's mobbed by his hometown's business leaders, who try to convince him to speculate on property, the value of which is surging.

When he resists, we understand the core of his character, and we gain a fore-shadowing of what's to come:

> *"I already got me a farm out in Zebu-lon," he said, and, grinning—"It's paid fer, too! … That's all I want. I couldn't use no more."*

You could write a character who does something as small as dropping pennies from his pocket because they're just too cumbersome to carry. Do we instantly know something about him without being told? You bet we do.

9. BESTOW A GIFT.

In *The Mists of Avalon*, Marion Zimmer Bradley's 1983 blockbuster retelling of the Arthurian legend from the perspective of women, she distinguishes the character of Morgaine by giving her special powers: Morgaine might be considered a sorceress or a seer.

Although part of the deal is the supernatural power itself, the developmental part comes when the character becomes aware of the gift. How does she react? Furthermore, the gift keeps on giving (to you as the author *and* to your readers) by sustaining your story as the character encounters new and unexpected uses—and potential abuses—for her gifts.

One way to hack this one fast: Simply endow a character with intuition a shade better than anybody else's. Throughout the story, then, the reader will know to expect that character to sense things before others do, and react—or manipulate the situation—accordingly.

10. ALL IN A GURU.

The role of mentor is a powerful one, and can help you steer your protagonist in new directions without having to lay much groundwork. The gentle relationship between the lonely child Mary and the gardener Ben, depicted by Frances Hodgson Burnett in the perennial (pun intended) favorite *The Secret Garden*, is simple as can be, yet powerful. Same with Professor Dumbledore and Harry Potter in *The Sorcerer's Stone*.

The beauty of this one is that a guru or mentor can turn up suddenly and help your protagonist mature and develop when nothing else seems to work.

11. TOSS A NET.

Throwing a net over a character is a way to give your readers instant insight into that player's self-control, courage, and competence (or lack thereof). George Saunders' protagonist in the blackly funny story "The Semplica Girl Diaries," for instance, is a family man who struggles in the net of his limited income and his family's expectations. Quickly enough, his struggles show that he's incapable of basic maturity. In fact, we perceive that he's a desperate loser, and damned in his quest to keep up with the richer folk by hyperextending his credit, not to mention his credibility.

In your own work, try thwarting a character and see what happens. This thwarting can be large—divorce papers—or small—a traffic ticket. For instance, someone slapped with a speeding violation might lose his temper and launch an obscene tirade against the cop, thus making everything worse, while a different character in a similar situation would keep composed and carry on. These psychological responses are powerful indicators of character. Something as small as a shrug in the face of difficulty can speak volumes.

12. KNOW THEIR NUMBER.

Even if you never discuss the birth order of your characters in your story, you can deepen their lives if you know how their place in their family has influenced their character. Most families have one kid—typically the youngest—who becomes the watcher: the one who figures out that Daddy is having an affair with Mrs. Thornside down the street before anybody else senses it. A younger child can observe an older one get in trouble, and learn how to fly under the radar and get away with a lot more.

Older children often learn bullying skills, naturally enough when the littler ones are so easy to push around. But they also can learn how to care for and nurture the small and the weak.

13. ENGINEER A TEMPTATION.

In Homer's Greek epic *The Odyssey*, a gang of sexy temptresses called the Sirens loudly attempt to lure Ulysses and his ship to an inglorious end on the rocks. To foil them, he bids his men to plug their ears and then tie him to his ship's mast so he cannot himself steer them toward destruction. This is great drama that still scans well today, and that single scene has served to cement the character of Ulysses in millions of readers' minds and hearts.

Temptation works so well because we all can relate to it. From that package of cookies sitting alluringly in the cupboard to the Jaguar we cannot possibly afford, everybody has felt the pull of forbidden fruit, and wondered about the self-destructive impulses behind it. Arrange for your characters to be tempted, to yield, to resist, to feel the slings and arrows of self-sabotage, and to experience the consequences.

14. GIVE YOUR NARRATOR AN OPINION.

Whether working in the first, second, or third person, you almost certainly have somebody doing bits of narration. Don't forget that your narrator has a point of view! Make use of it, as Alice Munro does in her story "Pictures of the Ice." A description of a female character in a photograph we see only this once:

> Short fair hair combed around her face in a businesslike way, brown slacks, white sweatshirt, with the fairly large bumps of her breasts and stomach plain to see, she meets the camera head-on and doesn't seem worried about what it will make of her.

We get it: She's not a knockout, and she's quite secure in herself. One sentence.

Your narrator, too, can notice telling details about your characters, and deliver the info just as decisively.

15. DIG DEEP.

This last hack is one you can work on yourself as an author. When you find yourself stumped for character-development ideas, step back and get humble. Here's the key: If you operate on the theory that your characters are deeper than you'll ever discover, you can't go wrong.

Explore these three things about each of your main characters:

1. What does he *say* he wants?
2. What does he *think* he wants?
3. What does he *really* (subconsciously) want?

You'll discover endless possibilities, and if you've given the previous hacks a try, you'll be able to figure out your own new ones as you go.

ELIZABETH SIMS's latest novel is *Left Field*, the fifth book in the Lillian Byrd Crime series. A WD contributing editor, she blogs on zestful writing and living at esimsauthor.blogspot.com.

9 WAYS TO A NONFICTION BOOK DEAL

Shortcuts to getting agents interested.

by Susan Shapiro

After 22 years of struggling to build a writing career, six months of rejections on the road to landing literary representation, and then another six months until that agent found a fantastic editor to take me on, I still had to wait 18 months for my debut book to come out. I was told this was fast. For a wildly impatient and broke 42-year-old journalist used to quickly seeing print in daily newspapers and webzines, that seemed like a lifetime. Since then, over the course of publishing nine books with some of the top houses in the country—and helping 80 of my writing students get book deals during the last decade—I've learned that, fortunately, there *are* ways to speed up the process while improving both your prose and your chances.

1. FINISH MORE PAGES FIRST.

Many aspiring authors think that while you must write an entire novel to sell it, you need complete only a short proposal to land a nonfiction deal. While that's sometimes true, it's also true that many agents

and publishers of memoir and narrative nonfiction prefer to see a complete manuscript—and that several first-timers I know who signed a contract based on a few sample chapters wound up choking, unable to cough up 200 more pages on deadline, and had to pay back their book advances.

Never forget: Cream rises. The sooner you write an entire great book, the easier it will be to entice an agent and book editor into publishing it. Your eventual agent might read your manuscript and then decide to submit only a "partial" to editors. But with more pages at least you—and your agent—will know you're for real, and be better positioned to craft a powerful pitch reflecting that.

2. HIRE YOUR OWN GHOST EDITOR.

Imagine if you could work on kicking your manuscript or proposal into shape with an expert who has been an agent or book editor for years—*before* showing it to anyone else. Guess what? You can! There are excellent, seasoned book doctors and editors you can hire to fix your pages, give you feedback and honest criticism, and let you know if or when your project is ready to go professional. True, it's an upfront investment, but this is my secret weapon for being prolific—and if you'd like to contact me personally, I'd be happy to recommend my favorites.

3. GET HEAT WITH AN ESSAY CLIP.

Insiders know one of the best ways to attract interest in a book is by first publishing a short excerpt or essay related to your book idea. One great provocative personal piece can lure professionals to call *you*, saving you a frustrating and lengthy search. My student Laura Zam's recent 1,500-word essay "Healing Sought (Bring Your Own Magic)" ran in *The New York Times* Modern Love column on a Sunday. By Monday three agents and two editors had contacted her. Similar experiences were also true of my protégés Liza Monroy (whose book *The Marriage Act* got its start in *Psychology Today*), Lisa L. Kirchner (her memoir *Hello American Lady Creature* was launched in the *Washington Post*), Maria E. Andreu (her YA novel *The Secret Side of Empty* began in *Newsweek*) and Abby Sher (whose book *Amen, Amen, Amen* started in *Self*). Lots of agents and editors routinely read these publications and others looking for prospective book projects.

4. GET MORE BANG FOR YOUR BLOG.

Several of my former students have landed meetings, agents and book deals through a hotly titled blog—including Leandra Medine's *Man Repeller* and Kayli Stollak's *Granny Is My Wingman*. In fact, free blog site Tumblr actually has a "literary liaison" now—it's my former student Rachel Fershleiser, and she says more than 100 traditional book publishers have bit from Tumblr bloggers so far (Liesl Schillinger's *Wordbirds: An Irreverent Lexicon for the 21st Century* is one example). You need a lot of hits to get attention, but sometimes a clever concept can go viral or catch the right person's eye—and push you toward publication quicker. It can't hurt to try.

5. LEVERAGE SOCIAL MEDIA.

It's well known that what would become the book and TV show "$#*! My Dad Says" started as then-struggling writer Justin Halpern's Twitter feed, but less sensational success stories are anything but anomalies these days. Consider ways to use Twitter, Tumblr, Facebook, LinkedIn and Instagram to help support your book concept (and while you're at it, take down any half-naked photos, unless your goal is to be a centerfold!). That way, the minute an agent or editor has a reason to search for your name online, good stuff pops up.

6. JOIN UP.

While for decades I prided myself on being a loner and an outsider, when I wanted to publish a Jewish-themed novel, I found that I needed a bigger platform and more of a connection to my audience. So I joined many organizations I thought might support my eventual book. I became a member of Hadassah, reached out to World ORT and the UJA-Federation of New York, and reconnected with old temples in my hometown Michigan neighborhood. I also joined the University of Michigan and New York University alumni associations, and it wasn't long before NYU invited me to give a speech at its annual alumni conference. The bigger your outreach, the easier it will be to prove to agents and editors you can effectively market yourself and your book, whether fiction or nonfiction.

7. PITCH LIKE HOLLYWOOD.

I described my first memoir *Five Men Who Broke My Heart* in a Hollywood movie sort of way, as a "book for anyone who has ever wondered what happened to their first love. Or second. Or third. Or fourth. Or fifth." Come up with a great title and a few lines to explain your concept quickly and get people excited. This will help you to land an agent, the agent to get a book editor, the editor to motivate the marketing people, the marketing people to entice the booksellers and mainstream media, and on and on.

8. GET ON THE AIR.

Dr. Diana Kirschner, a psychologist specializing in relationships, was a guest on a New York radio show the day her future agent, Wendy Sherman, happened to tune in. Sherman went on to sell her resulting book, *Love in 90 Days*. My former student Judy Batalion's appearance on "Anderson Cooper 360°," to talk about her family history of hoarding, helped her land a *New York Times* Motherlode columnist spot and a Penguin book deal. True, these are coveted appearances, but these days, news coverage is 24/7, so there's plenty of on-air time to fill. If you have *any* radio/TV contacts, use them. If not, see Nos. 3–6 to increase your odds of making these kinds of connections.

9. COLLECT ENDORSEMENTS.

When my friend Jackson Taylor finished his dazzling debut novel, *The Blue Orchard*, he asked colleagues at the graduate writing program where he worked if they'd recommend it. They did! So he handed in stellar blurbs by Sapphire, Vivian Gornick, Marie Ponsot, Hettie Jones, and Phillip Lopate along with the manuscript. The Simon & Schuster editor who bought it told me the first thing she saw was those blurbs—and she was already impressed before reading word one.

"Well, I'm not in a writing program with those kinds of contacts," someone I know lamented. While getting involved with a good writing program is worth considering, it's not as hard as you think to get endorsed. Ask your teachers, mentors, prominent members of organizations you belong to (see No. 6), even authors you admire. (I have recommended all 80 of my students' books, leading one of my editors to call me "a blurb whore.")

Still stumped? Go back to No. 3 and get some ink, and the blurbs may just come to you. After my student Aspen Matis published her beautiful Modern Love essay "A Hiker's Guide to Healing," *Wild* author Cheryl Strayed posted a laudatory comment on Facebook and *The New York Times* columnist Nicholas Kristof tweeted a tribute. At my urging, Matis asked Strayed and Kristof if she could quote them in her future book pitches—and they both said yes.

To paraphrase the philosopher Goethe: *Upon the moment of commitment, the world conspires to help you.* Always remember: The harder you work, the luckier you'll get.

SUSAN SHAPIRO is a Manhattan writing teacher, author of 8 books, and most recently coauthor of *The Bosnia List*. Follow her on Twitter @susanshapiro or her website at susanshaprio.net.

HOW NOT TO START YOUR BOOK

Learn agents' chapter 1 pet peeves.

by Chuck Sambuchino

Ask literary agents what they're looking for in a first chapter and they'll all say the same thing: "Good writing that hooks me in." Agents appreciate the same elements of good writing that readers do. They want action; they want compelling characters and a reason to read on; they want to see your voice come through in the work and feel an immediate connection with your writing style.

Sure, the fact that agents look for great writing and a unique voice is nothing new. But, for as much as you know about what agents *want* to see in chapter one, what about all those things they *don't* want to see? Obvious mistakes such as grammatical errors and awkward writing aside, writers need to be conscious of first-chapter clichés and agent pet peeves—any of which can sink a manuscript and send a form rejection letter your way.

Have you ever begun a story with a character waking up from a dream? Or opened chapter one with a line of salacious dialogue? Both clichés! Chances are, you've started a story with a cliché or touched on a pet peeve (or many!) in your writing and you don't even know it—and nothing turns off an agent like what agent Cricket Freeman of The August Agency calls "nerve-gangling, major turn-off, ugly-as-sin, nails-on-the-blackboard pet peeves."

To help compile a grand list of these poisonous chapter 1 no-no's, plenty of established literary agents were more than happy to chime in and vent about everything that they can't stand to see in that all-important first chapter. Here's what they had to say.

DESCRIPTION

"I dislike endless 'laundry list' character descriptions. For example: 'She had eyes the color of a summer sky and long blonde hair that fell in ringlets past her shoulders. Her petite nose was the perfect size for her heart-shaped face. Her azure dress—with the empire waist and long, tight sleeves—sported tiny pearl buttons down the bodice and ivory lace peeked out of the hem in front, blah, blah, blah.' Who cares! Work it into the story."

—LAURIE MCLEAN, Fuse Literary

"Slow writing with a lot of description will put me off very quickly. I personally like a first chapter that moves quickly and draws me in so I'm immediately hooked and want to read more."

—ANDREA HURST, Andrea Hurst & Associates Literary Management

VOICE AND POINT-OF-VIEW

"A pet peeve of mine is ragged, fuzzy point-of-view. How can a reader follow what's happening? I also dislike beginning with a killer's POV. What reader would want to be in such an ugly place? I feel like a nasty voyeur."

—CRICKET FREEMAN, The August Agency

"An opening that's predictable will not hook me in. If the average person could have come up with the characters and situations, I'll pass. I'm looking for a unique outlook, voice, or character and situation."

—DEBBIE CARTER, formerly of Muse Literary Management

"Avoid the opening line 'My name is …,' introducing the narrator to the reader so blatantly. There are far better ways in chapter one to establish an instant connection between narrator and reader."

—MICHELLE ANDELMAN, Regal Literary

"I hate reading purple prose, taking the time to set up—to describe something so beautifully and that has nothing to do with the ac-tual story. I also hate when an author starts something and then says '(the main character) would find out later.' I hate gratuitous sex and violence anywhere in the manuscript. If it is not crucial to the story then I don't want to see it in there, in any chapters."

—CHERRY WEINER, Cherry Weiner Literary

"I recently read a manuscript when the second line was something like, 'Let me tell you this, Dear Reader …' What do *you* think of that?"

—SHEREE BYKOFSKY, Sheree Bykofsky Literary

ACTION (OR LACK THEREOF)

"I don't really like first-day-of-school beginnings, or the 'From the beginning of time,' or 'Once upon a time' starts. Specifically, I dislike a chapter one where nothing happens."

—JESSICA REGEL, Foundry Literary + Media

" 'The Weather' is always a problem—the author feels he has to take time to set up the scene completely and tell us who the characters are. I like starting a story *in media res*."

—ELIZABETH POMADA, Larsen/Pomada, Literary Agents

"I want to feel as if I'm in the hands of a master storyteller, and starting a story with long, flowery, overly descriptive sentences (kind of like this one) makes the writer seem amateurish and the story contrived. Of course, an equally jarring beginning can be nearly as off-putting, and I hesitate to read on if I'm feeling disoriented by the fifth page. I enjoy when writers can find a good balance between exposition and mystery. Too much accounting always ruins the mystery of a novel, and the unknown is what propels us to read further. It is what keeps me up at night saying, 'Just one more chapter, then I'll sleep.' If everything is explained away in the first chapter, I'm probably putting the book down and going to sleep."

—PETER MILLER,
Global Lion Management

"Characters that are moving around doing little things, but essentially nothing. Washing dishes and thinking, staring out the window and thinking, tying shoes, thinking. Authors often do this to transmit information, but the result is action in a literal sense but no real energy in a narrative sense. The best rule of thumb is always to start the story where the story starts."

—DAN LAZAR, Writers House

CLICHÉS AND FALSE BEGINNINGS

"I *hate* it when a book begins with an adventure that turns out to be a dream at the end of the chapter."

—MOLLIE GLICK,
Foundry Literary + Media

"Anything cliché such as 'It was a dark and stormy night' will turn me off. I hate when a narrator or author addresses the reader (e.g., 'Gentle reader')."

—JENNIE DUNHAM, Dunham Literary

"Sometimes a reasonably good writer will create an interesting character and describe him in a compelling way, but then he'll turn out to be some unimportant bit

player. I also don't want to read about anyone sleeping, dreaming, waking up, or staring at anything. Other annoying, unoriginal things I see too often: some young person going home to a small town for a funeral, someone getting a phone call about a death, a description of a psycho lurking in the shadows or a terrorist planting a bomb."

—ELLEN PEPUS,
Signature Literary Agency

"I don't like it when the main character dies at the end of chapter one. Why did I just spend all this time with this character? I feel cheated."

—CRICKET FREEMAN,
The August Agency

"1) Squinting into the sunlight with a hangover in a crime novel. Good grief—been done a million times. 2) A sci-fi novel that spends the first two pages describing the strange landscape. 3) A trite statement ('Get with the program' or 'Houston, we have a problem' or 'You go girl' or 'Earth to Michael' or 'Are we all on the same page?'), said by a weenie sales guy, usually in the opening paragraph. 4) A rape scene in a Christian novel, especially in the first chapter. 5) 'Years later, Monica would look back and laugh ...' 6) 'The [adjective] [adjective] sun rose in the [adjective] [adjective] sky, shedding its [adjective] light across the [adjective] [adjective] [adjective] land.'"

—CHIP MACGREGOR,
MacGregor Literary

"A cheesy 'hook' drives me nuts. I know that they say 'Open with a hook!'—something to grab the reader. While that's true, there's a fine line between a hook that's intriguing and a hook that's just silly. An example of a silly hook would be opening with a line of overtly sexual dialogue. Or opening with a hook that's just too convoluted to be truly interesting."

—Dan Lazar, Writers House

"Here are things I can't stand: Cliché openings in fantasy novels can include an opening scene set in a battle (and my peeve is that I don't know any of the characters yet so why should I care about this battle) or with a pastoral scene where the protagonist is gathering herbs (I didn't realize how common this is). Opening chapters where a main protagonist is in the middle of a bodily function (jerking off, vomiting, peeing or what have you) is usually a firm *no* right from the get-go. Gross. Long prologues that often don't have anything to do with the story. (So common in fantasy, again.) Opening scenes that are all dialogue without any context. I could probably go on ..."

—Kristin Nelson, Nelson Literary

CHARACTERS AND BACKSTORY

"I don't like descriptions of the characters where writers make the characters seem too perfect. Heroines (and heroes) who are described physically as being unflawed come across as unrelatable and boring. No 'flowing, windswept golden locks'; no 'eyes as blue as the sky'; no 'willowy, perfect figures.'"

—Laura Bradford, Bradford Literary Agency

"Many writers express the character's backstory before they get to the plot. Good writers will go back and cut that stuff out and get right to the plot. The character's backstory stays with them—it's in their DNA—even after the cut. To paraphrase Bruno Bettelheim: The more the character in a fairy tale is described, the less the audience will identify with him ... The less the character is characterized and described, the more likely the reader is to identify with him."

—Adam Chromy, Movable Type Management

"I'm really turned off when a writer feels the need to fill in all the backstory before starting the story; a story that opens on the protagonist's mental reflection of their situation is (usually) a red flag."

—Stephany Evans, FinePrint Literary Management

"One of the biggest problems I encounter is the 'information dump' in the first few pages, where the author is trying to tell us everything we supposedly need to know to understand the story. Getting to know characters in a story is like getting to know people in real life. You find out their personality and details of their life over time."

—Rachelle Gardner, Books & Such Literary

OTHER PET PEEVES

"The most common opening is a grisly murder scene told from the killer's point of view. While this usually holds the reader's attention, the narrative drive often doesn't last once we get into the meat of the story. A catchy opening scene is great, but all too often it falls apart after the initial pages. I often refer people to the opening of *Rosemary's Baby* by Ira Levin, which is about nothing more than a young couple getting an apartment. It is masterfully written and yet it doesn't appear to be about anything sinister at all. And it keeps you reading."

—IRENE GOODMAN,
Irene Goodman Literary

"Things I dislike include: 1) Telling me what the weather's like in order to set atmosphere. OK, it was raining. It's *always* raining. 2) Not starting with action. I want to have a sense of dread quite quickly—and not from rain! 3) Sending me anything but the beginning of the book; if you tell me that it 'starts getting good' on page 35, then I will tell you to start the book on page 35, because if even you don't like the first 34, neither will I or any other reader."

—JOSH GETZLER,
Hannigan Salky Getzler Agency.

"One of my biggest pet peeves is when writers try to stuff too much exposition into dialogue rather than trusting their abilities as storytellers to get information across. I'm talking stuff like the mom saying, 'Listen, Jimmy, I know you've missed your father ever since he died in that mysterious boating accident last year on the lake, but I'm telling you, you'll love this summer camp!'"

—CHRIS RICHMAN,
Upstart Crow Literary

"I hate to see a whiny character who's in the middle of a fight with one of their parents, slamming doors, rolling eyes, and displaying all sorts of other stereotypical behavior. I also tend to have a hard time bonding with characters who address the reader directly."

—KELLY SONNACK,
Andrea Brown Literary

....

CHUCK SAMBUCHINO (chucksambuchino.com, @chucksambuchino) edits the *Guide to Literary Agents* (guidetoliteraryagents.com/blog) as well as the *Children's Writer's & Illustrator's Market*. His pop humor books include *How to Survive a Garden Gnome Attack* (film rights optioned by Sony) and *When Clowns Attack: A Survival Guide* (Sept. 2015, Ten Speed Press). Chuck's other writing guides include *Formatting & Submitting Your Manuscript (3rd. Ed.), Create Your Writer Platform*, and *Get a Literary Agent*. Besides that, he is a husband, guitarist, father, dog owner, and cookie addict.

....

CREATE YOUR WRITER PLATFORM

8 quick tips to sell your books and yourself.

by Chuck Sambuchino

The chatter about the importance of a writer platform builds each year. Having an effective platform has never been more important than right now. With so many books available and few publicists left to help promote, the burden now lies upon the author to make sure copies of their book fly off bookshelves. In other words, the pressure is on for writers to act as their own publicist and chief marketer, and very few can do this successfully.

Know that if you're writing nonfiction, a damn good idea won't cut it. You need to prove that people will buy your book by showing a comprehensive ability to market yourself through different channels such as social networking sites and traditional media. If you can't do that, a publisher won't even consider your idea.

WHAT IS PLATFORM?

Platform, simply put, is your visibility as an author. It's your personal ability to sell books right this instant. Better yet, I've always thought of platform like this: When you speak, who listens? In other words, when you have a something to say, what legitimate channels exist for you to release your message to audiences who will consider buying your books/services?

Platform will be your key to finding success as an author, especially if you're writing nonfiction. Breaking the definition down, realize that platform is your personal ability to sell books through:

1. Who you are

2. Personal and professional connections you have

3. Any media outlets (including personal blogs and social networks) that you can utilize to sell books

In my opinion, the following are the most frequent building blocks of a platform:

1. A blog of impressive size

2. A newsletter of impressive size

3. Article/column writing (or correspondent involvement) for the media—preferably for larger publications, radio, and TV shows

4. Contributions to successful websites, blogs and periodicals helmed by others

5. A track record of strong past book sales that ensures past readers will buy your future titles

6. Networking, and your ability to meet power players in your community and subject area

7. Public speaking appearances—especially national ones; the bigger the better

8. An impressive social media presence (such as on Twitter or Facebook)

9. Membership in organizations that support the successes of their own

10. Recurring media appearances and interviews—in print, on the radio, on TV, or online

11. Personal contacts (organizational, media, celebrity, relatives) who can help you market at no cost to yourself, whether through blurbs, promotion, or other means.

Not all of these methods will be of interest/ relevance to you. As you learn more about to how to find success in each one, some will jump out at you as practical and feasible, while others will not. And to learn what constitutes "impressive size" in a platform plank, check out this article: tinyurl. com/8d2hnrj.

"PLATFORM" VS. "PUBLICITY"

Platform and publicity are interconnected yet very different. Platform is what you do before a book comes out to make sure that when it hits shelves, it doesn't stay there long. Publicity is an active effort to acquire media attention for a book that already exists. In other words, platform falls upon the author, whereas (hopefully) publicity will be handled by a publicist, either in-house or contracted for money.

Do something right now: Go to Amazon.com and find a book for sale that promises to teach you how to sell more books. Look at the comparable titles below it and start scrolling left to right using the arrows. (Do it now. I'll wait.) Tons of them, aren't there? It's because so many authors are looking for any way possible to promote their work, especially the many self-published writers out there. They've got a book out—and now they realize copies aren't selling. Apparently having your work online to buy at places like Amazon isn't enough to have success as a writer. That's why we must take the reins on our own platform and marketing.

As a last thought, perhaps consider it like this: Publicity is about asking and wanting: gimme gimme gimme. Platform is about giving first, then receiving because of what you've given and the goodwill it's earned you.

THE FUNDAMENTAL PRINCIPLES OF PLATFORM

1. It is in giving that we receive.

In my experience, this concept—*it is in giving that we receive*—is the fundamental rule of platform. Building a platform means that people follow your updates, listen to your words, respect and trust you, and, yes, will consider buying whatever it is you're selling. But they will only do that if they like you—and the way you get readers to like you is by legitimately helping them. Answer their questions. Give them stuff for free. Share sources of good, helpful information. Make them laugh and smile. Inform them and make their lives easier and/or better. Do what they cannot: cull together information or entertainment of value. Access people and places they want to learn more about. Help them achieve their goals. Enrich their lives. After they have seen the value you provide, they will want to stay in contact with you for more information. They begin to like you, and become a follower. And the more followers you have, the bigger your platform becomes.

2. You don't have to go it alone.

Creating a large and effective platform from scratch is, to say the least, a daunting task. But you don't have to swim out in the ocean alone; you can—and are encouraged to—work with others. There are many opportunities to latch on to bigger publications and groups in getting your words out. And when your own platform outlets—such as a blog—get large enough, they will be a popular source for others seeking to contribute guest content. You will find yourself constantly teaming with others on your way up, and even after you've found some success.

3. Platform is what you are *able* to do, not what you are *willing* to do.

I review nonfiction book proposals for writers, and in each of these proposals there is a marketing section. Whenever I start to read a marketing section and see bullet points such as "I am happy to go on a book tour" or "I believe that Fox News and MSNBC will be interested in this book because it is controversial," then I stop reading—because the proposal has a big problem. Understand this immediately: Your platform is not pie-in-the-sky thinking. It is not what you hope will happen or maybe could possibly hopefully happen sometime if you're lucky and all the stars align when your publicist works really hard. It's also not what you are willing to do, such as "be interviewed by the media" or "sign books at trade events." (Everyone is willing to do these things, so by mentioning them, you are making no case for your book because you're demonstrating no value.) The true distinction for writer platform is that it must be absolutely what you can make happen right now.

4. You can only learn so much about writer platform by instruction, which is why you should study what others do well and learn by example.

I don't know about you, but, personally, I learn from watching and doing better than I learn from reading. On that note, don't be afraid to study and mimic what others are doing. If you are looking for totally original ideas on how to blog and build your platform, I'll just tell you right now there likely are few or none left. So if you want to see what's working, go to the blogs and websites and Twitter feeds and newspaper columns of those you admire—then take a page from what they're doing. If you start to notice your favorite large blogs include all their social networking links at the top ("Find me on Twitter," "Find me on Facebook"), then guess what? Do the same. If people are getting large followings doing book reviews of young adult fantasy novels, why not do the same?

5. You must make yourself easy to contact.

I have no idea why people make themselves difficult to contact without a website and/or e-mail listed online. Besides "visibility," another way to think about platform is to examine your reach. And if your goal is reach, you do not want to limit people's abilities to find and contact you much if at all. You want people to contact you. You want other writers to e-mail from out of the blue. I love it when a member of the media finds my info online and writes me. I don't even mind it when a writer sends me an e-mail with a random question. I've made long-term friends that way—friends who have bought my book and sung my praises to others. It's called networking—and networking starts by simply making yourself available, and taking the next step to encourage people with similar interests or questions to contact you.

6. Start small and start early.

A true writer platform is something that's built before your book comes out, so that when the book hits your hands, you will be above the masses for all to see. I won't lie—the beginning is hard. It's full of a lot of effort and not a whole lot of return. Fear not; this will pass. Building a platform is like building a structure—every brick helps. Every brick counts. Small steps are not bad. You must always be considering what an action has to offer and if it can lead to bigger and better things. "What frustrates most people is that they want to have platform now," says literary agent Roseanne Wells of the Marianne Strong Literary Agency. "It takes time and a lot of effort, and it builds on itself. You can always have more platform, but trying to sell a book before you have it will not help you."

7. Have a plan, but feel free to make tweaks.

At first, uncertainty will overwhelm you. What are you going to blog about? How should you present yourself when networking? Should your Twitter handle be your name or the title of your book/brand? All these important questions deserve careful thought early on. The earlier you have a plan, the better off you will be in the long run—so don't just jump in blind. The more you can diagram and strategize at the beginning, the clearer your road will be.

As you step out and begin creating a writer platform, make sure to analyze how you're doing, then slowly transition so you're playing to your strengths and eliminating your weakest elements. No matter what you want to write about, no matter what platform elements you hone in on, don't ignore the importance of analysis and evolution in your journey. Take a look at what you're doing right and wrong to make sure you're not throwing good money after bad. And feel free to make all kinds of necessary tweaks and changes along the way to better your route.

8. Numbers matter—so quantify your platform.

If you don't include specific numbers or details, editors and agents will be forced to assume the element of platform is unimpressive, which is why you left out the crucial detail of its size/reach. Details are sexy; don't tease us. Try these right and wrong approaches below:

WRONG: "I am on Twitter and just love it."
CORRECT: "I have more than 10,000 followers on Twitter."

WRONG: "I do public speaking on this subject."
CORRECT: "I present to at least 10 events a year—sometimes as a keynote. The largest events have up to 1,200 attendees."

WRONG: "I run a blog that has won awards from other friendly bloggers."
CORRECT: "My blog averages 75,000 page views each month and has grown at a rate of 8 percent each month over the past year."

Also, analyzing numbers will help you see what's working and not working in your platform plan—allowing you to make healthy changes and let the strategy evolve. Numbers reflect the success you're having, and it's up to you to figure out why you're having that success.

"PLATFORM" VS. "CREDENTIALS"

The most important question you will be asked as you try to get your nonfiction book published is: "Why are you the best person to write this book?" This question is two-fold, as it speaks to both your credentials and your platform. To be a successful author, you will need both, not just the former.

Your credentials encompass your education and experience to be considered as an expert in your category. For example, if you want to write a book called *How to Lose 10 Pounds in 10 Weeks*, then my first thought would be to wonder if you are a doctor or a dietician. If not, what position do you hold that would give you solid authority to speak on your subject and have others not question the advice you're presenting? Or maybe you want to write a book on how to sell real estate in a challenging market. To have the necessary gravitas to compose such a book, you would likely have to have worked as an agent for decades and excelled in your field—hopefully winning awards over the years and acting in leadership roles within the real estate agent community.

Would you buy a book on how to train a puppy from someone whose only credential was that they owned a dog? I wouldn't. I want to see accolades, leadership positions, endorsements, educational notes, and more. I need to make sure I'm learning from an expert before I stop questioning the text and take it as helpful fact.

All this—all your authority—comes from your credentials. That's why they're so necessary. But believe it or not, credentials are often easier to come by than platform.

Platform, as we now know, is your ability to sell books and market yourself to target audience(s). There are likely many dieticians out there who can teach people interesting ways to lower their weight. But a publishing company is not interested in the 90 percent of them who lack any platform. They want the 10 percent of experts who have the ability to reach readers. Publishing houses seek experts who possess websites, mailing lists, media contacts, a healthy number of Twitter followers, and a plan for how to grow their visibility.

It's where credentials meet platform—*that's* where book authors are born.

CHUCK SAMBUCHINO (chucksambuchino.com, @chucksambuchino) edits the *Guide to Literary Agents* (guidetoliteraryagents.com/blog) as well as the *Children's Writer's & Illustrator's Market*. His pop humor books include *How to Survive a Garden Gnome Attack* (film rights optioned by Sony) and *When Clowns Attack: A Survival Guide* (Sept. 2015, Ten Speed Press). Chuck's other writing guides include *Formatting & Submitting Your Manuscript (3rd. Ed.)*, *Create Your Writer Platform*, and *Get a Literary Agent*. Besides that, he is a husband, guitarist, father, dog owner, and cookie addict.

DEBUT AUTHORS TELL ALL

Learn how first-time authors got published.

compiled by Chuck Sambuchino

YOUNG ADULT

① SABAA TAHIR
SABAATAHIR.COM

An Ember in the Ashes (APRIL 2015, RAZORBILL)

QUICK TAKE: The story of an orphan girl fighting for her family and a tormented soldier fighting for his freedom.

WRITES FROM: San Francisco

PRE-BOOK: Before I began writing, I was an editor at the *Washington Post*. I wrote very rarely for the newspaper, and *Ember* is actually my first novel.

TIME FRAME: It took me about six years to write. During that time, I did a great deal of research to enrich the world I was creating. One of my characters is a warrior, so part of my research included interviews with modern-day warriors. What I learned in the interviews helped me write characters who (I hope) are more authentic and three-dimensional.

ENTER THE AGENT: A friend of mine in publishing told me about Alexandra Machinist [of ICM Partners], and said that she might be a good fit for me and for the book. I queried her, and she offered.

WHAT I LEARNED: You don't have to write alone. I was really isolated while writing *Ember*. It wasn't until after I got my book deal that I realized there's a huge, wonderful YA writing community online. It's supportive, fun, and a great place to find a sympathetic ear or advice when you're struggling.

WHAT I DID RIGHT: I revised the heck out of my book so that by the time I sent it in, it was in good shape. I also did a ton of agent research before I began querying. I figured out what my comps were and which agents were looking for what. I read the "Successful Queries" series on the Guide to Literary Agents Blog, as well as the Query Shark's entire archive of letters.

ADVICE FOR WRITERS: Never give up. Keep writing through the rejections, the revisions, the never-ending explanations to your friends about why you aren't published yet. Keep writing when you hear that other people have gotten agents and book deals. Keep writing, even if it takes you years to finally accomplish your goal.

WOMEN'S FICTION

❷ ELIZA KENNEDY
LILYWILDER.COM

I Take You (MAY 2015, CROWN)

QUICK TAKE: The story of Lily Wilder, a bride who is profoundly conflicted about getting married because she can't stop sleeping with other people.

WRITES FROM: New York City

PRE-BOOK: Like my narrator, I used to be a lawyer at a big firm in New York City. I got burned out, as lawyers do, and my family moved to the country. After a few years of raising a child and some chickens, a return to paid employment loomed. I gave myself a year to write a book. If I failed, it was back to law for me.

TIME FRAME: In 2008, I tried writing a novel about a wedding set in Key West. I eventually gave up. Five years later, I found myself thinking about that old idea. Then a voice popped into my head—funny, profane, libidinous. It was my narrator, Lily. I wrote the first chapter that afternoon and finished the book ten months later.

ENTER THE AGENT: I queried a few dozen agents directly. I also reached out to an acquaintance at William Morris Endeavor who doesn't work on this type of book, but who offered to pass it on to an agent who did. To my great good fortune, he handed it to co-agent Suzanne Gluck, who signed me.

BIGGEST SURPRISE: The biggest surprise was that anyone actually wanted to buy the book. It's a traditional topic—"The Big Wedding"—but my bride is about as untraditional as you can get. My husband and I both liked it, but it was possible that everyone else would recoil in horror. Fortunately, only my mother did that.

WHAT I DID RIGHT: I wasn't strategic. I didn't worry about what type of book I was writing, or whether it would find an audience. I wrote the book I wanted to write.

WHAT I WISH I WOULD HAVE DONE DIFFERENT: I would have agonized less about the early rejections. Not everybody is going to like every book, and a rejection does not spell eternal doom.

ADVICE FOR WRITERS: Choose enthusiasm. If you are lucky enough to have more than one agent or editor interested in your work, don't automatically choose the bigger name or even the most money. Go with the person who loves your book and is dying to work with you.

NEXT UP: Another novel. I work on it every day. Terror of returning to the legal profession is a great motivator.

ADVENTURE ROMANCE

③ CLAIRE KELLS
CLAIREKELLS.COM

Girl Underwater **(MARCH 2015, PENGUIN/DUTTON)**

QUICK TAKE: A young woman struggles to cope with the aftermath of a plane crash in the wilderness.

WRITES FROM: San Francisco

PRE-BOOK: I started writing fiction in medical school. This was not my first attempt to write a novel—far from it. But for me, it took several years to understand the concept of story and how to put one together in a cohesive, satisfying way.

TIME FRAME: I wrote the first draft in my final year of medical school over a period of about four months.

ENTER THE AGENT: My agent is the incomparable Stefanie Lieberman at Janklow & Nesbit. I actually queried a different agent at her agency, and my query was passed along.

WHAT I LEARNED: I had my laptop stolen from a hotel room and lost three novels on my hard drive; I have since learned to back up my work! I also learned that trends are not worth chasing. I spent a long time trying to guess what publishers wanted so that I could write a book that would sell, which, of course, ended in a lot of frustration and heartache.

WHAT I DID RIGHT: I read a lot. I also sought out other writers online—forums, blogs, social media—and read as much as I could about the writing process and, later, the publishing industry. Information is power! But really, I just wrote my heart out. Whenever I sat down to draft a new story or revise an old one, I would think, You can do better.

ADVICE FOR WRITERS: Read, write, and stay informed. The only thing you can control is how hard you're willing to work at becoming a better writer. I never realized how much work it would be when I first started, and it continues to be a challenge.

NEXT UP: I'm working on another novel.

SOUTHERN GOTHIC SUSPENSE

4 JAMIE KORNEGAY
TURNROWBOOKS.COM

Soil **(MARCH 2015, SIMON & SCHUSTER)**

QUICK TAKE: A young farmer, whose ambition and paranoia are getting the better of him, finds a dead body in the retreating waters of his flooded field, and rather than report it to the dubious local deputy, he mounts a cover-up and must contend with the repercussions while attempting to win back his estranged family.

WRITES FROM: Mississippi

PRE-BOOK: I wrote two novels, which I tried half-heartedly to publish. Rather than face rewrites, I started a new story, inspired by my daily drives through the rural backcountry of Mississippi.

TIME FRAME: I started this novel about ten years ago. Then my wife and I opened an independent bookstore, Turnrow Book Co. It took years to get it up and running, and it wasn't until five years ago that I gave the novel a serious attempt. It took two years to get the novel into [shape].

ENTER THE AGENT: I found Jim Rutman of Sterling Lord Literistic by reading an industry magazine. I liked what he had to say, and when I reached out to him, he was interested in my pitch.

WHAT I DID RIGHT: Just never quit. A successful writer friend recently told me that's the only difference between a published writer and someone who used to/wanted to be a writer. And certainly, my fifteen years as an independent bookseller has helped—giving me contacts in the industry, a working knowledge of the market, and daily interaction with the audience.

WHAT I WISH I WOULD HAVE DONE DIFFERENT: I wasted so much time early on waiting for the muse to strike. Finally, when I just sat down and treated it like a job, the pages piled up.

ADVICE FOR WRITERS: You can turn rejection and disappointment into a serious motivator if you're determined enough to be published. But you must also understand why the work is not accepted. Have the discipline and subjectivity to look at your work and say, "Yeah, that's not good enough," and then sit down and make it better.

NEXT UP: I'm hard at work on a new novel.

LITERARY FICTION

❺ BROOKE DAVIS

MILLIEBIRD.COM

Lost & Found **(JANUARY 2015, DUTTON)**

QUICK TAKE: A seven-year-old girl named Millie is abandoned by her mother, so two octogenarian friends follow Millie on a road trip across the Australian desert to help find her mom.

WRITES FROM: Perth, Australia

PRE-BOOK: I had some short stories and nonfiction pieces published in Australia, but this is my first novel. Though, I did attempt a novel when I was ten! It was basically just a rip-off of *The Babysitters Club*, and luckily—because it was abominable!—I gave up about 20 pages in.

TIME FRAME: I wrote it in five years as part of a Ph.D. in Creative Writing at Curtin University in Western Australia.

ENTER THE AGENT: I was put in touch with my Australian agent—Benython Oldfield from Zeitgeist Media Group Agency—through a friend in Australia. I sent Benython a copy of my manuscript the day after I'd been made an offer from an Australian publisher.

BIGGEST SURPRISE: I was actually amazed at how many people worked on my book. So much work goes into the one book.

WHAT I DID RIGHT: I work as a bookseller in Australia, and the account managers from the publishers were always asking me about the book I was writing. When I finished, one of them read it, and liked it, and took it to the head office of Hachette Australia. They ended up publishing my book. So being involved in the industry was really helpful for me.

ADVICE FOR WRITERS: Work hard, be patient, and become part of a writing community. Get involved in the industry in some capacity—even as a volunteer—to gain a better understanding as to how it all works.

NEXT UP: As soon as I get some time, I'll start writing the second book. I'll never have a first book out again, so, for now, I'm just enjoying the feeling of completing that goal.

NONFICTION REFERENCE

⑥ ADAM PLANTINGA
400 Things Cops Know (**OCTOBER 2014, QUILL DRIVER BOOKS**)

QUICK TAKE: A collection of reflections, anecdotes, and facts from a San Francisco police sergeant's 13 years in urban law enforcement.

WRITES FROM: San Francisco

PRE-BOOK: I had a short story included in the anthology *25 and Under: Fiction.* I've written a dozen or so nonfiction articles on police work. I have also scribed five novels, all of which are unpublished and some of which should probably remain that way.

TIME FRAME: I basically wrote this book over the course of my police career. I have accumulated plenty of material from law enforcement trainings, my own work experiences, and from my more seasoned colleagues. I scribbled diligent notes in the margins of my notebooks and later assembled it all in book form.

ENTER THE AGENT: I started out with an agent, who did due diligence, but we couldn't quite make the book happen. So, on my own, I scouted for smaller, independent publishers that had put out police-themed books in the past. I found one in Linden Publishing/Quill Driver Books.

BIGGEST SURPRISE: How gracious [crime fiction] author Joseph Wambaugh was in reading an advance copy of my book and supplying a generous blurb.

WHAT I DID RIGHT: This is nothing revolutionary, but what helped was just a healthy dose of stubbornness. I tried ninety different agents before I landed one, and then when that didn't work out, I went through a couple more independent publishers before I got on with Linden. I also sent the book to trusted friends, family, and co-workers, and received invaluable feedback.

INSPIRATIONAL HISTORICAL ROMANCE

⑦ BRANDY VALLANCE
BRANDYVALLANCE.COM
The Covered Deep (**OCTOBER 2014, WORTHY PUBLISHING**)

QUICK TAKE: In 1877, an incurably romantic bookworm from Appalachia wins an essay contest and travels to England and the Holy Land in search of the perfect romantic hero.

WRITES FROM: Colorado Springs, Colorado

PRE-BOOK: I was a freelance writer for six years and was on staff with a few magazines and newspapers. I had fifty articles published, most of them relating to the Victorian time period.

TIME FRAME: *The Covered Deep* took fourteen years and eleven drafts. I began by taking the Christian Writers Guild Apprenticeship Course. Throughout the years, I read every book I saw on writing. I attended fifteen writers' conferences. In 2009, I quit freelancing to focus on *The Covered Deep*. In 2012, I won the American Christian Fiction Writers Genesis Contest for historical romance. A year later, the novel contract came when I won the 2013 Christian Writers Guild Operation First Novel Contest.

ENTER THE AGENT: I met Rachelle Gardner of Books and Such Literary Management at a local writers' meeting. Everything she said clicked with me, and I knew she was my dream agent. I sent her a query letter and then followed up at another conference. When we were both [in Colorado Springs], we met for coffee. I've happily been her client ever since.

WHAT I DID RIGHT: Learning how to write newspaper and magazine articles trained me to write a novel. I learned discipline, structure, and how to meet a deadline.

PLATFORM: I'm on Facebook, YouTube, Goodreads, Pinterest, and Twitter. I try to use the 90/10 rule, which is to give your audience something unrelated to your book 90 percent of the time and then only talk about your book the other 10.

BEST ADVICE FOR WRITERS: My cousin used to tell me that if you throw enough stuff against the wall, something's bound to stick. Don't be afraid to put yourself and your writing out there. Take colossal risks. The publishing world rewards bravery.

NEXT UP: I recently finished my second book, *Within the Veil*, a sweeping Scottish romance set in 1885.

MYSTERY

8 MELISSA LENHARDT
MELISSALENHARDT.COM
Stillwater (**OCTOBER 2015, SKYHORSE PUBLISHING**)

QUICK TAKE: A city-boy outsider takes over as Stillwater Chief of Police from a long-tenured local and, through investigating two murders fifty years apart, uncovers corruption and long-buried secrets that rattle the small town to its core.

WRITES FROM: Texas

PRE-BOOK: Before finishing *Stillwater*, I started and stopped dozens of stories in all types of genres. In 2012, I queried agents with a historical fiction novel set in Texas and didn't make much progress. I decided a traditional mystery might be easier to pitch. I polished *Stillwater* and pitched it at the 2013 DFW Writers Conference.

TIME FRAME: *Stillwater* started as a modern day retelling of Jane Austen's *Persuasion*. While that story didn't work, I kept the town and the main female character and turned it into a mystery. I wrote the first draft during NaNo one year—honestly can't remember which one—but I knew the story still wasn't completely working. It all came together when my mother told me about a recurring dream she had that my father had buried a body in our woods. I kissed her and said, "Oh my God! I have to use that. Can I use that?" She said yes.

ENTER THE AGENT: I met my agent, Alice Speilburg [of Speilburg Literary Agency], at the 2013 DFW Writers Conference. I decided to treat the con as more of a networking opportunity than constantly shilling my book. Agents and editors ate lunch with the attendees and I randomly picked the table where Alice sat. Fate! We talked through lunch and hit it off, but pitching didn't come up. Nor did it the last day when I ate lunch at a table with her again. At the very end of the conference I was loitering near the doors, trying to find her in the crowd and thinking, *I'll just e-mail her. She'll remember me*, when she saw me, came over and asked me to pitch.

WHAT I LEARNED: Patience. You, the writer, are focused on one thing (your book), but your agent/editor have dozens of balls in the air. Including yours.

I WISH I WOULD HAVE DONE DIFFERENT: Nothing. I wrote for over ten years before I tried to get an agent. I needed all those years to build my confidence and hone my craft so the book I pitched was good enough to land an agent and good enough to sell to a publisher.

PLATFORM: All the main social media sites, a blog and, more recently, a newsletter. I post regularly, with a mixture of industry information, writing advice, and enough personal stuff to show a bit of personality.

BEST ADVICE FOR WRITERS: Finish. Don't keep tinkering with the same book for years. Put it aside and start another one. You won't improve as a writer by writing the same book over and over.

NEXT UP: I am working on the sequel to *Stillwater*.

SPECULATIVE (DYSTOPIAN / SCIENCE FICTION)

⑨ M.E. PARKER
MEPARKER.COM
Jonesbridge: Echoes of Hinterland (**JULY 2015, DIVERSION BOOKS**)

QUICK TAKE: In a fight for metal resources to fuel the war effort against the E'sters, the secretive Jonesbridge Industrial Complex enslaves a young dreamer whose escape plans are threatened when he falls for a pregnant railwalker on the salvage line.

WRITES FROM: McKinney, Texas

PRE-BOOK: I have published numerous short stories in literary journals and gathered some awards along the way. I also served as the editor-in-chief of the Camera Obscura Journal of Literature & Photography from 2009 to 2014.

TIME FRAME: A short story of mine, "The Harlot of Baltimore," that appeared in a literary journal in 2009 intrigued a literary agent who read it. (Yes, apparently some agents read literary journals.) This agent reached out to me and asked if I had a novel of a similar vein. As we all know, literary agents are hard to come by, so, instead of saying "no," my response was that I would have one very soon. Even though she'd solicited me out of the blue, this agent declined the hurried project, so I began the long process of revision before sending it anywhere else.

ENTER THE AGENT: Once I allowed the manuscript to percolate and tug at me from the deeply nested folder on my hard drive, I revisited it, revised it, gave it a nip and tuck, and sent it to Kimberley Cameron & Associates where Elizabeth Kracht fished it out of the slush pile. And she has been a joy to work with as we hammered the dents out of the manuscript and found it a home.

WHAT I LEARNED: 1) When to revise vs. when to start over. Sometimes it's faster to take it from the top than get mired in revisions of a manuscript with too many problems. 2) Over-revising in the first place can lead to number 1.

PLATFORM: I have a platform in short story writing, editing, blogs, and across social media, Facebook, Twitter, Instagram, LinkedIn (and yes Google+). Part of a writer's job in 2015 is to be proactive in getting your work to the world. But it's important for writers to know that if you're just now showing up on social media when it's time to tout your work, that is probably too late.

BEST ADVICE FOR WRITERS: Don't write for publication. Write the story that calls you. When you do seek publication, be confident in your work, but keep your ego in check—cinch it up in a straitjacket if you have to. The publication process is vast and fierce and feeds on a diet of aspiring writers and hope.

NEXT UP: *Jonesbridge* is the first of three books in the series, so I am hard at work on the other two books, as well as another unrelated novel.

HISTORICAL MYSTERY

⑩ TESSA ARLEN
TESSAARLEN.COM

Death of a Dishonorable Gentleman (**JANUARY 2015, MINOTAUR**)

QUICK TAKE: A story of blackmail, betrayal, and revenge, set in an elegant country house in England in 1912.

WRITES FROM: the Pacific Northwest

PRE-GENTLEMAN: I've always enjoyed writing; I wrote stories for my children when they were younger. When our youngest daughter left for college, I decided to write a novel. The idea for a story had been brewing in my head for months.

TIME FRAME: I started the novel in October of 2009. I wrote throughout the next five months and ended up with a vast first draft—145,000 words! I put it to one side and read a few things about story and structure and goodness knows what else. I worked [on it until] I had a workable book. In March 2013, I started to look for a literary agent.

ENTER THE AGENT: I have the most wonderful agent: Kevan Lyon of Marsal Lyon Literary Agency. I read absolutely everything I could find on the business of finding an agent, and overall, I submitted 127 e-mail queries! There were so many rejects. Just as I was telling myself that I would have to start the business all over again, I had two offers of representation.

WHAT I DID RIGHT: Writing and crafting a novel requires immense effort and focus. I think the thing I did right was completely focusing the best hours of my day on the work. I was given the gift of time and I used it.

ADVICE FOR WRITERS: Lay your first draft aside for a few months and then go back and revise. It's amazing how, with a bit of distance, you can see exactly what has to go, and where your plot sags or doesn't maintain momentum. Above all, be prepared to ditch things that just don't move your story along, even if you love them.

NEXT UP: The second book in the Lady Montfort series: *A Party For Winston*, which takes place in London in 1913.

NONFICTION BUSINESS

⑪ THOMAS LEE

Rebuilding Empires (**DECEMBER 2014, PALGRAVE MACMILLAN TRADE**)

QUICK TAKE: An examination of how big-box retailers like Best Buy and Target will adapt to the digital age.

TIME FRAME: I started writing *Rebuilding Empires* in September 2013 and took a three-month unpaid leave of absence from my job as business reporter at the *Star Tribune* in Minneapolis [to research the book]. When finishing the book, I took a new job at the *San Francisco Chronicle*. So I obviously had a lot on my plate with a new job, new home, and my first book to complete.

ENTER THE AGENT: I found my agent John Willig [of Literary Services, Inc.]at the Writer's Digest Conference in New York City in 2013. I attended the pitch slam and spoke to eight agents. All eight expressed interest in the project, and I ultimately chose John.

BIGGEST SURPRISE: Believe it or not, I found the writing and editing process of the book to be relatively easy, partly I suppose because of my background as a journalist. But I was surprised by the conservative nature of the publishing business, that a good deal of the economic risk of the project falls on the author. People should realize that an author is not only selling a project to the publisher but selling himself/herself. That the author must do most of the promotion and develop a marketing strategy, using every single contact and platform at his/her disposal.

WHAT I DID RIGHT: It sounds like a cliché but just taking the initiative is probably the biggest factor that allowed me to succeed. I'm pretty sure there are plenty of journalists out there who are way more talented than myself and who want to write books. But many of them don't take the risk and actually do the damn thing.

PLATFORM: Since I am a journalist, I already have a natural platform in place. I've been using my column at the *San Francisco Chronicle* to promote the book. I also enjoy a deep list of connections within the news media to help get the word out about *Rebuilding Empires*. I've already done a lot of interviews with radio and television stations, so I'm pretty comfortable in front of the camera or behind the microphone.

BEST ADVICE FOR WRITERS: Always use active verbs. Avoid passive voice if you can.

NEXT UP: A second book I hope!

CHILDREN'S PICTURE BOOK

⑫ VAL JONES
Who Wants Broccoli? **(JUNE 2015, HARPERCOLLINS)**

QUICK TAKE: Broccoli is a big, fun dog who has spent most of his life in Beezely's Animal Shelter among cute little animals but seems to have trouble being picked as someone's perfect pet.

WRITES FROM: Skippack, Pennsylvania

PRE-BOOK: In 2010, I was laid off at a large pharmaceutical company. I had some background in art and always loved children stories, so I decided to make the gigantic leap from the corporate world into the land of children's books. The first thing I did was join the Society of Children's Book Writers & Illustrators (SCBWI) and sign up for local workshops to learn about the industry. In 2011, I was invited into a wonderful "illustrators who want to write" critique group. This group of talented and published artists generously shared their experience with me and gave me so much support along the way.

TIME FRAME: When I started, I had no portfolio as an illustrator and had never even attempted to write. I started writing *Broccoli* in Fall 2011 and brought the dummy to a Highlights workshop in November 2012 for a critique (the weekend of Superstorm Sandy). The feedback from that critique was applied to the next version, which was picked up in April 2013 by HarperCollins.

ENTER THE AGENT: In November 2012 while attending Highlights' "Crash Course in the Business of Children's Publishing," I met my wonderful Agent, Karen Grencik of Red Fox Literary Agency.

BIGGEST SURPRISES: How long it takes from signing to when you actually get to hold your book in your hands. For me, it will be just under two years from signing my contract in July 2013 to the release of *Broccoli* in June 2015.

WHAT I DID RIGHT: I focused on what I really wanted to do, which is to write and illustrate my stories. And because I didn't know about the publishing industry, I created a roadmap of what I thought were the most important things I needed to do and learn, such as joining SCBWI, choosing relevant workshops, joining a good critique group, and learning Photoshop.

BEST ADVICE FOR WRITERS: Write what you know—and don't teach children any lessons with your writing that feel like you did it on purpose.

NEXT UP: If *Who Wants Broccoli?* does well and kids like the characters, perhaps there will be more Broccolis in the future ... you can never have enough Broccoli, right? I'm also working on a kitty book that I hope will find a home.

FANTASY

⑬ KARINA SUMNER-SMITH
Radiant (SEPTEMBER 2014, HARPERCOLLINS)

QUICK TAKE: A homeless young woman in a magic-run society attempts to rescue the ghost of a girl who hasn't died.

WRITES FROM: Ontario, Canada

PRE-BOOK: When I started writing, I followed the advice to write short fiction before attempting a novel. I wrote and published science fiction and fantasy short stories off and on for more than a decade before getting up the nerve to attempt a novel. *Radiant* actually started as a short story called "An End to All Things," which was nominated for the Nebula Award. I loved those characters and found I had to write the book to find out what happened to them.

TIME FRAME: I wrote the first draft of *Radiant* in a year (with many missteps and false turns along the way), and then took almost three years to rewrite and revise the book into something I felt was ready to send out. In retrospect, for much of that time it was perfectionism and fear that kept me from submitting rather than any big problems with the book itself.

ENTER THE AGENT: My agent is the awesome Sara Megibow of KT Literary. I researched literary agents online for years, and when my book was finally ready to head out into the world, Sara was my top choice—and I was thrilled beyond words that my work connected with her!

BIGGEST SURPRISES: Agents and editors are huge book nerds—and they really want to fall in love with your book. It can be hard to feel that way when querying and on submission (especially when the rejections are piling up!), but I think professionals feel the same way readers do when picking up a new book: They just really want to find that next great read.

WHAT I DID RIGHT: I tried to treat writing and publishing like a career, even when it couldn't even pay for a coffee. That meant being serious about my efforts, investing in ways to improve my craft, and approaching other publishing professionals with courtesy and respect. I also always tried to remember that publishing is a long game—getting rejected or having to put a novel aside doesn't mean inevitable failure, only that it's not the right project at this moment, for this market.

BEST ADVICE FOR WRITERS: Focus on developing your craft and writing your best work. Trends come and go, and the industry is always changing—but your writing is the one thing that you can control.

NEXT UP: The final two novels in the Towers Trilogy, *Defiant* and *Towers Fall*, are both due out from Talos Press in 2015.

CHUCK SAMBUCHINO (chucksambuchino.com, @chucksambuchino) edits the *Guide to Literary Agents* (guidetoliteraryagents.com/blog) as well as the *Children's Writer's & Illustrator's Market*. His pop humor books include *How to Survive a Garden Gnome Attack* (film rights optioned by Sony) and *When Clowns Attack: A Survival Guide* (Sept. 2015, Ten Speed Press). Chuck's other writing guides include *Formatting & Submitting Your Manuscript (3rd. Ed.), Create Your Writer Platform*, and *Get a Literary Agent*. Besides that, he is a husband, guitarist, father, dog owner, and cookie addict.

GLA SUCCESS STORIES

Those who have come before and succeeded.

I realize there are other places you can turn to for information on agents, but the *Guide to Literary Agents* has always prided itself as being the biggest (we list almost every agent) and the most thorough (guidelines, sales, agent-by-agent breakdowns, etc.). That's why it's sold more than 250,000 copies. It *works*—and if you keep reading, I'll prove it to you. Here are testimonials from a handful of writers who have used this book to find an agent and publishing success.

1 MARISHA CHAMBERLAIN, The Rose Variations (Soho)
"*Guide to Literary Agents* oriented me, the lowly first-time novelist, embarking on an agent search. The articles and the listings gave insight into the world of literary agents that allowed me to comport myself professionally and to persist. And I did find a terrific agent."

② **EUGENIA KIM,** *The Calligrapher's Daughter* (Holt)
"After so many years working on the novel, the relative speed of creating the query package prodded the impetus to send it out ... As a fail-safe measure, I bought the *Guide to Literary Agents* [and] checked who might be a good fit for my novel..."

③ **EVE BROWN-WAITE,** *First Comes Love, Then Comes Malaria* (Broadway)
"I bought the *Guide To Literary Agents* ... and came across Laney Katz Becker. So I sent off a very funny query. On March 15, 2007, Laney called. 'I love your book,' she said. 'I'd like to represent you.' Three months later, Laney sold my book—at auction—in a six-figure deal."

④ **MARA PURNHAGEN,** *Tagged* (Harlequin Teen)
"I trusted the *Guide to Literary Agents* to provide solid, up-to-date information to help me with the process. I now have a wonderful agent and a four-book deal."

⑤ **RICHARD HARVELL,** *The Bells* (Crown)
"*Guide to Literary Agents* was crucial in my successful search for an agent. I found a great agent and my book has now been translated into a dozen languages."

⑥ **PATRICK LEE,** *The Breach* (Harper)
"The *GLA* has all the info you need for narrowing down a list of agencies to query."

⑦ **KAREN DIONNE,** *Freezing Point* and *Boiling Point* (Jove)
"I'm smiling as I type this, because I actually got my agent via the *Guide to Literary Agents*. I certainly never dreamed that I'd tell my [success] story in the same publication!"

⑧ **HEATHER NEWTON,** *Under the Mercy Trees* (Harper)
"I found my literary agent through the *Guide to Literary Agents!*"

⑨ **MICHAEL WILEY,** *The Last Striptease* and *The Bad Kitty Lounge* (Minotaur)

"*GLA* was very useful to me when I started. I always recommend it to writers."

⑩ LES EDGERTON, *Hooked* and 11 more books

"Just signed with literary agent Chip Mac-Gregor and I came upon him through the *Guide to Literary Agents.* If not for *GLA,* I'd probably still be looking."

⑪ JENNIFER CERVANTES, *Tortilla Sun* (Chronicle)

"Within 10 days of submitting, I found an amazing agent—and it's all thanks to *GLA.*"

⑫ CARSON MORTON, *Stealing Mona Lisa* (St. Martin's / Minotaur)

"I wanted to thank you for the *Guide to Literary Agents.* After contacting 16 literary agencies, number 17 requested my historical novel. Within a few weeks, they offered to represent me. Hard work and good, solid, accurate information makes all the difference. Thanks again."

⑬ DARIEN GEE, *Friendship Bread: A Novel* (Ballantine)

"The *Guide to Literary Agents* was an indispensable tool for me when I was querying agents. I highly recommend it for any aspiring author."

⑭ LEXI GEORGE, *Demon Hunting in Dixie* (Brava)

"The *Guide to Literary Agents* is an invaluable resource for writers."

⑮ STEPHANIE BARDEN, *Cinderella Smith* (HarperCollins)

"When I felt my book was finally ready for eyes other than mine to see it, I got some terrific advice: Go buy the *Guide to Literary Agents.* By the time I was through with it, it looked like it had gone to battle—it was battered and dog-eared and highlighted and Post-It-Noted. But it was victorious; I had an agent. Huge thanks, *GLA*—I couldn't have done it without you!"

⑯ BILL PESCHEL, *Writers Gone Wild: The Feuds, Frolics, and Follies of Literature's Great Adventurers, Drunkards, Lovers, Iconoclasts, and Misanthropes* (Perigee)

"The *Guide to Literary Agents* gave me everything I needed to sell *Writers Gone Wild*. It was the personal assistant who found me the right agents to pitch, the publicist who suggested conferences to attend and the trusted adviser who helped me negotiate the path to publication."

17 **LAURA GRIFFIN**, *Unforgivable* (Pocket Books)

"Writing the book is only the first step. Then it's time to find a home for it. The *Guide to Literary Agents* is filled with practical advice about how to contact literary agents who can help you market your work."

18 **DEREK TAYLOR KENT (A.K.A. DEREK THE GHOST)**, *Scary School* (HarperCollins)

"The *Guide to Literary Agents* was absolutely instrumental to my getting an agent and subsequent three-book deal with Harper-Collins."

19 **TAMORA PIERCE**, *Alanna: The First Adventure: The Song of the Lioness* (Atheneum)

"The best guide to literary agents is the *Guide to Literary Agents*, published by Writer's Market Books … These listings will tell you the names and addresses of the agencies; if an agency is made up of more than one agent, they will list the different agents and what kinds of book they represent; they will include whether or not the agent will accept simultaneous submissions (submitting a manuscript to more agents than one)."

20 **WADE ROUSE**, *It's All Relative: Two Families, Three Dogs, 34 Holidays, and 50 Boxes of Wine: A Memoir* (Crown)

"And when you think you're done writing your book? Write some more. And when you think you're finished? Set it aside for a while, go back, redraft, edit, rewrite, and redraft … Then pick up the Writer's Digest *Guide to Literary Agents*."

21 **DIANNA DORISI WINGET**, *A Smidgen of Sky* (Harcourt)
"*Guide to Literary Agents* is simply the best writing reference book out there. I don't think I would have landed an agent without it."

22 **CAROLE BRODY FLEET**, *Happily Even After: A Guide to Getting Through (and Beyond!) the Grief of Widowhood* (Viva Editions)
"I am not overstating it when I say that *Guide to Literary Agents* was absolutely instrumental in my landing an agent. Moreover, I wound up with numerous agents from which to choose—how often does *that* happen to an unknown and unpublished author? Thank you again for this book. It not only changed my life forever, but it led to our being able to serve the widowed community around the world."

23 **GUINEVERE DURHAM**, *Teaching Test-Taking Skills: Proven Techniques to Boost Your Student's Scores* (R&L Education)
"I was looking for an agent for my book. I had been trying for 7 years. I have enough

rejection letters to wallpaper my office. Finally, I researched the *Guide to Literary Agents*. Three months later I had a contract."

24 **ADAM BROWNLEE**, *Building a Small Business That Warren Buffett Would Love* (John Wiley and Sons)
"The *Guide to Literary Agents* was invaluable for me in many ways. Specifically, the sections on 'Write a Killer Query Letter' and 'Nonfiction Book Proposals' enabled me to put together a package that led to the publication of my book."

25 **KIM BAKER**, *Pickle: The (Formerly) Anonymous Prank Club of Fountain Point Middle School* (Roaring Brook)
"I read the *Guide to Literary Agents* religiously when I was planning submissions."

26 **JERI WESTERSON**, *Blood Lance: A Medieval Noir* (Pocket Books)
"The whole writing industry is so confusing. Where to start? I started with the Writer's

Digest *Guide to Literary Agents,* where I not only created my list of agents and game plan, I received all sorts of excellent information in crafting my winning query letter. I recommend it to anyone starting out. And yes, I did get an agent through the Guide."

㉗ NOELLE STERNE, *Trust Your Life: Forgive Yourself and Go After Your Dreams* (Unity)
"Your *Guide to Literary Agents* and the features from authors on the often-hard lessons learned from the dream of publishing have helped me immensely to keep my feet on the ground, butt in the chair, and fingers on the keyboard. Thank you, Chuck, for taking all the time and effort and for caring."

㉘ LYNNE RAIMONDO, *Dante's Wood: A Mark Angelotti Novel* (Seventh Street Books)
"*Guide to Literary Agents* is how I found my agent, so I owe you one."

㉙ GENNIFER ALBIN, *Crewel* (Pocket Books)
"I got a lot of mileage out of *Guide to Literary Agents* when I was looking for an agent, and I frequently recommend it."

NEW AGENT SPOTLIGHTS

Learn about new reps seeking clients.

by Chuck Sambuchino

One of the most common recurring blog items I get complimented on is my "New Agent Alerts," a series where I spotlight new/newer literary reps who are open to queries and looking for clients right now.

This is due to the fact that newer agents are golden opportunities for aspiring authors because they are actively building their client lists. They're hungry to sign new clients and start the ball rolling with submissions to editors and get books sold. Whereas an established agent with 40 clients may have little to no time to consider new writers' work (let alone help them shape it), a newer agent may be willing to sign a promising writer whose work is not a guaranteed huge payday.

THE CONS AND PROS OF NEWER AGENTS

At writing conferences, a frequent question I get is "Is it OK to sign with a new agent?" The question comes about because people value experience and wonder about the skill of someone who's new to the scene. The concern is an interesting one, so let me try to list the downsides and upsides to choosing a rep who's in her first few years agenting.

Probable cons

- They are less experienced in contract negotiations.
- They know fewer editors at this point than a rep who's been in business a while, meaning there is a less likely chance they can help you get published. This is a big, justified point—and writers' foremost concern.
- They are in a weaker position to demand a high advance for you.
- New agents come and some go. This means if your agent is in business for a year or two and doesn't find the success for which they hoped, they could bail on the biz altogether. That leaves you without a home. If you sign with an agent who's been in business for 14 years, however, chances are they won't quit tomorrow.

Probable pros

- They are actively building their client lists—and that means they are anxious to sign new writers and lock in those first several sales.
- They are willing to give your work a longer look. They may be willing to work with you on a project to get it ready for submission, whereas a more established agent has lots of clients and no time—meaning they have no spare moments to help you with shaping your novel or proposal.
- With fewer clients under their wing, you will get more attention than you would with an established rep.
- If they've found their calling and don't seem like they're giving up any time soon (and keep in mind, most do continue on as agents), you can have a decades-long relationship that pays off with lots of books.
- They have little going against them. An established agent once told me that a new agent is in a unique position because they have no duds under their belt. Their slates are clean.

HOW CAN YOU DECIDE FOR YOURSELF?

1. Factor in if they're part of a larger agency. Agents share contacts and resources. If your agent is the new girl at an agency with five people, those other four agents will help her (and you) with submissions. In other words, she's new, but not alone.

2. Learn where the agent came from. Has she been an apprentice at the agency for two years? Was she an editor for seven years and just switched to agenting? If they already have a few years in publishing under their belt, they're not as green as you may think. Agents don't become agents overnight.

3. Ask where she will submit the work. This is a big one. If you fear the agent lacks proper contacts to move your work, ask straight out: "What editors do you see us submitting this book to, and have you sold to them before?" The question tests their plan for where to send the manuscript and get it in print.

4. Ask them, "Why should I sign with you?" This is another straight-up question that gets right to the point. If she's new and has little/no sales at that point, she can't respond with "I sell tons of books and I make it rain cash money!! Dolla dolla bills, y'all!!!" She can't rely on her track record to entice you. So what's her sales pitch? Weigh her enthusiasm, her plan for the book, her promises of hard work and anything else she tells you. In the publishing business, you want communication and enthusiasm from agents (and editors). Both are invaluable. What's the point of signing with a huge agent when they don't return your e-mails and consider your book last on their list of priorities for the day?

5. If you're not sold, you can always say no. It's as simple as that. Always query new/newer agents because, at the end of the day, just because they offer representation doesn't mean you have to accept.

NEW AGENT SPOTLIGHTS

Peppered throughout this book's large number of agency listings are sporadic "New Agent Alert" sidebars. Look them over to see if these newer reps would be a good fit for your work. Always read personal information and submission guidelines carefully. Don't let an agent reject you because you submitted work incorrectly.

Wherever possible, we have included a website address for their agency, as well as their Twitter handle for those reps that tweet.

Also please note that as of when this book went to press in 2015, all these agents were still active and looking for writers. That said, I cannot guarantee every one is still in their respective position when you read this, nor that they have kept their query inboxes open. I urge you to visit agency websites and double check before you query. (This is always a good idea in any case.) Good luck!

....

CHUCK SAMBUCHINO (chucksambuchino.com, @chucksambuchino) edits the *Guide to Literary Agents* (guidetoliteraryagents.com/blog) as well as the *Children's Writer's & Illustrator's Market*. His pop humor books include *How to Survive a Garden Gnome Attack* (film rights optioned by Sony) and *When Clowns Attack: A Survival Guide* (Sept. 2015, Ten Speed Press). Chuck's other writing guides include *Formatting & Submitting Your Manuscript (3rd. Ed.), Create Your Writer Platform,* and *Get a Literary Agent.* Besides that, he is a husband, guitarist, father, dog owner, and cookie addict.

....

GLOSSARY OF INDUSTRY TERMS

Your guide to every need-to-know term.

#10 ENVELOPE. A standard, business-size envelope.

ACKNOWLEDGMENTS PAGE. The page of a book on which the author credits sources of assistance—both individuals and organizations.

ACQUISITIONS EDITOR. The person responsible for originating and/or acquiring new publishing projects.

ADAPTATION. The process of rewriting a composition (novel, story, film, article, play) into a form suitable for some other medium, such as TV or the stage.

ADVANCE. Money a publisher pays a writer prior to book publication, usually paid in installments, such as one-half upon signing the contract and one-half upon delivery of the complete, satisfactory manuscript. An advance is paid against the royalty money to be earned by the book. Agents take their percentage off the top of the advance as well as from the royalties earned.

ADVENTURE. A genre of fiction in which action is the key element, overshadowing characters, theme and setting.

AUCTION. Publishers sometimes bid for the acquisition of a book manuscript with excellent sales prospects. The bids are for the amount of the author's advance, guaranteed dollar amounts, advertising and promotional expenses, royalty percentage, etc. Auctions are conducted by agents.

AUTHOR'S COPIES. An author usually receives about 10 free copies of his hardcover book from the publisher; more from a paperback firm. He can obtain additional copies at a price that has been reduced by an author's discount (usually 50 percent of the retail price).

AUTOBIOGRAPHY. A book-length account of a person's entire life written by the subject himself.

BACKLIST. A publisher's list of books that were not published during the current season, but that are still in print.

BACKSTORY. The history of what has happened before the action in your story takes place, affecting a character's current behavior.

BIO. A sentence or brief paragraph about the writer; includes work and educational experience.

BIOGRAPHY. An account of a person's life (or the lives of a family or close-knit group) written by someone other than the subject(s). The work is set within the historical framework (i.e., the unique economic, social and political conditions) existing during the subject's life.

BLURB. The copy on paperback book covers or hardcover book dust jackets, either promoting the book and the author or featuring testimonials from book reviewers or well-known people in the book's field. Also called flap copy or jacket copy.

BOILERPLATE. A standardized publishing contract. Most authors and agents make many changes on the boilerplate before accepting the contract.

BOOK DOCTOR. A freelance editor hired by a writer, agent or book editor who analyzes problems that exist in a book manuscript or proposal, and offers solutions to those problems.

BOOK PACKAGER. Someone who draws elements of a book together—from initial concept to writing and marketing strategies—and then sells the book package to a book publisher and/or movie producer. Also known as book producer or book developer.

BOUND GALLEYS. A prepublication, often paperbound, edition of a book, usually prepared from photocopies of the final galley proofs. Designed for promotional purposes, bound galleys serve as the first set of review copies to be mailed out. Also called bound proofs.

CATEGORY FICTION. A term used to include all types of fiction. See *genre*.

CLIMAX. The most intense point in the story line of a fictional work.

CLIPS. Samples, usually from newspapers or magazines, of your published work. Also called tearsheets.

COMMERCIAL FICTION. Novels designed to appeal to a broad audience. These are often broken down into categories such as western, mystery and romance. See *genre*.

CONFESSION. A first-person story in which the narrator is involved in an emotional situation that encourages sympathetic reader identification, concluding with the affirmation of a morally acceptable theme.

CONFLICT. A prime ingredient of fiction that usually represents some obstacle to the main character's (i.e., the protagonist's) goals.

CONTRIBUTOR'S COPIES. Copies of the book sent to the author. The number of contributor's copies is often negotiated in the publishing contract.

CO-PUBLISHING. Arrangement where author and publisher share publication costs and profits of a book. Also called co-operative publishing.

COPYEDITING. Editing of a manuscript for writing style, grammar, punctuation, and factual accuracy.

COPYRIGHT. A means to protect an author's work. A copyright is a proprietary right designed to give the creator of a work the power to control that work's reproduction, distribution, and public display or performance, as well as its adaptation to other forms.

COVER LETTER. A brief letter that accompanies the manuscript being sent to an agent or publisher.

CREATIVE NONFICTION. Type of writing where true stories are told by employing the techniques usually reserved for novelists and poets, such as scenes, character arc, a three-act structure and detailed descriptions. This category is also called narrative nonfiction or literary journalism.

CRITIQUING SERVICE. An editing service offered by some agents in which writers pay a fee for comments on the salability or other qualities of their manuscript. Sometimes the critique includes suggestions on how to improve the work. Fees vary, as does the quality of the critique.

CURRICULUM VITAE (CV). Short account of one's career or qualifications.

DEADLINE. A specified date and/or time that a project or draft must be turned into the editor. A deadline factors into a pre-production schedule, which involves copyediting, typesetting and production.

DEAL MEMO. The memorandum of agreement between a publisher and author that precedes the actual contract and includes important issues such as royalty, advance, rights, distribution and option clauses.

DEUS EX MACHINA. A term meaning "God from the machine" that refers to any unlikely, contrived or trick resolution of a plot in any type of fiction.

DIALOGUE. An essential element of fiction. Dialogue consists of conversations between two or more people, and can be used heavily or sparsely.

DIVISION. An unincorporated branch of a publishing house/company.

ELECTRONIC RIGHTS. Secondary or subsidiary rights dealing with electronic/multimedia formats (the Internet, CD-ROMs, electronic magazines).

EL-HI. Elementary to high school. A term used to indicate reading or interest level.

EROTICA. A form of literature or film dealing with the sexual aspects of love. Erotic content ranges from subtle sexual innuendo to explicit descriptions of sexual acts.

ETHNIC. Stories and novels whose central characters are African American, Native American, Italian American, Jewish, Appalachian or members of some other specific cultural group. Ethnic fiction usually deals with a protagonist caught between two conflicting ways of life: mainstream American culture and his ethnic heritage.

EVALUATION FEES. Fees an agent may charge to simply evaluate or consider material without further guarantees of representation. Paying upfront evaluation fees to agents is never recommended and strictly forbidden by the Association of Authors' Representations. An agent makes money through a standard commission—taking 15 percent of what you earn through advances, sales of subsidiary rights, and, if applicable, royalties.

EXCLUSIVE. Offering a manuscript, usually for a set period of time such as one month, to just one agent and guaranteeing that agent is the only one looking at the manuscript.

EXPERIMENTAL. Type of fiction that focuses on style, structure, narrative technique, setting and strong characterization rather than plot. This form depends largely on the revelation of a character's inner being, which elicits an emotional response from the reader.

FAMILY SAGA. A story that chronicles the lives of a family or a number of related or interconnected families over a period of time.

FANTASY. Stories set in fanciful, invented worlds or in a legendary, mythic past that rely on outright invention or magic for conflict and setting.

FILM RIGHTS. May be sold or optioned by the agent/author to a person in the film industry, enabling the book to be made into a movie.

FLOOR BID. If a publisher is very interested in a manuscript, he may offer to enter a floor bid when the book goes to auction. The publisher sits out of the auction, but agrees to take the book by topping the highest bid by an agreed-upon percentage (usually 10 percent).

FOREIGN RIGHTS. Translation or reprint rights to be sold abroad.

FOREIGN RIGHTS AGENT. An agent who handles selling the rights to a country other than that of the first book agent. Usually an additional percentage (about 5 percent) will be added on to the first book agent's commission to cover the foreign rights agent.

GENRE. Refers to either a general classification of writing, such as a novel, poem or short story, or to the categories within those classifications, such as problem novels or sonnets.

GENRE FICTION. A term that covers various types of commercial novels, such as mystery, romance, Western, science fiction, fantasy, thriller, and horror.

GHOSTWRITING. A writer puts into literary form the words, ideas or knowledge of another person under that person's name. Some agents offer this service; others pair ghostwriters with celebrities or experts.

GOTHIC. Novels characterized by historical settings and featuring young, beautiful women who win the favor of handsome, brooding heroes while simultaneously dealing with some life-threatening menace—either natural or supernatural.

GRAPHIC NOVEL. Contains comic-like drawings and captions, but deals more with everyday events and issues than with superheroes.

HIGH CONCEPT. A story idea easily expressed in a quick, one-line description.

HI-LO. A type of fiction that offers a high level of interest for readers at a low reading level.

HISTORICAL. A story set in a recognizable period of history. In addition to telling the stories of ordinary people's lives, historical fiction may involve political or social events of the time.

HOOK. Aspect of the work that sets it apart from others and draws in the reader/viewer.

HORROR. A story that aims to evoke some combination of fear, fascination and revulsion in its readers—either through supernatural or psychological circumstances.

HOW-TO. A book that offers the reader a description of how something can be accomplished. It includes both information and advice.

IMPRINT. The name applied to a publisher's specific line of books.

IN MEDIAS RES. A Latin term, meaning "into the midst of things," that refers to the literary device of beginning a narrative at a dramatic point in a story well along in the sequence of events to immediately convey action and capture reader interest.

IRC. International Reply Coupon. Buy at a post office to enclose with material sent outside the country to cover the cost of return postage. The recipient turns them in for stamps in their own country.

ISBN. This acronym stands for International Standard Book Number. ISBN is a tool used for both ordering and cataloging purposes.

JOINT CONTRACT. A legal agreement between a publisher and two or more authors that establishes provisions for the division of royalties their co-written book generates.

JUVENILE. Category of children's writing that can be broken down into easy-to-read books (ages 7–9), which run 2,000–10,000 words, and middle-grade books (ages 9–12), which run 20,000–40,000 words.

LIBEL. A form of defamation, or injury to a person's name or reputation. Written or published defamation is called *libel*, whereas spoken defamation is known as *slander*.

LITERARY. A book where style and technique are often as important as subject matter. In literary fiction, character is typically more important than plot, and the writer's voice and skill with words are both very essential. Also called serious fiction.

LOGLINE. A one-sentence description of a plot.

MAINSTREAM FICTION. Fiction on subjects or trends that transcend popular novel categories like mystery or romance. Using conventional methods, this kind of fiction tells stories about people and their conflicts.

MARKETING FEE. Fee charged by some agents to cover marketing expenses. It may be used to cover postage, telephone calls, faxes, photocopying or any other legitimate expense incurred in marketing a manuscript. Recouping expenses associated with submissions and marketing is the one and only time agents should ask for out-of-pocket money from writers.

MASS MARKET PAPERBACKS. Softcover books, usually 4×7 inches, on a popular subject directed at a general audience and sold in groceries, drugstores and bookstores.

MEMOIR. An author's commentary on the personalities and events that have significantly influenced one phase of his life.

MIDLIST. Those titles on a publisher's list expected to have limited sales. Midlist books are mainstream, not literary, scholarly or genre, and are usually written by new or relatively unknown writers.

MULTIPLE CONTRACT. Book contract that includes an agreement for a future book(s).

MYSTERY. A form of narration in which one or more elements remain unknown or unexplained until the end of the story. Subgenres include: amateur sleuth, caper, cozy, heist, malice domestic, police procedural, etc.

NET RECEIPTS. One method of royalty payment based on the amount of money a book publisher receives on the sale of the book after the booksellers' discounts, special sales discounts and returned copies.

NOVELIZATION. A novel created from the script of a popular movie and published in paperback. Also called a movie tie-in.

NOVELLA. A short novel or long short story, usually 20,000–50,000 words. Also called a novelette.

OCCULT. Supernatural phenomena, including ghosts, ESP, astrology, demonic possession, paranormal elements, and witchcraft.

ONE-TIME RIGHTS. This right allows a short story or portions of a fiction or nonfiction book to be published again without violating the contract.

OPTION. The act of a producer buying film rights to a book for a limited period of time (usually six months or one year) rather than purchasing said rights in full. A book can be optioned multiple times by different production companies.

OPTION CLAUSE. A contract clause giving a publisher the right to publish an author's next book.

OUTLINE. A summary of a book's content (up to 15 double-spaced pages); often in the form of chapter headings with a descriptive sentence or two under each one to show the scope of the book.

PICTURE BOOK. A type of book aimed at ages 2–9 that tells the story partially or entirely with artwork, with up to 1,000 words. Agents interested in selling to publishers of these books often handle both artists and writers.

PLATFORM. A writer's speaking experience, interview skills, website and other abilities that help form a following of potential buyers for his book.

PROOFREADING. Close reading and correction of a manuscript's typographical errors.

PROPOSAL. An offer to an editor or publisher to write a specific work, usually a package consisting of an outline and sample chapters.

PROSPECTUS. A preliminary written description of a book, usually one page in length.

PSYCHIC/SUPERNATURAL. Fiction exploiting—or requiring as plot devices or themes—some contradictions of the commonplace natural world and materialist assumptions about it (including the traditional ghost story).

QUERY. A letter written to an agent or a potential market to elicit interest in a writer's work.

READER. A person employed by an agent or buyer to go through the slush pile of manuscripts and scripts, and select those worth considering.

REGIONAL. A book faithful to a particular geographic region and its people, including behavior, customs, speech and history.

RELEASE. A statement that your idea is original, has never been sold to anyone else, and that you are selling negotiated rights to the idea upon payment. Some agents may ask that you sign a release before they request pages and review your work.

REMAINDERS. Leftover copies of an out-of-print or slow-selling book purchased from the publisher at a reduced rate. Depending on the contract, a reduced royalty or no royalty is paid to the author on remaindered books.

REPRINT RIGHTS. The right to republish a book after its initial printing.

ROMANCE. A type of category fiction in which the love relationship between a man and a woman pervades the plot. The story is told from the viewpoint of the heroine, who meets a man (the hero), falls in love with him, encounters a conflict that hinders their relationship, and then resolves the conflict with a happy ending.

ROYALTIES. A percentage of the retail price paid to the author for each copy of the book that is sold. Agents take their percentage from the royalties earned and from the advance.

SASE. Self-addressed, stamped envelope. It should be included with all mailed correspondence.

SCHOLARLY BOOKS. Books written for an academic or research audience. These are usually heavily researched, technical and often contain terms used only within a specific field.

SCIENCE FICTION. Literature involving elements of science and technology as a basis for conflict, or as the setting for a story.

SERIAL RIGHTS. The right for a newspaper or magazine to publish sections of a manuscript.

SIMULTANEOUS SUBMISSION. Sending the same query or manuscript to several agents or publishers at the same time.

SLICE OF LIFE. A type of short story, novel, play or film that takes a strong thematic approach, depending less on plot than on vivid detail in describing the setting and/or environment, and the environment's effect on characters involved in it.

SLUSH PILE. A stack of unsolicited submissions in the office of an editor, agent or publisher.

STANDARD COMMISSION. The commission an agent earns on the sales of a manuscript. The commission percentage (usually 15 percent) is taken from the advance and royalties paid to the writer.

SUBAGENT. An agent handling certain subsidiary rights, usually working in conjunction with the agent who handled the book rights. The percentage paid the book agent is increased to pay the subagent.

SUBSIDIARY. An incorporated branch of a company or conglomerate (for example, Crown Publishing Group is a subsidiary of Random House, Inc.).

SUBSIDIARY RIGHTS. All rights other than book publishing rights included in a book publishing contract, such as paperback rights, book club rights and movie rights. Part of an agent's job is to negotiate those rights and advise you on which to sell and which to keep.

SUSPENSE. The element of both fiction and some nonfiction that makes the reader uncertain about the outcome. Suspense can be created through almost any element of a story, including the title, characters, plot, time restrictions and word choice.

SYNOPSIS. A brief summary of a story, novel or play. As a part of a book proposal, it is a comprehensive summary condensed in a page or page-and-a-half, single-spaced. Unlike a query letter or logline, a synopsis is a front-to-back explanation of the work—and will give away the story's ending.

TERMS. Financial provisions agreed upon in a contract, whether between writer and agent, or writer and editor.

TEXTBOOK. Book used in school classrooms at the elementary, high school or college level.

THEME. The point a writer wishes to make. It poses a question—a human problem.

THRILLER. A story intended to arouse feelings of excitement or suspense. Works in this genre are highly sensational, usually focusing on illegal activities, international espionage, sex, and violence.

TOC. Table of Contents. A listing at the beginning of a book indicating chapter titles and their corresponding page numbers. It can also include chapter descriptions.

TRADE BOOK. Either a hardcover or softcover book sold mainly in bookstores. The subject matter frequently concerns a special interest for a more general audience.

TRADE PAPERBACK. A soft-bound volume, usually 5×8 inches, published and designed for the general public; available mainly in bookstores.

TRANSLATION RIGHTS. Sold to a foreign agent or foreign publisher.

UNSOLICITED MANUSCRIPT. An unrequested full manuscript sent to an editor, agent or publisher.

VET. A term used by editors when referring to the procedure of submitting a book manuscript to an outside expert (such as a lawyer) for review before publication. Memoirs are frequently vetted to confirm factually accuracy before the book is published.

WESTERNS/FRONTIER. Stories set in the American West, almost always in the 19th century, generally between the antebellum period and the turn of the century.

YOUNG ADULT (YA). The general classification of books written for ages 12–15. They run 40,000–80,000 words and include category novels—adventure, sports, paranormal, science fiction, fantasy, multicultural, mysteries, romance, etc.

LITERARY AGENTS

Literary Agents listed in this section do not charge for reading or considering your manuscript or book proposal. It's the goal of an agent to find salable manuscripts: Her income depends on finding the best publisher for your manuscript.

Since an agent's time is better spent meeting with editors, she will have little or no time to critique your writing. Agents who don't charge fees must be selective and often prefer to work with established authors, celebrities or those with professional credentials in a particular field.

Some agents in this section may charge clients for office expenses such as photocopying, foreign postage, long-distance phone calls or express mail services. Make sure you have a clear understanding of what these expenses are before signing any agency agreement.

SUBHEADS

Each agency listing is broken down into subheads to make locating specific information easier. In the first section, you'll find contact information for each agency. Additional information in this section includes the size of each agency, its willingness to work with new or unpublished writers, and its general areas of interest.

Member Agents: Agencies comprised of more than one agent list member agents and their individual specialties. This information will help you determine the appropriate person to whom you should send your query letter.

Represents: This section allows agencies to specify what nonfiction and fiction subjects they represent. Make sure you query only those agents who represent the type of material you write.

Look for the key icon to quickly learn an agent's areas of specialization. In this portion of the listing, agents mention the specific subject areas they're currently seeking, as well as those subject areas they do not consider.

How to Contact: Most agents open to submissions prefer an initial query letter that briefly describes your work. You should send additional material only if the agent requests them. In this section, agents also mention if they accept queries by fax or e-mail, if they consider simultaneous submissions, and how they prefer to obtain new clients.

Terms: Provided here are details of an agent's commission, whether a contract is offered and for how long, and what additional office expenses you might have to pay if the agent agrees to represent you. Standard commissions range from 10–15 percent for domestic sales and 15–25 percent for foreign or dramatic sales (with the difference going to the co-agent who places the work).

Writers' Conferences: A great way to meet an agent is at a writers' conference. Here agents list the conferences they usually attend. For more information about a specific conference, check the Conferences section starting on page 264.

Tips: In this section, agents offer advice and additional instructions for writers.

SPECIAL INDEXES

Literary Agents Specialties Index: This index (page 303) organizes agencies according to the subjects they are interested in re-

At the beginning of some listings, you will find one or more of the following symbols:

✚ agency new to this addition

⊘ agency not currently seeking new clients

◑ Canadian agency

◓ agency located outside of the U.S. and Canada

◗ comment from the editor of *Guide to Literary Agents*

○ newer agency actively seeking clients

◐ agency seeking both new and established writers

● agency seeking mostly established writers through referrals

◎ agency has a specialized focus

⌐ tips on agency's specializations

Find a pull-out bookmark with a key to symbols on the inside cover of this book.

ceiving. This index should help you compose a list of agents specializing in your areas. Cross-referencing categories and concentrating on agents interested in two or more aspects of your manuscript might increase your chances of success.

Agents Index: This index (page 325) provides a list of agents' names in alphabetical order, along with the name of the agency for which they work. Find the name of the person you would like to contact, and then check the agency listing.

USING THE LISTINGS

It is especially important that you read individual listings carefully before contacting these busy agents. The first information after the company name includes the address and phone, fax, e-mail address (when available), and website. **Member Agents** gives the names of individual agents working at that company. (Specific types of fiction an agent handles are indicated in parentheses after that agent's name). The **Represents** section lists the types of fiction the agency works with. Reading the **Recent Sales** gives you the names of writers an agent is currently working with and, very important, publishers the agent has placed manuscripts with. **Tips** presents advice directly from the agent to authors.

Also, look closely at the openness to submissions icon that precedes most listings. It indicates how willing an agency is to take on new writers.

DOMINICK ABEL LITERARY AGENCY, INC.

146 W. 82nd St., #1A, New York NY 10024. (212)877-0710. **E-mail:** agency@dalainc.com. **Website:** http://dalainc.com/. Estab. 1975. Member AAR. Represents 100 clients. Currently handles: adult fiction and nonfiction.

HOW TO CONTACT Query via e-mail. Check website to learn when this agency reopens to new submissions.

TERMS Agent receives 15% commission on domestic sales. Agent receives 20% commission on foreign sales.

ADAMS LITERARY

7845 Colony Rd., C4 #215, Charlotte NC 28226. (704)542-1440. **Fax:** (704)542-1450. **E-mail:** info@adamsliterary.com. **Website:** www.adamsliterary.com. **Contact:** Tracey Adams, Josh Adams. Member of AAR. Other memberships include SCBWI and WNBA. Currently handles: juvenile books.

MEMBER AGENTS Tracey Adams, Josh Adams, Samantha Bagood (assistant).

REPRESENTS Considers these fiction areas: middle grade, picture books, young adult.

➥ Represents "the finest children's book authors and artists."

HOW TO CONTACT Contact through online form on website only. Send e-mail if that is not operating correctly. All submissions and queries should first be made through the online form on website. Will not review—and will promptly recycle—any unsolicited submissions or queries received by mail. Before submitting work for consideration, review complete guidelines online, as the agency sometimes shuts off to new submissions. "While we have an established client list, we do seek new talent—and we accept submissions from both published and aspiring authors and artists."

TERMS Agent receives 15% commission on domestic sales; 20% on foreign sales. Offers written contract.

RECENT SALES *Exposed*, by Kimberly Marcus (Random House); *The Lemonade Crime*, by Jacqueline Davies (Houghton Mifflin); *Jane Jones: Worst Vampire Ever*, by Caissie St. Onge (Random House).

TIPS "Guidelines are posted (and frequently updated) on our website."

○◉ BRET ADAMS LTD. AGENCY

448 W. 44th St., New York NY 10036. (212)765-5630. **E-mail:** literary@bretadamsltd.net. **Website:** http://bretadamsltd.net. **Contact:** Aislinn Frantz. Member of AAR. Currently handles: stage plays.

MEMBER AGENTS Bruce Ostler, Mark Orsini; Alexis Williams.

REPRESENTS theatrical stage play.

➥ Handles theatre/film and TV projects. No books. Cannot accept unsolicited material.

HOW TO CONTACT Use the online submission form. Because of this agency's submission policy and interests, it's best to approach with a professional recommendation from a client.

THE AGENCY GROUP, LLC

142 W 57th St., 6th Floor, New York NY 10019. (212)581-3100. **Website:** www.theagencygroup.com. **Contact:** Marc Gerald, agent.

○ Prior to becoming an agent, Mr. Gerald owned and ran an independent publishing and entertainment agency.

MEMBER AGENTS Marc Gerald (no queries); Juliet Mushens, UK Literary division, JulietMushens@theagencygroup.com (fiction submissions, in all genres except picture books, middle grade, and erotica); Sasha Raskin, litsubmissions@theagencygroup.com (popular science, business books, historical narrative nonfiction, narrative and/or literary nonfiction, historical fiction, and genre fiction like sci-fi but when it fits the crossover space and isn't strictly confined to its genre).

REPRESENTS nonfiction books, novels. **Considers these nonfiction areas:** anthropology, archeology, architecture, art, autobiography, biography, business, child guidance, cooking, cultural interests, dance, decorating, design, economics, environment, ethnic, finance, foods, government, health, history, how-to, humor, interior design, investigative, law, medicine, memoirs, money, nature, nutrition, parenting, personal improvement, popular culture, politics, psychology, satire, self-help, sports, true crime. **Considers these fiction areas:** action, adventure, cartoon, comic books, commercial, confession, contemporary issues, crime, detective, erotica, ethnic, experimental, family saga, feminist, frontier, gay, glitz, hi-lo, historical, horror, humor, inspirational, juvenile, lesbian, literary, mainstream, metaphysical, military, multicultural, multimedia, mystery, New Age, occult, picture books, plays, poetry, poetry in translation, police, psychic, regional, religious, romance, satire, short story collections, spiritual, sports, supernatural, suspense, thriller, translation, war, Westerns, women's, young adult.

HOW TO CONTACT To query Juliet: "Please send your cover letter, first 3 chapters, and synopsis by e-mail. Juliet replies to all submissions, and aims to respond within 8-12 weeks of receipt of e-mail." To query Sasha: "e-query." Accepts simultaneous submissions. Obtains most new clients through recommendations from others.

TERMS Agent receives 15% commission on domestic sales. Agent receives 20% commission on foreign sales. Offers written contract.

THE AHEARN AGENCY, INC.

2021 Pine St., New Orleans LA 70118. (504)861-8395. **Fax:** (504)866-6434. **E-mail:** pahearn@aol.com. **Website:** www.ahearnagency.com. **Contact:** Pamela G. Ahearn. Other memberships include MWA, RWA, ITW. Represents 35 clients. 20% of clients are new/unpublished writers.

○ Prior to opening her agency, Ms. Ahearn was an agent for 8 years and an editor with Bantam Books.

REPRESENTS Considers these fiction areas: romance, suspense, thriller, women's.

☛ Handles women's fiction and suspense fiction only. Does not want to receive category romance, science fiction, or fantasy.

HOW TO CONTACT Query with SASE or via e-mail. Please send a one-page query letter stating the type of book you're writing, word length, where you feel your book fits into the current market, and any writing credentials you may possess. Please do not send ms pages or synopses if they haven't been previously requested. If you're querying via e-mail, send no attachments. Accepts simultaneous submissions. Responds in 2-3 months to queries & mss. Obtains most new clients through recommendations from others, solicitations, conferences.

TERMS Agent receives 15% commission on domestic sales. Agent receives 20% commission on foreign sales. Offers written contract, binding for 1 year; renewable by mutual consent.

RECENT SALES *Black-Eyed Susans*, by Julia Heaberlin; *The Art of Sinning*, by Sabrina Jeffries; *The Comfort of Black*, by Carter Wilson; *Flirting with Felicity*, by Gerri Russell; *The Iris Fan*, by Laura Joh Rowland.

TIPS "Be professional! Always send in exactly what an agent/editor asks for—no more, no less. Keep query letters brief and to the point, giving your writing credentials and a very brief summary of your book. If 1 agent rejects you, keep trying—there are a lot of us out there!"

AITKEN ALEXANDER ASSOCIATES

18-21 Cavaye Place, London England SW10 9PT United Kingdom. (020)7373-8672. **Fax:** (020)7373-6002. **E-mail:** reception@aitkenalexander.co.uk; reception@aitkenalexander.com. **Website:** www.aitkenalexander.co.uk. Estab. 1976.

MEMBER AGENTS Gillon Aitken; Clare Alexander (literary, commercial, memoir, narrative nonfiction); **Matthew Hamilton** (literary fiction, memoir, music, politics and sports); **Gillie Russell** (middle grade, young adult); **Anna Stein O'Sullivan; Imogen Pelham** (literary, commercial, serious narrative nonfiction, short stories); **Mary Pachnos; Anthony Sheil; Lucy Luck** (quality fiction and nonfiction); **Lesley Thorne; Matias Lopez Portillo** (high end commercial thrillers and literary fiction [with a particular focus on Latin America]; **Shruti Debi.**

REPRESENTS nonfiction books, novels. **Considers these nonfiction areas:** creative nonfiction, memoirs, music, politics, sports. **Considers these fiction areas:** commercial, literary, mainstream, middle grade, thriller, young adult.

☛ "We specialize in literary fiction and nonfiction." Does not represent illustrated children's books, poetry, or screenplays.

HOW TO CONTACT "If you would like to submit your work to us, please e-mail your covering letter with a short synopsis and the first 30 pages (as a Word Document) to submissions@aitkenalexander.co.uk indicating if there is a specific agent who you would like to consider your work. Submissions for the attention of the US Office should be sent to reception@aitkenalexander.com. Please note that the Indian Office does not accept unsolicited submissions." Accepts simultaneous submissions. Obtains most new clients through recommendations from others, solicitations.

TERMS Agent receives 15% commission on domestic sales. Agent receives 20% commission on foreign sales. Offers written contract; 28-day notice must be given to terminate contract. Charges for photocopying and postage.

RECENT SALES Sold 50 titles in the last year. *My Life with George*, by Judith Summers (Voice); *The Separate Heart*, by Simon Robinson (Bloomsbury); *The*

Fall of the House of Wittgenstein, by Alexander Waugh (Bloomsbury); *Shakespeare's Life*, by Germane Greer (Picador); *Occupational Hazards*, by Rory Stewart.

TIPS "Before submitting to us, we advise you to look at our existing client list to establish whether your work will be of interest. Equally, you should consider whether the material you have written is ready to submit to a literary agency. If you feel your work qualifies, then send us a letter introducing yourself. Keep it relevant to your writing (e.g., tell us about any previously published work, be it a short story or journalism; you may be studying or have completed a post graduate qualification in creative writing; when it comes to nonfiction, we would want to know what qualifies you to write about the subject)."

ALIVE COMMUNICATIONS, INC.

7680 Goddard St., Suite 200, Colorado Springs CO 80920. (719)260-7080. **Fax:** (719)260-8223. **E-mail:** submissions@alivecom.com. **Website:** www.alivecom.com. **Contact:** Rick Christian. Member of AAR. Other memberships include Authors Guild.

MEMBER AGENTS Rick Christian, president (blockbusters, bestsellers); Lee Hough (popular/commercial nonfiction and fiction, thoughtful spirituality, children's); **Andrea Heinecke** (thoughtful/inspirational nonfiction, women's fiction/nonfiction, popular/commercial nonfiction & fiction); **Bryan Norman**; **Lisa Jackson**.

REPRESENTS nonfiction books, novels, short story collections, novellas. **Considers these nonfiction areas:** autobiography, biography, business, child guidance, economics, how-to, inspirational, parenting, personal improvement, religious, self-help, women's issues, women's studies. **Considers these fiction areas:** adventure, contemporary issues, crime, family saga, historical, humor, inspirational, literary, mainstream, mystery, police, religious, satire, suspense, thriller.

This agency specializes in fiction, Christian living, how-to, and commercial nonfiction. Actively seeking inspirational, literary and mainstream fiction, and work from authors with established track records and platforms. Does not want to receive poetry, scripts, or dark themes.

HOW TO CONTACT "Because all our agents have full client loads, they are only considering queries from authors referred by clients and close contacts." New clients come through recommendations from others.

TERMS Agent receives 15% commission on domestic sales. Offers written contract; 2-month notice must be given to terminate contract.

TIPS Rewrite and polish until the words on the page shine. Endorsements and great connections may help, provided you can write with power and passion. Network with publishing professionals by making contacts, joining critique groups, and attending writers' conferences in order to make personal connections and to get feedback. Alive Communications, Inc., has established itself as a premiere literary agency. We serve an elite group of authors who are critically acclaimed and commercially successful in both Christian and general markets.

ALLEN O'SHEA LITERARY AGENCY

615 Westover Rd., Stamford CT 06902. (203)359-9965. **Fax:** (203)357-9909. **E-mail:** marilyn@allenoshea; coleen@allenoshea.com. **Website:** www.allenoshea.com. **Contact:** Marilyn Allen. Currently handles: nonfiction books 99%.

Prior to becoming agents, both Ms. Allen and Ms. O'Shea held senior positions in publishing.

MEMBER AGENTS Marilyn Allen; Coleen O'Shea.

REPRESENTS nonfiction books. **Considers these nonfiction areas:** biography, business, cooking, crafts, current affairs, health, history, how-to, humor, military, money, popular culture, psychology, science, interior design/decorating.

"This agency specializes in practical nonfiction including health, cooking, business, pop culture, etc. We look for clients with strong marketing platforms and new ideas coupled with strong writing ability." Actively seeking narrative nonfiction, health, popular science, cookbooks, and history writers; very interested in writers who have large media platforms following and interesting topics. Does not want to receive fiction, memoirs, poetry, textbooks, or children's.

HOW TO CONTACT Query via e-mail or mail with SASE. Submit book proposal with sample chapters, competitive analysis, outline, author bio, marketing page. No phone or fax queries. Accepts simultaneous submissions. Obtains most new clients through recommendations from others, conferences.

NEW AGENT SPOTLIGHT

DAN BALOW
STEVE LAUBE LITERARY AGENCY

Stevelaube.com

@danbalow

ABOUT DAN: Dan is a 30-year veteran of the Christian publishing industry. He was former director of marketing for Tyndale House Publishers. Beginning in 1995, he led the publisher's marketing team for the successful Jerry Jenkins & Tim LaHaye Left Behind series, becoming director of business development for the series (which has sold more than 60 million copies to date). In 2002, he added the role of director of international publishing until leaving Tyndale in 2006. After stints as publisher for two audio book companies and some publisher consulting, Dan joined the Steve Laube Agency.

HE IS SEEKING: Mostly nonfiction for the Christian market, but he represents a select number of novelists working in Christian historical, contemporary, Biblical, and futuristic genres.

HOW TO SUBMIT: E-query Dan through his assistant at vseem@stevelaube.com. A submission process and form is available at the agency website at stevelaube.com/guidelines/.

TERMS Agent receives 15% commission on domestic sales. Offers written contract, binding for 2 years; 1-month notice must be given to terminate contract.
TIPS "Prepare a strong overview, with competition, marketing and bio. We will consider when your proposal is ready."

◑ MIRIAM ALTSHULER LITERARY AGENCY

53 Old Post Rd. N, Red Hook NY 12571. (845)758-9408. **E-mail:** query@maliterary.com. **Website:** www.miriamaltshulerliteraryagency.com. **Contact:** Miriam Altshuler. Estab. 1994. Member of AAR. Represents 40 clients.
○ Ms. Altshuler has been an agent since 1982.
MEMBER AGENTS Miriam Altshuler (literary and commercial fiction, nonfiction, and children's books); **Reiko Davis** (literary fiction, well-told commercial fiction, narrative nonfiction, and young adult).

REPRESENTS nonfiction books, novels, short story collections, juvenile. **Considers these nonfiction areas:** creative nonfiction, how-to, memoirs, self-help, spirituality, women's issues. **Considers these fiction areas:** commercial, literary, middle grade, picture books, young adult.
⚷ Literary commercial fiction and general nonfiction. Does not want mystery, romance, horror, spiritual, fantasy, poetry, screenplays, science fiction or techno-thriller, western.

HOW TO CONTACT Query through e-mail or snail mail. "A query should include a brief author bio, a synopsis of the work, and the first chapter pasted within the body of the e-mail only. (For security purposes, we do not open attachments.)" Accepts simultaneous submissions. Obtains most new clients through recommendations from others.

TERMS Agent receives 15% commission on domestic sales. Agent receives 20% commission on foreign sales. Charges clients for overseas mailing, photocopies, overnight mail when requested by author.

WRITERS CONFERENCES Bread Loaf Writers' Conference; Washington Independent Writers Conference; North Carolina Writers' Network Conference.

TIPS See the website for specific submission details.

AMBASSADOR LITERARY AGENCY & SPEAKERS BUREAU

P.O. Box 50358, Nashville TN 37205. (615)370-4700. **Website:** www.ambassadoragency.com. **Contact:** Wes Yoder. Represents 25-30 clients. 10% of clients are new/unpublished writers. Currently handles: nonfiction books 95%, novels 5%.

○ Prior to becoming an agent, Mr. Yoder founded a music artist agency in 1973; he established a speakers bureau division of the company in 1984.

REPRESENTS nonfiction books, novels. **Considers these nonfiction areas:** biography, current affairs, ethnic, government, history, inspirational, memoirs, popular culture.

⚷ "This agency specializes in religious market publishing dealing primarily with A-level publishers." Actively seeking popular nonfiction themes, including the following: practical living, Christian spirituality, literary fiction. Does not want to receive short stories, children's books, screenplays, or poetry.

HOW TO CONTACT Authors should e-mail a short description of their manuscript with a request to submit their work for review. Official submission guidelines will be sent if we agree to review a manuscript. Speakers should submit a bio, headshot, and speaking demo. Direct all inquiries and submissions to info@ambassadorspeakers.com. Accepts simultaneous submissions. Obtains most new clients through recommendations from others.

TERMS Agent receives 15% commission on domestic sales. Agent receives 20% commission on foreign sales. Offers written contract.

BETSY AMSTER LITERARY ENTERPRISES

6312 SW Capitol Hwy #503, Portland OR 97239. **Website:** www.amsterlit.com. **Contact:** Betsy Amster (adult); Mary Cummings (children's and YA). Estab. 1992. Member of AAR. Represents more than 65 clients. 35% of clients are new/unpublished writers. Currently handles: nonfiction books 65%, novels 35%.

○ Prior to opening her agency, Ms. Amster was an editor at Pantheon and Vintage for 10 years, and served as editorial director for the Globe Pequot Press for 2 years.

REPRESENTS nonfiction books, novels. **Considers these nonfiction areas:** art & design, biography, business, child guidance, cooking/nutrition, current affairs, ethnic, gardening, health/medicine, history, memoirs, money, parenting, popular culture, psychology, science/technology, self-help, sociology, travelogues, social issues, women's issues. **Considers these fiction areas:** ethnic, literary, women's, high quality.

⚷ "Actively seeking strong narrative nonfiction, particularly by journalists; outstanding literary fiction (the next Jennifer Haigh or Jess Walter); witty, intelligent commerical women's fiction (the next Elinor Lipman); mysteries that open new worlds to us; and high-profile self-help and psychology, preferably research based." Does not want to receive poetry, children's books, romances, western, science fiction, action/adventure, screenplays, fantasy, techno-thrillers, spy capers, apocalyptic scenarios, or political or religious arguments.

HOW TO CONTACT For adult titles: b.amster.assistant@gmail.com. "For fiction or memoirs, please embed the first three pages in the body of your e-mail. For nonfiction, please embed your proposal." For children's and YA: b.amster.kidsbooks@gmail.com. See submission requirements online at website. "For picture books, please embed the entire text in the body of your e-mail. For novels, please embed the first three pages." Accepts simultaneous submissions. Responds in 1 month to queries. Responds in 2 months to mss. Obtains most new clients through recommendations from others, solicitations, conferences.

TERMS Agent receives 15% commission on domestic sales. Agent receives 20% commission on foreign sales. Offers written contract, binding for 1 year; 3-month notice must be given to terminate contract. Charges for photocopying, postage, messengers, galleys/books used in submissions to foreign and film agents and to magazines for first serial rights.

ANDERSON LITERARY MANAGEMENT, LLC

12 W. 19th St., New York NY 10011. (212)645-6045. **Fax:** (212)741-1936. **E-mail:** info@andersonliterary. com; kathleen@andersonliterary.com; adam@andersonliterary.com. **Website:** www.andersonliterary.com. **Contact:** Kathleen Anderson. Estab. 2006. Member of AAR. Represents 100+ clients. 20% of clients are new/unpublished writers. Currently handles: nonfiction books 50%, novels 50%.

MEMBER AGENTS Kathleen Anderson, Claire Wheeler.

REPRESENTS nonfiction books, novels, short story collections, juvenile. **Considers these nonfiction areas:** anthropology, archeology, architecture, art, autobiography, biography, cultural interests, current affairs, dance, design, education, environment, ethnic, gay, government, history, law, lesbian, memoirs, music, nature, politics, psychology, women's issues, women's studies. **Considers these fiction areas:** action, adventure, ethnic, family saga, feminist, frontier, gay, historical, lesbian, literary, mystery, suspense, thriller, westerns, women's, young adult.

⚭ ⌐ "Specializes in adult and young adult literary and commercial fiction, narrative nonfiction, American and European history, literary journalism, nature and travel writing, memoir, and biography. We do not represent science fiction, cookbooks, gardening, craft books, or children's picture books. While we love literature in translation, we cannot accept samples of work written in languages other than English."

HOW TO CONTACT Query with SASE. Submit synopsis, first 3 sample chapters, proposal (for nonfiction). Snail mail queries only. Accepts simultaneous submissions. Responds in 6 weeks to queries. Obtains most new clients through recommendations from others, solicitations, conferences.

TERMS Agent receives 15% commission on domestic sales. Offers written contract.

WRITERS CONFERENCES Squaw Valley Conference.

TIPS "We do not represent plays or screenplays."

APONTE LITERARY AGENCY

E-mail: apontelit@gmail.com. **E-mail:** agents@aponteliterary.com. **Website:** http://aponteliterary.com. **Contact:** Natalia Aponte.

MEMBER AGENTS Natalia Aponte (any genre of mainstream fiction and nonfiction, but she is especially seeking women's novels, historical novels, supernatural and paranormal fiction, fantasy novels, political and science thrillers); **Victoria Lea** (any category—especially interested in women's fiction, science fiction, and speculative fiction).

⚭ ⌐ Actively seeking women's novels, historical novels, supernatural and paranormal fiction, fantasy novels, political and science thrillers, science fiction and speculative fiction.

HOW TO CONTACT E-query. Responds in 8 weeks if interested.

ARCADIA

31 Lake Place N., Danbury CT 06810. **E-mail:** arcadialit@sbcglobal.net. **Contact:** Victoria Gould Pryor. Member of AAR.

REPRESENTS nonfiction books. **Considers these nonfiction areas:** biography, current affairs, health, history, psychology, science, investigative journalism, culture, classical music, life-transforming self-help.

⚭ ⌐ "I'm a very hands-on agent, which is necessary in this competitive marketplace. I work with authors on revisions until whatever we present to publishers is as strong as possible. Arcadia represents talented, dedicated, intelligent and ambitious writers who are looking for a long-term relationship based on professional success and mutual respect." Does not want to receive fiction, true crime, business, science fiction/fantasy, horror, memoirs about addiction or abuse, humor, or children's/YA.

HOW TO CONTACT No unsolicited submissions. Query with SASE. This agency accepts e-queries (no attachments).

THE AXELROD AGENCY

55 Main St., P.O. Box 357, Chatham NY 12037. (518)392-2100. **E-mail:** steve@axelrodagency.com. **Website:** www.axelrodagency.com. **Contact:** Steven Axelrod. Member of AAR. Represents 15-20 clients. Currently handles: novels 95%.

◓ Prior to becoming an agent, Mr. Axelrod was a book club editor.

REPRESENTS novels. **Considers these fiction areas:** crime, mystery, new adult, romance, women's.

☛ This agency specializes in women's fiction and romance.

HOW TO CONTACT Query. Accepts simultaneous submissions. Obtains most new clients through recommendations from others.

TERMS Agent receives 15% commission on domestic sales. Agent receives 20% commission on foreign sales. No written contract.

WRITERS CONFERENCES RWA National Conference.

AZANTIAN LITERARY AGENCY

E-mail: queries@azantianlitagency.com. **Website:** www.azantianlitagency.com. Estab. 2014.

○ Prior to her current position, Jennifer Azantian was with Sandra Dijkstra Literary Agency.

☛ Actively seeking fantasy, science fiction and psychological horror for adult, young adult, and middle grade readers. Does not want to receive nonfiction or picture books.

HOW TO CONTACT To submit, send your query letter, 1-2 page synopsis, and first 10-15 pages all pasted in an e-mail (no attachments) to queries@azantianlitagency.com. Please note in the e-mail subject line if your work was requested at a conference, is an exclusive submission, or if your work was referred by a current client. Accepts simultaneous submissions. Responds within 6 weeks. Check the website before submitting to make sure Jennifer is currently open to queries.

BARONE LITERARY AGENCY

385 North St., Batavia OH 45103. (513)732-6740. **Fax:** (513)297-7208. **E-mail:** baroneliteraryagency@road runner.com. **Website:** www.baroneliteraryagency. com. **Contact:** Denise Barone. Estab. 2010. RWA

REPRESENTS Considers these nonfiction areas: memoirs. **Considers these fiction areas:** action, adventure, cartoon, comic books, commercial, confession, contemporary issues, crime, detective, erotica, ethnic, experimental, family saga, fantasy, feminist, frontier, gay, glitz, hi-lo, historical, horror, humor, inspirational, juvenile, lesbian, literary, mainstream, metaphysical, military, multicultural, multimedia, mystery, New Age, occult, plays, psychic, regional, religious, romance, science fiction, sports, thriller, women's, young adult. **Considers these script areas:** action, adventure, animation, cartoon, comedy, contemporary issues, crime, detective, erotica, ethnic, experimental, family saga, fantasy, feminist, gay, glitz, historical, horror, juvenile, lesbian, mainstream, mystery, police, psychic, religious, romantic comedy, romantic drama, science fiction, sports, supernatural, teen, thriller, western.

☛ Actively seeking adult contemporary romance. Does not want textbooks.

HOW TO CONTACT "We are no longer accepting snail mail submissions; send a query letter via e-mail. If I like your query letter, I will ask for the first three chapters and a synopsis as attachments." Accepts simultaneous submissions. Obtains new clients by queries/submissions, Facebook, recommendations from others.

TERMS 15% commission on domestic sales, 20% on foreign sales. Offers written contract.

RECENT SALES *All The Glittering Bones*, by Anna Snow (Entangled Publishing); *Melody Massacre to the Rescue*, by Anna Snow (Entangled Publishing); *A Taste of Terror*, by Anna Snow (Entangled Publishing); *Devon's Choice*, by Cathy Bennett (Astraea Press); *In Deep*, by Laurie Albano (Solstice Publishing); *Treading on Dandelions*, by Jennifer Petersen Fraser (Solstice Publishing); *Fire and Ice*, by Michele Barrow-Belisle (Astraea Press).

TIPS "In the immortal words of Sir Winston Churchill, if you want to get published, you must never give up!"

BAROR INTERNATIONAL, INC.

P.O. Box 868, Armonk NY 10504. **E-mail:** heather@ barorint.com. **Website:** www.barorint.com. **Contact:** Danny Baror; Heather Baror. Represents 300 clients.

MEMBER AGENTS Danny Baror; Heather Baror-Shapiro.

☛ This agency represents authors and publishers in the international market. Currently representing all genres ranging from thrillers to science fiction/fantasy, self-help, spiritual, young adult, commercial fiction, and more.

HOW TO CONTACT Submit by e-mail or mail (with SASE); include a cover letter.

BARRON'S LITERARY MANAGEMENT

4615 Rockland Dr., Arlington TX 76016. **E-mail:** bar ronsliterary@sbcglobal.net. **Contact:** Adele Brooks, president.

☛ Barron's Literary Management is a small Dallas/ Fort Worth-based agency with good publishing contacts. Seeks tightly written, fast moving fiction and nonfiction authors with a significant platform or subject area expertise. Considers legal, crime, techno, or medical thrillers. Considers all romance. Considers nonfiction: business, cooking, health, investing, psychology, and true crime.

HOW TO CONTACT Contact by e-mail initially. Send bio and a brief synopsis of story (fiction) or a nonfiction book proposal. Obtains most new clients through e-mail submissions.

TIPS "Have your book tightly edited, polished and ready-to-be-seen before contacting agents. I respond quickly and if interested may request an electronic or hard copy mailing."

LORELLA BELLI LITERARY AGENCY (LBLA)

54 Hartford House, 35 Tavistock Crescent, Notting Hill, London England W11 1AY United Kingdom. (44)(207)727-8547. **Fax:** (44)(870)787-4194. **E-mail:** info@lorellabelliagency.com. **Website:** www.lorella belliagency.com. **Contact:** Lorella Belli. Membership includes AAA, Crime Writers' Association, Romantic Novelists Association.

8→ This agency handles adult fiction, adult nonfiction, and YA. Does not want to receive children's picture books, fantasy, science fiction, screenplays, short stories, poetry, academic, or specialist books.

HOW TO CONTACT E-query. Do not send a proposal or ms before it's requested.

TERMS Agent receives 15% commission on domestic sales. Agent receives 20% commission on foreign sales.

THE BENT AGENCY

Bent Agency, The, 159 20th St., #2B, Brooklyn NY 11232. **E-mail:** info@thebentagency.com. **Website:** www.thebentagency.com. **Contact:** Jenny Bent; Susan Hawk; Molly Ker Hawn; Gemma Cooper; Louise Fury; Brooks Sherman; Beth Phelan; Victoria Lowes; Heather Flaherty. Estab. 2009.

○ Prior to forming her own agency, Ms. Bent was an agent and vice president at Trident Media.

MEMBER AGENTS Jenny Bent (adult fiction including women's fiction, romance and crime/suspense, she particularly likes novels with magical or fantasy elements that fall outside of genre fiction; young adult and middle grade fiction; memoir; humor); **Susan Hawk** (young adult and middle grade and picture books; within the realm of kids stories, she likes contemporary, mystery fantasy, science fiction, and historical fiction); **Molly Ker Hawn** (young adult and middle grade books, including contemporary, historical science fiction, fantasy, thrillers, mystery); **Gemma Cooper** (all ages of children's and young adult books, including picture books, likes historical, contemporary, thrillers, mystery, humor, and science fiction); **Louise Fury** (picture books, literary middle grade, all young adult, speculative fiction, suspense/thriller, commercial fiction, all sub-genres of romance including erotic, non-fiction: cookbooks, pop culture); **Brooks Sherman** (speculative and literary adult fiction, select narrative nonfiction; all ages of children's and young adult books, including picture books; likes historical, contemporary, thrillers, humor, fantasy, and horror); **Beth Phelan** (young adult, thrillers, suspense and mystery, romance and women's fiction, literary and general fiction, cookbooks, lifestyle and pets/animals); **Victoria Lowes** (romance and women's fiction, thrillers and mystery, and young adult); **Heather Flaherty** (young adult [fiction and nonfiction], middle grade [fiction and nonfiction]; in her juvenile stories, she likes contemporary, humor, horror, historical, sci-fi, fantasy, and thrillers; select pop culture & humor nonfiction).

REPRESENTS Considers these nonfiction areas: animals, cooking, creative nonfiction, popular culture. Considers these fiction areas: commercial, crime, fantasy, historical, horror, literary, mystery, picture books, romance, suspense, thriller, women's, young adult.

HOW TO CONTACT For Jenny Bent, e-mail: queries@thebentagency.com; for Susan Hawk, e-mail: kidsqueries@thebentagency.com; for Molly Ker Hawn, e-mail: hawnqueries@thebentagency.com; for Gemma Cooper, e-mail: cooperqueries@thebent agency.com; for Louise Fury, e-mail: furyqueries@ thebentagency.com; for Brooks Sherman, e-mail: shermanqueries@thebentagency.com; for Beth Phelan, e-mail: phelanagencies@thebentagency.com; for Victoria Lowes, e-mail: lowesqueries@thebentagency. com; for Heather Flaherty, e-mail: flahertyqueries@ thebentagency.com. "Tell us briefly who you are, what your book is, and why you're the one to write it. Then include the first 10 pages of your material in the body of your e-mail. We respond to all queries; please resend your query if you haven't had a response within 4 weeks." Accepts simultaneous submissions.

RECENT SALES *The Pocket Wife*, by Susan Crawford (Morrow); *The Smell of Other Peoples Houses*, by Bonnie-Sue Hitchcock (Wendy Lamb Books); *The Graham Cracker Plot*, by Shelley Tougas (Roaring Brook); *Murder is Bad Manners*, by Robin Stevens (Simon & Schuster); *The Inside Out Series*, by Lisa Renee Jones (Simon & Schuster); *True North*, by Liora Blake (Pocket Star)

BIDNICK & COMPANY

E-mail: bidnick@comcast.net. **Website:** www.publishersmarketplace.com/members/bidnick/. Currently handles: 100% nonfiction books.

○ Prior to her time as an agent, this agent was a founding member of Collins Publishers and vice president of HarperCollins, San Francisco.

MEMBER AGENTS Carole Bidnick.

REPRESENTS Considers these nonfiction areas: cooking, creative nonfiction.

➤ This agency specializes in cookbooks and narrative nonfiction.

HOW TO CONTACT Send queries via e-mail only.

RECENT SALES *The Diabetes Solution*, by Jorge Rodriguez, MD (Ten Speed); *Snack Girl to the Rescue*, by Lisa Cain (Harmony); *Williams-Sonoma Gluten-Free Baking*, by Kristine Kidd (Weldon Owen).

VICKY BIJUR LITERARY AGENCY

333 West End Ave., Suite 5B, New York NY 10023. **E-mail:** queries@vickybijuragency.com. **Website:** www.vickybijuragency.com. Estab. 1988. Member of AAR.

○ Vicky Bijur worked at Oxford University Press and with the Charlotte Sheedy Literary Agency. Books she represents have appeared on *the New York Times* bestseller list, in the *New York Times* Notable Books of the Year, *Los Angeles Times* Best Fiction of the Year, *Washington Post* Book World Rave Reviews of the Year.

MEMBER AGENTS Vicky Bijur; Shelby Sampsel.

REPRESENTS nonfiction books, novels. **Considers these nonfiction areas:** cooking, government, health, history, memoirs, psychology, science, sociology, biography; child care/development; environmental studies; journalism; social sciences. **Considers these fiction areas:** commercial, literary, mystery, new adult, thriller, young adult.

➤ "We do not represent children's books, poetry, science fiction, fantasy, horror, or romance."

HOW TO CONTACT "You can query us via e-mail to queries@vickybijuragency.com, or by regular mail. If you query by hard copy, please include an SASE for our response. If you want your material returned, include an SASE large enough to contain pages. To query us with fiction, please send a synopsis and the first chapter of your ms with your query letter (if e-mailed, please paste the chapter into body of e-mail, as we don't open attachments from unfamiliar senders). For nonfiction, please send a query letter and proposal. No phone or fax queries. We generally respond to all queries within 6 weeks of receipt."

RECENT SALES *Louise's Dilemma*, by Sarah Shaber; *After I'm Gone*, by Laura Lippman; *The Sleeping Dictionary*, by Sujata Massey.

DAVID BLACK LITERARY AGENCY

335 Adams St., Suite 2707, Brooklyn NY 11201. (718)852-5500. **Fax:** (718)852-5539. **Website:** www.davidblackagency.com. **Contact:** David Black, owner. Member of AAR. Represents 150 clients.

MEMBER AGENTS David Black; Gary Morris; Joy E. Tutela (general nonfiction, literary fiction, commercial fiction, YA, MG); Linda Loewenthal; Antonella Iannarino; Susan Raihofer; Sarah Smith.

REPRESENTS nonfiction books, novels. **Considers these nonfiction areas:** biography, business, creative nonfiction, current affairs, gay/lesbian, health, history, humor, memoirs, money, parenting, politics, self-help, women's issues. **Considers these fiction areas:** commercial, literary, middle grade, thriller, young adult.

HOW TO CONTACT "To query an individual agent, please follow the specific query guidelines outlined in the agent's profile on our website. Not all agents are currently accepting unsolicited queries. To query the agency, please send a 1-2 page query letter describing your book, and include information about any previously published works, your audience, and your platform." Note that some agents prefer e-queries whereas some prefer snail mail queries. Accepts simultaneous submissions. Responds in 2 months to queries.

TERMS Agent receives 15% commission on domestic sales. Charges clients for photocopying and books purchased for sale of foreign rights.

RECENT SALES Some of the agency's bestselling authors include: Mitch Albom, Erik Larson, Ken Davis, Bruce Feiler, Dan Coyle, Jane Leavy, Randy Pausch, Steve Lopez, Jenny Sanford, David Kidder, and Noah Oppenheim.

JUDY BOALS, INC.

307 W. 38th St., #812, New York NY 10018. (212)500-1424. **Fax:** (212)500-1426. **E-mail:** info@judyboals.com. **Website:** www.judyboals.com. **Contact:** Judy Boals.

HOW TO CONTACT Query by referral or invitation only.

BOND LITERARY AGENCY

4340 E. Kentucky Ave., Suite 471, Denver CO 80246. (303)781-9305. **E-mail:** queries@bondliteraryagency.com. **Website:** www.bondliteraryagency.com. **Contact:** Sandra Bond.

○ Prior to her current position, Ms. Bond worked with agent Jody Rein.

⚡ Actively seeking narrative nonfiction, history, science, business; commercial and literary fiction, mystery, women's, young adult. Does not represent romance, adult fantasy, poetry, sci-fi, or children's picture books.

HOW TO CONTACT Submit query by mail or e-mail (no attachments). "She will let you know if she is interested in seeing more material. *No unsolicited mss. No phone calls, please.*" Accepts simultaneous submissions.

RECENT SALES *Compassionate Careers* by Jeff Pryor and Alexandra Mitchell; *Wiki Management* by Rod Collins; *Book Of Colors, A Novel*, by Raymond Barfield; *Three Rivers, A Novel*, by Tiffany Tyson.

BOOK CENTS LITERARY AGENCY, LLC

P.O. Box 11826, Charleston WV 25339. **E-mail:** cw@bookcentsliteraryagency.com. **Website:** www.bookcentsliteraryagency.com. **Contact:** Christine Witthohn. Member of AAR. RWA, MWA, SinC, KOD

MEMBER AGENTS Christine Witthohn (represents both published and unpublished authors).

REPRESENTS **Considers these nonfiction areas:** cooking, gardening, travel, women's issues. **Considers these fiction areas:** literary, new adult, romance, thriller, women's, young adult.

⚡ "Single-title romance (contemporary, romantic comedy, paranormal, mystery/suspense), women's lit (must have a strong hook), mainstream mystery/suspense, thrillers (high octane, psychological), literary fiction and new adult. For nonfiction, seeking women's issues/experiences, fun/quirky topics (particularly those of interest to women), cookbooks (fun, ethnic, etc.), gardening (herbs, plants, flowers, etc.), books with a 'save-the-planet' theme, how-to books, travel and outdoor adventure." Does not want to receive category romance, erotica, inspirational, historical, sci-fi/fantasy, horror/dark thrillers (serial killers), short stories/novella, children's picture books, poetry, screenplays.

HOW TO CONTACT You can submit via this agency's online form.

TIPS "Sponsors *International Women's Fiction Festival* in Matera, Italy. See: www.womensfictionfestival.com for more information. Christine is also the US rights and licensing agent for leading French publisher, Bragelonne, Egmont-Germany. For a list of upcoming publications, leading clients and sales, visit: www.publishersmarketplace.com/members/BookCents."

BOOKENDS, LLC

Website: www.bookends-inc.com. **Contact:** Jessica Faust, Kim Lionetti, Jessica Alvarez, Beth Campbell. Member of AAR. RWA, MWA Represents 50+ clients. 10% of clients are new/unpublished writers. Currently handles: nonfiction books 50%, novels 50%.

MEMBER AGENTS Jessica Faust, JFaust@bookends-inc.com (fiction: women's fiction, mysteries and suspense; all other genres accepted by referral only); **Kim Lionetti**, klionetti@bookends-inc.com (only currently considering contemporary romance, women's fiction, cozies, new adult, and contemporary young adult); **Jessica Alvarez** (romance, women's fiction, erotica, romantic suspense); **Beth Campbell** (urban fantasy, science fiction, YA, suspense, romantic suspense, and mystery); **Moe Ferrara** (science fiction and fantasy for all age groups except picture books).

REPRESENTS nonfiction books, novels. **Considers these nonfiction areas:** business, ethnic, how-to, money, sex. **Considers these fiction areas:** mainstream, mystery, romance, women's.

⚡ "BookEnds is currently accepting queries from published and unpublished writers in the areas of romance (and all its sub-genres), erotica, mystery, suspense, women's fiction, and literary fiction." BookEnds does not want to receive children's books, screenplays, poetry, or technical/military thrillers.

HOW TO CONTACT Review website for guidelines, as they change. BookEnds is no longer accepting unsolicited proposal packages or snail mail queries. Send query in the body of e-mail to only 1 agent. No attachments.

THE BOOK GROUP

20 W. 20th St., Suite 601, New York, NY 10011. (212)803-3360 **Website:** www.thebookgroup.com.
MEMBER AGENTS Julie Barer, Faye Bender, Brettne Bloom (literary and commercial fiction, history, biography, memoir, psychology, and a handful of young adult titles; she also represents a number of cookbook and lifestyle writers); **Elisabeth Weed** (women's, upmarket, literary); **Rebecca Stead** (innovative forms, diverse voices, and open-hearted fiction for children, young adults, and adults).

8—⚼ Please do not send poetry or screenplays.

HOW TO CONTACT Send a query letter and 10 sample pages to submissions@thebookgroup.com, with the first and last name of the agent you are querying in the subject line. All material must be in the body of the email, as the agents do not open attachments.
RECENT SALES *The Family Fang*, by Kevin Wilson; *The Violets of March*, by Sarah Jio; *The Husband's Secret*, by Liane Moriarty; *Everything I Never Told You*, by Celeste Ng; *The Engagements*, by J Courtney Sullivan; *Home is Burning*, by Dan Marshall.

BOOKS & SUCH LITERARY AGENCY

52 Mission Circle, Suite 122, PMB 170, Santa Rosa CA 95409. **E-mail:** representation@booksandsuch.com. **Website:** www.booksandsuch.com. **Contact:** Janet Kobobel Grant, Wendy Lawton, Rachel Kent, Mary Keeley, Rachelle Gardner. Member of AAR. Member of CBA (associate), American Christian Fiction Writers. Currently handles: nonfiction books 50%, novels 50%.

◯ Prior to becoming an agent, Ms. Grant was an editor for Zondervan and managing editor for *Focus on the Family*; Ms. Lawton was an author, sculptor, and designer of porcelein dolls. Ms. Keeley accepts both nonfiction and adult fiction. She previously was an acquisition editor for Tyndale publishers.

REPRESENTS nonfiction books, novels. **Considers these nonfiction areas:** humor, religion, self help, women's. **Considers these fiction areas:** historical, literary, mainstream, new adult, religious, romance, young adult.

8—⚼ This agency specializes in general and inspirational fiction, romance, and in the Christian booksellers market. Actively seeking well-crafted material that presents Judeo-Christian values, if only subtly.

HOW TO CONTACT Query via e-mail only; no attachments. Accepts simultaneous submissions. Responds in 1 month to queries. "If you don't hear from us asking to see more of your writing within 30 days after you have sent your e-mail, please know that we have read and considered your submission but determined that it would not be a good fit for us." Obtains most new clients through recommendations from others, conferences.

TERMS Agent receives 15% commission on domestic sales. Agent receives 20% commission on foreign sales. Offers written contract; 2-month notice must be given to terminate contract. No additional charges.
RECENT SALES A full list of this agency's clients (and the awards they have won) is on the agency website.
WRITERS CONFERENCES Mount Hermon Christian Writers' Conference; Writing for the Soul; American Christian Fiction Writers' Conference; San Francisco Writers' Conference.
TIPS "Our agency highlights personal attention to individual clients that includes coaching on how to thrive in a rapidly changing publishing climate, grow a career, and get the best publishing offers possible."

BOOKSTOP LITERARY AGENCY

67 Meadow View Rd., Orinda CA 94563. (925)254-2664. **Fax:** (925)254-2668. **E-mail:** kendra@bookstopliterary.com; info@bookstopliterary.com. **Website:** www.bookstopliterary.com. Estab. 1983.

8—⚼ "Special interest in Hispanic, Asian American, African American, and multicultural writers; quirky picture books; clever adventure/mystery novels; eye-opening nonfiction; heartfelt middle grade; unusual teen romance."

HOW TO CONTACT Send: cover letter, entire ms for picture books; first 10 pages of novels; proposal and sample chapters OK for nonfiction. E-mail submissions: Paste cover letter and first 10 pages of ms into body of e-mail, send to info@bookstopliterary.com. Send sample illustrations only if you are an illustrator. Illustrators: send postcard or link to online portfolio. Do not send original artwork.

TERMS Agent receives 15% commission on domestic sales. Offers written contract, binding for 1 year.

NEW AGENT SPOTLIGHT

HEATHER ALEXANDER
PIPPIN PROPERTIES

Pippinproperties.com

@HeatherAlexand

ABOUT HEATHER: Heather came into publishing through editorial at Dial, working with such authors as Jenny Martin, Vin Vogel, Scott McCormick, and Jeanne Ryan. After six years at Penguin, she was asked a very interesting question: Had she ever considered becoming an agent? Many discussions later, she accepted a position at Pippin Properties, where she is building her roster of authors and illustrators, including A. N. Kang, Darren Farrell, and Jennifer Goldfinger.

SHE IS SEEKING: Picture books, middle grade, young adult, and literary graphic novels. She specifically seeks quirky picture books with a strong emotional core, middle grade about a moment that changes a kid forever, and beautifully written YA. She enjoys contemporary, historical, funny, high stakes, gothic style horror, and magical realism, but not high fantasy, medieval, or time travel. She favors literary over commercial and as an agent, she is excited to develop new talent and help shape careers, which is what she loves to do best.

HOW TO SUBMIT: Send a query addressed to Heather via e-mail along with your first chapter of your manuscript or the entire picture book in the body of the e-mail to info@pippinproperties.com. Please include a short synopsis of the work, your background and/or publishing history, and anything else you think is relevant. No attachments, please.

⊘ GEORGES BORCHARDT, INC.

136 E. 57th St., New York NY 10022. (212)753-5785.
Website: www.gbagency.com. Estab. 1967. Member of AAR. Represents 200+ clients.
MEMBER AGENTS Anne Borchardt; Georges Borchardt; Valerie Borchardt; Samantha Shea.
☛ This agency specializes in literary fiction and outstanding nonfiction.
HOW TO CONTACT *No unsolicited mss.* Obtains most new clients through recommendations from others.

TERMS Agent receives 15% commission on domestic sales. Agent receives 20% commission on foreign sales. Offers written contract.
RECENT SALES John Ashbery's *Selected Translations* (FSG); Evelyn Barish's *The Double Life of Paul de Man* (Norton); Louis Begley's *Memories of a Marriage* (Nan A. Talese); W. Michael Blumenthal's *From Exile to Leadership* (Overlook).

❶ BRADFORD LITERARY AGENCY

5694 Mission Center Rd., #347, San Diego CA 92108. (619)521-1201. **E-mail:** queries@bradfordlit.com.

Website: www.bradfordlit.com. **Contact:** Laura Bradford, Natalie Lakosil, Sarah LaPolla; Monica Odom. Estab. 2001. Member of AAR. RWA, SCBWI, ALA Represents 50 clients. 20% of clients are new/unpublished writers. Currently handles: nonfiction books 5%, novels 95%.

REPRESENTS Considers these nonfiction areas: biography, business, creative nonfiction, humor, memoirs, parenting, self-help. **Considers these fiction areas:** erotica, middle grade, mystery, paranormal, picture books, romance, thriller, women's, young adult.

⚷ Actively seeking many types of romance (historical, romantic suspense, paranormal, category, contemporary, erotic). Does not want to receive poetry, screenplays, short stories, westerns, horror, new age, religion, crafts, cookbooks, gift books.

HOW TO CONTACT Accepts e-mail queries only; send to queries@bradfordlit.com (or sarah@bradfordlit if contacting Sarah LaPolla). The entire submission must appear in the body of the e-mail and not as an attachment. The subject line should begin as follows: QUERY: (the title of the ms or any short message that is important should follow). For fiction: e-mail a query letter along with the first chapter of ms and a synopsis. Include the genre and word count in cover letter. Nonfiction: e-mail full nonfiction proposal including a query letter and a sample chapter. Accepts simultaneous submissions. Responds in 2-4 weeks to queries. Responds in 10 weeks to mss. Obtains most new clients through solicitations.

TERMS Agent receives 15% commission on domestic sales. Agent receives 20% commission on foreign sales. Offers written contract. Charges for extra copies of books for foreign submissions.

RECENT SALES Sold 93 titles in the last year. *The Sweetness of Honey,* by Alison Kent (Montlake); *Weave of Absence,* by Carol Ann Martin (NAL); *Pushing the Limit,* by Emmy Curtis (Forever Yours); *Voyage of the Heart,* by Soraya Lane (Amazon); *The Last Cowboy in Texas,* by Katie Lane (Grand Central); *Broken Open,* by Lauren Dane (HQN); *Lovely Wild,* by Megan Hart (Mira).

WRITERS CONFERENCES RWA National Conference; Romantic Times Booklovers Convention.

BRANDT & HOCHMAN LITERARY AGENTS, INC.

1501 Broadway, Suite 2310, New York NY 10036. (212)840-5760. **Fax:** (212)840-5776. **Website:** http://brandthochman.com. **Contact:** Gail Hochman. Member of AAR. Represents 200 clients.

MEMBER AGENTS Gail Hochman; Marianne Merola; Bill Contardi; Emily Forland; Emma Patterson (anything about the Yankees, stories set in Brooklyn); Jody Kahn; Henry Thayer. The e-mail addresses and specific likes of each of these agents is listed on the agency website.

REPRESENTS Considers these nonfiction areas: biography, cooking, creative nonfiction, foods, history, memoirs, music, sports, young adult. **Considers these fiction areas:** crime, family saga, fantasy, historical, literary, middle grade, mystery, suspense, thriller, women's.

⚷ No screenplays or textbooks.

HOW TO CONTACT "We accept queries by e-mail and regular mail; however, we cannot guarantee a response to e-mailed queries. For queries via regular mail, be sure to include a SASE for our reply. Query letters should be no more than two pages and should include a convincing overview of the book project and information about the author and his or her writing credits. Address queries to the specific Brandt & Hochman agent whom you would like to consider your work. Agent e-mail addresses and query preferences may be found at the end of each agent profile on the 'Agents' page of our website." Accepts simultaneous submissions. Obtains most new clients through recommendations from others.

TERMS Agent receives 15% commission on domestic sales. Agent receives 20% commission on foreign sales.

RECENT SALES This agency sells 40-60 new titles each year. A full list of their hundreds of clients is on the agency website.

TIPS "Write a letter which will give the agent a sense of you as a professional writer—your long-term interests as well as a short description of the work at hand."

THE JOAN BRANDT AGENCY

788 Wesley Dr., Atlanta GA 30305. (404)351-8877. **Contact:** Joan Brandt.

Prior to her current position, Ms. Brandt was with Sterling Lord Literistic.

REPRESENTS Considers these nonfiction areas: how-to. **Considers these fiction areas:** literary, mystery, suspense, women's.

HOW TO CONTACT Query letter with SASE. Accepts simultaneous submissions.

TERMS Agent receives 15% commission on domestic sales. Agent receives 20% commission on foreign sales. No written contract.

THE BRATTLE AGENCY

P.O. Box 380537, Cambridge MA 02238. (617)721-5375. **E-mail:** christopher.vyce@thebrattleagency.com. **E-mail:** submissions@thebrattleagency.com. **Website:** http://thebrattleagency.com/. **Contact:** Christopher Vyce.

○ Prior to being an agent Mr. Vyce worked for the Beacon Press in Boston as an acquisitions editor.

MEMBER AGENTS Christopher Vyce.

REPRESENTS Considers these nonfiction areas: history, politics.

HOW TO CONTACT Query by e-mail. Include cover letter, brief synopsis, brief CV.

○ BARBARA BRAUN ASSOCIATES, INC.

7 E. 14th St., Suite 19F, New York NY 10003. **Fax:** (212)604-9023. **E-mail:** bbasubmissions@gmail.com. **Website:** www.barbarabraunagency.com. **Contact:** Barbara Braun. Member of AAR.

MEMBER AGENTS Barbara Braun; John F. Baker.

REPRESENTS nonfiction books, novels. **Considers these nonfiction areas:** architecture, art, biography, design, film, history, photography, psychology, women's issues. **Considers these fiction areas:** commercial, literary.

⊶ "Our fiction is strong on women's stories, historical and multicultural stories, as well as mysteries and thrillers. We're interested in narrative nonfiction and books by journalists. Look online for more details." We do not represent poetry, science fiction, fantasy, horror, or screenplays.

HOW TO CONTACT "We no longer accept submissions by regular mail. Please send all queries via e-mail, marked 'Query' in the subject line. Your query should include: a brief summary of your book, word count, genre, any relevant publishing experience, and the first 5 pages of your ms pasted into the body of the e-mail. (No attachments—we will not open these.)"

TERMS Agent receives 15% commission on domestic sales. Agent receives 20% commission on foreign sales.

TIPS "Our clients' books are represented throughout Europe, Asia, and Latin America by various sub-agents. We are also active in selling motion picture rights to the books we represent, and work with various Hollywood agencies."

○ BRESNICK WEIL LITERARY AGENCY

115 W. 29th St., Third Floor, New York NY 10001. (212)239-3166. **Fax:** (212)239-3165. **E-mail:** query@bresnickagency.com. **Website:** http://bresnickagency.com. **Contact:** Paul Bresnick, Polly Bresnick.

○ Prior to becoming an agent, Mr. Bresnick spent 25 years as a trade book editor.

MEMBER AGENTS Paul Bresnick; Polly Bresnick; Susan Duff; Lisa Kopel (narrative nonfiction, memoir, pop culture and both commercial and literary fiction).

REPRESENTS nonfiction books, novels. **Considers these nonfiction areas:** autobiography/memoir, biography, health, history, humor, memoirs, multicultural, popular culture, sports, travel, true crime, celebrity-branded books, narrative nonfiction, pop psychology, relationship issues. **Considers these fiction areas:** general fiction.

HOW TO CONTACT For fiction, submit query and 2 chapters. For nonfiction, submit query with proposal. Electronic submissions only (for both).

⊘◉ M. COURTNEY BRIGGS

Derrick & Briggs, LLP, 100 N. Broadway Ave., 28th Floor, Oklahoma City OK 73102-8806. (405)235-1900. **Fax:** (405)235-1995. **Website:** www.derrickandbriggs.com.

○ Prior to becoming an agent, Ms. Briggs was in subsidiary rights at Random House for 3 years; an associate agent and film rights associate with Curtis Brown, Ltd.; and an attorney for 16 years.

REPRESENTS nonfiction books, novels, juvenile. **Considers these nonfiction areas:** young adult.

⊶ "I work primarily, but not exclusively, with children's book authors and illustrators. I will also consult or review a contract on an hourly basis." Actively seeking children's fiction, children's picture books (illustrations and text), young adult novels, fiction, nonfiction.

HOW TO CONTACT Query with SASE. Only published authors should submit queries. Obtains most new clients through recommendations from others. **TERMS** Agent receives 15% commission on domestic sales. Agent receives 25% commission on foreign sales. Offers written contract; 60-day notice must be given to terminate contract. **WRITERS CONFERENCES** SCBWI Annual Winter Conference.

☉◑ RICK BROADHEAD & ASSOCIATES LITERARY AGENCY

47 St. Clair Ave. W., Suite 501, Toronto ON M4V 3A5 Canada. (416)929-0516. **Fax:** (416)927-8732. **E-mail:** info@rbaliterary.com. **E-mail:** submissions@rbaliterary.com. **Website:** www.rbaliterary.com. **Contact:** Rick Broadhead, president. Estab. 2002. Membership includes Authors Guild. Represents 125 clients. 50% of clients are new/unpublished writers. Currently handles: nonfiction books 100%.

○ With an MBA from the Schulich School of Business, one of the world's leading business schools, Rick Broadhead is one of the few literary agents in the publishing industry with a business and entrepreneurial background, one that benefits his clients at every step of the book development and contract negotiation process. He is also a best-selling author, having authored and co-authored 35 books.

REPRESENTS nonfiction books. **Considers these nonfiction areas:** biography, business, current affairs, environment, health, history, humor, medicine, military, popular culture, politics, science, self-help.

✇➟The agency is actively seeking compelling proposals from experts in their fields, journalists, and authors with relevant credentials and an established media platform (TV, Web, radio, print experience/exposure). Does not want to receive fiction, screenplays, children's, or poetry at this time.

HOW TO CONTACT "Please send a short query letter by e-mail or via regular mail with a description of the project, your credentials, and contact info. E-mail queries are welcome. Please do not send entire mss or sample chapters unless requested. If I am interested, I will request a proposal." Accepts simultaneous submissions. Obtains most new clients through recommendations from others, solicitations.

TERMS Agent receives 15% commission on domestic sales. Agent receives 20% commission on foreign sales. Offers written contract. Charges for postage and photocopying expenses.

TIPS "Books rarely sell themselves these days, so I look for authors who have a 'platform' (media exposure/experience, university affiliation, recognized expertise, etc.). Remember that a literary agent has to sell your project to an editor, and then the editor has to sell your project internally to his/her colleagues (including the marketing and sales staff), and then the publisher has to sell your book to the book buyers at the chains and bookstores. You're most likely to get my attention if you write a succinct and persuasive query letter that demonstrates your platform/credentials, the market potential of your book, and why your book is different. I love finding great authors, pitching great book ideas, negotiating deals for my clients, and being a part of this exciting and dynamic industry."

○ MARIE BROWN ASSOCIATES, INC.

412 W. 154th St., New York NY 10032. (212)939-9725. **Fax:** (212)939-9728. **E-mail:** info@janellwaldenagyeman.com. **Website:** http://www.janellwaldenagyeman.com/. **Contact:** Marie Brown; Janell Walden Agyeman. Estab. 1984.

MEMBER AGENTS Marie Brown; Janell Walden Agyeman (young adult, middle grade, women's commercial fiction or literary fiction [especially stories that consider the intersection of race, class and/or gender in contemporary America], and adult nonfiction in the areas of health, well being, memoirs, popular culture, history [in the Americas], spirituality, environment and sustainable living, parenting and aging, contemporary affairs and cross-cultural studies.

HOW TO CONTACT E-queries only. "If it is a simultaneous submission to several agents, I would appreciate knowing this. If your work is a novel, include a brief synopsis within the e-mail, no more than 150 words, and the first 3 chapters, or up to the first 50 pages of the ms as an attachments to the same e-mail." Accepts simultaneous submissions. Obtains most new clients through recommendations from others.

TERMS Agent receives 15% commission on domestic sales. Agent receives 20% commission on foreign sales. Offers written contract.

ANDREA BROWN LITERARY AGENCY, INC.

1076 Eagle Dr., Salinas CA 93905. (831)422-5925. **E-mail:** andrea@andreabrownlit.com; caryn@andreabrownlit.com; lauraqueries@gmail.com; jennifer@andreabrownlit.com; kelly@andreabrownlit.com; jennL@andreabrownlit.com; jamie@andreabrownlit.com; jmatt@andreabrownlit.com; lara@andreabrownlit.com. **Website:** www.andreabrownlit.com. Member of AAR. 10% of clients are new/unpublished writers.

○ Prior to opening her agency, Ms. Brown served as an editorial assistant at Random House and Dell Publishing and as an editor with Knopf.

MEMBER AGENTS Andrea Brown (president); **Laura Rennert** (senior agent); **Caryn Wiseman** (senior agent); **Kelly Sonnack** (agent); **Jennifer Rofé** (agent); **Jennifer Laughran** (agent); **Jamie Weiss Chilton** (agent); **Jennifer Mattson** (agent); **Lara Perkins** (associate agent, digital manager).

REPRESENTS nonfiction, fiction, juvenile books. **Considers these nonfiction areas:** juvenile nonfiction, memoirs, young adult, narrative. **Considers these fiction areas:** juvenile, literary, picture books, women's, young adult, middle grade, all juvenile genres.

⚷ Specializes in "all kinds of children's books—illustrators and authors." 98% juvenile books. Considers: nonfiction, fiction, picture books, young adult.

HOW TO CONTACT For picture books, submit complete ms. For fiction, submit query letter, first 10 pages. For nonfiction, submit proposal, first 10 pages. Illustrators: submit a query letter and 2-3 illustration samples (in jpeg format), link to online portfolio, and text of picture book, if applicable. "We only accept queries via e-mail. No attachments, with the exception of jpeg illustrations from illustrators." Visit the agents' bios on our website and choose only *one* agent to whom you will submit your e-query. Send a short e-mail query letter to that agent with QUERY in the subject field. Accepts simultaneous submissions. If we are interested in your work, we will certainly follow up by e-mail or by phone. However, if you haven't heard from us within 6 to 8 weeks, please assume that we are passing on your project. Obtains most new clients through referrals from editors, clients and agents. Check website for guidelines and information.

TERMS Agent receives 15% commission on domestic sales. Agent receives 25% commission on foreign sales. Offers written contract.

RECENT SALES *The Scorpio Races*, by Maggie Stiefvater (Scholastic); *The Raven Boys*, by Maggie Stiefvater (Scholastic); *Wolves of Mercy Falls* series, by Maggie Stiefvater (Scholastic); *The Future of Us*, by Jay Asher; *Triangles*, by Ellen Hopkins (Atria); *Crank*, by Ellen Hopkins (McElderry/S&S); *Burned*, by Ellen Hopkins (McElderry/S&S); *Impulse*, by Ellen Hopkins (McElderry/S&S); *Glass*, by Ellen Hopkins (McElderry/S&S); *Tricks*, by Ellen Hopkins (McElderry/S&S); *Fallout*, by Ellen Hopkins (McElderry/S&S); *Perfect*, by Ellen Hopkins (McElderry/S&S); *The Strange Case of Origami Yoda*, by Tom Angleberger (Amulet/Abrams); *Darth Paper Strikes Back*, by Tom Angleberger (Amulet/Abrams); *Becoming Chloe*, by Catherine Ryan Hyde (Knopf); Sasha Cohen autobiography (HarperCollins); *The Five Ancestors*, by Jeff Stone (Random House); *Thirteen Reasons Why*, by Jay Asher (Penguin); *Identical*, by Ellen Hopkins (S&S).

WRITERS CONFERENCES SCBWI; Asilomar; Maui Writers' Conference; Southwest Writers' Conference; San Diego State University Writers' Conference; Big Sur Children's Writing Workshop; William Saroyan Writers' Conference; Columbus Writers' Conference; Willamette Writers' Conference; La Jolla Writers' Conference; San Francisco Writers' Conference; Hilton Head Writers' Conference; Pacific Northwest Conference; Pikes Peak Conference.

TRACY BROWN LITERARY AGENCY

P.O. Box 772, Nyack NY 10960. (914)400-4147. **Fax:** (914)931-1746. **E-mail:** tracy@brownlit.com. **Contact:** Tracy Brown. Represents 35 clients. Currently handles: nonfiction books 90%, novels 10%.

○ Prior to becoming an agent, Mr. Brown was a book editor for 25 years.

REPRESENTS Considers these nonfiction areas: biography, current affairs, health, history, psychology, travel, women's issues, travel, popular history. **Considers these fiction areas:** literary.

⚷ Specializes in thorough involvement with clients' books at every stage of the process from writing to proposals to publication. Actively seeking serious nonfiction and fiction. Does not want to receive YA, sci-fi or romance.

HOW TO CONTACT Submit outline/proposal, synopsis, author bio. Accepts simultaneous submissions. Responds in 2 weeks to queries. Obtains most new clients through referrals.

TERMS Agent receives 15% commission on domestic sales. Agent receives 20% commission on foreign sales. Offers written contract.

RECENT SALES *Why Have Kids?* by Jessica Valenti (HarperCollins); *Tapdancing to Work*, by Carol J. Loomis (Portfolio); *Mating in Captivity* by Esther Perel.

BROWNE & MILLER LITERARY ASSOCIATES, LLC

410 S. Michigan Ave., Suite 460, Chicago IL 60605. (312)922-3063. **Fax:** (312)922-1905. **E-mail:** mail@browneandmiller.com. **Website:** www.brownean dmiller.com. Estab. 1971. Member of AAR, RWA, MWA.

Prior to opening the agency, Danielle Egan-Miller worked as an editor.

MEMBER AGENTS Danielle Egan-Miller (heavy emphasis on commercial adult fiction); **Abby Saul** (runs the gamut from literary newbies and classics, to cozy mysteries, to sappy women's fiction, to dark and twisted thrillers); **Joanna MacKenzie** (women's fiction, thrillers, new adult, and young adult genres).

Browne & Miller is most interested in literary/commercial fiction/women's fiction, women's historical fiction, literary-leaning crime fiction, romance, and Amish fiction. We are also interested in time travel stories; Christian/inspirational fiction by established authors; literary and commercial young adult fiction; a broad array of nonfiction by nationally-recognized, platformed author/experts. "We do not represent children's picture books, horror or sci-fi novels, short stories, poetry, original screenplays, articles, or software."

HOW TO CONTACT E-query. No attachments. Responds in 2-4 weeks to queries; 4-6 months to mss. Obtains clients through recommendations from others.

TERMS Agent receives 15% commission on domestic sales; 20% on foreign sales. Offers written contract. Offers written contract, binding for 2 years. 30 days notice must be given to terminate contract.

RECENT SALES Sold 10 books for young readers in the last year.

TIPS "WE are very hands-on and do much editorial work with our clients. We are passionate about the books we represent and work hard to help clients reach their publishing goals."

THE BUKOWSKI AGENCY

14 Prince Arthur Ave., Suite 202, Toronto Ontario M5R 1A9 Canada. (416)928-6728. **Fax:** (416)963-9978. **E-mail:** assistant@thebukowskiagency.com; info@thebukowskiagency.com. **Website:** www.the bukowskiagency.com. **Contact:** Denise Bukowski. Estab. 1986.

Prior to becoming an agent, Ms. Bukowski was a book editor.

REPRESENTS nonfiction books, novels.

"The Bukowski Agency specializes in international literary fiction and upmarket nonfiction for adults. Bukowski looks for Canadian writers whose work can be marketed in many media and territories, and who have the potential to make a living from their work." Actively seeking nonfiction and fiction works from Canadian writers. Does not want submissions from American authors, nor genre fiction, poetry, children's literature, picture books, film scripts, or TV scripts.

HOW TO CONTACT "The Bukowski Agency is currently accepting nonfiction submissions, by mail only, from prospective authors who are resident in Canada. We ask for exclusivity for six weeks after receipt to allow time for proper consideration. Please see our nonfiction submission guidelines for more details on submitting proposals for nonfiction. You must include a SASE for return of your proposal; if you do not do so, we will not be able to respond to your enquiry. The Bukowski Agency is currently considering fiction submissions, also, by mail only, from prospective authors who are resident in Canada. Please send the first 50 pages of your novel (double-spaced in 12-point type, printed on one side of the sheet only) with a *brief* synopsis and a self-addressed stamped envelope (SASE). Note that if you do not include an SASE, a response to your submission will not be possible." Responds in 6 weeks to queries.

BURKEMAN & SERAFINA CLARKE LTD, BRIE

14 Neville Ct., Abbey Road, London England NW8 9DD United Kingdom. (44)(870)199-5002. **Fax:** (44)(870)199-1029. **E-mail:** info@burkemanandclarke.com. **Website:** www.burkemanandclarke.com.

REPRESENTS Considers these nonfiction areas: narrative history, popular science, celebrity memoirs, popular culture. **Considers these fiction areas:** commercial literary fiction, psychological thrillers, historial, children's.

8—➤ No academic text, poetry, short stories, musicals, or short films

HOW TO CONTACT Not accepting submissions at present. Please see website for details and updates.

✚⊘◎ THE BURSON AGENCY

E-mail: Jana@janaburson.com. **Website:** www.janaburson.com. **Contact:** Jana Burson. Estab. 2014.

◯ Prior to being an agent, Ms. Burson was an editor and publicity director.

HOW TO CONTACT This agency does not currently welcome unsolicited submissions.

◯ SHEREE BYKOFSKY ASSOCIATES, INC.

PO Box 706, Brigantine NJ 08203. **E-mail:** shereebee@aol.com. **E-mail:** submitbee@aol.com. **Website:** www.shereebee.com. **Contact:** Sheree Bykofsky. Member of AAR. Memberships include Author's Guild, Atlantic City Chamber of Commerce, WNBA. Currently handles: nonfiction books 80%, novels 20%.

◯ Prior to opening her agency, Ms. Bykofsky served as executive editor of the Stonesong Press and managing editor of Chiron Press. She is also the author or coauthor of more than 20 books, including *The Complete Idiot's Guide to Getting Published*. As an adjunct professor, Ms. Bykofsky teaches publishing at Rosemont College, NYU, and SEAK, Inc.

MEMBER AGENTS Janet Rosen, associate; Thomas V. Hartmann, associate.

REPRESENTS nonfiction, novels. **Considers these nonfiction areas:** Americana, animals, architecture, art, autobiography, biography, business, child guidance, cooking, crafts, creative nonfiction, cultural interests, current affairs, dance, design, economics, education, environment, ethnic, film, finance, foods, gardening, gay, government, health, history, hobbies, humor, language, law, lesbian, memoirs, metaphysics, military, money, multicultural, music, nature, New Age, nutrition, parenting, philosophy, photography, popular culture, politics, psychology, recreation, regional, religious, science, sex, sociology, spirituality, sports, translation, travel, true crime, war, anthropology; creative nonfiction. **Considers these fiction areas:** contemporary issues, literary, mainstream, mystery, suspense.

8—➤ This agency specializes in popular reference nonfiction, commercial fiction with a literary quality, and mysteries. "I have wide-ranging interests, but it really depends on quality of writing, originality, and how a particular project appeals to me (or not). I take on fiction when I completely love it—it doesn't matter what area or genre." Does not want to receive poetry, material for children, screenplays, westerns, horror, science fiction, or fantasy.

HOW TO CONTACT "We only accept e-queries now and will only respond to those in which we are interested. E-mail short queries to submitbee@aol.com. Please, no attachments, snail mail, or phone calls. One-page query, one-page synopsis, and first page of ms in the body of the e-mail. Nonfiction: One-page query in the body of the e-mail. We cannot open attached Word files or any other types of attached files. These will be deleted." Accepts simultaneous submissions. Responds in 1 month to requested mss. Obtains most new clients through recommendations from others.

TERMS Agent receives 15% commission on domestic sales. Agent receives 15% commission on foreign sales, plus international co-agent receives another 10%. Offers written contract, binding for 1 year. Charges for postage, photocopying, fax.

RECENT SALES *ADHD Does Not Exist*, by Dr. Richard Saul (Harper Collins); *Be Bold and Win the Sale*, by Jeff Shore (McGraw-Hill); *Idea to Invention*, by Patricia Nolan-Brown (Amacom); *The Hour of Lead*, by Bruce Holbert (Counterpoint); *Slimed! An Oral History of Nickelodeon's Golden Age*, by Matthew Klickstein (Plume); *Bang the Keys: Four Steps to a Lifelong Writing Practice*, by Jill Dearman (Alpha, Penguin); *Signed, Your Student: Celebrities on the Teachers Who Made Them Who They Are Today*, by Holly Holbert (Kaplan); *The Five Ways We Grieve*, by Susan Berger (Trumpeter/Shambhala).

WRITERS CONFERENCES Truckee Meadow Community College, Keynote; ASJA Writers Conference; Asilomar; Florida Suncoast Writers' Conference; Whidbey Island Writers' Conference; Florida First Coast Writers' Festival; Agents and Editors Conference; Columbus Writers' Conference; Southwest Writers' Conference; Willamette Writers' Conference; Dorothy Canfield Fisher Conference; Maui Writers'

Conference; Pacific Northwest Writers' Conference; IWWG.

TIPS "Read the agent listing carefully and comply with guidelines."

KIMBERLEY CAMERON & ASSOCIATES

1550 Tiburon Blvd., #704, Tiburon CA 94920. **Fax:** (415)789-9191. **Website:** www.kimberleycameron. com. **Contact:** Kimberley Cameron. Member of AAR.

Kimberley Cameron & Associates (formerly The Reece Halsey Agency) has had an illustrious client list of established writers, including the estate of Aldous Huxley, and has represented Upton Sinclair, William Faulkner, and Henry Miller.

MEMBER AGENTS Kimberley Cameron; **Elizabeth Kracht**, liz@kimberleycameron.com (literary, commercial, women's, thrillers, mysteries, and YA with crossover appeal); **Pooja Menon**, pooja@kimberleycameron.com (international stories, literary, historical, commercial, fantasy and high-end women's fiction; in nonfiction, she's looking for adventure & travel memoirs, journalism and human-interest stories, and self-help books addressing relationships and the human psychology from a fresh perspective); **Amy Cloughley**, amyc@kimberleycameron.com (literary and upmarket fiction, women's, mystery, narrative nonfiction); **Mary C. Moore** (literary fiction; she also loves a good commercial book; commercially she is looking for unusual fantasy, grounded science fiction, and atypical romance; strong female characters and unique cultures especially catch her eye).

REPRESENTS Considers these nonfiction areas: creative nonfiction, psychology, self-help, travel. **Considers these fiction areas:** commercial, fantasy, historical, literary, mystery, romance, science fiction, thriller, women's, young adult.

"We are looking for a unique and heartfelt voice that conveys a universal truth."

HOW TO CONTACT "We accept e-mail queries only. Please address all queries to one agent only. Please send a query letter in the body of the e-mail, written in a professional manner and clearly addressed to the agent of your choice. Attach a one-page synopsis and the first 50 pages of your ms as separate Word or PDF documents. We have difficulties opening other file formats. Include 'Author Submission' in the subject line. If submitting nonfiction, attach a nonfiction proposal." Obtains new clients through recommendations from others, solicitations.

TERMS Agent receives 15% on domestic sales; 10% on film sales. Offers written contract, binding for 1 year.

TIPS "Please consult our submission guidelines and send a polite, well-written query to our e-mail address."

CYNTHIA CANNELL LITERARY AGENCY

833 Madison Ave., New York NY 10021. (212)396-9595. **Website:** www.cannellagency.com. **Contact:** Cynthia Cannell. Estab. 1997. Member of AAR. Other memberships include the Women's Media Group.

Prior to forming the Cynthia Cannell Literary Agency, Ms. Cannell was, for 12 years, vice president of Janklow & Nesbit Associates.

REPRESENTS Considers these nonfiction areas: biography, history, memoirs, science, self-help, spirituality. **Considers these fiction areas:** literary.

Does not represent screenplays, children's books, illustrated books, cookbooks, romance, category mystery, or science fiction.

HOW TO CONTACT "Please query us with an e-mail or letter. If querying by e-mail, send a brief description of your project with relevant biographical information including publishing credits (if any) to info@cannellagency.com. Do not send attachments. If querying by conventional mail, enclose an SASE." Responds if interested.

RECENT SALES *Song of the Shank*, by Jeffery Renard Allen (Graywolf Press); *100 Places That Can Change Your Child's Life*, by Keith Bellows (Nat. Geo Books); *Brilliant: The Evolution of Artificial Light*, by Jane Brox (HMH).

CAPITAL TALENT AGENCY

1330 Connecticut Ave. NW, Suite 271, Washington DC 20036. (202)429-4785. **E-mail:** literary.submissions@capitaltalentagency.com. **Website:** http://capitaltalentagency.com/html/literary.shtml. **Contact:** Cynthia Kane. Estab. 2014.

Prior to joining CTA, Ms. Kane was involved in the publishing industry for more than 10 years. She has worked as a development editor for different publishing houses and individual authors and has seen more than 100 titles to market.

REPRESENTS Considers these nonfiction areas: memoirs. **Considers these fiction areas:** commer-

NEW AGENT SPOTLIGHT

LEON HUSOCK
L. PERKINS AGENCY

Lperkinsagency.com

@leonhusock

ABOUT LEON: Prior to joining the L. Perkins Agency, Leon was an associate agent at Anderson Literary Management. He has a BA in Literature from Bard College and attended the Columbia Publishing Course.

HE IS SEEKING: He has a particular interest in science fiction & fantasy, young adult and middle grade novels filled with strong characters and original premises, but keeps an open mind for anything that catches his eye. He is also looking for historical fiction set in the 20th century, particularly the 1980s or earlier. He is not interested in nonfiction at this time.

HOW TO CONTACT: E-query leon@lperkinsagency.com.

---

cial, literary, mainstream, middle grade, mystery, romance, thriller, young adult.

⛐ No science fiction or fantasy.

HOW TO CONTACT "Submissions should be sent via e-mail. For fiction and nonfiction submissions, send a query letter in the body of your e-mail. Attachments will not be opened. Please note that while we consider each query seriously, we are unable to respond to all of them. We endeavor to respond within 6 weeks to projects that interest us."

ⓘ MARIA CARVAINIS AGENCY, INC.
Rockefeller Center, 1270 Avenue of the Americas, Suite 2320, New York NY 10020. (212)245-6365. **Fax:** (212)245-7196. **E-mail:** mca@mariacarvainisagency. com. **Website:** http://mariacarvainisagency.com. Estab. 1977. Member of AAR. Signatory of WGA. Other memberships include Authors Guild, Women's Media Group, ABA, MWA, RWA. Represents 75 clients.

Ⓞ Prior to opening her agency, Ms. Carvainis spent more than 10 years in the publishing industry as a senior editor with Macmillan Publishing, Basic Books, Avon Books, and Crown Publishers. Ms. Carvainis has served as a member of the AAR Board of Directors and AAR Treasurer, as well as serving as chair of the AAR Contracts Committee. She presently serves on the AAR Royalty Committee.

MEMBER AGENTS Maria Carvainis, president/ literary agent.

REPRESENTS nonfiction books, novels. **Considers these nonfiction areas:** biography, business, history, memoirs, popular culture, psychology, science. **Considers these fiction areas:** historical, literary, mainstream, middle grade, mystery, suspense, thriller, women's, young adult.

⛐ The agency does not represent screenplays, children's picture books, science fiction, or poetry.

HOW TO CONTACT You can query via e-mail or snail mail. If by snail mail, send your submission "ATTN: Query Department." Please send a query letter, a synopsis of the work, two sample chapters, and note any writing credentials. Obtains most new clients through recommendations from others, conferences, query letters.

TERMS Agent receives 15% commission on domestic sales. Agent receives 20% commission on foreign sales. Offers written contract. Charges clients for foreign postage and bulk copying.

RECENT SALES *A Secret Affair*, by Mary Balogh (Delacorte); *Tough Customer*, by Sandra Brown (Simon & Schuster); *A Lady Never Tells*, by Candace Camp (Pocket Books); *The King James Conspiracy*, by Phillip Depoy (St. Martin's Press).

◑ CASTIGLIA LITERARY AGENCY

P.O. Box 1094, Sumerland CA 93067. **E-mail:** castigliaagency-query@yahoo.com. **Website:** www.castigliaagency.com. Member of AAR. Other memberships include PEN. Represents 65 clients. Currently handles: nonfiction books 55%, novels 45%.

MEMBER AGENTS Julie Castiglia (not accepting queries at this time); **Win Golden** (fiction: thrillers, mystery, crime, science fiction, YA, commercial/literary fiction; nonfiction: narrative nonfiction, current events, science, journalism).

REPRESENTS nonfiction books, novels. **Considers these nonfiction areas:** creative nonfiction, current affairs, investigative, science. **Considers these fiction areas:** commercial, crime, literary, mystery, science fiction, thriller, young adult.

⌇ "We'd particularly like to hear from you if you are a journalist or published writer in magazines." Does not want to receive horror, screenplays, poetry, or academic nonfiction.

HOW TO CONTACT Query via e-mail to CastigliaAgency-query@yahoo.com. Send no materials via first contact besides a one-page query. No snail mail submissions accepted. Obtains most new clients through recommendations from others, solicitations, conferences.

TERMS Agent receives 15% commission on domestic sales. Agent receives 25% commission on foreign sales. Offers written contract; 6-week notice must be given to terminate contract.

WRITERS CONFERENCES Santa Barbara Writers' Conference; Southern California Writers' Conference; Surrey International Writers' Conference; San Diego State University Writers' Conference; Willamette Writers' Conference.

TIPS "Be professional with submissions. Attend workshops and conferences before you approach an agent."

CHALBERG & SUSSMAN

115 West 29th St, Third Floor, New York NY 10001. (917)261-7550. **Website:** www.chalbergsussman.com.

◐ Prior to her current position, Terra Chalberg held a variety of editorial positions, and was an agent with The Susan Golomb Literary Agency. Rachel Sussman was an agent with Zachary Shuster Harmsworth. Nicole James was with The Aaron Priest Literary Agency.

MEMBER AGENTS New agent added in 2014 is **Lana Popovic** (young adult, middle grade, literary thrillers, sci-fi, horror, romance, erotica, women's literary fiction, pop culture, blog-to-book, literary memoir).

REPRESENTS **Considers these nonfiction areas:** history, how-to, humor, memoirs, popular culture, psychology, self-help. **Considers these fiction areas:** commercial, erotica, horror, literary, middle grade, romance, science fiction, thriller, women's, young adult.

⌇ "Rachel represents a wide range of voice- and idea-driven nonfiction and a select list of literary fiction. Her nonfiction list spans both serious and 'unserious' subject matter, from history, psychology, and memoir to humor and pop culture. Nicole is looking for novels celebrated in other countries but unknown here in the US as well as literary and commercial fiction, including action-packed thrillers with great heroes. She is eager to find a female-driven thriller; a fantastic beach read for women; and a smart and thoughtfully written young adult series. On the nonfiction side, Nicole is looking out for a book about weddings (how-to or memoir); a hip and intelligent self-help book; and anything topical that calls to her."

HOW TO CONTACT To query by e-mail, please contact one of the following: terra@chalbergsussman.com, rachel@chalbergsussman.com, nicole@chalbergsussman.com. To query by regular mail, please address your letter to one agent and include a self-addressed stamped envelope.

RECENT SALES The agents' sales and clients are listed on their website.

◑ CHASE LITERARY AGENCY

236 W. 26th St., Suite 801, New York NY 10001. (212)477-5100. **E-mail:** farley@chaseliterary.com. **Website:** www.chaseliterary.com. **Contact:** Farley Chase.

MEMBER AGENTS Farley Chase.

REPRESENTS Considers these nonfiction areas: biography, business, current affairs, foods, history, memoirs, military, science, sports. **Considers these fiction areas:** commercial, historical, literary, mystery, thriller.

☛ No romance, science fiction, or young adult.

HOW TO CONTACT E-query farley@chaseliterary. com. If submitting fiction, please include the first few pages of the ms with the query.

RECENT SALES Nonfiction: *Devil in the Grove: Thurgood Marshall, the Groveland Boys, and the Dawn of a New America* (Harper), by Gilbert King (a *New York Times* bestseller and winner of the Pulitzer Prize); *Heads in Beds: A Reckless Memoir of Hotels, Hustles, and So-Called Hospitality* (Doubleday), by Jacob Tomsky (a *New York Times* bestseller); *The End of Night: My Search for Natural Darkness in an Age of Artificial Light* (Little, Brown), by Paul Bogard; *The Bintel Brief: Love and Longing in Old New York* (Ecco), by Liana Finck. Fiction: *And Every Day Was Overcast* (Black Balloon), by Paul Kwiatowski; *The Badlands Saloon* (Scribner), by Jonathan Twingley; *The Baptism of Billy Bean* (Counterpoint), by Roger Alan Skipper; *The Afrika Rech* (Holt), by Guy Saville.

◑ JANE CHELIUS LITERARY AGENCY

548 Second St., Brooklyn NY 11215. (718)499-0236. **Fax:** (718)832-7335. **E-mail:** Jane@janechelius.com. **E-mail:** queries@janechelius.com. **Website:** www. janechelius.com. Member of AAR.

MEMBER AGENTS Jane Chelius, Mark Chelius.

REPRESENTS nonfiction books, novels. **Considers these nonfiction areas:** biography, humor, medicine, parenting, popular culture, satire, women's issues, women's studies, natural history; narrative. **Considers these fiction areas:** literary, mystery, suspense, women's.

☛ Does not want to receive children's books, fantasy, science fiction, children's books, stage plays, screenplays, or poetry.

HOW TO CONTACT E-query. Does not consider e-mail queries with attachments. No unsolicited sample chapters or mss. Responds if interested. Responds in 3-4-weeks usually.

◐ ELYSE CHENEY LITERARY ASSOCIATES, LLC

78 Fifth Avenue, 3rd Floor, New York NY 10011. (212)277-8007. **Fax:** (212)614-0728. **E-mail:** elyse@ cheneyliterary.com. **E-mail:** submissions@cheney- literary.com. **Website:** www.cheneyliterary.com. **Contact:** Elyse Cheney; Adam Eaglin; Alex Jacobs.

💬 Prior to her current position, Ms. Cheney was an agent at Sanford J. Greenburger Associates.

MEMBER AGENTS Elyse Cheney; Adam Eaglin (literary fiction and nonfiction, including history, politics, current events, narrative reportage, biography, memoir, and popular science); **Alexander Jacobs** (narrative nonfiction [particularly in the areas of history, science, politics, and culture], literary fiction, crime, and memoir); **Sam Freilich** (literary fiction, crime, biography, narrative nonfiction, and anything about Los Angeles).

REPRESENTS nonfiction, novels. **Considers these nonfiction areas:** biography, business, creative non-fiction, current affairs, economics, memoirs, politics, science, journalism. **Considers these fiction areas:** commercial, family saga, historical, literary, short story collections, suspense, women's.

HOW TO CONTACT Query by e-mail or snail mail. For a snail mail responses, include a SASE. If you e-query, feel free to paste up to 3 chapters of your work in the e-mail below your query. Do not query more than one agent.

RECENT SALES *Moonwalking with Einstein: The Art and Science of Remembering Everything*, by Joshua Foer; *The Possessed: Adventures with Russian Books and the People Who Read Them*, by Elif Batuman (Farrar, Strauss & Giroux); *The Coldest Winter Ever*, by Sister Souljah (Atria); *A Heartbreaking Work of Staggering Genius*, by Dave Eggers (Simon and Schuster); *No Easy Day*, by Mark Owen; *Malcom X: A Life of Reinvention*, by Manning Marable.

◐◉ THE CHUDNEY AGENCY

72 North State Rd., Suite 501, Briarcliff Manor NY 10510. (201)758-8739. **E-mail:** steven@thechudneya- gency.com. **Website:** www.thechudneyagency.com. **Contact:** Steven Chudney. Estab. 2001. Other memberships include SCBWI. 90% of clients are new/un-published writers.

💬 Prior to becoming an agent, Mr. Chudney held various sales positions with major publishers.

REPRESENTS novels, juvenile. **Considers these nonfiction areas:** juvenile. **Considers these fiction areas:** historical, juvenile, literary, mystery, suspense, young adult.

☞ **THIS AGENCY** specializes in children's and teens books, and wants to find authors who are illustrators as well. "At this time, the agency is only looking for author/illustrators (one individual), who can both write and illustrate wonderful picture books. The author/illustrator must really know and understand the prime audience's needs and wants of the child reader! Storylines should be engaging, fun, with a hint of a life lessons and cannot be longer than 800 words. With chapter books, middle grade and teen novels, I'm primarily looking for quality, contemporary literary fiction: novels that are exceedingly well-written, with wonderful settings and developed, unforgettable characters. I'm looking for historical fiction that will excite me, young readers, editors, and reviewers, and will introduce us to unique characters in settings and situations, countries, and eras we haven't encountered too often yet in children's and teen literature." Does not want to receive any fantasy or science fiction; board books or lift-the-flap books, fables, folklore, or traditional fairytales, poetry or mood pieces, stories for all ages (as these ultimately are too adult oriented), message-driven stories that are heavy-handed, didactic or pedantic.

HOW TO CONTACT No snail-mail submissions. Queries only. Submit proposal package, 4-6 sample chapters. For children's, submit full text and 3-5 illustrations. Accepts simultaneous submissions. Responds in 2-3 weeks to queries. Responds in 3-4 weeks to mss.

TERMS Agent receives 15% commission on domestic sales. Agent receives 20% commission on foreign sales. Offers written contract, binding for 1 year; 30-day notice must be given to terminate contract.

TIPS "If an agent has a website, review it carefully to make sure your material is appropriate for that agent. Read lots of books within the genre you are writing; work hard on your writing; don't follow trends—most likely, you'll be too late."

⊘◉ CINE/LIT REPRESENTATION

P.O. Box 802918, Santa Clarita CA 91380-2918. (661)513-0268. **Fax:** (661)513-0915. **Contact:** Mary Alice Kier. Member of AAR.
MEMBER AGENTS Mary Alice Kier; Anna Cottle.
HOW TO CONTACT Send query letter with SASE. Or e-query to cinelit@att.net. Note this agency's specialized nature.

○ WM CLARK ASSOCIATES

186 Fifth Ave., Second Floor, New York NY 10010. (212)675-2784. **Fax:** (347)-649-9262. **E-mail:** wmclark@wmclark.com. **E-mail:** general@wmclark.com. **Website:** www.wmclark.com. Estab. 1997. Member of AAR. 50% of clients are new/unpublished writers. Currently handles: nonfiction books 50%, novels 50%.
💬 Prior to opening WCA, Mr. Clark was an agent at the William Morris Agency.
REPRESENTS nonfiction books, novels. **Considers these nonfiction areas:** architecture, art, autobiography, biography, cultural interests, current affairs, dance, design, ethnic, film, history, inspirational, memoirs, music, politics, popular culture, religious, science, sociology, technology, theater, translation, travel memoir, Eastern philosophy. **Considers these fiction areas:** contemporary issues, ethnic, historical, literary, mainstream, Southern fiction.
☞ William Clark represents a wide range of titles across all formats to the publishing, motion picture, television, and new media fields on behalf of authors of first fiction and award-winning, best-selling narrative nonfiction, international authors in translation, chefs, musicians, and artists. Offering individual focus and a global presence, the agency undertakes to discover, develop, and market today's most interesting content and the talent that create it, and forge sophisticated and innovative plans for self-promotion, reliable revenue streams, and an enduring creative career. Referral partners are available to provide services including editorial consultation, media training, lecture booking, marketing support, and public relations. Agency does not respond to screenplays or screenplay pitches. It is advised that before querying you become familiar with the kinds of books we handle by browsing our Book List, which is available on our website.

HOW TO CONTACT Accepts queries via online form only. "We respond to all queries submitted via this form." Responds in 1-2 months to queries.

TERMS Agent receives 15% commission on domestic sales. Agent receives 20% commission on foreign sales. Offers written contract.

TIPS "WCA works on a reciprocal basis with Ed Victor Ltd. (UK) in representing select properties to the US market and vice versa. Translation rights are sold directly in the German, Italian, Spanish, Portuguese,

Latin American, French, Dutch, and Scandinavian territories in association with Andrew Nurnberg Associates Ltd. (UK); through offices in China, Bulgaria, Czech Republic, Latvia, Poland, Hungary, and Russia; and through corresponding agents in Japan, Greece, Israel, Turkey, Korea, Taiwan, and Thailand."

⊘ COLCHIE AGENCY, GP

8701 Shore Rd., #514, Brooklyn NY 11209. (718)921-7468. **E-mail:** colchieagency@gmail.com. **Contact:** Thomas Colchie; Elaine Colchie.

REPRESENTS novels.

☛ Does not want to receive nonfiction.

HOW TO CONTACT This listing does not take or respond to unsolicited queries or submissions.

RECENT SALES *Marina*, by Carlos Ruiz Zafon (Little Brown Books); *The Broken Mirrors*, by Elias Khoury (Maclehose Press); *The Prince*, by Vito Bruschini (Atria); *Hot Sur*, by Laura Restrepo (Amazon Crossing); *In The Beginning Was the Sea*, by Tomas Gonzalez (Pushkin Press).

◯ FRANCES COLLIN, LITERARY AGENT

P.O. Box 33, Wayne PA 19087-0033. **E-mail:** queries@francescollin.com. **Website:** www.francescollin.com. Member of AAR. Represents 90 clients. 1% of clients are new/unpublished writers.

☛ Does not want to receive cookbooks, craft books, poetry, screenplays, or books for young children.

HOW TO CONTACT Query via e-mail describing project (text in the body of the e-mail only, no attachments) to queries@francescollin.com. "Please note that all queries are reviewed by all agents at the agency." No phone or fax queries. Accepts simultaneous submissions.

TERMS Agent receives 15% commission on domestic sales. Agent receives 20% commission on foreign sales. Offers written contract.

⊘◯ COMPASS TALENT

6 East 32nd Street, 6th Floor, New York NY 10016. (646)376-7718. **E-mail:** query@compasstalent.com. **Website:** www.compasstalent.com. **Contact:** Heather Schroder.

REPRESENTS Considers these nonfiction areas: cooking, creative nonfiction, foods, history, memoirs, science. **Considers these fiction areas:** commercial, juvenile, literary, mainstream.

HOW TO CONTACT This agency is currently closed to unsolicited submissions.

RECENT SALES A full list of agency clients is available on the website.

◯ DON CONGDON ASSOCIATES INC.

110 William St., Suite 2202, New York NY 10038. (212)645-1229. **Fax:** (212)727-2688. **E-mail:** dca@doncongdon.com. **Website:** http://doncongdon.com. **Contact:** Michael Congdon, Susan Ramer, Cristina Concepcion, Maura Kye Casella, Katie Kotchman, Katie Grimm. Member of AAR. Represents 100 clients.

REPRESENTS Considers these nonfiction areas: anthropology, archeology, autobiography, biography, child guidance, cooking, creative nonfiction, current affairs, dance, environment, film, foods, government, health, history, humor, language, law, literature, medicine, memoirs, military, music, parenting, popular culture, politics, psychology, satire, science, technology, theater, travel, true crime, war, women's issues, women's studies. **Considers these fiction areas:** action, adventure, contemporary issues, crime, detective, literary, mainstream, middle grade, mystery, police, short story collections, suspense, thriller, women's, young adult.

☛ Especially interested in narrative nonfiction and literary fiction.

HOW TO CONTACT "For queries via e-mail, you must include the word 'Query' and the agent's full name in your subject heading. Please also include your query and sample chapter in the body of the e-mail, as we do not open attachments for security reasons. Please query only one agent within the agency at a time." Responds in 3 weeks to queries. Responds in 1 month to mss. Obtains most new clients through recommendations from other authors.

TERMS Agent receives 15% commission on domestic sales. Agent receives 20% commission on foreign sales. Charges client for extra shipping costs, photocopying, copyright fees, book purchases.

RECENT SALES This agency represents many bestselling clients such as David Sedaris and Kathryn Stockett.

TIPS "Writing a query letter with an SASE is a must. We cannot guarantee replies to foreign queries via standard mail. No phone calls. We never download attachments to e-mail queries for security reasons, so please copy and paste material into your e-mail."

CONNOR LITERARY AGENCY

2911 W. 71st St., Minneapolis MN 55423. (612)866-1486. **E-mail:** connoragency@aol.com; coolmkc@aol.com. **Website:** www.connorliteraryagency.webs.com. **Contact:** Marlene Connor Lynch; Deborah Connor Coker.

Prior to opening her agency, Ms. Connor served at the Literary Guild of America, Simon & Schuster, and Random House. She is author of *Welcome to the Family: Memories of the Past for a Bright Future* (Broadway Books) and *What is Cool: Understanding Black Manhood in America* (Crown).

MEMBER AGENTS Marlene Connor Lynch (all categories of mainstream nonfiction and fiction); **Deborah Coker** (young adult and mainstream fiction and nonfiction, suspense, historical fiction, humor, illustrated books, children's books).

REPRESENTS nonfiction books, novels. **Considers these fiction areas:** historical, literary, mainstream, picture books, suspense, young adult.

HOW TO CONTACT Query with 1 page and synopsis; include SASE if by mail. All unsolicited mss returned unopened. There is also an online submission form on the agency website. Obtains most new clients through recommendations from others, conferences, grapevine.

TERMS Agent receives 15% commission on domestic sales. Agent receives 25% commission on foreign sales. Offers written contract, binding for 1 year.

RECENT SALES *Beautiful Hair at Any Age*, by Lisa Akbari; *12 Months of Knitting*, by Joanne Yordanou; *The Warrior Path: Confessions of a Young Lord* by Felipe Luciano.

WRITERS CONFERENCES National Writers Union, Midwest Chapter; Agents, Agents, Agents; Texas Writers' Conference; Detroit Writers' Conference; Annual Gwendolyn Brooks Writers' Conference for Literature and Creative Writing; Wisconsin Writers' Festival.

TIPS "Previously published writers are preferred; new writers with national exposure or potential to have national exposure from their own efforts preferred."

THE DOE COOVER AGENCY

P.O. Box 668, Winchester MA 01890. (781)721-6000. **E-mail:** info@doecooveragency.com. **Website:** www.doecooveragency.com. Represents 150+ clients. Currently handles: nonfiction books 80%, novels 20%.

MEMBER AGENTS Doe Coover (general nonfiction, including business, cooking/food writing, health and science); **Colleen Mohyde** (literary, commercial fiction, general nonfiction); associate **Frances Kennedy**.

The agency specializes in narrative nonfiction, particularly biography, business, cooking and food writing, health, history, popular science, social issues, gardening, and humor; literary and commercial fiction. The agency does not represent poetry, screenplays, romance, fantasy, science fiction or unsolicited children's books.

HOW TO CONTACT Accepts queries by e-mail only. Check website for submission guidelines. No unsolicited mss. Accepts simultaneous submissions. Responds within 4-6 weeks, only if additional material is required. Obtains most new clients through solicitation and recommendation.

TERMS Agent receives 15% commission on domestic sales, 10% of original advance commission on foreign sales. No reading fees.

RECENT SALES *Vegetable Literacy*, by Deborah Madison (Ten Speed Press); *L.A. Son: My Life, My City, My Food*, by Roy Choi (Anthony Bourdain/Ecco); *The Big-Flavor Grill*, by Chris Schlesinger and John Willoughby (Ten Speed Press); *The Shape Of The Eye: A Memoir*, by George Estreich (Tarcher). *Frontera: Margaritas, Guacamoles, and Snacks*, by Rick Bayless and Deann Groen Bayless (W.W. Norton); *The Essay*, by Robin Yocum (Arcade Publishing); *The Flower of Empire*, by Tatiana Holway (Oxford University Press); Dulcie Schwartz mystery series, by Clea Simon (Severn House UK). Other clients include: WGBH, New England Aquarium, Duke University, Cheryl & Bill Jamison, Blue Balliett, David Allen, Jacques Pepin, Cindy Pawlcyn, Joann Weir, Suzanne Berne, Paula Poundstone, Anita Silvey, Marjorie Sandor, Tracy Daugherty, Carl Rollyson, and Joel Magnuson.

JILL CORCORAN LITERARY AGENCY

P.O. Box 4116, Palos Verdes Peninsula CA 90274. **Website:** http://jillcorcoranliteraryagency.com; http://jillcorcoran.blogspot.com. **Contact:** Jill Corcoran. Estab. 2013.

REPRESENTS Considers these fiction areas: juvenile, middle grade, picture books, young adult.

HOW TO CONTACT Jill is closed to submissions. New assistant Eve Porinchak is open to submissions for picture books, middle grade and young adult: eve@jillcorcoranliteraryagency.com.

RECENT SALES Recent titles: *Guy-Write: What Every Guy Writer Needs to Know*, by Ralph Fletcher; *Kiss, Kiss Good Night*, by Kenn Nesbitt; *The Plot Whisperer: Secrets of Story Structure Any Writer Can Master*, by Martha Alderson; *Blind Spot*, by Laura Ellen; *How I Lost You*, by Janet Gurtler.

◑ CORNERSTONE LITERARY, INC.

4525 Wilshire Blvd., Suite 208, Los Angeles CA 90010. (323)930-6039. **Fax:** (323)930-0407. **E-mail:** info@cornerstoneliterary.com. **Website:** www.cornerstoneliterary.com. **Contact:** Helen Breitwieser. Member of AAR. Other memberships include Author's Guild, MWA, RWA, PEN, Poets & Writers. Represents 40 clients. 30% of clients are new/unpublished writers.

○ Prior to founding her own boutique agency, Ms. Breitwieser was a literary agent at The William Morris Agency.

REPRESENTS novels. **Considers these nonfiction areas:** creative nonfiction. **Considers these fiction areas:** commercial, literary.

⌐☞ "We do not respond to unsolicited e-mail inquiries. All unsolicited snail mail mss will be returned unopened." Does not want to receive how-to, photography books, science fiction, Western, poetry, screenplays, fantasy, gay/lesbian, horror, self-help, psychology, business, or diet.

HOW TO CONTACT "Submissions should consist of a one-page query letter detailing the book as well as the qualifications of the author. For fiction, submissions may also include the first 10 pages of the novel pasted in the e-mail or one short story from a collection. We receive hundreds of queries each month, and make every effort to give each one careful consideration. We cannot guarantee a response to queries submitted electronically due to the volume of queries received." Obtains most new clients through recommendations from others.

TERMS Agent receives 15% commission on domestic sales. Agent receives 20% commission on foreign sales. Offers written contract, binding for 1 year; 2-month notice must be given to terminate contract.

○ CORVISIERO LITERARY AGENCY

275 Madison Ave., 14th Floor, New York NY 10016. (646)942-8396. **Fax:** (646)217-3758. **E-mail:** contact@corvisieroagency.com. **E-mail:** query@corvisieroagency.com. **Website:** www.corvisieroagency.com. **Contact:** Marisa A. Corvisiero, senior agent and literary attorney.

MEMBER AGENTS Marisa A. Corvisiero, senior agent and literary attorney (nonfiction, picture books, middle grade, new adult, young adult, romance, thrillers, adventure, paranormal, fantasy, science fiction, and Christmas themes; Saritza Hernandez, senior agent (all kinds of romance, GLBT young adult, erotica); Sarah Negovetich (young adult, middle grade); Doreen McDonald (do not query); Cate Hart (YA, MG, historical romance, erotica, LGBTQ, romance, steampunk, clockpunk, candlepunk); Samantha Bremekamp (children's, middle grade, young adult, and new adult); Ella Kennen (picture books, MG, YA, some nonfiction).

REPRESENTS Considers these fiction areas: adventure, commercial, erotica, fantasy, gay, historical, lesbian, middle grade, multicultural, mystery, new adult, paranormal, picture books, science fiction, thriller, urban fantasy, young adult.

HOW TO CONTACT Accepts submissions via e-mail only. Include 5 pages of complete and polished ms pasted into the body of an e-mail, and a 1-2 page synopsis. For nonfiction, include a proposal instead of the synopsis. Put "Query for [Agent]" in the e-mail subject line.

TIPS "For tips and discussions on what we look for in query letters and submissions, please take a look at Marisa A. Corvisiero's blog: Thoughts From A Literary Agent."

⊕ CREATIVE MEDIA AGENCY, INC.

1745 Broadway, 17th Floor, New York NY 10019. **E-mail:** paige@cmalit.com. **Website:** www.cmalit.com. **Contact:** Paige Wheeler.

○ Prior to starting this agency, Ms. Wheeler was with Folio Literary.

REPRESENTS nonfiction, fiction.

⌐☞ "Fiction: All commercial fiction and upscale (think book club) fiction, as well as women's fiction, romance (all types), mystery, thrillers, inspirational/Christian and psychological suspense. I enjoy both historical fiction as well as contemporary fiction, so do keep that in mind. Nonfiction: I'm looking for both narrative nonfiction and prescriptive nonfiction. I'm looking for books where the author has a huge platform and something new to say in a particular area. Some of the areas that I like are lifestyle, relationship, parenting, business/entrepreneurship, food-subsistence-homesteading topics, popular/trendy reference projects and women's issues. I'd like books that would be a good fit on the *Today* show." Does not want to receive children's books, science fiction, fantasy, or academic nonfiction.

HOW TO CONTACT E-query. Write "query" in your e-mail subject line. For fiction, paste in the first 5 pages of the ms after the query. For nonfiction, after the query, paste in an extended author bio as well as a marketing plan/sextion.

⊘⊙ CREATIVE TRUST, INC.

210 Jamestown Park, Suite 200, Brentwood TN 37027. (615)297-5010. **Fax:** (615)297-5020. **E-mail:** info@ creativetrust.com. **Website:** www.creativetrust.com. New York Office: 39 Broadway, 3rd Floor, New York NY 10006. Currently handles: novella Graphic Novels, movie scripts, multimedia, other Video Scripts.

HOW TO CONTACT "Creative Trust Literary Group does not accept unsolicited mss or book proposals from unpublished authors. We do accept unsolicited inquiries from previously published authors under the following requisites: e-mail inquiries only, which must not be accompanied by attachments of any kind. If we're interested, we'll e-mail you an invitation to submit additional materials and instructions on how to do so."

⊘ CRICHTON & ASSOCIATES

6940 Carroll Ave., Takoma Park MD 20912. (301)495-9663. **Fax:** (202)318-0050. **E-mail:** query@crichton-associates.com. **Website:** www.crichton-associates.com. **Contact:** Sha-Shana Crichton. 90% of clients are new/unpublished writers. Currently handles: nonfiction books 50%, fiction 50%.

○ Prior to becoming an agent, Ms. Crichton did commercial litigation for a major law firm.

REPRESENTS nonfiction books, novels. **Considers these nonfiction areas:** child guidance, cultural interests, ethnic, gay, government, investigative, law, lesbian, parenting, politics, true crime, women's issues, women's studies, African-American studies. **Considers these fiction areas:** ethnic, feminist, inspirational, literary, mainstream, mystery, religious, romance, suspense, chick lit.

⚡→Actively seeking women's fiction, romance, and chick lit. Looking also for multicultural fiction

and nonfiction. Does not want to receive poetry, children's, YA, science fiction, or screenplays.

HOW TO CONTACT "In the subject line of e-mail, please indicate whether your project is fiction or nonfiction. Please do not send attachments. Your query letter should include a description of the project and your biography. If you wish to send your query via snail mail, please include your telephone number and e-mail address. We will respond to you via e-mail. For fiction, include short synopsis and first 3 chapters with query. For nonfiction, send a book proposal." Responds in 3-5 weeks to queries.

TERMS Agent receives 15% commission on domestic sales. Agent receives 20% commission on foreign sales. Offers written contract, binding for 45 days. Only charges fees for postage and photocopying.

RECENT SALES *The African American Entrepreneur*, by W. Sherman Rogers (Praeger); *The Diversity Code*, by Michelle Johnson (Amacom); *Secret & Lies*, by Rhonda McKnight (Urban Books); *Love on the Rocks*, by Pamela Yaye (Harlequin). Other clients include Kimberley White, Beverley Long, Jessica Trap, Altonya Washington, Cheris Hodges.

WRITERS CONFERENCES Silicon Valley RWA; BookExpo America.

⊘ RICHARD CURTIS ASSOCIATES, INC.

171 E. 74th St., New York NY 10021. (212)772-7363. **Fax:** (212)772-7393. **Website:** www.curtisagency.com. Memberships include RWA, MWA, ITW, SFWA. Represents 100 clients. 1% of clients are new/unpublished writers.

○ Prior to being an agent, Mr. Curtis authored blogs, articles, and books in the publishing business.

REPRESENTS **Considers these fiction areas:** commercial, fantasy, romance, science fiction, thriller, young adult.

HOW TO CONTACT Considers only authors published by national houses.

TERMS Agent receives 15% commission on domestic sales. Agent receives 25% commission on foreign sales. Offers written contract. Charges for photocopying, express mail, international freight, book orders.

RECENT SALES Sold 100 titles in the last year: *Sylo*, by DJ MacHale; *War Dogs*, by Greg Bear; *Ever After*, by Kim Harrison.

WRITERS CONFERENCES RWA National Conference.

⚫🌓 CURTIS BROWN (AUST) PTY LTD

P.O. Box 19, Paddington NSW 2021 Australia. (+61)(2)9361-6161. **Fax:** (+61)(2)9360-3935. **E-mail:** reception@curtisbrown.com.au. **Website:** www.curtisbrown.com.au. 10% of clients are new/unpublished writers. Currently handles: nonfiction books 30%, novels 30%, juvenile books 25%, other 15% other.

◯ "Prior to joining Curtis Brown, most of our agents worked in publishing or the film/theatre industries in Australia and the United Kingdom."

MEMBER AGENTS Fiona Inglis (managing director/agent); **Fran Moore** (deputy managing director / agent); **Tara Wynne** (agent); **Pippa Masson** (agent); **Clare Forster** (agent); **Grace Heifetz** (agent).

🔑➤ "We are Australia's oldest and largest literary agency representing a diverse range of Australian and New Zealand writers and Estates."

HOW TO CONTACT "Please refer to our website for information regarding ms submissions, permissions, theatre rights requests, and the clients and Estates we represent. We are not currently looking to represent poetry, short stories, stage/screenplays, picture books, or translations. We do not accept e-mailed or faxed submissions. No responsibility is taken for the receipt or loss of mss."

CURTIS BROWN, LTD.

10 Astor Place, New York NY 10003-6935. (212)473-5400. **Website:** www.curtisbrown.com. **Contact:** Ginger Knowlton. Alternate address: Peter Ginsberg, president at CBSF, 1750 Montgomery St., San Francisco CA 94111; (415)954-8566. Member of AAR. Signatory of WGA.

MEMBER AGENTS Ginger Clark (science fiction, fantasy, paranormal romance, literary horror, and young adult and middle grade fiction); **Katherine Fausset** (adult fiction and nonfiction, including literary and commercial fiction, journalism, memoir, lifestyle, prescriptive and narrative nonfiction); **Holly Frederick**; **Peter Ginsberg**, president; **Elizabeth Harding**, vice president (represents authors and illustrators of juvenile, middle grade, and young adult fiction); **Steve Kasdin** (commercial fiction, including mysteries/thrillers, romantic suspense—emphasis on the suspense, and historical fiction; narrative nonfiction, including biography, history, and current affairs; and young adult fiction, particularly if it has adult crossover appeal); **Ginger Knowlton**, executive vice president (authors and illustrators of children's books in all genres); **Timothy Knowlton**, chief executive officer; **Jonathan Lyons** (biographies, history, science, pop culture, sports, general narrative nonfiction, mysteries, thrillers, science fiction and fantasy, and young adult fiction); **Laura Blake Peterson**, vice president (memoir and biography, natural history, literary fiction, mystery, suspense, women's fiction, health and fitness, children's and young adult, faith issues and popular culture); **Maureen Walters**, senior vice president (working primarily in women's fiction and nonfiction projects on subjects as eclectic as parenting & child care, popular psychology, inspirational/motivational volumes as well as a few medical/nutritional book); **Mitchell Waters** (literary and commercial fiction and nonfiction, including mystery, history, biography, memoir, young adult, cookbooks, self-help, and popular culture); **Kerry D'Agostino** (a wide range of literary and commercial fiction, as well as narrative nonfiction and memoir); **Noah Ballard** (literary debuts, upmarket thrillers and narrative nonfiction, and he is always on the look-out for honest and provocative new writers).

REPRESENTS nonfiction books, novels, short story collections, juvenile. **Considers these nonfiction areas:** animals, anthropology, art, biography, business, computers, cooking, crafts, creative nonfiction, current affairs, education, ethnic, film, gardening, government, health, history, how-to, humor, language, memoirs, military, money, multicultural, music, New Age, philosophy, photography, popular culture, psychology, recreation, regional, science, self-help, sex, sociology, software, spirituality, sports, translation, travel, true crime. **Considers these fiction areas:** adventure, confession, detective, erotica, ethnic, experimental, fantasy, feminist, gay, historical, horror, humor, juvenile, literary, mainstream, middle grade, military, multicultural, multimedia, mystery, New Age, occult, picture books, regional, religious, romance, spiritual, sports, thriller, translation, women's, young adult.

HOW TO CONTACT "Send us a query letter, a synopsis of the work, a sample chapter and a brief resume. Illustrators should send 1-2 samples of published work, along with 6-8 color copies (no original art). Please send all book queries to our address, Attn: Query Department. Please enclose a stamped,

NEW AGENT SPOTLIGHT

KIRSTEN CARLETON
WAXMAN LEAVELL LITERARY AGENCY

Waxmanleavell.com

@kirstencarleton

ABOUT KIRSTEN: Before joining Waxman Leavell, Kirsten worked at Sobel Weber Associates. She holds a B.A. in English with a creative writing concentration from Amherst College, and a graduate certificate in publishing from the Columbia Publishing Course.

SHE IS SEEKING: Upmarket young adult, speculative, and literary fiction with strong characters and storytelling. She's particularly interested in novels that bend and blur genres; literary takes on high concept worldbuilding; diverse characters in stories that are not just about diversity; antiheroes she find herself rooting for; characters with drive and passion; girls and women in STEM fields; settings outside the US/Europe; well-researched historical settings; YA noir/thriller/mystery; stories that introduces her to a new subculture and makes her feel like a native. She is *not* interested in horror, romance, erotica, poetry, or picture books.

HOW TO SUBMIT: Send a query letter with the first 5–10 pages of your manuscript in the body of the e-mail to kirstensubmit@waxmanleavell.com.

self-addressed envelope for our response and return postage if you wish to have your materials returned to you. We typically respond to queries within 6 to 8 weeks." Note that some agents list their e-mail on the agency website and are fine with e-mail submissions. Note in your submission if the query is being considered elsewhere. Responds in 3 weeks to queries; 5 weeks to mss. Obtains most new clients through recommendations from others, solicitations, conferences.

TERMS Agent receives 15% commission on domestic sales; 20% on foreign sales. Offers written contract. 75-day notice must be given to terminate contract. Offers written contract. Charges for some postage (overseas, etc.).

RECENT SALES This agency prefers not to share information on specific sales.

D4EO LITERARY AGENCY

7 Indian Valley Rd., Weston CT 06883. (203)544-7180. **Fax:** (203)544-7160. **Website:** www.d4eoliteraryagency.com. **Contact:** Bob Diforio.

Prior to opening his agency, Mr. Diforio was a publisher.

MEMBER AGENTS Bob Diforio (prefers referrals); **Mandy Hubbard** (middle grade, young adult, and genre romance); **Kristin Miller** (closed to queries); **Bree Odgen** (children's, young adult, juvenile nonfiction, graphic novels, pop culture, art books, genre horror, noir, genre romance, historical, hard sci-fi); **Joyce Holland; Pam van Hycklama Vlieg.**

REPRESENTS nonfiction books, novels. **Considers these nonfiction areas:** juvenile, art, biography, business, child, current affairs, gay, health, history, how-to, humor, memoirs, military, money, psychology, religion, science, self help, sports, true crime, women's. **Considers these fiction areas:** adventure, detective, erotica, historical, horror, humor, juvenile, literary, mainstream, middle grade, mystery, picture books, romance, sports, thriller.

HOW TO CONTACT Each of these agents has a different submission e-mail and different tastes regarding how they review material. See all on their individual agent pages on the agency website. Responds in 1 week to queries if interested. Obtains most new clients through recommendations from others.

TERMS Offers written contract, binding for 2 years; automatic renewal unless 60 days notice given prior to renewal date. Charges for photocopying and submission postage.

○ LAURA DAIL LITERARY AGENCY, INC.

350 Seventh Ave., Suite 2003, New York NY 10001. (212)239-7477. **Fax:** (212)947-0460. **E-mail:** ldail@ldlainc.com. **E-mail:** queries@ldlainc.com. **Website:** www.ldlainc.com. Member of AAR.

MEMBER AGENTS Laura Dail; Tamar Rydzinski.

REPRESENTS nonfiction books, novels. **Considers these nonfiction areas:** humor. **Considers these fiction areas:** commercial, historical, young adult.

➤ Specializes in historical, literary, and some young adult fiction, as well as both practical and idea-driven nonfiction. "Tamar is not interested in prescriptive or practical nonfiction, humor, coffee table books or children's books (meaning anything younger than middle grade). She is interested in everything else that is well-written and has great characters, including graphic novels. Due to the volume of queries and mss received, we apologize for not answering every e-mail and letter. None of us handles children's picture books or chapter books. No New Age. We do not handle screenplays or poetry."

HOW TO CONTACT "If you would like, you may include a synopsis and no more than 10 pages. If you are mailing your query, please be sure to include a self-addressed, stamped envelope; without it, you may not hear back from us. To save money, time and trees, we prefer queries by e-mail to queries@ldlainc.com. We get a lot of spam and are wary of computer viruses, so please use the word 'Query' in the subject line and include your detailed materials in the body of your message, not as an attachment."

◐ DANIEL LITERARY GROUP

1701 Kingsbury Dr., Suite 100, Nashville TN 37215. (615)730-8207. **E-mail:** submissions@danielliterarygroup.com. **Website:** www.danielliterarygroup.com. **Contact:** Greg Daniel. Represents 45 clients. 30% of clients are new/unpublished writers.

○ Prior to becoming an agent, Mr. Daniel spent 10 years in publishing—6 at the executive level at Thomas Nelson Publishers.

REPRESENTS nonfiction. **Considers these nonfiction areas:** autobiography, biography, business, child guidance, current affairs, economics, environment, film, health, history, how-to, humor, inspirational, medicine, memoirs, nature, parenting, personal improvement, popular culture, religious, satire, self-help, sports, theater, women's issues, women's studies.

➤ "We take pride in our ability to come alongside our authors and help strategize about where they want their writing to take them in both the near and long term. Forging close relationships with our authors, we help them with such critical factors as editorial refinement, branding, audience, and marketing." The agency is open to submissions in almost every popular category of nonfiction, especially if authors are recognized experts in their fields. No fiction, screenplays, poetry, science fiction/fantasy, romance, children's, or short stories.

HOW TO CONTACT Query via e-mail only. Submit publishing history, author bio, key selling points; no attachments. Check submissions guidelines before querying or submitting. Please do not query via telephone. Responds in 2-3 weeks to queries.

○ DARHANSOFF & VERRILL LITERARY AGENTS

133 West 72nd St., Room 304, New York NY 10023. (917)305-1300. **Fax:** (917)305-1400. **E-mail:** submissions@dvagency.com. **Website:** www.dvagency.com. Member of AAR.

MEMBER AGENTS Liz Darhansoff; Chuck Verrill; Michele Mortimer; Catherine Luttinger (science fiction, fantasy, historical fiction, thrillers, mysteries).

REPRESENTS **Considers these nonfiction areas:** creative nonfiction, memoirs. **Considers these fic-**

tion areas: fantasy, historical, literary, mystery, science fiction, suspense, thriller.

HOW TO CONTACT Send queries via e-mail (submissions@dvagency.com) or by snail mail with SASE. Obtains most new clients through recommendations from others.

RECENT SALES A full list of clients is available on their website.

⊗○ CAROLINE DAVIDSON LITERARY AGENCY

5 Queen Anne's Gardens, London England W4 1TU United Kingdom. (44)(208)995-5768. **Fax:** (44)(208)994-2770. **E-mail:** enquiries@cdla.co.uk. **Website:** www.cdla.co.uk. **Contact:** Ms. Caroline Davidson.

REPRESENTS nonfiction books, serious material only, novels.

- Does not consider autobiographies, chick lit, children's, crime, erotica, fantasy, horror, local history, murder mysteries, occult, self-help, short stories, sci-fi, thrillers, individual short stories, or memoir.

HOW TO CONTACT Handles novels and nonfiction of originality and high quality (12.5%). Send preliminary letter with CV and detailed well thought-out book proposal/synopsis and/or first 50 pages of novel in hard copy only. No e-mail submissions will be accepted or replied to. No reply without large SAE with correct return postage/IRC. No reading fee. CDLA does not consider plays, films scripts, poetry, children's/YA, thrillers, fantasy, horror, crime, erotica, occult or sci-fi. Obtains most new clients through recommendations from others. Please refer to website for further information. CDLA does not acknowledge or reply to e-mail enquiries. No telephone enquiries. Responds in 2 weeks to queries. Obtains most new clients through recommendations from others, solicitations.

TIPS "Please visit our website before submitting any work to us."

ⓘ LIZA DAWSON ASSOCIATES

350 Seventh Ave., Suite 2003, New York NY 10001. (212)465-9071. **Website:** www.lizadawsonassociates.com. **Contact:** Caitie Flum. Member of AAR. Other memberships include MWA, Women's Media Group. Represents 50+ clients. 30% of clients are new/unpublished writers.

- Prior to becoming an agent, Ms. Dawson was an editor for 20 years, spending 11 years at William Morrow as vice president and 2 years at Putnam as executive editor. Ms. Blasdell was a senior editor at HarperCollins and Avon.

MEMBER AGENTS Liza Dawson, queryliza@LizaDawsonAssociates.com (plot-driven literary and popular fiction, historicals, thrillers, suspense, history,psychology [both popular and clinical], politics, narrative nonfiction and memoirs); **Caitlin Blasdell**, queryCaitlin@LizaDawsonAssociates.com (science fiction, fantasy [both adult and young adult], parenting, business, thrillers and women's fiction; **Hannah Bowman**, queryHannah@LizaDawsonAssociates.com, West coast office; (commercial fiction—especially science fiction and fantasy, women's fiction, cozy mysteries, romance, young adult, also nonfiction in the areas of mathematics, science, and spirituality); **Caitie Flum**, querycaitie@LizaDawsonAssociates.com (commercial fiction, especially historical, women's fiction, mysteries, new adult and young adult, nonfiction in the areas of theater, memoir, current affairs and pop culture).

- This agency specializes in readable literary fiction, thrillers, mainstream historicals, women's fiction, academics, historians, journalists, and psychology.

HOW TO CONTACT Query by e-mail only. No phone calls. Each of these agents has their own specific submission requirements, which you can find online at their website. queryHannah@LizaDawsonAssociates.com; queryhavis@LizaDawsonAssociates.com; queryanna@LizaDawsonAssociates.com; queryCaitlin@LizaDawsonAssociates.com; queryliza@LizaDawsonAssociates.com. Responds in 4 weeks to queries; 8 weeks to mss. Obtains most new clients through recommendations from others, conferences.

TERMS Agent receives 15% commission on domestic sales. Agent receives 20% commission on foreign sales. Offers written contract.

ⓘ THE JENNIFER DECHIARA LITERARY AGENCY

31 East 32nd St., Suite 300, New York NY 10016. (212)481-8484. **Fax:** (212)481-9582. **Website:** www.jdlit.com.

MEMBER AGENTS Jennifer DeChiara, jenndec@aol.com (literary, commercial, women's fiction (no bodice-rippers, please), chick-lit, mysteries, suspense, thrillers, funny/quirky picture books, middle grade and young adult; for nonfiction: celebrity memoirs and biographies, GLBTQ, memoirs, books about the arts and performing arts, behind-the-scenes-type books, and books about popular culture); **Stephen Fraser**, fraserstephena@gmail.com (one-of-a-kind picture books; strong chapter book series; whimsical, dramatic, or humorous middle grade; dramatic or high-concept young adult; powerful and unusual nonfiction; nonfiction with a broad audience on topics as far reaching as art history, theater, film, literature, and travel); **Marie Lamba**, marie.jdlit@gmail.com (young adult and middle grade fiction, along with general and women's fiction, and some memoir; interested in established illustrators and picture book authors); **Linda Epstein**, linda.p.epstein@gmail.com (young adult, middle grade, literary fiction, quality upscale commercial fiction, vibrant narrative nonfiction, compelling memoirs, health and parenting books, cookbooks); **Roseanne Wells**, queryroseanne@gmail.com (literary fiction, YA, middle grade, narrative nonfiction, select memoir, science (popular or trade, not academic), history, religion (not inspirational), travel, humor, food/cooking, and similar subjects); **Victoria Selvaggio**, vselvaggio@windstream.net (lyrical picture books, middle grade and young adult fiction, mysteries, suspense, thrillers, paranormal, fantasy, narrative nonfiction).

REPRESENTS nonfiction books, novels, juvenile. **Considers these nonfiction areas:** art, cooking, creative nonfiction, film, foods, gay/lesbian, health, history, humor, literature, memoirs, parenting, popular culture, religious, science, theater, travel. **Considers these fiction areas:** commercial, literary, middle grade, mystery, picture books, suspense, thriller, women's, young adult.

HOW TO CONTACT Each agent has their own e-mail submission address and submission instructions. Accepts simultaneous submissions. Obtains most new clients through recommendations from others, conferences, query letters.

TERMS Agent receives 15% commission on domestic sales. Agent receives 20% commission on foreign sales. Offers written contract.

◑ DEFIORE & CO.

47 E. 19th St., 3rd Floor, New York NY 10003. (212)925-7744. **Fax:** (212)925-9803. **E-mail:** brian@defliterary.com. **E-mail:** info@defliterary.com; submissions@defliterary.com. **Website:** www.defioreandco.com. Member of AAR.

○ Prior to becoming an agent, Mr. DeFiore was publisher of Villard Books (1997-1998), editor-in-chief of Hyperion (1992-1997), and editorial director of Delacorte Press (1988-1992).

MEMBER AGENTS Brian DeFiore (popular nonfiction, business, pop culture, parenting, commercial fiction); **Laurie Abkemeier** (memoir, parenting, business, how-to/self-help, popular science); **Kate Garrick** (literary fiction, memoir, popular nonfiction); **Matthew Elblonk** (young adult, popular culture, narrative nonfiction); **Caryn Karmatz-Rudy** (popular fiction, self-help, narrative nonfiction); **Adam Schear** (commercial fiction, humor, YA, smart thrillers, historical fiction, and quirky debut literary novels. For nonfiction: popular science, politics, popular culture, and current events); **Meredith Kaffel** (smart upmarket women's fiction, literary fiction [especially debut] and literary thrillers, narrative nonfiction, nonfiction about science and tech, sophisticated pop culture/humor books); **Rebecca Strauss** (literary and commercial fiction, women's fiction, urban fantasy, romance, mystery, YA, memoir, pop culture, and select nonfiction); **Debra Goldstein** (nonfiction books on how to live better).

REPRESENTS nonfiction books, novels. **Considers these nonfiction areas:** autobiography, biography, business, child guidance, cooking, economics, foods, how-to, inspirational, money, multicultural, parenting, popular culture, politics, psychology, religious, science, self-help, sports, young adult. **Considers these fiction areas:** ethnic, literary, mainstream, middle grade, mystery, paranormal, romance, short story collections, suspense, thriller, women's, young adult.

⊶ "Please be advised that we are not considering poetry, adult science fiction and fantasy, or dramatic projects at this time."

HOW TO CONTACT Query with SASE or e-mail to submissions@defliterary.com. "Please include the word 'Query' in the subject line. All attachments will be deleted; please insert all text in the body of the e-mail. For more information about our agents, their individual interests, and their query guidelines, please visit our 'About Us' page on our website." There is more information (details, sales) for each agent on the agency website. Accepts simultaneous submissions. Obtains most new clients through recommendations from others.

TERMS Agent receives 15% commission on domestic sales. Agent receives 20% commission on foreign sales. Offers written contract; 10-day notice must be given to terminate contract. Charges clients for photocopying and overnight delivery (deducted only after a sale is made).

⦿ JOELLE DELBOURGO ASSOCIATES, INC.

101 Park St., 3rd Floor, Montclair NJ 07042. (973)773-0836. **Fax:** (973)783-6802. **E-mail:** joelle@delbourgo.com. **E-mail:** submissions@delbourgo.com. **Website:** www.delbourgo.com. Represents more than 100 clients. Currently handles: nonfiction books 75%, novels 25%.

○ Prior to becoming an agent, Ms. Delbourgo was an editor and senior publishing executive at HarperCollins and Random House.

MEMBER AGENTS Joelle Delbourgo; Jacqueline Flynn; Carrie Cantor.

REPRESENTS nonfiction books, novels. **Considers these nonfiction areas:** creative nonfiction, current affairs, history, memoirs, politics, psychology, science, self-help. **Considers these fiction areas:** fantasy, literary, mainstream, middle grade, science fiction, thriller, women's, young adult.

⚯ "We are former publishers and editors with deep knowledge and an insider perspective. We have a reputation for individualized attention to clients, strategic management of authors' careers, and creating strong partnerships with publishers for our clients."

HOW TO CONTACT It's preferable if you submit via e-mail to a specific agent. Query one agent only. No attachments. Put the word "Query" in the subject line. "While we do our best to respond to each query, if you have not received a response in 60 days you may consider that a pass. Please do not send us copies of self-published books unless requested. Let us know if you are sending your query to us exclusively or if this is a multiple submission. For nonfiction, let us know if a proposal and sample chapters are available. If not, you should probably wait to send your query when you have a completed proposal. For fiction and memoir, embed the *first* 10 pages of ms into the e-mail after your query letter. Please no attachments. If we like your first pages, we may ask to see your synopsis and

more ms. Both should be completed before you query us." Accepts simultaneous submissions.

TERMS Agent receives 15% commission on domestic sales. Agent receives 20% commission on foreign sales. Offers written contract. Charges clients for postage and photocopying.

RECENT SALES *Alexander the Great*, by Philip Freeman; *The Big Book of Parenting Solutions*, by Dr. Michele Borba; *The Secret Life of Ms. Finkelman*, by Ben H. Wintners; *Not Quite Adults*, by Richard Settersten Jr. and Barbara Ray; *Tabloid Medicine*, by Robert Goldberg, PhD; *Table of Contents*, by Judy Gerlman and Vicky Levi Krupp.

TIPS "Do your homework. Do not cold call. Read and follow submission guidelines before contacting us. Do not call to find out if we received your material. No e-mail queries. Treat agents with respect, as you would any other professional, such as a doctor, lawyer or financial advisor."

⦿ SANDRA DIJKSTRA LITERARY AGENCY

1155 Camino del Mar, PMB 515, Del Mar CA 92014. (858)755-3115. **Fax:** (858)794-2822. **E-mail:** elise@dijkstraagency.com. **Website:** www.dijkstraagency.com. Member of AAR. Other memberships include Authors Guild, PEN West, PEN USA, Organization of American Historians, Poets and Editors, MWA. Represents 100+ clients. 30% of clients are new/unpublished writers.

MEMBER AGENTS Sandra Dijkstra, president (adult only). Acquiring Sub-agents: **Elise Capron** (adult only), **Jill Marr** (adult only), **Thao Le** (adult and YA), **Roz Foster** (adult and YA), **Jessica Watterson** (subgenres of adult and new adult romance, and women's fiction).

REPRESENTS nonfiction books, novels. **Considers these nonfiction areas:** biography, business, creative nonfiction, design, history, memoirs, psychology, science, self-help, narrative. **Considers these fiction areas:** commercial, horror, literary, middle grade, new adult, romance, science fiction, suspense, thriller, women's, young adult.

HOW TO CONTACT "Please see guidelines on our website, and note that we only accept e-mail submissions. Due to the large number of unsolicited submissions we receive, we are only able to respond those submissions in which we are interested." Accepts simultaneous submissions. Responds to queries of interest within 6 weeks.

TERMS Works in conjunction with foreign and film agents. Agent receives 15% commission on domestic sales and 20% commission on foreign sales. Offers written contract. No reading fee.

TIPS "Remember that publishing is a business. Do your research and present your project in as professional a way as possible. Only submit your work when you are confident that it is polished and ready for prime-time. Make yourself a part of the active writing community by getting stories and articles published, networking with other writers, and getting a good sense of where your work fits in the market."

⊙ DONADIO & OLSON, INC.

121 W. 27th St., Suite 704, New York NY 10001. (212)691-8077. **Fax:** (212)633-2837. **E-mail:** neil@donadio.com. **E-mail:** mail@donadio.com. **Website:** http://donadio.com. **Contact:** Neil Olson. Member of AAR.

MEMBER AGENTS Neil Olson (no queries); Edward Hibbert (no queries); Carrie Howland (represents literary fiction and nonfiction as well as young adult fiction; she can be reached at carrie@donadio.com).

REPRESENTS nonfiction books, novels. **Considers these fiction areas:** literary, young adult.

8—⊸ This agency represents mostly fiction, and is very selective.

HOW TO CONTACT Please send a query letter, full synopsis, and the first three chapters/first 25 pages of the ms to mail@donadio.com. Please allow a few weeks for a reply. Obtains most new clients through recommendations from others.

⊕ DONAGHY LITERARY GROUP

(647)527-4353. **E-mail:** query@donaghyliterary.com. **Website:** www.donaghyliterary.com.

MEMBER AGENTS Stacey Donaghy (romantic suspense, LGBT stories standalone or series, mystery of all kinds, contemporary romance, erotica; Stacey also seeks nonfiction—authorized biographies, compelling stories written by celebrities, music industry professionals, pop culture, film/television, Canadian/international content; she is not seeking general nonfiction or memoirs unless you are a rock icon, or celebrity); Valerie Noble (science fiction and fantasy [think Kristin Cashore and Suzanne Collins] for young adults and adults.

REPRESENTS Considers these fiction areas: erotica, fantasy, mystery, romance, science fiction, young adult.

HOW TO CONTACT Check the website, because the agency can close to submissions at any time.

○ JANIS A. DONNAUD & ASSOCIATES, INC.

525 Broadway, Second Floor, New York NY 10012. (212)431-2664. **Fax:** (212)431-2667. **E-mail:** jdonnaud@aol.com; donnaudassociate@aol.com. **Website:** http://www.publishersmarketplace.com/members/JanisDonnaud/. **Contact:** Janis A. Donnaud. Member of AAR. Signatory of WGA. Represents 40 clients. 5% of clients are new/unpublished writers. Currently handles: nonfiction books 100%.

○ Prior to opening her agency, Ms. Donnaud was vice president and associate publisher of Random House Adult Trade Group.

REPRESENTS nonfiction books. **Considers these nonfiction areas:** biography, business, creative nonfiction, health, history, memoirs, money, psychology.

8—⊸ Seeks the following kinds of nonfiction books: culinary subjects, narrative nonfiction, wellness, medical topics for a general audience, contemporary issues, and "big idea" books. Does not want to receive "fiction, poetry, mysteries, juvenile books, romances, science fiction, young adult, religious or fantasy."

HOW TO CONTACT Query. For nonfiction, send a proposal; for fiction, paste a sample chapter into the e-mail. Prefers exclusive submissions. Responds in 1 month to queries and mss. Obtains most new clients through recommendations from others.

TERMS Agent receives 15% commission on domestic and film sales; 20% commission on foreign sales. Offers written contract; 1-month notice must be given to terminate contract.

RECENT SALES *New York Times* bestseller *The Skinnytaste Cookbook* by Gina Homolka; *Fat Chance* by Robert Lustig, M.D.; *50 Shades of Chicken: A Parody in a Cookbook,* by FL Fowler; *The Immune System Recovery Plan,* by Susan Blum, M.D.; *Buvette: The Pleasure of Good Food* by Jody Williams; *Staten Italy* by the Artichoke Pizza Guys, Francis Garcia & Sal Basille; *A Taste Of Cowboy* by Kent Rollins; *30 Lessons For Loving* by Karl Pillemer, Ph.D.; award winning, best-selling cookbooks by Melissa Clark, Amy Thielen, Suzanne Goin, Carla Hall, Donald Link, Nancy Silverton.

⦿⦿ JIM DONOVAN LITERARY

5635 SMU Blvd., Suite 201, Dallas TX 75206. **E-mail:** jdliterary@sbcglobal.net. **Contact:** Melissa Shultz, agent.

MEMBER AGENTS Jim Donovan (history—particularly American, military, and Western; biography; sports; popular reference; popular culture; fiction—literary, thrillers, and mystery); **Melissa Shultz** (all subjects listed above [like Jim], along with parenting and women's issues).

�—ℸ This agency specializes in commercial fiction and nonfiction. "Does not want to receive poetry, children's, sci-fi, fantasy, short stories, inspirational, or anything else not listed above."

HOW TO CONTACT "For nonfiction, I need a well thought out query letter telling me about the book: What it does, how it does it, why it's needed now, why it's better or different than what's out there on the subject, and why the author is the perfect writer for it. For fiction, the novel has to be finished, of course; a short (2 to 5 page) synopsis—not a teaser, but a summary of all the action, from first page to last—and the first 30-50 pages is enough. This material should be polished to as close to perfection as possible." Accepts simultaneous submissions. Responds in 2 weeks to queries. Responds in 1 month to mss. Obtains most new clients through recommendations from others.

TERMS Agent receives 15% commission on domestic sales. Agent receives 20% commission on foreign sales. Offers written contract, binding for 1 year; 30-day notice must be given to terminate contract. This agency charges for things such as overnight delivery and ms copying. Charges are discussed beforehand.

RECENT SALES *Manson* by Jeff Guinn (S&S); *The Last Outlaws* by Thom Hatch (NAL); *Rough Riders* by Mark Lee Gardner (Morrow); *James Monroe* by Tim McGrath (NAL); *What Lurks Beneath* by Ryan Lockwood (Kensington); *Battle for Hell's Island* by Stephen Moore (NAL); *Powerless* by Tim Washburn (Kensington).

TIPS "Get published in short form—magazine reviews, journals, etc.—first. This will increase your credibility considerably, and make it much easier to sell a full-length book."

⦿ DOYEN LITERARY SERVICES, INC.

1931-660th St., Newell IA 50568-7613. **E-mail:** bestseller@barbaradoyen.com. **Website:** www.barbaradoyen.com. **Contact:** (Ms.) B.J. Doyen, president. Currently handles: nonfiction books 100%.

⦿ Prior to opening her agency, Ms. Doyen worked as a published author, teacher, guest speaker, and wrote and appeared in her own weekly TV show airing in 7 states. She is also the coauthor of *The Everything Guide to Writing a Book Proposal* (Adams 2005) and *The Everything Guide to Getting Published* (Adams 2006).

REPRESENTS nonfiction for adults, no children's. **Considers these nonfiction areas:** agriculture, Americana, animals, anthropology, archeology, architecture, art, autobiography, biography, business, child guidance, computers, cooking, crafts, cultural interests, current affairs, diet/nutrition, design, economics, education, environment, ethnic, film, foods, gardening, government, health, history, hobbies, horticulture, language, law, medicine, memoirs, metaphysics, military, money, multicultural, music, parenting, photography, popular culture, politics, psychology, recreation, regional, science, self-help, sex, sociology, software, technology, theater, true crime, women's issues, women's studies, creative nonfiction, computers, electronics.

�—ℸ This agency specializes in nonfiction. Actively seeking business, health, science, how-to, self-help—all kinds of adult nonfiction suitable for the major trade publishers. Does not want to receive pornography, screenplays, children's books, fiction, or poetry.

HOW TO CONTACT Send a **query letter** initially. "Do not send us any attachments. Your text must be in the body of the e-mail. Please read the website before submitting a query. Include your background information in a bio. Send no unsolicited attachments." Accepts simultaneous submissions. Responds immediately to queries. Responds in 3 weeks to mss.

TERMS Agent receives 15% commission on domestic sales. Agent receives 20% commission on foreign sales. Offers written contract, binding for 2 years.

TIPS "Our authors receive personalized attention. We market aggressively, undeterred by rejection. We get the best possible publishing contracts. We are very interested in nonfiction book ideas at this time and will consider most topics. Many writers come to us from referrals, but we also get quite a few who initially approach us with query letters. Do not call us regarding queries. It is best if you do not collect editorial rejections prior to seeking an agent, but if you do, be upfront and honest about it. Do not submit your manuscript to more than 1 agent at a time—querying first can save you (and us) much time. We're open to established or beginning writers—just send us a terrific letter!"

DREISBACH LITERARY MANAGEMENT

PO Box 5379, El Dorado Hills CA 95762. (916)804-5016. **E-mail:** verna@dreisbachliterary.com. **Website:** www.dreisbachliterary.com. **Contact:** Verna Dreisbach. Estab. 2007.

Prior to opening her own agency, Ms. Dreisbach was with Andrea Hurst Literary.

REPRESENTS Considers these nonfiction areas: animals, biography, business, health, memoirs, multicultural, parenting, travel, true crime, women's issues. **Considers these fiction areas:** commercial, literary, mystery, thriller, young adult.

The agency has a particular interest in books with a political, economic, or social context. Open to most types of nonfiction. Fiction interests include literary, commercial, and YA. Verna's first career as a law enforcement officer gives her a genuine interest and expertise in the genres of mystery, thriller, and true crime. Does not want to receive sci-fi, fantasy, horror, poetry, screenplay, Christian, or children's books.

HOW TO CONTACT E-mail queries only. No attachments in the query; they will not be opened. No unsolicited mss. *Accepting new nonfiction clients only through a writers conference or a personal referral. Not accepting fiction.*

RECENT SALES *How to Blog a Book* (Writer's Digest Books); *Quest for Justice* (New Horizon Press); *Walnut Wine and Truffle Groves* (Running Press); *Coming to the Fire* (BenBella Books); *Off the Street* (Behler Publications); *Lowcountry Bribe* (Bell Bridge Books).

DUNHAM LITERARY, INC.

110 William St., Suite 2202, New York NY 10038. (212)929-0994. **E-mail:** query@dunhamlit.com. **Website:** www.dunhamlit.com. **Contact:** Jennie Dunham. Member of AAR. SCBWI Represents 50 clients. 15% of clients are new/unpublished writers. Currently handles: nonfiction books 25%, novels 25%, juvenile books 50%.

Prior to opening her agency, Ms. Dunham worked as a literary agent for Russell & Volkening. The Rhoda Weyr Agency is now a division of Dunham Literary, Inc.

REPRESENTS Considers these nonfiction areas: anthropology, archeology, biography, cultural interests, environment, ethnic, health, history, language, literature, medicine, popular culture, politics, psychology, science, technology, women's issues, women's studies. **Considers these fiction areas:** ethnic, juvenile, literary, mainstream, picture books, young adult.

HOW TO CONTACT Query with SASE. Responds in 3 weeks to queries; 2 months to mss. Obtains most new clients through recommendations from others, solicitations.

TERMS Agent receives 15% commission on domestic sales. Agent receives 20% commission on foreign sales.

RECENT SALES Sales include The Bad Kitty Series, by Nick Bruel (Macmillan); *The Little Mermaid*, by Robert Sabuda (Simon & Schuster); *The Gollywhopper Games* and Sequels, by Jody Feldman (HarperCollins); *Learning Not To Drown*, by Anna Shinoda (Simon & Schuster); *The Things You Kiss Goodbye*, by Leslie Connor (HarperCollins); *Gangsterland*, by Tod Goldberg (Counterpoint); *Ancestors and Others*, by Fred Chappell (Macmillan), *Forward From Here*, by Reeve Lindbergh (Simon & Schuster).

DUNOW, CARLSON, & LERNER AGENCY

27 W. 20th St., Suite 1107, New York NY 10011. (212)645-7606. **E-mail:** betsy@dclagency.com; jennifer@dclagency.com. **E-mail:** mail@dclagency.com. **Website:** www.dclagency.com. Member of AAR.

MEMBER AGENTS Jennifer Carlson (narrative nonfiction writers and journalists covering current events and ideas and cultural history, as well as literary and upmarket commercial novelists); **Henry Dunow** (quality fiction—literary, historical, strongly written commercial—and with voice-driven nonfiction across a range of areas – narrative history, biography, memoir, current affairs, cultural trends and criticism, science, sports); **Erin Hosier** (nonfiction: popular culture, music, sociology and memoir); **Betsy Lerner** (nonfiction writers in the areas of psychology, history, cultural studies, biography, current events, business; fiction: literary, dark, funny, voice driven); **Yishai Seidman** (broad range of fiction: literary, post-

NEW AGENT SPOTLIGHT

LANE HEYMONT
THE SEYMOUR AGENCY

Theseymouragency.com

@laneheymont

ABOUT LANE: Serving as a literary assistant for the past two years at The Seymour Agency, Lane Heymont has led the marketing efforts for their authors and enjoyed connecting clients with readers. As a lover of literature since childhood, he decided to pursue his passion as a literary agent to bring more excellent books to the masses. With a bachelor's degree in psychology, business and literature, Lane continued his education in creative writing and English, attending Harvard. Lane is a member of HWA, ITW, and his AAR membership is pending. He believes what John Gregory Dunne said: "Writing is manual labor of the mind."

HE IS SEEKING: science fiction and fantasy (exceptional world-building is a must), and nonfiction (the inspiring, intriguing, mysterious, and scientific).

HOW TO CONNECT: Send all queries to lane@theseymouragency.com. The subject line should be "QUERY: (Title)". Please past the first five pages in the body of the e-mail.

modern, and thrillers; nonfiction: sports, music, and pop culture); **Amy Hughes** (nonfiction in the areas of history, cultural studies, memoir, current events, wellness, health, food, pop culture, and biography; also literary fiction); **Eleanor Jackson** (literary, commercial, memoir, art, food, science and history); **Julia Kenny** (fiction—adult, middle grade and YA—and is especially interested in dark, literary thrillers and suspense); **Edward Necarsulmer IV** (strong new voices in teen and middle grade, as well as picture books). **REPRESENTS** nonfiction books, novels, juvenile. **Considers these nonfiction areas:** art, biography, creative nonfiction, cultural interests, current affairs, foods, health, history, memoirs, music, popular culture, psychology, science, sociology, sports. **Considers these fiction areas:** commercial, literary, mainstream, middle grade, mystery, picture books, thriller, young adult.

HOW TO CONTACT Query via snail mail with SASE, or by e-mail. No attachments. Responds if interested. **RECENT SALES** A full list of agency clients is on the website.

⊘ DUPREE/MILLER AND ASSOCIATES INC. LITERARY

100 Highland Park Village, Suite 350, Dallas TX 75205. (214)559-BOOK. **Fax:** (214)559-PAGE. **E-mail:** editorial@dupreemiller.com. **Website:** www. dupreemiller.com. Member of ABA. Represents 200 clients. 20% of clients are new/unpublished writers. Currently handles: nonfiction books 90%, novels 10%. **MEMBER AGENTS** Jan Miller, founder/CEO; **Shannon Miser-Marven,** president; **Nena Madonia,** senior lead agent; **Lacy Lynch,** senior lead agent; **Dabney Rice,** foreign rights director.

REPRESENTS nonfiction books, novels, scholarly, syndicated, religious.inspirational/spirituality. **Considers these nonfiction areas:** animals, anthropology, archeology, architecture, art, autobiography, biography, business, child guidance, cooking, crafts, current affairs, dance, diet/nutrition, design, economics, education, environment, ethnic, film, foods, gardening, government, health, history, how-to, humor, language, literature, medicine, memoirs, money, multicultural, music, parenting, philosophy, photography, popular culture, psychology, recreation, regional, satire, science, self-help, sex, sociology, sports, technology, theater, translation, true crime, women's issues, women's studies. **Considers these fiction areas:** action, adventure, crime, detective, ethnic, experimental, family saga, feminist, glitz, historical, humor, inspirational, literary, mainstream, mystery, picture books, police, psychic, religious, satire, sports, supernatural, suspense, thriller.

8—ℸ This agency specializes in commercial fiction and nonfiction.

HOW TO CONTACT This agency does not request unsolicited submissions, and meets their new clients through referrals or face-to-face events. Obtains all new clients through recommendations from current clients.

TERMS Agent receives 15% commission on domestic sales. Offers written contract.

WRITERS CONFERENCES Aspen Summer Words Literary Festival.

❶ DYSTEL & GODERICH LITERARY MANAGEMENT

1 Union Square W., Suite 904, New York NY 10003. (212)627-9100. **Fax:** (212)627-9313. **Website:** www.dystel.com. Estab. 1994. Member of AAR. Other membership includes SCBWI. Represents 600+ clients.

MEMBER AGENTS Jane Dystel; Miriam Goderich, miriam@dystel.com (literary and commercial fiction as well as some genre fiction, narrative nonfiction, pop culture, psychology, history, science, art, business books, and biography/memoir); **Stacey Kendall Glick**, sglick@dystel.com (narrative nonfiction including memoir, parenting, cooking and food, psychology, science, health and wellness, lifestyle, current events, pop culture, YA, middle grade, and select adult contemporary fiction); **Michael Bourret**, mbourret@dystel.com (middle grade and young adult fiction, commercial adult fiction, and all sorts of nonfiction, from practical to narrative; he's especially interested in food and cocktail related books, memoir, popular history, politics, religion [though not spirituality], popular science, and current events); **Jim McCarthy**, jmccarthy@dystel.com (literary women's fiction, underrepresented voices, mysteries, romance, paranormal fiction, narrative nonfiction, memoir, and paranormal nonfiction); **Jessica Papin**, jpapin@dystel.com (literary and smart commercial fiction, narrative nonfiction, history with a thesis, medicine, science and religion, health, psychology, women's issues); **Lauren E. Abramo**, labramo@dystel.com (smart commercial fiction and well-paced literary fiction with a unique voice, including middle grade, YA, and adult and a wide variety of narrative nonfiction including science, interdisciplinary cultural studies, pop culture, psychology, reportage, media, contemporary culture, and history); **John Rudolph**, jrudolph@dystel.com (picture book author/illustrators, middle grade, YA, commercial fiction for men, nonfiction); **Rachel Stout**, rstout@dystel.com (literary fiction, narrative nonfiction, and believable and thought-provoking YA as well as magical realism); **Sharon Pelletier**, spelletier@dystel.com (witty literary fiction and smart commercial fiction featuring female characters, narrative nonfiction).

REPRESENTS nonfiction books, novels, cookbooks. **Considers these nonfiction areas:** animals, anthropology, archeology, autobiography, biography, business, child guidance, cultural interests, current affairs, economics, ethnic, gay/lesbian, health, history, humor, inspirational, investigative, medicine, metaphysics, military, New Age, parenting, popular culture, psychology, religious, science, technology, true crime, women's issues, women's studies. **Considers these fiction areas:** action, adventure, commercial, crime, detective, ethnic, family saga, gay, lesbian, literary, mainstream, middle grade, mystery, picture books, police, suspense, thriller, women's, young adult.

8—ℸ "We are actively seeking fiction for all ages, in all genres." No plays, screenplays, or poetry.

HOW TO CONTACT Query via e-mail and put "Query" in the subject line. "Synopses, outlines, or sample chapters (say, one chapter or the first 25 pages of your ms) should either be included below the cover letter or attached as a separate document. We won't open attachments if they come with a blank e-mail." Accepts simultaneous submissions. Responds in 6 to 8 weeks to queries; within 8 weeks to mss. Obtains most new clients through recommendations from others, solicitations, conferences.

TERMS Agent receives 15% commission on domestic sales. Agent receives 19% commission on foreign sales. Offers written contract.

WRITERS CONFERENCES Backspace Writers' Conference; Pacific Northwest Writers' Association; Pike's Peak Writers' Conference; Writers League of Texas; Love Is Murder; Surrey International Writers Conference; Society of Children's Book Writers and Illustrators; International Thriller Writers; Willamette Writers Conference; The South Carolina Writers Workshop Conference; Las Vegas Writers Conference; Writer's Digest; Seton Hill Popular Fiction; Romance Writers of America; Geneva Writers Conference.

TIPS "DGLM prides itself on being a full-service agency. We're involved in every stage of the publishing process, from offering substantial editing on mss and proposals, to coming up with book ideas for authors looking for their next project, negotiating contracts and collecting monies for our clients. We follow a book from its inception through its sale to a publisher, its publication, and beyond. Our commitment to our writers does not, by any means, end when we have collected our commission. This is one of the many things that makes us unique in a very competitive business."

●◑ TOBY EADY ASSOCIATES

Third Floor, 9 Orme Court, London England W2 4RL United Kingdom. (44)(207)792-0092. **Fax:** (44)(207)792-0879. **E-mail:** toby@tobyeadyassociates.co.uk. **E-mail:** submissions@tobyeadyassociates.co.uk. **Website:** www.tobyeadyassociates.co.uk. **Contact:** Toby Eady. Estab. 1968. Represents 53 clients. 13% of clients are new/unpublished writers. Currently handles: nonfiction books 50%, novels 50%.

MEMBER AGENTS Toby Eady (China, the Middle East, Africa, politics of a Swiftian nature); **Laetitia Rutherford** (fiction and nonfiction from around the world).

REPRESENTS nonfiction books, novels, short story collections, novellas, anthologies. **Considers these nonfiction areas:** architecture, art, cooking, cultural interests, current affairs, diet/nutrition, design, ethnic, foods, government, health, history, law, medicine, memoirs, popular culture, politics. **Considers these**

fiction areas: action, adventure, confession, historical, literary, mainstream.

�—ᴨ "We handle fiction and nonfiction for adults and we specialize in China, the Middle East and Africa." Actively seeking "stories that demand to be heard." Does not want to receive poetry, screenplays or children's books.

HOW TO CONTACT Send the first 50 pages of your work, double-spaced and unbound, with a synopsis and a brief bio attn: Jamie Coleman. Accepts simultaneous submissions. Responds in 2 weeks to queries. Responds in 2 weeks to mss. Obtains most new clients through recommendations from others, solicitations, conferences.

TERMS Agent receives 15% commission on domestic sales. Agent receives 20% commission on foreign sales. Offers written contract; 3-month notice must be given to terminate contract.

WRITERS CONFERENCES City Lit; Winchester Writers' Festival.

TIPS "Send submissions to this address: Toby Eady, 9 Orme Court, London W2 4RL."

○ EAST/WEST LITERARY AGENCY, LLC

1158 26th St., Suite 462, Santa Monica CA 90403. (310)573-9303. **Fax:** (310)453-9008. **E-mail:** dwarren@eastwestliteraryagency.com. **Contact:** Deborah Warren. Estab. 2000. Currently handles: juvenile books 90%, adult books 10%.

MEMBER AGENTS Deborah Warren, founder.

REPRESENTS Considers these fiction areas: middle grade, picture books, young adult.

HOW TO CONTACT By referral only. Submit proposal and first 3 sample chapters, table of contents (2 pages or fewer), synopsis (1 page). For picture books, submit entire ms. Requested submissions should be sent by mail as a Word document in Courier, 12-pt., double-spaced with 1.20-inch margin on left, ragged right text, 25 lines per page, continuously paginated, with all your contact info on the first page. Only responds if interested, no need for SASE. Responds in 60 days. Obtains new clients through recommendations from others.

TERMS Agent receives 15% commission on domestic sales. Agent receives 25% commission on foreign sales. Offers written contract; 30-day notice must be given to terminate contract. Charges for out-of-pocket expenses, such as postage and copying.

EBELING & ASSOCIATES

P.O. Box 2529, Lyons CO 80540. (303)823-6963. **E-mail:** ebothat@yahoo.com. **Website:** www.ebelinga gency.com. **Contact:** Michael Ebeling. Represents 6 clients. 50% of clients are new/unpublished writers. Currently handles: nonfiction books 100%.

○ Prior to becoming an agent, Mr. Ebeling established a career in the publishing industry through long-term author management. He has expertise in sales, platforms, publicity and marketing.

REPRESENTS nonfiction books. **Considers these nonfiction areas:** animals, business, cooking, diet/nutrition, environment, foods, history, how-to, humor, inspirational, medicine, money, music, parenting, psychology, religious, satire, self-help, spirituality, sports.

⌖ "We accept very few clients for representation. To be considered, an author needs a very strong platform and a unique book concept. We represent nonfiction authors, most predominantly in the areas of business and self-help. We are very committed to our authors and their messages, which is a main reason we have such a high placement rate. We are always looking at new ways to help our authors gain the exposure they need to not only get published, but develop a successful literary career." Actively seeking well-written nonfiction material with fresh perspectives written by writers with established platforms. Does not want to receive fiction, poetry or children's lit.

HOW TO CONTACT We accept queries and proposals by e-mail only. Accepts simultaneous submissions. Responds in 4-6 weeks to queries. Obtains most new clients through referrals and queries.

TERMS Agent receives 15% commission on domestic sales. Agent receives 20% commission on foreign sales. Offers written contract; 60-day notice must be given to terminate contract. There is a charge for normal out-of-pocket fees, not to exceed $200 without client approval.

RECENT SALES *Naked: How to Find Your Perfect Partner by Revealing Your True Self* by David Wygant (Hay House 2012); *The One Command: Command Your Wealth* by Asara Lovejoy (Berkley/Penguin 2012); *Growing Happy Kids* by Maureen Healy (Health Communications, Inc. 2012).

WRITERS CONFERENCES BookExpo America; San Francisco Writers' Conference.

TIPS "Approach agents when you're already building your platform, you have a well-written book, you have a firm understanding of the publishing process, and you have come up with a complete competitive proposal. Know the name of the agent you are contacting. You're essentially selling a business plan to the publisher. Make sure you've made a convincing pitch throughout your proposal, as ultimately, publishers are taking a financial risk by investing in your project."

EDEN STREET LITERARY

P.O. Box 30, Billings NY 12510. **E-mail:** info@eden streetlit.com. **E-mail:** submissions@edenstreetlit. com. **Website:** www.edenstreetlit.com. **Contact:** Liza Voges.

REPRESENTS Considers these fiction areas: juvenile, middle grade, picture books, young adult.

HOW TO CONTACT Send an e-mail (to submissions@edenstreetlit.com) with a picture book ms or dummy; a synopsis and 3 chapters of a middle grade or YA novel; or a proposal and 3 sample chapters for nonfiction. Responds only to submissions of interest.

RECENT SALES Recent Titles: *Dream Dog*, by Lou Berger; *Biscuit Loves the Library*, by Alyssa Capucilli; *The Scraps Book*, by Lois Ehlert; *Two Bunny Buddies*, by Kathryn O. Galbraith; *Between Two Worlds*, by Katherine Kirkpatrick.

EDUCATIONAL DESIGN SERVICES LLC

5750 Bou Ave, Suite 1508, N. Bethesda MD 20852. **E-mail:** blinder@educationaldesignservices.com. **Website:** www.educationaldesignservices.com. **Contact:** B. Linder. Estab. 1981. 80% of clients are new/unpublished writers.

⌖ "We specialize in educational materials to be used in classrooms (in class sets), for staff development or in teacher education classes." Actively seeking educational, text materials. Not looking for picture books, story books, fiction; no illustrators.

HOW TO CONTACT Query by e-mail or with SASE or send outline and 1 sample chapter. Considers simultaneous queries and submissions if so indicated. Returns material only with SASE. Responds in 6-8 weeks to queries/mss. Obtains clients through recommendations from others, queries/solicitations, or through conferences.

TERMS Agent receives 15% commission on domestic sales; 25% on foreign sales. Offers written contract, binding until any party opts out. Terminate contract through certified letter.

RECENT SALES *How to Solve Word Problems in Mathematics*, by Wayne (McGraw-Hill*); Preparing for the 8th Grade Test in Social Studies*, by Farran-Paci (Amsco); *Minority Report*, by Gunn-Singh (Scarecrow Education); *No Parent Left Behind*, by Petrosino & Spiegel (Rowman & Littlefield); *Teaching Test-taking Skills* (R&L Education); *10 Languages You'll Need Most in the Classroom*, by Sundem, Krieger, Pickiewicz (Corwin Press*); Kids, Classrooms & Capital Hill*, by Flynn (R&L Education); *Bully Nation*, by Susan Eva Porter (Paragon House).

❶ JUDITH EHRLICH LITERARY MANAGEMENT, LLC

880 Third Ave., 8th Floor, New York NY 10022. (646)505-1570. **Fax:** (646)505-1570. **Website:** www.judithehrlichliterary.com. Member of the Author's Guild and the American Society of Journalists and Authors.

○ Prior to her current position, Ms. Ehrlich was a senior associate at the Linda Chester Agency and is an award-winning journalist; she is the co-author of *The New Crowd: The Changing of the Jewish Guard on Wall Street* (Little, Brown).

MEMBER AGENTS Judith Ehrlich, jehrlich@judithehrlichliterary.com (nonfiction—narrative, women's, business, prescriptive); **Sophia Seidner**: sseidner@judithehrlichliterary.com (upmarket fiction and nonfiction including prescriptive, narrative nonfiction, memoir, and biography; areas of special interest include medical and health-related topics, science [popular, political and social], animal welfare, current events, politics, law, history, ethics, parody and humor, sports, and business self-help).

REPRESENTS Considers these nonfiction areas: biography, business, creative nonfiction, cultural interests, current affairs, health, history, memoirs, parenting, psychology, science, women's issues. **Considers these fiction areas:** commercial, literary, Also seeks prescriptive books offering fresh information and advice.

✎ Does not want to receive novellas, poetry, textbooks, plays, or screenplays.

HOW TO CONTACT E-query, with a synopsis and some sample pages. The agency will respond only if interested.

RECENT SALES *Power Branding: Leveraging the Success of the World's Best Brands* by Steve McKee (Palgrave Macmillan); *What was the Underground Railroad?* by Yona Zeldis McDonough (Grosset & Dunlap); *Confessions of a Sociopath: A Life Spent Hiding in Plain Sight* by M.E. Thomas (Crown); *The Last Kiss* by Leslie Brody (TitleTown); *Love, Loss, and Laughter: Seeing Alzheimer's Differently* (Lyons Press); *Luck and Circumstance: A Coming of Age in New York, Hollywood, and Points Beyond* by Michael Lindsay-Hogg (Knopf); *Paris Under Water: How the City of Light Survived the Great Flood of 1910* by Jeffrey H. Jackson (Palgrave Macmillan). Fiction titles: *Two of a Kind* by Yona Zeldis McDonough (NAL, September 2013); *Once We Were* by Kat Zhang (HarperCollins, September 2013).

➕ EINSTEIN LITERARY MANAGEMENT

27 West 20th St., No. 1003, New York NY 10011. **E-mail:** submissions@einsteinliterary.com. **Website:** http://einsteinliterary.com. **Contact:** Susanna Einstein. Estab. 2015.

○ Prior to her current position, Ms. Einstein was with LJK Literary Management and the Einstein Thompson Agency.

MEMBER AGENTS Susanna Einstein; Molly Reese Lerner (cookbooks, narrative nonfiction, and literary fiction).

REPRESENTS Considers these nonfiction areas: cooking, creative nonfiction, memoirs. **Considers these fiction areas:** crime, historical, literary, mainstream, middle grade, romance, women's, young adult.

✎ Does not want picture books, poetry, textbooks, or screenplays.

HOW TO CONTACT Please submit a query letter and the first 10 double-spaced pages of your ms in the body of the e-mail (no attachments). "We do not respond to queries that are not specifically addressed to an agent by name. We do not accept or respond to queries by physical mail or phone." Responds in 6 weeks if interested.

◎ THE LISA EKUS GROUP, LLC

57 North St., Hatfield MA 01038. (413)247-9325. **Fax:** (413)247-9873. **E-mail:** info@lisaekus.com. **Website:**

www.lisaekus.com. **Contact:** Lisa Ekus-Saffer. Member of AAR.

MEMBER AGENTS Lisa Ekus; Sally Ekus.

REPRESENTS nonfiction books. **Considers these nonfiction areas:** cooking, diet/nutrition, foods, occasionally health/well-being and women's issues.

⚷— "Please note that we do not handle fiction, poetry, or children's books. If we receive a query for titles in these categories, please understand that we do not have the time or resources to respond."

HOW TO CONTACT Submit a one-page query via e-mail or submit complete hard copy proposal with title page, proposal contents, concept, bio, marketing, TOC, etc. Include SASE for the return of materials. The agency shares submissions tips at http://lisaekus.com/submission-requirements/.

RECENT SALES "Please see the regularly updated client listing on our website."

TIPS "Please do not call. No phone queries."

ⓘ ETHAN ELLENBERG LITERARY AGENCY

155 Suffolk St., No. 2R, New York NY 10002. (212)431-4554. **E-mail:** agent@ethanellenberg.com. **Website:** http://ethanellenberg.com. **Contact:** Ethan Ellenberg. Estab. 1984.

○ Prior to opening his agency, Mr. Ellenberg was contracts manager of Berkley/Jove and associate contracts manager for Bantam.

MEMBER AGENTS Evan Gregory, senior agent; **Bibi Lewis**, associate agent.

⚷— "We specialize in commercial fiction and children's books. In commercial fiction we want to see science fiction, fantasy, romance, mystery, thriller, women's fiction; all genres welcome. In children's books, we want to see everything: picture books, early reader, middle grade and young adult.We do some nonfiction: history, biography, military, popular science, and cutting edge books about any subject. Does not want to receive poetry, short stories, or screenplays.

HOW TO CONTACT Query by e-mail. Paste the query, synopsis and first 50 pages (or 3 chapters) into the e-mail. For nonfiction, paste the proposal. For picture books, paste the entire text. Accepts simultaneous submissions. Responds in 2 weeks to queries (no attachments); 4-6 weeks to mss.

TERMS Agent receives 15% commission on domestic sales. Agent receives 10% commission on foreign sales. Offers written contract. Charges clients (with their consent) for direct expenses limited to photocopying and postage.

WRITERS CONFERENCES RWA National Conference; Novelists, Inc.; and other regional conferences.

EMPIRE LITERARY

50 Davis Lane, Roslyn NY 11576. (917)213-7082. **E-mail:** abarzvi@empireliterary.com. **Website:** www.empireliterary.com. Estab. 2013.

○ Prior to opening her own agency, Ms. Barzvi was an agent at ICM Partners for 13 years.

REPRESENTS Considers these nonfiction areas: cooking, creative nonfiction, diet/nutrition, health, how-to, memoirs, parenting. **Considers these fiction areas:** women's.

⚷— This agency specializes in commercial nonfiction, and women's fiction.

HOW TO CONTACT E-query. No attachments. Put "Query" in the subject line.

⊘ THE ELAINE P. ENGLISH LITERARY AGENCY

4710 41st St. NW, Suite D, Washington DC 20016. (202)362-5190. **Fax:** (202)362-5192. **Website:** www.elaineenglish.com/. **Contact:** Elaine English. Member of AAR.

○ Ms. English has been working in publishing for more than 20 years. She is also an attorney specializing in media and publishing law.

MEMBER AGENTS Elaine English (novels).

REPRESENTS novels. **Considers these fiction areas:** historical, multicultural, mystery, suspense, thriller, women's, romance (single title, historical, contemporary, romantic, suspense, chick lit, erotic), general women's fiction. The agency is slowly but steadily acquiring in all mentioned areas.

⚷— Actively seeking women's fiction, including single-title romances. Does not want to receive any science fiction, time travel, or picture books.

HOW TO CONTACT Not accepting queries as of 2015. Keep checking the website for further information and updates. Responds in 4-8 weeks to queries; 3 months to requested submissions. Obtains most new clients through recommendations from others, conferences, submissions.

TERMS Agent receives 15% commission on domestic sales. Agent receives 20% commission on foreign sales. Offers written contract; 30-day notice must be given to terminate contract. Charges only for shipping expenses; generally taken from proceeds.

RECENT SALES Have been to Sourcebooks, Tor, Harlequin.

WRITERS CONFERENCES RWA National Conference; Novelists, Inc.; Malice Domestic; Washington Romance Writers Retreat, among others.

◑ FELICIA ETH LITERARY REPRESENTATION

555 Bryant St., Suite 350, Palo Alto CA 94301-1700. **E-mail:** feliciaeth.literary@gmail.com. **Website:** http://ethliterary.com. **Contact:** Felicia Eth. Member of AAR. Represents 25-35 clients. Currently handles: nonfiction books 75%, novels 25% adult.

REPRESENTS nonfiction books, novels. **Considers these nonfiction areas:** animals, anthropology, autobiography, biography, business, child guidance, cultural interests, current affairs, economics, health, history, investigative, law, medicine, parenting, popular culture, politics, psychology, science, sociology, technology, women's issues, women's studies. **Considers these fiction areas:** literary, mainstream.

○━┅ This agency specializes in high-quality fiction (preferably mainstream/contemporary) and provocative, intelligent, and thoughtful nonfiction on a wide array of commercial subjects.

HOW TO CONTACT Query with SASE. Accepts simultaneous submissions. Responds in 3 weeks to queries. Responds in 4-6 weeks to mss.

TERMS Agent receives 15% commission on domestic sales. Agent receives 20% commission on foreign sales. Agent receives 20% commission on film sales. Charges clients for photocopying and express mail service.

RECENT SALES *Bumper Sticker Philosophy*, by Jack Bowen (Random House); *Boys Adrift* by Leonard Sax (Basic Books; *The Memory Thief*, by Emily Colin (Ballantine Books); *The World is a Carpet*, by Anna Badkhen (Riverhead).

WRITERS CONFERENCES "Wide array—from Squaw Valley to Mills College."

TIPS "For nonfiction, established expertise is certainly a plus—as is magazine publication—though not a prerequisite. I am highly dedicated to those projects I represent, but highly selective in what I choose."

○ MARY EVANS INC.

242 E. Fifth St., New York NY 10003. (212)979-0880. **Fax:** (212)979-5344. **E-mail:** info@maryevansinc.com. **Website:** http://maryevansinc.com. Member of AAR.

MEMBER AGENTS Mary Evans (no unsolicited queries); **Julia Kardon** (literary and upmarket fiction, narrative nonfiction, journalism, and history); **Mary Gaule** (picture books, middle grade, and YA fiction).

REPRESENTS nonfiction books, novels.

○━┅ No screenplays or stage plays.

HOW TO CONTACT Query by mail or e-mail. If querying by mail, include a proper SASE. If querying by e-mail, put "Query" in the subject line. For fiction: Include the first few pages, or opening chapter of your novel as a single Word attachment. For nonfiction: Include your book proposal as a single Word attachment. Responds within 8 weeks. Obtains most new clients through recommendations from others, solicitations.

◑ EVATOPIA, INC.

8447 Wilshire Blvd., Suite 401, Beverly Hills CA 90211. **E-mail:** submissions@evatopia.com. **Website:** www.evatopia.com. **Contact:** Margery Walshaw. Represents 15 clients. 85% of clients are new/unpublished writers. Currently handles: movie scripts and book to film applications.

◐ Prior to becoming an agent, Ms. Walshaw was a writer and publicist for the entertainment industry.

MEMBER AGENTS Mary Kay (story development); **Jamie Davis** (story editor); **Jill Jones** (story editor).

REPRESENTS movies, book-to-film works. **Considers these fiction areas:** projects aimed at women, teens and children. **Considers these script areas:** projects aimed at women, teens and children. In addition to representing screenplays, this agency specializes in book-to-film adaptations with particular emphasis on young adult fiction, and women's fiction—along with helping authors self-publish and market their novels.

○━┅ "All of our staff members have strong writing and entertainment backgrounds, making us sympathetic to the needs of our clients." Actively seeking dedicated and hard-working writers.

HOW TO CONTACT Submit via online submission form. Accepts simultaneous submissions. Obtains

NEW AGENT SPOTLIGHT

SARAH NAGEL
WRITERS HOUSE

Writershouse.com

@SarahNagel14

ABOUT SARAH: Sarah joined Writers House in 2011 to work with senior vice president Merrilee Heifetz, and is now actively building her own client list. Previously, Sarah was a media lawyer in London and graduated with two separate degrees in English Language and Literature, and Law.

SHE IS SEEKING: Sarah is looking for psychological thrillers (those that mess with your head rather than high speed cross-country chases), horror, mystery, suspense and literary fiction. Sarah is especially interested in strong character-driven fiction and stories that explore the dynamics of a dysfunctional family unit / relationships. Sarah also represents realistic young adult and middle grade with a hint of magical realism. On the nonfiction side, Sarah is interested in medical ethics, true crime, humor books and memoir with a distinctive narrative voice with a universal resonance. Sarah is <u>not</u> looking for straight sci-fi, high fantasy, romance or picture books.

HOW TO SUBMIT: "I accept e-mail queries and will try to respond within 8 weeks. Please submit your query, including the first 10 pages of your manuscript pasted into the body of the e-mail (no attachments please!), to sarahsubmissions@ writershouse.com with "Query for Sarah Nagel: [Title Of Manuscript]" in the subject line. Please do not query multiple Writers House agents simultaneously."

most new clients through recommendations from others, solicitations.

TERMS Agent receives 15% commission on domestic sales. Agent receives 15% commission on foreign sales. Offers written contract; 30-day notice must be given to terminate contract.

TIPS "Remember that you only have 1 chance to make that important first impression. Make your loglines original and your synopses concise. The secret to a screenwriter's success is creating an original story and telling it in a manner that we haven't heard before."

⊙ FAIRBANK LITERARY REPRESENTATION

P.O. Box 6, Hudson NY 12534-0006. (617)576-0030. **Fax:** (617)576-0030. **E-mail:** queries@fairbankliter ary.com. **Website:** www.fairbankliterary.com. **Contact:** Sorche Fairbank. Member of AAR.

MEMBER AGENTS Sorche Fairbank (narrative nonfiction, commercial and literary fiction, memoir, food and wine); **Matthew Frederick**, matt@fairbankliterary.com (scout for sports nonfiction, architecture, design).

REPRESENTS nonfiction books, novels, short story collections. **Considers these nonfiction areas:** agriculture, architecture, art, autobiography, biography, cooking, crafts, cultural interests, current affairs, decorating, diet/nutrition, design, environment, ethnic, foods, gay/lesbian, government, hobbies, horticulture, how-to, interior design, investigative, law, memoirs, photography, popular culture, politics, science, sociology, sports, technology, true crime, women's issues, women's studies. **Considers these fiction areas:** action, adventure, feminist, gay, lesbian, literary, mainstream, mystery, sports, suspense, thriller, women's, Southern voices.

"I tend to gravitate toward literary fiction and narrative nonfiction, with a strong interest in women's issues and women's voices, international voices, class and race issues, and projects that simply teach me something new about the greater world and society around us. We have a good reputation for working closely and developmentally with our authors and love what we do." Actively seeking literary fiction, international and culturally diverse voices, narrative nonfiction, topical subjects (politics, current affairs), history, sports, architecture/design and pop culture. Does not want to receive romance, poetry, science fiction, pirates, vampire, young adult, or children's works.

HOW TO CONTACT Query with SASE. Submit author bio. Accepts simultaneous submissions. Obtains most new clients through recommendations from others, solicitations, conferences, ideas generated in-house.

TERMS Agent receives 15% commission on domestic sales. Agent receives 20% commission on foreign sales. Offers written contract, binding for 12 months; 45-day notice must be given to terminate contract.

RECENT SALES *When Clowns Attack: A Survival Guide*, by Chuck Sambuchino (10 Speed Press); 101 Things I Learned in School series, by Matthew Fredericks; all recent sales available on website.

TIPS "Be professional from the very first contact. There shouldn't be a single typo or grammatical flub in your query. Have a reason for contacting me about your project other than I was the next name listed on some website. Please do not use form query software! Believe me, we can get a dozen or so a day that look identical—we know when you are using a form. Show me that you know your audience—and your competition. Have the writing and/or proposal at the very, very best it can be before starting the querying process. Don't assume that if someone likes it enough they'll 'fix' it. The biggest mistake new writers make is starting the querying process before they—and the work—are ready. Take your time and do it right."

LEIGH FELDMAN LITERARY

E-mail: query@lfliterary.com. **Website:** www.publishersmarketplace.com/members/leighfeldman. **Contact:** Leigh Feldman. Estab. 2014.

Prior to her current position, Ms. Feldman was an agent at Writers House.

REPRESENTS Considers these nonfiction areas: creative nonfiction, memoirs. **Considers these fiction areas:** historical, literary, mystery, young adult.

HOW TO CONTACT E-query. "Please include 'query' in the subject line. Due to large volume of submissions, we regret that we can not respond to all queries individually. Please include the first chapter or the first 10 pages of your ms (or proposal) pasted after your query letter. I'd love to know what led you to query me in particular, and please let me know if you are querying other agents as well."

RECENT Sales List of recent sales and best known sales are available on the agency website.

THE FIELDING AGENCY, LLC

1550-G Tiburon Blvd., No. 528, Tiburon CA 94920. **E-mail:** wlee@fieldingagency.com; query@fieldingagency.com. **Website:** www.fieldingagency.com. **Contact:** Whitney Lee.

Prior to her current position, Ms. Lee worked at other agencies in different capacities.

REPRESENTS nonfiction books, novels, short story collections, juvenile. **Considers these nonfiction areas:** animals, anthropology, archeology, architecture, art, autobiography, biography, business, child guidance, cooking, crafts, cultural interests, current affairs, decorating, diet/nutrition, design, economics, education, environment, ethnic, foods, gay/lesbian, government, health, history, hobbies, how-to, humor, investigative, juvenile nonfiction, language, law, literature, medicine, memoirs, military, money, parenting, popular culture, politics, psychology, satire, science, self-help, sociology, sports, technology, translation, true crime, war, women's issues, women's studies. **Considers these fiction areas:** action, adventure, cartoon, comic books, crime, detective, ethnic, family saga, fantasy, feminist, gay, glitz, historical, horror, humor, juvenile, lesbian, literary, mainstream, mystery, picture books, police, romance, satire, suspense, thriller, women's, young adult.

⊶ "We specialize in representing books published abroad and have strong relationships with foreign co-agents and publishers. For books we represent in the US, we have to be head-over-heels passionate about it because we are involved every step of the way." Does not want to receive scripts for TV or film.

HOW TO CONTACT Query with SASE. Submit synopsis, author bio. Accepts queries by e-mail and snail mail. Accepts simultaneous submissions. Obtains most new clients through recommendations from others.

TERMS Agent receives 15% commission on domestic sales. Agent receives 20% commission on foreign sales. Offers written contract, binding for 9-12 months.

WRITERS CONFERENCES London Book Fair; Frankfurt Book Fair; Bologna Book Fair.

⦿ DIANA FINCH LITERARY AGENCY

116 W. 23rd St., Suite 500, New York NY 10011. (917)544-4470. **E-mail:** diana.finch@verizon.net. **Website:** http://dianafinchliteraryagency.blogspot.com. **Contact:** Diana Finch. Member of AAR.

○ Seeking to represent books that change lives. Prior to opening her agency in 2003, Ms. Finch worked at Ellen Levine Literary Agency for 18 years.

REPRESENTS nonfiction books, novels, scholarly. **Considers these nonfiction areas:** autobiography, biography, business, child guidance, computers, cultural interests, current affairs, dance, economics, environment, ethnic, film, government, health, history, how-to, humor, investigative, juvenile nonfiction, law, medicine, memoirs, military, money, music, parenting, photography, popular culture, politics, psychology, satire, science, self-help, sports, technology, theater, translation, true crime, war, women's issues, women's studies. **Considers these fiction areas:** action, adventure, crime, detective, ethnic, historical, literary, mainstream, police, thriller, young adult.

⊶ "Does not want romance, mysteries, or children's picture books."

HOW TO CONTACT This agency prefers submissions via its online form: https://dianafinchliteraryagency.submittable.com/submit Accepts simultaneous submissions. Obtains most new clients through recommendations from others.

TERMS Agent receives 15% commission on domestic sales. Agent receives 20% commission on foreign sales. Offers written contract. "I charge for overseas postage, galleys, and books purchased, and try to recoup these costs from earnings received for a client, rather than charging outright."

TIPS "Do as much research as you can on agents before you query. Have someone critique your query letter before you send it. It should be only 1 page and describe your book clearly—and why you are writing it—but also demonstrate creativity and a sense of your writing style."

FINEPRINT LITERARY MANAGEMENT

115 W. 29th, 3rd Floor, New York NY 10001. (212)279-1282. **Website:** www.fineprintlit.com. Member of AAR.

MEMBER AGENTS Peter Rubie, CEO, peter@fineprintlit.com (nonfiction interests include narrative nonfiction, popular science, spirituality, history, biography, pop culture, business, technology, parenting, health, self help, music, and food; fiction interests include literate thrillers, crime fiction, science fiction and fantasy, military fiction and literary fiction, middle grade and YA fiction and nonfiction for boys); **Stephany Evans**, stephany@fineprintlit.com (nonfiction: health and wellness, especially women's health; spirituality, environment/sustainability, food and wine, memoir, and narrative nonfiction; fiction interests include stories with a strong and interesting female protagonist, both literary and upmarket commercial/book club fiction, romance [all subgenres], mysteries); **Janet Reid** (crime fiction and narrative nonfiction); **Laura Wood**, laura@fineprintlit.com (serious nonfiction, especially in the areas of science and nature, along with substantial titles in business, history, religion, and other areas by academics, experienced professionals, and journalists); **June Clark** (see juneclark.com).

REPRESENTS Considers these nonfiction areas: biography, business, creative nonfiction, foods, health, history, humor, law, memoirs, music, parenting, popular culture, science, self-help, spirituality, technology. **Considers these fiction areas:** commercial, crime, fantasy, middle grade, military, mystery, romance, science fiction, suspense, thriller, women's, young adult.

HOW TO CONTACT E-query. For fiction, send a query, synopsis, bio, and 30 pages pasted into the e-mail. No attachments. For nonfiction, send a query only; proposal requested later if the agent is interested. Obtains most new clients through recommendations from others, solicitations.
TERMS Agent receives 15% commission on domestic sales. Agent receives 20% commission on foreign sales.

JAMES FITZGERALD AGENCY

118 Waverly Place #1B, New York NY 10011. (212)308-1122. **E-mail:** submissions@jfitzagency.com. **Website:** www.jfitzagency.com. **Contact:** James Fitzgerald.

Prior to his current position, Mr. Fitzgerald was an editor at St. Martin's Press, Doubleday, and the New York Times.

MEMBER AGENTS James Fitzgerald; Christopher Rhodes.

James is a nonfiction generalist, meaning that he doesn't represent certain nonfiction categories as much as he simply connects with projects. Does not want to receive poetry or screenplays.

HOW TO CONTACT Query via e-mail or snail mail. This agency's online submission guidelines page explains all the elements they want to see when you submit a nonfiction book proposal.
RECENT SALES *Gimme Something Better: The Profound, Progressive, and Occasionally Pointless History of Punk in the Bay Area,* by Jack Boulware and Silke Tudor (Viking/Penguin); *Black Dogs: The Possibly Story of Classic Rock's Greatest Robbery,* by Jason Buhrmester (Three Rivers/Crown); *Theo Gray's Med Science: Experiments You Can Do at Home—But Probably Shouldn't* (Black Dog and Loenthal).
TIPS "Please submit all information in English, even if your ms is in Spanish."

FLANNERY LITERARY

1140 Wickfield Ct., Naperville IL 60563. (630)428-2682. **E-mail:** jennifer@flanneryliterary.com. **Contact:** Jennifer Flannery. Represents 40 clients. 50% of clients are new/unpublished writers. Currently handles: juvenile books 100%.

REPRESENTS **Considers these fiction areas:** juvenile, middle grade, young adult.

This agency specializes in children's and young adult fiction and nonfiction. It also accepts picture books. 100% juvenile books.

HOW TO CONTACT Query by mail with SASE. "Multiple queries are fine, but please inform us. Mail that requires a signature will be returned to sender, as we are not always available to sign for mail." Responds in 2 weeks to queries; 1 month to mss. Obtains new clients through referrals and queries.
TERMS Agent receives 15% commission on domestic sales. Agent receives 20% commission on foreign sales. Offers written contract, binding for life of book in print.
TIPS "Write an engrossing, succinct query describing your work. We are always looking for a fresh new voice."

FLETCHER & COMPANY

78 Fifth Ave., 3rd Floor, New York NY 10011. (212)614-0778. **Fax:** (212)614-0728. **E-mail:** info@fletcherandco.com. **Website:** www.fletcherandco.com. **Contact:** Christy Fletcher. Estab. 2003. Member of AAR.
MEMBER AGENTS Christy Fletcher (referrals only); Melissa Chinchillo (predominantly nonfiction—psychology, popular philosophy, science, history, biography, investigative/narrative journalism, politics, current affairs, pop culture and self-help; some fiction—upmarket, commercial, literary horror/fantasy, mystery; very select children's and young adult); Rebecca Gradinger (literary fiction, upmarket commercial fiction, narrative nonfiction, self-help, memoir, women's studies, humor, and pop culture); Gráinne Fox (literary fiction and quality commercial authors, award-winning journalists and food writers); Lisa Grubka (fiction—literary, upmarket women's, and young adult; and nonfiction—narrative, food, science, and more); Donald Lamm (nonfiction—history, biography, investigative journalism, politics, current affairs, and business); Todd Sattersten (business books); Sylvie Greenberg (literary fiction, business, history, sports writing, science, investigative journalism); Rachel Crawford (literary fiction, especially if it's dark, experimental, or quirky; speculative fiction; YA; and great science writing).
REPRESENTS nonfiction books, novels. **Considers these nonfiction areas:** biography, business, creative nonfiction, foods, history, humor, investigative, memoirs, popular culture, politics, science, self-help, sports, women's issues, women's studies. **Considers these fiction areas:** commercial, fantasy, literary, science fiction, women's, young adult.

HOW TO CONTACT To query, please send a letter, brief synopsis, and an SASE to our address, or you may also send queries to info@fletcherandco.com. Please do not include e-mail attachments with your initial query, as they will be deleted. Address your query to a specific agent. No snail mail queries.

RECENT SALES *Better than Before* by Gretchen Rubin; *The Opposite of Spoiled* by Ron Lieber; *Astonish Me*, by Maggie Shipstead; *I'm Having So Much Fun Here Without You* by Courtney Maum; *The Whole 30* by Melissa Hartwig and Dallas Hartwig; *Whisky Tango Foxtrot* by David Shafer; *Elusion*, by Claudia Gabel & Cheryl Klam.

◐ FOLIO LITERARY MANAGEMENT, LLC

The Film Center Building, 630 Ninth Ave., Suite 1101, New York NY 10036. (212)400-1494. **Fax:** (212)967-0977. **Website:** www.foliolit.com. Member of AAR. Represents 100+ clients.

○ Prior to creating Folio Literary Management, Mr. Hoffman worked for several years at another agency; Mr. Kleinman was an agent at Graybill & English.

MEMBER AGENTS Claudia Cross, Scott Hoffman, Jeff Kleinman, Frank Weimann, Michelle Brower, Michael Harriot, Erin Harris, Molly Jaffa, Katherine Latshaw, Erin Niumata, Ruth Pomerance, Marcy Posner, Jeff Silberman, Michael Sterling, Steve Troha, Emily van Beek, Melissa Sarver White.

REPRESENTS nonfiction books, novels, short story collections. **Considers these nonfiction areas:** animals, art, biography, business, child guidance, cooking, creative nonfiction, economics, environment, foods, health, history, how-to, humor, inspirational, memoirs, military, parenting, popular culture, politics, psychology, religious, satire, science, self-help, technology, war, women's issues, women's studies. **Considers these fiction areas:** commercial, erotica, fantasy, horror, literary, middle grade, mystery, picture books, religious, romance, thriller, women's, young adult.

✂━ No poetry, stage plays, or screenplays.

HOW TO CONTACT Query via e-mail only (no attachments). Read agent bios online for specific submission guidelines and e-mail addresses.

TIPS "Please do not submit simultaneously to more than one agent at Folio. If you're not sure which of us is exactly right for your book, don't worry. We work closely as a team, and if one of our agents gets a query that might be more appropriate for someone else, we'll always pass it along. It's important that you check each agent's bio page for clear directions as to how to submit, as well as when to expect feedback."

◐ FOUNDRY LITERARY + MEDIA

33 West 17th St., PH, New York NY 10011. (212)929-5064. **Fax:** (212)929-5471. **Website:** www.foundry media.com.

MEMBER AGENTS Peter McGuigan, pmsubmissions@foundrymedia.com; Yfat Reiss Gendell, yrg submissions@foundrymedia.com (practical nonfiction projects in the areas of health and wellness, diet, lifestyle, how-to, and parenting and a broad range of narrative nonfiction that includes humor, memoir, history, science, pop culture, psychology, and adventure/travel stories); Mollie Glick, mgsubmissions@foundrymedia.com (literary fiction, young adult fiction, narrative nonfiction, and a bit of practical nonfiction in the areas of popular science, medicine, psychology, cultural history, memoir, and current events); Chris Park, cpsubmissions@foundrymedia.com (memoirs, narrative nonfiction, sports books, Christian nonfiction and character-driven fiction); Hannah Brown Gordon, hbgsubmissions@foundry media.com (stories and narratives that blend genres, including thriller, suspense, historical, literary, speculative, memoir, pop-science, psychology, humor, and pop culture); Brandi Bowles, bbsubmissions@foundrymedia.com (literary and commercial fiction, especially high-concept novels that feature strong female bonds and psychological or scientific themes); Kirsten Neuhaus, knsubmissions@foundrymedia.com (platform-driven narrative nonfiction, in the areas of lifestyle (beauty/fashion/relationships), memoir, business, current events, history and stories with strong female voices, as well as smart, upmarket, and commercial fiction); Jessica Regel, jrsubmissions@foundrymedia.com (young adult and middle grade books, as well as a select list of adult general fiction, women's fiction, and adult nonfiction); Anthony Mattero, amsubmissions@foundrymedia.com (smart, platform-driven, nonfiction particularly in the genres of pop-culture, humor, music, sports, and pop-business); Matt Wise, mwsubmissions@foundrymedia.com (a wide array of projects, from controversial narrative nonfiction to literary fiction to art and design projects); Peter Steinberg, pssubmissions@foundry media.com (narrative nonfiction, commercial and literary fiction, memoir, health, history, lifestyle, humor, sports and young adult); **Roger Freet**, rfsubmissions@foundrymedia.com (narrative and idea-driven nonfiction clients in the areas of religion, spirituality, memoir, and cultural issues by leading scholars, pastors, historians, activists and musicians).

REPRESENTS Considers these nonfiction areas: creative nonfiction, current affairs, diet/nutrition, health, history, how-to, humor, medicine, memoirs, music, parenting, popular culture, psychology, science, sports, travel. **Considers these fiction areas:** commercial, historical, humor, literary, middle grade, suspense, thriller, women's, young adult.

HOW TO CONTACT Target one agent only. Send queries to the specific submission e-mail of the agent. For fiction: send query, synopsis, author bio, first three chapters—all pasted in the e-mail. For nonfiction, send query, sample chapters, table of contents, author bio (all pasted).

RECENT SALES *Tell the Wolves I'm Home*, by Carol Rifka Blunt; *The Rathbones*, by Janice Clark; *This is Your Captain Speaking*, by Jon Methven; *The War Against the Assholes* and *The November Criminals*, by Sam Munson; *Ready Player One*, by Ernest Cline.

TIPS "Consult website for each agent's submission instructions."

FOX LITERARY

110 W. 40th St., Suite 410, New York NY 10018. **E-mail:** submissions@foxliterary.com. **Website:** www.publishersmarketplace.com/members/fox/.

REPRESENTS Considers these nonfiction areas: biography, creative nonfiction, history, memoirs, popular culture. **Considers these fiction areas:** fantasy, historical, literary, mainstream, romance, science fiction, thriller, young adult, graphic novels.

☛ Does not want to receive screenplays, poetry, category westerns, horror, Christian/inspirational, or children's picture books.

HOW TO CONTACT E-mail query and first 5 pages in body of e-mail. E-mail queries preferred. For snail mail queries, must include an e-mail address for response and no response means *no*. Do not send SASE. No e-mail attachments.

RECENT SALES *Black Ships* by Jo Graham (Orbit); Evernight series by Claudia Gray (HarperCollins); October Daye series by Seanan McGuire (DAW); *Salt and Silver* by Anna Katherine (Tor); *Alcestis* by Katharine Beutner (Soho Press); *Shadows Cast* by Stars by Catherine Knutsson (Atheneum); *Saving June* and *Speechless* by Hannah Harrington (Harlequin Teen); Spellcaster trilogy by Claudia Gray (HarperCollins).

⊙ LYNN C. FRANKLIN ASSOCIATES, LTD.

1350 Broadway, Suite 2015, New York NY 10018. (212)868-6311. **Fax:** (212)868-6312. **E-mail:** agency@franklinandsiegal.com. **Website:** www.publishersmarketplace.com/members/LynnCFranklin/. **Contact:** Lynn Franklin, president; Claudia Nys, foreign rights. Other memberships include PEN America.

REPRESENTS nonfiction books, novels. **Considers these nonfiction areas:** biography, current affairs, memoirs, psychology, self-help, spirituality, alternative medicine.

☛ Primary interest lies in nonfiction (memoir, biography, current affairs, spirituality, psychology/self-help, alternative medicine, etc.).

HOW TO CONTACT Query via e-mail to agency@franklinandsiegal.com. No unsolicited mss. No attachments. For nonfiction, query letter with short outline and synopsis. For fiction, query letter with short synopsis and a maximum of 10 sample pages (in the body of the e-mail). Please indicate "query adult" or "query children's" in the subject line. Accepts simultaneous submissions. Obtains most new clients through recommendations from others, solicitations.

TERMS Agent receives 15% commission on domestic sales. Agent receives 20% commission on foreign sales. Offers written contract.

RECENT SALES *The Wahls Protocol: How I Beat Progressive MS Using Paleo Principles And Functional Medicine* by Terry Wahls, M.D. (Avery/Penguin); *The Book Of Forgiving: The Four-Fold Path To Healing For Ourselves And Our World* by Archbishop Desmond Tutu and Reverend Mpho Tutu (US: HarperOne, UK: Collins); *The Customer Rules: 39 Essential Practices For Delivering Sensational Service* by Lee Cockerell (Crown Business/Random House); *My Name Is Jody Williams* by Jody Williams (University of California Press-Berkeley); *Everybody Matters: A Memoir* by Mary Robinson (US: Bloomsbury, UK and Ireland: Hodder).

❶ JEANNE FREDERICKS LITERARY AGENCY, INC.

221 Benedict Hill Rd., New Canaan CT 06840. (203)972-3011. **Fax:** (203)972-3011. **E-mail:** jeanne.fredericks@gmail.com. **Website:** www.jeannefredericks.com. **Contact:** Jeanne Fredericks. Estab. 1997.

Member of AAR. Other memberships include Authors Guild. Currently handles: nonfiction books 100%.

○ Prior to opening her agency in 1997, Ms. Fredericks was an agent and acting director with the Susan P. Urstadt Agency.

REPRESENTS nonfiction books. **Considers these nonfiction areas:** animals, autobiography, biography, child guidance, cooking, decorating, foods, gardening, health, history, how-to, interior design, medicine, parenting, photography, psychology, self-help, women's issues.

⊶ This agency specializes in quality adult nonfiction by authorities in their fields. We do **not** handle: fiction, true crime, juvenile, textbooks, poetry, essays, screenplays, short stories, science fiction, pop culture, guides to computers and software, politics, horror, pornography, books on overly depressing or violent topics, romance, teacher's manuals, or memoirs.

HOW TO CONTACT Query first by e-mail, then send outline/proposal, 1-2 sample chapters, if requested. If you do send requested submission materials, note the word "Requested" in the subject line. See submission guidelines online first. Accepts simultaneous submissions. Responds in 3-5 weeks to queries. Responds in 2-4 months to mss. Obtains most new clients through recommendations from others, solicitations, conferences.

TERMS Agent receives 15% commission on domestic sales. Agent receives 25% commission on foreign sales with co-agent. Offers written contract, binding for 9 months; 2-month notice must be given to terminate contract. Charges client for photocopying of whole proposals and mss, overseas postage, priority mail, express mail services.

RECENT SALES *Yoga Therapy*, by Larry Payne, PH.D., Terra Gold, D.O.M. and Eden Goldman, D.C. (Basic Health); *The Creativity Cure*, by Carrie Alton, M.D., and Alton Barron, M.D. (Scribner); *For Sale—America's Paradise*, by Willie Drye (Lyons); *Lilias! Yoga*, by Lilias Folan (Skyhorse); *Greenhouse Gardener's Manual*, by Roger Marshall (Timber); *M.D.'s Guide to Alternative Medicine*, by Lloyd May, M.D. (Basic Health); *Yoga Nidra for Stress Relief*, by Julie Lusk (New Harbinger); *The Epidural Book*, by Rich Siegenfeld, M.D. (Johns Hopkins University Press); *A Place in the Sun*, by Stephen Snyder (Rizzoli).

WRITERS CONFERENCES Connecticut Authors and Publishers Association-University Conference; ASJA Writers' Conference; BookExpo America; Garden Writers' Association Annual Symposium; Harvard Medical School CME Course in Publishing.

TIPS "Be sure to research competition for your work and be able to justify why there's a need for your book. I enjoy building an author's career, particularly if he/she is professional, hardworking, and courteous. Aside from 20 years of agenting experience, I've had 10 years of editorial experience in adult trade book publishing that enables me to help an author polish a proposal so that it's more appealing to prospective editors. My MBA in marketing also distinguishes me from other agents."

○ GRACE FREEDSON'S PUBLISHING NETWORK

7600 Jericho Turnpike, Suite 300, Woodbury NY 11797. (516)931-7757. **Fax:** (516)931-7759. **E-mail:** gfreedson@gmail.com. **Contact:** Grace Freedson. 17 Center Dr., Syosset NY 11791. Represents 100 clients. 10% of clients are new/unpublished writers.

○ Prior to becoming an agent, Ms. Freedson was a managing editor and director of acquisition for Barron's Educational Series.

REPRESENTS Considers these nonfiction areas: animals, business, cooking, crafts, current affairs, diet/nutrition, economics, education, environment, foods, health, history, hobbies, how-to, humor, medicine, money, popular culture, psychology, satire, science, self-help, sports, technology.

⊶ "In addition to representing many qualified authors, I work with publishers as a packager of unique projects—mostly series." Does not want to receive fiction.

HOW TO CONTACT Query with SASE. Submit synopsis, SASE. Responds in 2-6 weeks to queries. Obtains most new clients through recommendations from others.

TERMS Agent receives 15% commission on domestic sales. Offers written contract; 30-day notice must be given to terminate contract.

WRITERS CONFERENCES BookExpo of America.

TIPS "At this point, I am only reviewing proposals on nonfiction topics by credentialed authors with platforms."

NEW AGENT SPOTLIGHT

HEATHER FLAHERTY
THE BENT AGENCY

Thebentagency.com

@heddaflaherty

ABOUT HEATHER: "I grew up in Massachusetts, between Boston and the Cape, and started working in New York City as a playwright during college. This pushed me towards English as a focus, and I wound up finally beginning my publishing career in editorial, specifically at Random House in the UK. That's also where I became a YA and children's literary scout, which finally landed me back in NYC, consulting with foreign publishers and Hollywood regarding what the next big book will be. Now as an agent, I'm thrilled to turn my focus on growing authors for that same success."

SHE IS SEEKING: Authors who write children's, middle grade, and young adult fiction and nonfiction, as well as select new adult fiction, and pop-culture or humorous nonfiction. "Currently I'm looking for YA fiction across-the-board, though my heart does sway towards issue-related YA with humor and heart— not depressing, or mopey. I also love hard, punchy, contemporary YA that's got no hesitations when it comes to crazy. I'm also always up for seeing contemporary stories with sci-fi or fantasy elements, as well as a clever respin of an old or classic tale. And then, I seek lastly, really good horror and ghost stories. As for the middle grade I'm looking for, I want it stark, honest, and even dark; either contemporary or period, as long as it's accessible. Coming-of-age stories, dealing-with-difficulty stories, witness stories (adult issues seen through the child's POV kinda thing), anything that makes you want to hold the narrator's hand. On the nonfiction side, I'm looking for strong teen memoirs about overcoming crushing situations."

HOW TO SUBMIT: Review The Bent Agency's updated submissions guidelines online, and then e-mail flahertyqueries@thebentagency.com.

◖◗ ◉ FRESH BOOKS LITERARY AGENCY
231 Diana St., Placerville CA 95667. **E-mail:** matt@
fresh-books.com. **Website:** www.fresh-books.com.
Contact: Matt Wagner.

Prior to becoming an agent, Mr. Wagner was with Waterside Productions for 15 years.
REPRESENTS Considers these nonfiction areas:
animals, anthropology, archeology, architecture, art,

business, child guidance, computers, cooking, crafts, cultural interests, current affairs, dance, design, economics, education, environment, ethnic, gay/lesbian, government, health, history, hobbies, humor, law, medicine, military, money, music, parenting, photography, popular culture, politics, psychology, satire, science, sports, technology. **Considers these fiction areas:** crime, thriller.

☛ "I specialize in tech and how-to. I love working with books and authors, and I've repped many of my clients for upwards of 15 years now." Actively seeking popular science, natural history, adventure, how-to, business, education and reference. Does not want to receive fiction (except crime and thrillers), children's books, screenplays, or poetry.

HOW TO CONTACT Plain text e-mail query (with no attachments) to matt@fresh-books.com. Accepts simultaneous submissions. Responds in 1-4 weeks to queries. Responds in 1-4 weeks to mss. Obtains most new clients through recommendations from others.

TERMS Agent receives 15% commission on domestic sales. Agent receives 20% commission on foreign sales.

RECENT SALES *Creating HDR Photos* (Amphoto); *Android Tablets for Dummies* (Wiley); *The Zombie Combat Field Guide Coloring Book* (Berkley); *How to Get a Meeting with Anyone* (BenBella).

TIPS "Do your research. Find out what sorts of books and authors an agent represents. Go to conferences and follow social media. Make friends with other writers—most of my clients come from referrals."

○ SARAH JANE FREYMANN LITERARY AGENCY

59 W. 71st St., Suite 9B, New York NY 10023. (212)362-9277. **E-mail:** sarah@sarahjanefreymann.com; Submissions@SarahJaneFreymann.com. **Website:** www.sarahjanefreymann.com. **Contact:** Sarah Jane Freymann, Steve Schwartz.

MEMBER AGENTS Sarah Jane Freymann (nonfiction books, novels, illustrated books); Jessica Sinsheimer, jessica@sarahjanefreymann.com (young adult fiction, literary fiction); Steven Schwartz, steve@sarahjanefreymann.com; Katharine Sands.

REPRESENTS Considers these nonfiction areas: animals, anthropology, architecture, art, autobiography, biography, business, child guidance, cooking,

current affairs, decorating, diet/nutrition, design, economics, ethnic, foods, health, history, interior design, medicine, memoirs, parenting, psychology, self-help, women's issues, women's studies, lifestyle. **Considers these fiction areas:** ethnic, literary, mainstream, young adult.

HOW TO CONTACT Query. Responds in 2 weeks to queries. Responds in 6 weeks to mss. Obtains most new clients through recommendations from others.

TERMS Agent receives 15% commission on domestic sales. Agent receives 20% commission on foreign sales. Offers written contract. Charges clients for long distance, overseas postage, photocopying. 100% of business is derived from commissions on ms sales.

RECENT SALES *How to Make Love to a Plastic Cup: And Other Things I Learned While Trying to Knock Up My Wife*, by Greg Wolfe (Harper Collins); *I Want to Be Left Behind: Rapture Here on Earth*, by Brenda Peterson (a Merloyd Lawrence book); *That Bird Has My Name: The Autobiography of an Innocent Man on Death Row*, by Jarvis Jay Masters with an introduction by Pema Chodrun (HarperOne); *Perfect One-Dish Meals*, by Pam Anderson (Houghton Mifflin); *Birdology*, by Sy Montgomery (Simon & Schuster); *Emptying the Nest: Launching Your Reluctant Young Adult*, by Dr. Brad Sachs (Macmillan); *Tossed & Found*, by Linda and John Meyers (Steward, Tabori & Chang); *32 Candles*, by Ernessa Carter; *God and Dog*, by Wendy Francisco.

TIPS "I love fresh, new, passionate works by authors who love what they are doing and have both natural talent and carefully honed skill."

◑ REBECCA FRIEDMAN LITERARY AGENCY

E-mail: Abby@rfliterary.com. **Website:** www.rfliterary.com/. Estab. 2013.

○ Prior to opening her own agency in 2013, Ms. Friedman was with Sterling Lord Literistic from 2006 to 2011, then with Frederick Hill Bonnie Nadell.

MEMBER AGENTS Rebecca Friedman, brandie@rfliterary.com (literary novels of suspense, women's fiction, contemporary romance, and young adult, as well as journalistic nonfiction and memoir); Kimberly Brower, kimberly@rfliterary.com (commercial and literary fiction, with an emphasis in women's fiction, contemporary romance, mysteries/thrillers, new adult and young adult, as well as certain areas of nonfiction, including business, diet, and fitness); **Rachel Marks,** rachel@rfliterary.com (young adult, fantasy, science fiction, new adult and romance).

REPRESENTS Considers these nonfiction areas: business, diet/nutrition, memoirs. **Considers these fiction areas:** commercial, fantasy, literary, new adult, romance, science fiction, suspense, women's, young adult.

✎→ The agency is interested in commercial and literary fiction with a focus on literary novels of suspense, women's fiction, contemporary romance, and young adult, as well as journalistic nonfiction and memoir. Most of all, we are looking for great stories told in strong voices.

HOW TO CONTACT Please submit your query letter and first chapter (no more than 15 pages, double-spaced). If querying Kimberly, paste a synopsis and the book's first 50 pages into the e-mail submission.

RECENT SALES *So Much Pretty*, by Cara Hoffman; *The Black Nile*, by Dan Morrison; *Maybe One Day*, by Melissa Kantor; *Devoured*, by Emily Snow. A complete list of agency authors is available online.

ⓘ FREDRICA S. FRIEDMAN AND CO., INC.

136 E. 57th St., 14th Floor, New York NY 10022. (212)829-9600. **Fax:** (212)829-9669. **E-mail:** submissions@fredricafriedman.com. **Website:** www.fredricafriedman.com. **Contact:** Ms. Chandler Smith.

◯ Prior to establishing her own literary management firm, Ms. Friedman was the editorial director, associate publisher and vice president of Little, Brown & Co., a division of Time Warner, and the first woman to hold those positions.

REPRESENTS nonfiction books, novels, anthologies. **Considers these nonfiction areas:** art, biography, business, child, cooking, current affairs, education, ethnic, gay, government, health, history, how to, humor, language, memoirs, money, music, photography, popular culture, psychology, self help, sociology, film, true crime, women's, interior design/decorating. **Considers these fiction areas:** literary.

✎→ "We represent a select group of outstanding nonfiction and fiction writers. We are particularly interested in helping writers expand their readership and develop their careers." Does not want poetry, plays, screenplays, children's books, sci-fi/fantasy, or horror.

HOW TO CONTACT Submit e-query, synopsis; be concise, and include any pertinent author information, including relevant writing history. If you are a fiction writer, we also request a one-page sample from your manuscript to provide its voice. We ask that you keep all material in the body of the e-mail. Accepts simultaneous submissions. Responds in 4-6 weeks to queries. Responds in 4-6 weeks to mss. Obtains most new clients through recommendations from others.

TERMS Agent receives 15% commission on domestic sales. Agent receives 25% commission on foreign sales. Offers written contract. Charges for photocopying and messenger/shipping fees for proposals.

TIPS "Spell the agent's name correctly on your query letter."

ⓘ THE FRIEDRICH AGENCY

19 W. 21st St., Suite 201, New York NY 10010. **E-mail:** mfriedrich@friedrichagency.com; lcarson@friedrichagency.com; nichole@friedrichagency.com. **Website:** www.friedrichagency.com. **Contact:** Molly Friedrich; Lucy Carson. Member of AAR. Signatory of WGA. Represents 50+ clients.

◯ Prior to her current position, Ms. Friedrich was an agent at the Aaron Priest Literary Agency.

MEMBER AGENTS Molly Friedrich, founder and agent (open to queries); **Lucy Carson,** foreign rights director and agent (open to queries); **Nichole LeFebvre** (foreign rights manager; open to queries).

REPRESENTS full-length fiction and nonfiction. **Considers these nonfiction areas:** creative nonfiction, memoirs. **Considers these fiction areas:** commercial, literary.

HOW TO CONTACT Query by e-mail only. Please query only one agent at this agency.

RECENT SALES *W is For Wasted*, by Sue Grafton; *Olive Kitteridge,* by Elizabeth Strout. Other clients include Frank McCourt, Jane Smiley, Esmeralda Santiago, Terry McMillan, Cathy Schine, Ruth Ozeki, Karen Joy Fowler and more.

ⓘ FULL CIRCLE LITERARY, LLC

7676 Hazard Center Dr., Suite 500, San Diego CA 92108. **E-mail:** submissions@fullcircleliterary.com. **Website:** www.fullcircleliterary.com. **Contact:** Stefanie Von Borstel. Member of AAR. Represents 55 clients. 60% of clients are new/unpublished writers.

MEMBER AGENTS Lilly Ghahremani; Stefanie Von Borstel; Adriana Dominguez; Taylor Martindale (multicultural voices, young adult fiction).

REPRESENTS nonfiction books, juvenile. **Considers these nonfiction areas:** creative nonfiction, design, how-to, popular culture, women's issues. **Considers these fiction areas:** literary, middle grade, picture books, women's, young adult.

8—➤ "Our full-service boutique agency, representing a range of nonfiction and children's books (limited fiction), provides a one-stop resource for authors. Our extensive experience in the realms of law and marketing provide Full Circle clients with a unique edge." Actively seeking nonfiction by authors with a unique and strong platform, projects that offer new and diverse viewpoints, and literature with a global or multicultural perspective. We are particularly interested in books with a Latino or Middle Eastern angle and books related to pop culture.

HOW TO CONTACT Agency accepts e-queries. Put "Query for [Agent]" in the subject line. Send a 1-page query letter (in the body of the e-mail) including a description of your book, writing credentials and author highlights. Following your query, please include the first 10 pages or complete picture book manuscript text within the body of the e-mail. For nonfiction, include a proposal with one sample chapter. Accepts simultaneous submissions. Obtains most new clients through recommendations from others, solicitations, conferences.

TERMS Agent receives 15% commission on domestic sales. Agent receives 20% commission on foreign sales. Offers written contract; up to 30-day notice must be given to terminate contract. Charges for copying and postage.

TIPS "Put your best foot forward. Contact us when you simply can't make your project any better on your own, and please be sure your work fits with what the agent you're approaching represents. Little things count, so copyedit your work. Join a writing group and attend conferences to get objective and constructive feedback before submitting. Be active about building your platform as an author before, during, and after publication. Remember this is a business and your agent is a business partner."

⊕ FUSE LITERARY

Website: www.fuseliterary.com.

MEMBER AGENTS Laurie McLean (only accepting referral inquiries and submissions from writers she meets at conferences); **Gordon Warnock,** query gordon@fuseliterary.com (high-concept commercial fiction, literary fiction, new adult, contemporary YA, graphic novels, memoir, cookbooks and food, politics, current events, pop science, pop culture, self-help, how-to, humor, pets, business, career); **Connor Goldsmith,** queryconnor@fuseliterary.com (in fiction: sci-fi/fantasy/horror, thrillers, upmarket commercial Fiction, and literary fiction with a unique and memorable hook; he is especially interested in books by and about people from marginalized perspectives, such as LGBT people and/or racial minorities; in nonfiction: history [particularly of the ancient world], theater, cinema, music, television, mass media, popular culture, feminism and gender studies, LGBT issues, race relations, and the sex industry); **Sara Sciuto,** querysara@fuseliterary.com (middle grade, young adult, standout picture books); **Michelle Richter,** querymichelle@fuseliterary.com (primarily seeking fiction, specifically book club reads, literary fiction, and well-crafted women's commercial fiction, thrillers and mysteries [amateur sleuth, police procedurals and smart cozies]); **Jen Karsbeak** (women's fiction, upmarket commercial fiction, historical fiction, and literary fiction); **Emily S. Keyes,** queryemily@fuseliterary.com (young adult, middle grade, and also a select list of commercial fiction which includes fantasy & science fiction, women's fiction, new adult fiction, along with pop culture and humor titles); **Jennifer Chen Tran,** queryjennifer@fuseliterary.com (literary, commercial, women's, upmarket, contemporary romance, mature young adult, new adult, suspense/thriller and select graphic novels [adult, YA or MG]; "As a second-generation Taiwanese-American, I am particularly interested in voices from underrepresented and marginalized communities, strong and conflicted female characters, war and post-war fiction, and writers who are adept at creating a developed sense of place"; nonfiction areas of interest include memoir [but writers must have a sizable platform], narrative nonfiction in the areas of adventure, biography, business, current affairs, medical, history, how-to, pop-culture, psychology, social entrepreneurism, social justice, and travel).

HOW TO CONTACT E-query an individual agent. Check the website to see if any individual agent has closed themselves to submissions, as well as each agent's individual submission preferences.

WRITERS CONFERENCES Agents from this agency attend many conferences. A full list of their appearances is available on the agency website.

◑ THE G AGENCY, LLC

P.O. Box 374, Bronx NY 10471. (718)664-4505. **E-mail:** gagencyquery@gmail.com. **Website:** www.publishersmarketplace.com/members/jeffg/. **Contact:** Jeff Gerecke. Estab. 2012.

MEMBER AGENTS Jeff Gerecke.

REPRESENTS Considers these nonfiction areas: biography, business, computers, history, military, money, popular culture, technology. **Considers these fiction areas:** mainstream, mystery.

➣━ "I am interested in commercial and literary fiction, as well as serious nonfiction and pop culture. My focus as an agent has always been on working with writers to shape their work for its greatest commercial potential. I provide lots of editorial advice in sharpening manuscripts and proposals before submission." Does not want screenplays, sci-fi/fantasy or romance.

HOW TO CONTACT E-mail submissions preferred - attach sample chapters or proposal if you wish. Enter "QUERY" along with the title in the subject line of e-mails or on the envelope of snail mail.

RECENT SALES *Killing The Cranes,* by Edward Girardet (Chelsea Green); *Islam Without Extremes,* by Mustafa Akyol (Norton); *The Race to the New World,* by Douglas Hunter (Palgrave); *Intelligence and US Foreign Policy,* by Paul Pillar (Columbia UP); *Transforming Darkness to Light,* by Travis Vining (Bella Rosa); *Faith Misplaced: The Broken Promise of US-Arab Relations,* by Ussama Makdisi (Public Affairs); *Drinking Arak Off An Ayatollah's Beard,* by Nick Jubber (DaCapo); *The Rule of Empires,* by Tim Parsons (Oxford).

TIPS "I am interested in commercial and literary fiction, as well as serious nonfiction and pop culture. My focus as an agent has always been on working with writers to shape their work for its greatest commercial potential. I provide lots of editorial advice in sharpening mss and proposals before submission. I've been a member of the Royalty Committee of the Association of Authors Representatives since its founding and am always keen to challenge publishers for their willfully obscure royalty reporting. Also I have recently taken over the position of Treasurer of the A.A.R. My publishing background includes working at the University of California Press so I am always intrigued by academic subjects which are given a commercial spin to reach an audience outside academia. I've also worked as a foreign scout for publishers like Hodder & Stoughton in England and Wilhelm Heyne in Germany, which gives me a good sense of how American books can be successfully translated overseas."

◎ NANCY GALLT LITERARY AGENCY

273 Charlton Ave., South Orange NJ 07079. (973)761-6358. **Website:** www.nancygallt.com. **Contact:** Nancy Gallt, Marietta Zacker. Represents 40 clients. 30% of clients are new/unpublished writers.

◔ Prior to opening her agency, Ms. Gallt was subsidiary rights director of the children's book division at Morrow, Harper and Viking.

MEMBER AGENTS Nancy Gallt; Marietta Zacker.

REPRESENTS juvenile. **Considers these fiction areas:** juvenile, middle grade, picture books, young adult.

➣━ "We only handle children's books." Actively seeking picture books, middle grade, and young adult novels.

HOW TO CONTACT Submit through online submission for on agency website. No e-mail queries, please. Accepts simultaneous submissions. Obtains new clients through recommendations from others.

TERMS Agent receives 15% commission on domestic sales. Agent receives 20% commission on foreign sales. Offers written contract; 30-day notice must be given to terminate contract.

RECENT SALES *Toya,* by Randi Revill; Rick Riordan's Books (Hyperion); *Something Extraordinary* by Ben Clanton (Simon & Schuster); *The Baby Tree* by Sophie Blackall (Nancy Paulsen Books/Penguin); *Fenway And Hattie* by Victoria J Coe (Putnam/Penguin); *The Meaning Of Maggie* by Megan Jean Sovern (Chronicle); *The Misadventures Of The Family Fletcher* by Dana Alison Levy (Random House); *Abrakapow!* by Isaiah Campbell (Simon & Schuster); *Subway Love* by Nora Raleigh Baskin (Candlewick).

TIPS "Writing and illustrations stand on their own, so submissions should tell the most compelling stories possible—whether visually, in words, or both."

◎ THE GARAMOND AGENCY, INC.

1840 Columbia Rd. NW, #503, Washington DC 20009. **E-mail:** query@garamondagency.com. **Website:** www.garamondagency.com. Other memberships include Author's Guild.

MEMBER AGENTS Lisa Adams; David Miller.

REPRESENTS nonfiction books. **Considers these nonfiction areas:** business, current affairs, economics, history, law, politics, psychology, science, technology, social science, narrative nonfiction.

8—☛ "We work closely with our authors through each stage of the publishing process, first in developing their books and then in presenting themselves and their ideas effectively to publishers and to readers. We represent our clients throughout the world in all languages, media, and territories through an extensive network of subagents." No proposals for children's or young adult books, fiction, poetry, or memoir.

HOW TO CONTACT Queries sent by e-mail may not make it through the spam filters on our server. Please e-mail a brief query letter only, we do not read unsolicited mss submitted by e-mail under any circumstances. See website.

RECENT SALES *Big Data*, by Viktor Mayer-Schoenberger and Kenneth Cukier (Houghton Mifflin Harcourt); *West of the Revolution*, by Laudio Saunt (Norton); *Market Madness,* by Blake Clayton (Oxford University Press); *The Depths* by Jonathan Rottenberg (Basic Books); *Outsiders* by William Thorndike (Harvard Business Press); *Personal Intelligence* by John D. Mayer, (Scientific American/Farrar, Straus & Giroux). See website for other clients.

TIPS "Query us first if you have any questions about whether we are the right agency for your work."

MAX GARTENBERG LITERARY AGENCY

912 N. Pennsylvania Ave., Yardley PA 19067. (215)295-9230. **Website:** www.maxgartenberg.com. **Contact:** Anne Devlin (fiction and nonfiction). Estab. 1954. Represents 100 clients. 20% of clients are new/unpublished writers. Currently handles: nonfiction books 80%, novels 20%.

MEMBER AGENTS Anne G. Devlin (current events, politics, true crime, women's issues, sports, parenting, biography, environment, narrative nonfiction, health, lifestyle, literary fiction, romance, and celebrity); **Dirk Devlin** (thrillers, science fiction, mysteries, and humor).

REPRESENTS nonfiction books, novels. **Considers these nonfiction areas:** agriculture horticulture, animals, art, biography, child, current affairs, health, history, money, music, nature, psychology, science, self help, sports, film, true crime, women's.

HOW TO CONTACT Writers desirous of having their work handled by this agency may query by e-mail to agdevlin@aol.com. Accepts simultaneous submissions. Responds in 2 weeks to queries. Responds in 6 weeks to mss. Obtains most new clients through recommendations from others, following up on good query letters.

TERMS Agent receives 15% commission on domestic sales. Agent receives 20% commission on foreign sales.

RECENT SALES *Blazing Ice: Pioneering the 21st Century's Road to the South Pole*, by John H. Wright; *Beethoven for Kids: His Life and Music*, by Helen Bauer; *Slaughter on North LaSalle*, by Robert L. Snow; *What Patients Taught Me*, by Audrey Young, M.D. (Sasquatch Books); *Unorthodox Warfare: The Chinese Experience*, by Ralph D. Sawyer (Westview Press); *Encyclopedia of Earthquakes and Volcanoes*, by Alexander E. Gates (Facts on File); *Homebirth in the Hospital*, by Stacey Kerr, M.D. (Sentient Publications).

TIPS "We have recently expanded to allow more access for new writers."

Ⓓ GELFMAN SCHNEIDER / ICM PARTNERS

850 7th Ave., Suite 903, New York NY 10019. (212)245-1993. **Fax:** (212)245-8678. **E-mail:** mail@gelfmanschneider.com. **Website:** www.gelfmanschneider.com. **Contact:** Jane Gelfman, Deborah Schneider. Member of AAR. Represents 300+ clients. 10% of clients are new/unpublished writers.

MEMBER AGENTS Deborah Schneider, Jane Gelfman, Victoria Marini, Heather Mitchell.

REPRESENTS fiction and nonfiction books. **Considers these nonfiction areas:** creative nonfiction, popular culture. **Considers these fiction areas:** historical, literary, mainstream, middle grade, mystery, science fiction, suspense, westerns, women's, young adult.

8—☛ Does not want to receive romance or illustrated children's books.

HOW TO CONTACT Query. Send queries via snail mail only. No unsolicited mss. Please send a query letter, a synopsis, and a sample chapter only. Consult website for each agent's submission requirements. Note that Ms. Marini is the only agent at this agency who accepts e-queries: victoria.gsliterary@gmail.com. If querying Marini, put "Query" in the subject line and paste all materials (query, 1-3 sample chapters) in the body of the e-mail. Responds in 1 month to queries. Responds in 2 months to mss.

TERMS Agent receives 15% commission on domestic sales. Agent receives 20% commission on foreign sales. Agent receives 15% commission on film sales. Offers written contract. Charges clients for photocopying and messengers/couriers.

○ THE GERNERT COMPANY

136 East 57th St., 18th Floor, New York NY 10022. (212)838-7777. **Fax:** (212)838-6020. **E-mail:** info@ thegernertco.com. **Website:** www.thegernertco.com. **Contact:** Sarah Burnes.

○ Prior to her current position, Ms. Burnes was with Burnes & Clegg, Inc.

MEMBER AGENTS Sarah Burnes (commercial fiction, adventure and true story); **Stephanie Cabot** (literary fiction, commercial fiction, historical fiction); **Chris Parris-Lamb**; **Seth Fishman** (accepts graphic novels); **Logan Garrison**; **Will Roberts**; **Erika Storella**; **Flora Hackett**; **Andy Kifer** (literary fiction, smart genre fiction (in particular, high-concept thrillers or sci-fi), and nonfiction with a strong narrative bent); **Ellen Goodson**. At this time, **Courtney Gatewood** and **Rebecca Gardner** are closed to queries. See the website to find out the tastes of each agent.

REPRESENTS nonfiction books, novels. **Considers these nonfiction areas:** art, crafts, creative nonfiction, foods, history, memoirs, politics, sociology, travel. **Considers these fiction areas:** fantasy, historical, literary, middle grade, science fiction, thriller, women's, young adult.

HOW TO CONTACT Queries should be addressed to a specific agent via the e-mail subject line. Please send a query letter, either by mail or e-mail, describing the work you'd like to submit, along with some information about yourself and a sample chapter if appropriate. Please do not send e-mails to individual agents; use info@thegernertco.com and indicate which agent you're querying. See company website for more instructions. Obtains most new clients through recommendations from others, solicitations.

RECENT SALES *Sycamore Row* by John Grisham; *The Night Guest* by Fiona McFarlane; *Someone* by Alice Mcdermott; *Ancillary Justice* by Ann Leckie; *Beatles Vs Stones* by John Mcmillian; *Bargain Fever* by Mark Ellwood.

⊕ GHOSH LITERARY

E-mail: submissions@ghoshliterary.com. **Website:** www.ghoshliterary.com/about.

○ Prior to opening her own agency, Ms. Ghosh was previously a partner at Scovil Galen Ghosh.

REPRESENTS Considers these nonfiction areas: creative nonfiction.

HOW TO CONTACT E-query.

⊕ GLASS LITERARY MANAGEMENT

138 West 25th St., 10th Floor, New York NY 10001. (646)237-4881. **E-mail:** submissions@glassliterary. com. **Website:** www.glassliterary.com. Estab. 2014. Member of AAR.

HOW TO CONTACT "Please send your query letter in the body of an e-mail and if we are interested, we will respond and ask for the complete manuscript or proposal. No attachments."

RECENT SALES *So That Happened: A Memoir*, by Jon Cryer; *Lawless*, by Matt Bondurant; *Bad Kid*, by David Crabb.

⊕ GLOBAL LION INTELLECTUAL PROPERTY MANAGEMENT

PO BOX 669238, Pompano Beach FL 33066. **E-mail:** queriesgloballionmgt@gmail.com. **Website:** www. globallionmanagement.com. **Contact:** Peter Miller. Estab. 2013.

○ Prior to his current position, Mr. Miller was formerly the founder of previously PMA Literary & Film Management Inc. of New York.

⌗ "I look for cutting-edge authors of both fiction and nonfiction with global marketing and motion picture/television production potential."

HOW TO CONTACT E-query. Below the query, paste a synopsis, a sample of your book (20 pages is fine), an author bio, and any impressive social media links. Prefers an exclusive submission.

BARRY GOLDBLATT LITERARY LLC

320 Seventh Ave. #266, Brooklyn NY 11215. (718)832-8787. **E-mail:** query@bgliterary.com. **Website:** www. bgliterary.com/. **Contact:** Barry Goldblatt. Estab. 2000.

MEMBER AGENTS Barry Goldblatt.

REPRESENTS Considers these fiction areas: middle grade, young adult.

8—☞"Please see our website for specific submission guidelines and information on our particular tastes."

HOW TO CONTACT "E-mail queries can be sent to query@bgliterary.com and should include the word 'query' in the subject line. Please know that we will read and respond to every e-query that we receive, provided it is properly addressed and follows the submission guidelines below. We will not respond to e-queries that are addressed to no one, or to multiple recipients. While we do not require exclusivity, exclusive submissions will receive priority review. If your submission is exclusive to Barry Goldblatt Literary, please indicate so by including the word 'Exclusive' in the subject line of your e-mail. Your e-query should include the following within the body of the e-mail: your query letter, a synopsis of the book, and the first 5 pages of your ms. We will not open or respond to any e-mails that have attachments." Obtains clients through referrals, queries, and conferences.

TERMS Agent receives 15% commission on domestic sales; 20% on foreign and dramatic sales. Offers written contract. 60 days notice must be given to terminate contract.

RECENT SALES *Read Between the Lines*, by Jo Knowles; *Bright Before Sunrise*, by Tiffany Schmidt; *The Infamous Ratsos*, by Kara LaReau; *Wonders of the Invisible World*, by Christopher Barzak.

TIPS "We're a hands-on agency, focused on building an author's career, not just making an initial sale. We don't care about trends or what's hot; we just want to sign great writers."

⭕ FRANCES GOLDIN LITERARY AGENCY, INC.

57 E. 11th St., Suite 5B, New York NY 10003. (212)777-0047. **Fax:** (212)228-1660. **Website:** www.goldinlit.com. Estab. 1977. Member of AAR.

MEMBER AGENTS Frances Goldin, principal/agent; **Ellen Geiger**, agent (commercial and literary fiction and nonfiction, cutting-edge topics of all kinds); Matt McGowan, agent/rights director (innovative works of fiction and nonfiction); **Sam Stoloff**, agent, (literary fiction, memoir, history, accessible sociology and philosophy, cultural studies, serious journalism, narrative and topical nonfiction with a progressive orientation); **Sarah Bridgins**, agent/office

manager, sb@goldinlit.com (voice-driven fiction and narrative nonfiction); **Ria Julien**; **Matt McGowan**.

REPRESENTS nonfiction books, novels. **Considers these nonfiction areas:** creative nonfiction, cultural interests, investigative, memoirs, philosophy, sociology. **Considers these fiction areas:** literary, mainstream.

8—☞"We are hands on and we work intensively with clients on proposal and manuscript development." Does not want anything that is racist, sexist, agist, homophobic, or pornographic. No screenplays, children's books, art books, cookbooks, business books, diet books, romance, self-help, or genre fiction.

HOW TO CONTACT There is an online submission process you can find here: www.goldinlit.com/contact.html Responds in 4-6 weeks to queries.

⭕ THE SUSAN GOLOMB LITERARY AGENCY

540 President St., 3rd Floor, Brooklyn NY 11215. **Fax:** (212)239-9503. **E-mail:** queries@sgolombagency.com. **Contact:** Susan Golomb; Krista Ingebretson.

MEMBER AGENTS Susan Golomb (accepts queries); **Krista Ingebretson** (accepts queries); **Soumeya Bendimerad** (literary fiction, upmarket/book club fiction, and select young adult and middle grade; in nonfiction, she is seeking topics in popular culture, music and art history, unconventional business, politics, narrative nonfiction, sociology, cooking, travel, and memoir).

REPRESENTS novels, short story collections. **Considers these nonfiction areas:** animals, anthropology, biography, business, current affairs, economics, environment, health, history, law, memoirs, military, money, popular culture, politics, psychology, science, sociology, technology, women's issues, women's studies. **Considers these fiction areas:** ethnic, historical, humor, literary, mainstream, middle grade, satire, thriller, women's, young adult.

8—☞"We specialize in literary and upmarket fiction and nonfiction that is original, vibrant and of excellent quality and craft. Nonfiction should be edifying, paradigm-shifting, fresh and entertaining." Actively seeking writers with strong voices.

HOW TO CONTACT Query by e-mail. Will respond if interested. Obtains most new clients through rec-

NEW AGENT SPOTLIGHT

VICTORIA SELVAGGIO
JENNIFER DE CHIARA LITERARY AGENCY

Jdlit.com

@vselvaggio1

ABOUT VICTORIA: Victoria joins The Jennifer De Chiara Literary Agency as an Associate Agent with a strong background in business ownership and over six years of actively working as a volunteer and Regional Advisor for SCBWI: Northern Ohio.

SHE IS SEEKING: "I am currently looking for many genres—lyrical picture books, middle grade and young adult fiction, new adult, mysteries, suspense, thrillers, paranormal, fantasy, narrative nonfiction, adult fiction—but find I'm drawn to middle grade and young adult. I especially love thrillers and all elements of weird, creepy stuff. If it's out of the box, and it will make me think and think, long after I'm done reading, send it to me. On the flip side, I yearn for books that make me laugh, cry and wonder about the world."

HOW TO SUBMIT: Please e-query vselvaggio@windstream.net. Put "Query" in the subject line of your e-mail. For queries regarding children's and adult fiction, please send the first 20 pages in the body of your e-mail, along with a one-paragraph bio and a one-paragraph pitch. For queries regarding a nonfiction book, please attach the entire proposal as a Word document (the proposal should include a sample chapter or two), along with a one-paragraph bio and a one-paragraph pitch of your book in the body of your e-mail. "I usually respond within three to six months. If you haven't received a response after six months, feel free to query me again."

---

ommendations from others, solicitations, and unsolicited queries.

TERMS Offers written contract.

GOODMAN ASSOCIATES

500 West End Ave., New York NY 10024. (212)873-4806. **Contact:** Arnold P. Goodman. Member of AAR. Accepting new clients by recommendation only.

IRENE GOODMAN LITERARY AGENCY

27 W. 24th St., Suite 700B, New York NY 10010. **Website:** www.irenegoodman.com. Member of AAR.

MEMBER AGENTS Irene Goodman (her fiction list includes upmarket women's fiction, middle grade, young adult, thrillers, historical fiction, and mysteries; her nonfiction list includes pop culture, science, Francophilia, and lifestyle); **Beth Vesel** (narrative nonfiction, cultural criticism, psychology, science and memoir; **Miriam Kriss** (commercial fiction and she represents everything from hardcover historical mysteries to all subgenres of romance, from young adult fiction to kick ass urban fantasies, and everything in between); **Barbara Poelle** (thrillers, literary suspense, young adult and upmarket fiction); **Rachel Ekstrom** (young adult, women's fiction, new adult, mysteries, thrillers, romance, and the occasional quirky work of nonfiction).

REPRESENTS nonfiction, novels. **Considers these nonfiction areas:** narrative nonfiction dealing with social, cultural and historical issues; an occasional memoir and current affairs book, parenting, social issues, francophilia, anglophilia, Judaica, lifestyles, cooking, memoir. **Considers these fiction areas:** crime, detective, historical, mystery, romance, thriller, women's, young adult.

8—¬ "Specializes in the finest in commercial fiction and nonfiction. We have a strong background in women's voices, including mysteries, romance, women's fiction, thrillers, suspense. Historical fiction is one of Irene's particular passions and Miriam is fanatical about modern urban fantasies. In nonfiction, Irene is looking for topics on narrative history, social issues and trends, education, Judaica, Francophilia, Anglophilia, other cultures, animals, food, crafts, and memoir." Barbara is looking for commercial thrillers with strong female protagonists; Miriam is looking for urban fantasy and edgy sci-fi/young adult. No children's picture books, screenplays, poetry, or inspirational fiction.

HOW TO CONTACT Query. Submit synopsis, first 10 pages. E-mail queries only! See the website submission page. No e-mail attachments. Query one agent only. Responds in 2 months to queries. Consult website for each agent's submission guidelines.

RECENT SALES *The Ark*, by Boyd Morrison; *Isolation*, by C.J. Lyons; *The Sleepwalkers*, by Paul Grossman; *Dead Man's Moon*, by Devon Monk; *Becoming Marie Antoinette*, by Juliet Grey; *What's Up Down There*, by Lissa Rankin; *Beg for Mercy*, by Toni Andrews; *The Devil Inside*, by Jenna Black.

TIPS "We are receiving an unprecedented amount of e-mail queries. If you find that the mailbox is full, please try again in two weeks. E-mail queries to our personal addresses will not be answered. E-mails to our personal inboxes will be deleted."

DOUG GRAD LITERARY AGENCY, INC.

68 Jay Street, Suite N3, Brooklyn NY 11201. (718)788-6067. **E-mail:** doug.grad@dgliterary.com. **E-mail:** query@dgliterary.com. **Website:** www.dgliterary.com. **Contact:** Doug Grad. Estab. 2008.

○ Prior to being an agent, Doug Grad spent the last 22 years as an editor at 4 major publishing houses.

MEMBER AGENTS Doug Grad (narrative nonfiction, military, sports, celebrity memoir, thrillers, mysteries, historical fiction, music, style, business, home improvement, cookbooks, self-help, science and theater).

REPRESENTS Considers these nonfiction areas: business, cooking, creative nonfiction, military, music, popular culture, science, self-help, sports, theater, travel. **Considers these fiction areas:** historical, mystery, science fiction, thriller, young adult.

HOW TO CONTACT Query by e-mail first at query@dgliterary.com. No sample material unless requested; no printed submissions by mail.

RECENT SALES *The Earthend Saga*, by Gillian Anderson and Jeff Rovin (Simon451); *Abandoned In Hell: The Fight for Vietnam's Fire Base Kate*, by William Albracht and Marvin Wolf (Berkley/Caliber); *Bounty* by Michael Byrnes (Bantam); *Sports Idioms and Words* by Josh Chetwynd (Ten Speed Press).

GRAHAM MAW CHRISTIE LITERARY AGENCY

37 Highbury Place, London England N5 1QP United Kingdom. (44)(207)812-9937; 0(207) 609 1326. **E-mail:** enquiries@grahammawchristie.com. **E-mail:** submissions@grahammawchristie.com. **Website:** www.grahammawchristie.com. Represents 40 clients. 30% of clients are new/unpublished writers. Currently handles: nonfiction books 100%.

○ Prior to opening her agency, Ms. Graham Maw was a publishing director at HarperCollins and worked in rights, publicity and editorial. She has ghostwritten several nonfiction books, which gives her an insider's knowledge of both the publishing industry and the pleasures and pitfalls of authorships. Ms. Christie has a background in advertising and journalism.

MEMBER AGENTS Jane Graham Maw; Jennifer Christie.

REPRESENTS nonfiction books. **Considers these nonfiction areas:** autobiography, biography, child guidance, cooking, diet/nutrition, foods, health, how-to, medicine, memoirs, parenting, popular culture, psychology, self-help.

☛ "We aim to make the publishing process easier and smoother for authors. We work hard to ensure that publishing proposals are watertight before submission. We aim for collaborative relationships with publishers so that we provide the right books to the right editor at the right time. We represent ghostwriters as well as authors." Actively seeking work from UK writers only. Does not want to receive fiction, poetry, children's books, plays or e-mail submissions.

HOW TO CONTACT E-queries only. This agency only accepts nonfiction. Query with synopsis, chapter outline, bio, SASE. Responds in 2 weeks to queries. Obtains most new clients through recommendations from others.

TERMS Agent receives 15% commission on domestic sales. Agent receives 20% commission on foreign sales. Offers written contract; 30-day notice must be given to terminate contract.

WRITERS CONFERENCES London Book Fair, Frankfurt Book Fair.

TIPS "UK clients only!"

○ ASHLEY GRAYSON LITERARY AGENCY

1342 W. 18th St., San Pedro CA 90732. **E-mail:** graysonagent@earthlink.net. **Website:** www.publishersmarketplace.com/members/CGrayson/. Estab. 1976. Member of AAR.

MEMBER AGENTS Ashley Grayson (fantasy, mystery, thrillers, young adult); **Carolyn Grayson** (chick lit, mystery, children's, nonfiction, women's fiction, romance, thrillers); **Lois Winston** (women's fiction, chick lit, mystery).

REPRESENTS nonfiction books, novels. **Considers these nonfiction areas:** business, computers, economics, history, investigative, popular culture, science, self-help, sports, technology, true crime. **Considers these fiction areas:** fantasy, juvenile, middle grade, multicultural, mystery, romance, science fiction, suspense, women's, young adult.

☛ "We represent literary and commercial fiction, as well as nonfiction for adults (self-help, parenting, pop culture, mind/body/spirit, true crime, business, science). We also represent fiction for younger readers (chapter books through YA). We are seeking more mysteries

and thrillers." Actively seeking previously published fiction authors.

HOW TO CONTACT The agency is temporarily closed to queries from *fiction* writers who are not previously published at book length (self published or print-on-demand do not count). There are only three exceptions to this policy: (1) Unpublished authors who have received an offer from a reputable publisher, who need an agent before beginning contract negotiations; (2) Authors who are recommended by a published author, editor or agent who has read the work in question; (3) Authors whom we have met at conferences and from whom we have requested submissions. Nonfiction authors who are recognized within their field or area may still query with proposals. Note: We cannot review self-published, subsidy-published, and POD-published works to evaluate moving them to mainstream publishers.

TERMS Agent receives 15% commission on domestic sales. Agent receives 20% commission on foreign sales.

TIPS "We do request revisions as they are required. We are long-time agents, professional and known in the business. We perform professionally for our clients and we ask the same of them."

○ SANFORD J. GREENBURGER ASSOCIATES, INC.

55 Fifth Ave., New York NY 10003. (212)206-5600. **Fax:** (212)463-8718. **Website:** www.greenburger.com. Member of AAR. Represents 500 clients.

MEMBER AGENTS Matt Bialer, LRibar@sjga.com (fantasy, science fiction, thrillers, and mysteries as well as a select group of literary writers, and also loves smart narrative nonfiction including books about current events, popular culture, biography, history, music, race, and sports); **Brenda Bowen**, queryBB@sjga.com (literary fiction, writers and illustrators of picture books, chapter books, and middle grade and teen fiction); **Lisa Gallagher**, lgsubmissions@sjga.com (accessible literary fiction, quality commercial women's fiction, crime fiction, lively narrative nonfiction); **Faith Hamlin**, fhamlin@sjga.com (receives submissions by referral); **Heide Lange**, queryHL@sjga.com; **Daniel Mandel**, querydm@sjga.com (literary and commercial fiction, as well as memoirs and nonfiction about business, art, history, politics, sports, and popular culture); **Courtney Miller-Callihan**, cmiller@sjga.com (YA, middle grade, women's fiction, romance, and historical novels, as well as non-fiction projects on unusual topics, humor, pop culture, and lifestyle books); **Nicholas Ellison**, nellison@sjga.com; **Chelsea Lindman**, clindman@sjga.com (playful literary fiction, upmarket crime fiction, and forward thinking or boundary-pushing nonfiction); **Rachael Dillon Fried**, rfried@sjga.com (both fiction and nonfiction authors, with a keen interest in unique literary voices, women's fiction, narrative nonfiction, memoir, and comedy); **Lindsay Ribar**, co-agents with Matt Bailer (young adult and middle grade fiction); **Thomas Miller** (primarily nonfiction projects in the areas of wellness and health, popular culture, psychology and self-help, business, diet, spirituality, cooking, and narrative nonfiction).

REPRESENTS nonfiction books and novels. **Considers these nonfiction areas:** art, biography, business, creative nonfiction, current affairs, ethnic, history, humor, memoirs, music, popular culture, politics, sports. **Considers these fiction areas:** crime, fantasy, historical, literary, middle grade, mystery, picture books, romance, science fiction, thriller, women's, young adult.

⚷ No Westerns. No screenplays.

HOW TO CONTACT E-query. "Please look at each agent's profile page for current information about what each agent is looking for and for the correct e-mail address to use for queries to that agent. Please be sure to use the correct query e-mail address for each agent." Accepts simultaneous submissions. Responds in 2 months to queries and mss. Obtains most new clients through recommendations from others.

TERMS Agent receives 15% commission on domestic sales. Agent receives 20% commission on foreign sales. Charges for photocopying and books for foreign and subsidiary rights submissions.

RECENT SALES *Inferno*, by Dan Brown; *Hidden Order*, by Brad Thor; *The Chalice*, by Nancy Bilveau; *Horns*, by Joe Hill.

◐◑ THE GREENHOUSE LITERARY AGENCY

4035 Ridge Top Road, Suite 550, Fairfax VA 22030. **E-mail:** submissions@greenhouseliterary.com. **Website:** www.greenhouseliterary.com. Member of AAR. Other memberships include SCBWI. Represents 20 clients. 100% of clients are new/unpublished writers. Currently handles: juvenile books 100%.

◯ Sarah Davies has had an editorial and management career in children's publishing spanning 25 years; for 5 years prior to launching the Greenhouse she was Publishing Director of Macmillan Children's Books in London, and publishing leading authors from both sides of the Atlantic.

MEMBER AGENTS **Sarah Davies**, vice president (middle grade and young adult); **John M. Cusick**, agent (picture books, chapter books, middle grade, YA); **Polly Nolan**, agent (fiction by UK, Irish, Commonwealth—including Australia, NZ and India—authors, from picture books to young fiction series, through middle grade and young adult).

REPRESENTS juvenile. **Considers these fiction areas:** juvenile, middle grade, picture books, young adult.

⚷ "We exclusively represent authors writing fiction for children and teens. The agency has offices in both the US and UK, and Sarah Davies (who is British) personally represents authors to both markets. The agency's commission structure reflects this—taking 15% for sales to both US and UK, thus treating both as 'domestic' market.'" All genres of children's and YA fiction—ages 5+. Does not want to receive nonfiction, poetry, picture books (text or illustration) or work aimed at adults; short stories, educational or religious/inspirational work, pre-school/novelty material, or screenplays.

HOW TO CONTACT Query one agent only. Put the target agent's name in the subject line. Paste the first 5 pages of your story (or your complete picture book) after the query. Obtains most new clients through recommendations from others, solicitations, conferences.

TERMS Agent receives 15% commission on domestic sales. Agent receives 25% commission on foreign sales. Offers written contract. This agency occasionally charges for submission copies to film agents or foreign publishers.

RECENT SALES *Vengeance*, by Megan Miranda (Bloomsbury); *Fiendish*, by Brenna Yovanoff (Razorbill); *The Very Nearly Honorable League Of Pirates*, by Caroline Carlson (Harpercollins); *We All Looked Up*, by Tommy Wallach (Simon & Schuster); *Shutter* by Courtney Alameda (Feiwel/Macmillan); *Can't Look Away*, by Donna Cooner (Scholastic); *Moonpenny Island*, by Tricia Springstubb (Harpercollins); *The Cha-*

pel Wars, by Lindsey Leavitt (Bloomsbury); *The Third Twin*, by C.J.Omololu (Delacorte).

WRITERS CONFERENCES Bologna Children's Book Fair, ALA and SCBWI conferences, BookExpo America.

TIPS "Before submitting material, authors should read the Greenhouse's 'Top 10 Tips for Authors of Children's Fiction' and carefully follow our submission guidelines which can be found on the website."

ⓘ KATHRYN GREEN LITERARY AGENCY, LLC

250 West 57th St., Suite 2302, New York NY 10107. (212)245-4225. **Fax:** (212)245-4042. **E-mail:** query@kgreenagency.com. **Contact:** Kathy Green. Other memberships include Women's Media Group. Represents approximately 20 clients. 50% of clients are new/unpublished writers.

Prior to becoming an agent, Ms. Green was a book and magazine editor.

REPRESENTS Considers these nonfiction areas: autobiography, biography, business, child guidance, cooking, current affairs, diet/nutrition, economics, education, foods, history, how-to, humor, interior design, investigative, juvenile nonfiction, memoirs, parenting, popular culture, psychology, satire, self-help, sports, true crime, women's issues, women's studies, juvenile. **Considers these fiction areas:** crime, detective, family saga, historical, humor, juvenile, literary, mainstream, middle grade, mystery, police, romance, satire, suspense, thriller, women's, young adult.

⚷ Keeping the client list small means that writers receive my full attention throughout the process of getting their project published. Does not want to receive science fiction or fantasy.

HOW TO CONTACT Query to query@kgreenagency.com. Send no samples unless requested. Accepts simultaneous submissions. Responds in 1-2 months to mss. Obtains most new clients through recommendations from others, solicitations, conferences.

TERMS Agent receives 15% commission on domestic sales. Agent receives 20% commission on foreign sales.

ⓘ GREGORY & COMPANY AUTHORS' AGENTS

3 Barb Mews, Hammersmith, London W6 7PA England. (44)(207)610-4676. **Fax:** (44)(207)610-4686. **E-mail:** info@gregoryandcompany.co.uk. **Website:** www.gregoryandcompany.co.uk. Other memberships include AAA.

MEMBER AGENTS Jane Gregory, Stephanie Glencross, Claire Morris.

REPRESENTS Considers these fiction areas: crime, detective, historical, literary, thriller, women's.

⚷ As a British agency, we do not generally take on American authors. Actively seeking well-written, accessible novels. Does not want to receive horror, science fiction, fantasy, mind/body/spirit, children's books, screenplays, plays, short stories or poetry.

HOW TO CONTACT Query with SASE. Submit outline, first 10 pages by e-mail or post, publishing history, author bio. Send submissions to Mary Jones, submissions editor: maryjones@gregoryandcompany.co.uk. Accepts simultaneous submissions. Returns materials only with SASE. Obtains most new clients through recommendations from others, conferences.

TERMS Agent receives 15% commission on domestic sales. Agent receives 20% commission on foreign sales. Offers written contract; 1-month notice must be given to terminate contract. Charges clients for photocopying of whole typescripts and copies of book for submissions.

ⓘ GREYHAUS LITERARY

3021 20th St., PL SW, Puyallup WA 98373. **E-mail:** scott@greyhausagency.com. **Website:** www.greyhausagency.com. **Contact:** Scott Eagan, member RWA. Estab. 2003.

REPRESENTS Considers these fiction areas: romance, women's.

⚷ "Greyhaus only focuses on romance and women's fiction. Please review submission information found on the website to know exactly what Greyhaus is looking for. Stories should be 75,000-120,000 words in length or meet the word count requirements for Harlequin or Entangled found on their respective websites." Does not want sci-fi, fantasy, literary, futuristic, erotica, writers targeting e-pubs, young adult, nonfiction, memoirs, how-to books, self-help, screenplays, novellas, or poetry.

HOW TO CONTACT Submissions to Greyhaus can be done in one of three ways: 1) Send a query, the first 3 pages and a synopsis of no more than 3 pages (and a SASE), using a snail mail submission. 2) A standard query letter via e-mail. If using this method, do not attach documents or send anything else other than a query letter. Or 3) use the Submission Form found on the website on the Contact page.

JILL GRINBERG LITERARY AGENCY

392 Vanderbilt Ave., Brooklyn NY 11238. (212)620-5883. **Fax:** (212)627-4725. **E-mail:** info@jillgrinbergliterary.com. **Website:** www.jillgrinbergliterary.com. Estab. 1999.

○ Prior to her current position, Ms. Grinberg was at Anderson Grinberg Literary Management.

MEMBER AGENTS Jill Grinberg, jill@jillgrinbergliterary.com; **Cheryl Pientka**, cheryl@jillgrinbergliterary.com; **Katelyn Detweiler**, katelyn@jillgrinbergliterary.com.

REPRESENTS nonfiction books, novels. **Considers these nonfiction areas:** biography, cooking, ethnic, history, science, travel. **Considers these fiction areas:** fantasy, juvenile, literary, mainstream, romance, science fiction, young adult.

HOW TO CONTACT Please send your query letter to info@jillgrinbergliterary.com and attach the first 50 pages (fiction) or proposal (nonfiction) as a Word doc file. All submissions will be read, but electronic mail is preferred.

RECENT SALES *Cinder*, Marissa Meyer; *The Hero's Guide to Saving Your Kingdom*, Christopher Healy; *Kiss and Make Up*, Katie Anderson; i, T.J. Stiles; *Eon* and *Eona*, Alison Goodman; *American Nations*, Colin Woodard; HALO Trilogy, Alexandra Adornetto; *Babymouse*, Jennifer & Matthew Holm; Uglies/Leviathan Trilogy, Scott Westerfeld; *Liar*, Justine Larbalestier; *Turtle in Paradise*, Jennifer Holm; *Wisdom's Kiss* and *Dairy Queen*, Catherine Gilbert Murdock.

TIPS "We prefer submissions by mail."

JILL GROSJEAN LITERARY AGENCY

1390 Millstone Rd., Sag Harbor NY 11963. (631)725-7419. **E-mail:** JillLit310@aol.com. **Contact:** Jill Grosjean. Estab. 1999. No No

○ Prior to becoming an agent, Ms. Grosjean managed an independent bookstore. She also worked in publishing and advertising.

REPRESENTS Considers these fiction areas: literary, mainstream, mystery.

➤ Actively seeking literary novels and mysteries.

HOW TO CONTACT E-mail queries preferred, no attachments. No cold calls, please. Accepts simultaneous submissions, though when manuscript requested, requires exclusive reading time. Accepts simultaneous

submissions. Responds in 1 week to queries; month to mss. Obtains most new clients through recommendations and solicitations.

TERMS Agent receives 15% commission on domestic sales; 20% commission on foreign and film sales.

RECENT SALES *A Spark of Death*, *Fatal Induction*, and *Capacity for Murder*, by Bernadette Pajer (Poison Pen Press); *Neutral Ground*, by Greg Garrett (Bondfire Books); *Threading the Needle*, by Marie Bostwick (Kensington Publishing); *Tim Cratchit's Christmas Carol: A Novel of Scrooge's Legacy*, by Jim Piecuch (Simon & Schuster).

WRITERS CONFERENCES Thrillerfest; Texas Writer's League; Book Passage Mystery's Writer's Conference.

LAURA GROSS LITERARY AGENCY

P.O. Box 610326, Newton Highlands MA 02461. (617)964-2977. **E-mail:** query@lg-la.com. **Website:** www.lg-la.com. Estab. 1988. Represents 30 clients.

○ Prior to becoming an agent, Ms. Gross was an editor and ran a reading series.

REPRESENTS nonfiction books, novels.

➤ Actively seeking high quality fiction—including mystery and suspense—as well as biography, books on cultural, social issues, currently affairs, history. Does not want romance, erotica, how-to, children's, screenplays.

HOW TO CONTACT Queries accepted online via online form on LGLA website. No e-mail queries. Responds in several days to queries.

TERMS Agent receives 15% commission on domestic sales. Agent receives 20% commission on foreign sales. Offers written contract.

THE JOY HARRIS LITERARY AGENCY, INC.

381 Park Avenue S, Suite 428, New York NY 10016. (212)924-6269. **Fax:** (212)725-5275. **E-mail:** submissions@jhlitagent.com. **Website:** joyharrisliterary.com. **Contact:** Joy Harris. Estab. 1990. Member of AAR. Represents more than 100 clients. Currently handles: nonfiction books 50%, novels 50%.

MEMBER AGENTS Joy Harris (most interested in literary fiction and narrative nonfiction); **Adam Reed** (arts, literary fiction, science and technology, and pop culture).

REPRESENTS Considers these nonfiction areas: art, creative nonfiction, popular culture, science, technology. **Considers these fiction areas:** literary.

We do not accept unsolicited manuscripts, and are not accepting poetry, screenplays, or self-help submissions at this time.

HOW TO CONTACT "Please e-mail your submission to submissions@joyharrisliterary.com; however, we will only reply if interested. Do not send your full manuscript before it is requested." Accepts simultaneous submissions. Responds in 2 months to queries. Obtains most new clients through recommendations from clients and editors.

TERMS Agent receives 15% commission on domestic sales. Agent receives 20% commission on foreign sales. Charges clients for some office expenses.

RECENT SALES *One Kick*, by Chelsea Cain; *Fire in the Belly*, by Cynthia Carr; *Rainey Royal* by Dylan Landis; *The Price of Silence*, William D. Cohan.

HARTLINE LITERARY AGENCY

123 Queenston Dr., Pittsburgh PA 15235-5429. (412)829-2483. **Fax:** (412)829-2432. **E-mail:** joyce@hartlineliterary.com. **Website:** www.hartlineliterary.com. **Contact:** Joyce A. Hart. Represents 40 clients. 20% of clients are new/unpublished writers. Currently handles: nonfiction books 40%, novels 60%.

MEMBER AGENTS Joyce A. Hart, principal agent (no unsolicited queries); **Jim Hart**, jim@hartlineliterary.com; **Terry Burns**: terry@hartlineliterary.com (some YA and middle grade along with his other interests); **Diana Flegal**: diana@hartlineliterary.com; **Linda Glaz**, linda@hartlineliterary.com; **Andy Scheer**, andy@hartlineliterary.com.

REPRESENTS nonfiction books, novels.

"This agency specializes in the Christian bookseller market." Actively seeking adult fiction, self-help, nutritional books, Christian living, devotional, and business. Does not want to receive erotica, gay/lesbian, fantasy, horror, etc.

HOW TO CONTACT E-query only. Target one agent only. "All e-mail submissions sent to Hartline Agents should be sent as a MS Word doc (or in rich text file format from another word processing program) attached to an e-mail with "submission: title, authors name and word count" in the subject line. A proposal is a single document, not a collection of files. Place the query letter in the e-mail itself. Do not send the entire proposal in the body of the e-mail or send PDF files." Further guidelines online. Accepts simultaneous submissions. Responds in 2 months to queries. Responds in 3 months to mss. Obtains most new clients through recommendations from others.

TERMS Agent receives 15% commission on domestic sales. Offers written contract.

ANTONY HARWOOD LIMITED

103 Walton St., Oxford OX2 6EB England. +44 01865 559 615. **Fax:** +44 01865 310 660. **E-mail:** ant@antonyharwood.com. **E-mail:** mail@antonyharwood.com. **Website:** www.antonyharwood.com. **Contact:** Antony Harwood; James Macdonald Lockhart; Jo Williamson. Estab. 2000. Represents 52 clients.

Prior to starting this agency, Mr. Harwood and Mr. Lockhart worked at publishing houses and other literary agencies.

MEMBER AGENTS Antony Harwood, James Macdonald Lockhart, Jo Williamson (children's).

REPRESENTS nonfiction books, novels. **Considers these nonfiction areas:** Americana, animals, anthropology, archeology, architecture, art, autobiography, biography, business, child guidance, computers, cooking, current affairs, design, economics, education, environment, ethnic, film, gardening, gay/lesbian, government, health, history, horticulture, how-to, humor, language, memoirs, military, money, multicultural, music, parenting, philosophy, photography, popular culture, psychology, recreation, regional, science, self-help, sex, sociology, software, spirituality, sports, technology, translation, travel, true crime, war, women's issues, women's studies. **Considers these fiction areas:** action, adventure, cartoon, comic books, confession, crime, detective, erotica, ethnic, experimental, family saga, fantasy, feminist, frontier, gay, hi-lo, historical, horror, humor, lesbian, literary, mainstream, military, multicultural, multimedia, mystery, occult, picture books, plays, police, regional, religious, romance, satire, science fiction, spiritual, sports, suspense, thriller, translation, war, westerns, young adult, gothic.

"We accept every genre of fiction and nonfiction except for children's fiction for readers ages 10 and younger." No poetry or screenplays.

HOW TO CONTACT "We are happy to consider submissions of fiction and nonfiction in every genre and category except for screenwriting and poetry. If you wish to submit your work to us for consideration, please send a covering letter, brief outline and the opening 50 pages by e-mail. If you want to post your material to us, please be sure to enclose an SAE

NEW AGENT SPOTLIGHT

AMANDA LEUCK
SPENCERHILL ASSOCIATES

Spencerhillassociates.com

@MandiLeone

ABOUT AMANDA: Amanda started her career in various facets of the media, including work on a TV talk show, at a fashion magazine, as a print journalist, and as an on-air traffic reporter. After graduating from New York University, Amanda went on to study literacy and literature at the post-graduate level. It was then that she developed a passion for the publishing industry.

SHE IS SEEKING: strong, character-driven stories. She's looking for literary and commercial young adult, new adult fiction, urban fantasy, and romance in all genres (including edgy romantic suspense, contemporary and paranormal with a fresh twist).

HOW TO SUBMIT: submission@spencerhillassociates.com. Send the query letter in the body of the e-mail. Address the query to Amanda. Include the pitch, and information about past publishing credits in the letter. Attach a detailed synopsis, and attach the first three chapters in .doc, rtf or txt format to the e-mail.

---

or the cost of return postage." Responds in 2 months to queries.

TERMS Agent receives 15% commission on domestic sales. Agent receives 20% commission on foreign sales.

JOHN HAWKINS & ASSOCIATES, INC.

80 Maiden Lane, Suite 1503, New York NY 10038. (212)807-7040. **Fax:** (212)807-9555. **E-mail:** jha@jhalit.com. **Website:** www.jhalit.com. **Contact:** Moses Cardona (rights and translations); Liz Free (permissions); Warren Frazier, literary agent; Anne Hawkins, literary agent. Member of AAR. Represents 100+ clients. 5-10% of clients are new/unpublished writers. Currently handles: nonfiction books 40%, novels 40%, juvenile books 20%.

MEMBER AGENTS Moses Cardona, moses@jhalit.com (commercial fiction, suspense, business, science, and multicultural fiction); **Warren Frazier**, frazier@jhalit.com (nonfiction—technology, history, world affairs and foreign policy); **Anne Hawkins** ahawkins@jhalit.com (thrillers to literary fiction to serious nonfiction; she also has particular interests in science, history, public policy, medicine and women's issues).

REPRESENTS nonfiction books, novels. **Considers these nonfiction areas:** biography, business, history, medicine, politics, science, technology, women's issues. **Considers these fiction areas:** commercial, historical, literary, multicultural, suspense, thriller.

HOW TO CONTACT Query. Include the word "Query" in the subject line. For fiction, include 1-3 chapters of your book as a single Word attachment. For nonfiction, include your proposal as a single attachment. E-mail a particular agent directly if you are targeting one. Accepts simultaneous submissions. Responds in

1 month to queries. Obtains most new clients through recommendations from others.

TERMS Agent receives 15% commission on domestic sales. Agent receives 20% commission on foreign sales. Charges clients for photocopying.

RECENT SALES *Publishing,* by Gail Godwin; *Interesting Facts: Stories,* by Adam Johnson; *The Sacrifice,* by Joyce Carol Oates; *Thin Air,* by Ann Cleeves; *The Dead Student,* by John Katzenbach; *The Catch,* by Taylor Stevens.

⭕ HEACOCK HILL LITERARY AGENCY, INC.

West Coast Office, 1020 Hollywood Way, #439, Burbank CA 91505. (818)951-6788. **E-mail:** agent@hea cockhill.com. **Website:** www.heacockhill.com. **Contact:** Catt LeBaigue or Tom Dark. Estab. 2009. Member of AAR. Other memberships include SCBWI.

◑ Prior to becoming an agent, Ms. LeBaigue spent 18 years with Sony Pictures and Warner Bros.

MEMBER AGENTS Tom Dark (adult fiction, nonfiction); Catt LeBaigue (juvenile fiction, adult nonfiction including arts, crafts, anthropology, astronomy, nature studies, ecology, body/mind/spirit, humanities, self-help).

REPRESENTS nonfiction, fiction. **Considers these nonfiction areas:** art, business, gardening, politics. **Considers these fiction areas:** juvenile, middle grade, picture books, young adult.

⚬➤ Not presently accepting new clients for adult fiction. Please check the website for updates.

HOW TO CONTACT E-mail queries only. No unsolicited manuscripts. No e-mail attachments. Responds in 1 week to queries. Obtains most new clients through recommendations from others, solicitations.

TERMS Offers written contract.

TIPS "Write an informative original e-query expressing your book idea, your qualifications, and short excerpts of the work. No unfinished work, please."

◔ HELEN HELLER AGENCY INC.

4-216 Heath Street W, Toronto Ontario M5P 1N7 Canada. (416)489-0396. **E-mail:** info@helenhelle ragency.com. **Website:** www.helenhelleragency.com. **Contact:** Helen Heller. Represents 30+ clients.

◑ Prior to her current position, Ms. Heller worked for Cassell & Co. (England), was an editor for Harlequin Books, a senior editor for Avon Books, and editor-in-chief for Fitzhenry & Whiteside.

MEMBER AGENTS Helen Heller, helen@helenhelle ragency.com (thrillers and front-list general fiction); Sarah Heller, sarah@helenhelleragency.com (front list commercial YA and adult fiction, with a particular interest in high concept historical fiction).

REPRESENTS nonfiction books, novels. **Considers these fiction areas:** commercial, crime, historical, literary, mainstream, young adult.

⚬➤ Actively seeking adult fiction and nonfiction (excluding children's literature, screenplays or genre fiction). Does not want to receive screenplays, poetry, or young children's picture books.

HOW TO CONTACT Submit synopsis, publishing history, author bio. Online submission form available at website. No attachments with e-queries. Responds in 6 weeks. Obtains most new clients through recommendations from others, solicitations.

RECENT SALES *Break on Through,* by Jill Murray (Doubleday Canada); *Womankind: Faces of Change Around the World,* by Donna Nebenzahl (Raincoast Books); *One Dead Indian: The Premier, The Police, and the Ipperwash Crisis,* by Peter Edwards (McClelland & Stewart); a full list of deals is available online.

TIPS "Whether you are an author searching for an agent, or whether an agent has approached you, it is in your best interest to first find out who the agent represents, what publishing houses has that agent sold to recently and what foreign sales have been made. You should be able to go to the bookstore, or search online and find the books the agent refers to. Many authors acknowledge their agents in the front or back or their books."

◑ RICHARD HENSHAW GROUP

145 W. 28th St., 12th Floor, New York NY 10001. (212)414-1172. **E-mail:** submissions@henshaw.com. **Website:** www.richardhenshawgroup.com. **Contact:** Rich Henshaw. Member of AAR.

◑ Prior to opening his agency, Mr. Henshaw served as an agent with Richard Curtis Associates, Inc.

MEMBER AGENTS Richard Henshaw; Susannah Taylor.

REPRESENTS nonfiction books, novels. **Considers these nonfiction areas:** animals, autobiography, biography, business, child guidance, cooking, current affairs, dance, economics, environment, foods, gay/lesbian, health, humor, investigative, money, music, New Age, parenting, popular culture, politics, psychology, science, self-help, sociology, sports, technology, true crime, women's issues, women's studies. **Considers these fiction areas:** crime, detective, fantasy, historical, horror, literary, mainstream, mystery, police, science fiction, supernatural, suspense, thriller, young adult.

8—¬ This agency specializes in thrillers, mysteries, science fiction, fantasy and horror. "We only consider works between 65,000-150,000 words. We do not represent children's books, screenplays, short fiction, poetry, textbooks, scholarly works or coffee-table books."

HOW TO CONTACT "Please feel free to submit a query letter in the form of an e-mail of fewer than 250 words to submissions@henshaw.com address." No snail mail queries. Responds in 3 weeks to queries. Responds in 6 weeks to mss. Obtains most new clients through recommendations from others, solicitations, conferences.

TERMS Agent receives 15% commission on domestic sales. Agent receives 20% commission on foreign sales. No written contract. Charges clients for photocopying and book orders.

RECENT SALES *Though Not Dead*, by Dana Stabenow; *The Perfect Suspect*, by Margaret Coel; *City of Ruins*, by Kristine Kathryn Rusch; *A Dead Man's Tale*, by James D. Doss, *Wickedly Charming*, by Kristine Grayson, History of the World series by Susan Wise Bauer; *Notorious Pleasures*, by Elizabeth Hoyt.

TIPS "While we do not have any reason to believe that our submission guidelines will change in the near future, writers can find up-to-date submission policy information on our website. Always include a SASE with correct return postage."

HERMAN AGENCY

350 Central Park West, New York NY 10025. (212)749-4907. **E-mail:** Ronnie@hermanagencyinc.com. **Website:** www.hermanagencyinc.com. Estab. 1999.
MEMBER AGENTS Ronnie Ann Herman.
REPRESENTS children's. **Considers these fiction areas:** picture books by author/artists only, not looking for manuscripts or artists and middle grade fiction and nonfiction.
HOW TO CONTACT Submit via e-mail

TIPS "Check our website to see if you belong with our agency."

THE JEFF HERMAN AGENCY, LLC

P.O. Box 1522, Stockbridge MA 01262. (413)298-0077. **Fax:** (413)298-8188. **E-mail:** jeff@jeffherman.com. **Website:** www.jeffherman.com. **Contact:** Jeffrey H. Herman. Represents 100 clients. 10% of clients are new/unpublished writers. Currently handles: nonfiction books 85%, scholarly books 5%, textbooks 5%.

O   Prior to opening his agency, Mr. Herman served as a public relations executive.

MEMBER AGENTS Deborah Levine, vice president (nonfiction book doctor); **Jeff Herman**.
REPRESENTS nonfiction books. **Considers these nonfiction areas:** business, economics, government, health, history, how-to, law, medicine, politics, psychology, self-help, spirituality, technology, popular reference.

8—¬ This agency specializes in adult nonfiction.
HOW TO CONTACT Query with SASE. Accepts simultaneous submissions.
TERMS Agent receives 15% commission on domestic sales. Offers written contract. Charges clients for copying and postage.
RECENT SALES *Days of Our Lives* book series; *H&R Block* book series. Sold 35 titles in the last year.

HIDDEN VALUE GROUP

27758 Santa Margarita Pkwy #361, Mission Viejo CA 92691. **E-mail:** bookquery@hiddenvaluegroup.com. **Website:** www.hiddenvaluegroup.com. **Contact:** Nancy Jernigan. Represents 55 clients. 10% of clients are new/unpublished writers.
MEMBER AGENTS Jeff Jernigan, jjernigan@hiddenvaluegroup.com (men's nonfiction, fiction, Bible studies/curriculum, marriage and family); **Nancy Jernigan**, njernigan@hiddenvaluegroup.com (nonfiction, women's issues, inspiration, marriage and family, fiction).
REPRESENTS nonfiction books and adult fiction; no poetry.

8—¬ We are currently interested in receiving proposals in a variety of genres such as family/parenting/marriage, inspirational, self-help, men's and women's issues, business and fiction. No poetry or short stories. Actively seeking established fiction authors, and authors who are focusing on women's issues. Does not want to receive poetry or short stories.

HOW TO CONTACT Query with SASE. Submit synopsis, 2 sample chapters, author bio, and marketing and speaking summary. Accepts queries to bookquery@hiddenvaluegroup.com. No fax queries. Responds in 1 month to queries. Responds in 1 month to mss. Obtains most new clients through recommendations from others, solicitations.

TERMS Agent receives 15% commission on domestic sales. Agent receives 15% commission on foreign sales. Offers written contract.

WRITERS CONFERENCES Glorieta Christian Writers' Conference; CLASS Publishing Conference.

O JULIE A. HILL AND ASSOCIATES, LLC

12997 Caminto del Pasaje, #530, Del Mar CA 92014. (858)259-2595. **Fax:** (858)259-2777. **E-mail:** Hillagent@aol.com. **Website:** www.publishersmarketplace/members/hillagent. **Contact:** Julie Hill.

MEMBER AGENTS Julie Hill, agent and principal.

REPRESENTS nonfiction books. **Considers these nonfiction areas:** biography, cooking, ethnic, health, history, how-to, language, memoirs, music, New Age, popular culture, psychology, religious, self-help, travel, women's issues, technology books, both for professionals and laypersons.

Actively seeking travel, health, and media tie-ins. Does not want to receive horror, juvenile, sci-fi, thrillers or autobiographies of any kind.

HOW TO CONTACT E-query or query via snail mail with SASE. Responds in 4-6 weeks to queries. Accepts simultaneous submissions. Responds in 4-6 weeks to queries. Obtains most new clients through recommendations from other authors, editors, and agents.

TIPS A secondary website for this agency is www.publishersmarketplace.com/members/destiny, titled "Astrology for Writers."

◐ HILL NADELL LITERARY AGENCY

6442 Santa Monica Blvd., Suite 201, Los Angeles CA 90038. (310)860-9605. **E-mail:** queries.hillnadell@gmail.com. **Website:** www.hillnadell.com. Represents 100 clients.

MEMBER AGENTS **Bonnie Nadell** (Her nonfiction books include works on current affairs and food as well as memoirs and other narrative nonfiction. In fiction, she represents thrillers along with upmarket women's and literary fiction); **Dara Hyde** (literary and genre fiction, narrative nonfiction, graphic novels, memoir and the occasional young adult novel).

REPRESENTS nonfiction books, novels. **Considers these nonfiction areas:** biography, current affairs, environment, government, health, history, language, literature, medicine, popular culture, politics, science, technology, biography; government/politics, narrative. **Considers these fiction areas:** literary, mainstream, thriller, women's, young adult.

HOW TO CONTACT Send a query and SASE. If you would like your materials returned, please include adequate postage. To submit electronically: Send your query letter and the first chapter (no more than 15 pages double-spaced) to queries@hillnadell.com. No attachments. Due to the high volume of submissions the agency receives, it cannot guarantee a response to all e-mailed queries. Accepts simultaneous submissions.

TERMS Agent receives 15% commission on domestic sales. Agent receives 20% commission on foreign sales. Agent receives 15% commission on film sales. Charges clients for photocopying and foreign mailings.

RECENT SALES *S Street Rising* by Ruben Castaneda; *Spare Parts* by Joshua Davis; *Men Explain Things to Me* by Rebecca Solnit; *Bellweather Rhapsody* by Kate Racculia.

◐ THE HOLMES AGENCY

1942 Broadway, Suite 314, Boulder CO 80302. (720)443-8550. **E-mail:** kristina@holmesliterary.com. **Website:** www.holmesliterary.com. **Contact:** Kristina A. Holmes.

MEMBER AGENTS Kristina A. Holmes.

REPRESENTS **Considers these nonfiction areas:** business, cooking, environment, foods, health, memoirs, psychology, science, sex, spirituality, women's issues.

HOW TO CONTACT To submit your book for consideration, please e-mail your query and full book proposal to submissions@holmesliterary.com. (Please note that this agency does not represent fiction of any kind, true crime, poetry, or children's books.) In your query, please briefly describe your book (content, vision, purpose, and audience), as well as a bit about your background as an author—including notable platform highlights such as national media, a popular blog or website, speaking career, etc.

RECENT SALES *Virtual Freedom: How To Work With Virtual Assistants To Create More Time, Increase Your Productivity, And Build Your Dream Business,* by Chris Ducker (Benbella Books 2014); *Recipes For A Sacred Life: True Stories and a Few Miracles*, by Rivvy Neshama (Divine Arts, Fall 2013); *50 Ways To Say You're Awesome*, by Alexandra Franzen (Sourcebooks, Fall 2013); *The Cosmic View Of Albert Einstein: His Reflections On Humanity And The Universe*, by Editors Walt Martin and Magda Ott (Sterling, Fall 2013); *Go Green, Spend Less, Live Better: The Ultimate Guide To Saving The Planet, Saving Money, And Protecting Your Health*, by Crissy Trask (Skyhorse, Spring 2013); *Pinfluence: The Complete Guide To Marketing Your Business With Pinterest*, by Beth Hayden (John Wiley & Sons, Summer 2012); *Stillpower: Excellence with Ease in Sports—and Life*, by Garret Kramer (Beyond Words/Atria/Simon & Schuster, Summer 2012); *Kissed by a Fox: And Other Stories of Friendship in Nature*, by Priscilla Stuckey (Counterpoint Press, Fall 2012); *The Mother's Wisdom Deck*, by Niki Dewart and Elizabeth Marglin (Sterling Publishing, Spring 2012).

TIPS "With years of experience as a literary agent, I have had the privilege of working with many gifted and inspiring writers. Some of them are bestselling authors and well-known experts in their field, but what makes them truly special, from my perspective, is their deep passion for their work, and their commitment to guiding, educating, and inspiring people around the world. At The Holmes Agency, I'm looking for considered and intelligent writing on a variety of nonfiction subjects. I am seeking authors focused on inspiring and helping positively transform readers' lives. I am open to queries, including from first time authors. However, please be aware that I don't generally represent authors without a platform."

HOPKINS LITERARY ASSOCIATES

2117 Buffalo Rd., Suite 327, Rochester NY 14624-1507. (585)352-6268. **Contact:** Pam Hopkins. Member of AAR. Other memberships include RWA.

REPRESENTS novels. **Considers these fiction areas:** romance, women's.

This agency specializes in women's fiction, particularly historical, contemporary, and category romance, as well as mainstream work.

HOW TO CONTACT Regular mail with synopsis, 3 sample chapters (or first 50 pages), SASE. Accepts simultaneous submissions. Obtains most new clients through recommendations from others, solicitations, conferences.

TERMS Agent receives 15% commission on domestic sales. Agent receives 20% commission on foreign sales. No written contract.

WRITERS CONFERENCES RWA National Conference.

HORNFISCHER LITERARY MANAGEMENT

P.O. Box 50544, Austin TX 78763. **E-mail:** queries@hornfischerlit.com. **Website:** www.hornfischerlit.com. **Contact:** James D. Hornfischer, president. Currently handles: nonfiction books 100%.

Prior to opening his agency, Mr. Hornfischer held editorial positions at HarperCollins and McGraw-Hill. "My New York editorial background is useful in this regard. In 17 years as an agent, I've handled 12 *New York Times* nonfiction bestsellers, including 3 No. 1's."

REPRESENTS nonfiction books. **Considers these nonfiction areas:** anthropology, archeology, autobiography, biography, business, child guidance, current affairs, economics, environment, government, health, history, how-to, humor, inspirational, investigative, law, medicine, memoirs, military, money, multicultural, parenting, popular culture, politics, psychology, religious, satire, science, self-help, sociology, sports, technology, true crime, war.

Actively seeking commercial nonfiction. Does not want poetry or genre fiction.

HOW TO CONTACT E-mail queries only. Responds if interested. Accepts simultaneous submissions. Responds in 5-6 weeks to submissions. Obtains most new clients through referrals from clients, reading books and magazines, pursuing ideas with New York editors.

TERMS Agent receives 15% commission on domestic sales. Agent receives 25% commission on foreign sales. Offers written contract.

TIPS "When you query agents and send out proposals, present yourself as someone who's in command of his material and comfortable in his own skin. Too many writers have a palpable sense of anxiety and insecurity. Take a deep breath and realize that—if you're good—someone in the publishing world will want you."

HSG AGENCY

287 Spring St., New York NY 10013. **E-mail:** channigan@hsgagency.com; jsalky@hsgagency.com; jgetzler@hsgagency.com; dburby@hsgagency.com. **Web-**

site: http://hsgagency.com. **Contact:** Carrie Hannigan; Jesseca Salky; Josh Getzler; Danielle Burby. Estab. 2011.

○ Prior to opening HSG Agency, Ms. Hannigan, Ms. Salky. and Mr. Getzler were agents at Russell & Volkening.

MEMBER AGENTS Carrie Hannigan, **Jesseca Salky** (literary and mainstream fiction), **Josh Getzler** (foreign and historical fiction; both women's fiction, straight ahead historical fiction, and thrillers and mysteries); **Danielle Burby** (YA, women's fiction, mysteries).

REPRESENTS Considers these nonfiction areas: business, creative nonfiction, current affairs, education, foods, memoirs, photography, politics, psychology, science. **Considers these fiction areas:** commercial, crime, historical, literary, middle grade, mystery, picture books, thriller, women's, young adult.

⌇ Ms. Hannigan is actively seeking both fiction and nonfiction children's books in the picture book and middle grade age range, as well as adult women's fiction and select photography projects that would appeal to a large audience. Ms. Salky is actively seeking literary and commercial fiction that appeals to women and men; "all types of nonfiction, with a particular interest in memoir and narrative nonfiction in the areas of science, pop-psychology, politics, current affairs, business, education, food, and any other topic that is the vehicle for a great story." Mr. Getzler is actively seeking adult historical and crime-related fiction (mystery, thriller), select nonfiction and YA projects (particularly those that fit within historical or crime fiction). He is also interested in smart women's fiction.

HOW TO CONTACT Electronic submissions only. Send query letter, first 5 pages of ms within e-mail to appropriate agent. Avoid submitting to multiple agents within the agency. Picture books: include entire ms. Responds in 4-6 weeks.

RECENT SALES *The Beginner's Goodbye*, by Anne Tyler (Knopf); *Blue Sea Burning*, by Geoff Rodkey (Putnam); *The Partner Track,* by Helen Wan (St. Martin's Press); *The Thrill of the Haunt*, by E.J. Copperman (Berkley) *Aces Wild*, by Erica Perl (Knopf Books for Young Readers); *Steve & Wessley: The Sea Monster*, by Jennifer Morris (Scholastic); *Infinite Worlds*, by Michael Soluri (Simon & Schuster).

◑ ANDREA HURST & ASSOCIATES

P.O. Box 1467, Coupeville WA 98239. **E-mail:** andrea@andreahurst.com. **Website:** www.andreahurst.com/literary-management/. **Contact:** Andrea Hurst. Represents 100+ clients. 50% of clients are new/unpublished writers.

○ Prior to becoming an agent, Ms. Hurst was an acquisitions editor as well as a freelance editor and published writer.

MEMBER AGENTS Andrea Hurst, queryandrea@andreahurst.com (adult fiction, women's fiction, nonfiction, including personal growth, health and wellness, science, business, parenting, relationships, women's issues, animals, spirituality, women's issues, metaphysical, psychological, cookbooks, and self-help); **Katie Reed**, querykate@andreahurst.com, (represents YA fiction and nonfiction and adult nonfiction); **Genevieve Nine**, querygenevieve@andreahurst.com (young adult, middle grade, mystery, thriller, historical, romantic comedy, magical realism, food memoir, travel memoir); **Amberly Finarelli** (not accepting new queries).

REPRESENTS nonfiction, novels, juvenile books. **Considers these nonfiction areas:** business, crafts, health, how-to, humor, inspirational, memoirs, parenting, popular culture, psychology, science, self-help, travel, true crime, women's issues. **Considers these fiction areas:** fantasy, historical, literary, mainstream, mystery, romance, science fiction, suspense, thriller, women's, young adult.

⌇ "We work directly with our signed authors to help them polish their work and their platform for optimum marketability. Our staff is always available to answer phone calls and e-mails from our authors and we stay with a project until we have exhausted all publishing avenues." Actively seeking "well written nonfiction by authors with a strong platform; superbly crafted fiction with depth that touches the mind and heart and all of our listed subjects." Does not want to receive horror, Western, poetry, or screenplays.

HOW TO CONTACT E-mail query with SASE. Submit outline/proposal, synopsis, 2 sample chapters, author bio. Query a specific agent after reviewing website. Use (agentfirstname)@andreahurst.com. Accepts simultaneous submissions. Obtains most new clients through recommendations from others, solicitations, conferences.

TERMS Agent receives 15% commission on domestic sales. Agent receives 20% commission on foreign sales. Offers written contract, binding for 6 to 12 months; 30-day notice must be given to terminate contract. This agency charges for postage. No reading fees.

RECENT SALES *Art of Healing*, by Bernie Siegel; *Truly, Madly, Deadly*, by Hannah Jayne; *Ultimate Poultry Cookbook*, by Chef John Ash; *The Guestbook*, by Andrea Hurst; *No Buddy Left Behind*, by Terrir Crisp and Cindy Hurn, Lyons Press; *A Year of Miracles* Dr. Bernie Siegel, NWL; *Selling Your Crafts on Etsy* (St. Martin's); *The Underground Detective Agency* (Kensington); *Alaskan Seafood Cookbook* (Globe Pequot); *Faith, Hope and Healing*, by Dr. Bernie Siegel (Rodale); *Code Name: Polar Ice*, by Jean-Michel Cousteau and James Fraioli (Gibbs Smith); *How to Host a Killer Party*, by Penny Warner (Berkley/Penguin).

WRITERS CONFERENCES San Francisco Writers' Conference; Willamette Writers' Conference; PNWA; Whidbey Island Writers Conference.

TIPS "Do your homework and submit a professional package. Get to know the agent you are submitting to by researching their website or meeting them at a conference. Perfect your craft: Write well and edit ruthlessly over and over again before submitting to an agent. Be realistic: Understand that publishing is a business and be prepared to prove why your book is marketable and how you will market it on your own. Be persistent! Andrea Hurst is no longer accepting unsolicited query letters. Unless you have been referred by one of our authors, an agent or publisher, please check our website for another appropriate agent. www.andreahurst.com."

⊕ INKLINGS LITERARY AGENCY

8363 Highgate Drive, Jacksonville FL 32216. (904)527-1686. **Fax:** (904)758-5440. **Website:** www.inklingsliterary.com. Estab. 2013.

MEMBER AGENTS Michelle Johnson, michelle@inklingsliterary.com (in fiction, contemporary, suspense, thriller, mystery, horror, fantasy—including paranormal and supernatural elements within those genres), romance of every level, nonfiction in the areas of memoir and true crime); **Dr. Jamie Bodnar Drowley**, jamie@inklingsliterary.com (new adult fiction in the areas of romance [all subgenres], fantasy [urban fantasy, light sci-fi, steampunk], mystery and thrillers—as well as young adult [all subgenres] and

middle grade stories); **Margaret Bail**, margaret@inklingsliterary.com (romance, science fiction, mystery, thrillers, action adventure, historical fiction, Western, some fantasy, memoir, cookbooks, true crime); **Naomi Davis**, naomi@inklingsliterary.com (romance of any variety—including paranormal, fresh urban fantasy, general fantasy, new adult and light sci-fi; young adult in any of those same genres; memoirs about living with disabilities, facing criticism, and mental illness); **Whitley Abell**, whitley@inklingsliterary.com (young adult, middle grade, and select upmarket women's fiction); **Alex Barba**, alex@inklingsliterary.com (YA fiction).

HOW TO CONTACT E-queries only. To query, type "Query (Agent Name)" plus the title of your novel in the subject line, then please send the following pasted into the body of the e-mail to query@inklingsliterary.com. Check the agency website to make sure that your targeted agent is currently open to submissions.

ⓘ INKWELL MANAGEMENT, LLC

521 Fifth Ave., 26th Floor, New York NY 10175. (212)922-3500. **Fax:** (212)922-0535. **E-mail:** submissions@inkwellmanagement.com. **Website:** www.inkwellmanagement.com. Represents 500 clients.

MEMBER AGENTS Stephen Barbara (select adult fiction and nonfiction); **Lizz Blaise** (literary fiction, women's and young adult fiction, suspense, and psychological thriller); **William Callahan** (nonfiction of all stripes, especially American history and memoir, pop culture and illustrated books, as well as voice-driven fiction that stands out from the crowd); **Michael V Carlisle**; **Catherine Drayton** (bestselling authors of books for children, young adults and women readers); **David Forrer** (literary, commercial, historical and crime fiction to suspense/thriller, humorous nonfiction and popular history); **Alexis Hurley** (literary and commercial fiction, memoir, narrative nonfiction and more); **Nathaniel Jacks** (memoir, narrative nonfiction, social sciences, health, current affairs, business, religion, and popular history, as well as fiction—literary and commercial, women's, young adult, historical, short story, among others); **Alyssa Mozdzen**; **Jacqueline Murphy**; (fiction, children's books, graphic novels and illustrated works, and compelling narrative nonfiction); **Richard Pine**; **Eliza Rothstein** (literary and commercial fiction, narrative nonfiction, memoir, popular science, and food writing); **Emma Schlee** (literary fiction, the occasional thriller, travel and adventure books, and popular culture and philosophy books); **Hannah Schwartz**; **David Hale Smith**; **Lauren Smythe** (smart narrative nonfiction [narrative journalism, modern history, biography, cultural criticism, personal essay, humor], personality-driven practical nonfiction [cookbooks, fashion and style], and contemporary literary fiction); **Kimberly Witherspoon**; **Monika Woods** (literary and commercial fiction, young adult, memoir, and compelling nonfiction in popular culture, science, and current affairs); **Lena Yarbrough** (literary fiction, upmarket commercial fiction, memoir, narrative nonfiction, history, investigative journalism, and cultural criticism).

REPRESENTS nonfiction books, novels. **Considers these nonfiction areas:** biography, business, cooking, creative nonfiction, current affairs, foods, health, history, humor, memoirs, popular culture, religious, science. **Considers these fiction areas:** commercial, crime, historical, literary, middle grade, picture books, romance, short story collections, suspense, thriller, women's, young adult.

HOW TO CONTACT In the body of your e-mail, please include a query letter and a short writing sample (1-2 chapters). We currently accept submissions in all genres except screenplays. Due to the volume of queries we receive, our response time may take up to two months. Feel free to put "Query for [Agent Name]: [Your Book Title]" in the e-mail subject line. Obtains most new clients through recommendations from others.

TERMS Agent receives 15% commission on domestic sales. Agent receives 20% commission on foreign sales. Offers written contract.

TIPS "We will not read mss before receiving a letter of inquiry."

⊘⊚ ICM PARTNERS

730 Fifth Ave., New York NY 10019. (212)556-5600. **Website:** www.icmtalent.com. **Contact:** Literary Department. Member of AAR. Signatory of WGA.

REPRESENTS nonfiction, fiction, novels, juvenile books.

⽛ *"We do not accept unsolicited submissions."*

HOW TO CONTACT This agency is generally not open to unsolicited submissions. However, some agents do attend conferences and meet writers then. The agents take referrals, as well. Obtains most new clients through recommendations from others.

TERMS Agent receives 15% commission on domestic sales. Agent receives 20% commission on foreign sales.

⊘ INTERNATIONAL TRANSACTIONS, INC.

P.O. Box 97, Gila NM 88038-0097. (845)373-9696. **Fax:** (480)393-5162. **E-mail:** submission-nonfiction@intltrans.com; submission-fiction@intltrans.com. **Website:** www.intltrans.com. **Contact:** Peter Riva.

MEMBER AGENTS Peter Riva (nonfiction, fiction, illustrated; television and movie rights placement); **Sandra Riva** (fiction, juvenile, biographies); **JoAnn Collins** (fiction, women's fiction, medical fiction).

REPRESENTS nonfiction books, novels, short story collections, juvenile, scholarly, illustrated books, anthologies. **Considers these nonfiction areas:** anthropology, archeology, architecture, art, autobiography, biography, computers, cooking, cultural interests, current affairs, diet/nutrition, design, ethnic, foods, gay/lesbian, government, health, history, humor, investigative, language, law, literature, medicine, memoirs, military, music, photography, politics, satire, science, sports, translation, true crime, war, women's issues, women's studies. **Considers these fiction areas:** action, adventure, crime, detective, erotica, experimental, family saga, feminist, gay, historical, humor, lesbian, literary, mainstream, mystery, police, satire, spiritual, sports, suspense, thriller, women's, young adult, chick lit.

⽛ "We specialize in large and small projects, helping qualified authors perfect material for publication." Actively seeking intelligent, well-written innovative material that breaks new ground. Does not want to receive material influenced by TV (too much dialogue); a rehash of previous successful novels' themes, or poorly prepared material.

HOW TO CONTACT First, e-query with an outline or synopsis. E-queries only. Put "Query: [Title]" in the e-mail subject line. Responds in 3 weeks to queries. Responds in 5 weeks to mss. Obtains most new clients through recommendations from others, solicitations.

TERMS Agent receives 15% (25% on illustrated books) commission on domestic sales. Agent receives 20% commission on foreign sales. Offers written contract; 120-day notice must be given to terminate contract.

TIPS 'Book'—a published work of literature. That last word is the key. Not a string of words, not a book of

(TV or film) 'scenes,' and never a stream of consciousness unfathomable by anyone outside of the writer's coterie. A writer should only begin to get 'interested in getting an agent' if the work is polished, literate and ready to be presented to a publishing house. Anything less is either asking for a quick rejection or is a thinly disguised plea for creative assistance—which is often given but never fiscally sound for the agents involved. Writers, even published authors, have difficulty in being objective about their own work. Friends and family are of no assistance in that process either. Writers should attempt to get their work read by the most unlikely and stern critic as part of the editing process, months before any agent is approached. In another matter: the economics of our job have changed as well. As the publishing world goes through the transition to e-books (much as the music industry went through the change to downloadable music)—a transition we expect to see at 95% within 10 years—everyone is nervous and wants 'assured bestsellers' from which to eke out a living until they know what the new e-world will bring. This makes the sales rate and, especially, the advance royalty rates, plummet. Hence, our ability to take risks and take on new clients' work is increasingly perilous financially for us and all agents."

ⓓ JABBERWOCKY LITERARY AGENCY

49 West 45th St., New York NY 10036. (718)392-5985. **Website:** www.awfulagent.com. **Contact:** Joshua Bilmes. Other memberships include SFWA. Represents 40 clients. 15% of clients are new/unpublished writers. Currently handles: nonfiction books 15%, novels 75%, scholarly books 5%, other 5% other.

MEMBER AGENTS Joshua Bilmes; Eddie Schneider; Lisa Rodgers; Sam Morgan.

REPRESENTS novels. **Considers these nonfiction areas:** autobiography, biography, business, cooking, current affairs, diet/nutrition, economics, film, foods, gay/lesbian, government, health, history, humor, language, law, literature, medicine, money, popular culture, politics, satire, science, sociology, sports, theater, war, women's issues, women's studies, young adult. **Considers these fiction areas:** action, adventure, contemporary issues, crime, detective, ethnic, family saga, fantasy, gay, glitz, historical, horror, humor, lesbian, literary, mainstream, middle grade, police, psychic, regional, satire, science fiction, sports, supernatural, thriller, young adult.

⌐ This agency represents quite a lot of genre fiction and is actively seeking to increase the amount of nonfiction projects. It does not handle children's or picture books. Book-length material only—no poetry, articles, or short fiction.

HOW TO CONTACT "We are currently open to unsolicited queries. No e-mail, phone, or fax queries, please. Query with SASE. Please check our website, as there may be times during the year when we are not accepting queries. Query letter only; no ms material unless requested." Accepts simultaneous submissions. Responds in 3 weeks to queries. Obtains most new clients through solicitations, recommendation by current clients.

TERMS Agent receives 15% commission on domestic sales. Agent receives 20% commission on foreign sales. Offers written contract, binding for 1 year. Charges clients for book purchases, photocopying, international book/ms mailing.

RECENT SALES 188 individual deals done in 2014: 60 domestic and 128 foreign. *Alcatraz #5* by Brandon Sanderson; *Aurora Teagarden* by Charlaine Harris; *The Unnoticeables* by Robert Brockway; *Messenger's Legacy* by Peter V. Brett; *Slotter Key* by Elizabeth Moon. Other clients include Tanya Huff, Simon Green, Jack Campbell, Myke Cole, Marie Brennan, Daniel Jose Older, Jim Hines, Mark Hodder, Toni Kelner, Ari Marmell, Ellery Queen, Erin Tettensor, and Walter Jon Williams.

TIPS "In approaching with a query, the most important things to us are your credits and your biographical background to the extent it's relevant to your work. I (and most agents) will ignore the adjectives you may choose to describe your own work."

ⓓ JAMES PETER ASSOCIATES, INC.

P.O. Box 358, New Canaan CT 06840. (203)972-1070. **E-mail:** gene_brissie@msn.com. **Website:** www.jamespeterassociates.com. **Contact:** Gene Brissie. Represents 75 individual and 6 corporate clients. 15% of clients are new/unpublished writers. Currently handles: nonfiction books 100%.

REPRESENTS nonfiction books. **Considers these nonfiction areas:** anthropology, archeology, architecture, art, biography, business, current affairs, dance, design, ethnic, film, gay/lesbian, government, health, history, language, literature, medicine, mil-

NEW AGENT SPOTLIGHT

LEILA CAMPOLI
STONESONG LITERARY

Stonesong.com

@lwcampoli

ABOUT LEILA: Before joining Stonesong, she was an editor at Palgrave Macmillan. Some of her previous titles include: Mark D. White's *The Illusion of Wellbeing*, Gudrun Johnsen's *Bringing Down the Banking Industry*, Deborah Gregory's *Unmasking Financial Psychopaths*, and Matt Ragas and Ron Culp's *Business Essentials for Strategic Communicators*.

SHE IS SEEKING: prescriptive and narrative nonfiction projects in business, finance, investing, science, pop culture, and current events. Her ideal author has a strong platform, groundbreaking ideas, and unique style. She's particularly interested in books that offer a window into remarkable lives and little known operations. Please no fiction, poetry, or screenplays.

HOW TO SUBMIT: submissions@stonesong.com. Put "Query for Leila: [Title]" in the subject line of your e-mail. No attachments. "If you have not received a request from us within 12 weeks, consider that we have passed."

itary, money, music, popular culture, psychology, self-help, theater, travel, war, women's issues, women's studies, memoirs (political, business).

➤ "We are especially interested in general, trade, and reference nonfiction." Does not want to receive children's/young adult books, poetry, or fiction.

HOW TO CONTACT Submit proposal package, outline, SASE. Prefers to read materials exclusively. Responds in 1 month to queries. Obtains most new clients through recommendations from others, solicitations, contact with people who are doing interesting things.

TERMS Agent receives 15% commission on domestic sales. Agent receives 20% commission on foreign sales. Offers written contract.

⊙ JANKLOW & NESBIT ASSOCIATES

445 Park Ave., New York NY 10022. (212)421-1700. **Fax:** (212)980-3671. **E-mail:** submissions@janklow. com. **Website:** www.janklowandnesbit.com. Estab. 1989.

MEMBER AGENTS Morton L. Janklow; Anne Sibbald; Lynn Nesbit; Luke Janklow; Cullen Stanley; **PJ Mark** (interests are eclectic, including short stories and literary novels. His nonfiction interests include journalism, popular culture, memoir/narrative, essays and cultural criticism); **Richard Morris** (books that challenge our common assumptions, be it in the fields of cultural history, business, food, sports, science or faith); **Paul Lucas** (literary and commercial fiction, focusing on literary thrillers, science fiction and fantasy; also seeks narrative histories of ideas and objects, as well as biographies and popular science);

Emma Parry (nonfiction by experts, but will consider outstanding literary fiction and upmarket commercial fiction. I'm not looking for children's books, middle grade, or fantasy); **Alexandra Machinist**; **Kirby Kim** (formerly of WME).

REPRESENTS nonfiction, fiction.

HOW TO CONTACT Query via snail mail or e-mail. Include a synopsis and the first 10 pages if sending fiction (no attachments). For nonfiction, send a query and full outline. Address your submission to an individual agent. Accepts simultaneous submissions. Responds in 8 weeks to queries/mss. Obtains most new clients through recommendations from others.

TIPS "Please send a short query with first 10 pages or artwork."

J DE S ASSOCIATES, INC.

9 Shagbark Road, Wilson Point, South Norwalk CT 06854. (203)838-7571. **E-mail:** Jdespoel@aol.com. **Website:** www.jdesassociates.com. **Contact:** Jacques de Spoelberch.

 Prior to opening his agency, Mr. de Spoelberch was an editor with Houghton Mifflin.

REPRESENTS nonfiction books, novels. **Considers these nonfiction areas:** biography, business, cultural interests, current affairs, economics, ethnic, government, health, history, law, medicine, metaphysics, military, New Age, personal improvement, politics, self-help, sociology, sports, translation. **Considers these fiction areas:** crime, detective, frontier, historical, juvenile, literary, mainstream, mystery, New Age, police, suspense, westerns, young adult.

HOW TO CONTACT "Brief queries by regular mail and e-mail are welcomed for fiction and nonfiction, but kindly do not include sample proposals or other material unless specifically requested to do so." Responds in 2 months to queries. Obtains most new clients through recommendations from authors and other clients.

TERMS Agent receives 15% commission on domestic sales. Agent receives 20% commission on foreign sales. Charges clients for foreign postage and photocopying.

RECENT SALES Joshilyn Jackson's new novel *A Grown-Up Kind of Pretty* (Grand Central), Margaret George's final Tudor historical *Elizabeth I* (Penguin), the fifth in Leighton Gage's series of Brazilian thrillers *A Vine in the Blood* (Soho), Genevieve Graham's romance *Under the Same Sky* (Berkley Sensa-

tion), Hilary Holladay's biography of the early Beat Herbert Huncke, *American Hipster* (Magnus), Ron Rozelle's *My Boys and Girls Are In There: The 1937 New London School Explosion* (Texas A&M), the concluding novel in Dom Testa's YA science fiction series, *The Galahad Legacy* (Tor), and Bruce Coston's new collection of animal stories *The Gift of Pets* (St. Martin's Press).

◑ THE CAROLYN JENKS AGENCY

30 Cambridge Park Dr., #3150, Cambridge MA 02140. (617)354-5099. **E-mail:** queries@carolynjenksagency.com. **Website:** www.carolynjenksagency.com. **Contact:** Carolyn Jenks. Estab. 1987. Signatory of WGA

MEMBER AGENTS Carolyn Jenks; Eric Wing. "See agency website for current member preferences" as well as a list of junior agents.

REPRESENTS **Considers these nonfiction areas:** architecture, art, autobiography, biography, business, cultural interests, current affairs, design, education, ethnic, gay/lesbian, government, history, juvenile nonfiction, language, law, literature, memoirs, metaphysics, military, money, music, New Age, religious, science, technology, translation, true crime, women's issues, women's studies. **Considers these fiction areas:** action, adventure, ethnic, experimental, family saga, fantasy, feminist, frontier, gay, historical, horror, humor, inspirational, juvenile, lesbian, literary, mainstream, mystery, psychic, regional, religious, science fiction, supernatural, thriller, westerns, women's, young adult. **Considers these script areas:** autobiography, biography, contemporary issues, ethnic, experimental, family saga, fantasy, feminist, frontier, gay, historical, horror, inspirational, lesbian, mainstream, mystery, psychic, religious, romantic comedy, romantic drama, science fiction, supernatural, suspense, thriller, western.

HOW TO CONTACT Please submit a one page query including a brief bio via the form on the agency website. "Due to the high volume of queries we receive, we are unable to respond to everyone. Queries are reviewed on a rolling basis, and we will follow up directly with the author if there is interest in a full manuscript. Queries should not be addressed to specific agents. All queries go directly to the director for distribution." Accepts simultaneous submissions. Obtains new clients by recommendations from others, queries/submissions, agency outreach.

TERMS Offers written contract, 1-3 years depending on the project. Requires 60 day notice before terminating contract.

TIPS "Do not make cold calls to the agency. E-mail contact only. Do not query for more than one property at a time. If possible, have a professional photograph of yourself ready to submit with your query, as it is important to be media-genic in today's marketplace. Be ready to discuss platform."

JET LITERARY ASSOCIATES

941 Calle Mejia, #507, Santa Fe NM 87501. (505)780-0721. **E-mail:** etp@jetliterary.com. **Website:** www.jetliterary.com. **Contact:** Liz Trupin-Pulli. Represents 75 clients. 35% of clients are new/unpublished writers. **MEMBER AGENTS** Liz Trupin-Pulli (adult fiction/nonfiction; romance, mysteries, parenting); **Jim Trupin** (adult fiction/nonfiction, military history, pop culture).

REPRESENTS nonfiction books, novels, short story collections.

"JET was founded in New York in 1975, so we bring a wealth of knowledge and contacts, as well as quite a bit of expertise to our representation of writers." JET represents the full range of adult fiction and nonfiction, including humor and cookbooks Does not want to receive YA, sci-fi, fantasy, horror, poetry, children's, or religious books.

HOW TO CONTACT An e-query only is accepted. Responds in 1 week to queries. Responds in 8 weeks to mss. Obtains most new clients through recommendations from others, solicitations, conferences.

TERMS Agent receives 15% commission on domestic sales. Agent receives 10% commission on foreign sales, while foreign agent receives 10%. Offers written agency contract, binding for 3 years. This agency charges for reimbursement of mailing and any photocopying.

TIPS "Do not write cute queries; stick to a straightforward message that includes the title and what your book is about, why you are suited to write this particular book, and what you have written in the past (if anything), along with a bit of a bio."

KELLER MEDIA INC.

578 Washington Blvd., No. 745, Marina del Rey CA 90292. (800)278-8706. **Website:** www.KellerMedia.com. **Contact:** Wendy Keller, senior agent; Megan Close, associate agent; Elise Howard, query manager.

Estab. 1989. Member of the National Speakers Association. 25% of clients are new/unpublished writers. Currently handles: nonfiction books 100%.

Prior to becoming an agent, Ms. Keller was an award-winning journalist and worked for PR Newswire.

REPRESENTS nonfiction. **Considers these nonfiction areas:** business, current affairs, health, history, politics, psychology, science, self-help, sociology, women's issues.

All of our authors are highly credible experts, who have or want to create a significant platform in media, academia, politics, paid professional speaking, syndicated columns, and/or regular appearances on radio/TV. Does not want (and absolutely will not respond to) fiction, true crime, scripts, teleplays, poetry, juvenile, anything Christian, picture books, illustrated books, first-person stories of mental or physical illness, wrongful incarceration, abduction by aliens, books channeled by aliens, demons, or dead celebrities (I wish I was kidding!)."

HOW TO CONTACT "To query, just go to www.KellerMedia.com/query and fill in the simple form; it takes 1 minute or less. You'll get a fast, courteous response. Please do not mail us anything unless requested to do so by a staff member." Accepts simultaneous submissions. Responds in 7 days or less. Obtains most new clients through referrals.

TERMS Agent receives 15% commission on domestic sales. Agent receives 20% commission on foreign, dramatic, sponsorship, appearance fees, audio, and merchandising deals. "30% on speaking engagements we book for the author."

TIPS "Don't send a query to any agent (including us) unless you're certain they handle the type of book you're writing. 90% of all rejections happen because what someone offered us doesn't fit our established, advertised, printed, touted and shouted guidelines. Be organized! Have your proposal in order before you query. Never make apologies for 'bad writing' or sloppy content. Please just get it right before you waste your 1 shot with us. Have something new, different or interesting to say and be ready to dedicate your whole heart to marketing it. Marketing is everything in publishing these days."

🄐 NATASHA KERN LITERARY AGENCY

P.O. Box 1069, White Salmon WA 98672. (509)493-3803. **E-mail:** queries@natashakern.com. **Website:** www.natashakern.com. **Contact:** Natasha Kern. Other memberships include RWA, MWA, SinC, The Authors Guild, and American Society of Journalists and Authors

🄞 Prior to opening her agency, Ms. Kern worked as an editor and publicist for Simon & Schuster, Bantam, and Ballantine. This agency has sold more than 700 books.

MEMBER AGENTS Natasha Kern; Sue Brower.

REPRESENTS Considers these nonfiction areas: animals, child guidance, cultural interests, current affairs, environment, ethnic, gardening, health, inspirational, medicine, metaphysics, New Age, parenting, popular culture, psychology, religious, self-help, spirituality, women's issues, women's studies, investigative journalism. **Considers these fiction areas:** commercial, historical, inspirational, mainstream, multicultural, mystery, religious, romance, suspense, thriller, women's.

🗝 "This agency specializes in commercial fiction and nonfiction for adults, including historical novels from any country or time period; contemporary fiction including novels with romance or suspense elements; and multi-cultural fiction. We are also seeking inspirational fiction in a broad range of genres including: suspense and mysteries, historicals, romance, and contemporary novels. Does not represent horror, true crime, erotica, children's books, short stories or novellas, poetry, screenplays, technical, photography or art/craft books, cookbooks, travel, or sports books.

HOW TO CONTACT This agency is currently closed to unsolicited fiction and nonfiction submissions. Accepts simultaneous submissions.

TERMS Agent receives 15% commission on domestic sales. Agent receives 20% commission on foreign sales. Agent receives 15% commission on film sales.

RECENT SALES Sold 43 titles in the last year. *China Dolls*, by Michelle Yu and Blossom Kan (St. Martin's); *Bastard Tongues*, by Derek Bickerton (Farrar Strauss); *Bone Rattler*, by Eliot Pattison; *Wicked Pleasure*, by Nina Bangs (Berkley); *Inviting God In*, by David Aaron (Shambhala); *Unlawful Contact*, by Pamela Clare (Berkley); *Dead End Dating*, by Kimberly Raye (Ballantine); *A Scent of Roses*, by Nikki Arana (Baker Book House); *The Sexiest Man Alive*, by Diana Holquist (Warner Books).

WRITERS CONFERENCES RWA National Conference; MWA National Conference; ACFW Conference; and many regional conferences.

TIPS "Your chances of being accepted for representation will be greatly enhanced by going to our website first. Our idea of a dream client is someone who participates in a mutually respectful business relationship, is clear about needs and goals, and communicates about career planning. If we know what you need and want, we can help you achieve it. A dream client has a storytelling gift, a commitment to a writing career, a desire to learn and grow, and a passion for excellence. We want clients who are expressing their own unique voice and truly have something of their own to communicate. This client understands that many people have to work together for a book to succeed and that everything in publishing takes far longer than one imagines. Trust and communication are truly essential."

🄞 VIRGINIA KIDD LITERARY AGENCY, INC.

P.O. Box 278, Milford PA 18337. (570)296-6205. **Fax:** (570)296-7266. **Website:** www.vk-agency.com. Other memberships include SFWA, SFRA. Represents 80 clients.

REPRESENTS novels. **Considers these fiction areas:** fantasy, science fiction, speculative.

🗝 This agency specializes in science fiction and fantasy. "The Virginia Kidd Literary Agency is one of the longest established, science fiction specialized literary agencies in the world—with almost half a century of rich experience in the science fiction and fantasy genres. Our client list reads like a top notch 'who's-who' of science fiction: Beth Bernobich, Gene Wolfe, Anne McCaffrey, Ted Chiang, Alan Dean Foster and others set the bar very high indeed.Our authors have won Hugos, Nebulas, World Fantasy, Tiptree, National Book Award, PEN Malamud, SFWA Grandmaster, Gandalf, Locus Award, Margaret Edwards Award, IAMTW Lifetime Achievement Award (Grand Master), Rhysling Award, Author Emeritus SFWA, BSFA Award—and more. The point is, we represent the best of the best.We welcome queries from prospective and published authors."

HOW TO CONTACT Snail mail queries only.

TERMS Agent receives 15% commission on domestic sales. Agent receives 20-25% commission on foreign sales. Agent receives 20% commission on film sales. Offers written contract; 2-month notice must be given to terminate contract. Charges clients occasionally for extraordinary expenses.

RECENT SALES *Sagramanda*, by Alan Dean Foster (Pyr); *Incredible Good Fortune*, by Ursula K. Le Guin (Shambhala); *The Wizard and Soldier of Sidon*, by Gene Wolfe (Tor); *Voices and Powers*, by Ursula K. Le Guin (Harcourt); *Galileo's Children*, by Gardner Dozois (Pyr); *The Light Years Beneath My Feet* and *Running From the Deity*, by Alan Dean Foster (Del Ray); *Chasing Fire*, by Michelle Welch. Other clients include Eleanor Arnason, Ted Chiang, Jack Skillingstead, Daryl Gregory, Patricia Briggs, and the estates for James Tiptree, Jr., Murray Leinster, E.E. "Doc" Smith, R.A. Lafferty.

TIPS "If you have a completed novel that is of extraordinary quality, please send us a query."

◐ HARVEY KLINGER, INC.

300 W. 55th St., Suite 11V, New York NY 10019. (212)581-7068. **E-mail:** queries@harveyklinger.com. **Website:** www.harveyklinger.com. **Contact:** Harvey Klinger. Member of AAR. Represents 100 clients. 25% of clients are new/unpublished writers. Currently handles: nonfiction books 50%, novels 50%.

MEMBER AGENTS **Harvey Kliinger**; **David Dunton** (popular culture, music-related books, literary fiction, young adult, fiction, and memoirs); **Sara Crowe** (children's and young adult authors, adult fiction and nonfiction, foreign rights sales); **Andrea Somberg** (literary fiction, commercial fiction, romance, sci-fi/fantasy, mysteries/thrillers, young adult, middle grade, quality narrative nonfiction, popular culture, how-to, self-help, humor, interior design, cookbooks, health/fitness).

REPRESENTS nonfiction books, novels. **Considers these nonfiction areas:** autobiography, biography, cooking, diet/nutrition, foods, health, investigative, medicine, psychology, science, self-help, spirituality, sports, technology, true crime, women's issues, women's studies. **Considers these fiction areas:** action, adventure, crime, detective, family saga, glitz, literary, mainstream, mystery, police, suspense, thriller.

8— This agency specializes in big, mainstream, contemporary fiction and nonfiction.

HOW TO CONTACT Use online e-mail submission form on the website, or query with SASE via snail mail. No phone or fax queries. Don't send unsolicited manuscripts or e-mail attachments. Make submission letter to the point and as brief as possible. Responds in 2-4 weeks to queries, if interested. Obtains most new clients through recommendations from others.

TERMS Agent receives 15% commission on domestic sales. Agent receives 25% commission on foreign sales. Offers written contract. Charges for photocopying mss and overseas postage for mss.

RECENT SALES *Rainbows on the Moon*, by Barbara Wood; *I Am Not a Serial Killer*, by Dan Wells; *Me, Myself and Us*, by Brian Little; *The Secret of Magic*, by Deborah Johnson; *Children of the Mist*; by Paula Quinn. Other clients include: George Taber, Terry Kay, Scott Mebus, Jacqueline Kolosov, Jonathan Maberry, Tara Altebrando, Alex McAuley, Eva Nagorski, Greg Kot, Justine Musk, Michael Northrup, Nina LaCour, Ashley Kahn, Barbara De Angelis.

O KNEERIM & WILLIAMS

90 Canal St., Boston MA 02114. **Website:** http://www.kwblit.com. Also located in New York and Washington D.C. Estab. 1990.

MEMBER AGENTS **Katherine Flynn**, flynn@kwblit.com (history, biography, politics, current affairs, adventure, nature, pop culture, science, and psychology for nonfiction and particularly loves exciting narrative nonfiction; literary and commercial fiction with urban or foreign locales, crime novels, insight into women's lives, biting wit, and historical settings); **Jill Kneerim**, jill@kwblit.com (narrative history; sociology; psychology and anthropology; biography; women's issues; and good writing); **Ike Williams**, jtwilliams@kwblit.com (biography, history, politics, natural science, and anthropology); **Carol Franco**, carolfranco@comcast.net (business; nonfiction; distinguished self-help/how-to); **Gerald Gross**, ggreens336@comcast.net (array of nonfiction, serious history, and memoir).

8— Actively seeking distinguished authors, experts, professionals, intellectuals, and serious writers.

HOW TO CONTACT E-query an individual agent. Send no attachments. Put "Query" in the subject line. Accepts simultaneous submissions. Obtains most new clients through recommendations from others.

THE KNIGHT AGENCY

E-mail: submissions@knightagency.net. **Website:** http://knightagency.net/.

MEMBER AGENTS Deidre Knight (romance, women's fiction, commercial fiction, inspirational, memoir and nonfiction narrative, personal finance, business, popular culture, self-help, religion, health, and parenting); **Judson Knight**; **Pamela Harty** (contemporary and historical romance, romantic suspense, women's fiction, young adult, business, motivational, diet and health, memoir, parenting, pop culture, and true crime); **Elaine Spencer** (romance, women's fiction, young adult and middle grade material); **Lucienne Diver** (fantasy, science fiction, romance, romantica, suspense and young adult); **Nephele Tempest** (literary/commercial fiction, women's fiction, fantasy, science fiction, romantic suspense, paranormal romance, contemporary romance, historical fiction, young adult and middle grade fiction); **Melissa Jeglinski** (romance [contemporary, category, historical, inspirational], young adult, middle grade, women's fiction and mystery); **Travis Pennington** (young adult, middle grade, mysteries, thrillers, commercial fiction, and romance [nothing paranormal/fantasy in any genre for now]).

REPRESENTS Considers these fiction areas: commercial, fantasy, middle grade, new adult, romance, science fiction, thriller, women's, young adult.

⊶ Does not want to receive screenplays, short stories, poetry, essays, or children's picture books.

HOW TO CONTACT E-queries only. "Your submission should include a 1-page query letter and the first 5 pages of your ms. All text must be contained in the body of your e-mail. Attachments will not be opened nor included in the consideration of your work. Queries must be addressed to a specific agent. Please do not query multiple agents."

LINDA KONNER LITERARY AGENCY

10 W. 15th St., Suite 1918, New York NY 10011. (212)691-3419. **E-mail:** ldkonner@cs.com. **Website:** www.lindakonnerliteraryagency.com. **Contact:** Linda Konner. Member of AAR. Signatory of WGA. Other memberships include ASJA. Represents 85 clients. 30-35% of clients are new/unpublished writers. Currently handles: nonfiction books 100%.

REPRESENTS nonfiction books. **Considers these nonfiction areas:** gay/lesbian, health, medicine, money, parenting, popular culture, psychology, science, self-help, women's issues, biography (celebrity), African American and Latino issues, relationships, popular science.

⊶ This agency specializes in health, self-help, and how-to books. Authors/co-authors must be top experts in their field with a substantial media platform.

HOW TO CONTACT Query by e-mail or by mail with SASE, synopsis, author bio, sufficient return postage. Prefers to read materials exclusively for 2 weeks. Accepts simultaneous submissions. Obtains most new clients through recommendations from others, occasional solicitation among established authors/journalists.

TERMS Agent receives 15% commission on domestic sales. Agent receives 25% commission on foreign sales. Offers written contract. Charges one-time fee for domestic expenses; additional expenses may be incurred for foreign sales.

RECENT SALES *The Calorie Myth* (*New York Times* bestseller) by Jonathan Bailor (Harper Wave); *Outsmarting Anger* (winner, Books for a Better Life award) by Joseph Shrand, M.D., with Leigh Devine and the editors of Harvard Health Publications (Jossey-Bass/Wiley); *Lucky Me: My Life With And Without My Mother, Shirley Maclaine* by Sachi Parker with Frederick Stroppel (Gotham/Penguin); *80/20 Running* by Matt Fitzgerald (NAL/Penguin).

WRITERS CONFERENCES ASJA Writers Conference, Harvard Medical School's "Publishing Books, Memoirs, and Other Creative Nonfiction" Annual Conference.

BARBARA S. KOUTS, LITERARY AGENT

P.O. Box 560, Bellport NY 11713. (631)286-1278. **Fax:** (631) 286-1538. **Contact:** Barbara S. Kouts. Member of AAR. Represents 50 clients. 10% of clients are new/unpublished writers.

REPRESENTS juvenile.

⊶ This agency specializes in children's books.

HOW TO CONTACT Query with SASE. Accepts solicited queries by snail mail only. Accepts simultaneous submissions. Obtains most new clients through recommendations from others, solicitations, conferences.

TERMS Agent receives 10% commission on domestic sales. Agent receives 20% commission on foreign sales. This agency charges clients for photocopying.

RECENT SALES *Code Talker*, by Joseph Bruchac (Dial); *The Penderwicks*, by Jeanne Birdsall (Knopf); *Froggy's Baby Sister*, by Jonathan London (Viking).

TIPS "Write, do not call. Be professional in your writing."

◑ KRAAS LITERARY AGENCY

E-mail: ikraas@yahoo.com. **Website:** www.kraasliterarygency.com. **Contact:** Irene Kraas. Estab. 1990.

MEMBER AGENTS Irene Kraas, principal.

REPRESENTS Considers these fiction areas: mystery, thriller.

⌐ This agency is interested in working with published writers, but that does not mean self-published writers. Does not want to receive short stories, plays, or poetry. This agency no longer represents adult fantasy, or science fiction.

HOW TO CONTACT Query and e-mail the first 10 pages of a completed ms. Requires exclusive read on mss. Attachments aren't accepted. Accepts simultaneous submissions.

TERMS Offers written contract.

TIPS "I am interested in material—in any genre—that is truly, truly unique."

◑ STUART KRICHEVSKY LITERARY AGENCY, INC.

381 Park Ave. S., Suite 428, New York NY 10016. (212)725-5288. **Fax:** (212)725-5275. **Website:** www.skagency.com. Member of AAR.

MEMBER AGENTS Stuart Krichevsky, query@skagency.com (emphasis on narrative nonfiction, literary journalism, and literary and commercial fiction); **Allison Hunter**, AHquery@skagency.com (literary and commercial fiction, memoir, narrative nonfiction, cultural studies and pop culture; she is always looking for funny female writers, great love stories, family epics, and for nonfiction projects that speak to the current cultural climate); **Ross Harris**, RHquery@skagency.com (voice-driven humor and memoir, books on popular culture and our society, narrative nonfiction and literary fiction); **David Patterson**, dp@skagency.com (writers of upmarket narrative nonfiction and literary fiction, historians, journalists and thought leaders); **Shana Cohen**.

REPRESENTS nonfiction books, novels. **Considers these nonfiction areas:** creative nonfiction, humor, memoirs, popular culture. **Considers these fiction areas:** commercial, contemporary issues, literary.

HOW TO CONTACT Please send a query letter and the first few (up to 10) pages of your ms or proposal in the body of an e-mail (not an attachment) to one of the e-mail addresses. No attachments. Responds if interested. Obtains most new clients through recommendations from others, solicitations.

EDITE KROLL LITERARY AGENCY, INC.

20 Cross St., Saco ME 04072. (207)283-8797. **Fax:** (207)283-8799. **E-mail:** ekroll@maine.rr.com. **Contact:** Edite Kroll. Represents 45 clients. 20% of clients are new/unpublished writers.

○ Prior to opening her agency, Ms. Kroll served as a book editor and translator.

⌐ "We represent writers and writer-artists of both adult and children's books. We have a special focus on international feminist writers, women writers of nonfiction, and artists who write their own books (including children's and humor books)." Actively seeking artists who write their own books and international feminists who write in English. Does not represent genre fiction (mysteries, thrillers, diet, cookery, etc.), photography books, coffee table books, romance, or commercial fiction.

HOW TO CONTACT Query with SASE or by e-mail. Submit outline/proposal, synopsis, 1-2 sample chapters, author bio, entire ms (or dummy) if sending picture book. No phone queries. Responds in 2-4 weeks to queries. Responds in 4-8 weeks to mss. Obtains most new clients through recommendations from others.

TERMS Agent receives 15% commission on domestic sales. Agent receives 20% commission on foreign sales. Offers written contract; 30-day notice must be given to terminate contract. Charges clients for photocopying and legal fees with prior approval from writer.

RECENT SALES Sold 12 domestic/30 foreign titles in the last year. Clients include Shel Silverstein and Charlotte Zolotow estates.

TIPS "Please do your research so you won't send me books/proposals I specifically excluded."

◑ KT LITERARY, LLC

9249 S. Broadway, #200-543, Highlands Ranch CO 80129. (720)344-4728. **Fax:** (720)344-4728. **E-mail:** queries@ktliterary.com. **Website:** http://ktliterary.com. **Contact:** Kate Schafer Testerman. Member of AAR. Other memberships include SCBWI. Represents 20 clients. 60% of clients are new/unpublished writers.

○ Prior to her current position, Ms. Schafer was an agent with Janklow & Nesbit.

MEMBER AGENTS Kate Schafer (middle grade and young adult); **Renee Nyen** (middle grade and young adult); **Sara Megibow**, saraquery@ktliterary.com (middle grade, young adult, new adult, romance, erotica, science fiction and fantasy; LGBTQ and diversity friendly).

REPRESENTS Considers these fiction areas: middle grade, young adult.

⚷ "We're thrilled to be actively seeking new clients writing brilliant, funny, original middle grade and young adult fiction, both literary and commercial." Does not want picture books, serious nonfiction, and adult literary fiction.

HOW TO CONTACT "To submit to kt literary, please e-mail us a query letter with the first three pages of your ms in the body of the e-mail. The subject line of your e-mail should include the word 'Query' along with the title of your manuscript. Queries should not contain attachments. Attachments will not be read, and queries containing attachments will be deleted unread. We aim to reply to all queries within two weeks of receipt. No snail mail queries." Responds in 2 weeks to queries. Responds in 2 months to mss. Obtains most new clients through recommendations from others, solicitations, conferences.

TERMS Agent receives 15% commission on domestic sales. Agent receives 20% commission on foreign sales. Offers written contract; 30-day notice must be given to terminate contract.

RECENT SALES *Albatross*, by Julie Bloss; *The Last Good Place of Lily Odilon*, by Sara Beitia; *Texting the Underworld*, by Ellen Booraem. A full list of clients is available on the agency website.

WRITERS CONFERENCES Various SCBWI conferences, BookExpo.

TIPS "If we like your query, we'll ask for (more). Continuing advice is offered regularly on my blog 'Ask Daphne,' which can be accessed from my website."

○ THE LA LITERARY AGENCY

P.O. Box 46370, Los Angeles CA 90046. (323)654-5288. **E-mail:** ann@laliteraryagency.com; mail@laliteraryagency.com. **Website:** www.laliteraryagency.com. **Contact:** Ann Cashman.

○ Prior to becoming an agent, Eric Lasher worked in broadcasting and publishing in New York and Los Angeles. Prior to opening the agency, Maureen Lasher worked in New York at Prentice-Hall, Liveright, and Random House.

MEMBER AGENTS Ann Cashman, Eric Lasher, Maureen Lasher.

REPRESENTS nonfiction books, novels. **Considers these nonfiction areas:** biography, business, cooking, creative nonfiction, health, history, memoirs, parenting, psychology, science, sports. **Considers these fiction areas:** commercial, literary.

HOW TO CONTACT Prefers submissions by mail, but welcomes e-mail submissions as well. Nonfiction: query letter and book proposal. Fiction: Query with outline and first 50 pages as an attachment, 1 sample chapter. Please visit the agency website for more info. Accepts simultaneous submissions.

RECENT SALES *The Fourth Trimester*, by Susan Brink (University of California Press); *Rebels in Paradise*, by Hunter Drohojowska-Philp (Holt); *La Cucina Mexicana*, by Marilyn Tausend (UC Press); *The Orpheus Clock*, by Simon Goodman (Scribner).

○ PETER LAMPACK AGENCY, INC.

The Empire State Building, 350 Fifth Ave., Suite 5300, New York NY 10118. (212)687-9106. **Fax:** (212)687-9109. **E-mail:** andrew@peterlampackagency.com. **Website:** www.peterlampackagency.com. **Contact:** Andrew Lampack.

REPRESENTS nonfiction books, novels. **Considers these fiction areas:** action, adventure, commercial, crime, detective, family saga, literary, mainstream, mystery, police, suspense, thriller.

⚷ "This agency specializes in commercial fiction, and nonfiction by recognized experts." Actively seeking literary and commercial fiction in the following categories: adventure, action, thrillers, mysteries, suspense, and psychological thrillers. Does not want to receive horror, romance, science fiction, westerns, historical literary fiction, or academic material.

HOW TO CONTACT The Peter Lampack Agency no longer accepts material through conventional mail. E-queries only. When submitting, you should include a cover letter, author biography and a one or two page synopsis. Please do not send more than one sample chapter of your ms at a time. Due to the extremely high volume of submissions,we ask that you allow

4-6 weeks for a response. Accepts simultaneous submissions. Obtains most new clients through referrals made by clients.

TERMS Agent receives 15% commission on domestic sales. Agent receives 20% commission on foreign sales.

RECENT SALES *The Assassin,* by Clive Cussler and Justin Scott; *The Solomon Curse,* by Clive Cussler and Russell Blake; *Patriot,* by Ted Bell; *The Good Story,* by J.M. Coetzee And Arabella Kurtz; *Police State: How America's Cops Get Away With Murder,* by Gerry Spence.

WRITERS CONFERENCES BookExpo America; Mystery Writers of America.

TIPS "Submit only your best work for consideration. Have a very specific agenda of goals you wish your prospective agent to accomplish for you. Provide the agent with a comprehensive statement of your credentials— educational and professional accomplishments."

LAURA LANGLIE, LITERARY AGENT

147-149 Green St., Hudson NY 12534. (518)828-4708. **Fax:** (518)828-4787. **E-mail:** laura@lauralanglie.com. **Contact:** Laura Langlie. Represents 25 clients. 50% of clients are new/unpublished writers.

○ Prior to opening her agency, Ms. Langlie worked in publishing for 7 years and as an agent at Kidde, Hoyt & Picard for 6 years.

REPRESENTS Considers these nonfiction areas: autobiography, biography, cultural interests, current affairs, environment, film, history, language, law, literature, memoirs, popular culture, politics, psychology, theater, women's studies. **Considers these fiction areas:** crime, detective, ethnic, feminist, historical, humor, juvenile, literary, mainstream, mystery, police, suspense, thriller, young adult, mainstream.

○━ "I'm very involved with and committed to my clients. Most of my clients come to me via recommendations from other agents, clients and editors. I've met very few at conferences. I've often sought out writers for projects, and I still find new clients via the traditional query letter." Does not want to receive how-to, children's picture books, hardcore science fiction, poetry, men's adventure, or erotica.

HOW TO CONTACT Query with SASE. Accepts queries via fax. Accepts simultaneous submissions. Responds in 1 week to queries. Responds in 1 month to

mss. Obtains most new clients through recommendations, submissions.

TERMS Agent receives 15% commission on domestic sales. Agent receives 20% commission on foreign and dramatic sales. No written contract.

RECENT SALES Sold 15 titles in the last year. *The Evening Spider,* by Emily Arsenault (William Morrow); *The Swans of 5th Avenue,* by Melanie Benjamin (Delacorte Press).

TIPS "Be complete, forthright and clear in your communications. Do your research as to what a particular agent represents."

⊘ MICHAEL LARSEN/ELIZABETH POMADA, LITERARY AGENTS

1029 Jones St., San Francisco CA 94109. (415)673-0939. **E-mail:** larsenpoma@aol.com. **Website:** www.larsenpomada.com. **Contact:** Mike Larsen, Elizabeth Pomada. Member of AAR. Other memberships include Authors Guild, ASJA, WNBA, California Writers Club, National Speakers Association. Represents 100 clients. 40-45% of clients are new/unpublished writers. Currently handles: nonfiction books 70%, novels 30%.

○ Prior to opening their agency, Mr. Larsen and Ms. Pomada were promotion executives for major publishing houses. Mr. Larsen worked for Morrow, Bantam, and Pyramid (now part of Berkley); Ms. Pomada worked at Holt, David McKay and Dial Press. Mr. Larsen is the author of the 4th edition of *How to Write a Book Proposal* and *How to Get a Literary Agent* as well as the coauthor of *Guerilla Marketing for Writers: 100 Weapons for Selling Your Work,* which was republished in September 2009.

MEMBER AGENTS Michael Larsen (nonfiction); Elizabeth Pomada (fiction & narrative nonfiction).

REPRESENTS Considers these nonfiction areas: anthropology, archeology, architecture, art, autobiography, biography, business, current affairs, diet/nutrition, design, economics, environment, ethnic, film, foods, gay/lesbian, health, history, how-to, humor, inspirational, investigative, law, medicine, memoirs, metaphysics, money, music, New Age, popular culture, politics, psychology, religious, satire, science, self-help, sociology, sports, travel, women's issues, women's studies, futurism. **Considers these fiction areas:** action, adventure, contemporary issues, crime, detective, ethnic, experimental, family saga, feminist, gay, glitz, historical, humor, inspirational, lesbian, literary, mainstream, mystery, police, religious, romance, satire, suspense.

○—ᴍ "We have diverse tastes. We look for fresh voices and new ideas. We handle literary, commercial and genre fiction, and the full range of nonfiction books." Actively seeking commercial, genre, and literary fiction. Does not want to receive children's books, plays, short stories, screenplays, pornography, poetry or stories of abuse.

HOW TO CONTACT As of early 2015, this agency is closed to submissions for some time. Responds in 8 weeks to pages or submissions.

TERMS Agent receives 15% commission on domestic sales. Agent receives 20% (30% for Asia) commission on foreign sales. May charge for printing, postage for multiple submissions, foreign mail, foreign phone calls, galleys, books, legal fees.

WRITERS CONFERENCES This agency organizes the annual San Francisco Writers' Conference (www.sfwriters.org).

TIPS "We love helping writers get the rewards and recognition they deserve. If you can write books that meet the needs of the marketplace and you can promote your books, now is the best time ever to be a writer. We must find new writers to make a living, so we are very eager to hear from new writers whose work will interest large houses, and nonfiction writers who can promote their books. For a list of recent sales, helpful info, and three ways to make yourself irresistible to any publisher, please visit our website."

◎ THE STEVE LAUBE AGENCY

24 W. Camelback Rd., A-635, Phoenix, AZ 85013. (602)336-8910. **Website:** www.stevelaube.com. Other memberships include CBA. Represents 60+ clients. 5% of clients are new/unpublished writers.

○ Prior to becoming an agent, Mr. Laube worked 11 years as a Christian bookseller and 11 years as editorial director of nonfiction with Bethany House Publishers. Mrs. Murray was an accomplished novelist and agent. Mrs. Ball was an executive editor with Tyndale, Multnomah, Zondervan, and B&H. Mr. Balow was marketing director for the Left Behind series at Tyndale.

MEMBER AGENTS Steve Laube, president, **Tamela Hancock Murray, Karen Ball, Dan Balow**.

REPRESENTS nonfiction books, novels. **Considers these nonfiction areas:** religious. **Considers these fiction areas:** inspirational, religious.

○—ᴍ Primarily serves the Christian market (CBA). Actively seeking Christian fiction and religious nonfiction. Does not want to receive children's picture books, poetry, or cookbooks.

HOW TO CONTACT Submit proposal package, outline, 3 sample chapters, SASE. For e-mail submissions, attach as Word doc or PDF. Consult website for guidelines, because queries are sent to assistants, and the assistants' e-mail addresses must change. Accepts simultaneous submissions. Responds in 6-8 weeks to queries. Obtains most new clients through recommendations from others, solicitations, conferences.

TERMS Agent receives 15% commission on domestic sales. Agent receives 20% commission on foreign sales. Offers written contract; 30-day notice must be given to terminate contract.

RECENT SALES Sold 200 titles in the last year. Other clients include Deborah Raney, Allison Bottke, H. Norman Wright, Ellie Kay, Jack Cavanaugh, Karen Ball, Susan May Warren, Lisa Bergren, Cindy Woodsmall, Karol Ladd, Judith Pella, Margaret Daley, William Lane Craig, Ginny Aiken, Kim Vogel Sawyer, Mesu Andrews, Mary Hunt, Hugh Ross, Bill & Pam Farrel, Ronie Kendig.

WRITERS CONFERENCES Mount Hermon Christian Writers' Conference; American Christian Fiction Writers' Conference; ACFW.

◎ LAUNCHBOOKS LITERARY AGENCY

(760)944-9909. **E-mail:** david@launchbooks.com. **Website:** www.launchbooks.com. **Contact:** David Fugate. Represents 45 clients. 35% of clients are new/unpublished writers.

○ David Fugate has been an agent for 20 years and has successfully represented more than 1,000 book titles. He left another agency to found LaunchBooks in 2005.

REPRESENTS Considers these nonfiction areas: business, creative nonfiction, current affairs, environment, history, humor, popular culture, politics, science, sociology, sports, technology. **Considers these fiction areas:** mainstream.

○—ᴍ "We're looking for genre-breaking fiction. Do you have the next *The Martian*? Or maybe the next *The Remaining*, *Ready Player One*, *Ancillary Sword*, or *The Bone Clocks*? We're on the

NEW AGENT SPOTLIGHT

KURESTIN ARMADA
P.S. LITERARY

Psliterary.com

@kurestinarmada

ABOUT KURESTIN: Kurestin began her publishing career as an intern with Workman Publishing, and spent time as an assistant at The Lotts Agency before joining P.S. Literary. She holds a B.A. in English from Kenyon College, as well as a publishing certificate from Columbia University. Kurestin is based in New York City, and spends most of her time in the city's thriving indie bookstores.

SHE IS SEEKING: upmarket and commercial fiction, magical realism, science fiction, fantasy, alternative history, historical fiction, LGBTQ (any genre), select young adult and middle grade, graphic novels, mystery (including mystery with elements of sci-fi/fantasy), and romance. In nonfiction, she is looking for design, cooking, pop psychology, humor, narrative, photography, and pop science.

HOW TO SUBMIT: P.S. Literary only accepts queries via e-mail: query@psliterary.com. Limit your query to one page. Do not send attachments or submit a full-length manuscript/proposal unless requested. In your e-mail subject line, have it read "Query for Kurestin: [Book Title]."

---

lookout for fun, engaging, contemporary novels that appeal to a broad audience."

HOW TO CONTACT Query via e-mail. Submit outline/proposal, synopsis, 1 sample chapter, author bio. Accepts simultaneous submissions. Responds in 1 week to queries. Responds in 4 weeks to mss. Obtains most new clients through recommendations from others, solicitations.

TERMS Agent receives 15% commission on domestic sales. Agent receives 25% commission on foreign sales. Offers written contract; 30-day notice must be given to terminate contract. Charges occur very seldom. This agency's agreement limits any charges to $50 unless the author gives a written consent.

RECENT SALES *The Martian*, by Andy Weir (Random House); *The Remaining: Allegiance*, by DJ Molles (Orbit); *The Fold*, by Peter Clines (Crown); *Faster, Higher, Stronger*, by Mark McClusky (Hudson Street Press); *Fluent in Three Months*, by Benny Lewis (HarperOne); *Ex-Purgatory*, by Peter Clines (Crown);] *The $100 Startup*, by Chris Guillebeau (Crown); *Ghost in the Wires*, by Kevin Mitnick (Little, Brown).

◉ SARAH LAZIN BOOKS

121 W. 27th St., Suite 704, New York NY 10001. (212)989-5757. **Fax:** (212)989-1393. **E-mail:** amanda@lazinbooks.com; slazin@lazinbooks.com. **Website:** www.lazinbooks.com. **Contact:** Sarah Lazin. Estab. 1983. Member of AAR.

MEMBER AGENTS Sarah Lazin; Amanda Hartman (subsidiary rights).

REPRESENTS nonfiction books, novels. **Considers these nonfiction areas:** biography, history, investigative, memoirs, parenting, popular culture. **Considers these fiction areas:** commercial, literary, short story collections.

☛ Works with companies who package their books; handles some photography.

HOW TO CONTACT As of 2015: "We accept submissions through referral only." Only accepts queries on referral.

TERMS Agent receives 15% commission on domestic sales. Agent receives 20% commission on foreign sales.

● SUSANNA LEA ASSOCIATES

28, rue Bonaparte, 75006 Paris France. **E-mail:** US-submission@susannalea.com. **E-mail:** US-submission@susannalea.com; uk-submission@susannalea.com; fr-submission@susannalea.com. **Website:** www.susannaleaassociates.com. **Contact:** Submissions Department. 331 West 20th Street, New York, NY 10011.
REPRESENTS nonfiction books, novels.

☛ "Keeps list small; prefers to focus energies on a limited number of projects rather than spreading themselves too thinly. The company is currently developing new international projects—selective, yet broad in their reach, their slogan is: 'Published in Europe, Read by the World.'" Does not want to receive poetry, plays, screenplays, science fiction, educational text books, short stories or illustrated works.

HOW TO CONTACT To submit your work, please send the following by e-mail: a concise query letter, including your e-mail address, telephone number, any relevant information about yourself (previous publications, etc.), a brief synopsis, and the first three chapters and/or proposal.

TIPS "Your query letter should be concise and include any pertinent information about yourself, relevant writing history, etc."

⊘ THE NED LEAVITT AGENCY

70 Wooster St., Suite 4F, New York NY 10012. (212)334-0999. **Website:** www.nedleavittagency.com. **Contact:** Ned Leavitt; Jillian Sweeney. Member of AAR. Represents 40+ clients.
MEMBER AGENTS Ned Leavitt, founder and agent; Britta Alexander, agent; Jillian Sweeney, agent.
REPRESENTS nonfiction books, novels.

☛ "We are small in size, but intensely dedicated to our authors and to supporting excellent and unique writing."

HOW TO CONTACT This agency now only takes queries/submissions through referred clients. Do *not* cold query.

TIPS "Look online for this agency's recently changed submission guidelines." For guidance in the writing process we strongly recommend the following books: *Writing Down The Bones* by Nathalie Goldberg; *Bird By Bird* by Anne Lamott.

◑ ROBERT LECKER AGENCY

4055 Melrose Ave., Montreal QC H4A 2S5 Canada. **E-mail:** robert.lecker@gmail.com. **Website:** www.leckeragency.com. **Contact:** Robert Lecker. Represents 20 clients. 20% of clients are new/unpublished writers. Currently handles: nonfiction books 80%, novels 10%, scholarly books 10%.

💬 Prior to becoming an agent, Mr. Lecker was the cofounder and publisher of ECW Press and professor of English literature at McGill University. He has 30 years of experience in book and magazine publishing.

MEMBER AGENTS Robert Lecker (popular culture, music); **Mary Williams** (travel, food, popular science).

REPRESENTS nonfiction books, novels, scholarly, syndicated material. **Considers these nonfiction areas:** autobiography, biography, cooking, cultural interests, dance, diet/nutrition, ethnic, film, foods, how-to, language, literature, music, popular culture, science, technology, theater. **Considers these fiction areas:** action, adventure, crime, detective, erotica, literary, mainstream, mystery, police, suspense, thriller.

☛ RLA specializes in books about popular culture, popular science, music, entertainment, food, and travel. The agency responds to articulate, innovative proposals within 2 weeks. We do not represent children's literature, screenplays, poetry, self-help books, or spiritual guides.

HOW TO CONTACT E-query. In the subject line, write: "New Submission QUERY." Accepts simultaneous submissions. Responds in 2 weeks to queries. Responds in 1 month to mss. Obtains most new clients through recommendations from others, conferences, interest in website.

TERMS Agent receives 15% commission on domestic sales. Agent receives 15-20% commission on foreign sales. Offers written contract, binding for 1 year; 6-month notice must be given to terminate contract.

THE LESHNE AGENCY

16 W. 23rd St., 4th Floor, New York NY 10010. **E-mail:** info@leshneagency.com. **E-mail:** submissions@leshneagency.com. **Website:** www.leshneagency.com. **Contact:** Lisa Leshne, agent and owner.

○ Prior to founding the Leshne Agency, Lisa was a literary agent at LJK Literary.

MEMBER AGENTS Lisa Leshne, agent and owner; Sandy Hodgman, director of foreign rights.

REPRESENTS Considers these nonfiction areas: business, creative nonfiction, health, memoirs, parenting, politics, sports. **Considers these fiction areas:** commercial, middle grade, young adult.

⚮ Wants "authors across all genres. We are interested in narrative, memoir, and prescriptive nonfiction, with a particular interest in sports, wellness, business, political and parenting topics. We will also look at truly terrific commercial fiction and young adult and middle grade books."

HOW TO CONTACT "Submit all materials in the body of an e-mail; no attachments. Be sure to include the word 'QUERY' and the title of your ms in the subject line. Include brief synopsis, TOC or chapter outline, 10 sample pages, bio, any previous publications, word count, how much of the ms is complete, and the best way to reach you."

LEVELFIVEMEDIA, LLC

130 W. 42nd St., Suite 1901-02, New York NY 10036. (212)575-4600. **Fax:** (212)575-7797. **Contact:** Stephen Hanselman.

○ Prior to becoming an agent, Ms. Hemming served as president and publisher of Harper-Collins General Books. Mr. Hanselman served as senior VP and publisher of HarperBusiness, HarperResource and HarperSanFrancisco.

MEMBER AGENTS Stephen Hanselman; Cathy Hemming.

REPRESENTS nonfiction books, novels. **Considers these nonfiction areas:** business, cooking, diet/nutrition, economics, foods, health, history, how-to, inspirational, medicine, money, parenting, psychology, self-help, fitness/exercise, popular science, investigative journalism, lifestyle, popular reference, cultural studies.

HOW TO CONTACT Not currently taking submissions. Obtains most new clients through recommendations from others.

RECENT SALES *The 4-Hour Body*, by Timothy Ferriss; *A Complaint-Free World*, by Will Bowen.

LEVINE GREENBERG ROSTAN LITERARY AGENCY, INC.

307 Seventh Ave., Suite 2407, New York NY 10001. (212)337-0934. **Fax:** (212)337-0948. **E-mail:** submit@levinegreenberg.com. **Website:** www.levinegreenberg.com. Member of AAR. Represents 250 clients. 33% of clients are new/unpublished writers. Currently handles: nonfiction books 70%, novels 30%.

○ Prior to opening his agency, Mr. Levine served as vice president of the Bank Street College of Education.

MEMBER AGENTS Jim Levine; **Stephanie Rostan** (adult fiction, nonfiction, YA); **Melissa Rowland**; **Daniel Greenberg** (literary fiction; nonfiction: popular culture, narrative nonfiction, memoir, and humor); **Victoria Skurnick**; **Danielle Svetcov**; **Elizabeth Fisher**; **Lindsay Edgecombe** (narrative nonfiction, memoir, lifestyle and health, illustrated books, as well as literary fiction); **Monika Verma** (nonfiction: humor, pop culture, memoir, narrative nonfiction and style and fashion titles; some young adult fiction); **Kerry Sparks** (young adult and middle grade); **Tim Wojcik** (quirky adventures, as-yet untold oral histories, smart humor, anything sports, music and food-related, thrillers, mysteries, and literary fiction); **Arielle Eckstut** (no queries); **Kirsten Wolf** (adult and children's literature).

REPRESENTS nonfiction books, novels. **Considers these nonfiction areas:** animals, art, biography, business, computers, cooking, creative nonfiction, gardening, health, humor, memoirs, money, New Age, science, sociology, spirituality, sports. **Considers these fiction areas:** literary, mainstream, middle grade, mystery, thriller, women's, young adult.

⚮ This agency specializes in business, psychology, parenting, health/medicine, narrative nonfiction, spirituality, religion, women's issues, and commercial fiction.

HOW TO CONTACT E-query, or online submission form. Do not submit directly to agents. Prefers electronic submissions. Cannot respond to submissions by mail. Do not attach more than 50 pages. Obtains most new clients through recommendations from others.

TERMS Agent receives 15% commission on domestic sales. Agent receives 20% commission on foreign sales. Offers written contract. Charges clients for out-of-pocket expenses—telephone, fax, postage, photo-copying—directly connected to the project.

RECENT SALES *Gone Girl*, by Gillian Flynn; *Hyperbole and a Half*, by Allie Brosh; *Our Dumb Century*, by editors of The Onion; *Predictably Irrational*, by Dan Ariely.

WRITERS CONFERENCES ASJA Writers' Conference.

TIPS "We focus on editorial development, business representation, and publicity and marketing strategy."

PAUL S. LEVINE LITERARY AGENCY

1054 Superba Ave., Venice CA 90291. (310)450-6711. **Fax:** (310)450-0181. **E-mail:** paul@paulslevinelit.com. **Website:** www.paulslevinelit.com. **Contact:** Paul S. Levine. Other memberships include the State Bar of California. Represents over 100 clients. 75% of clients are new/unpublished writers. Currently handles: non-fiction books 60%, novels 10%, movie scripts 10%, TV scripts 5%, juvenile books 5%.

MEMBER AGENTS Paul S. Levine (children's and young adult fiction and nonfiction, adult fiction and nonfiction except sci-fi, fantasy, and horror); Loren R. Grossman (archaeology, art/photography/architecture, gardening, education, health, medicine, science).

REPRESENTS nonfiction books, novels, episodic drama, movie, TV, movie scripts, feature film, TV movie of the week, sitcom, animation, documentary, miniseries, syndicated material, reality show. **Considers these nonfiction areas:** architecture, art, autobiography, biography, business, child guidance, computers, cooking, crafts, cultural interests, current affairs, diet/nutrition, design, economics, education, ethnic, film, foods, gay/lesbian, government, health, history, hobbies, how-to, humor, investigative, language, law, medicine, memoirs, military, money, music, New Age, parenting, photography, popular culture, politics, psychology, science, self-help, sociology, sports, theater, true crime, women's issues, women's studies, creative nonfiction, animation. **Considers these fiction areas:** action, adventure, comic books, confession, crime, detective, erotica, ethnic, experimental, family saga, feminist, frontier, gay, glitz, historical, humor, inspirational, lesbian, literary, mainstream, mystery, police, regional, religious, romance, satire, sports, suspense, thriller, westerns. **Considers these script areas:** action, biography, cartoon, comedy, contemporary, detective, erotica, ethnic, experimental, family, feminist, gay, glitz, historical, hor-

ror, juvenile, mainstream, multimedia, mystery, religious, romantic comedy, romantic drama, sports, teen, thriller, western.

☛ Does not want to receive science fiction, fantasy, or horror.

HOW TO CONTACT Query with SASE. Accepts simultaneous submissions. Responds in 1 day to queries. Responds in 6-8 weeks to mss. Obtains most new clients through conferences, referrals, listings on various websites, and in directories.

TERMS Agent receives 15% commission on domestic sales. Offers written contract. Charges for postage and actual, out-of-pocket costs only.

RECENT SALES Sold 8 books in the last year.

WRITERS CONFERENCES Willamette Writers Conference; San Francisco Writers Conference; Santa Barbara Writers Conference and many others.

TIPS "Write good, sellable books."

LIPPINCOTT MASSIE MCQUILKIN

27 West 20th Street, Suite 305, New York NY 10011. **Fax:** (212)352-2059. **E-mail:** info@lmqlit.com. **Website:** www.lmqlit.com.

MEMBER AGENTS Laney Katz Becker, laney@lmqlit.com (book club fiction, smart thrillers and suspense, memoir and nonfiction from platform-heavy authors); Kent Wolf, kent@lmqlit.com (literary and commercial fiction, including young adult and select middle grade, narrative nonfiction, memoir, essays, and pop culture); Ethan Bassoff, ethan@lmqlit.com (literary fiction, crime fiction, and narrative nonfiction in the areas of history, sports writing, journalism, science writing, pop culture, humor, and food writing); Jason Anthony, jason@lmqlit.com (commercial fiction of all types, including young adult, and nonfiction in the areas of memoir, pop culture, true crime, and general psychology and sociology); Will Lippincott, will@lmqlit.com (narrative nonfiction and nonfiction in the areas of politics, history, biography, foreign affairs, and health. He is not looking for fiction at this time); Maria Massie, maria@lmqlit.com (literary and upmarket commercial fiction [including select young adult and middle grade], memoir, and narrative nonfiction); Rob McQuilkin, rob@lmqlit.com (literary fiction as well as narrative nonfiction and nonfiction in the areas of memoir, history, biography, art history, cultural criticism, and popular sociology and psychology); Amanda Panitch, amanda@lmqlit.com (young adult and middle grade); Rayhane

Sanders, rayhane@lmqlit.com (literary fiction, historical fiction, upmarket commercial fiction [including select YA], narrative nonfiction [including essays], and select memoir); **Stephanie Abou** (literary and upmarket novelists).

REPRESENTS nonfiction books, novels, short story collections, scholarly, graphic novels. **Considers these nonfiction areas:** animals, anthropology, archeology, architecture, art, autobiography, biography, business, child guidance, cultural interests, current affairs, design, economics, ethnic, film, gay/lesbian, government, health, history, inspirational, language, law, literature, medicine, memoirs, military, money, music, parenting, popular culture, politics, psychology, religious, science, self-help, sociology, technology, true crime, women's issues, women's studies, young adult. **Considers these fiction areas:** action, adventure, cartoon, comic books, confession, family saga, feminist, gay, historical, humor, lesbian, literary, mainstream, regional, satire.

⌘ "LMQ focuses on bringing new voices in literary and commercial fiction to the market, as well as popularizing the ideas and arguments of scholars in the fields of history, psychology, sociology, political science, and current affairs. Actively seeking fiction writers who already have credits in magazines and quarterlies, as well as nonfiction writers who already have a media platform or some kind of a university affiliation." Does not want to receive romance, genre fiction, or children's material.

HOW TO CONTACT E-query. Include the word 'Query' in the subject line of your e-mail. Review the agency's online page of agent bios (lmqlit.com/contact.html), as some agents want sample pages with their submissions and some no not. If you have not heard back from the agency in 4 weeks, assume they are not interested in seeing more. Accepts simultaneous submissions. Obtains most new clients through recommendations from others, solicitations, conferences.

TERMS Agent receives 15% commission on domestic sales. Agent receives 20% commission on foreign sales. Offers written contract; 30-day notice must be given to terminate contract. Only charges for reasonable business expenses upon successful sale.

RECENT SALES Clients include: Peter Ho Davies, Kim Addonizio, Natasha Trethewey, Anne Carson, David Sirota, Katie Crouch, Uwen Akpan, Lydia Millet, Tom Perrotta, Jonathan Lopez, Chris Hayes, Caroline Weber.

⊘⊙ **LITERARY AND CREATIVE ARTISTS, INC.**
3543 Albemarle St., N.W., Washington D.C. 20008-4213. (202)362-4688. **Fax:** (202)362-8875. **E-mail:** lca9643@lcadc.com. **Website:** www.lcadc.com. **Contact:** Muriel Nellis. Member of AAR. Other memberships include Authors Guild, American Bar Association, American Booksellers Association. Currently handles: nonfiction books 50%, novels 50%.

MEMBER AGENTS Prior to becoming an agent, Mr. Powell was in sales and contract negotiation.

REPRESENTS nonfiction books, novels, art, biography, business, photography, popular culture, religion, self help, literary, regional, religious, satire. **Considers these nonfiction areas:** autobiography, biography, business, cooking, diet/nutrition, economics, foods, government, health, how-to, law, medicine, memoirs, philosophy, politics.

⌘ "Actively seeking quality projects by authors with a vision of where they want to be in 10 years and a plan of how to get there. We do not handle poetry, or purely academic/technical work."

HOW TO CONTACT Query via e-mail first and include a synopsis. No attachments. "We do not accept unsolicited manuscripts, faxed manuscripts, manuscripts sent by e-mail, or manuscripts on computer disk." Accepts simultaneous submissions. Responds in 3 weeks to queries. Responds in 1 week to mss. Obtains new clients through recommendations from others.

TERMS Agent receives 15% commission on domestic sales. Agent receives 25% commission on foreign sales. Offers written contract. Charges clients for long-distance phone/fax, photocopying, shipping.

TIPS "If you are an unpublished author, join a writers group, even if it is on the Internet. You need good honest feedback. Don't send a ms that has not been read by at least 5 people. Don't send a manuscript cold to any agent without first asking if they want it. Try to meet the agent face to face before signing. Make sure the fit is right."

🄳 **THE LITERARY GROUP INTERNATIONAL**
1357 Broadway,, Suite 316, New York NY 10018. (212)400-1494, ext. 380. **Website:** www.theliter

arygroup.com. **Contact:** Frank Weimann. 1900 Ave. of the Stars, 25 Fl., Los Angeles, CA 90067; Tel: (310)282-8961; **Fax:** (310) 282-8903 65% of clients are new/unpublished writers.

MEMBER AGENTS Frank Weimann.

REPRESENTS nonfiction books, novels, graphic novels. **Considers these nonfiction areas:** animals, anthropology, biography, business, child guidance, crafts, creative nonfiction, current affairs, education, ethnic, film, government, health, history, humor, juvenile nonfiction, language, memoirs, military, multicultural, music, nature, popular culture, politics, psychology, religious, science, self-help, sociology, sports, travel, true crime, women's issues, women's studies. **Considers these fiction areas:** adventure, contemporary issues, detective, ethnic, experimental, family saga, fantasy, feminist, historical, horror, humor, literary, multicultural, mystery, psychic, regional, romance, sports, thriller, young adult.

☞ This agency specializes in nonfiction (memoir, military, history, biography, sports, how-to).

HOW TO CONTACT Query. Prefers to read materials exclusively. Only responds if interested. Obtains most new clients through referrals, writers conferences, query letters.

TERMS Agent receives 15% commission on domestic sales. Agent receives 20% commission on foreign sales. Offers written contract; 30-day notice must be given to terminate contract.

RECENT SALES *As You Wish* by Cary Elwes (Simon and Schuster); *Ginger and Elvis* by Ginger Alden (Berkley); *Indulge* by Kathy Wakile (St. Martin's Press).

WRITERS CONFERENCES San Diego State University Writers' Conference; Agents and Editors Conference; NAHJ Convention in Puerto Rico, others.

◯ LITERARY MANAGEMENT GROUP, INC.

16970 San Carlos Blvd., Suite 160-100, Fort Myers FL 33908. **E-mail:** brucebarbour@literarymanagement group.com; brb@brucebarbour.com. **Website:** http://literarymanagementgroup.com; www.brucebarbour.com. **Contact:** Bruce Barbour.

◑ Prior to becoming an agent, Mr. Barbour held executive positions at several publishing houses, including Revell, Barbour Books, Thomas Nelson, and Random House.

REPRESENTS nonfiction books, novels. **Considers these nonfiction areas:** biography, Christian living; spiritual growth; women's and men's issues; prayer; devotional; meditational; Bible study; marriage; business; family/parenting.

☞ "Although we specialize in the area of Christian publishing from an Evangelical perspective, we have editorial contacts and experience in general interest books as well." Does not want to receive gift books, poetry, children's books, short stories, or juvenile/young adult fiction. No unsolicited mss or proposals from unpublished authors.

HOW TO CONTACT Query with SASE. E-mail proposal as an attachment. Consult website for each agent's submission guidelines.

TERMS Agent receives 15% commission on domestic sales.

❶ LITERARY SERVICES, INC.

P.O. Box 888, Barnegat NJ 08005. **E-mail:** jwlitagent@msn.com; shane@literaryservicesinc.com. **Website:** www.LiteraryServicesInc.com. **Contact:** John Willig. Other memberships include Author's Guild. Represents 90 clients. 25% of clients are new/unpublished writers. Currently handles: nonfiction books 100%. Beginning to accept and consider historical, crime and literary fiction projects.

MEMBER AGENTS John Willig (business, personal growth, narratives, history, health, science and technology, politics, current events).

REPRESENTS nonfiction books. **Considers these nonfiction areas:** architecture, art, biography, business, child guidance, cooking, crafts, design, economics, health, history, humor, language, literature, money, popular culture, psychology, satire, science, self-help, sports, technology, true crime.

☞ Works primarily with nonfiction and historical crime fiction authors. "Our publishing experience and 'inside' knowledge of how companies and editors really work sets us apart from many agencies; our specialties are noted above, but we are open to unique research, approaches, and presentations in all nonfiction topic areas." Actively seeking science, history, business, work/life topics, story-driven narratives. Does not want to receive fiction (except historical crime fiction), children's books, science fiction, religion or memoirs.

HOW TO CONTACT Query with SASE. For starters, a one-page outline sent via e-mail is acceptable. See our website and our Submissions section to learn more about our questions. Do not send ms unless requested. Accepts simultaneous submissions. Obtains most new clients through recommendations from others, solicitations, conferences.

TERMS Agent receives 15% commission on domestic sales. Agent receives 15% commission on foreign sales. Offers written contract. This agency charges administrative fees for copying, postage, etc.

RECENT SALES Sold 20 titles in the last year. A full list of new and award-winning books is noted on the agency website.

WRITERS CONFERENCES ASJA; Publicity Summit; Writer's Digest Conference (NYC); Thrillerfest.

TIPS "Be focused. In all likelihood, your work is not going to be of interest to 'a very broad audience' or 'every parent,' so I appreciate when writers research and do some homework, i.e., positioning, special features and benefits of your work. Be a marketer. How have you tested your ideas and writing (beyond your inner circle of family and friends)? Have you received any key awards for your work or endorsements from influential persons in your field? What steps, especially social media and speaking, have you taken to increase your presence in the market?"

⬤ LIVING WORD LITERARY AGENCY

P.O. Box 40974, Eugene OR 97414. **E-mail:** living wordliterary@gmail.com. **Website:** livingwordlit erary.wordpress.com. **Contact:** Kimberly Shumate, agent. Estab. 2009. Member Evangelical Christian Publishers Association

○ Kimberly began her employment with Harvest House Publishers as the assistant to the National Sales Manager as well as the International Sales Director, and continued into the editorial department.

REPRESENTS Considers these nonfiction areas: health, parenting, self-help, relationships. **Considers these fiction areas:** inspirational, adult fiction, Christian living.

⊶ Does not want to receive YA fiction, cookbooks, children's books, science fiction or fantasy, memoirs, screenplays or poetry.

HOW TO CONTACT Submit a query with short synopsis and first chapter via Word document. Agency only responds if interested.

⊕ LKG AGENCY

465 West End Ave., 2A, New York NY 10024. **E-mail:** query@lkgagency.com. **Website:** http://lkgagency. com.

MEMBER AGENTS Lauren Galit (nonfiction topics); **Caitlen Rubino-Bradway** (middle grade and young adult).

REPRESENTS Considers these nonfiction areas: animals, creative nonfiction, health, memoirs, parenting, psychology, women's issues. **Considers these fiction areas:** middle grade, young adult.

⊶ "The LKG Agency specializes in nonfiction, both practical and narrative."

HOW TO CONTACT "Send a query letter to query@ lkgagency.com. For nonfiction, please make sure to mention any publicity you have at your disposal. For middle grade and young adult, please send a query, synopsis, and the first chapter, and address all submissions to **Caitlen Rubino-Bradway** at CRubinoBrad way@lkgagency.com."

⊕ THE LOTTS AGENCY

303 West 18th St., New York NY 10011. Estab. 2013.

○ Formerly, Mr. Lotts worked for agent Ralph M. Vicinanza, and sold titles for sci-fi, fantasy, women's/romance, young adult and international rights.

○ LOWENSTEIN ASSOCIATES INC.

15 East 23rd St., Floor 4, New York NY 10010. (212)206-1630. **Fax:** (212)727-0280. **E-mail:** assis tant@bookhaven.com. **Website:** www.lowensteinas sociates.com. **Contact:** Barbara Lowenstein. Member of AAR.

MEMBER AGENTS Barbara Lowenstein, president (nonfiction interests include narrative nonfiction, health, money, finance, travel, multicultural, popular culture, and memoir; fiction interests include literary fiction and women's fiction).

REPRESENTS nonfiction books, novels. **Considers these nonfiction areas:** creative nonfiction, health, memoirs, money, multicultural, popular culture, travel. **Considers these fiction areas:** commercial, fantasy, literary, middle grade, science fiction, women's, young adult.

⊶ Barbara Lowenstein is currently looking for writers who have a platform and are leading experts in their field, including business, women's issues, psychology, health, science and social issues, and is particularly interest-

NEW AGENT SPOTLIGHT

LYDIA SHAMAH
CAROL MANN AGENCY

Carolmannagency.com

@lydiablyf

ABOUT LYDIA: Lydia Shamah (nee Blyfield) is originally from London. After studying PR and Communications in the UK, she relocated to New York City where she gained a B.A. in English and American Literature at New York University. .

SHE IS SEEKING: adult, young adult and middle grade fiction, and nonfiction projects. Lydia is looking for timely plots inspired by the headlines, effortless magical realism, unreliable narrators, and mysteries/psychological thrillers set in small communities (no CIA/FBI/MI5, please). She is always on the hunt for intriguing female voices and characters. In YA and MG, she is looking for strong hooks and modern themes. Most importantly, she wants fiction that is impossible to put down. She is not looking for high fantasy, political thrillers or romance. In nonfiction, Lydia is looking for books that are both inspirational and modern in the areas of self-improvement, lifestyle, relationships and business. She is also looking for unique blogs, Tumblrs and Instagram profiles to transform into gift books. She is particularly interested in feminism and women's issues.

HOW TO SUBMIT: Please send a query letter (including a brief bio) and the first 25 pages of your manuscript to querylydia@carolmannagency.com. All material should be pasted into the body of the email message.

ed in strong new voices in fiction and narrative nonfiction. Does not want Westerns, textbooks, children's picture books and books in need of translation.

HOW TO CONTACT "For fiction, please send us a 1-page query letter, along with the first 10 pages pasted in the body of the message by e-mail to assistant@bookhaven.com. If nonfiction, please send a 1-page query letter, a table of contents, and, if available, a proposal pasted into the body of the e-mail. Please put the word 'QUERY' and the title of your project in the subject field of your e-mail and address it to the agent of your choice. Please do not send an attachment as the message will be deleted without being read and no reply will be sent." Accepts simultaneous submissions. Responds in 6 weeks to queries. Obtains most new clients through recommendations from others, solicitations, conferences.

TERMS Agent receives 15% commission on domestic sales. Agent receives 20% commission on foreign sales. Offers written contract. Charges for large photocopy batches, messenger service, international postage.

TIPS "Know the genre you are working in and read!"

🌑🌕 ANDREW LOWNIE LITERARY AGENCY, LTD.

36 Great Smith St., London SW1P 3BU England. (44) (207)222-7574. **Fax:** (44)(207)222-7576. **E-mail:** lownie@globalnet.co.uk; david.haviland@andrewlownie.co.uk. **Website:** www.andrewlownie.co.uk. **Contact:** Andrew Lownie (nonfiction); David Haviland (fiction). Member of AAA. Represents 130 clients. 20% of clients are new/unpublished writers. Currently handles: nonfiction books 90%, novels 10%.

○ Prior to becoming an agent, Mr. Lownie was a journalist, bookseller, publisher, author of 12 books, and director of the Curtis Brown Agency. Short-listed for Literary Agent of the Year 2013 and 2014 by *Bookseller Magazine* and the top selling agent in the world on Publishers Marketplace 2013-2015. Mr. Haviland is a bestselling writer and has worked in advertising, script development, and was cofounder of Sirius Television.

REPRESENTS nonfiction books. **Considers these nonfiction areas:** autobiography, biography, current affairs, government, history, investigative, law, memoirs, military, popular culture, politics, true crime, war. **Considers these fiction areas:** commercial, crime, horror, literary, science fiction, thriller, women's.

8—🖛 This agent has wide publishing experience, extensive journalistic contacts, and a specialty in showbiz/celebrity memoir. Showbiz memoirs, narrative histories, and biographies. No poetry, short stories, children's fiction, academic, or scripts.

HOW TO CONTACT Query with by e-mail only. Submit outline, 1 sample chapter. Accepts simultaneous submissions. Responds in 1 week to queries. Responds in 1 month to mss. Obtains most new clients through recommendations from others and unsolicited through website.

TERMS Agent receives 15% commission on domestic sales. Agent receives 20% commission on foreign sales. Offers written contract; 30-day notice must be given to terminate contract.

RECENT SALES Sold 60 titles in the last year, with over a dozen top 10 bestsellers including many number ones, as well as the memoirs of Queen Elizabeth 11's Press Officer Dickie Arbiter, Lance Armstrong's masseuse Emma O'Reilly, actor Warwick Davis, Multiple Personality Disorder sufferer Alice Jamieson, round-the-world yachtsman Mike Perham, poker player Dave 'Devilfish' Ulliott, David Hasselhoff, Sam Faiers and Kirk Norcross from TOWIE, Spencer Matthews from Made in Chelsea, singer Kerry Katona. Other clients: Juliet Barker, Guy Bellamy, Joyce Cary estate, Roger Crowley, Duncan Falconer, Marius Gabriel, Laurence Gardner, the actress Paula Hamilton, Cathy Glass, Timothy Good, Robert Hutchinson, Lawrence James, Leslie Kenton, Christopher Lloyd, Sian Rees, Desmond Seward, Daniel Tammet, Casey Watson, and Christian Wolmar.

⊕◎ LR CHILDREN'S LITERARY

(224)848-4559. **E-mail:** submissions@LRchildrensliterary.com. **Website:** www.lrchildrensliterary.com. **Contact:** Loretta Caravette.

REPRESENTS Considers these fiction areas: juvenile, middle grade, picture books, young adult.

8—🖛 "I am very interested in the easy readers and early chapter books. I will take on an author/illustrator combination."

HOW TO CONTACT E-query only. Alert this agent if you are contacting other agencies at the same time. If submitting young adult or middle grade, submit the first 3 chapters and a synopsis. If submitting a picture book, send no more than 2 mss. Illustrations (no more than 5MB) can be sent as .JPG or .PDF formats. Responds in up to 6 weeks.

TIPS "No phone calls please."

○ DONALD MAASS LITERARY AGENCY

121 W. 27th St., Suite 801, New York NY 10001. (212)727-8383. **Website:** www.maassagency.com. Estab. 1980. Member of AAR. Other memberships include SFWA, MWA, RWA. Represents more than 100 clients. 5% of clients are new/unpublished writers. Currently handles: novels 100%.

○ Prior to opening his agency, Mr. Maass served as an editor at Dell Publishing (New York) and as a reader at Gollancz (London). He also served as the president of AAR.

MEMBER AGENTS Donald Maass (mainstream, literary, mystery/suspense, science fiction, romance); **Jennifer Jackson** (commercial fiction, romance, science fiction, fantasy, mystery/suspense); **Cameron McClure** (literary, mystery/suspense, urban, fantasy, narrative nonfiction and projects with multicultural, international, and environmental themes, gay/lesbian); **Stacia Decker** (fiction, memoir, narrative nonfiction, pop-culture [cooking, fashion, style, music, art], smart humor, upscale erotica/erotic memoir and multicultural fiction/nonfiction); **Amy Boggs** (fantasy and science fiction, especially urban fantasy, paranormal romance, steampunk, YA/children's, and alternate history. historical fiction, multicultural fiction, westerns); **Katie Shea Boutillier** (women's fiction/book club; edgy/dark, realistic/contemporary YA; commercial-scale literary fiction; and celebrity memoir); **Jennifer Udden** (speculative fiction (both science fiction and fantasy), urban fantasy, and mysteries, as well as historical, erotic, contemporary, and paranormal romance).

REPRESENTS nonfiction, novels. **Considers these nonfiction areas:** creative nonfiction, memoirs, popular culture. **Considers these fiction areas:** crime, detective, fantasy, historical, horror, literary, mainstream, multicultural, mystery, paranormal, police, psychic, romance, science fiction, supernatural, suspense, thriller, westerns, women's, young adult.

8—m This agency specializes in commercial fiction, especially science fiction, fantasy, mystery, and suspense. Actively seeking to expand in literary fiction and women's fiction. We are fiction specialists. All genres are welcome.

HOW TO CONTACT E-query. All the agents have different submission addresses and instructions. See the website and each agent's online profile for exact submission instructions. Accepts simultaneous submissions.

TERMS Agent receives 15% commission on domestic sales. Agent receives 20% commission on foreign sales.

RECENT SALES *Codex Alera 5: Princep's Fury*, by Jim Butcher (Ace); *Fonseca 6: Bright Futures*, by Stuart Kaimsky (Forge): *Fathom*, by Cherie Priest (Tor); *Gospel Grrls 3: Be Strong and Curvaceous*, by Shelly Adina (Faith Words); *Ariane 1: Peacekeeper*, by Laura Reeve (Roc); *Execution Dock*, by Anne Perry (Random House).

WRITERS CONFERENCES Donald Maass: World Science Fiction Convention; Frankfurt Book Fair; Pacific Northwest Writers Conference; Bouchercon.

Jennifer Jackson: World Science Fiction Convention; RWA National Conference.

TIPS We are fiction specialists, also noted for our innovative approach to career planning. Few new clients are accepted, but interested authors should query with a SASE. Works with subagents in all principle foreign countries and Hollywood. No prescriptive nonfiction, picture books, or poetry will be considered.

O GINA MACCOBY LITERARY AGENCY

P.O. Box 60, Chappaqua NY 10514. (914)238-5630. **E-mail:** query@maccobylit.com. **Website:** www.publishersmarketplace.com/members/GinaMaccoby/. **Contact:** Gina Maccoby. Member of AAR. AAR Board of Directors; Royalties and Ethics and Contracts subcommittees; Authors Guild. Represents 25 clients. Currently handles: nonfiction books 33%, novels 33%, juvenile books 33%.

MEMBER AGENTS Gina Maccoby.

REPRESENTS nonfiction books, novels, juvenile. **Considers these nonfiction areas:** autobiography, biography, cultural interests, current affairs, ethnic, history, juvenile nonfiction, popular culture, women's issues, women's studies. **Considers these fiction areas:** juvenile, literary, mainstream, mystery, thriller, young adult.

HOW TO CONTACT Query by e-mail only. Accepts simultaneous submissions. Owing to volume of submissions, may not respond to queries unless interested. Obtains most new clients through recommendations from clients and publishers.

TERMS Agent receives 15% commission on domestic sales. Agent receives 20-25% commission on foreign sales, which includes subagents commissions. May recover certain costs, such as legal fees or the cost of shipping books by air to Europe or Japan.

⊘⊚ MACGREGOR LITERARY INC.

P.O. Box 1316, Manzanita OR 97130. (503)389-4803. **Website:** www.macgregorliterary.com. **Contact:** Chip MacGregor. Signatory of WGA. Represents 40 clients. 10% of clients are new/unpublished writers. Currently handles: nonfiction books 40%, novels 60%.

O Prior to his current position, Mr. MacGregor was the senior agent with Alive Communications. Most recently, he was associate publisher for Time-Warner Book Group's Faith Division, and helped put together their Center Street imprint.

MEMBER AGENTS Chip MacGregor, Amanda Luedeke; Holly Lorincz; Erin Buterbaugh.

REPRESENTS nonfiction books, novels. **Considers these nonfiction areas:** business, current affairs, economics, history, how-to, humor, inspirational, parenting, popular culture, satire, self-help, sports, marriage. **Considers these fiction areas:** crime, detective, historical, inspirational, mainstream, mystery, police, religious, romance, suspense, thriller, women's, chick lit.

8—⊸ "My specialty has been in career planning with authors—finding commercial ideas, then helping authors bring them to market, and in the midst of that assisting the authors as they get firmly established in their writing careers. I'm probably best known for my work with Christian books over the years, but I've done a fair amount of general market projects as well." Actively seeking authors with a Christian worldview and a growing platform. Does not want to receive fantasy, sci-fi, children's books, poetry or screenplays.

HOW TO CONTACT Do not query this agency without an invitation or referral. Accepts simultaneous submissions. Responds in 3 weeks to queries. Obtains most new clients through recommendations from others. Not looking to add unpublished authors except through referrals from current clients.

TERMS Agent receives 15% commission on domestic sales. Agent receives 15% commission on foreign sales. Offers written contract; 30-day notice must be given to terminate contract. Charges for exceptional fees after receiving authors' permission.

WRITERS CONFERENCES Blue Ridge Christian Writers' Conference; Write to Publish.

TIPS "Seriously consider attending a good writers' conference. It will give you the chance to be face-to-face with people in the industry. Also, if you're a novelist, consider joining one of the national writers' organizations. The American Christian Fiction Writers (ACFW) is a wonderful group for new as well as established writers. And if you're a Christian writer of any kind, check into The Writers View, an online writing group. All of these have proven helpful to writers."

⊘ KIRSTEN MANGES LITERARY AGENCY

115 W. 29th St., Third Floor, New York NY 10001. **Website:** www.mangeslit.com. **Contact:** Kirsten Manges.

◯ Prior to her current position, Ms. Manges was an agent at Curtis Brown.

REPRESENTS nonfiction books, novels.

HOW TO CONTACT Closed to submissions. Obtains most new clients through recommendations from others, solicitations.

◑ CAROL MANN AGENCY

55 Fifth Ave., New York NY 10003. (212)206-5635. **Fax:** (212)675-4809. **E-mail:** submissions@carolmannagency.com. **Website:** www.carolmannagency.com. **Contact:** Lydia Byfield. Member of AAR. Represents roughly 200 clients. 15% of clients are new/unpublished writers.

MEMBER AGENTS Carol Mann (health/medical, religion, spirituality, self-help,parenting, narrative nonfiction, current affairs); Laura Yorke; Gareth Esersky; Myrsini Stephanides (nonfiction areas of interest: pop culture and music, humor, narrative nonfiction and memoir, cookbooks; fiction areas of interest: offbeat literary fiction, graphic works, and edgy YA fiction); Joanne Wyckoff (nonfiction areas of interest: memoir, narrative nonfiction,personal narrative, psychology, women's issues, education, health and wellness, parenting, serious self-help, natural history; also accepts fiction).

REPRESENTS nonfiction books, novels. **Considers these nonfiction areas:** anthropology, archeology, architecture, art, autobiography, biography, business, child guidance, cultural interests, current affairs, design, ethnic, government, health, history, law, medicine, money, music, parenting, popular culture, politics, psychology, self-help, sociology, sports, women's issues, women's studies. **Considers these fiction areas:** commercial, literary, young adult, graphic works.

8—⊸ Does not want to receive genre fiction (romance, mystery, etc.).

HOW TO CONTACT Please see website for submission guidelines. Responds in 4 weeks to queries.

TERMS Agent receives 15% commission on domestic sales. Agent receives 20% commission on foreign sales. Offers written contract.

◑ MANSION STREET LITERARY MANAGEMENT

Website: http://mansionstreet.com. **Contact:** Jean Sagendorph; Michelle Witte.

MEMBER AGENTS Jean Sagendorph, querymansionstreet@gmail.com (pop culture, gift books, cookbooks, general nonfiction, lifestyle, design, brand extensions), **Michelle Witte**, querymichelle@man sionstreet.com (young adult, middle grade, juvenile nonfiction).

REPRESENTS Considers these nonfiction areas: cooking, design, popular culture. **Considers these fiction areas:** juvenile, middle grade, young adult.

HOW TO CONTACT Send a query letter and no more than the first 10 pages of your manuscript in the body of an e-mail. Query one specific agent at this agency. No attachments. You must list the genre in the subject line. If the genre is not in the subject line, your query will be deleted. Responds in up to 6 weeks.

RECENT SALES Authors: Paul Thurlby, Steve Ouch, Steve Seabury, Gina Hyams, Sam Pocker, Kim Siebold, Jean Sagendorph, Heidi Antman, Shannon O'Malley, Meg Bartholomy, Dawn Sokol, Hollister Hovey, Porter Hovey, Robb Pearlman.

ⓘ MANUS & ASSOCIATES LITERARY AGENCY, INC.

425 Sherman Ave., Suite 200, Palo Alto CA 94306. (650)470-5151. **Fax:** (650)470-5159. **Website:** www. manuslit.com. **Contact:** Jillian Manus, Jandy Nelson, Penny Nelson. NYC address: 444 Madison Ave., 29th Floor, New York, NY 10022 Member of AAR.

○ Prior to becoming an agent, Ms. Manus was associate publisher of two national magazines and director of development at Warner Bros. and Universal Studios; she has been a literary agent for 20 years.

MEMBER AGENTS Jandy Nelson (currently not taking on new clients). **Jillian Manus**, jillian@manuslit. com (political, memoirs, self-help, history, sports, women's issues, thrillers); **Penny Nelson,** penny@ manuslit.com (memoirs, self-help, sports, nonfiction).

REPRESENTS nonfiction books, novels. **Considers these nonfiction areas:** cooking, history, inspirational, memoirs, politics, psychology, religious, self-help, sports, women's issues. **Considers these fiction areas:** thriller.

⚙ "Our agency is unique in the way that we not only sell the material, but we edit, develop concepts, and participate in the marketing effort. We specialize in large, conceptual fiction and nonfiction, and always value a project that can be sold in the TV/feature film market." Actively seeking high-concept thrillers, commercial literary fiction, women's fiction, celebrity biographies, memoirs, multicultural fiction, popular

health, women's empowerment and mysteries. No horror, romance, science fiction, fantasy, western, young adult, children's, poetry, cookbooks, or magazine articles.

HOW TO CONTACT Snail mail submissions welcome. E-queries also accepted. For nonfiction, send a full proposal via snail mail. For fiction, send a query letter and 30 pages (unbound) if submitting via snail mail. Send only an e-query if submitting fiction via e-mail. If querying by e-mail, submit directly to one of the agents. Accepts simultaneous submissions. Responds in 3 months to queries. Responds in 3 months to mss. Obtains most new clients through recommendations from others, solicitations, conferences.

TERMS Agent receives 15% commission on domestic sales. Agent receives 20-25% commission on foreign sales. Offers written contract, binding for 2 years; 60-day notice must be given to terminate contract. Charges for photocopying and postage/UPS.

RECENT SALES *Nothing Down for the 2000s* and *Multiple Streams of Income for the 2000s*, by Robert Allen; *Missed Fortune 101*, by Doug Andrew; *Cracking the Millionaire Code*, by Mark Victor Hansen and Robert Allen; *Stress Free for Good*, by Dr. Fred Luskin and Dr. Ken Pelletier; *The Mercy of Thin Air*, by Ronlyn Domangue; *The Fine Art of Small Talk*, by Debra Fine; *Bone Men of Bonares*, by Terry Tamoff.

WRITERS CONFERENCES Maui Writers' Conference; San Diego State University Writers' Conference; Willamette Writers' Conference; BookExpo America; MEGA Book Marketing University.

TIPS "Research agents using a variety of sources."

○ MARCH TENTH, INC.

24 Hillside Terrace, Montvale NJ 07645. (201)387-6551. **Fax:** (201)387-6552. **E-mail:** hchoron@aol. com; schoron@aol.com. **Website:** www.marchten-thinc.com. **Contact:** Harry Choron, vice president. Represents 40 clients. 30% of clients are new/unpublished writers. Currently handles: nonfiction books 100%.

REPRESENTS nonfiction books. **Considers these nonfiction areas:** autobiography, biography, current affairs, film, health, history, humor, language, literature, medicine, music, popular culture, satire, theater.

⚙ "We prefer to work with published/established writers." Does not want to receive children's or young adult novels, plays, screenplays or poetry.

HOW TO CONTACT "Query with SASE. Include your proposal, a short bio, and contact information." You can also query via e-mail. Detailed submission guidelines on agency website. Accepts simultaneous submissions. Responds in 1 month to queries.

TERMS Agent receives 15% commission on domestic sales. Agent receives 20% commission on foreign sales. Agent receives 20% commission on film sales. Does not require expense money upfront.

○◉ THE DENISE MARCIL LITERARY AGENCY, LLC

483 Westover Road, Stamford CT 06902. (203)327-9970. **E-mail:** dmla@DeniseMarcilAgency.com; AnneMarie@denisemarcilagency.com. **Website:** www.denisemarcilagency.com. **Contact:** Denise Marcil, Anne Marie O'Farrell. Address for Anne Marie O'Farrell: 86 Dennis Street, Manhasset, NY 11030. Member of AAR.

○ Prior to opening her agency, Ms. Marcil served as an editorial assistant with Avon Books and as an assistant editor with Simon & Schuster.

MEMBER AGENTS Denise Marcil (self-help and popular reference books such as wellness, health, women's issues, self-help, and popular reference); **Anne Marie O'Farrell** (books that convey and promote innovative, practical and cutting edge information and ideas which help people increase their self-awareness and fulfillment and maximize their potential in whatever area they choose; she is dying to represent a great basketball book).

REPRESENTS Considers these nonfiction areas: business, health, parenting, self-help, women's issues. **Considers these fiction areas:** commercial, suspense, thriller, women's.

⌐ "In nonfiction we are looking for self-help, business, and popular reference; we want to represent books that help people's lives."

HOW TO CONTACT E-query.

TERMS Agent receives 15% commission on domestic sales. Agent receives 20% commission on foreign sales. Offers written contract, binding for 2 years.

RECENT SALES *Dogwood Hill,* by Sherryl Woods; *The Healthy Pregnancy Book,* by William Sears, M.D. and Martha Sears, R.N.; *The Allergy Book,* by Robert W. Sears, M.D. and William Sears, M.D.; *The Yellow House and The Linen Queen* by Patricia Falvey; *Irresistible Force* and *Force Of Attraction* by D.D. Ayres.

MARSAL LYON LITERARY AGENCY, LLC

PMB 121, 665 San Rodolfo Dr. 124, Solana Beach CA 92075. **Website:** www.marsallyonliteraryagency.com. **Contact:** Kevan Lyon, Jill Marsal.

MEMBER AGENTS Kevan Lyon (women's fiction, with an emphasis on commercial women's fiction, young adult fiction and all genres of romance); **Jill Marsal** (all types of women's fiction, stories of family, interesting relationships, Southern fiction, or multi-generations, and all types of romance, including romantic suspense, historical, contemporary, and category romance; she also is looking for mysteries, cozies, suspense, and thrillers); **Kathleen Rushall** (all types of women's fiction, stories of family, interesting relationships, Southern fiction, or multi-generations, and all types of romance, including romantic suspense, historical, contemporary, and category romance. She also is looking for mysteries, cozies, suspense, and thrillers, select nonfiction—mind/ body/ spirit topics, yoga, alternative medicine, parenting, crafts, business, women's interest, humor, pop-culture, and some how-to); **Patricia Nelson** (literary fiction and commercial fiction in the new adult, women's fiction, and romance genres, young adult [lots of subgenres], LGBTQ fiction for both YA and adult); **Deborah Ritchkin** (lifestyle books, specifically in the areas of food, design and entertaining; pop culture; women's issues; biography; and current events; her niche interest is projects about France, including fiction); **Shannon Hassan** (literary and commercial fiction, young adult and middle grade fiction, and select nonfiction).

REPRESENTS nonfiction books, novels. **Considers these nonfiction areas:** animals, biography, business, cooking, creative nonfiction, current affairs, diet/nutrition, history, investigative, memoirs, parenting, popular culture, politics, psychology, science, self-help, sports, women's issues, women's studies. **Considers these fiction areas:** commercial, mainstream, middle grade, mystery, new adult, paranormal, picture books, suspense, thriller, women's, young adult.

HOW TO CONTACT Query by e-mail. Query only one agent at this agency at a time. "Please visit our website to determine who is best suited for your work. Write 'query' in the subject line of your e-mail. Please allow up to several weeks to hear back on your query."

TIPS "Our agency's mission is to help writers achieve their publishing dreams. We want to work with authors not just for a book but for a career; we are dedicated to building long-term relationships with our authors and publishing partners. Our goal is to help find homes for books that engage, entertain, and make a difference."

THE EVAN MARSHALL AGENCY

07068-1121, Roseland NJ 07068-1121. (973)287-6216. **Fax:** (973)488-7910. **E-mail:** evan@evanmarshalla gency.com. **Contact:** Evan Marshall. Member of AAR. Currently handles: novels 100%.

REPRESENTS novels. **Considers these fiction areas:** action, adventure, erotica, ethnic, frontier, historical, horror, humor, inspirational, literary, mainstream, mystery, religious, satire, science fiction, suspense, western, romance (contemporary, gothic, historical, regency).

HOW TO CONTACT Do not query. Currently accepting clients only by referal from editors and our own clients. Responds in 1 week to queries. Responds in 1 month to mss. Obtains most new clients through recommendations from others.

TERMS Agent receives 15% commission on domestic sales. Agent receives 20% commission on foreign sales. Offers written contract.

RECENT SALES *My Very Best Friend,* by Cathy Lamb (Kensington); *Johanna's Bridegroom,* by Emma Miller (Love Inspired); *If He's Noble,* by Hannah Howell (Kensington); *Meet Me at the Beach,* by V. K. Sykes (Grand Central Forever; *Killing Cupid,* by Laura Levine (Kensington).

THE MARTELL AGENCY

1350 Avenue of the Americas, Suite 1205, New York NY 10019. **Fax:** (212)317-2676. **E-mail:** submissions@ themartellagency.com. **Website:** www.themartella gency.com. **Contact:** Alice Martell.

REPRESENTS nonfiction, novels. **Considers these nonfiction areas:** "big idea" books, business, current affairs, economics, health/diet, history, medicine, memoirs, multicultural, politics, personal finance, psychology, science for the general reader, self-help, women's issues.

➻ Seeks the following subjects in fiction: literary and commercial, including mystery, suspense and thrillers. Does not want to receive romance, genre mysteries, genre historical fiction, or children's books.

HOW TO CONTACT E-query Alice Martell. This should include a summary of the project and a short biography and any information, if appropriate, as to why you are qualified to write on the subject of your

book, including any publishing credits. Send to submissions@themartellagency.com.

RECENT SALES *New York Times* bestseller *Defending Jacob,* by William Landay; Pulitzer Finalist *The Forest Unseen: A Year's Watch in Nature,* by David Haskell; *How Paris Became Paris: The Birth Of The Modern City,* by Joan Dejean; National Book Award Winner *Waiting for Snow in Havana,* by Carlos Eire; National Book Award Finalist *The Boy Kings of Texas,* by Domingo Martinez.

MARTIN LITERARY MANAGEMENT

7683 SE 27th St., #307, Mercer Island WA 98040. (206)466-1773. **E-mail:** sharlene@martinliterary management.com. **Website:** www.MartinLiterary Management.com. **Contact:** Sharlene Martin.

○ Prior to becoming an agent, Ms. Martin worked in film/TV production and acquisitions.

MEMBER AGENTS Sharlene Martin (nonfiction); Clelia Gore (children's, middle grade, young adult).

REPRESENTS **Considers these nonfiction areas:** autobiography, biography, business, child guidance, current affairs, economics, health, history, how-to, humor, inspirational, investigative, medicine, memoirs, parenting, popular culture, psychology, satire, self-help, true crime, women's issues, women's studies. **Considers these fiction areas:** juvenile, middle grade, young adult.

➻ This agency has strong ties to film/TV. Actively seeking nonfiction that is highly commercial and that can be adapted to film. "We are being inundated with queries and submissions that are wrongfully being submitted to us, which only results in more frustration for the writers."

HOW TO CONTACT Query via e-mail with MS Word only. No attachments on queries; place letter in body of e-mail. Accepts simultaneous submissions. Responds in 2 weeks to queries. Responds in 3-4 weeks to mss. Obtains most new clients through recommendations from others.

TERMS Agent receives 15% commission on domestic sales. Agent receives 25% commission on foreign sales. Offers written contract, binding for 1 year; 1-month notice must be given to terminate contract. Charges author for postage and copying if material is not sent electronically. 99% of materials are sent electronically to minimize charges to author for postage and copying.

RECENT SALES *Breakthrough,* by Jack Andraka; *In the Matter of Nikola Tesla: A Romance of the Mind,* by Anthony Flacco; *Honor Bound: My Journey to Hell and Back with Amanda Knox,* by Raffaele Sollecito; *Impossible Odds: The Kidnapping of Jessica Buchanan and Dramatic Rescue by SEAL Team Six,* by Jessica Buchanan, Erik Landemalm and Anthony Flacco; *Walking on Eggshells,* by Lisa Chapman; *Newtown: An American Tragedy,* by Matthew Lysiak; *Publish Your Nonfiction Book,* by Sharlene Martin and Anthony Flacco.

TIPS "Have a strong platform for nonfiction. Please don't call. (I can't tell how well you write by the sound of your voice.) I welcome e-mail. I'm very responsive when I'm interested in a query and work hard to get my clients' materials in the best possible shape before submissions. Do your homework prior to submission and only submit your best efforts. Please review our website carefully to make sure we're a good match for your work. If you read my book, *Publish Your Nonfiction Book: Strategies For Learning the Industry, Selling Your Book and Building a Successful Career* (Writer's Digest Books) you'll know exactly how to charm me."

⊙ MARGRET MCBRIDE LITERARY AGENCY

P.O. Box 9128, La Jolla CA 92038. (858)454-1550. **Fax:** (858)454-2156. **E-mail:** staff@mcbridelit.com. **Website:** www.mcbrideliterary.com. **Contact:** Michael Daley, submissions manager. Member of AAR. Other memberships include Authors Guild.

○ Prior to opening her agency, Ms. McBride worked at Random House, Ballantine Books, and Warner Books.

MEMBER AGENTS Margret McBride; Faye Atchinson.

REPRESENTS nonfiction books, novels. **Considers these nonfiction areas:** autobiography, biography, business, cooking, cultural interests, current affairs, economics, ethnic, foods, government, health, history, how-to, law, medicine, money, popular culture, politics, psychology, science, self-help, sociology, technology, women's issues, style. **Considers these fiction areas:** action, adventure, crime, detective, historical, humor, literary, mainstream, mystery, police, satire, suspense, thriller.

⚷ This agency specializes in mainstream fiction and nonfiction. Actively seeking commercial fiction and nonfiction, business, health, self-

help. Please do not send: screenplays, romance, poetry, or children's.

HOW TO CONTACT "Submit a query letter to us via e-mail (staff@mcbridelit.com) or snail mail. In your letter, please provide a brief synopsis of your work, as well as any pertinent information about yourself." There are detailed nonfiction proposal guidelines online. Accepts simultaneous submissions. Responds in 8 weeks to queries. Responds in 6-8 weeks to mss.

TERMS Agent receives 15% commission on domestic sales. Agent receives 25% commission on foreign sales. Charges for overnight delivery and photocopying.

RECENT SALES *Value Tales Treasure: Stories for Growing Good People,* by Spencer Johnson, MD. (Simon & Schuster Children's); *The 6 Reasons You'll Get the Job: What Employers Really Want—Whether They Know it or Not,* by Debra MacDougall and Elisabeth Harney Sanders-Park (Tarcher); *The Solution: Conquer Your Fear, Control Your Future,* by Lucinda Bassett (Sterling).

TIPS "Our office does not accept e-mail queries!"

⊙ E.J. MCCARTHY AGENCY

(415)383-6639. **E-mail:** ejmagency@gmail.com. **Website:** http://www.publishersmarketplace.com/members/ejmccarthy/.

○ Prior to his current position, Mr. McCarthy was a former executive editor with more than 20 years book-publishing experience (Bantam Doubleday Dell, Presidio Press, Ballantine/Random House).

REPRESENTS Considers these nonfiction areas: biography, history, memoirs, military, sports.

⚷ This agency specializes in nonfiction.

HOW TO CONTACT Query first by e-mail.

RECENT SALES *One Bullet Away* by Nathaniel Fick; *The Unforgiving Minute* by Craig Mullaney; *The Sling And The Stone* by Thomas X. Hammes; *The Heart and the First,* by Eric Greitens; *When Books Went to War,* by Molly Guptill Manning.

THE MCCARTHY AGENCY, LLC

456 Ninth St., No. 28, Hoboken NJ 07030. **E-mail:** McCarthylit@aol.com. **Contact:** Shawna McCarthy. Member of AAR.

MEMBER AGENTS Shawna McCarthy.

REPRESENTS nonfiction books, novels. **Considers these fiction areas:** fantasy, middle grade, mystery, new adult, science fiction, women's, young adult.

☛ This agency represents mostly novels. No picture books.

HOW TO CONTACT E-queries only. Accepts simultaneous submissions.

SEAN McCARTHY LITERARY AGENCY

E-mail: submissions@mccarthylit.com. **Website:** www.mccarthylit.com. **Contact:** Sean McCarthy.

○ Prior to his current position, Sean McCarthy began his publishing career as an editorial intern at Overlook Press and then moved over to the Sheldon Fogelman Agency.

REPRESENTS Considers these fiction areas: juvenile, middle grade, picture books, young adult.

☛ Sean is drawn to flawed, multifaceted characters with devastatingly concise writing in YA, and boy-friendly mysteries or adventures in MG. In picture books, he looks more for unforgettable characters, off-beat humor, and especially clever endings. He is not currently interested in high fantasy, message-driven stories, or query letters that pose too many questions.

HOW TO CONTACT E-query. "Please include a brief description of your book, your biography, and any literary or relevant professional credits in your query letter. If you are a novelist: Please submit the first three chapters of your ms (or roughly 25 pages) and a one page synopsis in the body of the e-mail or as a Word or PDF attachment. If you are a picture book author: Please submit the complete text of your ms. We are not currently accepting picture book mss over 1,000 words. If you are an illustrator: Please attach up to 3 JPEGs or PDFs of your work, along with a link to your website."

McCARTHY CREATIVE SERVICES

625 Main St., Suite 834, New York NY 10044-0035. (212)832-3428. **Fax:** (212)829-9610. **E-mail:** paulmc carthy@mccarthycreative.com. **Website:** www.mc carthycreative.com. **Contact:** Paul D. McCarthy. Other memberships include the Authors Guild, American Society of Journalists & Authors, National Book Critics Circle, Authors League of America. Represents 5 clients. 0% of clients are new/unpublished writers. Currently handles: nonfiction books 95%, novels 5%.

○ Prior to his current position, Mr. McCarthy was a professional writer, literary agent at the Scott Meredith Literary Agency, senior editor at publishing companies (Simon & Schuster, HarperCollins and Doubleday) and a public speaker. Learn much more about Mr. McCarthy by visiting his website.

MEMBER AGENTS Paul D. McCarthy.

REPRESENTS nonfiction books, novels. **Considers these nonfiction areas:** animals, anthropology, art, biography, business, child, current affairs, education, ethnic, gay, government, health, history, how to, humor, language, memoirs, military, money, music, nature, popular culture, psychology, religion, science, self help, sociology, sports, translation, true crime, women's. **Considers these fiction areas:** glitz, adventure, confession, detective, erotica, ethnic, family, fantasy, feminist, gay, historical, horror, humor, literary, mainstream, mystery, regional, romance, science, sports, thriller, western, young, women's.

☛ "I deliberately founded my company to be unlimited in its range. That's what I offer, and the world has responded. My agency was founded so that I could maximize and build on the value of my combined experience for my authors and other clients, in all of my capacities and more. I think it's *very* important for authors to know that because I'm so exclusive as an agent, I may not be able to offer representation on the basis of the ms they submit. However, if they decide to invest in their book and lifetime career as authors, by engaging my professional, near-unique editorial services, there is the possibility that at the end of the process, when they've achieved the very best, most salable and competitive book they can write, I may see sufficient potential in the book and their next books, that I do offer to be their agent. Representation is never guaranteed."

HOW TO CONTACT Submit outline, one chapter (either first or best). Queries and submissions by e-mail only. Send as e-mail attachment. Responds in 3-4 weeks to queries. Obtains most new clients through recommendations from others.

TERMS Agent receives 15% commission on domestic sales. Agent receives 20% commission on foreign sales. Offers written contract; 30-day notice must be given to terminate contract. "All reading done in deciding whether or not to offer representation is free. Mailing and postage expenses that incurred on the author's behalf are always approved by them in advance."

TIPS "Always keep in mind that your query letter/proposal is only one of hundreds and thousands that are competing for the agent's attention. Therefore, your presentation of your book and yourself as author has to be immediate, intense, compelling, and concise. Make the query letter one-page, and after short, introductory paragraph, write a 150-word keynote description of your ms."

⊕ MCCORMICK LITERARY

37 West 20th St., New York NY 10011. (212)691-9726. **Website:** http://mccormicklit.com/.
MEMBER AGENTS David McCormick; Pilar Queen (narrative nonfiction, practical nonfiction, and commercial women's fiction); **Bridget McCarthy** (literary and commercial fiction, narrative nonfiction, memoir, and cookbooks); **Alia Hanna Habib** (literary fiction, narrative nonfiction, memoir and cookbooks); **Edward Orloff** (literary fiction and narrative nonfiction, especially cultural history, politics, biography, and the arts).
HOW TO CONTACT Snail mail queries only. Send an SASE.

✪⊘ ANNE MCDERMID & ASSOCIATES, LTD

64 Bloem Ave., Toronto ON M6E 1S1 Canada. (416)324-8845. **Fax:** (416)324-8870. **E-mail:** info@mcdermidagency.com. **Website:** www.mcdermidagency.com. **Contact:** Anne McDermid. Estab. 1996.
MEMBER AGENTS Anne McDermid, Martha Webb, Monica Pacheco, and Chris Bucci.
REPRESENTS nonfiction books, novels.
⊶ "The agency represents literary novelists and commercial novelists of high quality, and also writers of nonfiction in the areas of memoir, biography, history, literary travel, narrative science, and investigative journalism. We also represent a certain number of children's and YA writers and writers in the fields of science fiction and fantasy.
HOW TO CONTACT Query via e-mail or mail with a brief bio, description, and first 5 pages of project only. *No unsolicited mss.* Obtains most new clients through recommendations from others.

◑ THE MCGILL AGENCY, INC.

10000 N. Central Expressway, Suite 400, Dallas TX 75231. (214)390-5970. **E-mail:** info.mcgillagency@gmail.com. **Contact:** Jack Bollinger. Estab. 2009.

Represents 10 clients. 50% of clients are new/unpublished writers.
MEMBER AGENTS Jack Bollinger (eclectic tastes in nonfiction and fiction); **Amy Cohn** (nonfiction interests include women's issues, gay/lesbian, ethnic/cultural, memoirs, true crime; fiction interests include mystery, suspense and thriller).
REPRESENTS Considers these nonfiction areas: biography, business, child guidance, current affairs, education, ethnic, gay, health, history, how-to, memoirs, military, psychology, self-help, true crime, women's issues. **Considers these fiction areas:** historical, mainstream, mystery, romance, thriller.
HOW TO CONTACT Query via e-mail. Responds in 2 weeks to queries and 6 weeks to mss. Obtains new clients through conferences.
TERMS Agent receives 15% commission.

◯ SALLY HILL MCMILLAN & ASSOCIATES, INC.

429 E. Kingston Ave., Charlotte NC 28203. (704)334-0897. **E-mail:** mcmagency@aol.com. **Website:** www.publishersmarketplace.com/members/McMillanAgency/. **Contact:** Sally Hill McMillan. Member of AAR.
REPRESENTS Considers these nonfiction areas: creative nonfiction, health, history, women's issues, women's studies. **Considers these fiction areas:** commercial, literary, mainstream, mystery.
⊶ Do not send science fiction, military, horror, fantasy/adventure, children's or cookbooks.
HOW TO CONTACT "Please query first with SASE and await further instructions. E-mail queries will be read, but not necessarily answered."
RECENT SALES Clients include—Fiction: Lynne Hinton, Linda Lenhoff, Jennifer Manske Fenske, Joe Martin, Nancy Peacock, Mike Stewart. Nonfiction: Lois Trigg Chaplin, Rose Clayton, Tanya Denckla, Andrea Engber, Ray Jones, Dr. Leah Klungness, Dr. Sally Kneidel, Katie Lyle, Bruce Roberts, Nancy Roberts, Dr. Bryan Robinson, Martha Woodham, John Yow, Victoria Zak.

BOB MECOY LITERARY AGENCY

66 Grand St., Suite 1, New York NY 10013. (212)226-1398. **E-mail:** mecoy@aol.com. **Contact:** Bob Mecoy.
MEMBER AGENTS Bob Mecoy.
⊶ Seeking fiction (literary, crime, romance); nonfiction (true crime, finance, memoir, literary,

prescriptive self-help & graphic novelists). No Westerns.

HOW TO CONTACT Query with sample chapters and synopsis.

○ MENDEL MEDIA GROUP, LLC

115 W. 30th St., Suite 800, New York NY 10001. (646)239-9896. **Fax:** (212)685-4717. **E-mail:** scott@mendelmedia.com. **Website:** www.mendelmedia.com. Member of AAR. Represents 40-60 clients.

○ Prior to becoming an agent, Mr. Mendel was an academic. "I taught American literature, Yiddish, Jewish studies, and literary theory at the University of Chicago and the University of Illinois at Chicago while working on my PhD in English. I also worked as a freelance technical writer and as the managing editor of a healthcare magazine. In 1998, I began working for the late Jane Jordan Browne, a long-time agent in the book publishing world."

REPRESENTS nonfiction books, novels, scholarly, with potential for broad/popular appeal. **Considers these nonfiction areas:** Americana, animals, anthropology, architecture, art, biography, business, child guidance, cooking, current affairs, dance, diet/nutrition, education, environment, ethnic, foods, gardening, gay/lesbian, government, health, history, how-to, humor, investigative, language, medicine, memoirs, military, money, multicultural, music, parenting, philosophy, popular culture, psychology, recreation, regional, religious, science, self-help, sex, sociology, software, spirituality, sports, true crime, war, women's issues, women's studies, Jewish topics; creative nonfiction. **Considers these fiction areas:** action, adventure, contemporary issues, crime, detective, erotica, ethnic, feminist, gay, glitz, historical, humor, inspirational, juvenile, lesbian, literary, mainstream, mystery, picture books, police, religious, romance, satire, sports, thriller, young adult, Jewish fiction.

☚━☞ "I am interested in major works of history, current affairs, biography, business, politics, economics, science, major memoirs, narrative nonfiction, and other sorts of general nonfiction." Actively seeking new, major or definitive work on a subject of broad interest, or a controversial, but authoritative, new book on a subject that affects many people's lives. I also represent more light-hearted nonfiction projects, such as gift or novelty books, when they suit the market

particularly well." Does not want "queries about projects written years ago that were unsuccessfully shopped to a long list of trade publishers by either the author or another agent. I am specifically not interested in reading short, category romances (regency, time travel, paranormal, etc.), horror novels, supernatural stories, poetry, original plays, or film scripts."

HOW TO CONTACT Query with SASE. Do not e-mail or fax queries. For nonfiction, include a complete, fully edited book proposal with sample chapters. For fiction, include a complete synopsis and no more than 20 pages of sample text. Responds in 2 weeks to queries. Responds in 4-6 weeks to mss. Obtains most new clients through recommendations from others.

TERMS Agent receives 15% commission on domestic sales. Agent receives 20% commission on foreign sales.

WRITERS CONFERENCES BookExpo America; Frankfurt Book Fair; London Book Fair; RWA National Conference; Modern Language Association Convention; Jerusalem Book Fair.

TIPS "While I am not interested in being flattered by a prospective client, it does matter to me that she knows why she is writing to me in the first place. Is one of my clients a colleague of hers? Has she read a book by one of my clients that led her to believe I might be interested in her work? Authors of descriptive nonfiction should have real credentials and expertise in their subject areas, either as academics, journalists, or policy experts, and authors of prescriptive nonfiction should have legitimate expertise and considerable experience communicating their ideas in seminars and workshops, in a successful business, through the media, etc."

○ SCOTT MEREDITH LITERARY AGENCY

One Exchange Plaza, Suite 2002, 55 Broadway, New York NY 10006. (646)274-1970. **Fax:** (212)977-5997. **E-mail:** info@scottmeredith.com. **Website:** www.scottmeredith.com. **Contact:** Arthur Klebanoff, CEO. Adheres to the AAR canon of ethics. Represents 20 clients. 5% of clients are new/unpublished writers. Currently handles: nonfiction books 85%, novels 5%, textbooks 5%.

○ Prior to becoming an agent, Mr. Klebanoff was a lawyer.

REPRESENTS nonfiction books, textbooks.

NEW AGENT SPOTLIGHT

STEPHANIE DELMAN
SANFORD J. GREENBURGER ASSOCIATES

Greenburger.com

@imaginarysmd

ABOUT STEPHANIE: After graduating from Johns Hopkins University with a B.A. in Writing Seminars, Stephanie held editorial positions at a health website and a literary journal, and then happily joined Sanford J. Greenburger Associates. There, she works for the president, collaborates on foreign rights, and is now building her own list.

SHE IS SEEKING: Literary fiction, historical/book club fiction featuring stories that haven't been told, upmarket women's fiction, and smart psychological thrillers/suspense. In nonfiction, Stephanie looks for pop culture, and blog-to-book projects (from writers with established platforms). She does not represent children's books, sci-fi, fantasy, romance novels, erotica, or prescriptive nonfiction.

HOW TO SUBMIT: Query Stephanie at sdelman@sjga.com. Please send a query letter and the first few chapters of your manuscript in the body of your e-mail, and Stephanie will be in touch if she would like to read more.

This agency's specialty lies in category nonfiction publishing programs. Actively seeking category leading nonfiction. Does not want to receive first fiction projects.

HOW TO CONTACT Query with SASE. Submit proposal package, author bio. Accepts simultaneous submissions. Responds in 2 weeks to queries. Responds in 4 weeks to mss. Obtains most new clients through recommendations from others.

TERMS Agent receives 15% commission on domestic sales. Offers written contract.

RECENT SALES *The Conscience of a Liberal* and *End this Depression Now*, by Paul Krugman; *The King of Oil: The Secret Lives of Marc Rich*, by Daniel Ammann; *Ten*, by Sheila Lukins; *Peterson Field Guide to Birds of North America*.

⊘ DORIS S. MICHAELS LITERARY AGENCY, INC.

1841 Broadway, Suite 903, New York NY 10023. (212)265-9474. **Fax:** (212)265-9480. **Website:** www.dsmagency.com. **Contact:** Doris S. Michaels, President. Member of AAR. Other memberships include WNBA.

REPRESENTS novels. **Considers these fiction areas:** commercial, literary.

HOW TO CONTACT As of early 2015, they are not taking new clients. Check the website to see if this agency reopens to queries.

⊘ MARTHA MILLARD LITERARY AGENCY

50 W.67th St., #1G, New York NY 10023. **Contact:** Martha Millard. Estab. 1980. Member of AAR. Other memberships include SFWA.

Prior to becoming an agent, Ms. Millard worked in editorial departments of several publishers and was vice president at another agency for more than four years.

REPRESENTS nonfiction books, novels. **Considers these nonfiction areas:** architecture, art, autobiography, biography, business, child guidance, cooking, cultural interests, current affairs, design, economics, education, ethnic, film, health, history, how-to, memoirs, metaphysics, money, music, New Age, parenting, photography, popular culture, psychology, self-help, theater, true crime, women's issues, women's studies. **Considers these fiction areas:** fantasy, mystery, romance, science fiction, suspense.

HOW TO CONTACT No unsolicited queries. **Referrals only.** Obtains most new clients through recommendations from others.

TERMS Agent receives 15% commission on domestic sales. Agent receives 20% commission on foreign sales. Offers written contract.

HOWARD MORHAIM LITERARY AGENCY

30 Pierrepont St., Brooklyn NY 11201. (718)222-8400. **Fax:** (718)222-5056. **Website:** www.morhaimliterary.com. Member of AAR.

MEMBER AGENTS Howard Morhaim (no unsolicited submissions), Kate McKean, kmckean@morhaimliterary.com (adult fiction: contemporary romance, contemporary women's fiction, literary fiction, historical fiction set in the 20th Century, high fantasy, magical realism, science fiction, middle grade, young adult; in nonfiction, books by authors with demonstrable platforms in the areas of sports, food writing, humor, design, creativity, and craft [sewing, knitting, etc.], narrative nonfiction by authors with or without an established platform. Some memoir); Paul Lamb, paul@morhaimliterary.com (nonfiction in a wide variety of genres and subjects, notably business, political science, sociology, memoir, travel writing, sports, pop culture, and music; he is also interested in select literary fiction); Maria Ribas, maria@morhaimliterary.com (cookbooks, self-help, health, diet, home, parenting, and humor, all from authors with demonstrable platforms; she's also interested in narrative nonfiction and select memoir).

REPRESENTS Considers these nonfiction areas: business, cooking, crafts, creative nonfiction, design, health, humor, memoirs, parenting, self-help, sports. **Considers these fiction areas:** fantasy, historical, literary, middle grade, new adult, romance, science fiction, women's, young adult, LGBTQ young adult, magical realism, fantasy should be high fantasy, historical fiction should be no earlier than the 20th century.

Kate McKean is open to many subgenres and categories of YA and MG fiction. Check the website for the most details. Actively seeking fiction, nonfiction, and young adult novels.

HOW TO CONTACT Query via e-mail with cover letter and three sample chapters. See each agent's listing for specifics.

MOVEABLE TYPE MANAGEMENT

244 Madison Ave., Suite 334, New York NY 10016. (646)431-6134. **Website:** www.mtmgmt.net.

MEMBER AGENTS Adam Chromy.

REPRESENTS Considers these nonfiction areas: business, creative nonfiction, history, how-to, humor, memoirs, money, popular culture. **Considers these fiction areas:** commercial, literary, mainstream, romance, women's, young adult.

Mr. Chromy is a generalist, meaning that he accepts fiction submissions of virtually any kind (except juvenile books aimed for middle grade and younger) as well as nonfiction. He has sold books in the following categories: new adult, women's, romance, memoir, pop culture, young adult, lifestyle, horror, how-to, general fiction, and more.

HOW TO CONTACT E-queries only. Responds if interested. For nonfiction: Send a query letter in the body of an e-mail that precisely introduces your topic and approach, and includes a descriptive bio. For journalists and academics, please also feel free to include a CV. Fiction: Send your query letter and the first 10 pages of your novel in the body of an e-mail. Your subject line needs to contain the word "Query" or your message will not reach the agency. No attachments and no snail mail.

RECENT SALES *The Gin Lovers* by Jamie Brenner (St. Martin's Press); *Miss Chatterley* by Logan Belle (Pocket/S&S); *Sons Of Zeus*, by Noble Smith (Thomas Dunne Books); *World Made By Hand And Too Much Magic* by James Howard Kunstler (Grove/Atlantic Press); *Dirty Rocker Boys* by Bobbie Brown (Gallery/S&S).

DEE MURA LITERARY

P.O. Box 131, Massapequa NY 11762. (516)795-1616. **Fax:** (516)795-8797. **E-mail:** query@deemuraliterary.com. **Website:** www.deemuraliterary.com. **Contact:** Dee Mura. 50% of clients are new/unpublished writers.

Prior to opening her agency, Mura was a public relations executive with a roster of film and entertainment clients. She is the president and CEO of both Dee Mura Literary and Dee Mura Entertainment.

MEMBER AGENTS Dee Mura, Kimiko Nakamura, Kaylee Davis.

REPRESENTS Considers these nonfiction areas: animals, anthropology, archeology, art, biography, business, cooking, creative nonfiction, current affairs, environment, ethnic, gardening, health, history, humor, inspirational, medicine, memoirs, New Age, parenting, photography, popular culture, psychology, religious, science, self-help, spirituality, sports, technology, travel, entertainment, Jewish, LGBTQ, mind/body, nature. **Considers these fiction areas:** adventure, commercial, contemporary issues, crime, erotica, family saga, fantasy, historical, literary, middle grade, mystery, new adult, paranormal, romance, satire, science fiction, suspense, thriller, women's, young adult, espionage, magical realism, speculative fiction.

Fiction with crossover film potential. No screenplays, poetry, or children's picture books.

HOW TO CONTACT Query with SASE or e-mail query@deemuraliterary.com (e-mail queries are preferred). Please include the first 25 pages in the body of the e-mail as well as a short author bio and synopsis of the work. Responds to queries in 3-4 weeks. Responds to mss in 8 weeks. Obtains new clients through recommendations, solicitation, and conferences Accepts simultaneous submissions. Obtains new clients through recommendations, solicitation, and conferences.

TERMS Agent receives 15% commission on domestic sales. Agent receives 20% commission on foreign sales. Offers written contract.

RECENT SALES *An Infinite Number of Parallel Universes*, by Randy Ribay; *The Number 7*, by Jessica Lidh.

WRITERS CONFERENCES Alaska Writers Guild Conference, BookExpo America, Hampton Roads Writers Conference, NESCBWI Regional Conference, San Francisco Writers Conference, Books Alive! Conference, Writer's Digest Conference East, LVW's Writers Meet Agents Conference

ERIN MURPHY LITERARY AGENCY

2700 Woodlands Village, #300-458, Flagstaff AZ 86001. **Fax:** (928)525-2480. **Website:** http://emliterary.com. **Contact:** Erin Murphy, president; Ammi-Joan Paquette, senior agent; Tricia Lawrence, associate agent. 25% of clients are new/unpublished writers. Currently handles: juvenile books.

REPRESENTS Considers these fiction areas: middle grade, picture books, young adult.

Specializes in children's books only.

TERMS Agent receives 15% commission on domestic sales; 20-30% on foreign sales. Offers written contract. 30 days notice must be given to terminate contract.

JEAN V. NAGGAR LITERARY AGENCY, INC.

216 E. 75th St., Suite 1E, New York NY 10021. (212)794-1082. **E-mail:** jweltz@jvnla.com; atasman@jvnla.com. **Website:** www.jvnla.com. **Contact:** Jean Naggar. Member of AAR. Other memberships include Women's Media Group, SCBWI, Pace University's Masters in Publishing Board Member. Represents 450 clients. 20% of clients are new/unpublished writers.

Ms. Naggar has served as president of AAR.

MEMBER AGENTS Jennifer Weltz (well researched and original historicals, thrillers with a unique voice, wry dark humor, and magical realism; enthralling narrative nonfiction; young adult, middle grade); **Jean Naggar** (taking no new clients); **Alice Tasman** (literary, commercial, YA, middle grade, and nonfiction in the categories of narrative, biography, music or pop culture); **Elizabeth Evans** (narrative nonfiction [travel/adventure], memoir, current affairs, pop science, journalism, health and wellness, psychology, history, pop culture, cookbooks and humor); **Laura Biagi** (literary fiction, magical realism, psychological thrillers, young adult novels, middle grade novels, and picture books).

REPRESENTS nonfiction books, novels. **Considers these nonfiction areas:** biography, creative nonfiction, current affairs, health, history, humor, memoirs, music, popular culture, psychology, science. **Considers these fiction areas:** commercial, fantasy, literary, middle grade, picture books, thriller, young adult.

This agency specializes in mainstream fiction and nonfiction and literary fiction with commercial potential. Does not want to receive screenplays.

HOW TO CONTACT "Visit our website, www.jvnla. com, for complete, up-to-date submission guidelines. Please be advised that Jean Naggar is no longer accepting new clients." Accepts simultaneous submissions.

TERMS Agent receives 15% commission on domestic sales. Agent receives 20% commission on foreign sales. Offers written contract. Charges for overseas mailing, messenger services, book purchases, long-distance telephone, photocopying—all deductible from royalties received.

RECENT SALES *Mort(e)* by Robert Repino; *The Paying Guests* by Sarah Waters; *Woman with a Gun* by Phillip Margolin; *An Unseemly Wife* by E.B. Moore; *The Man Who Walked Away* by Maud Casey; *A Lige in Men* by Gina Frangello; *The Tudor Vendetta* by C.W. Gortner; *Prototype* by M.D. Waters.

TIPS "We recommend courage, fortitude, and patience: the courage to be true to your own vision, the fortitude to finish a novel and polish it again and again before sending it out, and the patience to accept rejection gracefully and wait for the stars to align themselves appropriately for success."

⬗ NELSON LITERARY AGENCY

1732 Wazee St., Suite 207, Denver CO 80202. (303)292-2805. **Website:** www.nelsonagency.com. **Contact:** Kristin Nelson, president. Estab. 2002. Member of AAR. RWA, SCBWI, SFWA.

- Prior to opening her own agency, Ms. Nelson worked as a literary scout and subrights agent for agent Jody Rein.

REPRESENTS Considers these fiction areas: commercial, fantasy, literary, mainstream, middle grade, romance, science fiction, women's, young adult.

- NLA specializes in representing commercial fiction and high-caliber literary fiction. They represent many pop genre categories, including things like historical romance, steampunk, and all subgenres of YA. Does not want short story collections, mysteries, thrillers, Christian, horror, children's picture books, or screenplays.

HOW TO CONTACT Query by e-mail. Put the word "Query" in the e-mail subject line. No attachments; querykristin@nelsonagency.com. Responds within 1 month.

RECENT SALES *Champion*, by Marie Lu (young adult); *Wool*, by Hugh Howey (science fiction); *The*

Whatnot, by Stefan Bachmann (middle grade); *Catching Jordan*, by Miranda Kenneally (young adult); *Broken Like This*, by Monica Trasandes (debut literary fiction); *The Darwin Elevator*, by Jason Hough (debut science fiction). A full list of clients is available online.

⊕ ◑ NEW LEAF LITERARY & MEDIA, INC.

110 W. 40th St., Suite 410, New York NY 10018. (646)248-7989. **Fax:** (646)861-4654. **E-mail:** query@newleafliterary.com. Member of AAR.

MEMBER AGENTS Joanna Volpe (women's fiction, thriller, horror, speculative fiction, literary fiction and historical fiction, young adult, middle grade, art-focused picture books); **Kathleen Ortiz**, Director of Subsidiary Rights and literary agent (new voices in YA nd animator/illustrator talent); **Suzie Townsend** (new adult, young adult, middle grade, romance [all subgenres], fantasy [urban fantasy, science fiction, steampunk, epic fantasy] and crime fiction [mysteries, thrillers]); **Pouya Shahbazian**, Director of Film and Television; **Mackenzie Brady** (her taste in nonfiction extends beyond science books to memoirs, lost histories, epic sports narratives, true crime and gift/lifestyle books; she represents select adult and YA fiction projects, as well).

REPRESENTS Considers these fiction areas: crime, fantasy, historical, horror, literary, mainstream, middle grade, mystery, new adult, paranormal, picture books, romance, thriller, women's, young adult.

HOW TO CONTACT "Only query us when your manuscript is complete. Do not query more than one agent at New Leaf Literary & Media, Inc. Put the word 'Query' in the subject line along with the target agent's name. No attachments. Responds if interested." Responds only if interested.

RECENT SALES *Four*, by Veronica Roth (HarperCollins); *The Little World of Liz Climo*, by Liz Climo (Running Press); *Ruin and Risin,g* by Leigh Bardugo (Henry Holt); *A Snicker of Magic*, by Natalie Lloyd (Scholastic).

DANA NEWMAN LITERARY

9720 Wilshire Blvd., 5th Floor, Beverly Hills CA 90212. (323)974-4334. **Fax:** (866)636-7585. **E-mail:** dananewmanliterary@gmail.com. **Website:** www.about.me/dananewman. **Contact:** Dana Newman. Estab. 2009. Member of AAR. Represents 15 clients. 50% of clients are new/unpublished writers. Currently handles: 85% nonfiction books, 15% novels.

○ Prior to being an agent, Ms. Newman was an attorney in the entertainment industry for 14 years.

MEMBER AGENTS Dana Newman (narrative nonfiction, business, biography, lifestyle, current affairs, parenting, memoir, pop culture, health, literary, and upmarket fiction).

REPRESENTS nonfiction, fiction. **Considers these nonfiction areas:** architecture, art, autobiography, biography, business, child guidance, cooking, cultural interests, current affairs, design, education, ethnic, film, foods, gay/lesbian, government, health, history, how-to, language, law, literature, medicine, memoirs, metaphysics, music, popular culture, politics, science, self-help, sociology, sports, technology, theater, women's issues, women's studies. **Considers these fiction areas:** historical, literary, women's.

⊶ Ms. Newman has a background in contracts, licensing, and intellectual property law. She is experienced in digital content creation and distribution and embraces the changing publishing environment. Actively seeking narrative nonfiction, historical, or upmarket fiction. Does not want religious, children's, poetry, horror, mystery, thriller, romance, or science fiction.

HOW TO CONTACT Submit query letter, outline, synopsis, 2 sample chapters, biography, and proposal. Accepts simultaneous submissions. Responds to queries/proposals in 2 weeks; mss in 1 month. Obtains new clients through recommendations from others, queries, submissions.

TERMS Obtains 15% commission on domestic sales; 20% on foreign sales. Offers 1 year written contract. Notice must be given 30 days prior to terminate a contract.

RECENT SALES *Just Add Water*, by Clay Marzo and Robert Yehling (Houghton Mifflin Harcourt); *Stray Cat Slim: Jim Phantom's memoir* (St. Martin's Press); *Targeted*, by Mike Smith (AMACOM); *Tuff Juice*, by Caron Butler and Steve Springer (Lyons Press); *Like a Woman*, by Debra Busman (Dzanc Books]; *Home Sweet Anywhere*, by Lynne Martin (Sourcebooks); *Cracked, Not Broken*, by Kevin Hines (Roman and Littlefield).

○ HAROLD OBER ASSOCIATES

425 Madison Ave., New York NY 10017. (212)759-8600. **Fax:** (212)759-9428. **Website:** www.haroldober.com. **Contact:** Appropriate agent. Member of AAR. Represents 250 clients. 10% of clients are new/unpublished writers. Currently handles: nonfiction books 35%, novels 50%, juvenile books 15%.

○ Mr. Elwell was previously with Elwell & Weiser.

MEMBER AGENTS Phyllis Westberg; Pamela Malpas; Craig Tenney (few new clients, mostly Ober backlist); Jake Elwell (previously with Elwell & Weiser).

HOW TO CONTACT Submit concise query letter addressed to a specific agent with the first 5 pages of the ms or proposal and SASE. No fax or e-mail. Does not handle filmscripts or plays. Responds as promptly as possible. Obtains most new clients through recommendations from others.

TERMS Agent receives 15% commission on domestic sales. Agent receives 20% commission on foreign sales. Charges clients for express mail/package services.

○ FIFI OSCARD AGENCY, INC.

110 W. 40th St., 16th Floor, New York NY 10018. (212)764-1100. **Fax:** (212)840-5019. **E-mail:** agency@fifioscard.com; psawyer@fifioscard.com. **Website:** www.fifioscard.com. **Contact:** Literary Department. Signatory of WGA.

MEMBER AGENTS Peter Sawyer; Carmen La Via.

REPRESENTS nonfiction books, novels, stage plays. **Considers these nonfiction areas:** biography, business, cooking, economics, health, history, inspirational, religious, science, sports, technology, women's issues, women's studies, African American, body/mind/spirit, lifestyle, cookbooks.

HOW TO CONTACT Use the agency's online submission form. Note if it is a simultaneous submission. Accepts simultaneous submissions. Responds in 2 weeks to queries.

TERMS Agent receives 15% commission on domestic sales. Agent receives 20% commission on foreign sales. Agent receives 10% commission on film sales. Charges clients for photocopying expenses.

⊘ PARADIGM TALENT AND LITERARY AGENCY

360 Park Avenue South, 16th floor, New York NY 10010. (212)897-6400. **Fax:** (212)764-8941. **Website:** www.paradigmagency.com.

MEMBER AGENTS Alyssa Reuben, others.

REPRESENTS movie, tv, movie scripts, feature film, theatrical stage play, stage plays.

☞ Paradigm Talent and Literary Agency is an Los-Angeles-based talent agency with additional offices in New York City, Nashville, and Monterey. The firm acquired Writers & Artists Group International in 2004. The acquisition of WAGI added both talent and agents to Paradigm's roster, bolstering its New York office with legit agents, representing playwrights and theatre directors.

HOW TO CONTACT *No unsolicited queries.* Do not query unless meeting an agent at an event, or through a referral.

◑ PARK LITERARY GROUP, LLC

270 Lafayette St., Suite 1504, New York NY 10012. (212)691-3500. **Fax:** (212)691-3540. **E-mail:** queries@parkliterary.com. **Website:** www.parkliterary.com. Estab. 2005.

MEMBER AGENTS Theresa Park (plot-driven fiction and serious nonfiction); **Abigail Koons** (popular science, history, politics, current affairs and art, and women's fiction); **Peter Knapp** (middle grade and young adult fiction).

REPRESENTS nonfiction books, novels. **Considers these nonfiction areas:** art, current affairs, history, politics, science. **Considers these fiction areas:** middle grade, suspense, thriller, women's, young adult.

☞ The Park Literary Group represents fiction and nonfiction with a boutique approach: an emphasis on servicing a relatively small number of clients, with the highest professional standards and focused personal attention. Does not want to receive poetry or screenplays.

HOW TO CONTACT Please specify the first and last name of the agent to whom you are submitting in the subject line of the e-mail and send your query letter and accompanying material to queries@parkliterary.com. All materials must be in the body of the e-mail. Responds if interested. For fiction submissions to Abigail Koons or Theresa Park, please include a query letter with short synopsis and the first three chapters of your work. For middle grade and young adult submissions to Peter Knapp, please include a query letter and the first three chapters of your novel (no synopsis necessary). For nonfiction submissions, please send a query letter, proposal, and sample chapter(s).

RECENT SALES This agency's client list is on their website. It includes bestsellers Nicholas Sparks, Soman Chainani, Emily Giffin, and Debbie Macomber.

◑ THE RICHARD PARKS AGENCY

P.O. Box 693, Salem NY 12865. (518)854-9466. **Fax:** (518)854-9466. **E-mail:** rp@richardparksagency.com. **Website:** www.richardparksagency.com. **Contact:** Richard Parks. Member of AAR. Currently handles: nonfiction books 55%, novels 40%, story collections 5%.

REPRESENTS nonfiction books, novels. **Considers these nonfiction areas:** animals, anthropology, archeology, art, autobiography, biography, business, child guidance, cooking, crafts, cultural interests, current affairs, dance, diet/nutrition, economics, environment, ethnic, film, foods, gardening, gay/lesbian, government, health, history, hobbies, how-to, humor, language, law, memoirs, military, money, music, parenting, popular culture, politics, psychology, science, self-help, sociology, technology, theater, travel, women's issues, women's studies.

☞ Actively seeking nonfiction. Considers fiction by referral only. Does not want to receive unsolicited material.

HOW TO CONTACT Query with SASE. Does not accept queries by e-mail or fax. Other Responds in 2 weeks to queries. Obtains most new clients through recommendations/referrals.

TERMS Agent receives 15% commission on domestic sales. Agent receives 20% commission on foreign sales. Charges clients for photocopying or any unusual expense incurred at the writer's request.

◐◉ PAVILION LITERARY MANAGEMENT

660 Massachusetts Ave., Suite 4, Boston MA 02118. (617)792-5218. **E-mail:** jeff@pavilionliterary.com. **Website:** www.pavilionliterary.com. **Contact:** Jeff Kellogg.

◖ Prior to his current position, Mr. Kellogg was a literary agent with The Stuart Agency, and an acquiring editor with HarperCollins.

REPRESENTS nonfiction books, novels. **Considers these nonfiction areas:** creative nonfiction, memoirs, science. **Considers these fiction areas:** adventure, fantasy, juvenile, mystery, thriller.

HOW TO CONTACT No unsolicited submissions. If the agency has requested your submission: Query first by e-mail (no attachments). The subject line should specify fiction or nonfiction and include the title of the work. If submitting nonfiction, include a book proposal (no longer than 75 pages), with sample chapters.

L. PERKINS AGENCY

5800 Arlington Ave., Riverdale NY 10471. (718)543-5344. **Fax:** (718)543-5354. **E-mail:** submissions@lperkinsagency.com. **Website:** http://lperkinsagency.com. Member of AAR. Represents 90 clients. 10% of clients are new/unpublished writers.

Ms. Perkins has been an agent for 20 years. She is also the author of *The Insider's Guide to Getting an Agent* (Writer's Digest Books), as well as three other nonfiction books. She has also edited 12 erotic anthologies, and is also the editorial director of Ravenousromance.com, an e-publisher.

MEMBER AGENTS Tish Beaty, ePub agent (erotic romance—including paranormal, historical, gay/lesbian/bisexual, and light-BDSM fiction; also, she seeks new adult and YA); **Sandy Lu**, sandy@lperkinsagency.com (fiction: she is looking for dark literary and commercial fiction, mystery, thriller, psychological horror, paranormal/urban fantasy, historical fiction, YA, historical thrillers or mysteries set in Victorian times; nonfiction: narrative nonfiction, history, biography, pop science, pop psychology, pop culture [music/theatre/film], humor, and food writing); **Lori Perkins** (not currently taking new clients); **Leon Husock** (science fiction & fantasy, as well as young adult and middle grade); **Rachel Brooks** (picture books, all genres of young adult and new adult fiction, as well as adult romance—especially romantic suspense).

REPRESENTS nonfiction books, novels. **Considers these nonfiction areas:** biography, creative nonfiction, film, foods, history, humor, music, popular culture, psychology, science, theater. **Considers these fiction areas:** commercial, erotica, fantasy, gay, historical, horror, lesbian, middle grade, mystery, new adult, paranormal, picture books, science fiction, thriller, urban fantasy, young adult.

"Most of my clients write both fiction and nonfiction. This combination keeps my clients publishing for years. I am also a published author, so I know what it takes to write a good book."

HOW TO CONTACT E-queries only. Include your query, a 1-page synopsis, and the first 5 pages from your novel pasted into the e-mail. No attachments. Submit to only one agent at the agency. No smail mail

queries. "If you are submitting to one of our agents, please be sure to check the submission status of the agent by visiting their social media accounts listed [on the agency website]." Accepts simultaneous submissions. Obtains most new clients through recommendations from others, solicitations, conferences.

TERMS Agent receives 15% commission on domestic sales. Agent receives 20% commission on foreign sales. No written contract. Charges clients for photocopying.

WRITERS CONFERENCES NECON; Killercon; BookExpo America; World Fantasy Convention, RWA, Romantic Times.

TIPS "Research your field and contact professional writers' organizations to see who is looking for what. Finish your novel before querying agents. Read my book, *An Insider's Guide to Getting an Agent*, to get a sense of how agents operate. Read our agency blogs: agentinthemiddle.blogspot.com and ravenousromance.blogspot.com."

RUBIN PFEFFER CONTENT

648 Hammond St., Chestnut Hill MA 02467. **E-mail:** info@rpcontent.com. **Website:** www.rpcontent.com. **Contact:** Rubin Pfeffer. Estab. 2014.

Rubin has previously worked as the vice-president and publisher of Simon & Schuster Children's Books and as an independent agent at East West Literary Agency.

REPRESENTS Considers these fiction areas: juvenile, middle grade, picture books, young adult.

HOW TO CONTACT Note: *This agent accepts submissions by referral only. Specify the contact information of your reference when submitting.* Authors/illustrators should send a query and a 1-3 chapter ms via e-mail (no postal submissions). The query, placed in the body of the e-mail, should include a synopsis of the piece, as well as any relevant information regarding previous publications, referrals, websites, and biographies. The ms may be attached as a .doc or a .pdf file. Specifically for illustrators, attach a PDF of the dummy or artwork to the e-mail. Responds within 6-8 weeks.

RECENT SALES *Marti Feels Proud*, by Micha Archer; *Burning*, by Elana K. Arnold; *Junkyard*, by Mike Austin; *Little Dog, Lost*, by Marion Dane Bauer; *Not Your Typical Dragon*, by Tim Bowers; *Ghost Hawk*, by Susan Cooper.

◉ PIPPIN PROPERTIES, INC.

110 w. 40th Street, Suite 1704, New York NY 10018. (212)338-9310. **Fax:** (212)338-9579. **E-mail:** info@pippinproperties.com. **Website:** www.pippinproperties.com. **Contact:** Holly McGhee. Currently handles: juvenile books 100%.

○ Prior to becoming an agent, Ms. McGhee was an editor for 7 years and in book marketing for 4 years.

MEMBER AGENTS Holly McGhee; Elena Giovinazzo; Heather Alexander. Although each of the agents take children's books, you can find in-depth preferences for each agency on their website.

REPRESENTS Juvenile. **Considers these fiction areas:** middle grade, picture books, young adult.

⌗ "We are strictly a children's literary agency devoted to the management of authors and artists in all media. We are small and discerning in choosing our clientele."

HOW TO CONTACT Query via e-mail. Include a synopsis of the work(s), your background and/or publishing history, and anything else you think is relevant. Accepts simultaneous submissions. Obtains most new clients through recommendations from others.

TERMS Agent receives 15% commission on domestic sales. Agent receives 25% commission on foreign sales. Offers written contract; 30-day notice must be given to terminate contract.

TIPS "Please do not start calling after sending a submission."

◐ PONTAS AGENCY

Sèneca, 31, principal 08006 Barcelona Spain., This agency has other offices in Germany. **Website:** www.pontas-agency.com.

REPRESENTS nonfiction books, novels, movies.

⌗ Does not want original film screenplays.

HOW TO CONTACT For book submissions send the following by air mail: curriculum vitae, with contact details, details of previously published works, short synopsis of the work, a printed and bound copy.

LINN PRENTIS LITERARY

155 East 116th St., #2F, New York NY 10029. **Fax:** (212)875-5565. **Website:** www.linnprentis.com. **Contact:** Amy Hayden, acquisitions; Linn Prentis, agent. Represents 18-20 clients. 25% of clients are new/unpublished writers. Currently handles: nonfiction books 5%, novels 65%, story collections 7%, novella 10%, juvenile books 10%, scholarly books 3%.

○ Prior to becoming an agent, Ms. Prentis was a nonfiction writer and editor, primarily in magazines. She also worked in book promotion in New York. Ms. Prentis then worked for and later ran the Virginia Kidd Agency. She is known particularly for her assistance with ms development.

REPRESENTS Considers these nonfiction areas: biography, current affairs, ethnic, humor, memoirs, popular culture, women's issues. **Considers these fiction areas:** adventure, ethnic, fantasy, gay, glitz, historical, horror, humor, lesbian, literary, mainstream, thriller.

⌗ "Because of the Virginia Kidd connection and the clients I brought with me at the start, I have a special interest in sci-fi and fantasy, but, really, fiction is what interests me. As for nonfiction projects, they are books I just couldn't resist." Actively seeking hard science fiction, family saga, mystery, memoir, mainstream, literary, women's. Does not want to "receive books for little kids."

HOW TO CONTACT Query. No phone or fax queries. No snail mail. E-mail queries to ahayden@linnprentis.com. Include first 10 pages and synopsis as either attachment or as text in the e-mail. Accepts simultaneous submissions. Obtains most new clients through recommendations from others, solicitations.

TERMS Agent receives 15% commission on domestic sales. Agent and partners take 20% commission on foreign sales. Offers written contract; 60-day notice must be given to terminate contract.

RECENT SALES Sales include *Vienna* for new author William Kirby; *Hunting Ground, Frost Burned* and *Night Broken* titles in two series for *NY Times* bestselling author Patricia Briggs (as well as a graphic novel *Homecoming*) and a story collection; with more coming; a duology of novels for A.M. Dellamonica whose first book, *Indigo Springs*, won Canada's annual award for best fantasy, as well as several books abroad for client Tachyon Publications.

TIPS "Consider query letters and synopses as writing assignments. Spell names correctly."

AARON M. PRIEST LITERARY AGENCY

708 3rd Ave., 23rd Floor, New York NY 10017. (212)818-0344. **Fax:** (212)573-9417. **E-mail:** info@aaronpriest.com. **Website:** www.aaronpriest.com. Estab.

1974. Member of AAR. Currently handles: nonfiction books 25%, novels 75%.

MEMBER AGENTS Aaron Priest, querypriest@aaronpriest.com (thrillers, commercial fiction, biographies); **Lisa Erbach Vance**, queryvance@aaronpriest.com (contemporary fiction, especially women's fiction, thoughtful fiction about families and friends, thrillers/suspense, psychological suspense, contemporary gothic fiction, unique ghost stories, international fiction [not translation], narrative nonfiction, current or historical topics); **Lucy Childs Baker**, querychilds@aaronpriest.com (commercial fiction [women's and mystery], and especially literary fiction [including historical], as well as narrative nonfiction); **Melissa Edwards**, queryedwards@aaronpriest.com (international thrillers with likeable and arresting protagonists, lighthearted women's fiction and YA, female-driven [possibly small-town] suspense, and completely immersive fantasy).

➟ Does not want to receive poetry, screenplays, horror, or sci-fi.

HOW TO CONTACT Query one of the agents using the appropriate e-mail listed on the website. "Please do not submit to more than 1 agent at this agency. We urge you to check our website and consider each agent's emphasis before submitting. Your query letter should be about one page long and describe your work as well as your background. You may also paste the first chapter of your work in the body of the e-mail. Do not send attachments." Accepts simultaneous submissions. Responds in 4 weeks, only if interested.

TERMS Agent receives 15% commission on domestic sales.

RECENT SALES *The Hit*, by David Baldacci; *Six Years*, by Harlan Coben; *Suspect*, by Robert Crais; *Permanent Record*, by Leslie Stella.

◑ PROSPECT AGENCY

551 Valley Road, PMB 377, Upper Montclair NJ 07043. (718)788-3217. **Fax:** (718)360-9582. **Website:** www.prospectagency.com. Estab. 2005. Member of AAR. Currently handles: 60% of material handled is books for young readers.

MEMBER AGENTS Emily Sylvan Kim, esk@prospectagency.com (romance, women's, commercial, young adult, new adult); **Rachel Orr**, rko@prospectagency.com (picture books, illustrators, middle grade, young adult); **Becca Stumpf**, becca@prospectagency.com (young adult, middle grade, fantasy, sci-fi, literary mysteries, literary thrillers, spicy romance); **Carrie Pestritto**, carrie@prospectagency.com (narrative nonfiction, general nonfiction, biography, and memoir; commercial fiction with a literary twist, women's fiction, romance, upmarket, historical fiction, new adult, YA, and upper middle grade); **Teresa Kietlinski**, tk@prospectagency.com (picture book artists and illustrators); **Linda Camacho** (adult, middle grade, and young adult fiction across all genres [romance, horror, fantasy, realistic, light sci-fi, and graphic novels]; select literary fiction [preferably with commercial bent] and picture books [both writers and illustrators welcome], select narrative nonfiction and memoir diversity of all types [ethnicity, disability, sexuality]).

REPRESENTS Considers these nonfiction areas: biography, memoirs. **Considers these fiction areas:** commercial, historical, juvenile, middle grade, mystery, new adult, picture books, romance, thriller, women's, young adult.

➟ "We're looking for strong, unique voices and unforgettable stories and characters."

HOW TO CONTACT Note that each agent at this agency has a different submission e-mail address and different submission policies. Check the agency website for the latest formal guideline per each agent. Obtains new clients through conferences, recommendations, queries, and some scouting.

TERMS Agent receives 15% on domestic sales, 20% on foreign sales sold directly and 25% on sales using a subagent. Offers written contract.

RECENT SALES Recent sales include: *Ollie and Claire* (Philomel), *Vicious* (Bloomsbury), *Temptest Rising* (Walker Books), *Where do Diggers Sleep at Night* (Random House Children's), *A DJ Called Tomorrow* (Little, Brown), *The Princesses of Iowa* (Candlewick).

◑ P.S LITERARY AGENCY

20033—520 Kerr St., Oakville ON L6K 3C7 Canada. **E-mail:** query@psliterary.com. **Website:** http://www.psliterary.com. **Contact:** Curtis Russell, principal agent; Carly Watters, agent; Maria Vicente, associate agent. Estab. 2005. Currently handles: nonfiction books 50%, novels 50%.

MEMBER AGENTS Curtis Russell (young adult and middle grade books); **Carly Watters** (young adult, book club fiction, commercial fiction, women's fiction, contemporary romance, cookbooks, unique memoirs, pop science and psychology, literary thrill-

NEW AGENT SPOTLIGHT

CARA MANNION
HAROLD OBER ASSOCIATES

Haroldober.com

@Cara_Mannion

ABOUT CARA: A graduate of New York University's Summer Publishing Institute, Cara is the newest addition to the legacy agency Harold Ober Associates. Before joining the agency world, she worked in editorial at Entangled Publishing's new adult imprint for two years. At HOA, she works in both the book and film/TV worlds as she assists with selling books' motion picture rights. Originally hailing from the sunny beaches of Florida, Cara is now enjoying seeing the seasons actually change while actively building her own client list.

SHE IS SEEKING: Mainly young adult and adult commercial fiction, including romance (and all its subgenres), historical fiction, women's fiction, paranormal, science fiction, horror, mysteries and thrillers. Limited interest in nonfiction includes humor and biography. Cara particularly enjoys strong female protagonists, juicy love triangles, subversive conspiracy plots, and opening lines that make you want to jump headfirst into the book. She does not want fantasy, memoirs, picture books, poetry, self-help books, screenplays and short story collections.

HOW TO SUBMIT: Please e-mail the first 10 pages of your manuscript, a concise query letter, and a detailed synopsis to cara@haroldober.com.

ers and mysteries, platform-heavy nonfiction); **Maria Vicente** (young adult, middle grade and illustrated picture books); **Kurestin Armada** (particular affection for science fiction and fantasy, especially books that recognize and subvert typical tropes of genre fiction).
REPRESENTS nonfiction, novels, juvenile books. **Considers these nonfiction areas:** autobiography, biography, business, child guidance, cooking, current affairs, diet/nutrition, economics, environment, foods, government, health, history, how-to, humor, law, memoirs, military, money, parenting, popular culture, politics, science, self-help, sports, technol-ogy, true crime, war, women's issues, women's studies. **Considers these fiction areas:** action, adventure, detective, erotica, ethnic, family saga, historical, horror, humor, juvenile, literary, mainstream, middle grade, mystery, new adult, picture books, romance, sports, thriller, women's, young adult, biography/autobiography, business, child guidance/parenting, cooking/food/nutrition, current affairs, government/politics/law, health/medicine, history, how-to, humor, memoirs, military/war, money/finance/economics, nature/environment, popular culture, science/technology, self-help/personal improvement, sports, true crime/investigative, women's issues/women's studies.

"What makes our agency distinct: We take on a small number of clients per year in order to provide focused, hands-on representation. We pride ourselves in providing industry-leading client service." Actively seeking both fiction and nonfiction. Seeking both new and established writers. Does not want to receive poetry or screenplays.

HOW TO CONTACT Queries by e-mail only. Submit query letter and bio. "Please limit your query to one page." Accepts simultaneous submissions. Responds in 4-6 weeks to queries/proposals; mss 4-8 weeks. Obtains most new clients through solicitations.

TERMS Agent receives 15% commission on domestic sales. Agent receives 25% commission on foreign sales. We offer a written contract, with 30-days notice terminate. Fees for postage/messenger services only if project is sold. "This agency charges for postage/messenger services only if a project is sold."

TIPS "Please review our website for the most up-to-date submission guidelines. We do not charge reading fees. We do not offer a critique service."

PUBLICATION RIOT GROUP

E-mail: submissions@priotgroup.com. **Website:** www.priotgroup.com. **Contact:** Donna Bagdasarian. Prior to being an agent, Ms. Bagdasarian worked as an acquisitions editor. Previously, she worked for the William Morris and Maria Carvainis agencies.

REPRESENTS nonfiction books, novels. **Considers these nonfiction areas:** memoirs, popular culture, politics, science, sociology. **Considers these fiction areas:** ethnic, historical, literary, mainstream, thriller, women's.

"The company is a literary management company, representing their authors in all processes of the entertainment trajectory: from book development, to book sales, to subsidiary sales in the foreign market, television and film." Does not want science fiction and fantasy.

HOW TO CONTACT Currently closed to all submissions.

RECENT SALES List of sales on agency website.

JOANNA PULCINI LITERARY MANAGEMENT

E-mail: info@jplm.com. **Website:** www.jplm.com. **Contact:** Joanna Pulcini.

"JPLM is not accepting submissions at this time; however, I do encourage those seeking representation to read the 'Advice to Writers' essay on our website for some guidance on finding an agent."

HOW TO CONTACT Do not query this agency until they open their client list.

RECENT SALES *TV*, by Brian Brown; *The Movies That Changed Us*, by Nick Clooney; *Strange, But True*, by John Searles; *The Intelligencer*, by Leslie Silbert; *In Her Shoes* and *The Guy Not Taken* by Jennifer Weiner.

THE PURCELL AGENCY

E-mail: TPAqueries@gmail.com. **Website:** www.thepurcellagency.com. **Contact:** Tina P. Schwartz. Estab. 2012.

REPRESENTS Considers these nonfiction areas: juvenile nonfiction. **Considers these fiction areas:** juvenile, middle grade, young adult.

This agency also takes juvenile nonfiction for MG and YA markets. At this point, the agency is not considering fantasy, science fiction, or picture book submissions.

HOW TO CONTACT E-query. Mention if you are part of SCBWI. For fiction, send a query, the first 3 chapters, and synopsis. No attachments. For nonfiction, send table of contents + intro and sample chapter, author's credentials. Accepts simultaneous submissions. Responds in 1-3 months.

QUEEN LITERARY AGENCY

47 E. 19th St., Third Floor, New York NY 10003. (212)974-8333. **Fax:** (212)974-8347. **E-mail:** submissions@queenliterary.com. **Website:** www.queenliterary.com. **Contact:** Lisa Queen. Prior to her current position, Ms. Queen was a former publishing executive and most recently head of IMG Worldwide's literary division.

REPRESENTS nonfiction books, novels. **Considers these nonfiction areas:** business, foods, psychology, science, sports. **Considers these fiction areas:** commercial, historical, literary, mystery, thriller.

Ms. Queen's specialties: "While our agency represents a wide range of nonfiction titles, we have a particular interest in business books, food writing, science and popular psychology, as well as books by well-known chefs, radio and television personalities, and sports figures."

HOW TO CONTACT E-query.

RECENT SALES A full list of this agency's clients and sales is available on their website.

🅓 LYNNE RABINOFF AGENCY

72-11 Austin St., No. 201, Forest Hills NY 11375. **E-mail:** Lynne@lynnerabinoff.com. **Contact:** Lynne Rabinoff. Represents 50 clients. 50% of clients are new/unpublished writers. Currently handles: nonfiction books 99%, novels 1%.

🅠 Prior to becoming an agent, Ms. Rabinoff was in publishing and dealt with foreign rights.

REPRESENTS nonfiction books. **Considers these nonfiction areas:** anthropology, archeology, autobiography, biography, business, cultural interests, current affairs, economics, ethnic, government, history, inspirational, law, memoirs, military, popular culture, politics, psychology, religious, science, technology, women's issues, women's studies.

8—🖝 "This agency specializes in history, political issues, current affairs and religion."

HOW TO CONTACT Query with SASE or e-mail. Submit proposal package, synopsis, 1 sample chapter, author bio. Responds in 3 weeks to queries. Responds in 1 month to mss. Obtains most new clients through recommendations from others.

TERMS Agent receives 15% commission on domestic sales. Agent receives 20% commission on foreign sales. Offers written contract; 60-day notice must be given to terminate contract. This agency charges for postage.

RECENT SALES *The Confrontation*, by Walid Phares (Palgrave); *Flying Solo*, by Robert Vaughn (Thomas Dunne); *Thugs*, by Micah Halpern (Thomas Nelson); *Size Sexy*, by Stella Ellis (Adams Media); *Cruel and Usual*, by Nonie Darwish (Thomas Nelson); *Now They Call Me Infidel*, by Nonie Darwish (Sentinel/Penguin); *34 Days*, by Avid Issacharoff (Palgrave).

🅓 RED SOFA LITERARY

2163 Grand Ave., #2, St. Paul MN 55105. (651)224-6670. **E-mail:** dawn@redsofaliterary.com; jennie@redsofaliterary.com; laura@redsofaliterary.com; amanda@redsofaliterary.com. **Website:** www.redsofaliterary.com. **Contact:** Dawn Frederick, literary agent and owner; Jennie Goloboy, agent; Laura Zats, associate agent; Amanda Rutter, associate agent. Red Sofa is a member of the Authors Guild and the MN Publishers Round Table Represents 20 clients. 80% of clients are new/unpublished writers.

🅠 Prior to her current position, Ms. Frederick spent 5 years at Sebastian Literary Agency. In addition, Ms. Frederick worked more than 10 years in indie and chain book stores, and at an independent children's book publisher. Ms. Frederick has a master's degree in library and information sciences from an ALA-accredited institution. In Fall 2011, Jennie Goloboy joined Red Sofa Literary as an associate agent. Jennie Goloboy has a PhD in the History of American Civilization from Harvard. She is also a published author of both history and fiction, and a member of SFWA, RWA, SHEAR, OAH, the AHA, and Codex Writer's Group. Her funny, spec-fic short stories appear under her pen name, Nora Fleischer. Laura Zats became an associate agent in December 2013; she graduated from Grinnell College with degrees in English and anthropology.

REPRESENTS nonfiction, fiction, juvenile books. **Considers these nonfiction areas:** animals, anthropology, archeology, crafts, cultural interests, current affairs, gay/lesbian, government, health, history, hobbies, humor, investigative, popular culture, politics, satire, sociology, true crime, women's issues, women's studies, extreme sports. **Considers these fiction areas:** erotica, fantasy, middle grade, romance, science fiction, young adult.

8—🖝 Does not want to receive any personal memoirs.

HOW TO CONTACT Query by e-mail or mail with SASE. No attachments, please. Submit full proposal plus 3 sample chapters and any other pertinent writing samples. Accepts simultaneous submissions. Obtains most new clients through recommendations from others, solicitations.

TERMS Agent receives 15% commission on domestic sales. Agent receives 20% commission on foreign sales. Offers written contract.

TIPS "Always remember the benefits of building an author platform, and the accessibility of accomplishing this task in today's industry. Most importantly, research the agents queried. Avoid contacting every literary agent about a book idea. Due to the large volume of queries received, the process of reading queries for unrepresented categories (by the agency) becomes quite the arduous task. Investigate online directories, printed guides (like *Writer's Market*), individual agent websites, and more, before beginning the query process. It's good to remember that each agent has a vision of what s/he wants to represent and will communicate this information accordingly. We're simply waiting for those specific book ideas to come in our direction."

RED TREE LITERARY AGENCY

403 12th St., #4, Brooklyn, NY 11215. **Website:** www.redtreeliterary.com. **Contact:** Elana Roth.

Elana is a graduate of Barnard College and the Jewish Theological Seminary, where she earned degrees in English literature and Bible.

REPRESENTS Considers these fiction areas: juvenile, middle grade, young adult.

HOW TO CONTACT E-query elana@redtreeliterary.com "Include 'QUERY: [title]' in the e-mail subject field. Please also include publisher submission history and previous publishing credits, if applicable. If you are a debut author, do not worry. After your query letter, paste the first 5-10 pages of your novel into the body of the email. If you are an author/illustrator and have not yet realized it's a necessity, I highly recommend creating an online portfolio, which you can link to in your query instead of attaching sample artwork to an email."

RECENT SALES *Doug-Dennis and the Flyaway Fib*, by Darren Farrel; *Juniper Berry*, by M.P. Kozlowsky; *The Selection*, by Kiera Cass; *Unison Spark*, by Andy Marino.

REES LITERARY AGENCY

14 Beacon St., Suite 710, Boston MA 02108. (617)227-9014. **Fax:** (617)227-8762. **Website:** http://reesagency.com. Estab. 1983. Member of AAR. Represents more than 100 clients. 50% of clients are new/unpublished writers.

MEMBER AGENTS Ann Collette, Agent10702@aol.com (literary, mystery, thrillers, suspense, vampire, and women's fiction; in nonfiction, she prefers true crime, narrative nonfiction, military and war, work to do with race and class, and work set in or about Southeast Asia); **Lorin Rees**, lorin@reesagency.com (literary fiction, memoirs, business books, self-help, science, history, psychology, and narrative nonfiction); **Rebecca Podos**, rebecca@reesagency.com (young adult fiction of all kinds, including contemporary, emotionally driven stories, mystery, romance, urban and historical fantasy, horror and sci-fi; occasionally, she considers literary and commercial adult fiction, new adult, and narrative nonfiction).

REPRESENTS nonfiction books, novels. **Considers these nonfiction areas:** business, creative nonfiction, health, history, memoirs, military, psychology, science, self-help, true crime, war. **Considers these fiction areas:** commercial, historical, horror, literary, mystery, new adult, romance, science fiction, suspense, thriller, urban fantasy, women's, young adult.

HOW TO CONTACT Consult website for each agent's submission guidelines and e-mail addresses, as they differ. Obtains most new clients through recommendations from others, conferences, submissions.

TERMS Agent receives 15% commission on domestic sales. Agent receives 20% commission on foreign sales.

RECENT SALES *The Art Forger,* by B.A. Shapiro; *Busy Monsters,* by William Giraldi; *Pitch Dark,* by Steven Sidor; *You Know When the Men Are Gone,* by Siobhan Fallon; and *Death Drops,* by Chrystle Fiedler; *Get Your Ship Together,* by Capt. D. Michael Abrashoff; *Overpromise and Overdeliver,* by Rick Berrara; *Opacity,* by Joel Kurtzman; *America the Broke,* by Gerald Swanson; *Murder at the B-School,* by Jeffrey Cruikshank; *Bone Factory,* by Steven Sidor; *Father Said,* by Hal Sirowitz; *Winning,* by Jack Welch; *The Case for Israel,* by Alan Dershowitz; *As the Future Catches You,* by Juan Enriquez; *Blood Makes the Grass Grow Green,* by Johnny Rico; *DVD Movie Guide,* by Mick Martin and Marsha Porter; *Words That Work,* by Frank Luntz; *Stirring It Up,* by Gary Hirshberg; *Hot Spots,* by Martin Fletcher; *Andy Grove: The Life and Times of an American,* by Richard Tedlow; *Girls Most Likely To,* by Poonam Sharma.

REGAL LITERARY AGENCY

236 W. 26th St., #801, New York NY 10001. (212)684-7900. **Fax:** (212)684-7906. **E-mail:** submissions@regal-literary.com. **Website:** www.regal-literary.com. London Office: 36 Gloucester Ave., Primrose Hill, London NW1 7BB, United Kingdom, uk@regal-literary.com Estab. 2002. Member of AAR. Represents 70 clients. 20% of clients are new/unpublished writers.

MEMBER AGENTS Michelle Andelman (all categories of children's books); **Claire Anderson-Wheeler**; **Markus Hoffmann** (international and literary fiction, crime, [pop] cultural studies, current affairs, economics, history, music, popular science, and travel literature); **Joseph Regal** (literary fiction, international thrillers, history, science, photography, music, culture, and whimsy).

REPRESENTS Considers these nonfiction areas: creative nonfiction, memoirs, psychology, science.

Considers these fiction areas: literary, middle grade, picture books, thriller, women's, young adult.

⚷→ Actively seeking literary fiction and narrative nonfiction. "We do not consider romance, science fiction, poetry, or screenplays."

HOW TO CONTACT "Query with SASE or via e-mail. No phone calls. Submissions should consist of a 1-page query letter detailing the book in question, as well as the qualifications of the author. For fiction, submissions may also include the first 10 pages of the novel or one short story from a collection." Responds if interested. Accepts simultaneous submissions. Responds in 4-8 weeks.

TERMS Agent receives 15% commission on domestic sales. Agent receives 20% commission on foreign sales. "We charge no reading fees."

RECENT SALES Audrey Niffenegger's *The Time Traveler's Wife* (Mariner) and *Her Fearful Symmetry* (Scribner), Gregory David Roberts' *Shantaram* (St. Martin's), Josh Bazell's *Beat the Reaper* (Little, Brown), John Twelve Hawks' *The Fourth Realm Trilogy* (Doubleday), James Reston, Jr.'s *The Conviction of Richard Nixon* (Three Rivers) and *Defenders of the Faith* (Penguin), Michael Psilakis' *How to Roast a Lamb: New Greek Classic Cooking* (Little, Brown), Colman Andrews' *Country Cooking of Ireland* (Chronicle) and *Reinventing Food: Ferran Adria and How He Changed the Way We Eat* (Phaidon).

TIPS "We are deeply committed to every aspect of our clients' careers, and are engaged in everything from the editorial work of developing a great book proposal or line editing a fiction ms to negotiating state-of-the-art book deals and working to promote and publicize the book when it's published. We are at the forefront of the effort to increase authors' rights in publishing contracts in a rapidly changing commercial environment. We deal directly with co-agents and publishers in every foreign territory and also work directly and with co-agents for feature film and television rights, with extraordinary success in both arenas. Many of our clients' works have sold in dozens of translation markets, and a high proportion of our books have been sold in Hollywood. We have strong relationships with speaking agents, who can assist in arranging author tours and other corporate and college speaking opportunities when appropriate. We also have a staff publicist and marketer to help promote our clients' and their work."

REID BOATES LITERARY AGENCY

69 Cooks Crossroad, Pittstown NJ 08867. (908)797-8087. **Fax:** (908)788-3667. **E-mail:** reid.boates@gmail.com; boatesliterary@att.net. **Contact:** Reid Boates. Represents 45 clients.

HOW TO CONTACT No unsolicited queries of any kind. Obtains new clients by personal referral only. This agency, at the current time, is handling 100% nonfiction.

TERMS Agent receives 15% commission on domestic sales. Agent receives 20% commission on foreign sales.

RECENT SALES New sales include placements at HarperCollins, Wiley, Random House, and other major general-interest publishers.

○ THE AMY RENNERT AGENCY

98 Main St., #302, Tiburon CA 94920. **E-mail:** queries@amyrennert.com. **Website:** www.publishersmarketplace.com/members/amyrennert/. **Contact:** Amy Rennert.

REPRESENTS nonfiction books, novels. **Considers these nonfiction areas:** biography, business, creative nonfiction, health, history, money, sports. **Considers these fiction areas:** literary, mainstream, mystery.

⚷→ "The Amy Rennert Agency specializes in books that matter. We provide career management for established and first-time authors, and our breadth of experience in many genres enables us to meet the needs of a diverse clientele."

HOW TO CONTACT Amy Rennert is not currently accepting unsolicited submissions. "Referrals are still welcome. Cover letter in e-mail and attached PDF proposal for nonfiction; cover letter and first 25 pages for fiction and sometimes memoir. For picture books, cover letter and ms. Please send to queries@amyrennert.com. We likely won't be able to respond unless interested. "

TIPS Due to the high volume of submissions, it is not possible to respond to each and every one. Please understand that we are only able to respond to queries that we feel may be a good fit with our agency.

◐ THE LISA RICHARDS AGENCY

108 Upper Leeson St., Dublin 4 Republic of Ireland Ireland. (03)(531)637-5000. **Fax:** (03)531)667-1256. **E-mail:** info@lisarichards.ie. **Website:** www.lisarichards.ie. Estab. 1989.

MEMBER AGENTS Faith O'Grady (literary).

REPRESENTS movie, tv, broadcast. **Considers these nonfiction areas:** biography, current affairs, history, memoirs, popular culture, travel, politics. **Considers these script areas:** comedy, general scripts.

8→ "For fiction, I am always looking for exciting new writing – distinctive voices, original, strong storylines, and intriguing characters."

HOW TO CONTACT If sending fiction, please limit your submission to the first three or four chapters, and include a covering letter and an SAE if required. If sending nonfiction, please send a detailed proposal about your book, a sample chapter and a cover letter. Every effort will be made to respond to submissions within 3 months of receipt.

RECENT SALES Clients include Denise Deegan, Arlene Hunt, Roisin Ingle, Declan Lynch, Jennifer McCann, Sarah O'Brien, Kevin Rafter.

◌ THE RIGHTS FACTORY

P.O. Box 499, Station C, Toronto ON M6J 3P6 Canada. (416)966-5367. **Website:** www.therightsfactory.com. Estab. 2004.

MEMBER AGENTS Sam Hiyate, Ali McDonald (children's literature of all kinds); Haskell Nussbaum; Drea Cohane (fiction, memoir, crime, nonfiction and YA; her roster consists of British, American, and Canadian clients; international talent is welcome); Olga Filina (commercial and historical fiction, great genre fiction in the area of romance and mystery, nonfiction in the field of business, wellness, lifestyle and memoir; and young adult and middle grade novels with memorable characters); Lydia Moed (science fiction and fantasy, though she also enjoys magic realism, historical fiction and stories inspired by folklore from around the world; for nonfiction, she is interested in narrative nonfiction on a wide variety of topics, including history, popular science, biography and memoir).

REPRESENTS Considers these nonfiction areas: biography, business, history, memoirs, science. **Considers these fiction areas:** commercial, crime, fantasy, historical, literary, mainstream, middle grade, mystery, picture books, romance, science fiction, young adult.

HOW TO CONTACT There is a submission form on this agency's website. You can also query via snail mail.

◑ ANGELA RINALDI LITERARY AGENCY

P.O. Box 7875, Beverly Hills CA 90212-7875. (310)842-7665. **Fax:** (310)837-8143. **E-mail:** amr@rinaldiliter

ary.com. **Website:** www.rinaldiliterary.com. **Contact:** Angela Rinaldi. Member of AAR.

◯ Prior to opening her agency, Ms. Rinaldi was an editor at NAL/Signet, Pocket Books and Bantam, and the manager of book development for *The Los Angeles Times.*

REPRESENTS nonfiction books, novels, TV and motion picture rights (for clients only). **Considers these nonfiction areas:** biography, business, cooking, current affairs, health, psychology, self-help, women's issues, food narratives, wine, lifestyle, career, personal finance, prescriptive and proactive self help books by journalists, academics, doctors and therapists, based on their research. **Considers these fiction areas:** commercial, literary, suspense, women's, upmarket women's fiction, book club women's fiction.

8→ Actively seeking commercial and literary fiction. Does not want to receive humor, pop culture,thrillers, category romances, science fiction, fantasy, horror, film scripts, poetry, category romances, magazine articles, religion, occult, paranormal, children's or middle grade fiction

HOW TO CONTACT E-queries only. For fiction, please send a brief e-mail inquiry with the first 10 pages pasted into the e-mail—no attachments unless asked for. For nonfiction, query with detailed letter or outline/proposal, no attachments unless asked for. Accepts simultaneous submissions. Responds in 2-4 weeks.

TERMS Agent receives 15% commission on domestic sales. Agent receives 25% commission on foreign sales. Offers written contract.

WRITERS CONFERENCES Writer's Digest Conference West (Los Angeles).

◯ ANN RITTENBERG LITERARY AGENCY, INC.

15 Maiden Lane, Suite 206, New York NY 10038. **Website:** www.rittlit.com. **Contact:** Ann Rittenberg, president. Member of AAR. Currently handles: fiction 75%, nonfiction 25%.

REPRESENTS Considers these nonfiction areas: creative nonfiction, women's issues.

8→ This agent specializes in specific fiction genres— upmarket thrillers, literary fiction and literary nonfiction. Does not want to receive screenplays, straight genre fiction, poetry, self-help.

HOW TO CONTACT Query with SASE. Submit outline, 3 sample chapters, SASE. Query via postal mail or e-mail to info@rittlit.com. Accepts simultaneous submissions. Responds in 6 weeks to queries. Responds in 2 months to mss. Obtains most new clients through referrals from established writers and editors.

TERMS Agent receives 15% commission on domestic sales. Agent receives 20% commission on foreign sales. Offers written contract. This agency charges clients for photocopying only.

RECENT SALES *World Gone By*, by Dennis Lehane; *Leaving Haven*, by Kathleen McCleary; *The Bone Orchard*, by Paul Doiron; *Endangered*, by C.J. Box.

RIVERSIDE LITERARY AGENCY

41 Simon Keets Rd., Leyden MA 01337. (413)772-0067. **Fax:** (413)772-0969. **E-mail:** rivlit@sover.net. **Website:** www.riversideliteraryagency.com. **Contact:** Susan Lee Cohen.

> This agency sells mostly adult nonfiction, and has sold books in the categories of religion, true crime, parenting, history/politics, and narrative.

HOW TO CONTACT E-query. Accepts simultaneous submissions. Obtains most new clients through referrals.

TERMS Agent receives 15% commission on domestic sales. Offers written contract. Charges clients for foreign postage, photocopying large mss, express mail deliveries, etc.

RLR ASSOCIATES, LTD.

Literary Department, 7 W. 51st St., New York NY 10019. (212)541-8641. **Fax:** (212)262-7084. **E-mail:** sgould@rlrassociates.net. **Website:** www.rlrassociates.net. **Contact:** Scott Gould. Member of AAR. Represents 50 clients. 25% of clients are new/unpublished writers. Currently handles: nonfiction books 70%, novels 25%, story collections 5%.

REPRESENTS nonfiction books, novels, short-story collections, scholarly. **Considers these nonfiction areas:** creative nonfiction. **Considers these fiction areas:** commercial, literary, mainstream, middle grade, picture books, romance, women's, young adult.

> "We provide a lot of editorial assistance to our clients and have connections." Actively seeking fiction, current affairs, history, art, popular culture, health and business. Does not want to receive screenplays.

HOW TO CONTACT Query by either e-mail or snail mail. For fiction, send a query and 1-3 chapters (pasted). For nonfiction, send query or proposal. Accepts simultaneous submissions. "If you do not hear from us within 3 months, please assume that your work is out of active consideration." Obtains most new clients through recommendations from others.

TERMS Agent receives 15% commission on domestic sales. Agent receives 20% commission on foreign sales. Offers written contract.

RECENT SALES Clients include Shelby Foote, The Grief Recovery Institute, Don Wade, Don Zimmer, The Knot.com, David Plowden, PGA of America, Danny Peary, George Kalinsky, Peter Hyman, Daniel Parker, Lee Miller, Elise Miller, Nina Planck, Karyn Bosnak, Christopher Pike, Gerald Carbone, Jason Lethcoe, Andy Crouch.

TIPS "Please check out our website for more details on our agency."

B.J. ROBBINS LITERARY AGENCY

5130 Bellaire Ave., North Hollywood CA 91607-2908. **E-mail:** Robbinsliterary@gmail.com. **Website:** www.publishersmarketplace.com/members/bjrobbins. **Contact:** (Ms.) B.J. Robbins, or Amy Maldonado. Estab. 1992. Member of AAR.

REPRESENTS nonfiction books, novels. **Considers these nonfiction areas:** autobiography, biography, cultural interests, current affairs, dance, ethnic, film, health, humor, investigative, medicine, memoirs, music, popular culture, psychology, self-help, sociology, sports, theater, travel, true crime, women's issues, women's studies. **Considers these fiction areas:** crime, detective, ethnic, literary, mainstream, mystery, police, sports, suspense, thriller.

> "We do not represent screenplays, plays, poetry, science fiction, horror, westerns, romance, techno-thrillers, religious tracts, dating books or anything with the word 'unicorn' in the title."

HOW TO CONTACT E-query with no attachments. Accepts simultaneous submissions. Only responds to projects if interested. Obtains most new clients through conferences, referrals.

TERMS Agent receives 15% commission on domestic sales. Agent receives 20% commission on foreign sales. Offers written contract; 3-month notice must be given to terminate contract.

THE ROBBINS OFFICE, INC.

405 Park Ave., 9th Floor, New York NY 10022. (212)223-0720. **Fax:** (212)223-2535. **Website:** www. robbinsoffice.com. **Contact:** Kathy P. Robbins, owner.
MEMBER AGENTS Kathy P. Robbins; David Halpern.
REPRESENTS nonfiction books, novels. **Considers these nonfiction areas:** history, politics, journalism, regional interest, memoirs.

➤ This agency specializes in selling serious nonfiction as well as commercial and literary fiction.

HOW TO CONTACT Accepts submissions by referral only. Do not cold query this market.
TERMS Agent receives 15% commission on domestic sales. Agent receives 15% commission on foreign sales. Agent receives 15% commission on film sales. Bills back specific expenses incurred in doing business for a client.

RODEEN LITERARY MANAGEMENT

3501 N. Southport #497, Chicago IL 60657. **E-mail:** submissions@rodeenliterary.com. **Website:** www.rodeenliterary.com. **Contact:** Paul Rodeen. Estab. 2009.

○ Paul Rodeen established Rodeen Literary Management in 2009 after 7 years of experience with the literary agency Sterling Lord Literistic, Inc.

REPRESENTS nonfiction books, novels, juvenile books, illustrations, graphic novels. **Considers these fiction areas:** juvenile, middle grade, picture books, young adult, graphic novels, comics.

➤ Actively seeking "writers and illustrators of all genres of children's literature including picture books, early readers, middle grade fiction and nonfiction, graphic novels and comic books, as well as young adult fiction and nonfiction." This is primarily an agency devoted to children's books.

HOW TO CONTACT Unsolicited submissions are accepted by e-mail only to submissions@rodeenliterary. com. Cover letters with synopsis and contact information should be included in the body of your e-mail. An initial submission of 50 pages from a novel or a longer work of nonfiction will suffice and should be pasted into the body of your e-mail. Electronic portfolios from illustrators are accepted but please keep the images at 72 dpi—a link to your website or blog is also helpful. Electronic picture book dummies and picture book texts are accepted. Graphic novels and comic books are accepted. Accepts simultaneous submissions. Response time varies.

ROGERS, COLERIDGE & WHITE

20 Powis Mews, London England W11 1JN United Kingdom. (44)(207)221-3717. **Fax:** (44)(207)229-9084. **E-mail:** info@rcwlitagency.co.uk. **Website:** www.rcwlitagency.co.uk. **Contact:** David Miller, agent. Estab. 1987.

○ Prior to opening the agency, Ms. Rogers was an agent with Peter Janson-Smith; Ms. Coleridge worked at Sidgwick & Jackson, Chatto & Windus, and Anthony Sheil Associates; Ms. White was an editor and rights director for Simon & Schuster; Mr. Straus worked at Hodder and Stoughton, Hamish Hamilton, and Macmillan; Mr. Miller worked as Ms. Rogers' assistant and was treasurer of the AAA; Ms. Waldie worked with Carole Smith.

MEMBER AGENTS Deborah Rogers; Gill Coleridge; Pat White (illustrated and children's books); Peter Straus; David Miller; Zoe Waldie (fiction, biography, current affairs, narrative history); Laurence Laluyaux (foreign rights); Stephen Edwards (foreign rights); Peter Robinson; Sam Copeland; Jenny Hewson; Jo Unwin; Rebecca Jones; Cara Jones.

REPRESENTS nonfiction books, novels, juvenile.

➤ This agency takes virtually all subjects and genres. Does not want to receive plays, screenplays, technical books or educational books.

HOW TO CONTACT "Submit synopsis, proposal, sample chapters, bio, SAE by mail. Submissions should include a cover letter with brief bio and the background to the book. In the case of fiction, they should consist of the first 3 chapters or approximately the first 50 pages of the work to a natural break, and a brief synopsis. Nonfiction submissions should take the form of a proposal up to 20 pages in length explaining what the work is about and why you are best placed to write it. Material should be printed out in 12 point font, in double-spacing and on one side only of A4 paper. YA and Children's fiction should be submitted via e-mail to clairewilson@rcwlitagency.com. We regret that this department cannot undertake to read submissions from the US due to the large volume received. We do not accept any other e-mail submissions unless by prior arrangement with individual agents." Responds in 6-8 weeks to queries. Obtains most new clients through recommendations from others, solicitations, conferences.

TERMS Agent receives 15% commission on domestic sales. Agent receives 20% commission on foreign sales. Offers written contract.

● LINDA ROGHAAR LITERARY AGENCY, LLC

133 High Point Dr., Amherst MA 01002. (413)256-1921. **E-mail:** linda@lindaroghaar.com. **E-mail:** contact@lindaroghaar.com. **Website:** www.lindaroghaar.com. **Contact:** Linda L. Roghaar. Member of AAR. Currently handles: nonfiction books 100%.

○ Prior to opening her agency, Ms. Roghaar worked in retail bookselling for 5 years and as a publishers' sales rep for 15 years.

REPRESENTS nonfiction books.

⊶ The Linda Roghaar Literary Agency represents authors with substantial messages and specializes in nonfiction. We sell to major, independent, and university presses.

HOW TO CONTACT "We prefer e-queries. Please mention 'query' in the subject line, and do not include attachments." Paste the first 5 pages of your ms below the query. Accepts simultaneous submissions. Responds within 12 weeks if interested.

TERMS Agent receives 15% commission on domestic sales. Agent receives negotiable commission on foreign sales. Offers written contract.

● THE ROSENBERG GROUP

23 Lincoln Ave., Marblehead MA 01945. (781)990-1341. **Fax:** (781)990-1344. **Website:** www.rosenberggroup.com. **Contact:** Barbara Collins Rosenberg. Estab. 1998. Member of AAR. Recognized agent of the RWA. Represents 25 clients. 15% of clients are new/unpublished writers. Currently handles: nonfiction books 30%, novels 30%, scholarly books 10%, 30% college textbooks.

○ Prior to becoming an agent, Ms. Rosenberg was a senior editor for Harcourt.

REPRESENTS nonfiction books, novels, textbooks, college textbooks only. **Considers these nonfiction areas:** current affairs, foods, popular culture, psychology, sports, women's issues, women's studies, women's health, wine/beverages. **Considers these fiction areas:** romance, women's, chick lit.

⊶ Ms. Rosenberg is well-versed in the romance market (both category and single title). She is a frequent speaker at romance conferences.

The Rosenberg Group is accepting new clients working in romance fiction, women's fiction, and chick lit. Does not want to receive inspirational, time travel, futuristic or paranormal.

HOW TO CONTACT Query via snail mail. Your query letter should not exceed one page in length. It should include the title of your work, the genre and/or sub-genre; the ms word count; and a brief description of the work. If you are writing category romance, please be certain to let her know the line for which your work is intended. Responds in 2 weeks to queries. Responds in 4-6 weeks to mss. Obtains most new clients through recommendations from others, solicitations, conferences.

TERMS Agent receives 15% commission on domestic sales. Agent receives 15% commission on foreign sales. Offers written contract; 1-month notice must be given to terminate contract. Charges maximum of $350/year for postage and photocopying.

RECENT SALES Sold 27 titles in the last year.

WRITERS CONFERENCES RWA National Conference; BookExpo America.

● RITA ROSENKRANZ LITERARY AGENCY

440 West End Ave., #15D, New York NY 10024. (212)873-6333. **Website:** www.ritarosenkranzliteraryagency.com. **Contact:** Rita Rosenkranz. Member of AAR. Represents 35 clients. 30% of clients are new/unpublished writers. Currently handles: nonfiction books 99%, novels 1%.

○ Prior to opening her agency, Ms. Rosenkranz worked as an editor at major New York publishing houses.

REPRESENTS nonfiction books. **Considers these nonfiction areas:** animals, anthropology, art, autobiography, biography, business, child guidance, computers, cooking, crafts, cultural interests, current affairs, dance, decorating, economics, ethnic, film, gay, government, health, history, hobbies, how-to, humor, inspirational, interior design, language, law, lesbian, literature, medicine, military, money, music, nature, parenting, personal improvement, photography, popular culture, politics, psychology, religious, satire, science, self-help, sports, technology, theater, war, women's issues, women's studies.

⊶ "This agency focuses on adult nonfiction, stresses strong editorial development and refinement before submitting to publishers, and brainstorms ideas with authors." Actively seeks authors who are well paired with their subject, either for professional or personal reasons.

HOW TO CONTACT Send query letter only (no proposal) via regular mail or e-mail. Submit proposal package with SASE only on request. No fax queries. Accepts simultaneous submissions. Responds in 2 weeks to queries. Obtains most new clients through directory listings, solicitations, conferences, word of mouth.

TERMS Agent receives 15% commission on domestic sales. Agent receives 20% commission on foreign sales. Offers written contract, binding for 3 years; 3-month written notice must be given to terminate contract. Charges clients for photocopying. Makes referrals to editing services.

RECENT SALES *A Mind For Numbers: How to Succeed at Math Even if You Flunked Algebra* by Barbara Oakley (Tarcher); *The Politics Of Promotion: How High Achieving Women Get Ahead and Stay Ahead* by Bonnie Marcus (Wiley); *If Joan Of Arc Had Cancer: Finding Courage, Faith, and Healing from History's Most Inspirational Woman Warrior* by Janet Lynn Roseman (New World Library); *A Triumph Of Genius: Edwin Land, Polaroid, and the Kodak Patent War* by Ron K. Fierstein (ABA Publishing).

TIPS "Identify the current competition for your project to make sure the project is valid. A strong cover letter is very important."

○ ANDY ROSS LITERARY AGENCY

767 Santa Ray Ave., Oakland CA 94610. (510)238-8965. **E-mail:** andyrossagency@hotmail.com. **Website:** www.andyrossagency.com. **Contact:** Andy Ross. Member of AAR.

REPRESENTS Considers these nonfiction areas: anthropology, autobiography, biography, child guidance, creative nonfiction, cultural interests, current affairs, education, environment, ethnic, government, history, language, law, literature, military, parenting, popular culture, politics, psychology, science, sociology, technology, war. **Considers these fiction areas:** commercial, juvenile, literary, young adult.

⌖ "This agency specializes in general nonfiction, politics and current events, history, biography, journalism and contemporary culture." Actively seeking literary, commercial, and young adult fiction. Does not want to receive poetry.

HOW TO CONTACT Queries should be less than half page. Please put the word "query" in the title header of the e-mail. In the first sentence, state the category of the project. Give a short description of the book and your qualifications for writing. Accepts simultaneous submissions. Responds in 1 week to queries.

TERMS Agent receives 15% commission on domestic sales. Agent receives 20% commission on foreign sales or other deals made through a sub-agent. Offers written contract.

○◉ ROSS YOON AGENCY

1666 Connecticut Ave. NW, Suite 500, Washington DC 20009. (202)328-3282. **Fax:** (202)328-9162. **E-mail:** submissions@rossyoon.com. **Website:** http://rossyoon.com. **Contact:** Jennifer Manguera. Member of AAR.

MEMBER AGENTS Gail Ross (represents important commercial nonfiction in a variety of areas and counts top doctors, CEO's, prize-winning journalists, and historians among her clients. She and her team work closely with first-time authors; gail@rossyoon.com); **Howard Yoon** (nonfiction topics ranging from current events and politics to culture to religion and history, to smart business; howard@rossyoon.com); **Anna Sproul-Latimer** (pop culture, science, humor, memoir, anything surprising; anna@rossyoon.com).

REPRESENTS nonfiction books.

⌖ "This agency specializes in adult trade nonfiction."

HOW TO CONTACT E-query submissions@rossyoon.com with a query letter briefly explaining your idea, media platform, and qualifications for writing on this topic; or send a complete book proposal featuring an overview of your idea, author bio, media and marketing strategy, chapter outline, and 1-3 sample chapters. Please send these as attachments in .doc or .docx format. Accepts simultaneous submissions. Responds in 4-6 weeks to queries. Obtains most new clients through referrals from current clients.

TERMS Agent receives 15% commission on domestic sales. Agent receives 20% commission on foreign sales. Reserves the right to bill clients for office expenses.

○ JANE ROTROSEN AGENCY LLC

318 E. 51st St., New York NY 10022. (212)593-4330. **Fax:** (212)935-6985. **Website:** www.janerotrosen.com. Estab. 1974. Member of AAR. Other member-

ships include Authors Guild. Represents more than 100 clients.

MEMBER AGENTS Jane Rotrosen Berkey (not taking on clients); **Andrea Cirillo**, acirillo@janerotrosen.com (suspense and women's fiction); **Annelise Robe**y, arobey@janerotrosen.com (women's fiction, suspense, mystery, literary fiction and the occasional nonfiction project); **Meg Ruley**, mruley@janerotrosen.com (women's fiction as well as suspense, thrillers, and mystery); **Christina Hogrebe**, chogrebe@janerotrosen.com (young adult, contemporary romance and new adult, women's fiction, historical fiction, mystery, fanfiction); **Amy Tannenbaum**, atannenbaum@janerotrosen.com (contemporary romance and new adult; Amy is particularly interested in those areas, as well as women's fiction that falls into that sweet spot between literary and commercial); **Rebecca Scherer** (women's fiction, mystery, suspense/thriller, romance, upmarket fiction at the cross between commercial and literary).

REPRESENTS nonfiction books, novels. **Considers these fiction areas:** literary, mystery, new adult, romance, suspense, thriller, women's.

HOW TO CONTACT Agent submission e-mail addresses are different. Send a query letter, a brief synopsis, and up to three chapters of your novel or the proposal for nonfiction. No attachments. Responds in 2 weeks to writers who have been referred by a client or colleague. Responds in 2 months to mss. Obtains most new clients through recommendations from others.

TERMS Agent receives 15% commission on domestic sales. Agent receives 20% commission on foreign sales. Offers written contract, binding for 3 years; 2-month notice must be given to terminate contract. Charges clients for photocopying, express mail, overseas postage, book purchase.

⊘ THE DAMARIS ROWLAND AGENCY

420 E. 23rd St., Suite 6F, New York NY 10010. **Contact:** Damaris Rowland. Member of AAR.

REPRESENTS nonfiction books, novels.

⊶ This agency specializes in women's fiction, literary fiction and nonfiction, and pop fiction.

HOW TO CONTACT Obtains most new clients through recommendations from others, solicitations, conferences.

TERMS Agent receives 15% commission on domestic sales. Agent receives 20% commission on foreign sales. Offers written contract.

◑ ◉ THE RUDY AGENCY

825 Wildlife Lane, Estes Park CO 80517. (970)577-8500. **Fax:** (970)577-8600. **E-mail:** mak@rudyagency.com; fred@rudyagency.com. **Website:** www.rudyagency.com. **Contact:** Maryann Karinch. Adheres to AAR canon of ethics. Represents 15 clients. 50% of clients are new/unpublished writers.

◗ Prior to becoming an agent, Ms. Karinch was, and continues to be, an author of nonfiction books—covering the subjects of health/medicine and human behavior. Prior to that, she was in public relations and marketing: areas of expertise she also applies in her practice as an agent.

MEMBER AGENTS Maryann Karinch; Fred Tribuzzo (fiction: thrillers, historical).

REPRESENTS nonfiction, novels. **Considers these nonfiction areas:** anthropology, archeology, autobiography, biography, business, child guidance, computers, cultural interests, current affairs, economics, education, ethnic, gay/lesbian, government, health, history, how-to, language, law, literature, medicine, memoirs, military, money, music, parenting, popular culture, politics, psychology, science, sociology, sports, technology, true crime, war, women's issues, women's studies. **Considers these fiction areas:** historical, thriller.

⊶ "We support authors from the proposal stage through promotion of the published work. We work in partnership with publishers to promote the published work and coach authors in their role in the marketing and public relations campaigns for the book." Actively seeking projects with social value, projects that open minds to new ideas and interesting lives, and projects that entertain through good storytelling. Does not want to receive poetry, children's/juvenile books, screenplays/plays, art/photo books, novellas, religion books, and joke books or books that fit in to the impulse buy/gift book category.

HOW TO CONTACT "Query us. If we like the query, we will invite a complete proposal (or complete ms if writing fiction). No phone queries." Accepts simultaneous submissions. Responds in 8 weeks to mss. Obtains most new clients through recommendations from others, solicitations.

TERMS Agent receives 15% commission on domestic sales. Offers written contract, binding for 1 year.

NEW AGENT SPOTLIGHT

NOAH BALLARD
CURTIS BROWN, LTD.

Curtisbrown.com

@noahballard

ABOUT NOAH: Noah received his BA in English from the University of Nebraska–Lincoln, and began his career in publishing at Emma Sweeney Agency where he sold foreign rights for the agency in addition to building his own client list. He has appeared across the country at graduate programs and writing conferences speaking about query letters, building nonfiction platforms and submission etiquette. He lives in Brooklyn.

HE IS SEEKING: Noah specializes in literary debuts, upmarket thrillers and narrative nonfiction, and he is always on the lookout for honest and provocative new writers. Noah mainly represents books geared toward adults, but is open to young adult and middle grade that breaks the mold.

HOW TO SUBMIT: E-queries only. Please send your query letter and contact information along with the first ten pages of your manuscript or proposal to nb@cbltd.com with the word "Query" in the subject line. He reviews all queries sent to him within three to four weeks, and responds if interested.

RECENT SALES *The Alchemists's Daugher,* by Mary Lawrence (Kensington); *Live It!* by Jairek Robbins (Grand Harbor/Amazon); *Parenting With A Story,* by Paul Smith (Amacom); *Toy Time!* by Christopher Byrne (Random House); *Find Out Anything From Anyone, Anytime,* by James O. Pyle (Career Press); *Prairie Man,* by Norm Matteoni (Lyons Press); *The Slaughter,* by EthanGutmann (Prometheus Books).

TIPS "Present yourself professionally. I tell people all the time: Subscribe to *Writer's Digest* (I do), because you will get good advice about how to approach an agent."

○ REGINA RYAN PUBLISHING ENTERPRISES, INC.

251 Central Park W., 7D, New York NY 10024. (212)787-5589. **E-mail:** queries@reginaryanbooks.com. **Website:** www.reginaryanbooks.com. **Contact:** Regina Ryan. Member of AAR. Currently handles: nonfiction books 100%.

○ Prior to becoming an agent, Ms. Ryan was an editor at Alfred A. Knopf, editor-in-chief of Macmillan Adult Trade, and a book producer.

REPRESENTS nonfiction books. **Considers these nonfiction areas:** animals, architecture, gardening, government, history, law, memoirs, parenting, politics, psychology, travel, women's issues, women's studies, narrative nonfiction; natural history (especially birds and birding); popular science, adventure, lifestyle, business, sustainability, mind-body-spirit, relationships.

⊶ "We are always looking for new and exciting books in our areas of interest, including well-written narrative nonfiction, architecture, history, politics, natural history (especially birds), science (especially the brain), the environment, women's issues, parenting, cooking, psychology, health, wellness, diet, lifestyle, sustainability, popular reference, and leisure activities including sports, narrative travel, and gardening. We represent books that have something new to say, are well-written and that will, if possible, make the world a better place."

HOW TO CONTACT E-query. If the agency is interested, they will request a proposal. Accepts simultaneous submissions. Tries to respond in 1 month to queries. Obtains most new clients through recommendations from others.

TERMS Agent receives 15% commission on domestic sales. Agent receives 15% commission on foreign sales. Offers written contract. Charges clients for all out-of-pocket expenses (e.g., long distance calls, messengers, freight, copying) if it's more than just a nominal amount.

TIPS "An analysis of why your proposed book is different and better than the competition is essential; a sample chapter is helpful."

⊕ SADLER CHILDREN'S LITERARY

(815)209-6252. **E-mail:** jodell.sadlerliterary@gmail.com. **E-mail:** submissions.sadlerliterary@gmail.com. **Website:** www.sadlercreativeliterary.com. **Contact:** Jodell Sadler.

REPRESENTS Considers these fiction areas: juvenile, middle grade, picture books, young adult.

HOW TO CONTACT E-query only. Your subject line should read "QUERY—Name or Title—Genre." Alert this agency if submitting to other agencies at the same time. Along with your query, include an attached Word doc with your complete picture book text or the first 10 pages or your book. If you are an illustrator, send a link to online portfolio, or send PDF with pictures.

❶ THE SAGALYN AGENCY / ICM PARTNERS

1250 Connecticut Ave., 7th Floor, Washington DC 20036. **E-mail:** query@sagalyn.com. **Website:** www.sagalyn.com. Estab. 1980. Member of AAR.

MEMBER AGENTS Raphael Sagalyn.

REPRESENTS Considers these nonfiction areas: biography, business, creative nonfiction, economics, popular culture, science, technology.

"Our list includes upmarket nonfiction books in these areas: narrative history, biography, business, economics, popular culture, science, technology." Actively seeking upmarket nonfiction and upmarket fiction. No stage plays, screenplays, poetry, science fiction, fantasy, romance, or children's books.

HOW TO CONTACT Please send e-mail queries only (no attachments).

TIPS "We receive 1,000-1,200 queries a year, which in turn lead to 2 or 3 new clients. See our website for sales information and recent projects."

❶ VICTORIA SANDERS & ASSOCIATES

40 Buck Rd., Stone Ridge NY 12484. (212)633-8811. **Fax:** (212)633-0525. **E-mail:** queriesvsa@gmail.com. **Website:** www.victoriasanders.com. **Contact:** Victoria Sanders. Estab. 1992. Member of AAR. Signatory of WGA. Represents 135 clients. 25% of clients are new/unpublished writers.

MEMBER AGENTS Victoria Sanders, Chris Kepner, Bernadette Baker-Baughman.

REPRESENTS nonfiction books, novels. **Considers these nonfiction areas:** autobiography, biography, cultural interests, current affairs, ethnic, film, gay/lesbian, government, history, humor, law, literature, music, popular culture, politics, psychology, satire, theater, translation, women's issues, women's studies. **Considers these fiction areas:** action, adventure, contemporary issues, crime, ethnic, family saga, feminist, lesbian, literary, mainstream, mystery, new adult, picture books, thriller, young adult.

HOW TO CONTACT Query by e-mail only. "We will not respond to e-mails with attachments or attached files."

TERMS Agent receives 15% commission on domestic sales. Agent receives 20% commission on foreign/film sales. Offers written contract. Charges for photocopying, messenger, express mail. If in excess of $100, client approval is required.

RECENT SALES Sold 20+ titles in the last year.

TIPS "Limit query to letter (no calls) and give it your best shot. A good query is going to get a good response."

◯ SCHIAVONE LITERARY AGENCY, INC.

236 Trails End, West Palm Beach FL 33413-2135. (561)966-9294. **Fax:** (561)966-9294. **E-mail:** profschia@aol.com. **Website:** www.publishersmarket

place.com/members/profschia; blog site: www.schi avoneliteraryagencyinc.blogspot.com. **Contact:** Dr. James Schiavone, CEO, corporate offices in Florida; Jennifer DuVall, president, New York office; Francine Edelman, senior executive VP. Other memberships include National Education Association.

○ Prior to opening his agency, Dr. Schiavone was a full professor of developmental skills at the City University of New York and author of 5 trade books and 3 textbooks. Jennifer DuVall has many years of combined experience in office management and agenting.

MEMBER AGENTS James Schiavone, profschia@ aol.com; **Jennifer DuVall**, jendu77@aol.com; **Kevin McAdams**, kvn.mcadams@yahoo.com.

REPRESENTS Considers these nonfiction areas: biography, business, cooking, health, history, politics, science, sports, true crime. **Considers these fiction areas:** fantasy, literary, mainstream, middle grade, mystery, romance, science fiction, suspense, thriller, young adult.

☛ This agency specializes in celebrity biography and autobiography and memoirs. Does not want to receive poetry.

HOW TO CONTACT "One-page e-mail queries only. Absolutely no attachments. Postal queries are not accepted. No phone calls. We do not consider poetry, short stories, anthologies or children's books. No scripts or screen plays. We handle dramatic, film and TV rights, options, and screen plays for books we have agented. We are NOT interested in work previously published in any format (e.g., self-published; online; ebooks; Print On Demand). E-mail queries may be addressed to any of the agency's agents." Accepts simultaneous submissions. Responds in 2 weeks to queries. Responds in 6 weeks to mss. Obtains most new clients through recommendations from others, solicitations, conferences.

TERMS Agent receives 15% commission on domestic sales. Agent receives 20% commission on foreign sales. Offers written contract. Charges clients for postage only.

WRITERS CONFERENCES Key West Literary Seminar; South Florida Writers' Conference; Tallahassee Writers' Conference, Million Dollar Writers' Conference; Alaska Writers Conference.

TIPS "We prefer to work with established authors published by major houses in New York. We will con-sider marketable proposals from new/previously unpublished writers."

WENDY SCHMALZ AGENCY

402 Union St., #831, Hudson NY 12534. (518)672-7697. **E-mail:** wendy@schmalzagency.com. **Website:** www. schmalzagency.com. **Contact:** Wendy Schmalz. Estab. 2002. Member of AAR.

REPRESENTS Considers these nonfiction areas: , Many nonfiction subjects are of interest to this agency. **Considers these fiction areas:** literary, mainstream, middle grade, young adult.

☛ Not looking for picture books, science fiction, or fantasy.

HOW TO CONTACT Accepts only e-mail queries. Paste all text into the e-mail. Do not attach the ms or sample chapters or synopsis. Replies to queries only if they want to read the ms. (2015: Not currently accepting submissions of genre fiction or children's picture books.) If you do not hear from this agency within 6 weeks, consider that a no. Obtains clients through recommendations from others.

TERMS Agent receives 15% commission on domestic sales; 20% on foreign sales; 25% for Asian sales.

⊘ HAROLD SCHMIDT LITERARY AGENCY

415 W. 23rd St., #6F, New York NY 10011. **Contact:** Harold Schmidt, acquisitions. Estab. 1984. Member of AAR. Represents 3 clients.

REPRESENTS nonfiction, fiction. **Considers these fiction areas:** contemporary issues, gay, literary, original quality fiction with unique narrative voices, high quality psychological suspense and thrillers, likes offbeat/quirky.

HOW TO CONTACT Query by mail with SASE or e-mail; do not send further material without being asked. No telephone or e-mail queries. We will respond if interested. Do not send material unless asked as it cannot be read or returned.

◑◎ SUSAN SCHULMAN LITERARY AGENCY

454 W. 44th St., New York NY 10036. (212)713-1633. **Fax:** (212)581-8830. **E-mail:** Susan@Schulmanagen cy.com. **Website:** www.publishersmarketplace.com/ members/Schulman/. **Contact:** Susan Schulman. Estab. 1980. Member of AAR. Signatory of WGA. Other memberships include Dramatists Guild. 10% of clients are new/unpublished writers. Currently handles: non-

fiction books 50%, novels 25%, juvenile books 15%, stage plays 10%.

REPRESENTS Considers these nonfiction areas: biography, business, cooking, ethnic, health, history, money, religious, science, travel, women's issues, women's studies. **Considers these fiction areas:** juvenile, literary, mainstream, women's.

⚷ "We specialize in books for, by and about women and women's issues including nonfiction self-help books, fiction and theater projects. We also handle the film, television and allied rights for several agencies as well as foreign rights for several publishing houses." Actively seeking new nonfiction. Considers plays. Does not want to receive poetry, television scripts or concepts for television.

HOW TO CONTACT "For fiction: query letter with outline and three sample chapters, résumé and SASE. For nonfiction: query letter with complete description of subject, at least one chapter, résumé and SASE. Queries may be sent via regular mail or e-mail. Please do not submit queries via UPS or Federal Express. Please do not send attachments with e-mail queries." Accepts simultaneous submissions. Responds in 6 weeks to queries/mss. Obtains most new clients through recommendations from others, solicitations, conferences.

TERMS Agent receives 15% commission on domestic sales. Agent receives 20% commission on foreign sales. Offers written contract; 30-day notice must be given to terminate contract.

RECENT SALES Sold 50 titles in the last year; hundred of subsidiary rights deals.

WRITERS CONFERENCES Geneva Writers' Conference (Switzerland); Columbus Writers' Conference; Skidmore Conference of the Independent Women's Writers Group.

TIPS "Keep writing!" Schulman describes her agency as "professional boutique, long-standing, eclectic."

◐ THE SCIENCE FACTORY

Scheideweg 34C, 20253 Hamburg, Germany. +49 40 4327 4959 (Germany); +44 (0)207 193 7296 (Skype). **E-mail:** info@sciencefactory.co.uk. **Website:** www.sciencefactory.co.uk. **Contact:** Peter Tallack. Estab. 2008.

○ Prior to his current position, Mr. Tallack was a director of the UK agency Conville & Walsh, publishing director at Weidenfeld & Nicolson, and on the editorial staff of the science journal *Nature.*

⚷ "This agency specializes in representing nonfiction authors aiming to satisfy the public's intellectual hunger for serious ideas. Experience of dealing directly in all markets, media and languages across the world." Actively seeking popular science nonfiction, particularly from public intellectuals, academics and journalists.

HOW TO CONTACT E-query. "In the subject line please include the word 'query' and the name of your project or your name. If you are attaching a file (sample chapter for fiction, or proposal for nonfiction), please name the file with your name (not ours)."

TIPS The Science Factory is the trading name of The Science Factory Ltd. Registered Office (not address for general correspondence): The Courtyard, Shoreham Road, Upper Beeding, Steyning, West Sussex BN44 3TN, UK. Registered in England and Wales: Company No. 06498410. German VAT Registration No. DE 274 9743 26.

◎ SCOVIL GALEN GHOSH LITERARY AGENCY, INC.

276 Fifth Ave., New York NY 10001. (212)679-8686. **Fax:** (212)679-6710. **Website:** www.sgglit.com. **Contact:** Russell Galen. Estab. 1992. Member of AAR. Represents 300 clients.

MEMBER AGENTS Russell Galen, russellgalen@sgglit.com (novels that stretch the bounds of reality; strong, serious nonfiction books on almost any subject that teach something new; no books that are merely entertaining, such as diet or pop psych books; serious interests include science, history, journalism, biography, business, memoir, nature, politics, sports, contemporary culture, literary nonfiction, etc.); **Ann Behar**, annbehar@sgglit.com (juvenile books for all ages).

HOW TO CONTACT E-mail queries only. Note how each agent at this agency has their own submission e-mail. Accepts simultaneous submissions.

◑ SCRIBE AGENCY, LLC

5508 Joylynne Dr., Madison WI 53716. **E-mail:** whattheshizzle@scribeagency.com. **E-mail:** submissions@scribeagency.com. **Website:** www.scribeagency.com. **Contact:** Kristopher O'Higgins. Represents 11 clients. 18% of clients are new/unpublished writers. Currently handles: novels 98%, story collections 2%.

○ "With more than 15 years experience in publishing, with time spent on both the agency and editorial sides, with marketing experience to boot, Scribe Agency is a full-service literary agency, working hands-on with its authors on their projects. Check the website (scribeagency.com) to make sure your work matches the Scribe aesthetic."

MEMBER AGENTS Kristopher O'Higgins.

REPRESENTS novels, anthologies. **Considers these fiction areas:** experimental, fantasy, feminist, horror, literary, mainstream, science fiction, thriller.

8—➤Actively seeking excellent writers with ideas and stories to tell.

HOW TO CONTACT E-queries only: submissions@scribeagency.com. See the website for submission info, as it may change. Responds in 3-4 weeks to queries. Responds in 5 months to mss.

TERMS Agent receives 15% commission on domestic sales. Agent receives 20% commission on foreign sales. Offers written contract. Charges for postage and photocopying.

WRITERS CONFERENCES BookExpo America; WisCon; Wisconsin Book Festival; World Fantasy Convention; WorldCon.

SECRET AGENT MAN

P.O. Box 1078, Lake Forest CA 92609. (949)698-6987. **E-mail:** query@secretagentman.net. **Website:** www.secretagentman.net. **Contact:** Scott Mortenson.

8—➤Selective mystery, thriller, suspense and detective fiction. Does not want to receive scripts or screenplays.

HOW TO CONTACT Query via e-mail only; include sample chapter(s), synopsis and/or outline. Prefers to read the real thing rather than a description of it. Obtains most new clients through recommendations from others.

➕ SELECTIC ARTISTS

127 W. 83rd St., No. 56, New York NY 10024. **E-mail:** query@selectricartists.com. **Website:** www.selectricartists.com.

HOW TO CONTACT E-mail your query letter with manuscript attached as .doc or .pdf. No snail mail of phone pitches. Feel free to follow up if you have not heard back in 6 weeks.

LYNN SELIGMAN, LITERARY AGENT

400 Highland Ave., Upper Montclair NJ 07043. (973)783-3631. **Contact:** Lynn Seligman.

○ Prior to opening her agency, Ms. Seligman worked in the subsidiary rights department of Doubleday and Simon & Schuster, and served as an agent with Julian Bach Literary Agency (which became IMG Literary Agency). Foreign rights are represented by Books Crossing Borders, Inc.

REPRESENTS nonfiction books, novels. **Considers these nonfiction areas:** interior, anthropology, art, biography, business, child guidance, cooking, current affairs, education, ethnic, government, health, history, how-to, humor, language, money, music, nature, photography, popular culture, psychology, science, self-help, sociology, film, true crime, women's. **Considers these fiction areas:** detective, ethnic, fantasy, feminist, historical, horror, humor, literary, mainstream, mystery, romance, contemporary, gothic, historical, regency, science fiction.

8—➤"This agency specializes in general nonfiction and fiction. I also do illustrated and photography books and have represented several photographers for books."

HOW TO CONTACT Query with SASE. Prefers to read materials exclusively. Accepts simultaneous submissions. Responds in 2 weeks to queries. Responds in 2 months to mss. Obtains most new clients through referrals from other writers and editors.

TERMS Agent receives 15% commission on domestic sales. Agent receives 25% commission on foreign sales. Charges clients for photocopying, unusual postage, express mail, telephone expenses (checks with author first).

RECENT SALES Sold 15 titles in the last year. Lords of Vice series, by Barbara Pierce; Untitled series, by Deborah Leblanc.

◑ SERENDIPITY LITERARY AGENCY, LLC

305 Gates Ave., Brooklyn NY 11216. (718)230-7689. **Fax:** (718)230-7829. **E-mail:** rbrooks@serendipitylit.com; info@serendipitylit.com. **Website:** www.serendipitylit.com; facebook.com/serendipitylit. **Contact:** Regina Brooks. Represents 50 clients. 50% of clients are new/unpublished writers. Currently handles: nonfiction books 50%, other 50% fiction.

○ Prior to becoming an agent, Ms. Brooks was an acquisitions editor for John Wiley & Sons, Inc. and McGraw-Hill Companies.

MEMBER AGENTS Regina Brooks; **Dawn Michelle Hardy** (sports, pop culture, blog and trend, music, lifestyle and social science), **Karen Thomas** (narrative nonfiction, celebrity, pop culture, memoir, general fiction, women's fiction, romance, mystery, self-help, inspirational, Christian based fiction and nonfiction including Evangelical), **John Weber** (unique YA and middle grade); **Folade Bell** (literary and commercial women's fiction, YA, literary mysteries & thrillers, historical fiction, African-American issues, gay/lesbian, Christian fiction, humor and books that deeply explore other cultures); **Nadeen Gayle** (romance, memoir, pop culture, inspirational/ religious, women's fiction, parenting young adult, mystery and political thrillers, and all forms of nonfiction).

REPRESENTS Considers these nonfiction areas: creative nonfiction, current affairs, humor, inspirational, investigative, memoirs, music, parenting, popular culture, religious, self-help, spirituality, sports. **Considers these fiction areas:** commercial, gay, historical, humor, lesbian, literary, middle grade, mystery, romance, thriller, women's, young adult.

⚓ African-American nonfiction, commercial fiction, young adult novels, and juvenile books. No stage plays, screenplays or poetry.

HOW TO CONTACT Check the website, as there are online submission forms for fiction, nonfiction and juvenile. Accepts simultaneous submissions. Obtains most new clients through conferences, referrals.

TERMS Agent receives 15% commission on domestic sales. Agent receives 20% commission on foreign sales. Offers written contract; 2-month notice must be given to terminate contract. Charges clients for office fees, which are taken from any advance.

RECENT SALES *How I Discovered Poetry* by Marilyn Nelson; *Cooking Allergy Free* by Jenna Short; *Cleo Edison Oliver* by Sundee Frazier; *Flight Of The Seahawks* by Jerry Brewer; *It's Not A Game* by Kent Babb; *Drop The Act: It's Exhausting* by Beth Thomas Cohen; *College, Quicker: The Fast-Track To a More Affordable College Degree* by Katherine Stephens; *Every Closed Eye Ain't Sleep* by Marita Teague Tips "

TIPS "See The books *Writing Great Books For Young Adults* and *You Should Really Write A Book: How To Write Sell And Market Your Memoir.* We are looking for high concept ideas with big hooks. If you get writer's block try possibiliteas.co, it's a muse in a cup."

◑○ SEVENTH AVENUE LITERARY AGENCY

2052-124th St., South Surrey BC Canada. (604)538-7252. **Fax:** (604)538-7252. **E-mail:** info@seventhavenuelit.com. **Website:** www.seventhavenuelit.com. **Contact:** Robert Mackwood, director. Currently handles: nonfiction books 100%.

REPRESENTS nonfiction books. **Considers these nonfiction areas:** autobiography, biography, business, computers, economics, health, history, medicine, science, sports, technology, travel.

⚓ Seventh Avenue Literary Agency is both a literary agency and personal management agency. (The agency was originally called Contemporary Management.)

HOW TO CONTACT Query with SASE. Submit outline, synopsis, 1 sample chapter (nonfiction), publishing history, author bio, table of contents with proposal or query. Provide full contact information. Let us know the submission history. No fiction Obtains most new clients through recommendations from others, some solicitations. Does not add many new clients.

TIPS "If you want your material returned, please include an SASE with adequate postage; otherwise, material will be recycled. (US stamps are not adequate; they do not work in Canada.)"

◑ THE SEYMOUR AGENCY

475 Miner St., Canton NY 13617. (315)386-1831. **E-mail:** marysue@twcny.rr.com; nicole@theseymouragency.com; julie@theseymouragency.com; lane@theseymouragency.com. **Website:** www.theseymouragency.com. Member of AAR. Signatory of WGA. Other memberships include RWA, Authors Guild.

○ Ms. Seymour is a retired New York State certified teacher. Ms. Resciniti was recently named "Agent of the Year" by the ACFW.

MEMBER AGENTS **Mary Sue Seymour** (accepts queries in Christian, inspirational, romance, and nonfiction); **Nicole Resciniti** (accepts all genres of romance, young adult, middle grade, new adult, suspense, thriller, mystery, sci-fi, fantasy); **Julie Gwinn** (Christian and inspirational fiction and nonfiction, women's fiction [contemporary and historical], new adult, Southern fiction, literary fiction and young adult); Lane Heymont (science fiction, fantasy, nonfiction).

REPRESENTS nonfiction books, novels. **Considers these nonfiction areas:** business, health, how-to, self help, Christian books; cookbooks; any well-written nonfiction that includes a proposal in standard format and 1 sample chapter. **Considers these fiction areas:** action, fantasy, inspirational, middle grade, mystery, new adult, religious, romance, science fiction, suspense, thriller, young adult.

HOW TO CONTACT For Mary Sue: E-query with synopsis, first 50 pages for romance. Accepts e-mail queries. For Nicole and Julie: E-mail the query plus first 5 pages of the manuscript pasted into the e-mail. Accepts simultaneous submissions. Responds in 1 month to queries. Responds in 3 months to mss.

TERMS Agent receives 12-15% commission on domestic sales.

ⓘ DENISE SHANNON LITERARY AGENCY, INC.

20 W. 22nd St., Suite 1603, New York NY 10010. (212)414-2911. **Fax:** (212)414-2930. **E-mail:** submissions@deniseshannonagency.com. **Website:** www.deniseshannonagency.com. **Contact:** Denise Shannon. Estab. 2002. Member of AAR.

    ○ Prior to opening her agency, Ms. Shannon worked for 16 years with Georges Borchardt and International Creative Management.

REPRESENTS nonfiction books, novels. **Considers these nonfiction areas:** biography, business, health, narrative nonfiction; politics; journalism; memoir; social history. **Considers these fiction areas:** literary.

    ⊶ "We are a boutique agency with a distinguished list of fiction and nonfiction authors."

HOW TO CONTACT "Queries may be submitted by post, accompanied by a SASE, or by e-mail to submissions@deniseshannonagency.com. Please include a description of the available book project and a brief bio including details of any prior publications. We will reply and request more material if we are interested. We request that you inform us if you are submitting material simultaneously to other agencies."

RECENT SALES *My New American Life*, by Francine Prose (Harper); *Swamplandia!*, by Karen Russell (Knopf); *The Girls of No Return*, by Erin Saldin (Scholastic); *Everyone But You*, by Sandra Novack (Random House).

TIPS "Please do not send queries regarding fiction projects until a complete ms is available for review. We request that you inform us if you are submitting material simultaneously to other agencies."

◎ KEN SHERMAN & ASSOCIATES

1275 N. Hayworth, Ste. 103, Los Angeles CA 90046. (310)273-8840. **Fax:** (310)271-2875. **Website:** www.kenshermanassociates.com. **Contact:** Ken Sherman.

    ○ Prior to opening his agency, Mr. Sherman was with The William Morris Agency, The Lantz Office and Paul Kohner, Inc. He has taught The Business of Writing For Film and Television and The Book Worlds at UCLA and USC. He also lectures extensively at writer's conferences and film festivals around the U.S. He is currently a Commissioner of Arts and Cultural Affairs in the City of West Hollywood, and is on the International Advisory Board of the Christopher Isherwood Foundation.

REPRESENTS nonfiction books, novels, movie, tv, not episodic drama, teleplays, life rights, film/TV rights to books and life rights. **Considers these nonfiction areas:** agriculture horticulture, americana, crafts, interior, newage, young, animals, anthropology, art, biography, business, child, computers, cooking, current affairs, education, ethnic, gardening, gay, government, health, history, how to, humor, language, memoirs, military, money, multicultural, music, nature, philosophy, photography, popular culture, psychology, recreation, regional, religion, science, self help, sex, sociology, software, spirituality, sports, film, translation, travel, true crime, womens, creative nonfiction. **Considers these fiction areas:** glitz, newage, psychic, adventure, comic, confession, detective, erotica, ethnic, experimental, family, fantasy, feminist, gay, gothic, hi lo, historical, horror, humor, literary, mainstream, military, multicultural, multimedia, mystery, occult, picture books, plays, poetry, poetry translation, regional, religious, romance, science, short, spiritual, sports, thriller, translation, western, young adult. **Considers these script areas:** action, biography, cartoon, comedy, contemporary, detective, erotica, ethnic, experimental, family, fantasy, feminist, gay, glitz, historical, horror, mainstream, multicultural, multimedia, mystery, psychic, regional, religious, romantic comedy, romantic drama, science, sports, teen, thriller, western.

HOW TO CONTACT Contact by referral only. Reports in approximately 1 month to mss. Obtains most new clients through recommendations from others.

TERMS Agent receives 15% commission on domestic sales. Agent receives 15% commission on foreign sales. Agent receives 10-15% commission on film sales. Offers written contract. Charges clients for reasonable office expenses (postage, photocopying, etc.)

RECENT SALES Sold more than 20 scripts in the last year. *Back Roads*, by Tawni O'Dell with Adrian Lyne set to direct; *Priscilla Salyers Story*, produced by Andrea Baynes (ABC); *Toys of Glass*, by Martin Booth (ABC/Saban Entertainment); *Brazil*, by John Updike (film rights to Glaucia Carmagos); *Fifth Sacred Thing*, by Starhawk (Bantam), with Starhawk adapting her book into a screenplay; *Questions From Dad*, by Dwight Twilly (Tuttle); *Snow Falling on Cedars* by David Guterson (Universal Pictures); *The Witches f Eastwick - The Musical*, by John Updike (Cameron Macintosh, Ltd.); *Rabbit"/HBO-1-Hr Series,* John Updike.

WRITERS CONFERENCES Maui Writers' Conference; Squaw Valley Writers' Workshop; Santa Barbara Writers' Conference; Screenwriting Conference in Santa Fe; Aspen Summer Words Literary Festival (The Aspen Institute and the San Francisco Writer's Conference). San Francisco Writers' Conference, Chautaq UA Writers' Conference.

ⓘ WENDY SHERMAN ASSOCIATES, INC.

27 W. 24th St., Suite 700B, New York NY 10010. (212)279-9027. **E-mail:** submissions@wsherman.com. **Website:** www.wsherman.com. **Contact:** Wendy Sherman; Kim Perel. Member of AAR.

Prior to opening the agency, Ms. Sherman served as vice president, executive director, associate publisher, subsidiary rights director, and sales and marketing director for major publishers.

MEMBER AGENTS Wendy Sherman (women's fiction that hits that sweet spot between literary and mainstream, Southern voices, historical dramas, suspense with a well-developed protagonist, and writing that illuminates the multicultural experience); **Kim Perel** (illustrated lifestyle books in the areas of fashion, home décor and food; she also loves unique memoir that reads like fiction, in-depth journalistic no-fiction, "big idea" books about why we think, live or process thoughts the way we do, and fiction that straddles literary and commercial with a strong story and beautifully crafted prose).

REPRESENTS Considers these nonfiction areas: creative nonfiction, foods, humor, memoirs, parenting, popular culture, psychology, self-help, narrative nonfiction. **Considers these fiction areas:** mainstream, Mainstream fiction that hits the sweet spot between literary and commercial.

> "We specialize in developing new writers, as well as working with more established writers. My experience as a publisher has proven to be a great asset to my clients."

HOW TO CONTACT Query via e-mail only. "We ask that you include your last name, title, and the name of the agent you are submitting to in the subject line. For fiction, please include a query letter and your first 10 pages copied and pasted in the body of the e-mail. We will not open attachments unless they have been requested. For nonfiction, please include your query letter and author bio. Due to the large number of e-mail submissions that we receive, we can only reply to e-mail queries in the affirmative. We respectfully ask that you do not send queries to our individual e-mail addresses." Accepts simultaneous submissions. Obtains most new clients through recommendations from other writers.

TERMS Agent receives standard 15% commission. Offers written contract.

RECENT SALES *Z, A Novel of Zelda Fitzgerald*, by Therese Anne Fowler; *The Silence of Bonaventure Arrow*, by Rita Leganski; *Together Tea*, by Marjan Kamali; *A Long Long Time Ago and Essentially True*, by Brigid Pasulka; *Illuminations*, by Mary Sharratt; *The Accounting,* by William Lashner; *Lunch in Paris*, by Elizabeth Bard; *The Rules of Inheritance*, by Claire Bidwell Smith; *Love in Ninety Days*, by Dr. Diana Kirschner; *The Wow Factor*, by Jacqui Stafford; *Humor Memoirs*, by Wade Rouse.

TIPS "The bottom line is: Do your homework. Be as well prepared as possible. Read the books that will help you present yourself and your work with polish. You want your submission to stand out."

⊘ ROSALIE SIEGEL, INTERNATIONAL LITERARY AGENCY, INC.

1 Abey Dr., Pennington NJ 08534. (609)737-1007. **Fax:** (609)737-3708. **Website:** http://rosaliesiegel.com. **Contact:** Rosalie Siegel. Member of AAR.

HOW TO CONTACT "Please note that we are no longer accepting submissions of new material." Obtains most new clients through referrals from writers and friends.

TERMS Agent receives 15% commission on domestic sales. Agent receives 20% commission on foreign sales. Offers written contract; 2-month notice must be given to terminate contract. Charges clients for photocopying.

RECENT SALES *Mud Season*, by Ellen Stimson.

🌑🌗 JEFFREY SIMMONS LITERARY AGENCY

15 Penn House, Mallory St., London NW8 8SX England. (44)(207)224-8917. **E-mail:** jasimmons@uni combox.co.uk. **Contact:** Jeffrey Simmons. Represents 43 clients. 40% of clients are new/unpublished writers. Currently handles: nonfiction books 65%, novels 35%.

○ Prior to becoming an agent, Mr. Simmons was a publisher. He is also an author.

REPRESENTS nonfiction books, novels. **Considers these nonfiction areas:** autobiography, biography, current affairs, film, government, history, language, memoirs, music, popular culture, sociology, sports, translation, true crime. **Considers these fiction areas:** action, adventure, confession, crime, detective, family saga, literary, mainstream, mystery, police, suspense, thriller.

8—ਜ "This agency seeks to handle good books and promising young writers. My long experience in publishing and as an author and ghostwriter means I can offer an excellent service all around, especially in terms of editorial experience where appropriate." Actively seeking quality fiction, biography, autobiography, showbiz, personality books, law, crime, politics, and world affairs. Does not want to receive science fiction, horror, fantasy, juvenile, academic books, or specialist subjects (e.g., cooking, gardening, religious).

HOW TO CONTACT Submit sample chapter, outline/proposal, SASE (IRCs if necessary).Prefers to read materials exclusively. Responds in one week to queries. Responds in one month to mss. Obtains most new clients through recommendations from others, solicitations.

TERMS Agent receives 10-15% commission on domestic sales. Agent receives 15% commission on foreign sales. Offers written contract, binding for lifetime of book in question or until it becomes out of print.

TIPS "When contacting us with an outline/proposal, include a brief biographical note (listing any previous publications, with publishers and dates). Preferably tell us if the book has already been offered elsewhere."

◯◯ BEVERLEY SLOPEN LITERARY AGENCY

131 Bloor St. W., Suite 711, Toronto ON M5S 1S3 Canada. (416)964-9598. **E-mail:** beverly@slopenagency.ca. **Website:** www.slopenagency.ca. **Contact:** Beverley Slopen. Represents 70 clients. 20% of clients are new/unpublished writers.

○ Prior to opening her agency, Ms. Slopen worked in publishing and as a journalist.

REPRESENTS nonfiction books, novels, scholarly. **Considers these nonfiction areas:** anthropology, archeology, autobiography, biography, business, creative nonfiction, current affairs, economics, investigative, psychology, sociology, true crime. **Considers these fiction areas:** commercial, literary, mystery, suspense.

8—ਜ "This agency has a strong bent toward Canadian writers." Actively seeking serious nonfiction that is accessible and appealing to the general reader. Does not want to receive fantasy, science fiction, or children's books.

HOW TO CONTACT Query by e-mail. Returns materials only with SASE (Canadian postage only). To submit a work for consideration, e-mail a short query letter and a few sample pages. Submit only one work at a time. If we want to see more, we will contact the writer by phone or e-mail. Accepts simultaneous submissions. Responds in 2 months to queries.

TERMS Agent receives 15% commission on domestic sales. Agent receives 10% commission on foreign sales. Offers written contract, binding for 2 years; 3-month notice must be given to terminate contract.

RECENT SALES *Solar Dance*, by Modris Eksteins (Knopf Canada, Harvard University Press US); *The Novels*, by Terry Fallis; *God's Brain*, by Lionel Tiger & Michael McGuire (Prometheus Books); *What They Wanted*, by Donna Morrissey (Penguin Canada, Premium/DTV Germany); *The Age of Persuasion*, by Terry O'Reilly & Mike Tennant (Knopf Canada, Counterpoint US); *Prisoner of Tehran*, by Marina Nemat (Penguin Canada, Free Press US, John Murray UK); *Race to the Polar Sea*, by Ken McGoogan (HarperCollins Canada, Counterpoint US); *Transgression*, by James Nichol (HarperCollins US, McArthur Canada, Goldmann Germany); *Midwife of Venice* and *The Harem Midwife*, by Roberta Rich; *Vermeer's Hat*, by Timothy

NEW AGENT SPOTLIGHT

LINDA CAMACHO
PROSPECT AGENCY

Prospectagency.com

@lindarandom

ABOUT LINDA: Linda joined Prospect Agency after nearly a decade in publishing. After graduating from Cornell University, Linda interned at Simon & Schuster and Writers House literary agency, and worked at Penguin before happily settling into children's marketing at Random House. She has an MFA in creative writing from the Vermont College of Fine Arts.

SHE IS SEEKING: She enjoys a variety of categories and genres, ranging from clean and lighthearted to edgy and dark. She is currently seeking: Adult, middle grade, and young adult fiction across many genres (romance, horror, fantasy, realistic, light sci-fi, and graphic novels); select literary fiction (preferably with commercial bent); diversity of all types (ethnicity, disability, sexuality, etc.). Linda is not seeking early readers/chapter books, screenplays, poetry, and short stories.

HOW TO SUBMIT: Linda is currently accepting queries through Prospect Agency's Submissions page (see the website). Please include three chapters and a brief synopsis. Do not query by e-mail or postal mail, and do not submit unsolicited manuscripts or inquire about the status of submissions via e-mail.

Brook (HarperCollins Canada, Bloomsbury US); *Distantly Related to Freud*, by Ann Charney (Cormorant).
TIPS "Please, no unsolicited mss."

⊙ SLW LITERARY AGENCY

4100 Ridgeland Ave., Northbrook IL 60062. (847)509-0999. **Fax:** (847)509-0996. **E-mail:** shariwenk@swenkagency.com. **Contact:** Shari Wenk. Currently handles: nonfiction books 100%.

REPRESENTS nonfiction books. **Considers these nonfiction areas:** sports.

⊶ "This agency specializes in representing books written by sports celebrities and sports writers."

HOW TO CONTACT Query via e-mail, but note the agency's specific specialty.

🗩🌑 ROBERT SMITH LITERARY AGENCY, LTD.

12 Bridge Wharf, 156 Caledonian Rd., London NI 9UU England. (44)(207)278-2444. **Fax:** (44)(207)833-5680. **E-mail:** robertsmith.literaryagency@virgin.net. **Contact:** Robert Smith. Other memberships include AAA. Represents 40 clients. 10% of clients are new/unpublished writers. Currently handles: nonfiction books 80%, syndicated material 20%.

🗩 Prior to becoming an agent, Mr. Smith was a book publisher (Ebury Press, Sidgwick & Jackson, Smith Gryphon).

REPRESENTS nonfiction books, syndicated material. **Considers these nonfiction areas:** autobiography, biography, cooking, diet/nutrition, film, foods, health, investigative, medicine, memoirs, music, popular culture, self-help, sports, theater, true crime, entertainment.

⊶ "This agency offers clients full management service in all media. Clients are not necessarily book authors. Our special expertise is in placing newspaper series internationally." Actively seeking autobiographies.

HOW TO CONTACT Submit outline/proposal, SASE (IRCs if necessary). Prefers to read materials exclusively. Responds in 2 weeks to queries. Obtains most new clients through recommendations from others, direct approaches to prospective authors.

TERMS Agent receives 15% commission on domestic sales. Agent receives 20% commission on foreign sales. Offers written contract, binding for 3 months; 3-month notice must be given to terminate contract. Charges clients for couriers, photocopying, overseas mailings of mss (subject to client authorization).

RECENT SALES *Naming Jack The Ripper*, by Russell Edwards (Macmillan); *Confessions of an Essex Girl*, by Becci Fox (Macmillan); *Before Marilyn*, by Astrid Franse and Michelle Morgan (The History Press); *The News Is Read*, by Charlotte Green (The Robson Press); *They Laughed At Galileo*, by Albert Jack (Constable & Robinson); *Forgotten Girl*, by Naomi Jacobs (Macmillan); *Dispatches From The Kabul Café*, by Heidi Kingstone (Advance Editions); *Bad Girl*, By Roberta Kray (Sphere); *The Murders At Whitehouse Farm*, by Carol Ann Lee (Macmillan); *Hitler's Valkyrie*, by David R.L. Litchfield (The History Press); *Down But Not Out*, by Maurice Mayne With Mark Ryan (The History Press); *History's Narrowest Escapes*, by James Moore And Paul Nero (The History Press); *The Ice Cream Blonde*, by Michelle Morgan (Chicago Review Press); *The High Fat Diet*, by Zana Morris And Helen Foster [Vermilion]; *All Of Me*, by Kim Noble (Piatkus); *Enter The Dragon*, By Theo Paphitis (Orion); *The Sixteen*, by John Urwin (John Blake Publishing).

MICHAEL SNELL LITERARY AGENCY

P.O. Box 1206, Truro MA 02666-1206. (508)349-3718. **E-mail:** query@michaelsnellagency.com. **Website:** http://michaelsnellagency.com. Represents 200 clients. 25% of clients are new/unpublished writers.

○ Prior to opening his agency in 1978, Mr. Snell served as an editor at Wadsworth and Addison-Wesley for 13 years.

MEMBER AGENTS Michael Snell (business, leadership, entrepreneurship, pets, sports); **Patricia Snell,** (business, business communications, parenting, relationships, health).

REPRESENTS nonfiction books. **Considers these nonfiction areas:** business (all categories, all levels), creative nonfiction, health, how-to, self-help, women's issues, fitness.

⊶ This agency specializes in how-to, self-help, and all types of business, business leadership, entrepreneurship, and books for small-business owners from low-level how-to to professional and reference. Especially interested in business management, strategy, culture building, performance enhancement, marketing and sales, finance and investment, marketing and sales, finance and investment, career development, executive skills, leadership, and organization development. Actively seeking strong book proposals in any area of business where a clear need exists for a new business book. Does not want to receive fiction, children's books, or complete mss (considers proposals only).

HOW TO CONTACT Query by mail with SASE, or e-mail. Visit the agency's website for Proposal Guidelines. Only considers new clients on an exclusive basis. Responds in 1 week to queries. Responds in 2 weeks to mss. Obtains most new clients through unsolicited mss, word of mouth, *Literary Market Place, Guide to Literary Agents*.

TERMS Agent receives 15% commission on domestic sales. Agent receives 15% commission on foreign sales.

TIPS "Visit the agency's website to view recent publications and guidelines for writing a book proposal. Prospective authors can also download model book proposals at the website. The agency only considers new clients on an exclusive basis. Simultaneous queries are OK; multiple submissions are not."

① SPECTRUM LITERARY AGENCY

320 Central Park W., Suite 1-D, New York NY 10025. **Fax:** (212)362-4562. **Website:** www.spectrumliteraryagency.com. **Contact:** Eleanor Wood, president. Estab. 1976. SFWA Represents 90 clients. Currently handles: nonfiction books 10%, novels 90%.

MEMBER AGENTS Eleanor Wood (referrals only), **Justin Bell** (science fiction, mysteries, nonfiction).

REPRESENTS nonfiction books, novels. **Considers these fiction areas:** mystery, science fiction.

HOW TO CONTACT Snail mail query with SASE. Submit author bio, publishing credits. No unsolicited mss will be read. Responds in 1-3 months to queries. Obtains most new clients through recommendations from authors.

TERMS Agent receives 15% commission on domestic sales. Deducts for photocopying and book orders.

TIPS "Spectrum's policy is to read only book-length mss that we have specifically asked to see. Unsolicited mss are not accepted. The letter should describe your book briefly and include publishing credits and background information or qualifications relating to your work, if any."

✪ SPEILBURG LITERARY AGENCY

E-mail: speilburgliterary@gmail.com. **Website:** speilburgliterary.com. Estab. 2012.

○ Alice Speilburg previously held publishing positions at John Wiley & Sons and Howard Morhaim Literary Agency

REPRESENTS Considers these nonfiction areas: biography, foods, health, history, investigative, music, popular culture, science, travel. **Considers these fiction areas:** historical, literary, mainstream, middle grade, mystery, science fiction, thriller, young adult.

HOW TO CONTACT If you are interested in submitting your manuscript or proposal for consideration, please e-mail a query letter along with either three sample chapters for fiction, or a TOC and proposal for nonfiction.

◐ SPENCERHILL ASSOCIATES

8131 Lakewood Main St., Building M, Suite 2015, Lakewood Ranch FL 34202. (518)392-9293. **Fax:** (518)392-9554. **E-mail:** submissions@spencerhillassociates.com. **Website:** www.spencerhillassociates.com. **Contact:** Karen Solem, Nalini Akolekar or Amanda Leuck. Member of AAR. Represents 96 clients. 10% of clients are new/unpublished writers.

○ Prior to becoming an agent, Ms. Solem was editor-in-chief at HarperCollins and an associate publisher.

MEMBER AGENTS Karen Solem; Nalini Akolekar; Amanda Leuck.

REPRESENTS novels. **Considers these fiction areas:** commercial, erotica, literary, mainstream, mystery, paranormal, romance, thriller.

☛ "We handle mostly commercial women's fiction, historical novels, romance (historical, contemporary, paranormal, urban fantasy), thrillers, and mysteries. We also represent Christian fiction only—no nonfiction." No nonfiction, poetry, science fiction, children's picture books, or scripts.

HOW TO CONTACT "We accept electronic submissions and are no longer accepting paper queries. Please send us a query letter in the body of an e-mail, pitch us your project and tell us about yourself: Do you have prior publishing credits? Attach the first three chapters and synopsis preferably in .doc, rtf or txt format to your e-mail. Send all queries to submission@spencerhillassociates.com. We do not have a preference for exclusive submissions, but do appreciate knowing if the submission is simultaneous. We receive thousands of submissions a year and each query receives our attention. Unfortunately, we are unable to respond to each query individually. If we are interested in your work, we will contact you within 8 weeks." Accepts simultaneous submissions.

TERMS Agent receives 15% commission on domestic sales. Agent receives 20% commission on foreign sales. Offers written contract; 3-month notice must be given to terminate contract.

RECENT SALES A full list of sales and clients is available on the agency website.

○ THE SPIELER AGENCY

27 W. 20 St., Suite 305, New York NY 10011. **E-mail:** thespieleragency@gmail.com. **Contact:** Joe Spieler. Represents 160 clients. 2% of clients are new/unpublished writers.

○ Prior to opening his agency, Mr. Spieler was a magazine editor.

MEMBER AGENTS Eric Myers, eric@TheSpielerAgency.com (pop culture, memoir, history, thrillers, young adult, middle grade, new adult, and picture books [text only]); **Victoria Shoemaker**, victoria@TheSpielerAgency.com (environment and natural history, popular culture, memoir, photography and film, literary fiction and poetry, and books on food and cooking); **John Thornton**, john@TheSpielerAgency.com (nonfiction); **Joe Spieler**, joe@TheSpielerAgen cy.com (nonfiction and fiction and books for children and young adults).

REPRESENTS novels, juvenile books. **Considers these nonfiction areas:** cooking, environment, film, foods, history, memoirs, photography, popular culture. **Considers these fiction areas:** literary, middle grade, New Age, picture books, thriller, young adult.

HOW TO CONTACT "Before submitting projects to the Spieler Agency, check the listings of our individual agents and see if any particular agent shows a general interest in your subject (e.g. history, memoir, YA, etc.). Please send all queries either by e-mail or regular mail. If you query us by regular mail, we can only reply to you if you include a self-addressed, stamped envelope." Accepts simultaneous submissions. Cannot guarantee a personal response to all queries. Obtains most new clients through recommendations, listing in *Guide to Literary Agents.*

TERMS Agent receives 15% commission on domestic sales. Charges clients for messenger bills, photocopying, postage.

WRITERS CONFERENCES London Book Fair.

TIPS "Check http://www.publishersmarketplace.com/members/spielerlit/."

PHILIP G. SPITZER LITERARY AGENCY, INC

50 Talmage Farm Lane, East Hampton NY 11937. (631)329-3650. **Fax:** (631)329-3651. **E-mail:** lukas.ortiz@spitzeragency.com; spitzer516@aol.com. **Website:** www.spitzeragency.com. **Contact:** Luc Hunt. Member of AAR.

○   Prior to opening his agency, Mr. Spitzer served at New York University Press, McGraw-Hill, and the John Cushman Associates Literary Agency.

MEMBER AGENTS Philip G. Spitzer; Lukas Ortiz.

REPRESENTS nonfiction books, novels. **Considers these nonfiction areas:** biography, current affairs, history, politics, sports, travel. **Considers these fiction areas:** juvenile, literary, mainstream, suspense, thriller.

⟶   This agency specializes in mystery/suspense, literary fiction, sports and general nonfiction (no how-to).

HOW TO CONTACT E-mail or snail mail query containing synopsis of work, brief biography, and two sample chapters (pasted into the e-mail). Be aware that this agency openly says their client list is quite full.

TERMS Agent receives 15% commission on domestic sales. Agent receives 20% commission on foreign sales. Charges clients for photocopying.

RECENT SALES *Creole Belle* by James Lee Burke (Simon & Schuster), *Never Tell* by Alafair Burke (HarperCollins), *Townie,* by Andre Dubus III (Norton), *The Black Box,* by Michael Connelly (Little, Brown & Co), *Headstone,* Ken Bruen (Mysterious Press/Grove-Atlantic), *Mean Town Blues* by Sam Reaves (Pegasus Books), *The Fifth Season,* by Donald Honig (Ivan Dee Publisher), *The Big Town,* by Monte Schulz (Fantagraphics Books), *Assume Nothing,* Gar Anthony Haywood (Severn House), *Midnight Alley* (Oceanview Publishing), *My Brother's Keeper,* by Keith Gilman (Severn House), *Fontana,* by Joshua Martino (Bold Stroke Books), *Everything Beautiful Began After,* by Simon Van Booy (HarperPerennial).

WRITERS CONFERENCES London Bookfair, Frankfurt, BookExpo America.

NANCY STAUFFER ASSOCIATES

P.O. Box 1203, Darien CT 06820. (203)202-2500. **E-mail:** nancy@staufferliterary.com. **Website:** www.publishersmarketplace.com/members/nstauffer. **Contact:** Nancy Stauffer Cahoon. Other memberships include Authors Guild. Currently handles: nonfiction books 10%, novels 90%.

○   "Over the course of my more than 20 year career, I've held positions in the editorial, marketing, business, and rights departments of the *New York Times,* McGraw-Hill, and Doubleday. Before founding Nancy Stauffer Associates, I was Director of Foreign and Performing Rights then Director, Subsidiary Rights, for Doubleday, where I was honored to have worked with a diverse range of internationally known and bestselling authors of all genres."

HOW TO CONTACT Accepts simultaneous submissions. Obtains most new clients through referrals from existing clients.

TERMS Agent receives 15% commission on domestic sales. Agent receives 20% commission on foreign sales.

RECENT SALES *Blasphemy,* by Sherman Alexie; *Benediction,* by Kent Haruf; *Bone Fire,* by Mark Spragg; *The Carry Home,* by Gary Ferguson.

STEELE-PERKINS LITERARY AGENCY

26 Island Ln., Canandaigua NY 14424. (585)396-9290. **Fax:** (585)396-3579. **E-mail:** pattiesp@aol.com. **Con-**

tact: Pattie Steele-Perkins. Member of AAR. Other memberships include RWA. Currently handles: novels 100%.

REPRESENTS novels. **Considers these fiction areas:** romance, women's, category romance, romantic suspense, historical, contemporary, multi-cultural, and inspirational.

HOW TO CONTACT Submit query along with synopsis and one chapter via e-mail (no attachments) or snail mail. Snail mail submissions require SASE. Accepts simultaneous submissions. Obtains most new clients through recommendations from others, queries/solicitations.

TERMS Agent receives 15% commission on domestic sales. Offers written contract, binding for 1 year; 1-month notice must be given to terminate contract.

RECENT SALES Sold 130 titles last year. This agency prefers not to share specific sales information.

TIPS "Be patient. E-mail rather than call. Make sure what you are sending is the best it can be."

○ STERLING LORD LITERISTIC, INC.

65 Bleecker St., 12th Floor, New York NY 10012. (212)780-6050. **Fax:** (212)780-6095. **E-mail:** info@ sll.com. **Website:** www.sll.com. Estab. 1987. Member of AAR. Signatory of WGA.

MEMBER AGENTS Philippa Brophy (represents journalists, nonfiction writers and novelists, and is most interested in current events, memoir, science, politics, biography, and women's issues); **Laurie Liss** (represents authors of commercial and literary fiction and nonfiction whose perspectives are well developed and unique); **Sterling Lord**; **Peter Matson**; **Douglas Stewart** (primarily fiction and memoir, running the gamut from the innovatively literary to the unabashedly commercial); **Neeti Madan** (memoir, journalism, popular culture, lifestyle, women's issues, multicultural books and virtually any intelligent writing on intriguing topics); **Robert Guinsler** (literary and commercial fiction (including YA), journalism, narrative nonfiction with an emphasis on pop culture, science and current events, memoirs and biographies); **Jim Rutman**; **Celeste Fine** (expert, celebrity, and corporate clients with strong national and international platforms, particularly in the health, science, self-help, food, business, and lifestyle fields); **Judy Heiblum** (literary fiction, narrative nonfiction, history, and popular science); **Erica Rand Silverman** (specializes in representing authors and illustrators

of children's literature, picture books through YA, and adult nonfiction, with a special interest in parenting, DIY, emotional health and education); **Caitlin McDonald**; **Mary Krienke** (literary fiction, creative nonfiction, and realistic YA that pays close attention to craft and voice); **Madeleine Clark** (commercial and literary fiction as well as narrative nonfiction; she is particularly drawn to realistic YA, literary thrillers, novels that can believably introduce a bit of fantasy/sci-fi, and books that draw heavily from their environment whether that is geographical or cultural); **Jenny Stephens** (some fiction, as well as food and travel-related narrative nonfiction, lifestyle, and cookbook projects).

REPRESENTS **Considers these nonfiction areas:** biography, cooking, creative nonfiction, current affairs, education, history, memoirs, multicultural, parenting, popular culture, politics, science, women's issues. **Considers these fiction areas:** commercial, juvenile, literary, middle grade, picture books, young adult.

HOW TO CONTACT Query via snail mail. "Please submit a query letter, a synopsis of the work, a brief proposal or the first three chapters of the ms, a brief bio or resume, and a stamped self-addressed envelope for reply. Original artwork is not accepted. Enclose sufficient postage if you wish to have your materials returned to you. We do not respond to unsolicited e-mail inquiries." Responds in approximately 1 month.

TERMS Agent receives 15% commission on domestic sales; 20% commission on foreign sales. Offers written contract.

○ STERNIG & BYRNE LITERARY AGENCY

2370 S. 107th St., Apt. #4, Milwaukee WI 53227. (414)328-8034. **Fax:** (414)328-8034. **E-mail:** jack byrne@hotmail.com. **Website:** www.sff.net/people/jackbyrne. **Contact:** Jack Byrne. Other memberships include SFWA, MWA.

REPRESENTS nonfiction books, novels, juvenile. **Considers these fiction areas:** fantasy, horror, mystery, science fiction, suspense.

⊶ "Our client list is comfortably full, and our current needs are therefore quite limited." Actively seeking science fiction/fantasy and mystery by established writers. Does not want to receive romance, poetry, textbooks, or highly specialized nonfiction.

HOW TO CONTACT Query with SASE. Prefers e-mail queries (no attachments); hard copy queries also acceptable.

TIPS "Don't send first drafts, have a professional presentation (including cover letter), and know your field. Read what's been done—good and bad."

STIMOLA LITERARY STUDIO

308 Livingston Ct., Edgewater NJ 07020. **E-mail:** info@stimolaliterarystudio.com. **Website:** www.stimolaliterarystudio.com. **Contact:** Rosemary B. Stimola. Estab. 1997. Member of AAR. Represents 45 clients. 15% of clients are new/unpublished writers. Currently handles: 10% novels, 90% juvenile books.

Ｏ Agency is owned and operated by a former educator and children's bookseller with a Ph.D in Linguistics.

MEMBER AGENTS Rosemary B. Stimola.

Actively seeking remarkable young adult fiction and debut picture book author/illustrators. No institutional books.

HOW TO CONTACT Query via e-mail. Author/illustrators of picture books may attach text and sample art. A PDF dummy is preferred. Accepts simultaneous submissions. Responds in 3 weeks to queries "we wish to pursue further." Responds in 2 months to requested mss. While unsolicited queries are welcome, most clients come through editor, agent, client referrals.

TERMS Agent receives 15% commission on domestic sales. Agent receives 20% (if subagents are employed) commission on foreign sales. Offers written contract, binding for all children's projects. 60 days notice must be given to terminate contract.

TIPS Agent is hands-on, no-nonsense. May request revisions. Does not line edit but may offer suggestions for improvement before submission. Well-respected by clients and editors. "A firm but reasonable deal negotiator."

STONESONG

270 W. 39th St. #201, New York NY 10018. (212)929-4600. **Fax:** (212)486-9123. **E-mail:** editors@stonesong.com. **E-mail:** submissions@stonesong.com. **Website:** http://stonesong.com.

MEMBER AGENTS Alison Fargis, Ellen Scordato, Judy Linden, Emmanuelle Morgen; Maria Ribas (cookbooks, self-help, health, diet, home, parenting, and humor, all from authors with demonstrable platforms; she's also interested in narrative nonfiction and select memoir).

Does not represent plays, screenplays, picture books, or poetry.

HOW TO CONTACT Accepts electronic queries for fiction and nonfiction. Submit query addressed to 1 agent. Include first chapter or first 10 pages of ms.

RECENT SALES *Revolutionary*, by Alex Myers; *Rebel*, by Amy Tintera; *Dangerous Curves Ahead*, by Sugar Jamison; *Sunday Suppers*, by Karen Mordechai; *Find Momo*, by Andrew Knapp; *Smitten Kitchen*, by by Deb Perelman.

Ｏ ROBIN STRAUS AGENCY, INC.

229 E. 79th St., Suite 5A, New York NY 10075. (212)472-3282. **Fax:** (212)472-3833. **E-mail:** info@robinstrausagency.com. **Website:** www.robinstrausagency.com. **Contact:** Ms. Robin Straus. Estab. 1983. Member of AAR.

Ｏ Prior to becoming an agent, Robin Straus served as a subsidiary rights manager at Random House and Doubleday. She began her career in the editorial department of Little, Brown.

REPRESENTS **Considers these nonfiction areas:** biography, cooking, creative nonfiction, current affairs, history, memoirs, parenting, popular culture, psychology, mainstream science. **Considers these fiction areas:** commercial, literary, mainstream, women's.

Does *not* represent juvenile, young adult, science fiction/fantasy, horror, romance, Westerns, poetry, or screenplays.

HOW TO CONTACT E-query or query via snail mail with SASE. "Send us a query letter with contact information, an autobiographical summary, a brief synopsis or description of your book project, submission history, and information on competition. If you wish, you may also include the opening chapter of your ms (pasted). We do not open attachments from people we don't know. Please let us know if you are showing the ms to other agents simultaneously."

TERMS Agent receives 15% commission on domestic sales. Agent receives 20% commission on foreign sales. Offers written contract.

THE STRINGER LITERARY AGENCY, LLC

E-mail: mstringer@stringerlit.com. **Website:** www.stringerlit.com. **Contact:** Marlene Stringer.

REPRESENTS **Considers these fiction areas:** fantasy, middle grade, mystery, romance, thriller, women's, young adult.

This agency specializes in fiction. This agency is seeking all kinds of romance, except inspirational or erotic. Does not want to receive picture books, plays, short stories, or poetry. The agency is also seeking nonfiction as of this time.

HOW TO CONTACT Electronic submissions through website submission form only. Accepts simultaneous submissions.

RECENT SALES *The Secret History*, by Stephanie Thornton (NAL); *The Bone Song*, by Alex Bledsoe (Tor); *Red*, by Alyxandra Harvey (Entangled); *Mer*, by Katie Schickel (Forge); The Paper Magician series, by Charlie Holmberg (47 North); *Fly by Night*, by Andrea Thalasinos (Forge); *Duty of Evil*, by April Taylor (Carina); The Joe Gale mysteries, by Brenda Buchanan (Carina); *Wreckage*, by Emily Bleeker (Lake Union); *A Wicked Way to Win an Earl*, by Anna Bradley (Berkley); *The Stilt House*, by Charlie Donlea (Kensington).

TIPS "If your ms falls between categories, or you are not sure of the category, query and we'll let you know if we'd like to take a look. We strive to respond as quickly as possible. If you have not received a response in the time period indicated on website, please re-query."

THE STROTHMAN AGENCY, LLC

63 East 9th St., 10X, New York NY 10003. **E-mail:** info@strothmanagency.com. **Website:** www.strothmanagency.com. **Contact:** Wendy Strothman, Lauren MacLeod. Member of AAR. Other memberships include Authors' Guild. Represents 50 clients.

Prior to becoming an agent, Ms. Strothman was head of Beacon Press (1983-1995) and executive vice president of Houghton Mifflin's Trade & Reference Division (1996-2002).

MEMBER AGENTS Wendy Strothman; Lauren MacLeod.

REPRESENTS nonfiction, juvenile books. **Considers these nonfiction areas:** business, current affairs, environment, government, history, language, law, literature, politics, travel. **Considers these fiction areas:** literary, middle grade, young adult.

"Because we are highly selective in the clients we represent, we increase the value publishers place on our properties. We specialize in narrative nonfiction, memoir, history, science and nature, arts and culture, literary travel, current affairs, young adult, middle grade, and some business." The Strothman Agency seeks out scholars, journalists, and other acknowledged and emerging experts in their fields. We are now actively looking for authors of well-written young adult fiction and nonfiction. Browse the Latest News to get an idea of the types of books that we represent. For more about what we're looking for, read Pitching an Agent: The Strothman Agency on the publishing website www.strothmanagency.com." Does not want to receive adult fiction or self-help.

HOW TO CONTACT Accepts queries only via e-mail at strothmanagency@gmail.com. See submission guidelines online. Accepts simultaneous submissions. Responds in 4 weeks to queries. Responds in 8 weeks to mss. Obtains most new clients through recommendations from others.

TERMS Agent receives 15% commission on domestic sales. Agent receives 20% commission on foreign sales. Offers written contract; 30-day notice must be given to terminate contract.

THE STUART AGENCY

260 W. 52 St., #24C, New York NY 10019. (212)586-2711. **Fax:** (212)977-1488. **E-mail:** andrew@stuartagency.com. **Website:** http://stuartagency.com. **Contact:** Andrew Stuart. Estab. 2002.

Prior to his current position, Mr. Stuart was an agent with Literary Group International for five years. Prior to becoming an agent, he was an editor at Random House and Simon & Schuster.

REPRESENTS nonfiction books, novels. **Considers these nonfiction areas:** business, creative nonfiction, current affairs, history, memoirs, psychology, science, sports. **Considers these fiction areas:** literary.

HOW TO CONTACT Query via online submission form on the agency website.

RECENT SALES Projects and clients include former Congressman Ron Paul's *New York Times* #1 bestseller *The Revolution*; publisher and free speech advocate Larry Flynt; Pulitzer Prize-winning journalists Kathleen Parker, William Dietrich and Carl Cannon; political scientist Alan Wolfe; Hollywood studio mogul Mike Medavoy; Mark Bauerlein, author of the national bestseller *The Dumbest Generation*; Christopher Ryan, author of the *New York Times* bestseller *Sex at Dawn*; renowned child psychiatrist Bruce Perry; *New*

York Times bestselling novelist Mary Monroe; and the *New York Times* bestseller *The Darwin Awards: Evolution in Action.*

◑ EMMA SWEENEY AGENCY, LLC

245 E 80th St., Suite 7E, New York NY 10075. **E-mail:** queries@emmasweeneyagency.com. **Website:** www.emmasweeneyagency.com. Member of AAR. Other memberships include Women's Media Group. Represents 80 clients. 5% of clients are new/unpublished writers. Currently handles: nonfiction books 50%, novels 50%.

○ Prior to becoming an agent, Ms. Sweeney was director of subsidiary rights at Grove Press. Since 1990, she has been a literary agent.

MEMBER AGENTS Emma Sweeney, president.
REPRESENTS nonfiction books, novels. **Considers these nonfiction areas:** biography, business, history, religious. **Considers these fiction areas:** literary, mainstream, mystery.

8→ Does not want to receive romance, Westerns or screenplays.

HOW TO CONTACT "We accept only electronic queries, and ask that all queries be sent to queries@emmasweeneyagency.com rather than to any agent directly. Please begin your query with a succinct (and hopefully catchy) description of your plot or proposal. Always include a brief cover letter telling us how you heard about ESA, your previous writing credits, and a few lines about yourself. We cannot open any attachments unless specifically requested, and ask that you paste the first 10 pages of your proposal or novel into the text of your e-mail."

TERMS Agent receives 15% commission on domestic sales. Agent receives 10% commission on foreign sales.

◑ THE SWETKY AGENCY

2150 Balboa Way, No. 29, St. George UT 84770. (435)313-8006. **E-mail:** fayeswetky@amsaw.org. **Website:** www.amsaw.org/swetkyagency/index.html. **Contact:** Faye M. Swetky. Other memberships include American Society of Authors and Writers. Represents 20+ clients. 90% of clients are new/unpublished writers. Currently handles: nonfiction books 45%, novels 45%, movie scripts 10%, TV scripts 20%.

○ Prior to becoming an agent, Ms. Swetky was an editor and corporate manager. She has also raised and raced thoroughbred horses.

REPRESENTS nonfiction books, novels, short story collections, juvenile, movie, TV, movie scripts, feature film, MOW (movie of the week), sitcom, documentary. **Considers these nonfiction areas:** All major genres. **Considers these fiction areas:** All major genres. **Considers these script areas:** action, biography, cartoon, comedy, contemporary, detective, erotica, ethnic, experimental, family, fantasy, feminist, gay, glitz, historical, horror, juvenile, mainstream, multicultural, multimedia, mystery, psychic, regional, religious, romantic comedy, romantic drama, science, sports, teen, thriller, Western.

8→ "We handle only book-length fiction and nonfiction and feature-length movie and television scripts. Please visit our website before submitting. All agency-related information is there, including a sample contract, e-mail submission forms, policies, clients, etc." Actively seeking marketable full-length material. Do not send unprofessionally prepared mss and/or scripts.

HOW TO CONTACT See website for submission instructions. Accepts e-mail queries only. Accepts simultaneous submissions. Response time varies. Obtains most new clients through queries.

TERMS Agent receives 15% commission on domestic sales; 20% commission on foreign sales; 20% commission on film sales. Offers written contract, binding for 6 months.

TIPS "Be professional. Have a professionally prepared product."

STEPHANIE TADE LITERARY AGENCY

P.O. Box 235, Durham PA 18039. (610)346-8667. **Contact:** Stephanie Tade.

○ Prior to becoming an agent, Ms. Tade was an executive editor at Rodale Press. She was also an agent with the Jane Rotrosen Agency.

MEMBER AGENTS Stephanie Tade.
REPRESENTS nonfiction.

8→ "Mostly commercial nonfiction, especially in categories of health/diet, spirituality and Eastern philosophy, relationships/dating, self-improvement, psychology, science, and women's issues.

HOW TO CONTACT Query by e-mail or mail with SASE.

◑ TALCOTT NOTCH LITERARY

2 Broad St., Second Floor, Suite 10, Milford CT 06460. (203)876-4959. **Fax:** (203)876-9517. **E-mail:** edito

rial@talcottnotch.net. **Website:** www.talcottnotch. net. **Contact:** Gina Panettieri, President. Represents 35 clients. 25% of clients are new/unpublished writers.

- Prior to becoming an agent, Ms. Panettieri was a freelance writer and editor.

MEMBER AGENTS Gina Panettieri, gpanettieri@ talcottnotch.net (history, business, self-help, science, gardening, cookbooks, crafts, parenting, memoir, true crime and travel, women's fiction, paranormal, urban fantasy, horror, science fiction, historical, mystery, thrillers and suspense); **Paula Munier**, pmunier@talc ottnotch.net (mystery/thriller, SF/fantasy, romance, YA, memoir, humor, pop culture, health & wellness, cooking, self-help, pop psych, New Age, inspirational, technology, science, and writing); **Rachael Dugas**, rdugas@talcottnotch.net (young adult, middle grade, romance, and women's fiction); **Jessica Negron**, jne gron@talcottnotch.net (commercial fiction, sci fi and fantasy (and all the little sub genres), psychological thrillers, cozy mysteries, romance, erotic romance, YA); **Suba Sulaiman**, ssulaiman@talcottnotch.net (upmarket literary and commercial fiction, romance [all subgenres except paranormal], character-driven psychological thrillers, cozy mysteries, memoir, young adult [except paranormal and sci-fi), middle grade, and nonfiction humor).

REPRESENTS Considers these nonfiction areas: business, cooking, crafts, gardening, health, history, humor, inspirational, memoirs, parenting, popular culture, psychology, science, self-help, technology, travel, true crime. **Considers these fiction areas:** commercial, fantasy, historical, horror, literary, mainstream, middle grade, mystery, New Age, paranormal, romance, science fiction, suspense, thriller, urban fantasy, women's, young adult.

HOW TO CONTACT Query via e-mail (preferred) with first 10 pages of the ms pasted within the body of the e-mail, not as an attachment. Accepts simultaneous submissions. Responds in 1 week to queries. Responds in 4-6 weeks to mss.

TERMS Agent receives 15% commission on domestic sales. Agent receives 20% commission on foreign sales. Offers written contract, binding for 1 year.

RECENT SALES Sold 36 titles in the last year. *Delivered From Evil*, by Ron Franscell (Fairwinds) and *Sourtoe* (Globe Pequot Press); *Hellforged*, by Nancy Holzner (Berkley Ace Science Fiction); *Welcoming Kitchen*; *200 Allergen- and Gluten-Free Vegan Recipes*, by Kim Lutz and Megan Hart (Sterling); *Dr. Seteh's*

Love Prescription, by Dr. Seth Meyers (Adams Media); *The Book of Ancient Bastards*, by Brian Thornton (Adams Media); *Hope in Courage*, by Beth Fehlbaum (Westside Books) and more.

TIPS "Know your market and how to reach them. A strong platform is essential in your book proposal. Can you effectively use social media/Are you a strong networker: Are you familiar with the book bloggers in your genre? Are you involved with the interest-specific groups that can help you? What can you do to break through the 'noise' and help present your book to your readers? Check our website for more tips and information on this topic."

TESSLER LITERARY AGENCY, LLC

27 W. 20th St., Suite 1003, New York NY 10011. (212)242-0466. **Fax:** (212)242-2366. **Website:** www. tessleragency.com. **Contact:** Michelle Tessler. Estab. 2004. Member of AAR.

- Prior to forming her own agency, Ms. Tessler worked at the prestigious literary agency Carlisle & Company (now Inkwell Management) and at the William Morris Agency.

REPRESENTS Considers these nonfiction areas: biography, business, creative nonfiction, foods, memoirs, science, travel. **Considers these fiction areas:** commercial, literary, women's.

- "Our list is diverse and far-reaching. In nonfiction, it includes narrative, popular science, memoir, history, psychology, business, biography, food, and travel. In many cases, we sign authors who are especially adept at writing books that cross many of these categories at once. In fiction, we represent literary, women's, and commercial. We do not take on genre fiction or children's books.If your project is in keeping with the kind of books we take on, we want to hear from you." Does not want genre fiction or children's books.

HOW TO CONTACT Submit query through online query form only. Accepts simultaneous submissions. New clients by queries/submissions through the website and recommendations from others.

TERMS Receives 15% commission on domestic sales; 20% on foreign sales. Offers written contract.

THE TFS LITERARY AGENCY

P.O. Box 46-031, Park Ave., Lower Hutt 5044 New Zealand. **E-mail:** tfs@elseware.co.nz. **Website:** www.

elseware.co.nz. **Contact:** Chris Else, Barbara Else. Other memberships include NZALA.

⚷—⇥General fiction, nonfiction, and children's books from New Zealand authors only. No poetry, individual short stories, or articles.

HOW TO CONTACT Send query and brief author bio via e-mail.

✛ THOMPSON LITERARY AGENCY

27 W. 20th St., No. 1003, New York NY 10011. (212)221-8797. **E-mail:** submissions@thompsonliterary.com. **Website:** http://thompsonliterary.com. **Contact:** Meg Thompson. Estab. 2014.

○ Before her current position, Ms. Thompson was with LJK Literary and the Einstein Thompson Agency.

⚷—⇥ The agency is always on the lookout for both commercial and literary fiction, as well as young adult and children's books. Nonfiction, however, is our specialty, and our interests include biography, memoir, music, popular science, politics, blog-to-book projects, cookbooks, sports, health and wellness, fashion, art, and popular culture. "Please note that we do not accept submissions for poetry collections or screenplays, and we only consider picture books by established illustrators."

HOW TO CONTACT "For fiction: Please send a query letter, including any salient biographical information or previous publications, and attach the first 25 pages of your manuscript. For nonfiction: Please send a query letter and a full proposal, including biographical information, previous publications, credentials that qualify you to write your book, marketing information, and sample material. You should address your query to whichever agent you think is best suited for your project." Responds in 6 weeks if interested.

◑ THREE SEAS LITERARY AGENCY

P.O. Box 8571, Madison WI 53708. (608)834-9317. **E-mail:** queries@threeseaslit.com. **Website:** http://threeseasagency.com. **Contact:** Michelle Grajkowski, Cori Deyoe. Estab. 2000. Member of AAR. Other memberships include RWA (Romance Writers of America), SCBWI Represents 55 clients. 10% of clients are new/unpublished writers.

○ Since its inception, 3 Seas has sold more than 500 titles worldwide. Ms. Grajkowski's authors have appeared on all the major lists including *The New York Times, USA Today* and *Publish-*

ers Weekly. Prior to joining the agency in 2006, Ms. Deyoe was a multi-published author. She represents a wide range of authors and has sold many projects at auction.

MEMBER AGENTS Michelle Grajkowski; Cori Deyoe (all sub-genres of romance, women's fiction, young adult, middle grade, picture books, thrillers, mysteries and select nonfiction); Linda Scalissi (women's fiction, thrillers, young adult, mysteries and romance).

REPRESENTS nonfiction, novels, juvenile. **Considers these fiction areas:** middle grade, romance, thriller, women's, young adult.

⚷—⇥ 3 Seas focuses primarily on romance (including contemporary, romantic suspense, paranormal, fantasy, historical and category), women's fiction, mysteries, nonfiction, young adult, and children's stories. "Currently, we are looking for fantastic authors with a voice of their own." 3 Seas does not represent poetry or screenplays.

HOW TO CONTACT E-mail queries only. For fiction titles, query with first chapter and synopsis embedded in the e-mail. For nonfiction, query with complete proposal and first chapter. For picture books, query with complete text. One sample illustration may be included. Accepts simultaneous submissions. Responds in 1 month to queries. Obtains most new clients through recommendations from others, conferences.

TERMS Agent receives 15% commission on domestic sales. Agent receives 20% commission on foreign sales. Offers written contract.

RECENT SALES Jennifer Brown and Alexis Morgan, both of whom are bestselling authors. Also: Laura Marie Altom, Lindsey Brookes, Carla Capshaw, P.A. DePaul, Anna DeStefano, Heather Doherty, Molly Evans, K.M. Fawcett, R. Barri Flowers, Kristi Gold, Winnie Griggs, Susan Gee Heino, Timothy Lewis, Lesli Muir Lytle, Donna MacMeans, Tracy Madison, Lori McDonald, Elizabeth Michels, Trish Milburn, Keri Mikulski, Tricia Mills, Lisa Mondello, Natalie Richards, Liz Talley and Norah Wilson.

◐○ TRANSATLANTIC LITERARY AGENCY

2 Bloor St., Suite 3500, Toronto ON M4W 1A8 Canada. (416)488-9214. **E-mail:** info@transatlanticagency.com. **Website:** http://transatlanticagency.com.

MEMBER AGENTS Trena White (nonfiction); Amy Tompkins (fiction, nonfiction, juvenile); Stephanie

Sinclair (fiction, nonfiction); **Fiona Kenshole** (juvenile, illustrators); **Samantha Haywood** (fiction, nonfiction, graphic novels); **Jesse Finkelstein** (nonfiction); **Marie Campbell** (middle grade fiction); **Shaun Bradley** (referrals only); **Sandra Bishop** (fiction, nonfiction, serious narratives to inspirational romance); **Barb Miller**; **Lynn Bennett**; **David Bennett**.

REPRESENTS nonfiction books, novels, juvenile.

ℰ━┓ "In both children's and adult literature, we market directly into the US, the United Kingdom and Canada." Actively seeking literary children's and adult fiction, nonfiction. Does not want to receive picture books, poetry, screenplays or stage plays.

HOW TO CONTACT Always refer to the website, as guidelines will change, and only various agents are open to new clients at any given time. Obtains most new clients through recommendations from others.

TERMS Agent receives 15% commission on domestic sales. Agent receives 20% commission on foreign sales. Offers written contract; 45-day notice must be given to terminate contract. This agency charges for photocopying and postage when it exceeds $100.

RECENT SALES Sold 250 titles in the last year.

⊘◎ S©OTT TREIMEL NY

434 Lafayette St., New York NY 10003. (212)505-8353. **E-mail:** general@scotttreimelny.com. **Website:** ScottTreimelNY.blogspot.com; www.ScottTreimelNY.com. Estab. 1995. Member of AAR. Other memberships include Authors Guild, SCBWI. 10% of clients are new/unpublished writers. Currently handles: other 100% junvenile/teen books.

◯ Prior to becoming an agent, Mr. Treimel was an assistant to Marilyn E. Marlow at Curtis Brown, a rights agent for Scholastic, a book packager and rights agent for United Feature Syndicate, a freelance editor, a rights consultant for HarperCollins Children's Books, and the founding director of Warner Bros. Worldwide Publishing.

MEMBER AGENTS Scott Treimel.

REPRESENTS nonfiction books, novels, juvenile, children's, picture books, young adult.

ℰ━┓ This agency specializes in tightly focused segments of the trade and institutional markets.

HOW TO CONTACT No longer accepts simultaneous submissions. Wants queries only from writers he has met at conferences.

TERMS Agent receives 15% commission on domestic sales. Agent receives 20% commission on foreign sales. Offers verbal or written contract. Charges clients for photocopying, express postage, messengers, and books needed to sell foreign, film and other rights.

RECENT SALES *The Hunchback Assignments*, by Arthur Slade (Random House, HarperCollins Canada; HarperCollins Australia); *Shotgun Serenade*, by Gail Giles (Little, Brown); *Laundry Day*, by Maurie Manning (Clarion); *The P.S. Brothers*, by Maribeth Boelts (Harcourt); *The First Five Fourths*, by Pat Hughes (Viking); *Old Robert and the Troubadour Cats*, by Barbara Joosse (Philomel); *Ends*, by David Ward (Abrams); *Dear Canada*, by Barbara Haworth-Attard (Scholastic); *Soccer Dreams*, by Maribeth Boelts (Candlewick); *Lucky Me*, by Richard Scrimger (Tundra); *Play, Louie, Play*, by Muriel Harris Weinstein (Bloomsbury).

WRITERS CONFERENCES SCBWI NY, NJ, PA, Bologna; The New School; Southwest Writers' Conference; Pikes Peak Writers' Conference.

TIPS "We look for dedicated authors and illustrators able to sustain longtime careers in our increasingly competitive field. I want fresh, not derivative story concepts with overly familiar characters. We look for gripping stories, characters, pacing, and themes. We remain mindful of an authentic (to the age) point-of-view, and look for original voices. We spend significant time hunting for the best new work, and do launch debut talent each year. It is best *not* to send mss with lengthy submission histories already."

◑ TRIADA U.S. LITERARY AGENCY, INC.

P.O. Box 561, Sewickley PA 15143. (412)401-3376. **E-mail:** uwe@triadaus.com; brent@triadaus.com; laura@triadaus.com. **Website:** www.triadaus.com. **Contact:** Dr. Uwe Stender. Member of AAR.

MEMBER AGENTS Uwe Stender; Brent Taylor (middle grade, young adult, new adult, and select mystery/crime and women's fiction); **Laura Crockett**.

REPRESENTS fiction, nonfiction. **Considers these nonfiction areas:** biography, business, cooking, diet/nutrition, economics, education, foods, health, how-to, memoirs, popular culture, science, sports. **Considers these fiction areas:** action, adventure, crime, detective, ethnic, historical, horror, juvenile, literary, mainstream, middle grade, mystery, new adult, occult, police, romance, women's, young adult.

ℰ━┓ "We are looking for great writing and story platforms. Our response time is fairly unique. We recognize that neither we nor the authors have time to waste, so we guarantee a 5-day response time. We usually respond within 24 hours. " Actively looking for both fiction and nonfiction in all areas.

HOW TO CONTACT E-mail queries preferred. Accepts simultaneous submissions. Obtains most new clients through recommendations from others, conferences.

TERMS Agent receives 15% commission on domestic sales. Agent receives 20% commission on foreign sales. Offers written contract; 30-day notice must be given to terminate contract.

RECENT SALES *The Man Whisperer*, by Samantha Brett and Donna Sozio (Adams Media); *Whatever Happened to Pudding Pops*, by Gael Fashingbauer Cooper and Brian Bellmont (Penguin/Perigee); *86'd*, by Dan Fante (Harper Perennial); *Hating Olivia*, by Mark SaFranko (Harper Perennial); *Everything I'm Not Made Me Everything I Am*, by Jeff Johnson (Smiley Books).

TIPS "I comment on all requested manuscripts that I reject."

◐ TRIDENT MEDIA GROUP

41 Madison Ave., 36th Floor, New York NY 10010. (212)333-1511. **Website:** www.tridentmediagroup. com. **Contact:** Ellen Levine. Member of AAR.

MEMBER AGENTS Kimberly Whalen, ws.assistant@tridentmediagroup (commercial fiction and nonfiction, women's fiction, suspense, paranormal, and pop culture); **Scott Miller**, smiller@tridentmediagroup.com (thrillers, crime fiction, women's and book club fiction, and a wide variety of nonfiction, such as military, celebrity and pop culture, narrative, sports, prescriptive, and current events); **Melissa Flashman**, mflashman@tridentmediagroup.com (pop culture, memoir, wellness, popular science, business and economics, and technology—also fiction in the genres of mystery, suspense or YA); **Alyssa Eisner Henkin**, ahenkin@tridentmediagroup.com (juvenile, children's, young adult); **Don Fehr**, dfehr@tridentmediagroup.com (literary and commercial fiction, narrative nonfiction, memoirs, travel, science, and health); **John Silbersack**, silbersack.assistant@tridentmediagroup.com (commercial and literary fiction, science fiction and fantasy, narrative nonfiction, young adult, thrillers); **Erica Spellman-Silverman**; **Ellen Levine**, levine.assistant@tridentmedia-

group.com (popular commercial fiction and compelling nonfiction—memoir, popular culture, narrative nonfiction, history, politics, biography, science, and the odd quirky book); **MacKenzie Fraser-Bub**, MFraserBub@tridentmediagroup.com (many genres of fiction—specializing in women's fiction); **Mark Gottlieb** (in fiction, he seeks science fiction, fantasy, young adult, comics, graphic novels, historical, history, horror, literary, middle grade, mystery, thrillers and new adult; in nonfiction, he seeks arts, cinema, photography, biography, memoir, self-help, sports, travel, world cultures, true crime, mind/body/spirit, narrative nonfiction, politics, current affairs, pop culture, entertainment, relationships, family, science, technology); **Alexander Slater**, aslater@tridentmdiagroup.com (children's, middle grade, and young adult fiction and nonfiction, from new and established authors).

REPRESENTS Considers these nonfiction areas: biography, business, creative nonfiction, current affairs, economics, health, history, memoirs, military, popular culture, politics, science, sports, technology, travel. **Considers these fiction areas:** commercial, crime, fantasy, juvenile, literary, middle grade, mystery, paranormal, science fiction, suspense, thriller, women's, young adult.

⚷—Actively seeking new or established authors in a variety of fiction and nonfiction genres.

HOW TO CONTACT While some agents are open to e-queries, all seem open to submissions through the agency's online submission form on the agency website. Query only one agent at a time. If you e-query, include no attachments.

RECENT SALES *Sacred River*, by Syl Cheney-Coker; *Saving Quinton*, by Jessica Sorensen; *The Secret History of Las Vegas*, by Chris Abani; *The Summer Wind*, by Mary Alice Munroe.

TIPS "If you have any questions, please check FAQ page before e-mailing us."

UNION LITERARY

30 Vandam St., Suite 5A, New York NY 10013. (212)255-2112. **E-mail:** info@unionliterary.com. **E-mail:** submissions@unionliterary.com. Member of AAR.

◑ "Prior to becoming an agent, Trena Keating was editor-in-chief of Dutton and associate publisher of Plume, both imprints of Penguin, senior editor at HarperCollins, and humanities assistant at Stanford University Press.

MEMBER AGENTS Trena Keating; Sally Wofford-Girand, swg@unionliterary.com (history, memoir, women's issues, cultural studies, fiction); **Jenni Ferrari-Adler**, jenni@unionliterary.com (fiction, cookbook/food, young adult, narrative nonfiction); **Shaun Dolan**, sd@unionliterary.com (muscular and lyrical literary fiction, narrative nonfiction, memoir, pop culture, and sports narratives).

⌖➤ The agency does not represent romance, poetry, science fiction, or illustrated books.

HOW TO CONTACT Nonfiction submissions: Include a query letter, a proposal and a sample chapter. Fiction submissions: should include a query letter, synopsis, and either sample pages or full ms. Responds in 1 month.

RECENT SALES *The Language of Flowers*, by Vanessa Diffenbaugh (Ballantine); *The Rebel Wife*, by Taylor M. Polites (Simon & Schuster).

ⓘ THE UNTER AGENCY

23 W. 73rd St., Suite 100, New York NY 10023. (212)401-4068. **E-mail:** Jennifer@theunteragency. com. **Website:** www.theunteragency.com. **Contact:** Jennifer Unter. Estab. 2008.

○ Ms. Unter began her book publishing career in the editorial department at Henry Holt & Co. She later worked at the Karpfinger Agency while she attended law school. She then became an associate at the entertainment firm of Cowan, DeBaets, Abrahams & Sheppard LLP where she practiced primarily in the areas of publishing and copyright law.

REPRESENTS Considers these nonfiction areas: biography, environment, foods, health, memoirs, popular culture, politics, travel, true crime, nature subjects. **Considers these fiction areas:** commercial, mainstream, middle grade, picture books, young adult.

⌖➤ This agency specializes in children's and nonfiction, but does take quality fiction.

HOW TO CONTACT Send an e-query. There is also an online submission form. If you do not hear back from this agency within 3 months, consider that a no.

RECENT SALES A full list of recent sales/titles is available on the agency website.

ⓘ UPSTART CROW LITERARY

244 Fifth Avenue, 11th Floor, New York NY 10001. **E-mail:** danielle.submission@gmail.com. **Website:** www.upstartcrowliterary.com. **Contact:** Danielle Chiotti, Alexandra Penfold. Estab. 2009.

MEMBER AGENTS Michael Stearns (not accepting submissions); **Danielle Chiotti** (young adult, middle grade, adult upmarket commercial that explores deep emotional relationships in an interesting or unusual way, and nonfiction in the areas of narrative/memoir, lifestyle, relationships, humor, current events, food, wine, and cooking); **Ted Malawer** (accepting queries only through conference submissions and client referrals); **Alexandra Penfold** (not accepting submissions).

REPRESENTS Considers these nonfiction areas: cooking, creative nonfiction, foods, humor, memoirs. **Considers these fiction areas:** middle grade, picture books, women's, young adult.

HOW TO CONTACT Submit a query and 20 pages pasted into an e-mail.

ⓘ VENTURE LITERARY

2683 Via de la Valle, G-714, Del Mar CA 92014. (619)807-1887. **Fax:** (772)365-8321. **E-mail:** submissions@ventureliterary.com. **Website:** www.ventureliterary.com. **Contact:** Frank R. Scatoni.

○ Prior to becoming an agent, Mr. Scatoni worked as an editor at Simon & Schuster.

MEMBER AGENTS Frank R. Scatoni (general nonfiction, biography, memoir, narrative nonfiction, sports, serious nonfiction, graphic novels, narratives).

REPRESENTS nonfiction books, novels, graphic novels, narratives. **Considers these nonfiction areas:** anthropology, biography, business, cultural interests, current affairs, dance, economics, environment, ethnic, government, history, investigative, law, memoirs, military, money, multicultural, music, popular culture, politics, psychology, science, sports, technology, true crime, women's issues, women's studies. **Considers these fiction areas:** action, adventure, crime, detective, literary, mainstream, mystery, police, sports, suspense, thriller, women's.

HOW TO CONTACT Considers e-mail queries only. *No unsolicited mss* and no snail mail whatsoever. See website for complete submission guidelines. Obtains most new clients through recommendations from others.

TERMS Agent receives 15% commission on domestic sales. Agent receives 20% commission on foreign sales. Offers written contract.

ⓘ VERITAS LITERARY AGENCY

601 Van Ness Ave., Opera Plaza, Suite E, San Francisco CA 94102. (415)647-6964. **Fax:** (415)647-6965. **E-mail:** submissions@veritasliterary.com. **Website:**

www.veritasliterary.com. **Contact:** Katherine Boyle. Member of AAR. Other memberships include Author's Guild and SCBWI.

MEMBER AGENTS Katherine Boyle, Michael Carr.
REPRESENTS nonfiction books, novels. **Considers these nonfiction areas:** current affairs, memoirs, popular culture, politics, true crime, women's issues, narrative nonfiction, art and music biography, natural history, health and wellness, psychology, serious religion (no New Age) and popular science. **Considers these fiction areas:** commercial, fantasy, literary, middle grade, mystery, science fiction, young adult.

8—➤ Does not want to receive poetry or Christian fiction.

HOW TO CONTACT This agency accepts short queries or proposals via e-mail only. "If you are sending a proposal or a ms after a positive response to a query, please write 'requested material' on the subject line and include the initial query letter." For fiction, send a query, synopsis, and the first 2 chapters pasted. For nonfiction, send a full, thorough book proposal. If you have not heard from this agency in 12 weeks, consider that a no.

RECENT SALES *Hedwig and Berti* by Frieda Arkin (St. Martin's); *Shadowdance* by David Dalglish (Orbit); *Sickened: A Memoir of a Lost Childhood* by Julie Gregory (Bantam); *If I Am Missing or Dead* by Janine Latus (Simon & Schuster); *Free Burning* by Bayo Ojikutu (Crown).

🌑🌕 WADE & CO. LITERARY AGENCY, LTD

33 Cormorant Lodge, Thomas Moore St., London E1W 1AU England. (44)(207)488-4171. **Fax:** (44)(207)488-4172. **E-mail:** rw@rwla.com. **Website:** www.rwla.com. **Contact:** Robin Wade. Estab. 2001.

◐ Prior to opening his agency, Mr. Wade was an author.

MEMBER AGENTS Robin Wade.
REPRESENTS fiction and nonfiction, including children's books.

8—➤ "We are young and dynamic, and actively seek new writers across the literary spectrum." Does not want to receive poetry, plays, screenplays or short stories. Is also currently closed to picture books.

HOW TO CONTACT New proposals for full length adult and young adult books (excluding children's picture books or poetry) are always welcome. We much prefer to receive queries and submissions by e-mail, although we do, of course, accept proposals by post. There is no need to telephone in advance. Please provide a few details about yourself, a synopsis (i.e. a clear narrative summary of the complete story, of between say 1 and 6 pages in length) and the first 10,000 words or so (ideally as word.doc or PDF attachments) over e-mail. Responds in 1 week to queries. Responds in 1 month to mss.

TERMS Agent receives 15% commission on domestic sales. Agent receives 20% commission on foreign sales. Offers written contract; 1-month notice must be given to terminate contract.

TIPS "We seek mss that are well written, with strong characters and an original narrative voice. Our absolute priority is giving the best possible service to the authors we choose to represent, as well as maintaining routine friendly contact with them as we help develop their careers."

◐ WALES LITERARY AGENCY, INC.

P.O. Box 9426, Seattle WA 98109. (206)284-7114. **E-mail:** waleslit@waleslit.com. **Website:** www.waleslit.com. **Contact:** Elizabeth Wales; Neal Swain. Member of AAR. Other memberships include Authors Guild, Pacific Northwest Writers Association.

◐ Prior to becoming an agent, Ms. Wales worked at Oxford University Press and Viking Penguin.

MEMBER AGENTS Elizabeth Wales; Neal Swain.
8—➤ This agency specializes in quality fiction and narrative nonfiction. Does not handle screenplays, children's picture books, genre fiction, or most category nonfiction.

HOW TO CONTACT E-query with no attachments. Accepts simultaneous submissions. Responds in 2 weeks to queries, 2 months to mss.

TERMS Agent receives 15% commission on domestic sales. Agent receives 20% commission on foreign sales.

TIPS "We are especially interested in work that espouses a progressive cultural or political view, projects a new voice, or simply shares an important, compelling story. We also encourage writers living in the Pacific Northwest, West Coast, Alaska, and Pacific Rim countries, and writers from historically underrepresented groups, such as gay and lesbian writers and writers of color, to submit work (but does not discourage writers outside these areas). Most importantly, whether in fiction or nonfiction, the agency is looking for talented storytellers."

○ WATERSIDE PRODUCTIONS, INC.

2055 Oxford Ave., Cardiff CA 92007. (760)632-9190. **Fax:** (760)632-9295. **E-mail:** bgladstone@waterside.com. **E-mail:** admin@waterside.com. **Website:** www.waterside.com. Estab. 1982.

MEMBER AGENTS Bill Gladstone (big nonfiction books); **Margot Maley Hutchinson** (computer, health, psychology, parenting, fitness, pop-culture, and business); **Carole Jelen**, carole@jelenpub.com (innovation and thought leaders especially in business, technology, lifestyle and self-help); **Neil Gudovitz** (neilg@earthlink.net); **David Nelson**; **Jill Kramer**, WatersideAgentJK@aol.com (quality fiction with empowering themes for adults and YA (including crossovers); she also represents nonfiction books in the areas of: mind-body-spirit, self-help, celebrity memoirs, relationships, sociology, finance, psychology, health and fitness, diet/nutrition, inspiration, business, family/parenting issues, and more); **Brad Schepp** (e-commerce, social media and social commerce, careers, entrepreneurship, general business, health and fitness).

REPRESENTS Considers these nonfiction areas: business, computers, diet/nutrition, health, inspirational, money, parenting, psychology, self-help, sociology, technology. **Considers these fiction areas:** mainstream, young adult.

↻ Specializes in computer books, how-to, business, and health titles. Note that most agents here are nonfiction only, so target your query to the appropriate agent.

HOW TO CONTACT "Please read each agent bio [on the website] to determine who you think would best represent your genre of work. When you have chosen your agent, please write his or her name in the subject line of your e-mail and send it to admin@waterside.com with your query letter in the body of the e-mail, and your proposal or sample material as an attached word document." Obtains most new clients through referrals from established client and publisher list.

TIPS "For new writers, a quality proposal and a strong knowledge of the market you're writing for goes a long way toward helping us turn you into a published author. We like to see a strong author platform. Two foreign rights agents on staff—Neil Gudovitz and Kimberly Brabec—help us with overseas sales."

⊘ ◎ WATKINS LOOMIS AGENCY, INC.

P.O. Box 20925, New York NY 10025. (212)532-0080. **Fax:** (646)383-2449. **E-mail:** assistant@watkinsloomis.com. **Website:** www.watkinsloomis.com. Estab. 1980. Represents 50+ clients.

MEMBER AGENTS Gloria Loomis, president, **Julia Masnik**, junior agent.

REPRESENTS nonfiction, novels. **Considers these nonfiction areas:** autobiography, biography, cultural interests, current affairs, environment, ethnic, history, popular culture, technology, investigative journalism. **Considers these fiction areas:** literary, short story collections.

↻ This agency specializes in literary fiction and nonfiction.

HOW TO CONTACT *No unsolicited mss.* This agency does not guarantee a response to queries.

TERMS Agent receives 15% commission on domestic sales. Agent receives 20% commission on foreign sales.

RECENT SALES Entire list of sales is available on the agency website.

◑ WAXMAN LEAVELL LITERARY AGENCY, INC.

443 Park Ave. S, Suite 1004, New York NY 10016. (212)675-5556. **Fax:** (212)675-1381. **Website:** www.waxmanleavell.com.

MEMBER AGENTS Scott Waxman (thrillers, mysteries, YA, middle grade, memoir, history, adventure nonfiction, sports, narrative); **Byrd Leavell** (narrative nonfiction, sports, humor, and select commercial fiction); Holly Root (commercial, middle grade, young adult, women's fiction, urban fantasy, romance); **Larry Kirschbaum** (fiction and nonfiction; select self-published breakout books); **Rachel Vogel** (nonfiction: subject-driven narratives, memoirs and biography, journalism, popular culture and the occasional humor and gift book); **Julie Stevenson**; **Taylor Haggerty** (young adult, historical, women's, new adult); **Cassie Hanjian** (new adult novels, plot-driven commercial and upmarket women's fiction, historical fiction, psychological suspense, cozy mysteries and contemporary romance; for nonfiction, parenting, mind/body/spirit, inspirational memoir, narrative nonfiction focusing on food-related topics and a limited number of accessible cookbooks); Fleetwood Robbins (fantasy and sci-fi—all subgenres); **Kirsten Carleton** (upmarket young adult, speculative, and literary fiction).

REPRESENTS Considers these nonfiction areas: prescriptive, historical, sports, narrative, pop culture, humor, memoir, biography, celebrity. **Considers these fiction areas:** historical, literary, mainstream, middle grade, mystery, paranormal, romance, thriller, women's, young adult.

∞➙ "We're looking for new novelists with non-published works."

HOW TO CONTACT To submit a project, please send a query letter ONLY via e-mail to one of the addresses included here. Do not send attachments, though for fiction you may include 5-10 pages of your ms in the body of your e-mail. Accepts simultaneous submissions.

TERMS Agent receives 15% commission on domestic sales. Agent receives 10% commission on foreign sales. Offers written contract; 2-month notice must be given to terminate contract.

⊕ CK WEBBER ASSOCIATES, LITERARY MANAGEMENT

E-mail: carlie@ckwebber.com. **Website:** http://ck-webber.com/.

🔾 Ms. Webber's professional publishing experience includes an internship at Writers House and work with the Publish or Perish Agency/New England Publishing Associates and the Jane Rotrosen Agency.

REPRESENTS Considers these nonfiction areas: memoirs. **Considers these fiction areas:** fantasy, literary, mainstream, middle grade, mystery, new adult, romance, science fiction, suspense, thriller, women's, young adult.

HOW TO CONTACT To submit your work for consideration, please send a query letter, synopsis, and the first 30 pages or three chapters of your work, whichever is more, to carlie@ckwebber.com and put the word "query" in the subject line of your e-mail. You may include your materials either in the body of your e-mail or as a Word or PDF attachment. Blank e-mails that include an attachment will be deleted unread. We only accept queries via e-mail.

CHERRY WEINER LITERARY AGENCY

925 Oak Bluff Ct., Dacula GA 30019. (732)446-2096. **Fax:** (732)792-0506. **E-mail:** cherry8486@aol.com. **Contact:** Cherry Weiner. Represents 40 clients. 10% of clients are new/unpublished writers.

REPRESENTS novels. **Considers these fiction areas:** action, adventure, contemporary issues, crime, detective, family saga, fantasy, frontier, historical, mainstream, mystery, police, psychic, romance, science fiction, supernatural, thriller, westerns.

∞➙ *This agency is currently not accepting new clients except by referral or by personal contact at writers' conferences.* Specializes in fantasy, science fiction, westerns, mysteries (both contemporary and historical), historical novels, Native-American works, mainstream, and all genre romances.

HOW TO CONTACT Accepts e-queries only. Only wishes to receive submissions from referrals and from writers she has met at conferences/events. Responds in 1 week to queries. Responds in 2 months to mss that I have asked for.

TERMS Agent receives 15% commission on domestic sales. Agent receives 15% commission on foreign sales. Offers written contract. Charges clients for extra copies of mss, first-class postage for author's copies of books, express mail for important documents/mss.

RECENT SALES Sold 65 titles in the last year. This agency prefers not to share information on specific sales.

TIPS "Meet agents and publishers at conferences. Establish a relationship, then get in touch with them and remind them of the meeting and conference."

○ THE WEINGEL-FIDEL AGENCY

310 E. 46th St., 21E, New York NY 10017. (212)599-2959. **Contact:** Loretta Weingel-Fidel. Currently handles: nonfiction books 75%, novels 25%.

🔾 Prior to opening her agency, Ms. Weingel-Fidel was a psychoeducational diagnostician.

REPRESENTS nonfiction books, novels. **Considers these nonfiction areas:** art, autobiography, biography, dance, memoirs, music, psychology, science, sociology, technology, women's issues, women's studies, investigative journalism. **Considers these fiction areas:** literary, mainstream.

∞➙ This agency specializes in commercial and literary fiction and nonfiction. Actively seeking investigative journalism. Does not want to receive genre fiction, self-help, science fiction, or fantasy.

HOW TO CONTACT Accepts writers by referral only. *No unsolicited mss.*

TERMS Agent receives 15% commission on domestic sales. Agent receives 20% commission on foreign sales. Offers written contract, binding for 1 year with automatic renewal. Bills sent back to clients are all reasonable expenses, such as UPS, express mail, photocopying, etc.

TIPS "A very small, selective list enables me to work very closely with my clients to develop and nurture talent. I only take on projects and writers about which I am extremely enthusiastic."

LARRY WEISSMAN LITERARY, LLC

526 8th St., #2R, Brooklyn NY 11215. **E-mail:** lwsubmissions@gmail.com. **Contact:** Larry Weissman.

REPRESENTS nonfiction books, novels, short story collections. **Considers these fiction areas:** literary.

"Very interested in established journalists with bold voices. Interested in anything to do with food. Fiction has to feel 'vital' and short stories are accepted, but only if you can sell us on an idea for a novel as well." Nonfiction, including food and lifestyle, politics, pop culture, narrative, cultural/social issues, journalism. No genre fiction, poetry or children's.

HOW TO CONTACT "Send e-queries only. If you don't hear back, your project was not right for our list."

TERMS Agent receives 15% commission on domestic sales. Agent receives 20% commission on foreign sales.

WELLS ARMS LITERARY

E-mail: info@wellsarms.com. **Website:** www.wellsarms.com. **Contact:** Victoria Wells Arms. Estab. 2013.

Prior to opening her agency, Victoria was a children's book editor for Dial Books.

REPRESENTS Considers these fiction areas: juvenile, middle grade, picture books, young adult.

We focus on books for readers of all ages, and we particularly love board books, picture books, readers, chapter books, middle grade, and young adult fiction—both authors and illustrators. We do not represent to the textbook, magazine, adult romance or fine art markets.

HOW TO CONTACT E-query. Put "Query" in your e-mail subject line. No attachments.

WERNICK & PRATT AGENCY

E-mail: info@wernickpratt.com. **Website:** www.wernickpratt.com. **Contact:** Marcia Wernick; Linda Pratt; Emily Mitchell. Member of AAR. SCBWI

Prior to co-founding Wernick & Pratt Agency, Ms. Wernick worked at the Sheldon Fogelman Agency, in subsidiary rights, advancing to director of subsidiary rights; Ms. Pratt also worked at the Sheldon Fogelman Agency.

MEMBER AGENTS Marcia Wernick, Linda Pratt, Emily Mitchell.

"Wernick & Pratt Agency specializes in children's books of all genres, from picture books through young adult literature and everything in between. We represent both authors and illustrators. We do not represent authors of adult books." Wants people who both write and illustrate in the picture book genre; humorous young chapter books with strong voice, and which are unique and compelling; middle grade/YA novels, both literary and commercial. No picture book mss of more than 750 words, or mood pieces; work specifically targeted to the educational market; fiction about the American Revolution, Civil War, or World War II unless it is told from a very unique perspective.

HOW TO CONTACT Submit via e-mail only. "Please indicate to which agent you are submitting." Detailed submission guidelines available on website. Responds in 6 weeks.

WHIMSY LITERARY AGENCY, LLC

49 North 8th St., G6, Brooklyn NY 11249. (212)674-7162. **E-mail:** whimsynyc@aol.com. **Website:** http://whimsyliteraryagency.com/. **Contact:** Jackie Meyer. Other memberships include Center for Independent Publishing Advisory Board. Represents 30 clients. 20% of clients are new/unpublished writers.

Prior to becoming an agent, Ms. Meyer was with Warner Books for 19 years.

MEMBER AGENTS Jackie Meyer; Lenore Skomal.

REPRESENTS nonfiction books. **Considers these nonfiction areas:** art, biography, business, child guidance, cooking, education, health, history, horticulture, how-to, humor, interior design, memoirs, money, New Age, popular culture, psychology, self-help, true crime, women's issues, women's studies. **Considers these fiction areas:** mainstream.

"Whimsy looks for projects that are concept- and platform-driven. We seek books that educate, inspire and entertain." Actively seeking experts in their field with good platforms.

HOW TO CONTACT Send a query letter via e-mail. Send a synopsis, bio, platform, and proposal. No snail mail submissions. Responds "quickly, but only if interested" to queries. *Does not accept unsolicited mss.* Obtains most new clients through recommendations from others, solicitations.

TERMS Agent receives 15% commission on domestic sales. Agent receives 20% commission on foreign sales. Offers written contract.

⊘⊙ WILLIAM MORRIS ENDEAVOR ENTERTAINMENT

1325 Avenue of the Americas, New York NY 10019. (212)586-5100. **Fax:** (212)246-3583. **Website:** www.wma.com. **Contact:** Literary Department Coordinator. Member of AAR.

REPRESENTS nonfiction books, novels, tv, movie scripts, feature film.

HOW TO CONTACT This agency is generally closed to unsolicited literary submissions. Meet an agent at a conference, or query through a referral. Accepts simultaneous submissions.

TERMS Agent receives 15% commission on domestic sales. Agent receives 20% commission on foreign sales.

TIPS "If you are a prospective writer interested in submitting to the William Morris Agency in **London**, please follow these guidelines: For all queries, please send a cover letter, synopsis, and the first three chapters (up to 50 pages) by e-mail only to: dkar@wmeentertainment.com."

WOLF LITERARY SERVICES, LLC

Website: http://wolflit.com. Estab. 2008.

MEMBER AGENTS Kirsten Wolf (no queries); **Adriann Ranta** (all genres for all age groups with a penchant for edgy, dark, quirky voices, unique settings, and everyman stories told with a new spin; she loves gritty, realistic, true-to-life stories with conflicts based in the real world; women's fiction and nonfiction; accessible, pop nonfiction in science, history, and craft; and smart, fresh, genre-bending works for children); **Kate Johnson** (literary fiction, particularly character-driven stories, psychological investigations, modern-day fables, and the occasional high-concept plot; she also represents memoir, cultural history and narrative nonfiction, and loves working with journalists); **Allison Devereux** (literary and upmarket commercial fiction, everyman characters in unlikely situations, debut voices, and psychologically adept narratives with a surreal bent; she loves narrative nonfiction, examinations of contemporary culture, pop science, cultural history, illustrated/graphic memoir, humor, and blog-to-book).

REPRESENTS Considers these nonfiction areas: art, crafts, creative nonfiction, history, memoirs, science, women's issues. **Considers these fiction areas:** literary, women's, young adult, magical realism.

HOW TO CONTACT To submit a project, please send a query letter along with a 50-page writing sample (for fiction) or a detailed proposal (for nonfiction) to queries@wolflit.com. Samples may be submitted as an attachment or embedded in the body of the e-mail.

RECENT SALES *Hoodoo*, by Ronald Smith (Clarion); *Binary Star*, by Sarah Gerard (Two Dollar Radio); *Conviction*, by Kelly Loy Gilbert (Hyperion); *The Empire Striketh Back*, by Ian Doescher (Quirk Books).

ⓘ WOLFSON LITERARY AGENCY

P.O. Box 266, New York NY 10276. **E-mail:** query@wolfsonliterary.com. **Website:** www.wolfsonliterary.com. **Contact:** Michelle Wolfson. Estab. 2007. Adheres to AAR canon of ethics.

- Prior to forming her own agency in December 2007, Ms. Wolfson spent two years with Artists & Artisans, Inc. and two years with Ralph Vicinanza, Ltd.
- Actively seeking commercial fiction: young adult, mainstream, mysteries, thrillers, suspense, women's fiction, romance, practical or narrative nonfiction (particularly of interest to women).

HOW TO CONTACT E-queries only. Accepts simultaneous submissions. Responds only if interested. Positive response is generally given within 2-4 weeks. Responds in 3 months to mss. Obtains most new clients through queries or recommendations from others.

TERMS Agent receives 15% commission on domestic sales. Agent receives 25% commission on foreign sales. Offers written contract; 30-day notice must be given to terminate contract.

TIPS "Be persistent."

⊙ WORDSERVE LITERARY GROUP

7061 S. University Blvd., Suite 307, Centennial CO 80122. **Website:** www.wordserveliterary.com. **Contact:** Greg Johnson. Represents 100 clients. 20% of clients are new/unpublished writers. Currently handles:

nonfiction books 50%, novels 35%, juvenile books 10%, multimedia 5%.

○ Prior to becoming an agent in 1994, Mr. Johnson was a magazine editor and freelance writer of more than 20 books and 200 articles.

MEMBER AGENTS Greg Johnson, Alice Crider, Sarah Freese.

REPRESENTS Considers these nonfiction areas: biography, inspirational, memoirs, parenting, self-help. **Considers these fiction areas:** historical, inspirational, mainstream, spiritual, thriller, women's.

8—₮ Seeks materials with a faith-based angle. This agency also seeks romantic suspense. No fantasy or sci-fi. Please do not send mss that are more than 120,000 words.

HOW TO CONTACT E-query admin@wordservelit erary.com. In the subject line, include the word "query." All queries should include the following three elements: a pitch for the book, information about you and your platform (for nonfiction) or writing background (for fiction), and the first 5 (or so) pages of the manuscript pasted into the e-mail. More submission guidelines available online. Accepts simultaneous submissions. Responds in 4 weeks to queries. Responds in 2 months to mss. Obtains most new clients through recommendations from others.

TERMS Agent receives 15% commission on domestic sales. Agent receives 10-15% commission on foreign sales. Offers written contract; up to 60-day notice must be given to terminate contract.

TIPS "We are looking for good proposals, great writing and authors willing to market their books, as appropriate. Also, we're only looking for projects with a faith element bent. See the website before submitting."

❶ WRITERS HOUSE

21 W. 26th St., New York NY 10010. (212)685-2400. **Fax:** (212)685-1781. **Website:** www.writershouse.com. Estab. 1973. Member of AAR.

MEMBER AGENTS Amy Berkower; Stephen Barr, sbarr@writershouse.com; Susan Cohen; Dan Conaway; Lisa DiMona; Susan Ginsburg; Merrilee Heifetz; Brianne Johnson; Daniel Lazar; Simon Lipskar; Steven Malk; Jodi Reamer, Esq.; Robin Rue; Rebecca Sherman; Geri Thoma; Albert Zuckerman; Alec Shane; Sarah Nagel, sarahsubmissions@writershouse.com (psychological thrillers, horror, mystery, suspense, literary fiction, young adult, middle grade; nonfiction in the areas of medical ethics, true crime, humor books and memoir); **Stacy Testa**, st-esta@writershouse.com (literary fiction, commercial fiction, young adult, some nonfiction); **Lisa DiMona**.

REPRESENTS nonfiction books, novels, juvenile. **Considers these nonfiction areas:** animals, art, autobiography, biography, business, child guidance, cooking, decorating, diet/nutrition, economics, film, foods, health, history, humor, interior design, juvenile nonfiction, medicine, military, money, music, parenting, psychology, satire, science, self-help, technology, theater, true crime, women's issues, women's studies. **Considers these fiction areas:** adventure, cartoon, contemporary issues, crime, detective, erotica, ethnic, family saga, fantasy, feminist, frontier, gay, hi-lo, historical, horror, humor, juvenile, literary, mainstream, middle grade, military, multicultural, mystery, New Age, occult, picture books, police, psychic, regional, romance, spiritual, sports, thriller, translation, war, women's, young adult.

8—₮ This agency specializes in all types of popular fiction and nonfiction. Does not want to receive scholarly, professional, poetry, plays, or screenplays.

HOW TO CONTACT Query with SASE. Do not contact two agents here at the same time. While snail mail is OK for all agents, some agents do accept e-queries (see below). Check the website for individual agent bios. "Please send us a query letter of no more than 2 pages, which includes your credentials, an explanation of what makes your book unique and special, and a synopsis. (If submitting to Steven Malk: Writers House, 7660 Fay Ave., #338H, La Jolla, CA 92037. Note that Malk only accepts queries on an exclusive basis.)" Accepts simultaneous submissions. Obtains most new clients through recommendations from authors and editors.

TERMS Agent receives 15% commission on domestic sales. Agent receives 20% commission on foreign sales. Offers written contract, binding for 1 year. Agency charges fees for copying mss/proposals and overseas airmail of books.

TIPS "Do not send mss. Write a compelling letter. If you do, we'll ask to see your work. Follow submission guidelines and please do not simultaneously submit your work to more than 1 Writers House agent."

○ WRITERS' REPRESENTATIVES, LLC

116 W. 14th St., 11th Floor, New York NY 10011-7305. **E-mail:** transom@writersreps.com. **Website:** www.

writersreps.com. Represents 100 clients. Currently handles: nonfiction books 90%, novels 10%.

○ Prior to becoming an agent, Ms. Chu was a lawyer; Mr. Hartley worked at Simon & Schuster, Harper & Row and Cornell University Press.

MEMBER AGENTS Lynn Chu, Glen Hartley.

REPRESENTS nonfiction books, novels. **Considers these fiction areas:** literary.

☛ Serious nonfiction and quality fiction. No motion picture or television screenplays.

HOW TO CONTACT Query with SASE. Prefers to read materials exclusively. Considers simultaneous queries, but must be informed at time of submission. Consult website section "FAQ" for detailed submission guidelines.

TERMS Agent receives 15% commission on domestic sales. Agent receives 20% commission on foreign sales.

TIPS "Always include a SASE; it will ensure a response from the agent and the return of your submitted material."

⊘ THE WYLIE AGENCY

250 West 57th St., Suite 2114, New York NY 10107. (212)246-0069. **Fax:** (212)586-8953. **E-mail:** mail@wylieagency.com. **Website:** www.wylieagency.com. Overseas address: 17 Bedford Square, London WC1B 3JA, United Kingdom; mail@wylieagency.co.uk.

MEMBER AGENTS Andrew Wylie; Jeff Posternak; Sarah Chalfant.

REPRESENTS nonfiction books, novels.

☛ **THIS AGENCY** is not currently accepting unsolicited submissions; do not query unless you are asked.

HOW TO CONTACT This agency does not currently take unsolicited queries/proposals.

⊕ JASON YARN LITERARY AGENCY

3544 Broadway, No. 68, New York NY 10031. **E-mail:** jasonyarnagency@gmail.com.

HOW TO CONTACT E-query.

◉ YATES & YATES

1551 N. Tustin Ave, Suite 710, Santa Ana CA 92705. (714)480-4000. **Fax:** (714)480-4001. **E-mail:** submissions@yates2.com. **E-mail:** e-mail@yates2.com. **Website:** www.yates2.com. Represents 60 clients.

REPRESENTS nonfiction books. **Considers these nonfiction areas:** autobiography, biography, business, current affairs, memoirs, politics, sports, religious.

RECENT SALES *No More Mondays*, by Dan Miller (Doubleday Currency).

⊘ ZACHARY SHUSTER HARMSWORTH

19 West 21st St., Suite 501, New York, NY 10010. (212)765-6900. **Fax:** (212)765-6490. **Website:** www.zshliterary.com. Alternate address: 535 Boylston St., 11th Floor, Boston MA 02116. (617)262-2400. **Fax:** (617)262-2468.

○ "Our principals include two former publishing and entertainment lawyers, a journalist and an editor/agent. Lane Zachary was an editor at Random House before becoming an agent."

MEMBER AGENTS Lane Zachary (memoir, current events, history, biography and psychology); **Todd Shuster** (current affairs, biography, true-crime, popular science, adventure, politics and civil rights, history, memoir, business, health, parenting, and psychology; his fiction list is comprised primarily of literary and "crossover" commercial novels, including mysteries and thrillers); **Esmond Harmsworth** (fiction and nonfiction); **Jennifer Gates** (a range of nonfiction, as well as literary and commercial fiction and children's); **Janet Silver** (literary fiction and nonfiction, including memoir, biography, history, science, philosophy, and poetry); **Bridget Wagner Matzie** (nonfiction and commercial fiction); **Jane Von Mehren**; **Rick Richter** (new adult, young adult, middle grade, picture books, nonfiction in the areas of history and military history); **Nan Thonrton** (literary and commercial fiction, narrative nonfiction, biography, memoir, and nonfiction in the areas of health, science, business, parenting, and education, as well as children's books); **Chelsey Heller** (subsidiary rights); **Elias Altman** (literary fiction, memoirs, and a broad range of narrative and expository nonfiction including works of history, science, travel, and cultural criticism).

REPRESENTS nonfiction books, novels.

☛ **CHECK THE** website for updated info.

HOW TO CONTACT *Cannot accept unsolicited submissions.* If you are invited to send material, use the online agency submission form. Obtains most new clients through recommendations from others.

TERMS Agent receives 15% commission on domestic sales. Agent receives 20% commission on foreign sales. Offers written contract, binding for 1 work only; 30-day notice must be given to terminate contract.

○ KAREN GANTZ ZAHLER LITERARY MANAGEMENT AND ATTORNEY AT LAW

860 Fifth Ave., Suite 7J, New York NY 10065. (212)734-3619. **E-mail:** karen@karengantzlit.com. **Website:** www.karengantzlit.com. **Contact:** Karen Gantz Zahler. Currently handles: nonfiction books 95%, novels 5%, film, TV scripts.

○ Prior to her current position, Ms. Gantz Zahler practiced law at two law firms, wrote two cookbooks, *Taste of New York* (Addison-Wesley) and *Superchefs* (John Wiley & Sons). She also participated in a Presidential Advisory Committee on Intellectual Property, U.S. Department of Commerce.

☛ **ACTIVELY SEEKING** nonfiction. "We assist with speaking engagements and publicity."

HOW TO CONTACT Accepting queries and summaries by e-mail only. Check the website for complete submission information (karengantzlit.com/submission.html), because it is intricate and specific. Responds in 4 weeks to queries. Obtains most new clients through recommendations from others, solicitations.

RECENT SALES *Extraordinary Hearts: A Journey of Cardiac Medicine and the Human Spirit* by Dr. John Elefteriades (Berkley Books); *Transplant* by Dr. John Elefteriades (Berkley Books); *The Lost Khrushchev: A Journey into the Gulag of the Russian Mind* by Nina L. Khrushcheva (Tate Publishing); *The Magic of Math: Solving for x and Figuring Out Why* by Arthur Benjamin (Basic Books); more sales can be found online.

TIPS "Our dream client is someone who is a professional writer and a great listener. What writers can do to increase the likelihood of our retainer is to write an excellent summary and provide a great marketing plan for their proposal in an excellent presentation. Any typos or grammatical mistakes do not resonate well. If we want to review your project, we will ask you to send a copy by snail mail with an envelope and return postage enclosed. We don't call people unless we have something to report."

① HELEN ZIMMERMANN LITERARY AGENCY

New Paltz NY 12561. **E-mail:** submit@ZimmAgency.com. **Website:** www.zimmermannliterary.com. **Contact:** Helen Zimmermann. Estab. 2003. Currently handles: nonfiction books 80%, other 20% fiction.

○ Prior to opening her agency, Ms. Zimmermann was the director of advertising and promotion at Random House and the events coordinator at an independent bookstore.

REPRESENTS Considers these nonfiction areas: diet/nutrition, health, memoirs, music, popular culture, sports, women's issues, relationships. **Considers these fiction areas:** literary.

☛ **"AS AN** agent who has experience at both a publishing house and a bookstore, I have a keen insight for viable projects. This experience also helps me ensure every client gets published well, through the whole process." Actively seeking memoirs, pop culture, women's issues, and accessible literary fiction. Does not want to receive horror, science fiction, poetry or romance.

HOW TO CONTACT Accepts e-mail queries only. E-mail should include a short description of project and bio, whether it be fiction or nonfiction. Accepts simultaneous submissions. Responds in 2 weeks to queries. Responds in 1 month to mss. Obtains most new clients through recommendations from others, solicitations.

TERMS Agent receives 15% commission on domestic sales. Offers written contract; 30-day notice must be given to terminate contract.

WRITERS CONFERENCES BEA/Writer's Digest Books Writers' Conference; Portland, ME Writers Conference; Berkshire Writers and Readers Conference; La Jolla Writers Conference; The New School Writers Conference; Vermont Writers Conference; ASJA Conference; Books Alive! Conference; Southeast Writers Conference; Kansas Writers Conference.

RENÈE ZUCKERBROT LITERARY AGENCY

115 West 29th St., 3rd Floor, New York NY 10001. (212)967-0072. **Fax:** (212)967-0073. **E-mail:** renee@rzagency.com. **E-mail:** submissions@rzagency.com. **Website:** rzagency.com. **Contact:** Renèe Zuckerbrot. Represents 30 clients. Currently handles: 30% nonfiction and 70% fiction.

○ Prior to becoming an agent, Ms. Zuckerbrot worked as an editor at Doubleday as well as in the editorial department at Putnam.

REPRESENTS Considers these fiction areas: science fiction, short story collections, women's.
☞ **NARRATIVE NONFICTION** (focusing on science, history and pop culture). No business books, self-help, spirituality or romance. No screenplays.

HOW TO CONTACT Query by e-mail: submissions@rzagency.com. Include a synopsis, publication history and a brief personal bio. You may include up to the first 3 chapters. Responds in approximately 4-6 weeks.

TERMS Agent receives 15% commission on domestic sales. Agent receives 25% commission on foreign sales (10% to RZA; 15% to foreign rights co-agent).

WRITERS' CONFERENCES

Attending a writers' conference that includes agents gives you the opportunity to learn more about what agents do and to show an agent your work. Ideally, a conference should include a panel or two with a number of agents to give writers a sense of the variety of personalities and tastes of different agents.

Not all agents are alike: Some are more personable, and sometimes you simply click better with one agent versus another. When only one agent attends a conference, there is a tendency for every writer at that conference to think, "Ah, this is the agent I've been looking for!" When the number of agents attending is larger, you have a wider group from which to choose, and you may have less competition for the agent's time.

Besides including panels of agents discussing what representation means and how to go about securing it, many of these gatherings also include time—either scheduled or impromptu—to meet briefly with an agent to discuss your work.

If they're impressed with what they see and hear about your work, they will invite you to submit a query, a proposal, a few sample chapters, or possibly your entire manuscript. Some conferences even arrange for agents to review manuscripts in advance and schedule one-on-one sessions during which you can receive specific feedback or advice regarding your work. Such meetings often cost a small fee, but the input you receive is usually worth the price.

Ask writers who attend conferences and they'll tell you that, at the very least, you'll walk away with new knowledge about the industry. At the very best, you'll receive an invitation to send an agent your material!

Many writers try to make it to at least one conference a year, but cost and location can count as much as subject matter when determining which one to attend. There are conferences in almost every state and province that can provide answers to your questions about writing and the publishing industry. Conferences also connect you with a community of other writers. Such connections help you learn about the pros and cons of different agents, and they can also give you a renewed sense of purpose and direction in your own writing.

SUBHEADS

Each listing is divided into subheads to make locating specific information easier. In the first section, you'll find contact information for conference contacts. You'll also learn conference dates, specific focus, and the average number of attendees. Finally, names of agents who will be speaking or have spoken in the past are listed along with details about their availability during the conference. Calling or e-mailing a conference director to verify the names of agents in attendance is always a good idea.

Costs: Looking at the price of events, plus room and board, may help writers on a tight budget narrow their choices.

Accommodations: Here conferences list overnight accommodations and travel information. Often conferences held in hotels will reserve rooms at a discount rate and may provide a shuttle bus to and from the local airport.

Additional Information: This section includes information on conference-sponsored contests, individual meetings, the availability of brochures, and more.

At the beginning of some listings, you will find one or more of the following symbols:

➕ Conference new to this addition

🔄 Canadian Conference

🔁 International Conference

Find a pull-out bookmark with a key to symbols on the inside cover of this book.

ABROAD WRITERS CONFERENCES

17363 Sutter Creek Rd., Sutter Creek CA 95685. (209)296-4050. **E-mail:** abroadwriters@yahoo.com; nancy@abroadwritersconference.com. **Website:** http://abroadwritersconference.com/. "Abroad Writers Conferences are devoted to introducing our participants to world views here in the US and Abroad. Throughout the world we invite several authors to come join us to give readings and to participate on a panel. Our discussion groups touch upon a wide range of topics from important issues of our times to publishing abroad and in the US. Our objective is to broaden our cultural and scientific perspectives of the world through discourse and writing." Conferences are held throughout the year in various places worldwide. See website for scheduling details. Conference duration: 7-10 days. "Instead of being lost in a crowd at a large conference, Abroad Writers' Conference prides itself on holding small group meetings where participants have personal contact with everyone. Stimulating talks, interviews, readings, Q&A's, writing workshops, film screenings, private consultations and social gatherings all take place within a week to ten days. Abroad Writers' Conference promises you true networking opportunities and full detailed feedback on your writing."

COSTS See website for pricing details.

ADDITIONAL INFORMATION Agents participate in conference. Application is online at website.

ALABAMA WRITING WORKSHOP

Website: www.alabamawritingworkshop.com. Estab. 2015. The 2016 event is set for Friday, February 19, 2016. Organized by Writing Day Workshops. The workshop is a one-day, all-day "How to Get Published" conference with instructional sessions and panels. Multiple literary agents are in attendance at the workshop to meet with writers and hear pitches.

COSTS Early-bird tuition is $129; later tuition is $149; agent meetings are $29 per appointment.

ACCOMMODATIONS Rooms available at the event hotels.

ADDITIONAL INFORMATION Query critique options available. Check the website for contact and registration information.

ALASKA WRITERS CONFERENCE

Alaska Writers Guild, PO Box 670014, Chugiak AK 99567. **E-mail:** alaskawritersguild.awg@gmail.com. **Website:** alaskawritersguild.com. Annual event held in the fall—usually September. Duration: 2 days. There are many workshops and instructional tracks of courses. This event sometimes teams up with SCBWI and Alaska Pacific University to offer courses at the event. Literary agents are in attendance each year to hear pitches and meet writers.

AMERICAN CHRISTIAN WRITERS CONFERENCES

P.O. Box 110390, Nashville TN 37222-0390. (800)219-7483. **Fax:** (615)834-7736. **E-mail:** acwriters@aol.com. **Website:** www.acwriters.com. **Contact:** Reg Forder, director. Estab. 1981. ACW hosts dozens of annual two-day writers conferences and mentoring retreats across America taught by editors and professional freelance writers. These events provide excellent instruction, networking opportunities, and valuable one-on-one time with editors. Annual conferences promoting all forms of Christian writing (fiction, nonfiction, scriptwriting). Conferences are held between March and November during each year.

COSTS Costs vary based on conference. Prices also depend on whether it is a conference or a mentoring retreat.

ACCOMMODATIONS Special rates are available at the host hotel (usually a major chain like Holiday Inn).

ADDITIONAL INFORMATION Send a SASE for conference brochures/guidelines.

ANAM CARA WRITER'S AND ARTIST'S RETREAT

Eyeries, Beara, Co. Cork Ireland. (353)(027)74441. **Fax:** (353)(027)74448. **E-mail:** anamcararetreat@gmail.com. **Website:** www.anamcararetreat.com. **Contact:** Sue Booth-Forbes, director.

ACCOMMODATIONS 2015 cost: residency fee ranges from 600-700 Euro/week for individual retreats (full room and board). The event also features editorial consulting, laundry, sauna, hot tub overlooking Coulagh Bay, 5 acres of gardens, meadows, riverbank and cascades, river island, swimming hole, and several unique working spots, such as the ruin of a stone mill and a sod-roofed beehive hut. Overflow from workshops stay in nearby B&Bs, a 10-minute walk or 2-minute drive away. Transportation provided if needed. Details regarding workshops scheduled for 2015 and their fees as well as transportation to Anam Cara are available on the website.

ADDITIONAL INFORMATION Requests for specific information about rates and availability can be made through the website.

ANNUAL SPRING POETRY FESTIVAL

City College, 160 Convent Ave., New York NY 10031. (212)650-6356. **Website:** www1.ccny.cuny.edu/pro spective/humanities/poetry. Writer workshops geared to all levels. **Open to students.** Annual poetry festival. 2015 dates: May 8, 2015. Registration limited to 325. Cost of workshops and festival: free. Write for more information. Site: Theater B of Aaron Davis Hall.

ANTIOCH WRITERS' WORKSHOP

c/o Antioch University Midwest, 900 Dayton St., Yellow Springs OH 45387. (937)769-1803. **E-mail:** info@ antiochwritersworkshop.com. **Website:** www.antio chwritersworkshop.com. **Contact:** Sharon Short, director. Estab. 1986. Average attendance: 80. Programs are offered year-round; see the website for details. The dates of the 2015 conference are July 11-17. Workshop concentration: fiction, poetry, personal essay, memoir. Workshop located at Antioch University Midwest in the Village of Yellow Springs. Literary agents attend. Writers of all levels (beginner to advanced) of fiction, memoir, personal essay, and poetry are warmly welcomed to discover their next steps on their writing paths--whether that's developing craft or preparing to submit for publication. An agent and an editor will be speaking and available for meetings with attendees.

ACCOMMODATIONS Accommodations are available at local hotels and bed & breakfasts.

ADDITIONAL INFORMATION The easiest way to contact this event is through the online website contact form.

ARKANSAS WRITERS' CONFERENCE

6817 Gingerbread Lane, Little Rock AR 72204. (501)833-2756. **E-mail:** breannacone1@yahoo.com. **Website:** www.arkansaswritersconference.org. 2015 dates: June 5-6. Held at Pulaski Technical College NLR Campus in Little Rock. There is a keynote speaker, events, contests, and more.

○☺⊕ ART WORKSHOPS IN GUATEMALA

4758 Lyndale Ave. S., Minneapolis MN 55419-5304. (612)825-0747. **E-mail:** info@artguat.org. **Website:** www.artguat.org. **Contact:** Liza Fourre, director. Estab. 1995. Art & cultural workshops held year-round. Maximim class size: 10 students per class.

COSTS See website. ncludes tuition, lodging, breakfast, ground transportation.

ACCOMMODATIONS All transportation and accommodations included in price of conference.

ADDITIONAL INFORMATION Conference information available now. For brochure/guidelines visit website, e-mail or call. Accepts inquiries by e-mail, phone.

ASJA ANNUAL WRITERS CONFERENCE

American Society of Journalists and Authors, 355 Lexington Ave., 15th Floor, New York NY 10017. (212)997-0947. **E-mail:** asjaoffice@asja.org; director@ asja.org. **Website:** www.asjaconferences.org. **Contact:** Alexandra Owens, executive director. Estab. 1971. Annual conference held in April. Conference duration: 3 days. Average attendance: 600. Covers nonfiction. Held at the Roosevelt in New York. Speakers have included Arianna Huffington, Kitty Kelley, Barbara Ehrenreich, and Stefan Fatsis.

COSTS $200 minimum, depending on when you sign up (includes lunch). Check website for updates.

ACCOMMODATIONS The hotel holding our conference always blocks out discounted rooms for attendees.

ADDITIONAL INFORMATION Conference program online by mid-January. Registration is online only. Sign up for e-mail updates online.

ASPEN SUMMER WORDS LITERARY FESTIVAL & WRITING RETREAT

Aspen Words, 110 E. Hallam St., #116, Aspen CO 81611. (970)925-3122. **Fax:** (970)925-5700. **E-mail:** as penwords@aspeninstitute.org. **Website:** www.aspen words.org. **Contact:** Caroline Tory, programs coordinator. Estab. 1976. 2015 dates: June 21-26. The 39th annual Aspen Summer Words Writing Retreat and Literary Festival offers workshops in fiction, memoir, novel editing, and playwriting. The faculty includes fiction writers Ann Hood, Richard Russo, Akhil Sharma, and Hannah Tinti; memoir writers Andre Dubus III and Dani Shapiro; and playwright Sharr White. Aspen Summer Words features lectures, readings, panel discussions, and the opportunity to meet with agents and editors. Tuition for the writing workshops ranges from $1,100 to $1,375, which includes some meals. Financial aid is available on a limited basis. To apply for a juried workshop, submit up to 10 pages of prose with a $30 application fee by February 27. Registration to non-juried workshops (Beginning

Fiction and Playwriting) is first-come, first-served. A pass to all the public panels is $150, tickets to individual events are $20. Call, e-mail, or visit the website for an application and complete guidelines.

ASSOCIATION OF WRITERS & WRITING PROGRAMS ANNUAL CONFERENCE

Association of Writers & Writing Programs, George Mason University, 4400 University Drive, MSN 1E3, Fairfax VA 22030-4444. (703)993-4317. **Fax:** (703)993-4302. **E-mail:** conference@awpwriter.org; events@awpwriter.org. **Website:** www.awpwriter.org/awp_conference. Estab. 1992. Each year, AWP holds its Annual Conference & Bookfair in a different city to celebrate the authors, teachers, writing programs, literary centers, and independent publishers of that region. The conference typically features hundreds of readings, lectures, panel discussions, and forums, as well as hundreds of book signings, receptions, dances, and informal gatherings. AWP's is now the largest literary conference in North America.

ADDITIONAL INFORMATION Upcoming conference locations include Minneapolis (2015), Los Angeles (March 30-April 2, 2016), and Washington, D.C. (February 8-11, 2017).

ATLANTA WRITERS CONFERENCE

E-mail: awconference@gmail.com. **E-mail:** gjweinstein@yahoo.com. **Website:** www.atlantawritersconference.com. **Contact:** George Weinstein. The Atlanta Writers Conference happens twice a year (May and October/November) with 10 agents and publishing editors who critique ms samples and query letters, and also respond to pitches. There also are sessions with authors and industry professionals.

ACCOMMODATIONS Westin Airport Atlanta Hotel

ADDITIONAL INFORMATION There is a free shuttle that runs between the airport and the hotel.

ATLANTA WRITING WORKSHOP

Website: www.atlantawritingworkshop.com. Estab. 2015. The 2016 event is set for Saturday, February 20, 2016. Organized by Writing Day Workshops. The workshop is a one-day, all-day "How to Get Published" conference with instructional sessions and panels. Multiple literary agents are in attendance at the workshop to meet with writers and hear pitches.

COSTS Early-bird tuition is $129; later tuition is $149; agent meetings are $29 per appointment.

ACCOMMODATIONS Rooms available at the event hotel: Hyatt Place Cobb Galleria (NW of Atlanta).

ADDITIONAL INFORMATION Query critique options available. Check the website for contact and registration information.

AUSTIN FILM FESTIVAL & CONFERENCE

1801 Salina St., Suite 210, Austin TX 78702. (512)478-4795; (800)310-FEST. **Fax:** (512)478-6205. **Website:** www.austinfilmfestival.com. **Contact:** Conference director. Estab. 1994. "Built around one of the most prestigious screenwriting contests in the country, the Conference attracts groundbreaking producers, agents, managers, and development execs, as well as countless working screenwriters and filmmakers. The speakers converging in Austin every October range from established A-listers like Steven Zaillian, Ron Howard, Judd Apatow, Caroline Thompson, Susannah Grant and John Lee Hancock to upstart writers and filmmakers who have just broken into the industry. The Conference is famous, like its host city, for a culture of progressive ideas, big heart and zero pretensions. You won't just watch your heroes speak from a podium—we want you to get up close and personal—so panels are designed for intimacy and interaction, workshops are hands-on dream opportunities for writers and filmmakers, and parties are grand and fun without the velvet ropes. AFF's combination of high-caliber talent with access is unmatched by any other film festival or conference." Runs in the final week of October each year.

COSTS Austin Film Festival offers 4 badge levels for entry into the October festival, which also features access to the conference, depending on the Badge level. Go online for offers, and to view the different options with available with each badge.

AUSTIN INTERNATIONAL POETRY FESTIVAL

P.O. Box 26455, Austin TX 78755. (512)777-1888. **E-mail:** joe@aipf.org; james@aipf.org. **Website:** www.aipf.org. **Contact:** Joe Brundidge or James Jacobs. Estab. 1993. The 24th Austin International Poetry Festival (AIPF) will be held April 7-10, 2016. Registration is required for all poets. Nikki Giovanni was featured April 11, 2015—additional ticket required for this special reading, AIPF registered poets get in free. All additional events are free to the general public. This four-day citywide, all-inclusive celebration of poetry and poets has grown to become "the largest non-juried poetry festival in the US." The festival will include a minimum of the following: 20 readings, one youth anthology read, 10 workshops, 5 open mics, 2 music and poetry presentations, 2 anthology competitions and complete readings, 2 poetry slams, an all-night open mic and a poetry panel symposium. Additional information available online at www.aipf. org. Discount registration fees available for retired, college students, and military poets.

ACCOMMODATIONS Includes anthology submission fee, program bio, scheduled reading at one of AIPF's 15 venues, participation in all events, 1 catered meal, workshop participation, and more.

ADDITIONAL INFORMATION Offers multiple poetry contests as part of festival. Guidelines available on website. Registration form available on website. "Largest non-juried poetry festival in the US."

BALTIMORE COMIC-CON

Baltimore Convention Center, One West Pratt St., Baltimore MD 21201. (410)526-7410. **E-mail:** general@baltimorecomiccon.com. **Website:** www.baltimorecomiccon.com. **Contact:** Marc Nathan. Estab. 1999. Annual. 2015 dates: September 25-27. Conference "promoting the wonderful world of comics to as many people as possible." The Baltimore Comic-Con welcomes the return of The Harvey Awards: "The Harvey Awards are one of the comic book industry's oldest and most respected awards. The Harveys recognize outstanding achievements in over 20 categories, ranging from Best Artist to The Hero Initiative Lifetime Achievement Award. They are the only industry awards both nominated by and selected by the full body of comic book professionals."

ACCOMMODATIONS Does not offer overnight accommodations. Provides list of area hotels and lodging options.

ADDITIONAL INFORMATION For brochure, visit website.

BALTIMORE WRITERS' CONFERENCE

English Department, Liberal Arts Bldg., Towson University, 8000 York Rd., Towson MD 21252. (410)704-3695. **E-mail:** prwr@towson.edu. **Website:** baltimorewritersconference.org. Estab. 1994. "Annual conference held in November at Towson University. Conference duration: 1 day. Average attendance: 150-200. Covers all areas of writing and getting published. Held at Towson University. Session topics include fiction, nonfiction, poetry, magazine and journals, agents and publishers. Sign up the day of the confer-

ence for quick critiques to improve your stories, essays, and poems."

ACCOMMODATIONS Hotels are close by, if required.

ADDITIONAL INFORMATION Writers may register through the BWA website. Send inquiries via e-mail.

BAY TO OCEAN WRITERS CONFERENCE

P.O. Box 1773, Easton MD 21601. (443)786-4536. **E-mail:** info@baytoocean.com. **Website:** www.baytoocean.com. Estab. 1998. Annual conference held the last Saturday in February. Average attendance: 200. Approximately 30 speakers conduct workshops on publishing, agents, editing, marketing, craft, the Internet, poetry, fiction, nonfiction, and freelance writing. Site: Chesapeake College, Rt. 213 and Rt. 50, Wye Mills, on Maryland's historic Eastern Shore. Accessible to individuals with disabilities.

COSTS Adults $115, students $55. A paid ms review is also available—details on website. Includes continental breakfast and networking lunch.

ADDITIONAL INFORMATION Registration is on website. Pre-registration is required; no registration at door. Conference usually sells out one month in advance. Conference is for all levels of writers.

BIG SUR WRITING WORKSHOP

Henry Miller Library, Highway One, Big Sur CA 93920. (831)667-2574. **E-mail:** writing@henrymiller.org. **Website:** bigsurwriting.wordpress.com. Annual workshops focusing on children's and young adult writing (picture books, middle grade, and young adult). (2015 dates were March 6-8.) Workshop held in Big Sur Lodge in Pfeiffer State Park. Cost of workshop includes meals, lodging, workshop, Saturday evening reception. This event is helmed by the literary agents of the Andrea Brown Literary Agency, which is the most successful agency nationwide in selling kids books. All attendees meet with at least 2 faculty members, so work is critiqued.

BLOCKBUSTER PLOT INTENSIVE WRITING WORKSHOPS (SANTA CRUZ)

Santa Cruz CA **E-mail:** contact@blockbusterplots.com. **Website:** www.blockbusterplots.com. **Contact:** Martha Alderson (also known as the Plot Whisperer), instructor. Estab. 2000. Held 4 times per year. Conference duration: 2 days. Average attendance: 20. Workshop is intended to help writers create an action, character, and thematic plotline for a screenplay, memoir, short story, novel, or creative nonfiction. Site: Conference hall.

COSTS Costs vary based on the time frame of the retreat/workshop.

ACCOMMODATIONS Updated website provides list of area hotels and lodging options.

ADDITIONAL INFORMATION Accepts inquiries by e-mail.

BLUE RIDGE MOUNTAIN CHRISTIAN WRITERS CONFERENCE

No public address available, (800)588-7222. **E-mail:** BlueRidgeCWC@aol.com. **Website:** ridgecrestconferencecenter.org/event/blueridgemountainchristianwritersconference. Annual conference held in May. 2015 dates: May 17-21. Conference duration: Sunday through lunch on Thursday. Average attendance: 400. The conference is a training and networking event for both seasoned and aspiring writers that allows attendees to interact with editors, agents, professional writers, and readers. Workshops and continuing classes in a variety of creative categories are also offered.

COSTS $325, meal package is $145.00 per person (12 meals beginning with dinner Sunday and ending with lunch on Thursday)

ADDITIONAL INFORMATION For a PDF of the complete BRMCWC schedule (typically posted in April) visit BRMCWC.com.

BOOKS-IN-PROGRESS CONFERENCE

Carnegie Center for Literacy and Learning, 251 West Second Street, Lexington KY 40507. (859)254-4175. **E-mail:** lwhitaker@carnegiecenterlex.org. **Website:** carnegiecenterlex.org/. **Contact:** Laura Whitaker. Estab. 2010. This is an annual writing conference at the Carnegie Center for Literacy and Learning in Lexington. "Each conference will offer writing and publishing workshops and includes a keynote presentation." Literary agents are flown in to meet with writers and hear pitches. Website is updated several months prior to each annual event.

ACCOMMODATIONS Several area hotels are nearby.

BOSTON WRITING WORKSHOP

Website: www.bostonwritingworkshop.com. The 2015 event is set for Saturday, November 14, 2015. Organized by Writing Day Workshops. The workshop is a one-day, all-day "How to Get Published" conference with instructional sessions and panels. At least 8 literary agents are in attendance at the workshop to meet with writers and hear pitches.

COSTS Early-bird tuition is $149; later tuition is $179; agent meetings are $29 per appointment.

ACCOMMODATIONS Rooms available at the event hotel: The Sheraton Boston in Back Bay.

ADDITIONAL INFORMATION Query critique options available. Check the website for contact and registration information.

BREAD LOAF IN SICILY WRITERS' CONFERENCE

Middlebury College, Middlebury VT 05753. (802)443-5286. **Fax:** (802)443-2087. **E-mail:** blwc@middlebury.edu. **Website:** www.middlebury.edu/bread-loaf-conferences/blSicily. Estab. 2011. Annual conference held in September in Erice, Sicily (western coast of the island). Conference duration: 7 days. Offers workshops for fiction, nonfiction, and poetry. Agents and editors will be in attendance. 2015 dates: Sept. 20-26. Average attendance: 32.

COSTS The fee (contributor, $2,820) includes the conference program, transfer to and from Palermo Airport, six nights of lodging, three meals daily (except for Wednesday), wine reception at the readings, and an excursion to the ancient ruins of Segesta. The charge for an additional person is $1,575.

ACCOMMODATIONS Accommodations are single rooms with private bath. Breakfast and lunch are served at the hotel and dinner is available at select Erice restaurants. A double room is possible for those who would like to be accompanied by a spouse or significant other.

ADDITIONAL INFORMATION "Application Period: November 1-March 15. Rolling admissions. Space is limited."

BREAD LOAF ORION ENVIRONMENTAL WRITERS' CONFERENCE

Middlebury College, Middlebury VT 05753. (802)443-5286. **Fax:** (802)443-2087. **E-mail:** blwc@middlebury.edu. **Website:** www.middlebury.edu/bread-loaf-conferences/BLOrion. Estab. 2014. Annual specialized conference held in June. Conference duration: 7 days. Offers workshops for fiction, nonfiction, and poetry. Agents and editors will be in attendance. 2015 dates: June 1-7. Average attendance: 60. "Application Period: November 1 - March 15. Rolling admissions. Space is limited."

ACCOMMODATIONS Mountain campus of Middlebury College in Vermont.

ADDITIONAL INFORMATION The event is designed to hone the skills of people interested in producing literary writing about the environment and the natural world. The conference is co-sponsored by the Bread Loaf Writers' Conference, Orion magazine, and Middlebury College's Environmental Studies Program.

BREAD LOAF WRITERS' CONFERENCE

Middlebury College, Middlebury College, Middlebury VT 05753. (802)443-5286. **Fax:** (802)443-2087. **E-mail:** blwc@middlebury.edu. **Website:** www.middle bury.edu/bread-loaf-conferences/bl_writers. Estab. 1926. Annual conference held in late August. Conference duration: 10 days. Offers workshops for fiction, nonfiction, and poetry. Agents and editors will be in attendance.

ACCOMMODATIONS Bread Loaf Campus in Ripton, Vermont.

ADDITIONAL INFORMATION 2015 Conference Dates: August 12-22. Location: mountain campus of Middlebury College in Vermont. Average attendance: 230. The application deadline for the 2015 event is March 1, 2015; there is $15 application fee.

BUSINESS OF WRITING INTERNATIONAL SUMMIT

P.O. Box 768, Simpsonville KY 40204. (502)303-7926. **E-mail:** larry@tbowt.com. **Website:** www.busines sofwritingsummit.com. **Contact:** Larry DeKay or Peggy DeKay. Estab. 2012. Learn how to grow your book sales and build your author platform at this annual 3-day event for writers and authors. The summit brings together industry experts from around the world and features multiple programming tracks, including publishing, book promotion and marketing, e-books and social media, and the craft of writing. More than 2 dozen exciting sessions to choose from each year, with great food, outstanding networking opportunities, and more.

COSTS $200-300.

ACCOMMODATIONS An official hotel is designated each year for attendees that offers a special money-saving room rate and is within close proximity of the event. Details available online.

ADDITIONAL INFORMATION This is a fun, exciting and energy-filled event which allows unprecedented access to speakers and exhibitors. Event organizers Larry and Peggy DeKay pride themselves on creating a warm and hospitable environment where attendees feel welcome and have the opportunity to make new and lasting friendships and business relationships.

BYRDCLIFFE ARTS COLONY

34 Tinker St., Woodstock NY 12498. (845)679-2079. **Fax:** (845)679-4529. **E-mail:** info@woodstockguild. org. **Website:** www.woodstockguild.org. Estab. 1991. Offers 1-month residencies June-September. Open to composers, writers, and visual artists. Accommodates 15 at 1 time. Personal living quarters include single rooms, shared baths, and kitchen facilities. Offers separate private studio space. Composers must provide their own keyboard with headphone. Activities include open studio and readings for the Woodstock community at the end of each session. The Woodstock Guild, parent organization, offers music and dance performances and gallery exhibits.

COSTS $600/month; fellowships available. Residents are responsible for own meals and transportation. $40 application fee.

ADDITIONAL INFORMATION Deadline: March of each year. (2015 deadline was March 20.) Online application; visit woodstockguild.org for submission guidelines. Download application fee and online payment from website.

CALIFORNIA CRIME WRITERS CONFERENCE

Co-sponsored by Sisters in Crime/Los Angeles and the Southern California Chapter of Mystery Writers of America, **E-mail:** sistersincrimela@gmail.com. **Website:** www.ccwconference.org. Estab. 1995. Biennial. 2015 conference dates: June 6-7. Average attendance: 200. Two-day conference on mystery and crime writing. Offers craft, forensic, industry news, marketing, and career-buildings sessions, 2 keynote speakers, author, editor, and agent panels and book signings. 2015 Keynote speakers are Charlaine Harris and Anne Perry. Breakfast and lunch both days included.

ADDITIONAL INFORMATION Conference information is available at www.ccwconference.org.

CAPE COD WRITERS CENTER ANNUAL CONFERENCE

P.O. Box 408, Osterville MA 02655. **E-mail:** writers@ capecodwriterscenter.org. **Website:** www.capecod writerscenter.org. **Contact:** Nancy Rubin Stuart, executive director. Duration: 3 days; held during first week in August. Offers workshops in fiction, commercial fiction, nonfiction, poetry, writing for children, memoir, pitching your book, screenwriting, digital communications, and getting published. There are ms evaluation and mentoring sessions with faculty.

COSTS Vary, depending on the number of courses selected.

ACCOMMODATIONS Held at Resort and Conference Center of Hyannis, Hyannis, MA.

CAPON SPRINGS WRITERS' WORKSHOP

2836 Westbrook Dr., Cincinnati OH 45211-7617. (513)481-9884. **E-mail:** whbeckman@gmail.com. **Website:** wendyonwriting.com. Estab. 2000. Event will be in October 2015. Conference duration: 2.5 days. Covers fiction, creative nonfiction, and publishing basics. Conference is held at Capon Springs and Farms Resort, a secluded 5,000-acre mountain resort in West Virginia.

COSTS Check website.

ACCOMMODATIONS Facility has swimming, hiking, fishing, tennis, badminton, volleyball, basketball, ping pong, etc. A 9-hole golf course is available for an additional fee.

ADDITIONAL INFORMATION Brochures available for SASE. Inquire via e-mail.

CAT WRITERS' ASSOCIATION ANNUAL WRITERS CONFERENCE

66 Adams St., Jamestown NY 14701. **E-mail:** lorie huston@pet-health-care-gazette.com. **Website:** www.catwriters.org. **Contact:** President Lorie Huston, DVM. Conference in the fall. The Cat Writers' Association holds an annual conference at varying locations around the US. The agenda for the conference is filled with seminars, editor appointments, an autograph party, networking breakfast, reception and annual awards banquet, as well as the annual meeting of the association. As of 2014, the event merged with BarkWorld Pet Expo to present BarkWorld/Meow-World. See website for details.

CELEBRATION OF SOUTHERN LITERATURE

Southern Lit Alliance, 3069 S. Broad St., Suite 2, Chattanooga TN 37408-3056. (423)267-1218. **Fax:** (866)483-6831. **E-mail:** srobinson@southernlitalliance.org. **Website:** www.southernlitalliance.org. **Contact:** Susan Robinson. "The Celebration of Southern Literature stands out because of its unique collaboration with the Fellowship of Southern Writers, an organization founded by towering literary figures like Eudora Welty, Cleanth Brooks, Walker Percy, and Robert Penn Warren to recognize and encourage literature in the South. The 2015 celebration marked 26 years since the Fellowship selected Chattanooga for its headquarters and chose to collaborate with the Celebration of Southern Literature. The Fellowship awards 11 literary prizes and induct new members, making this event the place to discover up-and-coming voices in Southern literature. The Southern Lit Alliance's Celebration of Southern Literature attracts more than 1,000 readers and writers from all over the US. It strives to maintain an informal atmosphere where conversations will thrive, inspired by a common passion for the written word. The Southern Lit Alliance (formerly The Arts & Education Council) started as 1 of 12 pilot agencies founded by a Ford Foundation grant in 1952. The Alliance is the only organization of the 12 still in existence. The Southern Lit Alliance celebrates southern writers and readers through community education and innovative literary arts experiences."

CENTRAL OHIO FICTION WRITERS ANNUAL CONFERENCE

A chapter of the Romance Writers of America, P.O. Box 4213, Newark OH 43058. **E-mail:** susan_gee_heino@yahoo.com; msgigimorgan@gmail.com. **Website:** www.cofw.org. **Contact:** Susan Gee Heino, current president; Gigi Morgan, conference chair. Estab. 1990. Conferences currently planned for even years only (2014, 2016). Events held in central Ohio in the greater Columbus area. The conference hosts up to 100 authors and industry professionals, has a list of outstanding breakout sessions, and brings in agents and editors.

COSTS Costs will be decided as the next event draws near.

CHICAGO WRITERS CONFERENCE

E-mail: ines@chicagowritersconference.org; mare@chicagowritersconference.org. **Website:** chicagowritersconference.org. **Contact:** Mare Swallow. Estab. 2011. This conference happens every year in October. Find them on Twitter at @ChiWritersConf. The conference brings together a variety of publishing professionals (agents, editors, authors) and brings together several Chicago literary, writing, and bookselling groups. The conference often sells out. Past speakers have included *New York Times* bestselling author Sara Paretsky, children's author Allan Woodrow, YA author Erica O'Rourke, novelist Eric Charles May, and novelist Loretta Nyhan.

CHRISTOPHER NEWPORT UNIVERSITY WRITERS' CONFERENCE & WRITING CONTEST

(757)269-4368. **E-mail:** eleanor.taylor@cnu.edu. **Website:** www.facebook.com/cnuwriters. Estab. 1981. Conference held in the first few months of each year. This is a working conference. Presentations made by editors, agents, fiction writers, poets, and more. Breakout sessions in fiction, nonfiction, poetry, juvenile fiction, and publishing. Previous panels included "Publishing," "Proposal Writing," "Internet Research."
ACCOMMODATIONS Provides list of area hotels.
ADDITIONAL INFORMATION 2016 conference dates are set for May 6-7.

CLARKSVILLE WRITERS CONFERENCE

1123 Madison St., Clarksville TN 37040. (931)551-8870. **E-mail:** artsandheritage@cdelightband.net; burawac@apsu.edu. **E-mail:** artsandheritage@cdelightband.net; burawac@apsu.edu. **Website:** www.artsandheritage.us/writers. **Contact:** Ellen Kanervo. Annual conference held in the summer at Austin Peay State University. The conference features a variety of presentations on fiction, nonfiction, and more. Past presenting authors include Tom Franklin, Frye Gaillard, William Gay, Susan Gregg Gilmore, Will Campbell, John Seigenthaler Sr., Alice Randall, George Singleton, Alanna Nash, and Robert Hicks. Our presentations and workshops are valuable to writers and interesting to readers.
COSTS Costs available online; prices vary depending on how long attendees stay and if they attend the banquet dinner.
ADDITIONAL INFORMATION Multiple literary agents are flown in to the event every year to meet with writers and take pitches.

THE COLRAIN POETRY MANUSCRIPT CONFERENCE

Concord Poetry Center, 40 Stow St., Concord MA 01742. **Website:** www.colrainpoetry.com. Estab. 2000. "Colrain is the original, one-of-a-kind ms conference. Faculty includes nationally-renowned poet-editors and publishers. Work with the best for the best results. Our unique, realistic method of ms evaluation sets poets with a ms-in-progress on a path toward publication. Poets also get a look into the publication

world and make important contacts with leading editors, teachers, and publishers."
ACCOMMODATIONS The Colrain Practicum is April 25-26, 2015 in Massachusetts. The Colarin Classic is May 15-18, 2015 in Vermont. The second Colrain Classic is June 5-8, 2015 in New Mexico.
ADDITIONAL INFORMATION Details, application, and registration form available on website.

CONFERENCE FOR WRITERS & ILLUSTRATORS OF CHILDREN'S BOOKS

Book Passage, 51 Tamal Vista Blvd., Corte Madera CA 94925. (415)927-0960, ext. 234. **E-mail:** lberkler@bookpassage.com. **Website:** www.bookpassage.com. Conference for writers and illustrators geared toward beginner and intermediate levels. Sessions cover such topics as the nuts and bolts of writing and illustrating, publisher's spotlight, market trends, developing characters, finding voice in your writing, and the author/agent relationship. Held each summer with a conference length of 4 days. Includes opening night dinner, 3 lunches and a closing reception. 2015 dates: June 18-21.

CONNECTICUT WRITING WORKSHOP

Website: www.connecticutwritingworkshop.com. The 2015 event is set for Friday, November 13, 2015. Organized by Writing Day Workshops. The workshop is a one-day, all-day "How to Get Published" conference with instructional sessions and panels. Multiple literary agents are in attendance at the workshop to meet with writers and hear pitches.
COSTS Early-bird tuition is $129; later tuition is $149; agent meetings are $29 per appointment.
ACCOMMODATIONS Rooms available at the event hotel.
ADDITIONAL INFORMATION Query critique options available. Check the website for contact and registration information.

CRESTED BUTTE WRITERS CONFERENCE

P.O. Box 1361, Crested Butte CO 81224. **E-mail:** coordinator@conf.crestedbuttewriters.org. **Website:** www.crestedbuttewriters.org/conf.php. **Contact:** Barbara Crawford or Theresa Rizzo, co-coordinators. Estab. 2006. Annual conference held in June.
COSTS $330 nonmembers; $300 members; $297 Early Bird; The Sandy Writing Contest Finalist $280; and groups of 5 or more $280.
ACCOMMODATIONS The conference is held at The Elevation Hotel, located at the Crested Butte Moun-

tain Resort at the base of the ski mountain. The quaint historic town lies nestled in a stunning mountain valley 3 short miles from the resort area of Mt. Crested Butte. A free bus runs frequently between the 2 towns. The closest airport is 30 miles away, in Gunnison. The conference website lists 3 lodging options besides rooms at the event facility. All condos, motels, and hotel options offer special conference rates. No special travel arrangements are made through the conference; however, information for car rental from Gunnison airport or the Alpine Express shuttle is listed on the online conference FAQ page.

ADDITIONAL INFORMATION "Our conference workshops address a wide variety of writing craft and business. Our most popular workshop is Our First Pages Readings—with a twist. Agents and editors read opening pages volunteered by attendees-with a few best selling authors' openings mixed in. Think the A/E can identify the bestsellers? Not so much. Each year one of our attendees has been mistaken for a bestseller and obviously garnered requests from some on the panel. Writers may request additional information by e-mail."

DESERT DREAMS CONFERENCE: REALIZING THE DREAM

P.O. Box 27407, Tempe AZ 85285. **E-mail:** desertdreams@desertroserwa.org; desertdreamsconference@gmail.com. **Website:** www.desertroserwa.org. **Contact:** Conference coordinator. Estab. 1986. Conference held every 2 years (even years). 2016 dates: April 7-10. Average attendance: 250. Desert Dreams Writers' Conference provides authors of all skill levels, from beginner to multi-published, with the tools necessary to take their writing to the next level. Sessions will include general writing, career development, genre-specific, agent/publisher spotlights, as well as an agent/editor panel. There will also be one-on-one appointments with editors or agents, a book signing, and keynote addresses.

ADDITIONAL INFORMATION Agents and editors participate in conference.

DETROIT WORKING WRITERS ANNUAL WRITERS CONFERENCE

Detroit Working Writers, Box 82395, Rochester MI 48308. **E-mail:** conference@detworkingwriters.org. **Website:** dww-writers-conference.org. Estab. 1961. 2015 dates: May 16. The theme in 2015 was "Craft: Getting it Write." Location: MSU Management Education Center, Troy, Michigan. Conference is 1 day, with breakfast, luncheon and keynote speaker, 4 breakout sessions, and three choices of workshop sessions. Much more info available online. Detroit Working Writers was founded on June 5, 1900, as the Detroit Press Club, The City of Detroit's first press club. Today, more than a century later, it is a 501 (c)(6) organization, and the State of Michigan's oldest writer's organization. There are 5 writing competitions with cash prizes in different categories: young adult/new adult, creative nonfiction, poetry, children's, adult fiction. Registration and Competition entry begins January 5, 2015, online.

COSTS Costs $65-155, depending on early bird registration and membership status within the organization.

EAST TEXAS CHRISTIAN WRITERS CONFERENCE

The School of Humanities, Dr. Jerry L. Summers, Dean, Scarborough Hall, East Texas Baptist University, 1 Tiger Dr., Marshall TX 75670. (903)923-2083. **E-mail:** jhopkins@etbu.edu; contest@etbu.edu. **Website:** www.etbu.edu/News/CWC. **Contact:** Elizabeth Hoyer, humanities secretary. Estab. 2002. Annual conference held the last weekend in October. 2015 dates: October 30-31, 2015. Duration: 2 days (Friday and Saturday). Average attendance: 160. Site: East Texas Baptist University. "Primarily, we are interested in promoting quality Christian writing that would be accepted in mainstream publishing." Past conference themes were Back to Basics, Getting Started in Fiction, Writers & Agents, Writing Short Stories, Writing for Newspapers, The Significance of Style, Writing Fillers and Articles, Writing Devotionals, Blogging for Writers, Christian Nonfiction, Inspirational Writing, E-Publishing, Publishing on Demand, and Editor and Author Relations. Conference offers contact, conversation, and exchange of ideas with other aspiring writers; outstanding presentations and workshop experiences with established authors, agents, editors, and publishers; potential publishing and writing opportunities; networking with other writers with related interests, acquisitions editors; promotion of both craft and faith; and one-on-one consultations with agents, editors, and publishers. Past conference speakers/workshop leaders were Marlene Bagnull, Bill Keith, Mary Lou Redding, Marie Chapian, Vickie Phelps, Michael Farris, Pamela Dowd, Donn Taylor, Terry Burns, Donna Walker-Nixon, Lexie Smith,

Marv Knox, Don Piper Jim Pence, Andrea Chevalier, Cecil Murphey, and Sally Stuart. Offers an advanced track, a beginner's track, and a teen track. There is a writing contest with cash awards for winners. Partial scholarships available for students only.

ACCOMMODATIONS Visit website for a list of local hotels offering a discounted rate.

WRITERS IN PARADISE

Eckerd College, 4200 54th Ave. South, St. Petersburg FL 33711. (727) 864-7994. **Fax:** (727) 864-7575. **E-mail:** wip@eckerd.edu. **Website:** writersinparadise. eckerd.edu/. Estab. 2005. Annual. January. 2015 dates: Jan 16-23. Conference duration: 8 days. Average attendance: 84 maximum. Workshop. Offers college credit. "Writers in Paradise Conference offers workshop classes in fiction (novel and short story), poetry, and nonfiction. Working closely with our award-winning faculty, students will have stimulating opportunities to ask questions and learn valuable skills from fellow students and authors at the top of their form. Most importantly, the intimate size and secluded location of the Writers in Paradise experience allows you the time and opportunity to share your mss, critique one another's work, and discuss the craft of writing with experts and peers who can help guide you to the next level." Previous faculty includes Andre Dubus III (*House of Sand and Fog*), Michael Koryta (*So Cold the River*), Dennis Lehane (*The Given Day*), Laura Lippman (*I'd Know You Anywhere*), Seth Fishman (literary agent), Johnny Temple (Akashic Books), and more." Editors and agents attend the conference.

ADDITIONAL INFORMATION Application (December deadline) materials are required of all attendees.

ERMA BOMBECK WRITERS' WORKSHOP

University of Dayton, 300 College Park, Dayton OH 45469. **E-mail:** erma@udayton.edu. **Website:** humorwriters.org. **Contact:** Teri Rizvi. This is a specialized writing conference for writers of humor (books, articles, essays, blogs, film/TV). It happens every 2 years. The 2016 conference dates are March 31-April 2. The Bombeck Workshop is the only one in the country devoted to both humor and human interest writing. Through the workshop, the University of Dayton and the Bombeck family honor one of America's most celebrated storytellers and humorists. Over the past decade, the workshop has attracted such household names as Dave Barry, Art Buchwald, Phil Donahue,

Nancy Cartwright, Don Novello, Garrison Keillor, Gail Collins, Connie Schultz, Adriana Trigiani and Alan Zweibel. The workshop draws approximately 350 writers from around the country and typically sells out very quickly, so don't wait once registration opens.

ADDITIONAL INFORMATION Connect with the event on social media: facebook.com/ermabombeck, and @ebww.

FLATHEAD RIVER WRITERS CONFERENCE

P.O. Box 7711, Kalispell MT 59904-7711. (406)881-4066. **E-mail:** answers@authorsoftheflathead.org. **Website:** www.authorsoftheflathead.org/conference. asp. Estab. 1990. Two-day conference packed with energizing speakers. Highlights include 2 literary agents who will review 12 ms one-on-one with the first 24 paid attendees requesting this opportunity, a synopsis writing workshop, a screenwriting workshop, and more.

COSTS Check the website for updated cost information and more.

ACCOMMODATIONS Rooms are available at a discounted rate.

ADDITIONAL INFORMATION Watch website for additional speakers and other details. Register early as seating is limited.

FLORIDA CHRISTIAN WRITERS CONFERENCE

530 Lake Kathryn Circle, Casselberry FL 32707. (386)295-3902. **E-mail:** FloridaCWC@aol.com. **Website:** floridacwc.net. **Contact:** Eva Marie Everson & Mark T. Hancock. Estab. 1988. Annual conference during the last Wednesday of February to the first Sunday in March at Lake Yale Conference Center, Leesburg, FL. Workshops/classes geared toward all levels, from beginners to published authors. Open to students. FCWC offers 6 keynote addresses, 8 continuing classes, and a number of 3-hour workshops, 1-hour workshops, and after hours workshops. FCWC brings in the finest the industry as to offer in editors, agents, freelancers, and marketing/media experts. Additionally, FCWC provides a book proposal studio and a pitch studio. For those flying in to Orlando or Sanford, FCWC provides a shuttle from and to the conference center. Accommodations for both single and double-room occupancy. Meals provided. Awards banquet, Saturday p.m. Advanced critique services offered. Scholarships offered. For more information or to register, go to the conference website.

FLORIDA ROMANCE WRIITERS FUN IN THE SUN CONFERENCE

Florida Romance Writers, P.O. Box 550562, Fort Lauderdale FL 33355. **E-mail:** FRWfuninthesun@yahoo. com. **Website:** frwfuninthesunmain.blogspot.com. Estab. 1986. "Cruise With Your Muse 2015" happens Feb. 5-9, 2015. Conference with the Florida Romance Writers and *New York Times* bestselling author and keynote speaker, Julia Quinn, a slue of talented writers, and wonderful industry professionals. Inspiring workshops and panels will keep your muse buzzing with plot turns. For those with a well behaved muse who continues to do her job, schedule an appointment with our guests: Nalini Akolekar with Spencerhill Associates, Ltd., Beth Campbell with Bookends, LLC, Leah Hultenschmidt with Grand Central Publishing, Rhonda Penders with The Wild Rose Press, Peter Senftleben with Kensington Books, or Deb Werksman with Sourcebooks. Also, take advantage of the opportunities to build a website and create a marketing plan while at sea. Space is limited.

FLORIDA WRITING WORKSHOPS

Website: www.floridawritingworkshops.com. Estab. 2015. The 2016 calendar year includes events in the Tampa area (Friday, Match 25, 2016) and the Fort Lauderdale area (Saturday, March 26, 2016) at hotel locations. Organized by Writing Day Workshops. The workshops are separate yet identical "How to Get Published" one-day conferences with instructional sessions all day. Multiple literary agents are in attendance at both events to meet with writers and hear pitches.

COSTS Early-bird tuition is $129; later tuition is $149; agent meetings are $29 per appointment.

ACCOMMODATIONS Rooms available at the event hotels.

ADDITIONAL INFORMATION Query critique options available. Check the website for contact and registration information.

● GENEVA WRITERS CONFERENCE

Geneva Writers Group, Switzerland. **E-mail:** info@ GenevaWritersGroup.org. **Website:** www.genevaw ritersgroup.org. Estab. 1993. Biennial conference (even years) held at Webster University in Bellevue/ Geneva, Switzerland. (The 2014 dates were January 31-February 2.) Conference duration: 2.5 days, welcoming more than 200 writers from around the world. Speakers and presenters have included Peter Ho Davies, Jane Alison, Russell Celyn Jones, Patricia Hampl,

Robert Root, Brett Lott, Dinty W. Moore, Naomi Shihab Nye, Jo Shapcott, Wallis Wilde Menozzi, Susan Tiberghien, Jane Dystel, Laura Longrigg, and Colin Harrison.

GREATER LEHIGH VALLEY WRITERS GROUP 'THE WRITE STUFF' WRITERS CONFERENCE

3650 Nazareth Pike, PMB #136, Bethlehem PA 18020-1115. **E-mail:** writestuffchair@glvwg.org. **Website:** www.glvwg.org. Estab. 1993. 2015 dates: March 26-28. Annual conference.

ADDITIONAL INFORMATION "The Writer's Flash contest is judged by conference participants. Write 100 words or less in fiction, creative nonfiction, or poetry. Brochures available in January by SASE, or by phone, e-mail, or on website. Accepts inquiries by SASE, e-mail or phone. Agents and editors attend conference. For updated info refer to the website. Greater Lehigh Valley Writers Group hosts a friendly conference and gives you the most for your money. Breakout rooms offer craft topics, business of publishing, editor and agent panels. Book fair with book signing by published authors and presenters."

GREEN MOUNTAIN WRITERS CONFERENCE

47 Hazel St., Rutland VT 05701. (802)236-6133. **E-mail:** ydaley@sbcglobal.net. **E-mail:** yvonnedaley@ me.com. **Website:** vermontwriters.com. **Contact:** Yvonne Daley, director. Estab. 1998. "Annual conference held in the summer. Covers fiction, creative nonfiction, poetry, young adult fiction, journalism, nature writing, essay, memoir, personal narrative, and biography. Held at The Mountain Top Inn and Resort, a beautiful lakeside inn located in Chittenden, VT. Speakers have included Grace Paley, Ruth Stone, Howard Frank Mosher, Chris Bohjalian, Yvonne Daley, David Huddle, David Budbill, Jeffrey Lent, Verandah Porche, Tom Smith, and Chuck Clarino."

COSTS $500 before May 1; $550 minimum after May 1. Partial scholarships are available

ACCOMMODATIONS Dramatically reduced rates at The Mountain Top Inn and Resort for attendees. Close to other area hotels, B&Bs in Rutland County, Vermont.

ADDITIONAL INFORMATION Participants' mss can be read and commented on at a cost. Sponsors contests. Conference publishes a literary magazine featuring work of participants. Brochures available on website or e-mail. "We offer the opportunity to learn from some of the nation's best writers at a small, supportive conference in a lakeside setting that allows one-to-one feedback. Participants often continue to correspond and share work after conferences."

GULF COAST WRITERS CONFERENCE

P.O. Box 35038, Panama City FL 32412. (800)628-6028. **E-mail:** PulpwoodPress@gmail.com. **Website:** www.gulfcoastwritersconference.com. Estab. 1999. Annual conference held in September in Panama City, Fla. Conference duration: 1 day. Average attendance: 100+. This conference is deliberately small and writer-centric with an affordable attendance price. (As of this listing being updated, the conference is completely free.) Speakers include writers, editors and agents. Cricket Freeman of the August Agency is often in attendance. A former keynote speaker was mystery writer Michael Connelly.

HAIKU NORTH AMERICA CONFERENCE

1275 Fourth St., PMB 365, Santa Rosa CA 95404. **E-mail:** welchm@aol.com. **Website:** www.haiku northamerica.com. **Contact:** Michael Dylan Welch. Estab. 1991. Biennial conference. 2015 dates: Oct 15-18, 2015. Haiku North America (HNA) is the largest and oldest gathering of haiku poets in the US and Canada. There are no membership fees and HNA provides breaking news and interaction at the HNA blog. All haiku poets and interested parties are welcome. HNA is a long weekend of papers, panels, workshops, readings, performances, book sales, and much socialization with fellow poets, translators, scholars, editors, and publishers. Both established and aspiring haiku poets are welcome.

COSTS Typically around $200, including a banquet and a conference anthology

ACCOMMODATIONS Accommodations at discounted hotels nearby are an additional cost. Information available on website as details are finalized closer to the conference date.

HAMPTON ROADS WRITERS CONFERENCE

P.O. Box 56228, Virginia Beach VA 23456. **E-mail:** hrwriters@cox.net. **Website:** hamptonroadswriters. org. 2015 dates: Sept. 17-20, 2015. Workshops cover fiction, nonfiction, memoir, poetry, and the business of getting published. A bookshop, 3 free contests with cash prizes, free evening networking social, and many networking opportunities will be available. Multiple literary agents are in attendance each year to meet with writers and hear 10-minute pitches. Much more information available on the website.

COSTS Maximum of $255. Costs vary. There are discounts for members, for early bird registration, for students and more

HIGHLAND SUMMER CONFERENCE

Box 7014, Radford University, Radford VA 24142-7014. **E-mail:** tburriss@radford.edu; rbderrick@radford.edu. **Website:** tinyurl.com/q8z8ej9. **Contact:** Dr. Theresa Burriss, Ruth Derrick. Estab. 1978. 2015 dates: June 15-19. The Highland Summer Writers' Conference is a 4-day lecture-seminar workshop combination conducted by well-known guest writers. It offers the opportunity to study and practice creative and expository writing within the context of regional culture. The course is graded on Pass/Fail basis for undergraduates and letter grades for graduate students. It may be taken twice for credit. The evening readings are free and open to the public. Services at a reduced rate for continuing education credits or to simply participate.

HIGHLIGHTS FOUNDATION FOUNDERS WORKSHOPS

814 Court St., Honesdale PA 18431. (570)253-1122. **Fax:** (570)253-0179. **E-mail:** klbrown@highlights foundation.org. **E-mail:** jo.lloy@highlightsfounda tion.org. **Website:** highlightsfoundation.org. **Contact:** Kent L. Brown, Jr. Estab. 2000. Offers more than three dozen workshops per year. Conference duration: 3-7 days. Average attendance: limited to 10-14. Genre specific workshops and retreats on children's writing: fiction, nonfiction, poetry, promotions. "Our goal is to improve, over time, the quality of literature for children by educating future generations of children's authors." Highlights Founders' home in Boyds Mills, Pa.

COSTS Prices vary based on workshop. Check website for details.

ACCOMMODATIONS Coordinates pickup at local airport. Offers overnight accommodations. Participants stay in guest cabins on the wooded grounds surrounding Highlights Founders' home adjacent to the house/conference center.

ADDITIONAL INFORMATION Some workshops require pre-workshop assignment. Brochure available for SASE, by e-mail, on website, by phone, by fax. Accepts inquiries by phone, fax, e-mail, SASE. Editors attend conference. "Applications will be reviewed and accepted on a first-come, first-served basis, applicants must demonstrate specific experience in writing area of workshop they are applying for—writing samples are required for many of the workshops."

HOUSTON WRITERS GUILD CONFERENCE

P.O. Box 42255, Houston TX 77242. (281)736-7168. E-mail: HoustonWritersGuild@Hotmail.com. **Website:** houstonwritersguild.org/annual-conference. 2015 dates: Saturday, April 24-26. This annual conference, organized by the Houston Writers Guild, happens in the spring, and has concurrent sessions and tracks on the craft and business of writing. Each year, multiple agents are in attendance taking pitches from writers. The 2015 keynote speaker was Jane Friedman.

COSTS Costs are different for members and non-members. Costs depend on how many days and events you sign up for.

ADDITIONAL INFORMATION There is a writing contest at the event. There is also a for-pay pre-conference workshop the day before the conference.

IDAHO WRITERS LEAGUE WRITERS' CONFERENCE

601 W. 75 S., Blackfoot ID 83221-6153. (208)684-4200. **Website:** www.idahowritersleague.com. Estab. 1940. Annual floating conference, usually held in September. This conference has at least one agent in attendance every year, along with other writers and presenters.

COSTS A minimum of $145, depending on early bird pricing and membership. Check the website for updates on cost.

INDIANA UNIVERSITY WRITERS' CONFERENCE

464 Ballantine Hall, 1020 E. Kirkwood Ave., Bloomington IN 47405-7103. (812)855-1877. **Fax:** (812)855-9535. **E-mail:** writecon@indiana.edu. **Website:** www.indiana.edu/~writecon. Estab. 1940. Annual. Conference/workshops held in May. 2015 dates: May 30-June 3. Average attendance: 115. "The Indiana University Writers' Conference believes in a craft-based teaching of fiction writing. We emphasize an exploration of creativity through a variety of approaches, offering workshop-based craft discussions, classes focusing on technique, and talks about the careers and concerns of a writing life."

ACCOMMODATIONS Information on accommodations available on website.

ADDITIONAL INFORMATION Connect on Twitter at @iuwritecon.

INTERNATIONAL MUSIC CAMP CREATIVE WRITING WORKSHOP

111 11th Ave. SW, Minot ND 58701. (701)838-8472. **Fax:** (701)838-1351. **E-mail:** info@internationalmu siccamp.com. **Website:** www.internationalmusic camp.com. **Contact:** Christine Baumann and Tim Baumann, camp directors. Estab. 1956. Annual. Conference held in June. Average attendance: 35. "The workshop offers students the opportunity to refine their skills in thinking, composing, and writing in an environment that is conducive to positive reinforcement. In addition to writing poems, essays, and stories, individuals are encouraged to work on their own area of interest with conferencing and feedback from the course instructor." Site: International Peace Garden on the border between the US and Canada. "Similar to a university campus, several dormitories, classrooms, lecture halls, and cafeteria provide the perfect site for such a workshop. The beautiful and picturesque International Peace Garden provides additional inspiration to creative thinking." Instructors: Melissa Cournia & Andrea Nell.

COSTS $395, includes tuition, room and board. Early bird registration (postmarked by May 1) is $380.

ACCOMMODATIONS Airline and depot shuttles are available upon request. Housing is included in the fee.

ADDITIONAL INFORMATION Conference information is available on the website. Welcomes questions via e-mail.

🌎 INTERNATIONAL WOMEN'S FICTION FESTIVAL

Via Cappuccini 8E, Matera 75100 Italy. (39)0835-312044. **Fax:** (39)0835-312093. **E-mail:** e.jennings@womensfictionfestival.com. **Website:** www.wom ensfictionfestival.com. **Contact:** Elizabeth Jennings. Estab. 2004. Annual conference usually held in September. 2015 dates: Sept. 24-27. Conference duration: 3.5 days. Average attendance: 100. International writers' conference with a strong focus on fiction and a strong focus on marketing to international markets. Numerous literary agents and editors are in attendance—both from the US and Europe.

COSTS 220 euros.

ACCOMMODATIONS Le Monacelle, a restored 17th century convent. Conference travel agency will find reasonably priced accommodation. A paid shuttle is available from the Bari Airport to the hotel in Matera.

IOWA SUMMER WRITING FESTIVAL

The University of Iowa, C215 Seashore Hall, University of Iowa, Iowa City IA 52242. (319)335-4160. **Fax:** (319)335-4743. **E-mail:** iswfestival@uiowa.edu. **Website:** uiowa.edu/~iswfest. Estab. 1987. Annual festival held in June and July. 2015 event will have 138 workshops with 72 instructors. Conference duration: Workshops are 1 week or a weekend. Average attendance: Limited to 12 people/class, with over 1,500 participants throughout the summer. "We offer courses across the genres: novel, short story, poetry, essay, memoir, humor, travel, playwriting, screenwriting, writing for children, and women's writing. Held at the University of Iowa campus." Speakers have included Marvin Bell, Lan Samantha Chang, John Dalton, Hope Edelman, Katie Ford, Patricia Foster, Bret Anthony Johnston, Barbara Robinette Moss, among others.

ACCOMMODATIONS Accommodations available at area hotels. Information on overnight accommodations available by phone or on website.

ADDITIONAL INFORMATION Brochures are available in February. Inquire via e-mail or on website.

IWWG ANNUAL CONFERENCE

International Women's Writing Guild Conference, International Women's Writing Guild, P.O. Box 810, Gracie Station, New York NY 10028. (212)737-7536. **Fax:** (212)737-9469. **E-mail:** iwwgquestions@gmail.com. **Website:** www.iwwg.org. Writer and illustrator workshops geared toward all levels. Offers over 50 different workshops—some are for children's book writers and illustrators. Also sponsors other events throughout the US. Annual workshops. Workshops held every summer for a week. Length of each session: 90 minutes; sessions take place for an entire week. Registration limited to 500. Write for more information. The 2015 spring conference was March 15 in Los Angeles.

JACKSON HOLE WRITERS CONFERENCE

PO Box 1974, Jackson WY 83001. (307)413-3332. **E-mail:** nicole@jacksonholewritersconference.com. **Website:** jacksonholewritersconference.com. Estab. 1991. Annual conference held in late June. Conference duration: 4 days. Average attendance: 110. Covers fiction, creative nonfiction, and young adult and offers ms critiques from authors, agents, and editors.

Agents in attendance will take pitches from writers. Paid manuscript critique programs are available.

COSTS $365 if registered by May 12. Accompanying teen writer: $175. Pre-Conference Writing Workshop: $150.

ADDITIONAL INFORMATION Held at the Center for the Arts in Jackson, Wyoming and online.

JAMES RIVER WRITERS CONFERENCE

2319 East Broad St., Richmond VA 23223. (804)433-3790. **Fax:** (804)291-1466. **E-mail:** info@jamesriverwriters.com; fallconference@jamesriverwriters.com. **Website:** www.jamesriverwriters.com. Estab. 2003. Annual conference held in October. The event has master classes, agent pitching, editor pitching, critiques, sessions, panels, and more. Previous attending agents have included Kimiko Nakamura, Kaylee Davis, Peter Knapp, and more.

COSTS $240-290.

ACCOMMODATIONS Hilton Garden Inn, 501 E. Broad St.

KACHEMAK BAY WRITERS' CONFERENCE

Kenai Peninsula College - Kachemak Bay Campus, 533 East Pioneer Ave., Homer AK 99603. (907)235-7743. **E-mail:** iyconf@uaa.alaska.edu. **Website:** writersconference.uaa.alaska.edu. Annual writers conference held in June. 2015 dates: June 12-16. 2015 keynote speaker was Andre Dubus III. Sponsored by Kachemak Bay Campus-Kenai Peninsula College / UAA. This nationally recognized writing conference features workshops, readings and panel presentations in fiction, poetry, nonfiction, and the business of writing. There are "open mic" sessions for conference registrants; evening readings open to the public; agent/editor consultations, and more.

COSTS See the website. Some scholarships available.

ACCOMMODATIONS Homer is 225 miles south of Anchorage, Alaska on the southern tip of the Kenai Peninsula and the shores of Kachemak Bay. There are multiple hotels in the area.

KENTUCKY WOMEN WRITERS CONFERENCE

University of Kentucky College of Arts & Sciences, 232 E. Maxwell St., Lexington KY 40506. (859)257-2874. **E-mail:** kentuckywomenwriters@gmail.com. **Website:** kentuckywomenwriters.org. **Contact:** Julie Wrinn, director. Estab. 1979. Conference held in second or third weekend of September. The 2015 dates were Sept. 11-12. The location is the Carnegie Center for Literacy in Lexington, Kentucky. Conference duration: 2 days. Average attendance: 150-200. Conference covers poetry, fiction, creative nonfiction, playwriting. Writing workshops, panels, and readings featuring contemporary women writers. The 2015 conference featured novelist and short story writer Anne Beattie as its keynote speaker.

COSTS $175 early bird discount, $200 thereafter; $125 without workshop; $30 for students; includes boxed lunch on Friday; $20 for writers' reception. Other meals and accommodations are not included.

ADDITIONAL INFORMATION Sponsors prizes in poetry ($200), fiction ($200), nonfiction ($200), playwriting ($500), and spoken word ($500). Winners also invited to read during the conference. Pre-registration opens May 1.

KENTUCKY WRITERS CONFERENCE

Southern Kentucky Book Fest, Knicely Conference Center, 2355 Nashville Road, Bowling Green KY 42101. (270)745-4502. **E-mail:** kristie.lowry@wku.edu. **Website:** www.sokybookfest.org/KYWriter sConf. **Contact:** Kristie Lowry. This event is entirely free to the public. 2015 date: April 17. Duration: 1 day. Precedes the Southern Kentucky Book Fest the next day. Authors who will be participating in the Book Fest on Saturday will give attendees at the writers' conference the benefit of their wisdom on Friday. Free workshops on a variety of writing topics will be presented during this day-long event. Sessions run for 75 minutes and the day begins at 9 a.m. and ends at 3:30 p.m. The conference is open to anyone who would like to attend, including high school students, college students, teachers, and the general public.

KENYON REVIEW WRITERS WORKSHOP

Kenyon College, Gambier OH 43022. (740)427-5207. **Fax:** (740)427-5417. **E-mail:** kenyonreview@kenyon.edu; writers@kenyonreview.org. **Website:** www.kenyonreview.org. **Contact:** Anna Duke Reach, director. Estab. 1990. Annual 8-day workshop held in June. Participants apply in poetry, fiction, creative nonfiction, literary hybrid/book arts or writing online, and then participate in intensive daily workshops which focus on the generation and revision of significant new work. Held on the campus of Kenyon College in the rural village of Gambier, Ohio. Workshop leaders have included David Baker, Carl Phillips, Mary Szybist, Rebecca McClanahan, Dinty Moore, Caitlin Horrocks, Lee K. Abbott, and Nancy Zafris.

COSTS $1,995; includes tuition, room and board.

ACCOMMODATIONS The workshop operates a shuttle to and from Gambier and the airport in Columbus, Ohio. Offers overnight accommodations. Participants are housed in Kenyon College student housing. The cost is covered in the tuition.

ADDITIONAL INFORMATION Application includes a writing sample. Admission decisions are made on a rolling basis. Workshop information is available online at www.kenyonreview.org/work shops in November. For brochure send e-mail, visit website, call, or fax. Accepts inquiries by SASE, e-mail, phone, fax.

KEY WEST LITERARY SEMINAR

717 Love Lane, Key West FL 33040. (305)293-9291. **E-mail:** mail@kwls.org; arlo@kwls.org. **Website:** www.kwls.org. "The mission of KWLS is to promote the understanding and discussion of important literary works and their authors, to recognize and support new voices in American literature, and to preserve and promote Key West's literary heritage while providing resources that strengthen literary culture." The annual seminar and writers' workshop program are held in January. Scholarships are available to teachers, librarians, and students. Awards are given to emerging writers. See website for details.

COSTS $575/seminar; $575/writers' workshops.

ACCOMMODATIONS A list of nearby lodging establishments is made available.

KILLALOE HEDGE-SCHOOL OF WRITING

4 Riverview, Ballina, Killaloe Co. Clare Ireland. (353)(61)375-217. **E-mail:** KHS@killaloe.ie. **Website:** www.killaloe.ie/khs. Estab. 1999. Conference duration: 1 day. Holds workshops on 6 different topics.

COSTS €125/course. Courses resume spring 2015.

ACCOMMODATIONS There is a list of hotels and bed and breakfasts on the official website.

KILLER NASHVILLE

P.O. Box 680759, Franklin TN 37068-0686. (615)599-4032. **E-mail:** contact@killernashville.com. **Website:** www.killernashville.com. Jaden Terrell, Executive Director **Contact:** Maria Giordano. Estab. 2006. Annual. 2015 dates: October 29-November 1. Conference duration: 4 days. Average attendance: 400+. Conference designed for writers and fans of mysteries and thrillers, including fiction and nonfiction authors, playwrights, and screenwriters. There are many opportunities for authors to sign books. Killer Nashville's

2015 writers conference had over 60 sessions, 2 guests of honor, agent / editor / publisher roundtables, 5 distinct session tracks (general writing, genre specific writing, publishing, publicity & promotion, and forensics, breakout sessions for intense study, special sessions, ms critiques (fiction, nonfiction, short story, screenplay, marketing, query), realistic mock crime scene for guests to solve, networking with bestselling authors, agents, editors, publishers, attorneys, publicists, representatives from law and emergency services, mystery games, authors' bar, wine tasting event, two cocktail receptions, guest of honor dinner and awards program, prizes, free giveaways, free book signings, and more.

COSTS Early Bird Registration: $210 (February 15); Advanced Registration: $230 (April 30); $230 for three day full registration.

ACCOMMODATIONS The Omni Nashville Hotel has all rooms available for the Killer Nashville Writers' Conference.

ADDITIONAL INFORMATION Additional information about registration is provided online.

KINDLING WORDS EAST

VT **Website:** www.kindlingwords.org. Annual retreat held early in the year near Burlington, Vermont. 2015 dates: February 5-8. A retreat with three strands: writer, illustrator and editor; professional level. Intensive workshops for each strand, and an open schedule for conversations and networking. Registration limited to approximately 70. Hosted by the 4-star Inn at Essex (room and board extra). Participants must be published by a CCBC listed publisher, or if in publishing, occupy a professional position. Registration opens August 1 or as posted on the website, and fills quickly. Check website to see if spaces are available, to sign up to be notified when registration opens each year, or for more information. No contact e-mail is available for this organization, but there is a contact form on the website.

KINDLING WORDS WEST

Breckenridge CO **Website:** www.KindlingWords.org. Annual retreat specifically for children's book writers held in late April/early May out west. 2015 location was in Marble Falls, TX. 2015 dates are April 7-14. KWW is an artist's colony-style week with workshops by gifted teachers followed by a working retreat. Participants gather just before dinner to have white-space discussions; evenings include fireside readings, star gazing and songs. Participants must be published by CBC-recognized publisher.

KUNDIMAN POETRY RETREAT

P.O. Box 4248, Sunnyside NY 11104. **E-mail:** info@kundiman.org. **Website:** kundiman.org/retreat. **Contact:** June W. Choi, executive director. Held annually. 2015 dates: June 24-28. Held at Fordham University's Rose Hill campus. "This is a special event for Asian American poets. Renowned faculty will conduct workshops and provide one-on-one mentorship sessions with fellows. Readings and informal social gatherings will also be scheduled. Fellows selected based on sample of 6-8 poems and short essay answer.

ACCOMMODATIONS Room and board is free to accepted Fellows.

ADDITIONAL INFORMATION Additional information, guidelines, and online application available on website.

LA JOLLA WRITERS CONFERENCE

P.O. Box 178122, San Diego CA 92177. **E-mail:** akuritz@san.rr.com. **Website:** www.lajollawritersconference.com. **Contact:** Jared Kuritz, director. Estab. 2001. Annual conference held in November. 2015 dates: November 6-8. Conference duration: 3 days. Average attendance: 200. The LJWC covers all genres and both fiction and nonfiction as well as the business of writing. "We take particular pride in educating our attendees on the business aspect of the book industry and have agents, editors, publishers, publicists, and distributors teach classes. There is unprecedented access to faculty at the LJWC. Our conference offers lecture sessions that run for 50 minutes, and workshops that run for 110 minutes. Each block period is dedicated to either workshop or lecture-style classes, with 6-8 classes on various topics available each block. For most workshop classes, you are encouraged to bring written work for review. Literary agents from prestigious agencies such as The Andrea Brown Literary Agency, The Dijkstra Agency, The McBride Agency and Full Circle Literary Group, the Zimmerman Literary Agency, the Van Haitsma Literary Agency, the Farris Literary Agency, and more have participated in the past, teaching workshops in which they are familiarized with attendee work. Late night and early bird sessions are also available. The conference creates a strong sense of community, and it has seen many of its attendees successfully published."

COSTS $295 early bird registration for 2015. Conference limited to 200 attendees.

LAS VEGAS WRITERS CONFERENCE

Henderson Writers' Group, PO Box 92032, Henderson NV 89009. (702)564-2488; or, toll-free, (866)869-7842. **E-mail:** lasvegaswritersconference@gmail.com. **Website:** www.lasvegaswritersconference.com. Annual. Held April 28-30. Conference duration: 3 days. Average attendance: 150 maximum. "Join writing professionals, agents, industry experts, and your colleagues for 3 days in Las Vegas as they share their knowledge on all aspects of the writer's craft. While there are formal pitch sessions, panels, workshops, and seminars, the faculty is also available throughout the conference for informal discussions and advice. Workshops, seminars, and expert panels cover topics in both fiction and nonfiction, screenwriting, marketing, indie-publishing and the craft of writing itself. There will be many Q&A panels for you to ask the experts all your questions." Site: Sam's Town Hotel and Gambling Hall in Las Vegas (Henderson, Nevada). **COSTS** 2015 prices: $375 until October 31, 2015; $450 starting February 1, 2015; $500 at door; $300 for one day.

ADDITIONAL INFORMATION Sponsors contest. Agents and editors participate in conference.

LEAGUE OF UTAH WRITERS' ANNUAL WRITER'S CONFERENCE

Dianne Hardy, League of Utah Writers, 420 W. 750 N., Logan UT 84321. **E-mail:** Luwriters@gmail.com. **Website:** www.luwriters.org/index.html. **Contact:** Tim Keller. Annual spring and fall conferences. Faculty includes novelists, screenwriters, agents, and editors. Writer workshops geared toward beginner, intermediate or advanced. Annual conference.

THE MACDOWELL COLONY

100 High St., Peterborough NH 03458. (603)924-3886. **Fax:** (603)924-9142. **E-mail:** admissions@macdowellcolony.org. **Website:** www.macdowellcolony.org. Estab. 1907. Open to writers, playwrights, composers, visual artists, film/video artists, interdisciplinary artists and architects. Applicants submit information and work samples for review by a panel of experts in each discipline. Application form submitted online at www.macdowellcolony.org/apply.html.

COSTS Travel reimbursement and stipends are available for participants of the residency, based on need. There are no residency fees.

MENDOCINO COAST WRITERS CONFERENCE

1211 Del Mar Dr., second address is P.O. Box 2087, Fort Bragg CA 95437. (707)485-4032. **E-mail:** info@mcwc.org. **Website:** www.mcwc.org. Estab. 1988. Annual summer conference. 2015 dates: August 6-8, 2015. Average attendance: 90. Offers intensive workshops in fiction, creative nonfiction, poetry, YA, and seminars/panels about writing and publishing. Located at a community college on the Northern California Coast. Workshop leaders at the 2015 event: Ellen Bass, David Corbett, Catherine Ryan Hyde, Albert DeSilver, Lisa Locascio. Opportunities to meet informally or in private manuscript consultations with agents and editors.

COSTS $525 (minimum) includes morning intensives, afternoon panels and seminars, social events, and most meals. Scholarships available. Early application advised.

ADDITIONAL INFORMATION Emphasis is on encouragement, expertise and inspiration in a literary community where authors are also fantastic teachers. Registration opens March 15.

MIDWEST WRITERS WORKSHOP

Ball State University, Department of Journalism, Muncie IN 47306. (765)282-1055. **E-mail:** midwestwriters@yahoo.com. **Website:** www.midwestwriters.org. **Contact:** Jama Kehoe Bigger, director. Annual workshop held in late July in eastern Indiana. Writer workshops geared toward writers of all levels. Topics include most genres. Faculty/speakers have included Joyce Carol Oates, George Plimpton, Clive Cussler, Haven Kimmel, William Kent Krueger, Wiliam Zinsser, John Gilstrap, Lee Martin, Jane Friedman, Chuck Sambuchino, and numerous bestselling mystery, literary fiction, young adult, and children's authors. Workshop also includes agent pitch sessions ms evaluation and a writing contest. Registration tentatively limited to 200.

COSTS $185-395. Most meals included.

ADDITIONAL INFORMATION Offers scholarships. See website for more information. Keep in touch with the MWW at facebook.com/MidwestWriters and twitter.com/MidwestWriters.

MISSOURI WRITERS' GUILD CONFERENCE

St. Louis MO **E-mail:** mwgconferenceinfo@gmail.com. **Website:** www.missouriwritersguild.org. **Contact:** Tricia Sanders, vice president/conference chairman. Writer and illustrator workshops geared to all levels. **Open to students.** Conference "gives writers the opportunity to hear outstanding speakers and to receive information on marketing, research, and writing techniques." Agents, editors, and published authors in attendance. There will be no 2015 event, but keep checking the guild website for future events because a return is planned. The keynote speaker in 2014 was Writer's Digest Books editor Chuck Sambuchino. **ADDITIONAL INFORMATION** The primary contact individual changes every year, because the conference chair changes every year. See the website for contact info.

MONTEVALLO LITERARY FESTIVAL

Sta. 6420, University of Montevallo, Montevallo AL 35115. (205)665-6420. **Fax:** (205)665-6422. **E-mail:** murphyj@montevallo.edu. **Website:** http://www.montevallo.edu/arts-sciences/college-of-arts-sciences/departments/english-foreign-languages/student-organizations/montevallo-literary-festival/. **Contact:** Dr. Jim Murphy, director. Estab. 2003. 2015 dates: March 20. "Each April, the University of Montevallo's Department of English and Foreign Languages hosts the annual Montevallo Literary Festival, a celebration of creative writing dedicated to bringing literary writers and readers together on a personal scale. Our friendly, relaxed festival runs all day into the evening featuring readings by all invited writers, book signings, a Q&A panel, social gatherings and dinner with live music."

MONTROSE CHRISTIAN WRITERS' CONFERENCE

218 Locust St., Montrose PA 18801. (570)278-1001 or (800)598-5030. **Fax:** (570)278-3061. **E-mail:** mbc@montrosebible.org. **Website:** montrosebible.org. Estab. 1990. "Annual conference held in July. Offers workshops, editorial appointments, and professional critiques. We try to meet writing needs, for beginners and advanced, covering fiction, poetry, and writing for children. It is small enough to allow personal interaction between attendees and faculty. Speakers have included William Petersen, Mona Hodgson, Jim Fletcher, and Terri Gibbs." Held in Montrose, with the 2015 event planned for July 19-24, 2015.
COSTS Tuition is $180.
ACCOMMODATIONS Will meet planes in Binghamton, N.Y. and Scranton, Pa. On-site accommodations: room and board $340-475/conference, including food (2015 rates). RV court available.
ADDITIONAL INFORMATION "Writers can send work ahead of time and have it critiqued for a small fee." The attendees are usually church related. The writing has a Christian emphasis. Conference information available in April. For brochure, visit website, e-mail or call. Accepts inquiries by phone or e-mail.

MOONLIGHT AND MAGNOLIAS WRITER'S CONFERENCE

Georgia Romance Writers, 3741 Casteel Park Dr., Marietta GA 30064. **Website:** www.georgiaromance writers.org/mm-conference/. Estab. 1982. Georgia Romance Writers Annual Conference. 2015 dates: October 1-4. "Conference focuses on writing of women's fiction with emphasis on romance. Includes agents and editors from major publishing houses. Previous workshops have included: beginning writer sessions, research topics, writing basics and professional issues for the published author; plus specialty sessions on writing young adult, multicultural, paranormal, and Regency. Speakers have included experts in law enforcement, screenwriting and research. Literary raffle and advertised speaker and GRW member autographing open to the public. Please note the Maggies are now 100% electronic. Published authors make up first round, editors judge final."

JENNY MCKEAN MOORE COMMUNITY WORKSHOPS

English Department, George Washington University, 801 22nd St. NW, Rome Hall, Suite 760, Washington DC 20052. (202)994-6180. **Fax:** (202)994-7915. **E-mail:** lpageinc@gwu.edu. **Website:** www.gwu.edu/~english/creative_jennymckeanmoore.html. **Contact:** Lisa Page, acting director of creative writing. Estab. 1976. Workshop held each semester at the university. Average attendance: 15. Concentration varies depending on professor—usually fiction or poetry. The Creative Writing department brings an established poet or novelist to campus each year to teach a writing workshop for GW students and a free community workshop for adults in the larger Washington community. Details posted on website in June, with an application deadline at the end of August or in early September.
ADDITIONAL INFORMATION Admission is competitive and by decided by the quality of a submitted ms.

MOUNT HERMON CHRISTIAN WRITERS CONFERENCE

PO Box 413, Mount Hermon CA 95041. **E-mail:** info@mounthermon.org. **Website:** writers.mounthermon.org. Estab. 1970. Annual professional conference. 2015 dates: March 18-22. Average attendance: 450. Sponsored by and held at the 440-acre Mount Hermon Christian Conference Center near San Jose, California in the heart of the coastal redwoods, we are a broad-ranging conference for all areas of Christian writing, including fiction, nonfiction, fantasy, children's, teen, young adult, poetry, magazines, inspirational and devotional writing. This is a working, how-to conference, with Major Morning tracks in all genres (including a track especially for teen writers), and as many as 20 optional workshops each afternoon. Faculty-to-student ratio is about 1 to 6. The bulk of our more than 70 faculty members are editors and publisher representatives from major Christian publishing houses nationwide. Speakers have included T. Davis Bunn, Debbie Macomber, Jerry Jenkins, Bill Butterworth, Dick Foth and others.

MUSE AND THE MARKETPLACE

Grub Street, 162 Boylston St., 5th Floor, Boston MA 02116. (617)695-0075. **E-mail:** info@grubstreet.org. **Website:** www.grubstreet.org/muse. The conferences are held in the late spring, such as early May. (2015 dates were May 1-3.) Conference duration: 3 days. Average attendance: 400. Dozens of agents are in attendance to meet writers and take pitches. The conference has workshops on all aspects of writing.
ACCOMMODATIONS Boston Park Plaza Hotel.

NAPA VALLEY WRITERS' CONFERENCE

Napa Valley College, 1088 College Ave., St. Helena CA 94574. (707)967-2900. **E-mail:** writecon@napavalley.edu. **Website:** www.napawritersconference.org. **Contact:** Andrea Bewick, managing director. Estab. 1981. Established 1981. Annual weeklong event. 2015 dates: July 26 - July 31. Location: Upper Valley Campus in the historic town of St. Helena, 25 miles north of Napa in the heart of the valley's wine growing community. Average attendance: 48 in poetry and 48 in fiction. "Serious writers of all backgrounds and experience are welcome to apply." Offers poets and fiction writers workshops, lectures, faculty readings at Napa Valley wineries, and one-on-one faculty counseling. "Poetry session provides the opportunity to work both on generating new poems and on revising previously written ones."
COSTS $975; $25 application fee.

NASHVILLE SCREENWRITERS CONFERENCE

(615)254-2049. **E-mail:** info@nashscreen.com. **Website:** www.nashscreen.com. Annual conference held in May or June, though not necessarily ever year. The entire lineup of speakers and panelists is online. This is a 3-day conference dedicated to those who write for the screen. Nashville is a city that celebrates its writers and its creative community, and every writer wants to have a choice of avenues to increase their potential for success. During the event, conference participants will have the opportunity to attend various writing panels led by working professionals and participate in several special events.

NEW JERSEY ROMANCE WRITERS PUT YOUR HEART IN A BOOK CONFERENCE

P.O. Box 513, Plainsboro NJ 08536. **Website:** www.njromancewriters.org/conference.html. Estab. 1984. Annual conference held in October. Average attendance: 500. Workshops are offered on various topics for all writers of romance, from beginner to multi-published. Speakers have included Nora Roberts, Kathleen Woodiwiss, Patricia Gaffney, Jill Barnett and Kay Hooper. Appointments are offered with editors/agents.

NIMROD ANNUAL WRITERS' WORKSHOP

800 S. Tucker Dr., Tulsa OK 74104. (918)631-3080. **E-mail:** nimrod@utulsa.edu. **Website:** www.utulsa.edu/nimrod. **Contact:** Eilis O'Neal, editor-in-chief. Estab. 1978. Annual conference held in October. Conference duration: 1 day. Offers one-on-one editing sessions, readings, panel discussions, and master classes in fiction, poetry, nonfiction, memoir, and fantasy writing. Speakers have included Ted Kooser, Colum McCann, Molly Peacock, Peter S. Beagle, Aimee Nezhukumatathil, Philip Levine, and Linda Pastan. Full conference details are online in August.
COSTS Approximately $50. Lunch provided. Scholarships available for students.
ADDITIONAL INFORMATION *Nimrod International Journal* sponsors literary awards: The Katherine Anne Porter Prize for fiction and The Pablo Neruda Prize for poetry. Poetry and fiction prizes: $2,000 each and publication (top prize); $1,000 each

and publication (other winners). Deadline: must be postmarked no later than April 30.

NORTH CAROLINA WRITERS' NETWORK FALL CONFERENCE

P.O. Box 21591, Winston-Salem NC 27120. (336)293-8844. **E-mail:** mail@ncwriters.org. **Website:** www.ncwriters.org. Estab. 1985. Annual conference held in November in different NC venues. Average attendance: 250. This organization hosts 2 conferences: 1 in the spring and 1 in the fall. Each conference is a weekend full of workshops, panels, book signings, and readings (including open mic). There will be a keynote speaker, a variety of sessions on the craft and business of writing, and opportunities to meet with agents and editors.

COSTS Approximately $250 (includes 4 meals).

ACCOMMODATIONS Special rates are usually available at the conference hotel, but conferees must make their own reservations.

ADDITIONAL INFORMATION Available at www.ncwriters.org.

NORTHERN COLORADO WRITERS CONFERENCE

2107 Thunderstone Court, Fort Collins CO 80525. (970)556-0908. **E-mail:** kerrie@northerncoloradow riters.com. **Website:** www.northerncoloradowriters.com. Estab. 2006. Annual conference held in March in Fort Collins. 2015 dates: March 27-28. Conference duration: 2-3 days. The conference features a variety of speakers, agents and editors. There are workshops and presentations on fiction, nonfiction, screenwriting, children's books, marketing, magazine writing, staying inspired, and more. Previous agents who have attended and taken pitches from writers include Jessica Regel, Kristen Nelson, Rachelle Gardner, Andrea Brown, Ken Sherman, Jessica Faust, Gordon Warnock, and Taylor Martindale. Each conference features more than 30 workshops from which to choose from. Previous keynotes include Chuck Sambuchino, Andrew McCarthy, and Stephen J. Cannell.

COSTS $255-541, depending on what package the attendee selects, whether you're a member or nonmember, and whether you're renewing your NCW membership.

ACCOMMODATIONS The conference is hosted at the Fort Collins Hilton, where rooms are available at a special rate.

NORWESCON

100 Andover Park W. PMB 150-165, Tukwila WA 98188-2828. (425)243-4692. **Fax:** (520)244-0142. **E-mail:** info@norwescon.org. **Website:** www.norwescon.org. Estab. 1978. Annual conference held on Easter weekend. Average attendance: 2,800. General convention (with multiple tracks) focusing on science fiction and fantasy literature with wide coverage of other media. Tracks cover science, sociocultural, literary, publishing, editing, writing, art, and other media of a science fiction/fantasy orientation. Literary agents will be speaking and available for meetings with attendees.

ACCOMMODATIONS Conference is held at the Doubletree Hotel Seattle Airport.

ADDITIONAL INFORMATION Brochures are available online or for a SASE. Send inquiries via e-mail.

ODYSSEY FANTASY WRITING WORKSHOP

P.O. Box 75, Mont Vernon NH 03057. (603)673-6234. **E-mail:** jcavelos@sff.net. **Website:** www.sff.net/odyssey/. Saint Anselm College 100 Saint Anselm Drive, Manchester, New Hampshire, 03102. Estab. 1996. Annual workshop held in June (through July). Conference duration: 6 weeks. Average attendance: 15. A workshop for fantasy, science fiction, and horror writers that combines an intensive learning and writing experience with in-depth feedback on students' mss. Held on the campus of Saint Anselm College in Manchester, New Hampshire. Speakers have included George R.R. Martin, Elizabeth Hand, Jane Yolen, Harlan Ellison, Melissa Scott, and Dan Simmons.

COSTS In 2015: $1,995 tuition, $830 housing (double room), $1,660 (single room); $35 application fee, $600 food (approximate), $650 processing fee to receive college credit.

ADDITIONAL INFORMATION Students must apply and include a writing sample. Application deadline for 2015: April 8. Students' works are critiqued throughout the 6 weeks. Workshop information available in October. For brochure/guidelines, send SASE, e-mail, visit website, or call. Accepts inquiries by SASE, e-mail, phone.

OHIO KENTUCKY INDIANA CHILDREN'S LITERATURE CONFERENCE

Northern Kentucky University, 405 Steely Library, Highland Heights KY 41099. (859)572-6620. **Fax:** (859)572-5390. **E-mail:** smithjen@nku.edu. **Website:** http://oki.nku.edu. **Contact:** Jennifer Smith. Annual conference for writers and illustrators geared toward all levels. **Open to all.** Emphasizes multicultural literature for children and young adults. Conference held annually in November. Contact Jennifer Smith for more information.

COSTS $75; includes registration/attendance at all workshop sessions, *Tri-state Authors and Illustrators of Childrens Books Directory*, continental breakfast, lunch, author/illustrator signings. Manuscript critiques are available for an additional cost. E-mail or call for more information.

OKLAHOMA WRITERS' FEDERATION, INC. ANNUAL CONFERENCE

9800 South Hwy. 137, Miami OK 74354. **Website:** www.owfi.org. Annual conference held just outside Oklahoma City. Held first weekend in May each year. Writer workshops geared toward all levels. The goal of theconference is to create good stories with strong bones. We will be exploring cultural writing and cultural sensitivity in writing. Several literary agents are in attendance each year to meet with writers and hear pitches.

COSTS Costs vary depending on when registrants sign up. Cost includes awards banquet and famous author banquet. Three extra sessions are available for an extra fee. Visit the eventwebsite for a complete faculty list and conference information

OREGON CHRISTIAN WRITERS SUMMER CONFERENCE

Red Lion Hotel on the River, 909 N. Hayden Island Dr., Portland OR 97217-8118. **E-mail:** summerconf@oregonchristianwriters.org. **Website:** www.oregonchristianwriters.org. **Contact:** Lindy Jacobs, OCW Summer Conference Director. Estab. 1989. Held annually in August at the Red Lion Hotel on the River, a full-service hotel. Conference duration: 4 days. 2015 dates: August 10-13. 2016 dates: August 15-19. Average attendance: 225 (175 writers, 50 faculty). Top national editors, agents, and authors in the field of Christian publishing teach 12 intensive coaching classes and 30 workshops plus critique sessions. Published authors as well as emerging writers have opportunities to improve their craft, get feedback through ms reviews, meet one-on-one with editors and agents, and have half-hour mentoring appointments with published authors. Classes include fiction, nonfiction, memoir, young adult, poetry, magazine articles, devotional writing, children's books, and marketing. Daily general sessions include worship and an inspirational keynote address. Each year contacts made during the OCW summer conference lead to publishing contracts. 2015 conference theme was "Being Salt and Light," based on Matthew 6:13. 2015 Keynote speakers were: Ed Underwood and Jane Kirkpatrick. Agents: Chip MacGregor, Greg Johnson of WordServe Agency, Sally Apokedak of Les Stobbe Agency, Mary Keeley and Wendy Lawton of Books & Such Literary, Tamela Hancock Murray of the Steve Laube Agency. Editors: Revell, a division of Baker Books, Bethany/Chosen, LIVE, Harvest House, Grace Publishing, Focus on the Family Clubhouse, The Upper Room, Bible Advocate and *Splickety Magazine.*

COSTS $500 for OCW members, $535 for nonmembers. Registration fee includes all classes, workshops, and 2 lunches and 3 dinners. Lodging additional. Full-time registered registrants may also pre-submit three proposals for review by an editor (or agent) through the conference, plus sign up for a half-hour mentoring appointment with an author.

ACCOMMODATIONS Conference is held at the Red Lion on the River Hotel. Conferees wishing to stay at the hotel must make a reservation through the hotel. A block of rooms has been reserved at the hotel at a special rate for conferees and held until mid-July. The hotel reservation link will be posted on the website in late spring. Shuttle bus transportation will be provided by the hotel for conferees from Portland Airport (PDX) to the hotel, which is 20 minutes away.

ADDITIONAL INFORMATION Conference details will be posted online beginning in January. All conferees are welcome to attend the Cascade Awards ceremony, which takes place Wednesday evening during the conference. For more information about the Cascade Writing Contest, please check the website.

OUTDOOR WRITERS ASSOCIATION OF AMERICA ANNUAL CONFERENCE

615 Oak St., Suite 201, Missoula MT 59801. (406)728-7434. **E-mail:** info@owaa.org. **Website:** http://owaa.org. **Contact:** Jessica Seitz, conference and membership coordinator. Outdoor communicator workshops geared toward all levels. Annual three-day conference. Craft improvement seminars; newsmaker sessions. 2015 conference was held in Knoxville, TN. Cost includes attendance at all workshops and most meals. Visit owaa.org/2016conference for additional information on the 2016 event.

COSTS $425-449.

OZARK CREATIVE WRITERS, INC. CONFERENCE

P.O. Box 9076, Fayetteville AR 72703. **E-mail:** ozark creativewriters1@gmail.com. **Website:** www.ozark creativewriters.org. The annual event is held in October at the Inn of the Ozarks, in the resort town of Eureka Springs, Arkansas. Approximately 200 attend each year; many also enter the creative writing competitions. Open to professional and amateur writers, workshops are geared to all levels and all forms of the creative process and literary arts. Sessions sometimes include songwriting, with presentations by best-selling authors, editors, and agents. The OCW Conference promotes writing by offering writing competitions in all genres.

PACIFIC COAST CHILDREN'S WRITERS WHOLE-NOVEL WORKSHOP: FOR ADULTS AND TEENS

P.O. Box 244, Aptos CA 95001. **Website:** www.chil drenswritersworkshop.com. Estab. 2003. 2015 dates: Oct. 2-4. "Our seminar offers semi-advanced through published adult writers an editor and/or agent critique on their full novel or 15-30 page partial. (Midbook and synopsis critique may be included with the partial.) A concurrent workshop is open to students age 13 and up, who give adults target-reader feedback. There is a focus on craft as a marketing tool. Team-taught master classes (open clinics for manuscript critiques) explore such topics as "Story Architecture and Arcs." Continuous close contact with faculty, who have included Andrea Brown, agent, and Simon Boughton, VP/executive editor at 3 Macmillan imprints. **Past seminars**: Annually, the first weekend of October. Registration limited to 16 adults and 10 teens. For the most critique options, submit sample chapters and synopsis with e-application by mid May; open until filled. **Content:** Character-driven novels with protagonists ages 11 and older. Collegial format; 90% hands-on. Our pre-workshop anthology of peer manuscripts maximizes learning and networking. Several past attendees have landed contracts as a direct result of our seminar. **Details:** visit our website and e-mail Director Nancy Sondel via the contact form."

🌑 PARIS WRITERS WORKSHOP

WICE, 10 rue Tiphaine, 75015, Paris France. (33) (14)566-7550. **Fax:** (33)(14)065-9653. **E-mail:** pww@ wice-paris.org. **Website:** pariswritersworkshop.org.

Estab. 1987. Annual conference held in July. Conference duration: 1 week. Average attendance: 12/section. Each participant chooses one workshop section - creative nonfiction, novel, screenwriting, novella or short story - which meets for a total of 15 classroom hours. Writers in residence have included Vivian Gornick, Lynne Sharon Schwartz, Liam Rector, Ellen Sussman, and Katharine Weber. Literary agents in attendance.

PENNWRITERS CONFERENCE

5706 Sonoma Ridge, Missouri City TX 77459. **E-mail:** conferenceco@pennwriters.org. **Website:** www.pen nwriters.org/prod. **Contact:** Carol A. Silvis, conference coordinator. Estab. 1987. The Mission of Pennwriters Inc. is to help writers of all levels, from the novice to the award-winning and multi-published, improve and succeed in their craft. The annual Pennwriters conference is held every year in May in Pennsylvania, switching between locations—Lancaster in even years and Pittsburgh in odd years. 2015 event dates: May 15-17 in Pittsburgh.

ACCOMMODATIONS $289 for members, $324 for nonmembers.

ADDITIONAL INFORMATION Sponsors contest. Published authors judge fiction in various categories. Agent/editor appointments are available on a first-come, first serve basis.

PHILADELPHIA WRITERS' CONFERENCE

P.O. Box 7171, Elkins Park PA 19027-0171. (215) 619-7422. **E-mail:** info@pwcwriters.org. **E-mail:** info@ pwcwriters.org. **Website:** pwcwriters.org. Estab. 1949. Annual. Conference held in June. Average attendance: 160-200. Conference covers many forms of writing: novel, short story, genre fiction, nonfiction book, magazine writing, blogging, juvenile, poetry.

ACCOMMODATIONS Wyndham Hotel (formerly the Holiday Inn), Independence Mall, Fourth and Arch Streets, Philadelphia, PA 19106-2170. Hotel offers discount for early registration.

ADDITIONAL INFORMATION Accepts inquiries by e-mail. Agents and editors attend the conference. Many questions are answered online.

PHOTOGRAPHERS' FORMULARY

P.O. Box 950, 7079 Hwy. 83 N., Condon MT 59826-0950. (800)922-5255. **Fax:** (406)754-2896. **E-mail:** lynnw@blackfoot.net; formulary@blackfoot.net. **Website:** www.photoformulary.com; www.work shopsinmt.com. **Contact:** Lynn Wilson, workshop program director. Photographers' Formulary workshops include a wide variety of alternative processes, and many focus on the traditional darkroom. Located in Montana's Swan Valley, some of the best wilderness lands in the Rocky Mountains. See website for details on costs and lodging. Open to all skill levels. Workshops held frequently throughout the year. See website for listing of dates and registration.

PIKES PEAK WRITERS CONFERENCE

Pikes Peak Writers, PO Box 64273, Colorado Springs CO 80962. (719)244-6220. **Website:** www.pikespeak writers.com/ppwc/. Estab. 1993. Annual conference held in April. 2016 dates: April 15-17. Conference duration: 3 days. Average attendance: 300. Workshops, presentations, and panels focus on writing and publishing mainstream and genre fiction (romance, science fiction/fantasy, suspense/thrillers, action/adventure, mysteries, children's, young adult). Agents and editors are available for meetings with attendees on Saturday. 2015 speakers included R.L. Stine and Mary Kay Andrews.

COSTS $300-500 (includes all meals).

ACCOMMODATIONS Marriott Colorado Springs holds a block of rooms at a special rate for attendees until late March.

ADDITIONAL INFORMATION Readings with critiques are available on Friday afternoon. Also offers a contest for unpublished manuscripts; entrants need not attend the conference. Deadline: November 1. Registration and contest entry forms are online; brochures are available in January. Send inquiries via e-mail.

PIMA WRITERS' WORKSHOP

Pima College, 2202 W. Anklam Rd., Tucson AZ 85709. (520)206-6084. **Fax:** (520)206-6020. **E-mail:** mfiles@pima.edu. **Contact:** Meg Files, director. Annual conference geared toward beginner, intermediate and advanced levels. **Open to students.** The conference features presentations and writing exercises on writing and publishing stories for children and young adults, among other genres. Participants may attend for college credit. Meals and accommodations not included. Features a dozen authors, editors, and agents talking about writing and publishing fiction, nonfiction, poetry, and stories for children. E-mail us for more info, or check the website.

PNWA SUMMER WRITERS CONFERENCE

317 NW Gilman Blvd., Suite 8, Issaquah WA 98027. (425)673-2665. **E-mail:** pnwa@pnwa.org. **Website:** www.pnwa.org. Estab. 1955. Annual conference held in July. 2015 dates: july 16-19. Conference duration: 4 days. Average attendance: 400. Attendees have the chance to meet agents and editors, learn craft from authors and uncover marketing secrets. Speakers have included J.A. Jance, Sheree Bykofsky, Kimberley Cameron, Jennie Dunham, Donald Maass, Jandy Nelson, Robert Dugoni, and Terry Brooks.

ACCOMMODATIONS SeaTac Hilton Hotel and Conference Center.

ROCKY MOUNTAIN FICTION WRITERS COLORADO GOLD

Rocky Mountain Fiction Writers, P.O. Box 735, Confier CO 80433. **E-mail:** conference@rmfw.org. **Website:** www.rmfw.org. Estab. 1982. Annual conference held in September. Conference duration: 3 days. Average attendance: 350. Themes include general fiction, genre fiction, contemporary romance, mystery, science fiction/fantasy, mainstream, young adult, screenwriting, short stories, and historical fiction. 2015 keynote speakers were Jeffery Deaver and Jack Ketchum. Past speakers have included William Kent Krueger, Margaret George, Jodi Thomas, Bernard Cornwell, Terry Brooks, Dorothy Cannell, Patricia Gardner Evans, Diane Mott Davidson, Constance O'Day, and Connie Willis. Approximately 8 editors and 5 agents attend annually.

COSTS Available online.

ACCOMMODATIONS Special rates will be available at conference hotel.

ADDITIONAL INFORMATION Editor-conducted critiques are limited to 8 participants, with auditing available. Pitch appointments available at no charge. Friday morning master classes available. Pitch coaching is available. Special critiques are available. Craft workshops include beginner through professional levels.

ROMANCE WRITERS OF AMERICA NATIONAL CONFERENCE

14615 Benfer Road, Houston TX 77069. (832)717-5200. **Fax:** (832)717-5201. **E-mail:** info@rwa.org. **Website:** www.rwa.org/conference. Estab. 1981. Annual conference held in July. (2015 conference: July 22-25 in New York.) Average attendance: 2,000. More than 100 workshops on writing, researching, and the business side of being a working writer. Publishing professionals attend and accept appointments. The keynote speaker is a renowned romance writer. "Romance Writers of America (RWA) is a nonprofit trade association, with a membership of more than 10,000 romance writers and related industry professionals, whose mission is to advance the professional interests of career-focused romance writers through networking and advocacy."

COSTS $450-675 depending on your membership status as well as when you register.

ADDITIONAL INFORMATION Annual RTA awards are presented for romance authors. Annual Golden Heart awards are presented for unpublished writers. Numerous literary agents are in attendance to meet with writers and hear book pitches.

RT BOOKLOVERS CONVENTION

55 Bergen St., Brooklyn NY 11201. **Website:** rtconvention.com. Annual conference with a varying location. 2016 details: April 12-16 in Las Vegas. Features 125 workshops, agent and editor appointments, a book fair, and more. More than 800 authors were at the 2015 event.

COSTS $489 normal registration; $425 for industry professionals (agents, editors). Many other pricing options available. See website.

ACCOMMODATIONS Rooms available nearby.

SALT CAY WRITERS RETREAT

Salt Cay Bahamas. (732)267-6449. **E-mail:** admin@ saltcaywritersretreat.com. **Website:** www.saltcay writersretreat.com. **Contact:** Karen Dionne and Christopher Graham. 5-day retreat held in the Bahamas in October. "The Salt Cay Writers Retreat is particularly suited for novelists (especially those writing literary, upmarket commercial fiction, or genre novelists wanting to write a break-out book), memoirists and narrative nonfiction writers. However, any author (published or not-yet-published) who wishes to take their writing to the next level is welcome to apply." Speakers have included or will include editors Chuck Adams (Algonquin Books) and Amy Einhorn (Amy Einhorn Books); agents Jeff Kleinman, Michelle Brower, Erin Niumata, and Erin Harris (all of Folio Literary Management); authors Robert Goolrick and Jacquelyn Mitchard.

COSTS $2,450 through May 1; $2,950 after.

ACCOMMODATIONS Comfort Suites, Paradise Island, Nassau, Bahamas.

SAN DIEGO STATE UNIVERSITY WRITERS' CONFERENCE

SDSU College of Extended Studies, 5250 Campanile Dr., San Diego State University, San Diego CA 92182-1920. (619)594-3946. **Fax:** (619)594-8566. **E-mail:** sd suwritersconference@mail.sdsu.edu. **Website:** ces. sdsu.edu/writers. Estab. 1984. Annual conference held in January. Conference duration: 2.5 days. Average attendance: 350. Covers fiction, nonfiction, scriptwriting and e-books. Held at the San Diego Marriott Mission Valley Hotel. Each year the conference offers a variety of workshops for the beginner and advanced writers. This conference allows the individual writer to choose which workshop best suits his/her needs. In addition to the workshops, editor reading appointments and agent/editor consultation appointments are provided so attendees may meet with editors and agents one-on-one to discuss specific questions. A reception is offered Saturday immediately following the workshops, offering attendees the opportunity to socialize with the faculty in a relaxed atmosphere. Last year, approximately 60 faculty members attended.

COSTS Approximately $399-435. Parking is available for $8/day.

ACCOMMODATIONS Attendees must make their own travel arrangements. A conference rate for attendees is available at the event hotel (Marriott Mission Valley Hotel).

SAN DIEGO WRITING WORKSHOP

Website: www.sandiegowritingworkshop.com. The 2016 event is set for Friday, October 9, 2015. Organized by Writing Day Workshops. The workshop is a one-day, all-day "How to Get Published" conference with instructional sessions and panels. Multiple literary agents are in attendance at the workshop to meet with writers and hear pitches.

COSTS Early-bird tuition is $149; later tuition is $179; agent meetings are $29 per appointment.

ACCOMMODATIONS Rooms available at the event hotel: The Crowne Plaza in Mission Valley.

ADDITIONAL INFORMATION Query critique options available. Check the website for contact and registration information.

SAN FRANCISCO WRITERS CONFERENCE

1029 Jones St., San Francisco CA 94109. (415)673-0939. **E-mail:** Barbara@sfwriters.org. **Website:** sfwriters. org. **Contact:** Barbara Santos, marketing director. Estab. 2003. "Annual conference held President's Day weekend in February. Average attendance: 500 minimum. More than 100 top authors, respected literary agents, and major publishing houses are at the event so attendees can make face-to-face contact with all the right people. Writers of nonfiction, fiction, poetry, and specialty writing (children's books, cookbooks, travel, etc.) will all benefit from the event. There are important sessions on marketing, self-publishing, technology, and trends in the publishing industry. Plus, there's an optional 4-hour session called Speed Dating for Agents where attendees can meet with 20+ agents. Speakers have included Jennifer Crusie, R.L. Stine, Richard Paul Evans, Jamie Raab, Mary Roach, Jane Smiley, Debbie Macomber, Clive Cussler, Guy Kawasaki, Lisa See, Steve Berry, and Jacquelyn Mitchard. More than 20 agents and editors participate each year, many of whom will be available for meetings with attendees."

COSTS Check the website for pricing on later dates. 2015 pricing was $650-795 depending on when you signed up and early bird registration, etc.

ACCOMMODATIONS The Intercontinental Mark Hopkins Hotel is a historic landmark at the top of Nob Hill in San Francisco. The hotel is located so that everyone arriving at the Oakland or San Francisco airport can take BART to either the Embarcadero or Powell Street exits, then walk or take a cable car or taxi directly to the hotel.

ADDITIONAL INFORMATION "Present yourself in a professional manner and the contacts you will make will be invaluable to your writing career. Fliers, details and registration information are online."

SAN FRANCISCO WRITING FOR CHANGE CONFERENCE

1029 Jones St., San Francisco CA 94109. (415)673-0939. **E-mail:** Barbara@sfwriters.org. **Website:** SFWriting forChange.org. **Contact:** Barbara Santos, marketing director; Michael Larsen, co-director. Estab. 2004. Annual conference. 2015 dates: September 12, 2015, at Unitarian Universalist Center in San Francisco. Average attendance: 100. Early discounts available. Includes panels, workshops, keynote address, editor, and agent consultations.

COSTS Costs to be announced. Please visit the website.

ACCOMMODATIONS Check website for event details, accommodations, directions, and parking.

ADDITIONAL INFORMATION "The limited number of attendees (150 or fewer) and excellent presenter-to-attendee ratio make this a highly effective and productive conference. The presenters are major names in the publishing business, but take personal interest in the projects discovered at this event each year." Guidelines available on website.

🌑 SAN MIGUEL WRITERS' CONFERENCE AND LITERARY FESTIVAL

220 N. Zapata Hwy. #11, Laredo TX 78043. (510)295-4097. **E-mail:** susan@susanpage.com. **Website:** www.sanmiguelwritersconference.org. Estab. 2005. Annual conference held in February. 3 days with 2-day intensive retreats on either end of the conference. 2016 dates: Feb. 10-14. Average attendance: 150. Covers poetry, fiction, nonfiction, memoir, screenwriting. "San Miguel de Allende is a magical town, a UNESCO World Heritage Site filled with charm and history. It is completely safe and very far from any of the border violence." 2015 keynote speakers were: Alice Walker, Scott Turow, and more.

COSTS $325 before January 20th; $375 after Jan. 20th for 2011, includes meals sessions, workshops, open mic and readings, planned excursions. Optional fee consultations and two-day Intensives not included.

ACCOMMODATIONS Consultants work with attendees to arrange accommodations. Cost in the conference hotel is $75/night, double occupancy. "We assist with making airline reservations and transportation arrangements from airport."

ADDITIONAL INFORMATION "The entire conference is simultaneously translated into Spanish. We offer workshops in a broad range of writing topics. We offer seven general session speakers or panels, 90-minute workshops from a choice of 36, 2 optional 2-day intensive workshops, open mic sessions, author readings, individual consultations, and a spectacular Mexican fiesta." Guidelines available as of November 1.

SANTA BARBARA WRITERS CONFERENCE

27 W. Anapamu St., Suite 305, Santa Barbara CA 93101. (805)568-1516. **E-mail:** info@sbwriters.com. **Website:** www.sbwriters.com. Estab. 1972. Annual conference held in June. 2015 dates: June 7-12. Average attendance: 200. Covers fiction, nonfiction, journalism, memoir, poetry, playwriting, screenwriting, travel writing, young adult, children's literature, humor, and marketing. Speakers have included Ray Bradbury, William Styron, Eudora Welty, James Michener, Sue Grafton, Charles M. Schulz, Clive Cussler,

Fannie Flagg, Elmore Leonard, and T.C. Boyle. Agents will appear on a panel; in addition, there will be an agents and editors day that allows writers to pitch their projects in one-on-one meetings.

COSTS Early conference registration is $575, and regular registration is $650.

ACCOMMODATIONS Hyatt Santa Barbara.

ADDITIONAL INFORMATION Register online or contact for brochure and registration forms.

☼ SASKATCHEWAN FESTIVAL OF WORDS

217 Main St. N., Moose Jaw SK S6J 0W1 Canada. **Website:** www.festivalofwords.com. Estab. 1997. Annual 4-day event, third week of July (2015 dates: July 16-19). Location: Moose Jaw Library/Art Museum complex in Crescent Park. Average attendance: about 4,000 admissions. "Canadian authors up close and personal for readers and writers of all ages in mystery, poetry, memoir, fantasy, graphic novels, history, and novel. Each summer festival includes more than 60 events within 2 blocks of historic Main Street. Audience favorite activities include workshops for writers, audience readings, drama,performance poetry, concerts, panels, and music."

ACCOMMODATIONS Information available at www.templegardens.sk.ca, campgrounds, and bed and breakfast establishments. Complete information about festival presenters, events, costs, and schedule also available on website.

✚ SCBWI–AUSTIN CONFERENCE

E-mail: austin@scbwi.org. **Website:** https://austin.scbwi.org. **Contact:** Samantha Clark, regional advisor. Annual conference. 2015 dates: March 7-8. Features a faculty of published authors and illustrators. Editors and agents are in attendance to meet with writers. The schedule consists of keynotes and breakout sessions with writing, illustrating and professional development tracks. Session topics include publishing, diversity, social media, contracts, picture books, nonfiction, the hero's journey, editor acquisitions, and more

COSTS Check the website for costs. There is early bird pricing for early sign-ups.

☼ SCBWI–CANADA EAST

Canada. **E-mail:** canadaeast@scbwi.org; almafullerton@almafullerton.com. **Website:** www.canadaeast.scbwi.org. **Contact:** Alma Fullerton, regional advisor. Writer and illustrator events geared toward all levels. Usually offers one event in spring and another

in the fall. Check website Events pages for updated information.

SCBWI COLORADO/WYOMING (ROCKY MOUNTAIN); EVENTS

E-mail: lindsayeland@me.com; todd.tuell@rmc scbwi.org. **Website:** www.rmc.scbwi.org. **Contact:** Todd Tuell and Lindsay Eland, co-regional advisors. SCBWI Rocky Mountain chapter (CO/WY) offers special events, schmoozes, meetings, and conferences throughout the year. Major events: Fall Conference (annually, September); Summer Retreat, "Big Sur in the Rockies" (bi- and tri-annually). More info on website.

SCBWI EASTERN NEW YORK FALLING LEAVES MASTER CLASS RETREAT

Silver Bay NY **E-mail:** ntcastaldo@taconic.net. **Website:** http://easternny.scbwi.org; http://scbwi-easternny.org. **Contact:** Nancy Castaldo, regional advisor. Annual master class retreat hosted by the SCBWI Eastern New York and held in Silver Bay on Lake George in November. Holds ms and portfolio critiques, Q&A and speaker sessions, intensives, and more, with respected authors and editors. Theme varies each year between picture books, novels and nonfiction. See website for more information.

SCBWI–MIDATLANTIC; ANNUAL FALL CONFERENCE

P.O. Box 3215, Reston VA 20195. **E-mail:** scbwimidatlantic@gmail.com. **Website:** midatlantic.scbwi.org/. For updates and details visit website. Registration limited to 275. Conference fills quickly.Includes continental breakfast and boxed lunch. Optional craft-focused workshops and individual consultations with conference faculty are available for additional fees.

SCBWI NEW ENGLAND WHISPERING PINES WRITER'S RETREAT

West Greenwich RI **E-mail:** lyndamullalyhunt@yahoo.com; momeraths@verizon.net. **Website:** http://lyndamullalyhunt.com. **Contact:** Lynda Mullaly Hunt, co-director; Mary Pierce, co-director. Three-day retreat (with stays overnight) that offers the opportunity to work intimately with professionals in an idyllic setting. Attendees will work with others who are committed to quality children's literature in small groups and will benefit from a 30-minute one-on-one critique with a mentor. Also includes mentors' presentations and an intimate Q&A session, Team Kid Lit

Jeopardy with prizes, and more. Retreat limited to 32 full-time participants. Held annually in late March.

SCBWI—NEW JERSEY; ANNUAL SUMMER CONFERENCE

SCBWI-New Jersey: Society of Children's Book Writers & Illustrators, New Jersey NJ **Website:** http://njscbwi.com. **Contact:** Leeza Hernandez, regional advisor. This weekend conference is held in thesummer. Multiple one-on-one critiques; "how to" workshops for every level, first page sessions, agent pitches and interaction with the faculty of editors, agents, art director and authors are some of the highlights of the weekend. On Friday attendees can sign up for writing intensives or register for illustrators' day with the art directors. Published authors attending the conference can sign up to participate in the bookfair to sell and autograph their books; illustrators have the opportunity to display their artwork. Attendees have the option to participate in group critiques after dinner on Saturday evening and attend a mix and mingle with the faculty on Friday night. Meals are included with the cost of admission. Conference is known for its high ratio of faculty to attendees and interaction opportunities.

SCBWI WINTER CONFERENCE ON WRITING AND ILLUSTRATING FOR CHILDREN

8271 Beverly Blvd., Los Angeles CA 90048. (323)782-1010. **Fax:** (323)782-1892. **E-mail:** scbwi@scbwi.org. **Website:** www.scbwi.org. **Contact:** Stephen Mooser. Estab. 2000. Annual. Conference held in February. Average attendance: 1,000. Conference is to promote writing and illustrating for children: picture books; fiction; nonfiction; middle grade and young adult; network with professionals; financial planning for writers; marketing your book; art exhibition; etc. Site: Manhattan.

COSTS See website for current cost and conference information .

ADDITIONAL INFORMATION SCBWI also holds an annual summer conference in August in Los Angeles.

✪ THE SCHOOL FOR WRITERS FALL WORKSHOP

The Humber School for Writers, Humber Institute of Technology & Advanced Learning, 3199 Lake Shore Blvd. W., Toronto ON M8V 1K8 Canada. (416)675-6622. **E-mail:** antanas.sileika@humber.ca; hilary.

higgins@humber.ca. **Website:** www.humber.ca/scapa/programs/school-writers. The School for Writers Workshop has moved to the fall with the International Festival of Authors. The workshop runs during the last week in October. Conference duration: 1 week. Average attendance: 60. New writers from around the world gather to study with faculty members to work on their novels, short stories, poetry, or creative nonfiction. Agents and editors participate in the conference. Include a work-in-progress with your registration. Faculty has included Martin Amis, David Mitchell, Kevin Barry, Rachel Kuschner, Peter Carey, Roddy Doyle, Tim O'Brien, Andrea Levy, Barry Unsworth, Edward Albee, Ha Jin, Julia Glass, Mavis Gallant, Bruce Jay Friedman, Isabel Huggan, Alistair MacLeod, Lisa Moore, Kim Moritsugu, Francine Prose, Paul Quarrington, Olive Senior, D.M. Thomas, Annabel Lyon, Mary Gaitskill, and M.G. Vassanji.

COSTS around $850 (in 2014). Some limited scholarships are available.

ADDITIONAL INFORMATION Accepts inquiries by e-mail, phone, and fax.

SEWANEE WRITERS' CONFERENCE

735 University Ave., 119 Gailor Hall, Stamler Center, Sewanee TN 37383-1000. (931)598-1654. **E-mail:** allatham@sewanee.edu. **Website:** www.sewaneewriters.org. **Contact:** Adam Latham. Estab. 1990. Annual conference. 2015 dates: July 21-Aug. 2. Average attendance: 150. "The University of the South will host the 26th session of the Sewanee Writers' Conference. Thanks to the generosity of the Walter E. Dakin Memorial Fund, supported by the estate of the late Tennessee Williams, the Conference will gather a distinguished faculty to provide instruction and criticism through workshops and craft lectures in poetry, fiction, and playwriting. During an intense 12-day period, participants will read and critique each other's mss under the leadership of some of our country's finest fiction writers, poets, and playwrights. All faculty members and fellows give scheduled readings; senior faculty members offer craft lectures; open-mic readings accommodate many others. Additional writers, along with a host of writing professionals, visit to give readings, participate in panel discussions, and entertain questions from the audience. Receptions and mealtimes offer opportunities for informal exchange. This year's faculty includes fiction writers Richard Bausch, Tony Earley, Adrianne Harun, Randall Ke-

nan, Jill McCorkle, Alice McDermott, Tim O'Brien, Christine Schutt, Allen Wier, and Steve Yarbrough; and poets Daniel Anderson, Claudia Emerson, B.H. Fairchild, Andrew Hudgins, Maurice Manning, Charles Martin, Mary Jo Salter, and A.E. Stallings. Dan O'Brien and Paula Vogel will lead the playwriting workshop. Erin McGraw and Wyatt Prunty will read from their work. The conference fee reflects but two-thirds of the actual cost to attend. Additional funding is awarded to fellows and scholars."

COSTS $1,000 for tuition and $800 for room, board, and activity costs.

ACCOMMODATIONS Participants are housed in single rooms in university dormitories. Bathrooms are shared by small groups.

SLEUTHFEST

MWA Florida Chapter, **E-mail:** Sleuthfestinfo@yahoo.com. **Website:** sleuthfest.com. Annual conference held in Feb/March, at the Deerfield Beach Hilton, Florida. 2015 dates: Feb. 26 - March 1. Conference duration: 4 days. Hands-on workshops, 4 tracks of writing and business panels, and 2 keynote speakers for writers of mystery and crime fiction. 2015 keynote speaker was James Patterson. Also offers agent and editor appointments and paid ms critiques. A full list of attending speakers as well as agents and editors is online. This event is put on by the local chapter of the Mystery Writers of America.

ACCOMMODATIONS Doubletree by Hilton in Deerfield Beach.

THE SOUTHAMPTON WRITERS CONFERENCE

239 Montauk Highway, Southampton NY 11968. (631)632-5030. **E-mail:** southamptonarts@stony brook.edu. **Website:** www.stonybrook.edu/south ampton/mfa/summer/cwl_home.html. Estab. 1975. 2015 dates: July 8-19. "Since 1976, the Southampton Writers Conference has brought together writers at all stages of their careers with world-class novelists, essayists, editors, poets and children's book authors for lectures, readings, panels and workshops. All writers are welcome to attend the Conference, including those who seek a 12-day writers residency in the Hamptons. This year's offerings include a 5-part craft lecture series with Roger Rosenblatt. Admission to a 5-day writing workshop is competitive and requires additional application materials."

SOUTH CAROLINA WRITERS WORKSHOP

4840 Forest Drive, Suite 6B: PMB 189, Columbia SC 29206. **E-mail:** scwwliaison@gmail.com; scww2013@gmail.com. **Website:** www.myscww.org. Estab. 1991. Conference in October held at the Hilton Myrtle Beach Resort in Myrtle Beach, SC. Held almost every year. Conference duration: 3 days. The conference features critique sessions, open mic readings, presentations from agents and editors and more. The conference features more than 50 different workshops for writers to choose from, dealing with all subjects of writing craft, writing business, getting an agent and more. Agents will be in attendance.

SOUTH COAST WRITERS CONFERENCE

Southwestern Oregon Community College, P.O. Box 590, 29392 Ellensburg Ave., Gold Beach OR 97444. (541)247-2741. **Fax:** (541)247-6247. **E-mail:** scwc@socc.edu. **Website:** www.socc.edu/scwriters. Estab. 1996. Annual conference held Presidents Day weekend in February. Conference duration: 2 days. Covers fiction, poetry, children's, nature, songwriting, and marketing. Melissa Hart was the keynote speaker in 2014, and presenters include Stevan Allred, Mark Bennion, Dan Berne, Mark Graham, Nina Kiriki Hoffman, Elena Passarello, Liz Prato, Jeffrey Shultz, Tess Thompson.

ADDITIONAL INFORMATION See website for cost and additional details.

SOUTHEASTERN WRITERS ASSOCIATION—ANNUAL WRITERS WORKSHOP

161 Woodstone, Athens GA 30605. **E-mail:** purple@southeasternwriters.org. **Website:** www.southeast ernwriters.com. Estab. 1975. **Open to all writers**. (2015 dates: June 19-23.) Contests with cash prizes. Instruction offered for novel and short fiction, non-fiction, writing for children, humor, inspirational writing, and poetry. Manuscript deadline April 1; includes free evaluation conference(s) with instructor(s). Agent in residence. Annual 4-day workshop held in June. Cost of workshop: $445 for 4 days or lower prices for daily tuition. (See online.) Accommodations: Offers overnight accommodations on workshop site. Visit website for more information and cost of overnight accommodations. Tuition pricing online.

ACCOMMODATIONS Multiple hotels available in St. Simon's Island, GA.

SPACE COAST WRITERS GUILD ANNUAL CONFERENCE

No public address available, **E-mail:** stilley@scwg.org. **Website:** www.scwg.org/conference.asp. Annual conference held last weekend of January along the east coast of central Florida, though the event is not necessarily held every year. Conference duration: 2 days. Average attendance: 150+. This conference is hosted in Florida and features a variety of presenters on all topics writing. Critiques are available for a price, and agents in attendance will take pitches from writers. Previous presenters have included Debra Dixon, Davis Bunn (writer), Ellen Pepus (agent), Jennifer Crusie, Chuck Sambuchino, Madeline Smoot, Mike Resnick, Christina York, Ben Bova, and Elizabeth Sinclair. **COSTS** $180-220. Agent and editor appointments cost more.

ACCOMMODATIONS The conference is hosted on a beachside hotel, with special room rates available.

😊 SPACE (SMALL PRESS AND ALTERNATIVE COMICS EXPO)

Back Porch Comics, P.O. Box 20550, Columbus OH 43220. **E-mail:** bpc13@earthlink.net. **Website:** www.backporchcomics.com/space.htm. 2015 conference/trade show to be held July 18-19, 2015. Conference duration: 2 days. "The Midwest's largest exhibition of small press, alternative, and creator-owned comics." Site: Held at Ramada Plaza Hotel and Conference Center, 4900 Sinclair Rd., Columbus, OH 43229. Over 150 small press artists, writers, and publishers will be in attendance.

COSTS Admission: $5 per day or $8 for weekend.

ADDITIONAL INFORMATION For brochure, visit website. Editors participate in conference.

SQUAW VALLEY COMMUNITY OF WRITERS

P.O. Box 1416, Nevada City CA 95959-1416. (530)470-8440. **E-mail:** info@squawvalleywriters.org. **Website:** www.squawvalleywriters.org. **Contact:** Brett Hall Jones, executive director. Estab. 1969.

COSTS Tuition is $1,075, which includes 6 dinners. Limited financial aid is available.

ACCOMMODATIONS The Community of Writers rents houses and condominiums in the Valley for participants to live in during the week of the conference. Single room (1 participant): $700/week. Double room (twin beds, room shared by conference participant of the same sex): $465/week. Multiple room (bunk beds, room shared with 2 or more participants of the same sex): $295/week. All rooms subject to availability; early requests are recommended. Can arrange airport shuttle pick-ups for a fee.

ADDITIONAL INFORMATION Online submittal process, see squawvalleywriters.org/writers_ws.htm#APPLY for instructions and application form. Send inquiries via e-mail to info@squawvalleywriters.org.

STEAMBOAT SPRINGS WRITERS CONFERENCE

Steamboat Springs Arts Council, Eleanor Bliss Center for the Arts at the Depot, 1001 13th St., Steamboat Springs CO 80487. (970)879-9008. **Fax:** (970)879-8138. **E-mail:** info@steamboatwriters.com. **Website:** www.steamboatwriters.com. **Contact:** Susan de Wardt. Estab. 1982. Writers' workshops geared toward intermediate levels. Open to professionals and amateurs alike.

COSTS Tuition: $60 early registration, $75 after May 16.

ADDITIONAL INFORMATION For additional information, please consult the website.

SUMMER WRITING PROGRAM

Naropa University, 2130 Arapahoe Ave., Boulder CO 80302. (303)245-4862. **Fax:** (303)546-5287. **E-mail:** swpr@naropa.edu. **Website:** www.naropa.edu/swp. **Contact:** Kyle Pivarnik, special projects manager. Estab. 1974. Annual event in summer. Workshop duration: 4 weeks. Average attendance: 250. Offers college credit. Accepts inquiries by e-mail, phone. With 13 workshops to choose from each of the 4 weeks of the program, students may study poetry, prose, hybrid/cross-genre writing, small press printing, or book arts. Site: All workshops, panels, lectures and readings are hosted on the Naropa University main campus. Located in downtown Boulder, the campus is within easy walking distance of restaurants, shopping, and the scenic Pearl Street Mall.

ADDITIONAL INFORMATION Writers can elect to take the Summer Writing Program for noncredit, graduate, or undergraduate credit. The registration procedure varies, so consider whether or not you'll be taking the SWP for academic credit. All participants can elect to take any combination of the first, second, third, and/or fourth weeks. To request a catalog of upcoming program or to find additional information, visit naropa.edu/swp. Naropa University also welcomes participants with disabilities.

○ SURREY INTERNATIONAL WRITERS' CONFERENCE

151-10090 152 St., Suite 544, Surrey BC V3R 8X8 Canada. **E-mail:** kathychung@siwc.ca. **Website:** www.siwc.ca. **Contact:** Kathy Chung, proposals contact and conference coordinator. Annual writing conference outside Vancouver, Canada, held every October. Writing workshops geared toward beginner, intermediate, and advanced levels. More than 70 workshops and panels, on all topics and genres, plus pre-conference master classes. Blue Pencil and agent/editor pitch sessions included. Different conference price packages available. Check the conference website for more information. This event has many literary agents in attendance taking pitches.

TAOS SUMMER WRITERS' CONFERENCE

Department of English Language and Literature, MSC 03 2170, 1 University of New Mexico, Albuquerque NM 87131-0001. **E-mail:** swarner@unm.edu. **Website:** taosconf.unm.edu. **Contact:** Sharon Oard Warner. Estab. 1999. Annual conference held in July. 2015 dates: July 12-19. Offers workshops and master classes in the novel, short story, poetry, creative nonfiction, memoir, prose style, screenwriting, humor writing, yoga and writing, literary translation, book proposal, the query letter and revision.Participants may also schedule a consultation with a visiting agent/editor.

COSTS Week-long workshop registration $700, weekend workshop registration $400, master classes between $1,350 and $1,625, publishing consultations are $175.

TEXAS CHRISTIAN WRITERS' CONFERENCE

1108 Valerie, Pasadena TX 77502. **E-mail:** patav@aol.com. **Website:** http://tcwhouston.blogspot.com. Martha Rogers (marthalrogers@sbcqlobal.net) **Contact:** Pat Vance, conference registration. Estab. 1990. Open conference for all interested writers, held the first Saturday in August. Fiction and nonfiction workshops offered. 2016 dates are not set as of early 2015.

TEXAS WRITING RETREAT

Grimes County TX **E-mail:** PaulTCuclis@gmail.com. **E-mail:** PaulTCuclis@gmail.com. **Website:** www.texaswritingretreat.com. **Contact:** Paul Cuclis, coordinator. Estab. 2013. The Texas Writing Retreat is an intimate event with a limited number of attendees. Held on a private residence ranch an hour outside of Houston, it has an agent and editor in attendance teaching. All attendees get to pitch the attending agent. Meals and excursions and amenities included. This is a unique event that combines craft sessions, business sessions, time for writing, relaxation, and more. The retreat is not held every year. It's best to check the website and see if there is a retreat this year.

COSTS Costs vary per event. There are different pricing options for those staying onsite vs. commuters.

ACCOMMODATIONS Private ranch residence in Texas.

THRILLERFEST

P.O. Box 311, Eureka CA 95502. **E-mail:** infocentral@thrillerwriters.org. **Website:** www.thrillerfest.com. **Contact:** Kimberley Howe, executive director. Grand Hyatt New York, 109 E. 42nd St., New York, NY 10017. Estab. 2006. Annual. 2015 dates: July 7-11 in Manhattan. Conference duration: 5 days. Average attendance: 1,000. Workshop/conference/festival. "A great place to learn the craft of writing the thriller. Classes taught by bestselling authors." Speakers have included David Morrell, James Patterson, Sandra Brown, Ken Follett, Eric Van Lustbader, David Baldacci, Brad Meltzer, Steve Martini, R.L. Stine, Steve Berry, Kathleen Antrim, Douglas Preston, Gayle Lynds, Harlan Coben, Lee Child, Lisa Scottolini, Katherine Neville, Robin Cook, Andrew Gross, Kathy Reichs, Brad Thor, Clive Cussler, Donald Maass, M.J. Rose, and Al Zuckerman. Three days of the conference are CraftFest, where the focus is on the craft of writing, and 2 days are ThrillerFest, which showcase the author-fan relationship. Also featured: PitchFest—a unique event where authors can pitch their work face-to-face to 50 top literary agents. Lastly, there is the International Thriller Awards and Banquet.

COSTS Price will vary from $330-1,100, depending on which events are selected. Various package deals are available offering savings, and Early Bird pricing is offered beginning September of each year.

ACCOMMODATIONS Grand Hyatt in Manhattan.

TIN HOUSE SUMMER WRITERS WORKSHOP

P.O. Box 10500, Portland OR 97296. (503)219-0622. **Website:** http://www.tinhouse.com/blog/workshop. Estab. 2003. Annual workshops held in Oregon. 2015 dates: fiction workshop is Jan. 30 - Feb. 2; nonfiction workshop is Feb. 6-9. Full list of faculty members is available online.

COSTS $40 application fee; $1,200 for program + room and board (breakfast and one dinner).

ACCOMMODATIONS Sylvia Beach Hotel.

ADDITIONAL INFORMATION Attendees must apply; all information available online. "A board composed of Tin House editorial staff members decides upon applications. Acceptance is based on the strength and promise of the submitted writing sample, as well as how much the board feels an applicant might benefit from the Winter Workshop. We will notify applicants of acceptance or rejection within 4 weeks of the application's receipt. Once accepted, enrollment into the program is granted on a first-come, first-serve basis (meaning you need to register in-order to guarantee your spot). We encourage you to apply early, as workshops can fill quickly."

TMCC WRITERS' CONFERENCE

Truckee Meadows Community College, 7000 Dandini Blvd., Reno NV 89512. (775)673-7111. **E-mail:** wdce@tmcc.edu. **Website:** wdce.tmcc.edu. Estab. 1991. Annual conference held in April. 2015 date: April 18. Average attendance: 150. Conference focuses on strengthening mainstream/literary fiction and nonfiction works and how to market them to agents and publishers. Site: Truckee Meadows Community College in Reno. "There is always an array of speakers and presenters with impressive literary credentials, including agents and editors." Speakers have included Chuck Sambuchino, Sheree Bykofsky, Andrea Brown, Dorothy Allison, Karen Joy Fowler, James D. Houston, James N. Frey, Gary Short, Jane Hirschfield, Dorrianne Laux, and Kim Addonizio. Literary agents are onsite to take pitches from writers.

COSTS $119 for a full-day seminar; $32 for a 10-minute one-on-one appointment with an agent or editor; $12 for lunch.

ACCOMMODATIONS Contact the conference manager to learn about accommodation discounts.

ADDITIONAL INFORMATION "The conference is open to all writers, regardless of their level of experience. Brochures are available online and mailed in January. Send inquiries via e-mail."

TONY HILLERMAN WRITERS CONFERENCE

1063 Willow Way, Santa FE NM 87505. (505)471-1565. **E-mail:** wordharvest@wordharvest.com. **Website:** www.wordharvest.com. **Contact:** Anne Hillerman and Jean Schaumberg, co-founders. Estab. 2004. An-

nual event held in November. Conference duration: 3 days. Average attendance: 100. Site: Hilton Santa Fe Historic Plaza. Full days of presentations on the craft of writing. We honor the winner of the $10,000 Tony Hillerman Prize for best first mystery at the Hillerman luncheon. A flash critique session-"Writing With the Stars"-is open to any interested attendee and adds to the fun and information. A book signing/reception is followed by the keynote dinner.

COSTS A full registration is $695, but there are many options in terms of lower prices if the attendee only comes 1-2 days. All information available on website.

ACCOMMODATIONS Hilton Santa Fe Historic Plaza.

UNICORN WRITERS CONFERENCE

P.O. Box 176, Redding CT 06876. (203)938-7405. **E-mail:** unicornwritersconference@gmail.com. **Website:** www.unicornwritersconference.com. This writers conference draws upon its close proximity to New York City and pulls in many literary agents and editors to pitch each year. There are ms review sessions (40 pages equals 30 minutes with an agent/editor), query/ms review sessions, and five different workshops every hour. $300 cost includes all workshops and 3 meals.

ACCOMMODATIONS Held at Reid Castle, Purchase, N.Y. Directions available on event website.

UNIVERSITY OF NORTH DAKOTA WRITERS CONFERENCE

Department of English, 110 Merrifield Hall, 276 Centennial Dr., Stop 7209, Grand Forks ND 58202. (701)777-2393. **Fax:** (701)777-2373. **E-mail:** crystal.alberts@e-mail.und.edu. **Website:** http://und.edu/orgs/writers-conference. **Contact:** Crystal Alberts, director. Estab. 1970. Annual event of 3-5 days. 2016 dates: April 6-8. Offers panels, readings, and films focused around a specific theme. Almost all events take place in the UND Memorial Union, which has a variety of small rooms and a 1,000-seat main hall. Past speakers include Art Spiegelman, Truman Capote, Sir Salman Rushdie, Allen Ginsberg, Alice Walker, and Louise Erdrich.

COSTS All events are free and open to the public. Donations accepted.

ACCOMMODATIONS Accommodations available at area hotels. Information on overnight accommodations available on website.

ADDITIONAL INFORMATION Schedule and other information available on website.

UNIVERSITY OF WISCONSIN AT MADISON WRITERS INSTITUTE

21 N. Park St., Madison WI 53715-1218. (608)262-3447. **Website:** https://uwwritersinstitute.wisc.edu/. Estab. 1990. Annual conference. 2016 dates: April 15-17. Conference on fiction and nonfiction held at the University of Wisconsin at Madison. Guest speakers are published authors, editors, and agents.

COSTS $125-260, depending on discounts and if you attend one day or multiple days.

ACCOMMODATIONS The 2016 location is at the Madison Concourse Hotel.

UW-MADISON WRITERS' INSTITUTE

21 North Park St., Room 7331, Madison WI 53715. (608)265-3972. **Fax:** (608)265-2475. **E-mail:** lscheer@dcs.wisc.edu. **Website:** www.uwwritersinstitute.org. **Contact:** Laurie Scheer. Estab. 1989. Annual. Conference usually held in the spring. Site: Madison Concourse Hotel, downtown Madison. Average attendance: 600. Conference speakers provide workshops and consultations. For information, send e-mail, visit website, call, fax. Accepts inquiries by SASE, e-mail, phone, fax. Agents and editors participate in conference.

COSTS $260-310; includes materials, breaks.

ACCOMMODATIONS Provides a list of area hotels or lodging options.

ADDITIONAL INFORMATION Sponsors contest.

WESLEYAN WRITERS CONFERENCE

Wesleyan University, 294 High St., Room 207, Middletown CT 06459. (860)685-3604. **Fax:** (860)685-2441. **E-mail:** agreene@wesleyan.edu. **Website:** www.wesleyan.edu/writing/conference. Estab. 1956. Annual conference. 2015 dates: June 10-14. Average attendance: 100. Focuses on the novel, fiction techniques, short stories, poetry, screenwriting, nonfiction, literary journalism, memoir, mixed media work and publishing. The conference is held on the campus of Wesleyan University, in the hills overlooking the Connecticut River. Features a faculty of award-winning writers, seminars and readings of new fiction, poetry, nonfiction and mixed media forms - as well as guest lectures on a range of topics including publishing. Both new and experienced writers are welcome. Participants may attend seminars in all genres. Speakers have included Esmond Harmsworth (Zachary Schuster Agency), Daniel Mandel (Sanford J. Greenburger Associates), Amy Williams (ICM and Collins McCormick), and many others. Agents will be speaking and available for meetings with attendees. Participants are often successful in finding agents and publishers for their mss. Wesleyan participants are also frequently featured in the anthology *Best New American Voices*.

ACCOMMODATIONS Meals are provided on campus. Lodging is available on campus or in town.

ADDITIONAL INFORMATION Ms critiques are available, but not required.

WESTERN RESERVE WRITERS & FREELANCE CONFERENCE

7700 Clocktower Dr., Kirtland OH 44094. (440)525-7812. **E-mail:** deencr@aol.com. **Website:** www.deannaadams.com. **Contact:** Deanna Adams, director/conference coordinator. Estab. 1983. Biannual. Last conference held September 26, 2015. Conference duration: 1 day or half-day. Average attendance: 120. "The Western Reserve Writers Conferences are designed for all writers, aspiring and professional, and offer presentations in all genres—nonfiction, fiction, poetry, essays, creative nonfiction, and the business of writing, including Web writing and successful freelance writing." Site: "Located in the main building of Lakeland Community College, the conference is easy to find and just off the I-90 freeway. The Fall 2013 conference featured top-notch presenters from newspapers and magazines, along with published authors, freelance writers, and professional editors. Presentations included 'Writing Believable Dialogue,' 'Creating a Sense of Place,' 'Writing Your Life Story,' 'First Fiction,' 'Writing and Researching Crime Stories,' as well as tips on submissions, getting books into stores, and storytelling for both fiction and nonfiction writers. Included throughout the day are one-on-one editing consults, Q&A panel, and book sale/author signings."

COSTS Fall all-day conference includes lunch: $105. Spring half-day conference, no lunch: $69.

ADDITIONAL INFORMATION Brochures for the conferences are available by January (for spring conference) and July (for fall). Also accepts inquiries by e-mail and phone. Check Deanna Adams' website for all updates. Editors always attend the conferences. Private editing consultations are available, as well.

WHIDBEY ISLAND WRITERS' CONFERENCE

P.O. Box 1289, Langley WA 98260. (360)331-0307. **E-mail:** http://writeonwhidbey.org. **Website:** http://writeonwhidbey.org. Annual conference held in early spring. Registration limited to 290. Registration includes workshops, fireside chats, book-signing reception, various activities, and daily luncheons. The conference offers consultation appointments with editors and agents. Registrants may reduce the cost of their conference by volunteering. See the website for more information. "The uniquely personal and friendly weekend is designed to be highly interactive." There are a variety of sessions on topics such as fiction, craft, poetry, platform, agents, screenwriting, and much more. Topics are varied, and there is something for all writers. Multiple agents and editors are in attendance. The schedule and faculty change every year, and those changes are reflected online

COSTS Cost: $395; early bird and member discounts available

WILDACRES WRITERS WORKSHOP

233 S. Elm St., Greensboro NC 27401. (336)255-8210. **E-mail:** judihill@aol.com. **Website:** www.wildacres-writers.com. **Contact:** Judi Hill, Director. Estab. 1985. 2015 summer workshop dates: July 4-11. Conference duration: 1 week. Average attendance: 100. Workshop focuses on novel, short story, flash fiction, poetry, and nonfiction. 10 on faculty include Ron Rash, Carrie Brown, Dr. Janice Fuller, Phillip Gerard, Luke Whisnant, Dr. Joe Clark, John Gregory Brown, Dr. Phebe Davidson, Lee Zacharias, and Vicki Lane. This group also has a week-long writing retreat that is different from the workshop.

COSTS The current price is $790. Check the website for more info.

ADDITIONAL INFORMATION Include a 1-page writing sample with your registration. See the website for information.

WILLAMETTE WRITERS CONFERENCE

2108 Buck St., West Linn OR 97068. (503)305-6729. **Fax:** (503)344-6174. **Website:** willamettewriters.com/wwcon/. Estab. 1981. Annual conference held in August. 2015 dates: Aug. 7-9. Conference duration: 3 days. Average attendance: 600. "Willamette Writers is open to all writers, and we plan our conference accordingly. We offer workshops on all aspects of fiction, nonfiction, marketing, the creative process, screen-writing, etc. Also, we invite top-notch inspirational speakers for keynote addresses. We always include at least 1 agent or editor panel and offer a variety of topics of interest to both fiction and nonfiction writers and screenwriters." Agents will be speaking and available for meetings with attendees.

COSTS Pricing schedule available online.

ACCOMMODATIONS If necessary, arrangements can be made on an individual basis through the conference hotel. Special rates may be available. 2015 location was the Lloyd Center DoubleTree Hotel.

ADDITIONAL INFORMATION Brochure/guidelines are available for a catalog-sized SASE.

◉ THE UNIVERSITY OF WINCHESTER WRITERS' FESTIVAL

University of Winchester, Winchester Hampshire WA S022 4NR United Kingdom. 44(0)1962-827238. **E-mail:** judith.heneghan@winchester.ac.uk. **Website:** www.writersfestival.co.uk. The dates for the 35th Winchester Writers' Festival (2015) are June 19-21, held at the University of Winchester. Sebastian Faulks, internationally acclaimed author of *Birdsong, A Possible Life* and *Human Traces* will give the keynote address and will lead an outstanding team of 60 best-selling authors, commissioning editors and literary agents offering day-long workshops, 32 talks and 700 one-to-one appointments to help writers harness their creative ideas, turn them into marketable work and pitch to publishing professionals. Participate by entering some of the 11 writing competitions, even if you can't attend. More than 130 writers have now reported major publishing successes as a direct result of their attendance at past festivals. This leading international literary event offers a magnificent source of support, advice, inspiration and networking opportunities for new and published writers working in all genres. Enjoy a creative writing weekend in Winchester, the oldest city in England and only one hour from London. To view Festival details, including all the competition details please go to the official event website.

WINTER POETRY & PROSE GETAWAY

18 N. Richards Ave., Ventnor NJ 08406. (888)887-2105. **E-mail:** info@wintergetaway.com; amanda@murphywriting.com. **Website:** www.wintergetaway.com. **Contact:** Peter Murphy. Estab. 1994. Annual January conference at the Jersey Shore. 2016 dates: January 15-18. "This is not your typical writers' conference. Advance your craft and energize your writing at the

Winter Getaway. Enjoy challenging and supportive workshops, insightful feedback, and encouraging community. Choose from small, intensive workshops in memoir, novel, YA, nonfiction, and poetry."

ACCOMMODATIONS See website or call for current fee information.

ADDITIONAL INFORMATION Previous faculty has included Julianna Baggott, Christian Bauman, Laure-Anne Bosselaar, Kurt Brown, Mark Doty (National Book Award winner), Stephen Dunn (Pulitzer Prize winner), Dorianne Laux, Carol Plum-Ucci, James Richardson, Mimi Schwartz, Terese Svoboda, and more.

WISCONSIN BOOK FESTIVAL

Madison Public Library, 201 W. Mifflin St., Madison WI 53703. (608)266-6300. **E-mail:** bookfest@mplfoundation.org. **Website:** www.wisconsinbookfestival.org. Estab. 2002. Annual festival held in October. Conference duration: 4 days. The festival features readings, lectures, book discussions, writing workshops, live interviews, children's events, and more. Speakers have included Isabel Allende, Jonathan Alter, Paul Auster, Michael Chabon, Billy Collins, Phillip Gourevitch, Ian Frazier, Tim O'Brien, Elizabeth Strout.

COSTS All festival events are free.

WOMEN WRITERS WINTER RETREAT

Homestead House B&B, 38111 West Spaulding, Willoughby OH 44094. (440)946-1902. **E-mail:** deencr@aol.com. **Website:** www.deannaadams.com. Estab. 2007. Annual —always happens the last weekend in February. Conference duration: 3 days. Average attendance: 35-40."The Women Writers' Winter Retreat was designed for aspiring and professional women writers who cannot seem to find enough time to devote to honing their craft. Each retreat offers class time and workshops facilitated by successful women writers, as well as allows time to do some actual writing, alone or in a group. A Friday night dinner and keynote kickstarts the weekend, followed by Saturday workshops, free time, meals, and an open mic to read your works. Sunday wraps up with 1 more workshop and fellowship. All genres welcome. Choice of overnight stay or commuting." Door prizes and book sale/author signings throughout the weekend.

COSTS Single room: $315; shared room: $235 (includes complete weekend package, with B&B stay and all meals and workshops); weekend commute: $165; Saturday only: $125 (prices include lunch and dinner).

ADDITIONAL INFORMATION Brochures for the writers retreat are available by December. Accepts inquiries and reservations by e-mail or phone. See Deanna's website for additional information and updates.

WOMEN WRITING THE WEST

8547 E. Araphoe Rd., Box J-541, Greenwood Village CO 80112-1436. **E-mail:** conference@womenwritingthewest.org; jane@jkbooks.com. **Website:** www.womenwritingthewest.org. 2015 dates: October 8-11. "Women Writing the West is a nonprofit association of writers, editors, publishers, agents, booksellers, and other professionals writing and promoting the women's west. As such, women writing their stories in the American West in a way that illuminates them authentically. In addition, the organization provides support, encouragement, and inspiration to all women writing about any facet of the American West. Membership is open to all interested persons worldwide. Open to students. Members actively exchange ideas on a list e-bulletin board. WWW membership also allows the choice of participation in our marketing marvel, the annual WWW Catalog of Author's Books. An annual conference is held every fall. Our blog, Facebook and ListServ publish current WWW activities; features market research, and experience articles of interest pertaining to American West literature and member news. Sponsors annual WILLA Literary Award, which is given in several categories for outstanding literature featuring women's stories, set in the West. The winner of a WILLA literary Award receives a cash award and a trophy at the annual conference. Contest open to non-members. Annual conference held in third weekend in October. Covers research, writing techniques, multiple genres, marketing/promotion, and more. Agents and editors will be speaking and available for one-on-one meetings with attendees. Conference location changes each year."

COSTS See website. Discounts available for members, and for specific days only.

ACCOMMODATIONS See website for location and accommodation details.

WORDS & MUSIC

624 Pirate's Alley, New Orleans LA 70116. (504)586-1609. **Fax:** (504)522-9725. **E-mail:** info@wordsandmusic.org; Faulkhouse@aol.com. **Website:** www.

wordsandmusic.org. Estab. 1997. Annual conference held in November. Conference duration: 5 days. Average attendance: 300. Presenters include authors, agents, editors and publishers. Past speakers included agents Deborah Grosvenor, Judith Weber, Stuart Bernstein, Nat Sobel, Jeff Kleinman, Emma Sweeney, Liza Dawson, and Michael Murphy; editors Lauren Marino, Webster Younce, Ann Patty, Will Murphy, Jofie Ferrari-Adler, and Elizabeth Stein; critics Marie Arana, Jonathan Yardley, and Michael Dirda; fiction writers Oscar Hijuelos, Robert Olen Butler, Shirley Ann Grau, Mayra Montero, Ana Castillo, and H.G. Carrillo. Agents and editors critique mss in advance; meet with them one-on-one during the conference. A full, detailed schedule of workshops is available online.

COSTS See website for a costs and additional information on accommodations. Website will update closer to date of conference.

ACCOMMODATIONS Hotel Monteleone in New Orleans.

WRITE-BY-THE-LAKE WRITER'S WORKSHOP & RETREAT

21 N. Park St., 7th Floor, Madison WI 53715. (608)262-3447. **E-mail:** cdesmet@dcs.wisc.edu. **Website:** www.dcs.wisc.edu/lsa/writing. **Contact:** Christine DeSmet, director. Open to all writers and students; 12 workshops for all levels. Includes classes for full-novel critique and one Master Class for 50 pages. Held the third week of June on UW-Madison campus. Registration limited to 15 each section; fewer in Master Classes. Writing facilities available; computer labs, wi-fi in all buildings and on the outdoor lakeside terrace. E-mail for more information. "Registration opens every January for following June."

COSTS Costs $365 before May 18; $415 after May 18. Additional cost for Master Classes and college credits. Cost includes instruction, welcome luncheon, and pastry/coffee each day.

☯ WRITE CANADA

The Word Guild, Suite 226, 245 King George Rd., Brantford ON N3R 7N7 Canada. **E-mail:** writecanada@thewordguild.com. **Website:** thewordguild.com/events/write-canada/. Conference duration: 3 days. Annual conference in Ontario for writers who are Christian of all types and at all stages. Offers solid instruction, stimulating interaction, exciting challenges, and worshipful community.

ADDITIONAL INFORMATION Write Canada is the nation's largest Christian writers' conference held annually. Each year hundreds of writers and editors–authors, journalists, columnists, bloggers, poets and playwrights–gather to hone their craft at the three-day conference.Over the past three decades, Write Canada has successfully equipped writers and editors, beginner to professional, from all across North America.

WRITE ON THE SOUND WRITERS' CONFERENCE

Edmonds Arts Commission, Frances Anderson Center, 700 Main St., Edmonds WA 98020. (425)771-0228. **Fax:** (425)771-0253. **E-mail:** wots@edmondswa.gov. **Website:** www.writeonthesound.com. Estab. 1985. Annual conference held in October. 2015 dates: 2-4. Conference duration: 2.5 days. Average attendance: 200. Features over 30 presenters, a literary contest, ms critiques, a reception and book signing, onsite bookstore, and a variety of evening activities. Held at the Frances Anderson Center in Edmonds, just north of Seattle on the Puget Sound. Speakers have included Elizabeth George, Dan Hurley, Marcia Woodard, Holly Hughes, Greg Bear, Timothy Egan, Joe McHugh, Frances Wood, Garth Stein and Max Grover.

COSTS See website for more information on applying to view costs.

ADDITIONAL INFORMATION Brochures are available in July. Accepts inquiries via phone, e-mail, and fax.

WRITERS' CONFERENCE AT OCEAN PARK

P.O. Box 172, Assonet ME 02702. (401)598-1424. **E-mail:** jbrosnan@jwu.edu. **Website:** www.oceanpark.org. Estab. 1941. Annual conference held in mid-August. Conference duration: 4 days. Average attendance: 50. "We try to present a balanced and eclectic conference. In addition to time and attention given to poetry, we also have children's literature, mystery writing, travel, fiction, nonfiction, journalism, and other issues of interest to writers. Our speakers are editors, writers, and other professionals. Our concentration is, by intention, a general view of writing to publish with supportive encouragement. We are located in Ocean Park, a small seashore village 14 miles south of Portland. Ours is a summer assembly center with many buildings from the Victorian age. The conference meets in Porter Hall, one of the assembly buildings which is listed in the National

Register of Historic Places. Speakers have included Michael C. White (novelist/short story writer), Betsy Shool (poet), Suzanne Strempek Shea (novelist), John Perrault (poet), Josh Williamson (newspaper editor), Dawn Potter (poet), Bruce Pratt (fiction writer), Amy McDonald (children's author), Anne Wescott Dodd (nonfiction writer), Kate Chadbourne (singer/songwriter), Wesley McNair (poet/Maine faculty member), and others. We usually have about 8 guest presenters each year." Writers/editors will be speaking, leading workshops, and available for meetings with attendees. Workshops start at 8:30 a.m. on Tuesday and continue through Friday until early afternoon.

COSTS $200. The fee does not include housing or meals, which must be arranged separately by conferees.

ACCOMMODATIONS "An accommodations list is available. We are in a summer resort area where motels, guest houses, and restaurants abound."

ADDITIONAL INFORMATION 2015 marked the conference's 75th anniversary.

WRITER'S DIGEST CONFERENCES

F+W Media, Inc., 10151 Carver Rd., Suite 200, Blue Ash OH 45242. **E-mail:** jill.ruesch@fwmedia.com. **E-mail:** phil.sexton@fwmedia.com. **Website:** www. writersdigestconference.com. Estab. 1995. The Writer's Digest conferences feature an amazing line up of speakers to help writers with the craft and business of writing. Each calendar year typically features multiple conferences around the country. In 2015, the New York conference will be July 31 - Aug 2, while the Los Angeles conference will be in October. The most popular feature of the east coast conference is the agent pitch slam, in which potential authors are given the ability to pitch their books directly to agents. For the 2015 conference, there will be more than 50 agents in attendance. For more details, see the website.

COSTS Cost varies by location and year. There are typically different pricing options for those who wish to stay for the entire event vs. daylong passes.

ACCOMMODATIONS A block of rooms at the event hotel are reserved for guests.

WRITERS' LEAGUE OF TEXAS AGENTS CONFERENCE

Writers' League of Texas, 611 S. Congress Ave., Suite 200 A-3, Austin TX 78704. (512)499-8914. **Fax:** Shool (poet), Suzanne Strempek Shea (novelist), John Perrault (poet), Josh Williamson (newspaper editor), Dawn Potter (poet), Bruce Pratt (fiction writer), Amy McDonald (children's author), Anne Wescott Dodd (nonfiction writer), Kate Chadbourne (singer/songwriter), Wesley McNair (poet/Maine faculty member), and others. We usually have about 8 guest presenters each year." Writers/editors will be speaking, leading workshops, and available for meetings with attendees. Workshops start at 8:30 a.m. on Tuesday and continue through Friday until early afternoon.

COSTS $200. The fee does not include housing or meals, which must be arranged separately by conferees.

ACCOMMODATIONS "An accommodations list is available. We are in a summer resort area where motels, guest houses, and restaurants abound."

ADDITIONAL INFORMATION 2015 marked the conference's 75th anniversary.

WRITERS WEEKEND AT THE BEACH

P.O. Box 877, Ocean Park WA 98640. (360)665-4367. **E-mail:** director@opretreat.org. **Contact:** Brandon Scheer; Tracie Heskett. Estab. 1992. Annual conference held in March. Conference duration: 2 days. Average attendance: 45. A retreat for writers with an emphasis on poetry, fiction, and nonfiction. Held at the Ocean Park Methodist Retreat Center & Camp. Speakers have included Miralee Ferrell, Leslie Gould, Linda Clare, Birdie Etchison, Colette Tennant, Gail Denham, Patricia Rushford, and Marion Duckworth.

COSTS $200 for full registration before Feb. 15 and $215 after Feb. 15.

ACCOMMODATIONS Offers on-site overnight lodging.

WRITE-TO-PUBLISH CONFERENCE

WordPro Communication Services, 9118 W. Elmwood Dr., Suite 1G, Niles IL 60714-5820. (847)296-3964. **Fax:** (847)296-0754. **E-mail:** lin@writetopublish.com. **Website:** www.writetopublish.com. **Contact:** Lin Johnson, director. Estab. 1971. Annual. 2015 Conference dates: June 3-6. Average attendance: 200. Conference is focused for the Christian market and includes classes on writing for children. Writer workshops geared toward all levels. Open to students. Site: Wheaton College, Wheaton, IL (Chicago).

COSTS $475; includes conference and banquet.

ACCOMMODATIONS Attendees stay in campus residence halls. Cost is $280-360.

ADDITIONAL INFORMATION Optional ms evaluation available. College credit available. Conference information available in January. For details, visit website, or e-mail brochure@writetopublish.com. Accepts inquiries by e-mail, fax, phone.

THE WRITING CONFERENCE OF LOS ANGELES

Website: www.writingconferenceoflosangeles.com. The 2015 event is set for Saturday, October 10, 2015. Organized by Writing Day Workshops. The workshop is a one-day, all-day "How to Get Published" conference with instructional sessions and panels. Multiple literary agents are in attendance at the workshop to meet with writers and hear pitches.

COSTS Early-bird tuition is $149; later tuition is $179; agent meetings are $29 per appointment.

ACCOMMODATIONS Rooms available at the event hotel: The Four Points Sheraton in Culver City.

ADDITIONAL INFORMATION Query critique options available. Check the website for contact and registration information.

WRITING AND ILLUSTRATING FOR YOUNG READERS CONFERENCE

1480 East 9400 South, Sandy UT 84093. **E-mail:** staff@wifyr.com. **Website:** www.wifyr.com. Estab. 2000. Annual workshop. June 2015 dates: June 15-19. Conference duration: 5 days. Average attendance: 100+. Learn how to write, illustrate, and publish in the children's and young adult markets. Beginning and advanced writers and illustrators are tutored in a small-group workshop setting by published authors and artists and receive instruction from and network with editors, major publishing house representatives, and literary agents. Afternoon attendees get to hear practical writing and publishing tips from published authors, literary agents, and editors. Held at the Waterford School in Sandy, UT. Speakers have included John Cusick, Stephen Fraser, Alyson Heller, and Ruth Katcher.

COSTS Costs available online.

ACCOMMODATIONS A block of rooms are available at the Best Western Cotton Tree Inn in Sandy, UT at a discounted rate. This rate is good as long as there are available rooms.

ADDITIONAL INFORMATION There is an online form to contact this event.

WRITING FOR THE SOUL

Jerry B. Jenkins Christian Writers Guild, P.O. Box 88288, Black Forest CO 80908. (866)495-7551. **Fax:** (719)494-1299. **E-mail:** Jerry@JerryJenkins.com.

Website: www.Jerry-Jenkins.com. Conferences as announced, covering fiction, nonfiction, and online writing. Nationally known, bestselling authors as keynote speakers, hosted by Jerry B. Jenkins. See website for pricing, locations, dates, and accommodations.

WRITING WORKSHOPS AT CASTLE HILL

10 Meetinghouse Rd., P.O. Box 756, Truro MA 02666. (508)349-7511. **Fax:** (508)349-7513. **E-mail:** info@castlehill.org. **Website:** www.castlehill.org/workshop-writing.html. Workshops about poetry, fiction, narrative nonfiction, memoir, and more; these writing workshops are geared toward intermediate and advanced levels. **Open to students.** The dates, courses, and instructors change each year, so check the website for individual details of upcoming events. Held at the Truro Center for the Arts at Castle Hill in Massachusetts.

THE HELENE WURLITZER FOUNDATION

P.O. Box 1891, Taos NM 87571. (575)758-2413. **Fax:** (575)758-2559. **E-mail:** hwf@taosnet.com. **Website:** www.wurlitzerfoundation.org. **Contact:** Michael A. Knight, executive director. Estab. 1954.

ACCOMMODATIONS "Provides individual housing in fully furnished studio/houses (casitas), rent and utility free. Artists are responsible for transportation to and from Taos, their meals, and materials for their work. Bicycles are provided upon request."

WYOMING WRITERS CONFERENCE

Cheyenne WY **E-mail:** president@wyowriters.org. **Website:** wyowriters.org. **Contact:** Chris Williams. This is a statewide writing conference for writers of Wyoming and neighboring states. 2015 conference dates: June 5-7, 2015 in Cheyenne, WY. Each year, multiple published authors, editors, and literary agents are in attendance to meet with writers and take pitches.

LITERARY AGENT SPECIALTIES INDEX

///

FICTION:

ACTION
Agency Group LLC, The 111
Anderson Literary Management, LLC 116
Barone Literary Agency 117
Diana Finch Literary Agency 156
Don Congdon Associates Inc. 134
Dupree/Miller and Associates Literary 147
Dystel & Goderich Literary Management 148
Fairbank Literary Representation 154
Fielding Agency, LLC, The 155
Harwood Limited, Antony 175
International Transactions, Inc. 183
Jabberwocky Literary Agency 184
Jenks Agency, The Carolyn 186
Klinger, Inc., Harvey 189
Lampack Agency, Inc., Peter 192
Larsen/Elizabeth Pomada, Literary Agents,
Michael 193
Lecker Agency, Robert 196
Levine Literary Agency, Paul S. 198
Lippincott Massie McQuilkin 198
Marshall Agency, The Evan 208
McBride Literary Agency, Margret 209
Mendel Media Group, LLC 212
P.S. Literary Agency 221
Sanders & Associates, Victoria 234
Seymour Agency, The 238
Simmons Literary Agency, Jeffrey 241
Toby Eady Associates 149
Triada U.S. Literary Agency, Inc. 252
Venture Literary 254
Weiner Literary Agency, Cherry 257

ADVENTURE
Agency Group LLC, The 111
Alive Communications, Inc. 113
Anderson Literary Management, LLC 116
Barone Literary Agency 117
Corvisiero Literary Agency 136
Curtis Brown, Ltd. 138
D4EO Literary Agency 139
Diana Finch Literary Agency 156
Don Congdon Associates Inc. 134
Dupree/Miller and Associates Literary 147
Dystel & Goderich Literary Management 148
Fairbank Literary Representation 154
Fielding Agency, LLC, The 155
Harwood Limited, Antony 175
International Transactions, Inc. 183
Jabberwocky Literary Agency 184
Jenks Agency, The Carolyn 186
Klinger, Inc., Harvey 189
Lampack Agency, Inc., Peter 192

Larsen/Elizabeth Pomada, Literary Agents,
Michael 193
Lecker Agency, Robert 196
Levine Literary Agency, Paul S. 198
Lippincott Massie McQuilkin 198
Literary Group International, The 199
Marshall Agency, The Evan 208
McBride Literary Agency, Margret 209
McCarthy Creative Services 210
Mendel Media Group, LLC 212
Mura Literary, Dee 215
Pavilion Literary Management 218
Prentis Literary, Linn 220
P.S. Literary Agency 221
Sanders & Associates, Victoria 234
Sherman & Associates, Ken 239
Simmons Literary Agency, Jeffrey 241
Toby Eady Associates 149
Triada U.S. Literary Agency, Inc. 252
Venture Literary 254
Weiner Literary Agency, Cherry 257
Writers House 260

COMIC BOOKS
Agency Group LLC, The 111
Barone Literary Agency 117
Fielding Agency, LLC, The 155
Harwood Limited, Antony 175
Levine Literary Agency, Paul S. 198
Lippincott Massie McQuilkin 198

COMMERCIAL
Agency Group LLC, The 111
Aitken Alexander Associates 112
Barone Literary Agency 117
Bent Agency, The 118
Braun Associates, Inc., Barbara 124
Cameron & Associates, Kimberley 129
Capital Talent Agency 129
Castiglia Literary Agency 131
Chalberg & Sussman 131
Chase Literary Agency 131
Cheney Literary Associates, LLC, Elyse 132
Compass Talent 134
Cornerstone Literary, Inc. 136
Corvisiero Literary Agency 136
Curtis Associates, Inc., Richard 137
David Black Literary Agency 119
DeChiara Literary Agency, The Jennifer 141
Dijkstra Literary Agency, Sandra 143
Dreisbach Literary Management 146
Dunow, Carlson, & Lerner Agency 146
Dystel & Goderich Literary Management 148
FinePrint Literary Management 156
Fletcher & Company 157
Folio Literary Management, LLC 158

Foundry Literary + Media 158
Friedrich Agency, The 163
Hawkins & Associates, Inc., John 176
Heller Agency Inc., Helen 177
HSG Agency 180
InkWell Management, LLC 182
Judith Ehrlich Literary Management, LLC
151
Kern Literary Agency, The Natasha 188
Krichevsky Literary Agency, Inc., Stuart 191
LA Literary Agency, The 192
Lampack Agency, Inc., Peter 192
Laura Dail Literary Agency, Inc. 140
Lazin Books, Sarah 195
Leshne Agency, The 197
Lowenstein Associates Inc. 201
Lownie Literary Agency, Ltd., Andrew 203
Mann Agency, Carol 205
Marcil Literary Agency, Inc., The Denise 207
Marsal Lyon Literary Agency, LLC 207
McMillan & Associates, Inc., Sally Hill 211
Michaels Literary Agency, Inc., Doris S. 213
Miriam Altshuler Literary Agency 114
Moveable Type Management 214
Mura Literary, Dee 215
Naggar Literary Agency, Inc. Jean V. 215
Nelson Literary Agency 216
Perkins Agency, L. 219
Prospect Agency 221
Queen Literary Agency 223
Rebecca Friedman Literary Agency 162
Rees Literary Agency, Helen 225
Rights Factory, The 227
Rinaldi Literary Agency, Angela 227
RLR Associates, Ltd. 228
Ross Literary Agency, Andy 231
Serendipity Literary Agency, LLC 237
Slopen Literary Agency, Beverley 241
Spencerhill Associates 244
Sterling Lord Literistic, Inc. 246
Straus Agency, Inc., Robin 247
Talcott Notch Literary 249
Tessler Literary Agency, LLC 250
The Knight Agency 190
Trident Media Group 253
Unter Agency, The 254
Veritas Literary Agency 254
Vicky Bijur Literary Agency 119

CONTEMPORARY ISSUES
Agency Group LLC, The 111
Alive Communications, Inc. 113
Barone Literary Agency 117
Don Congdon Associates Inc. 134
Jabberwocky Literary Agency 184
Krichevsky Literary Agency, Inc., Stuart 191

Larsen/Elizabeth Pomada, Literary Agents,
Michael 193
Literary Group International, The 199
Mendel Media Group, LLC 212
Mura Literary, Dee 215
Sanders & Associates, Victoria 234
Schmidt Literary Agency, Harold 235
Sheree Bykofsky Associates, Inc. 128
Weiner Literary Agency, Cherry 257
Wm Clark Associates 133
Writers House 260

CRIME
Agency Group LLC, The 111
Alive Communications, Inc. 113
Axelrod Agency, The 116
Barone Literary Agency 117
Bent Agency, The 118
Brandt & Hochman Literary Agents, Inc. 123
Castiglia Literary Agency 131
Diana Finch Literary Agency 156
Don Congdon Associates Inc. 134
Dupree/Miller and Associates Literary 147
Dystel & Goderich Literary Management 148
Einstein Literary Management 151
Fielding Agency, LLC, The 155
FinePrint Literary Management 156
Fresh Books Literary Agency 161
Goodman Literary Agency, Irene 169
Greenburger Associates, Inc., Sanford J. 171
Green Literary Agency, LLC, Kathryn 173
Gregory & Co. Authors' Agents 173
Harwood Limited, Antony 175
Heller Agency Inc., Helen 177
Henshaw Group, Richard 177
HSG Agency 180
InkWell Management, LLC 182
International Transactions, Inc. 183
Jabberwocky Literary Agency 184
J de S Associates, Inc. 186
Klinger, Inc., Harvey 189
Lampack Agency, Inc., Peter 192
Langlie, Literary Agent, Laura 193
Larsen/Elizabeth Pomada, Literary Agents,
Michael 193
Lecker Agency, Robert 196
Levine Literary Agency, Paul S. 198
Lownie Literary Agency, Ltd., Andrew 203
Maass Literary Agency, Donald 203
MacGregor Literary Inc. 204
McBride Literary Agency, Margret 209
Mendel Media Group, LLC 212
Mura Literary, Dee 215
New Leaf Literary & Media, Inc. 216
Rights Factory, The 227
Robbins Literary Agency, B.J. 228
Sanders & Associates, Victoria 234
Simmons Literary Agency, Jeffrey 241
Triada U.S. Literary Agency, Inc. 252
Trident Media Group 253
Venture Literary 254
Weiner Literary Agency, Cherry 257
Writers House 260

DETECTIVE
Agency Group LLC, The 111
Barone Literary Agency 117
Curtis Brown, Ltd. 138
D4EO Literary Agency 139
Diana Finch Literary Agency 156
Don Congdon Associates Inc. 134
Dupree/Miller and Associates Literary 147
Dystel & Goderich Literary Management 148
Fielding Agency, LLC, The 155
Goodman Literary Agency, Irene 169
Green Literary Agency, LLC, Kathryn 173
Gregory & Co. Authors' Agents 173
Harwood Limited, Antony 175
Henshaw Group, Richard 177
International Transactions, Inc. 183
Jabberwocky Literary Agency 184
J de S Associates, Inc. 186
Klinger, Inc., Harvey 189
Lampack Agency, Inc., Peter 192
Langlie, Literary Agent, Laura 193

Larsen/Elizabeth Pomada, Literary Agents,
Michael 193
Lecker Agency, Robert 196
Levine Literary Agency, Paul S. 198
Literary Group International, The 199
Maass Literary Agency, Donald 203
MacGregor Literary Inc. 204
McBride Literary Agency, Margret 209
McCarthy Creative Services 210
Mendel Media Group, LLC 212
P.S. Literary Agency 221
Robbins Literary Agency, B.J. 228
Seligman, Literary Agent, Lynn 237
Sherman & Associates, Ken 239
Simmons Literary Agency, Jeffrey 241
Triada U.S. Literary Agency, Inc. 252
Venture Literary 254
Weiner Literary Agency, Cherry 257
Writers House 260

EROTICA
Agency Group LLC, The 111
Barone Literary Agency 117
Bradford Literary Agency 122
Chalberg & Sussman 131
Corvisiero Literary Agency 136
Curtis Brown, Ltd. 138
D4EO Literary Agency 139
Donaghy Literary Group 144
Folio Literary Management, LLC 158
Harwood Limited, Antony 175
International Transactions, Inc. 183
Lecker Agency, Robert 196
Levine Literary Agency, Paul S. 198
Marshall Agency, The Evan 208
McCarthy Creative Services 210
Mendel Media Group, LLC 212
Mura Literary, Dee 215
Perkins Agency, L. 219
P.S. Literary Agency 221
Red Sofa Literary 224
Sherman & Associates, Ken 239
Spencerhill Associates 244
Writers House 260

ETHNIC
Agency Group LLC, The 111
Amster Literary Enterprises, Betsy 115
Anderson Literary Management, LLC 116
Barone Literary Agency 117
Crichton & Associates 137
Curtis Brown, Ltd. 138
DeFiore & Co. 142
Diana Finch Literary Agency 156
Dunham Literary, Inc. 146
Dupree/Miller and Associates Literary 147
Dystel & Goderich Literary Management 148
Fielding Agency, LLC, The 155
Freymann Literary Agency, Sarah Jane 162
Golomb Literary Agency, The Susan 168
Harwood Limited, Antony 175
Jabberwocky Literary Agency 184
Jenks Agency, The Carolyn 186
Langlie, Literary Agent, Laura 193
Larsen/Elizabeth Pomada, Literary Agents,
Michael 193
Levine Literary Agency, Paul S. 198
Literary Group International, The 199
Marshall Agency, The Evan 208
McCarthy Creative Services 210
Mendel Media Group, LLC 212
Prentis Literary, Linn 220
P.S. Literary Agency 221
Publication Riot Group 223
Robbins Literary Agency, B.J. 228
Sanders & Associates, Victoria 234
Seligman, Literary Agent, Lynn 237
Sherman & Associates, Ken 239
Triada U.S. Literary Agency, Inc. 252
Wm Clark Associates 133
Writers House 260

EXPERIMENTAL
Agency Group LLC, The 111
Barone Literary Agency 117

Curtis Brown, Ltd. 138
Dupree/Miller and Associates Literary 147
Harwood Limited, Antony 175
International Transactions, Inc. 183
Jenks Agency, The Carolyn 186
Larsen/Elizabeth Pomada, Literary Agents,
Michael 193
Levine Literary Agency, Paul S. 198
Literary Group International, The 199
Scribe Agency, LLC 236
Sherman & Associates, Ken 239

FAMILY SAGA
Agency Group LLC, The 111
Alive Communications, Inc. 113
Anderson Literary Management, LLC 116
Barone Literary Agency 117
Brandt & Hochman Literary Agents, Inc. 123
Cheney Literary Associates, LLC, Elyse 132
Dupree/Miller and Associates Literary 147
Dystel & Goderich Literary Management 148
Fielding Agency, LLC, The 155
Green Literary Agency, LLC, Kathryn 173
Harwood Limited, Antony 175
International Transactions, Inc. 183
Jabberwocky Literary Agency 184
Jenks Agency, The Carolyn 186
Klinger, Inc., Harvey 189
Lampack Agency, Inc., Peter 192
Larsen/Elizabeth Pomada, Literary Agents,
Michael 193
Levine Literary Agency, Paul S. 198
Lippincott Massie McQuilkin 198
Literary Group International, The 199
Mura Literary, Dee 215
P.S. Literary Agency 221
Sanders & Associates, Victoria 234
Simmons Literary Agency, Jeffrey 241
Weiner Literary Agency, Cherry 257
Writers House 260

FANTASY
Barone Literary Agency 117
Bent Agency, The 118
Brandt & Hochman Literary Agents, Inc. 123
Cameron & Associates, Kimberley 129
CK Webber Associates Literary Management
257
Corvisiero Literary Agency 136
Curtis Associates, Inc., Richard 137
Curtis Brown, Ltd. 138
Darhansoff & Verrill Literary Agents 140
Donaghy Literary Group 144
Fielding Agency, LLC, The 155
FinePrint Literary Management 156
Fletcher & Company 157
Folio Literary Management, LLC 158
Fox Literary 159
Gernert Company, The 167
Grayson Literary Agency, Ashley 171
Greenburger Associates, Inc., Sanford J. 171
Grinberg Literary Agency, Jill 174
Harwood Limited, Antony 175
Henshaw Group, Richard 177
Hurst Literary Management, Andrea 181
Jabberwocky Literary Agency 184
Jenks Agency, The Carolyn 186
Joelle Delbourgo Associates, Inc. 143
Kidd Agency, Inc., Virginia 188
Literary Group International, The 199
Lowenstein Associates Inc. 201
Maass Literary Agency, Donald 203
McCarthy Agency, LLC, The 209
McCarthy Creative Services 210
Millard Literary Agency, Martha 213
Morhaim Literary Agency, Howard 214
Mura Literary, Dee 215
Naggar Literary Agency, Inc. Jean V. 215
Nelson Literary Agency 216
New Leaf Literary & Media, Inc. 216
Pavilion Literary Management 218
Perkins Agency, L. 219
Prentis Literary, Linn 220
Rebecca Friedman Literary Agency 162
Red Sofa Literary 224

Rights Factory, The 227
Schiavone Literary Agency, Inc. 234
Scribe Agency, LLC 236
Seligman, Literary Agent, Lynn 237
Seymour Agency, The 238
Sherman & Associates, Ken 239
Sternig & Byrne Literary Agency 246
Stringer Literary Agency, LLC, The 247
Talcott Notch Literary 249
The Knight Agency 190
Trident Media Group 253
Veritas Literary Agency 254
Weiner Literary Agency, Cherry 257
Writers House 260

FEMINIST

Agency Group LLC, The 111
Anderson Literary Management, LLC 116
Barone Literary Agency 117
Crichton & Associates 137
Curtis Brown, Ltd. 138
Dupree/Miller and Associates Literary 147
Fairbank Literary Representation 154
Fielding Agency, LLC, The 155
Harwood Limited, Antony 175
International Transactions, Inc. 183
Jenks Agency, The Carolyn 186
Langlie, Literary Agent, Laura 193
Larsen/Elizabeth Pomada, Literary Agents,
Michael 193
Levine Literary Agency, Paul S. 198
Lippincott Massie McQuilkin 198
Literary Group International, The 199
McCarthy Creative Services 210
Mendel Media Group, LLC 212
Sanders & Associates, Victoria 234
Scribe Agency, LLC 236
Seligman, Literary Agent, Lynn 237
Sherman & Associates, Ken 239
Writers House 260

GAY

Agency Group LLC, The 111
Anderson Literary Management, LLC 116
Barone Literary Agency 117
Corvisiero Literary Agency 136
Curtis Brown, Ltd. 138
Dystel & Goderich Literary Management 148
Fairbank Literary Representation 154
Fielding Agency, LLC, The 155
Harwood Limited, Antony 175
International Transactions, Inc. 183
Jabberwocky Literary Agency 184
Jenks Agency, The Carolyn 186
Larsen/Elizabeth Pomada, Literary Agents,
Michael 193
Levine Literary Agency, Paul S. 198
Lippincott Massie McQuilkin 198
McCarthy Creative Services 210
Mendel Media Group, LLC 212
Perkins Agency, L. 219
Prentis Literary, Linn 220
Schmidt Literary Agency, Harold 235
Serendipity Literary Agency, LLC 237
Sherman & Associates, Ken 239
Writers House 260

GLITZ

Agency Group LLC, The 111
Barone Literary Agency 117
Dupree/Miller and Associates Literary 147
Fielding Agency, LLC, The 155
Jabberwocky Literary Agency 184
Klinger, Inc., Harvey 189
Larsen/Elizabeth Pomada, Literary Agents,
Michael 193
Levine Literary Agency, Paul S. 198
McCarthy Creative Services 210
Mendel Media Group, LLC 212
Prentis Literary, Linn 220
Sherman & Associates, Ken 239

HISTORICAL

Agency Group LLC, The 111
Alive Communications, Inc. 113

Anderson Literary Management, LLC 116
Barone Literary Agency 117
Bent Agency, The 118
Books & Such Literary Agency 121
Brandt & Hochman Literary Agents, Inc. 123
Cameron & Associates, Kimberley 129
Chase Literary Agency 131
Cheney Literary Associates, LLC, Elyse 132
Chudney Agency, The 132
Connor Literary Agency 135
Corvisiero Literary Agency 136
Curtis Brown, Ltd. 138
D4EO Literary Agency 139
Darhansoff & Verrill Literary Agents 140
Diana Finch Literary Agency 156
Dupree/Miller and Associates Literary 147
Einstein Literary Management 151
English Literary Agency, The Elaine P. 152
Fielding Agency, LLC, The 155
Foundry Literary + Media 158
Fox Literary 159
Gelfman Schneider Literary Agents, Inc. 166
Gernert Company, The 167
Golomb Literary Agency, The Susan 168
Goodman Literary Agency, Irene 169
Grad Literary Agency, Inc., Doug 170
Greenburger Associates, Inc., Sanford J. 171
Green Literary Agency, LLC, Kathryn 173
Gregory & Co. Authors' Agents 173
Harwood Limited, Antony 175
Hawkins & Associates, Inc., John 176
Heller Agency Inc., Helen 177
Henshaw Group, Richard 177
HSG Agency 180
Hurst Literary Management, Andrea 181
InkWell Management, LLC 182
International Transactions, Inc. 183
Jabberwocky Literary Agency 184
J de S Associates, Inc. 186
Jenks Agency, The Carolyn 186
Kern Literary Agency, The Natasha 188
Langlie, Literary Agent, Laura 193
Larsen/Elizabeth Pomada, Literary Agents,
Michael 193
Laura Dail Literary Agency, Inc. 140
Leigh Feldman Literary 155
Levine Literary Agency, Paul S. 198
Lippincott Massie McQuilkin 198
Literary Group International, The 199
Maass Literary Agency, Donald 203
MacGregor Literary Inc. 204
Maria Carvainis Agency, Inc. 130
Marshall Agency, The Evan 208
McBride Literary Agency, Margret 209
McCarthy Creative Services 210
McGill Literary Agency, Inc., The 211
Mendel Media Group, LLC 212
Morhaim Literary Agency, Howard 214
Mura Literary, Dee 215
New Leaf Literary & Media, Inc. 216
Newman Literary, Dana 216
Perkins Agency, L. 219
Prentis Literary, Linn 220
Prospect Agency 221
P.S. Literary Agency 221
Publication Riot Group 223
Queen Literary Agency 223
Rees Literary Agency, Helen 225
Rights Factory, The 227
Rudy Agency, The 232
Seligman, Literary Agent, Lynn 237
Serendipity Literary Agency, LLC 237
Sherman & Associates, Ken 239
Speilburg Literary Agency 244
Talcott Notch Literary 249
Toby Eady Associates 149
Triada U.S. Literary Agency, Inc. 252
Waxman Leavell Literary Agency, Inc. 256
Weiner Literary Agency, Cherry 257
Wm Clark Associates 133
Wordserve Literary Group 259
Writers House 260

HORROR

Agency Group LLC, The 111

Barone Literary Agency 117
Bent Agency, The 118
Chalberg & Sussman 131
Curtis Brown, Ltd. 138
D4EO Literary Agency 139
Dijkstra Literary Agency, Sandra 143
Fielding Agency, LLC, The 155
Folio Literary Management, LLC 158
Harwood Limited, Antony 175
Henshaw Group, Richard 177
Jabberwocky Literary Agency 184
Jenks Agency, The Carolyn 186
Literary Group International, The 199
Lownie Literary Agency, Ltd., Andrew 203
Maass Literary Agency, Donald 203
Marshall Agency, The Evan 208
McCarthy Creative Services 210
New Leaf Literary & Media, Inc. 216
Perkins Agency, L. 219
Prentis Literary, Linn 220
P.S. Literary Agency 221
Rees Literary Agency, Helen 225
Scribe Agency, LLC 236
Seligman, Literary Agent, Lynn 237
Sherman & Associates, Ken 239
Sternig & Byrne Literary Agency 246
Talcott Notch Literary 249
Triada U.S. Literary Agency, Inc. 252
Writers House 260

HUMOR

Agency Group LLC, The 111
Alive Communications, Inc. 113
Barone Literary Agency 117
Curtis Brown, Ltd. 138
D4EO Literary Agency 139
Dupree/Miller and Associates Literary 147
Fielding Agency, LLC, The 155
Foundry Literary + Media 158
Golomb Literary Agency, The Susan 168
Green Literary Agency, LLC, Kathryn 173
Harwood Limited, Antony 175
International Transactions, Inc. 183
Jabberwocky Literary Agency 184
Jenks Agency, The Carolyn 186
Langlie, Literary Agent, Laura 193
Larsen/Elizabeth Pomada, Literary Agents,
Michael 193
Levine Literary Agency, Paul S. 198
Lippincott Massie McQuilkin 198
Literary Group International, The 199
Marshall Agency, The Evan 208
McBride Literary Agency, Margret 209
McCarthy Creative Services 210
Mendel Media Group, LLC 212
Prentis Literary, Linn 220
P.S. Literary Agency 221
Seligman, Literary Agent, Lynn 237
Serendipity Literary Agency, LLC 237
Sherman & Associates, Ken 239
Writers House 260

INSPIRATIONAL

Agency Group LLC, The 111
Alive Communications, Inc. 113
Barone Literary Agency 117
Crichton & Associates 137
Dupree/Miller and Associates Literary 147
Jenks Agency, The Carolyn 186
Kern Literary Agency, The Natasha 188
Larsen/Elizabeth Pomada, Literary Agents,
Michael 193
Laube Agency, The Steve 194
Levine Literary Agency, Paul S. 198
Living Word Literary Agency 201
MacGregor Literary Inc. 204
Marshall Agency, The Evan 208
Mendel Media Group, LLC 212
Seymour Agency, The 238
Wordserve Literary Group 259

JUVENILE

Agency Group LLC, The 111
Barone Literary Agency 117
Brown Literary Agency, Inc., Andrea 126

Chudney Agency, The 132
Compass Talent 134
Corcoran Literary Agency, Jill 135
Curtis Brown, Ltd. 138
D4EO Literary Agency 139
Dunham Literary, Inc. 146
Eden Street Literary 150
Fielding Agency, LLC, The 155
Flannery Literary 157
Gallt Literary Agency, Nancy 165
Grayson Literary Agency, Ashley 171
Greenhouse Literary Agency, The 172
Green Literary Agency, LLC, Kathryn 173
Grinberg Literary Agency, Jill 174
Heacock Hill Literary Agency, Inc. 177
J de S Associates, Inc. 186
Jenks Agency, The Carolyn 186
Langlie, Literary Agent, Laura 193
LR Children's Literary 203
Maccoby Literary Agency, Gina 204
Mansion Street Literary Management 205
Martin Literary Management 208
Mendel Media Group, LLC 212
Pavilion Literary Management 218
Pfeffer Content, Rubin 219
Prospect Agency 221
P.S. Literary Agency 221
Red Tree Literary Agency 225
Rodeen Literary Management 229
Ross Literary Agency, Andy 231
Sadler Children's Literary 234
Schulman Literary Agency, Susan 235
Sean McCarthy Literary Agency 210
Spitzer Literary Agency, Inc., Philip G. 245
Sterling Lord Literistic, Inc. 246
The Purcell Agency, LLC 223
Triada U.S. Literary Agency, Inc. 252
Trident Media Group 253
Wells Arms Literary 258
Writers House 260

LESBIAN

Agency Group LLC, The 111
Anderson Literary Management, LLC 116
Barone Literary Agency 117
Corvisiero Literary Agency 136
Dystel & Goderich Literary Management 148
Fairbank Literary Representation 154
Fielding Agency, LLC, The 155
Harwood Limited, Antony 175
International Transactions, Inc. 183
Jabberwocky Literary Agency 184
Jenks Agency, The Carolyn 186
Larsen/Elizabeth Pomada, Literary Agents, Michael 193
Levine Literary Agency, Paul S. 198
Lippincott Massie McQuilkin 198
Mendel Media Group, LLC 212
Perkins Agency, L. 219
Prentis Literary, Linn 220
Sanders & Associates, Victoria 234
Serendipity Literary Agency, LLC 237

LITERARY

Agency Group LLC, The 111
Aitken Alexander Associates 112
Alive Communications, Inc. 113
Amster Literary Enterprises, Betsy 115
Anderson Literary Management, LLC 116
Barone Literary Agency 117
Bent Agency, The 118
Book Cents Literary Agency, LLC 120
Books & Such Literary Agency 121
Brandt Agency, The Joan 123
Brandt & Hochman Literary Agents, Inc. 123
Braun Associates, Inc., Barbara 124
Brown Literary Agency, Inc., Andrea 126
Cameron & Associates, Kimberley 129
Capital Talent Agency 129
Castiglia Literary Agency 131
Chalberg & Sussman 131
Chase Literary Agency 131
Chelius Literary Agency, Jane 132
Cheney Literary Associates, LLC, Elyse 132
Chudney Agency, The 132

CK Webber Associates Literary Management 257
Compass Talent 134
Connor Literary Agency 135
Cornerstone Literary, Inc. 136
Crichton & Associates 137
Curtis Brown, Ltd. 138
Cynthia Cannell Literary Agency 129
D4EO Literary Agency 139
Darhansoff & Verrill Literary Agents 140
David Black Literary Agency 119
DeChiara Literary Agency, The Jennifer 141
DeFiore & Co. 142
Diana Finch Literary Agency 156
Dijkstra Literary Agency, Sandra 143
Donadio & Olson, Inc. 144
Don Congdon Associates Inc. 134
Dreisbach Literary Management 146
Dunham Literary, Inc. 146
Dunow, Carlson, & Lerner Agency 146
Dupree/Miller and Associates Literary 147
Dystel & Goderich Literary Management 148
Einstein Literary Management 151
Fairbank Literary Representation 154
Felicia Eth Literary Representation 153
Fielding Agency, LLC, The 155
Fletcher & Company 157
Folio Literary Management, LLC 158
Foundry Literary + Media 158
Fox Literary 159
Freymann Literary Agency, Sarah Jane 162
Friedman and Co., Inc., Frederica 163
Friedrich Agency, The 163
Full Circle Literary, LLC 163
Gelfman Schneider Literary Agents, Inc. 166
Gernert Company, The 167
Goldin Literary Agency, Inc., Frances 168
Golomb Literary Agency, The Susan 168
Greenburger Associates, Inc., Sanford J. 171
Green Literary Agency, LLC, Kathryn 173
Gregory & Co. Authors' Agents 173
Grinberg Literary Agency, Jill 174
Grosjean Literary Agency, Jill 174
Harris Literary Agency, Inc., The Joy 174
Harwood Limited, Antony 175
Hawkins & Associates, Inc., John 176
Heller Agency Inc., Helen 177
Henshaw Group, Richard 177
Hill Bonnie Nadell, Inc., Frederick 179
HSG Agency 180
Hurst Literary Management, Andrea 181
InkWell Management, LLC 182
International Transactions, Inc. 183
Jabberwocky Literary Agency 184
J de S Associates, Inc. 186
Jenks Agency, The Carolyn 186
Joelle Delbourgo Associates, Inc. 143
Judith Ehrlich Literary Management, LLC 151
Klinger, Inc., Harvey 189
Krichevsky Literary Agency, Inc., Stuart 191
LA Literary Agency, The 192
Lampack Agency, Inc., Peter 192
Langlie, Literary Agent, Laura 193
Larsen/Elizabeth Pomada, Literary Agents, Michael 193
Lazin Books, Sarah 195
Lecker Agency, Robert 196
Leigh Feldman Literary 155
Levine Greenberg Literary Agency, Inc. 197
Levine Literary Agency, Paul S. 198
Lippincott Massie McQuilkin 198
Literary Group International, The 199
Lowenstein Associates Inc. 201
Lownie Literary Agency, Ltd., Andrew 203
Maass Literary Agency, Donald 203
Maccoby Literary Agency, Gina 204
Mann Agency, Carol 205
Maria Carvainis Agency, Inc. 130
Marshall Agency, The Evan 208
McBride Literary Agency, Margret 209
McCarthy Creative Services 210
McMillan & Associates, Inc., Sally Hill 211
Mendel Media Group, LLC 212
Michaels Literary Agency, Inc., Doris S. 213

Miriam Altshuler Literary Agency 114
Morhaim Literary Agency, Howard 214
Moveable Type Management 214
Mura Literary, Dee 215
Naggar Literary Agency, Inc. Jean V. 215
Nelson Literary Agency 216
New Leaf Literary & Media, Inc. 216
Newman Literary, Dana 216
Prentis Literary, Linn 220
P.S. Literary Agency 221
Publication Riot Group 223
Queen Literary Agency 223
Rebecca Friedman Literary Agency 162
Rees Literary Agency, Helen 225
Regal Literary Agency 225
Rennert Agency, The Amy 226
Rights Factory, The 227
Rinaldi Literary Agency, Angela 227
RLR Associates, Ltd. 228
Robbins Literary Agency, B.J. 228
Ross Literary Agency, Andy 231
Rotrosen Agency LLC, Jane 231
Sanders & Associates, Victoria 234
sazTracy Brown Literary Agency 126
Schiavone Literary Agency, Inc. 234
Schmalz Agency, Wendy 235
Schmidt Literary Agency, Harold 235
Schulman Literary Agency, Susan 235
Scribe Agency, LLC 236
Seligman, Literary Agent, Lynn 237
Serendipity Literary Agency, LLC 237
Shannon Literary Agency, Inc., Denise 239
Sheree Bykofsky Associates, Inc. 128
Sherman & Associates, Ken 239
Simmons Literary Agency, Jeffrey 241
Slopen Literary Agency, Beverley 241
Speilburg Literary Agency 244
Spencerhill Associates 244
Spieler Agency, The 244
Spitzer Literary Agency, Inc., Philip G. 245
Sterling Lord Literistic, Inc. 246
Straus Agency, Inc., Robin 247
Strothman Agency, LLC, The 248
Stuart Agency, The 248
Sweeney Agency, LLC, Emma 249
Talcott Notch Literary 249
Tessler Literary Agency, LLC 250
Toby Eady Associates 149
Triada U.S. Literary Agency, Inc. 252
Trident Media Group 253
Venture Literary 254
Veritas Literary Agency 254
Vicky Bijur Literary Agency 119
Watkins Loomis Agency, Inc. 256
Waxman Leavell Literary Agency, Inc. 256
Weingel-Fidel Agency, The 257
Weissman Literary, LLC, Larry 258
Wm Clark Associates 133
Wolf Literary Services 259
Writers House 260
Writers' Representatives, LLC 260
Zimmermann Literary Agency, Helen 262

MAINSTREAM

Agency Group LLC, The 111
Aitken Alexander Associates 112
Alive Communications, Inc. 113
Barone Literary Agency 117
BookEnds, LLC 120
Books & Such Literary Agency 121
Capital Talent Agency 129
CK Webber Associates Literary Management 257
Compass Talent 134
Connor Literary Agency 135
Crichton & Associates 137
Curtis Brown, Ltd. 138
D4EO Literary Agency 139
DeFiore & Co. 142
Diana Finch Literary Agency 156
Don Congdon Associates Inc. 134
Dunham Literary, Inc. 146
Dunow, Carlson, & Lerner Agency 146
Dupree/Miller and Associates Literary 147
Dystel & Goderich Literary Management 148

Einstein Literary Management 151
Fairbank Literary Representation 154
Felicia Eth Literary Representation 153
Fielding Agency, LLC, The 155
Fox Literary 159
Freymann Literary Agency, Sarah Jane 162
G Agency, LLC, The 165
Gelfman Schneider Literary Agents, Inc. 166
Goldin Literary Agency, Inc., Frances 168
Golomb Literary Agency, The Susan 168
Green Literary Agency, LLC, Kathryn 173
Grinberg Literary Agency, Jill 174
Grosjean Literary Agency, Jill 174
Harwood Limited, Antony 175
Heller Agency Inc., Helen 177
Henshaw Group, Richard 177
Hill Bonnie Nadell, Inc., Frederick 179
Hurst Literary Management, Andrea 181
International Transactions, Inc. 183
Jabberwocky Literary Agency 184
J de S Associates, Inc. 186
Jenks Agency, The Carolyn 186
Joelle Delbourgo Associates, Inc. 143
Kern Literary Agency, The Natasha 188
Klinger, Inc., Harvey 189
Lampack Agency, Inc., Peter 192
Langlie, Literary Agent, Laura 193
Larsen/Elizabeth Pomada, Literary Agents,
Michael 193
LaunchBooks Literary Agency 194
Lecker Agency, Robert 196
Levine Greenberg Literary Agency, Inc. 197
Levine Literary Agency, Paul S. 198
Lippincott Massie McQuilkin 198
Maass Literary Agency, Donald 203
Maccoby Literary Agency, Gina 204
MacGregor Literary Inc. 204
Maria Carvainis Agency, Inc. 130
Marsal Lyon Literary Agency, LLC 207
Marshall Agency, The Evan 208
McBride Literary Agency, Margret 209
McCarthy Creative Services 210
McGill Agency, Inc., The 211
McMillan & Associates, Inc., Sally Hill 211
Mendel Media Group, LLC 212
Moveable Type Management 214
Nelson Literary Agency 216
New Leaf Literary & Media, Inc. 216
Prentis Literary, Linn 220
P.S. Literary Agency 221
Publication Riot Group 223
Rennert Agency, The Amy 226
Rights Factory, The 227
RLR Associates, Ltd. 228
Robbins Literary Agency, B.J. 228
Sanders & Associates, Victoria 234
Schiavone Literary Agency, Inc. 234
Schmalz Agency, Wendy 235
Schulman Literary Agency, Susan 235
Scribe Agency, LLC 236
Seligman, Literary Agent, Lynn 237
Sheree Bykofsky Associates, Inc. 128
Sherman Associates, Inc., Wendy 240
Sherman & Associates, Ken 239
Simmons Literary Agency, Jeffrey 241
Speilburg Literary Agency 244
Spencerhill Associates 244
Spitzer Literary Agency, Inc., Philip G. 245
Straus Agency, Inc., Robin 247
Sweeney Agency, LLC, Emma 249
Talcott Notch Literary 249
Toby Eady Associates 149
Triada U.S. Literary Agency, Inc. 252
Unter Agency, The 254
Venture Literary 254
Waterside Productions, Inc. 256
Waxman Leavell Literary Agency, Inc. 256
Weiner Literary Agency, Cherry 257
Weingel-Fidel Agency, The 257
Whimsy Literary Agency, LLC 258
Wm Clark Associates 133
Wordserve Literary Group 259
Writers House 260

MIDDLE GRADE

Adams Literary 111
Aitken Alexander Associates 112
Bradford Literary Agency 122
Brandt & Hochman Literary Agents, Inc. 123
Capital Talent Agency 129
Chalberg & Sussman 131
CK Webber Associates Literary Management
257
Corcoran Literary Agency, Jill 135
Corvisiero Literary Agency 136
Curtis Brown, Ltd. 138
D4EO Literary Agency 139
David Black Literary Agency 119
DeChiara Literary Agency, The Jennifer 141
DeFiore & Co. 142
Dijkstra Literary Agency, Sandra 143
Don Congdon Associates Inc. 134
Dunow, Carlson, & Lerner Agency 146
Dystel & Goderich Literary Management 148
East/West Literary Agency, LLC 149
Eden Street Literary 150
Einstein Literary Management 151
FinePrint Literary Management 156
Flannery Literary 157
Folio Literary Management, LLC 158
Foundry Literary + Media 158
Full Circle Literary, LLC 163
Gallt Literary Agency, Nancy 165
Gelfman Schneider Literary Agents, Inc. 166
Gernert Company, The 167
Goldblatt Literary LLC, Barry 167
Golomb Literary Agency, The Susan 168
Grayson Literary Agency, Ashley 171
Greenburger Associates, Inc., Sanford J. 171
Greenhouse Literary Agency, The 172
Green Literary Agency, LLC, Kathryn 173
Heacock Hill Literary Agency, Inc. 177
HSG Agency 180
InkWell Management, LLC 182
Jabberwocky Literary Agency 184
Joelle Delbourgo Associates, Inc. 143
KT Literary, LLC 191
Leshne Agency, The 197
Levine Greenberg Literary Agency, Inc. 197
LKG Agency 201
Lowenstein Associates Inc. 201
LR Children's Literary 203
Mansion Street Literary Management 205
Maria Carvainis Agency, Inc. 130
Marsal Lyon Literary Agency, LLC 207
Martin Literary Management 208
McCarthy Agency, LLC, The 209
Miriam Altshuler Literary Agency 114
Morhaim Literary Agency, Howard 214
Mura Literary, Dee 215
Murphy Literary Agency, Erin 215
Naggar Literary Agency, Inc. Jean V. 215
Nelson Literary Agency 216
New Leaf Literary & Media, Inc. 216
Park Literary Group, LLC 218
Perkins Agency, L. 219
Pfeffer Content, Rubin 219
Pippin Properties, Inc. 220
Prospect Agency 221
P.S. Literary Agency 221
Red Sofa Literary 224
Red Tree Literary Agency 225
Regal Literary Agency 225
Rights Factory, The 227
RLR Associates, Ltd. 228
Rodeen Literary Management 229
Sadler Children's Literary 234
Schiavone Literary Agency, Inc. 234
Schmalz Agency, Wendy 235
Sean McCarthy Literary Agency 210
Serendipity Literary Agency, LLC 237
Seymour Agency, The 238
Speilburg Literary Agency 244
Spieler Agency, The 244
Sterling Lord Literistic, Inc. 246
Stringer Literary Agency, LLC, The 247
Strothman Agency, LLC, The 248
Talcott Notch Literary 249
The Knight Agency 190
The Purcell Agency, LLC 223

Three Seas Literary Agency 251
Triada U.S. Literary Agency, Inc. 252
Trident Media Group 253
Unter Agency, The 254
Upstart Crow Literary 254
Veritas Literary Agency 254
Waxman Leavell Literary Agency, Inc. 256
Wells Arms Literary 258
Writers House 260

MILITARY

Agency Group LLC, The 111
Barone Literary Agency 117
Curtis Brown, Ltd. 138
FinePrint Literary Management 156
Harwood Limited, Antony 175
Sherman & Associates, Ken 239
Writers House 260

MULTICULTURAL

Agency Group LLC, The 111
Barone Literary Agency 117
Corvisiero Literary Agency 136
Curtis Brown, Ltd. 138
English Literary Agency, The Elaine P. 152
Grayson Literary Agency, Ashley 171
Harwood Limited, Antony 175
Hawkins & Associates, Inc., John 176
Kern Literary Agency, The Natasha 188
Literary Group International, The 199
Maass Literary Agency, Donald 203
Sherman & Associates, Ken 239
Writers House 260

MYSTERY

Agency Group LLC, The 111
Alive Communications, Inc. 113
Anderson Literary Management, LLC 116
Axelrod Agency, The 116
Barone Literary Agency 117
Bent Agency, The 118
BookEnds, LLC 120
Bradford Literary Agency 122
Brandt Agency, The Joan 123
Brandt & Hochman Literary Agents, Inc. 123
Cameron & Associates, Kimberley 129
Capital Talent Agency 129
Castiglia Literary Agency 131
Chase Literary Agency 131
Chelius Literary Agency, Jane 132
Chudney Agency, The 132
CK Webber Associates Literary Management
257
Corvisiero Literary Agency 136
Crichton & Associates 137
Curtis Brown, Ltd. 138
D4EO Literary Agency 139
Darhansoff & Verrill Literary Agents 140
DeChiara Literary Agency, The Jennifer 141
DeFiore & Co. 142
Donaghy Literary Group 144
Don Congdon Associates Inc. 134
Dreisbach Literary Management 146
Dunow, Carlson, & Lerner Agency 146
Dupree/Miller and Associates Literary 147
Dystel & Goderich Literary Management 148
English Literary Agency, The Elaine P. 152
Fairbank Literary Representation 154
Fielding Agency, LLC, The 155
FinePrint Literary Management 156
Folio Literary Management, LLC 158
G Agency, LLC, The 165
Gelfman Schneider Literary Agents, Inc. 166
Goodman Literary Agency, Irene 169
Grad Literary Agency, Inc., Doug 170
Grayson Literary Agency, Ashley 171
Greenburger Associates, Inc., Sanford J. 171
Green Literary Agency, LLC, Kathryn 173
Grosjean Literary Agency, Jill 174
Harwood Limited, Antony 175
Henshaw Group, Richard 177
HSG Agency 180
Hurst Literary Management, Andrea 181
International Transactions, Inc. 183
J de S Associates, Inc. 186

Jenks Agency, The Carolyn 186
Kern Literary Agency, The Natasha 188
Klinger, Inc., Harvey 189
Kraas Literary Agency 191
Lampack Agency, Inc., Peter 192
Langlie, Literary Agent, Laura 193
Larsen/Elizabeth Pomada, Literary Agents, Michael 193
Lecker Agency, Robert 196
Leigh Feldman Literary 155
Levine Greenberg Literary Agency, Inc. 197
Levine Literary Agency, Paul S. 198
Literary Group International, The 199
Maass Literary Agency, Donald 203
Maccoby Literary Agency, Gina 204
MacGregor Literary Inc. 204
Maria Carvainis Agency, Inc. 130
Marsal Lyon Literary Agency, LLC 207
Marshall Agency, The Evan 208
McBride Literary Agency, Margret 209
McCarthy Agency, LLC, The 209
McCarthy Creative Services 210
McGill Agency, Inc., The 211
McMillan & Associates, Inc., Sally Hill 211
Mendel Media Group, LLC 212
Millard Literary Agency, Martha 213
Mura Literary, Dee 215
New Leaf Literary & Media, Inc. 216
Pavilion Literary Management 218
Perkins Agency, L. 219
Prospect Agency 221
P.S. Literary Agency 221
Queen Literary Agency 223
Rees Literary Agency, Helen 225
Rennert Agency, The Amy 226
Rights Factory, The 227
Robbins Literary Agency, B.J. 228
Rotrosen Agency LLC, Jane 231
Sanders & Associates, Victoria 234
Schiavone Literary Agency, Inc. 234
Seligman, Literary Agent, Lynn 237
Serendipity Literary Agency, LLC 237
Seymour Agency, The 238
Sheree Bykofsky Associates, Inc. 128
Sherman & Associates, Ken 239
Simmons Literary Agency, Jeffrey 241
Slopen Literary Agency, Beverley 241
Spectrum Literary Agency 243
Speilburg Literary Agency 244
Spencerhill Associates 244
Sternig & Byrne Literary Agency 246
Stringer Literary Agency, LLC, The 247
Sweeney Agency, LLC, Emma 249
Talcott Notch Literary 249
Triada U.S. Literary Agency, Inc. 252
Trident Media Group 253
Venture Literary 254
Veritas Literary Agency 254
Vicky Bijur Literary Agency 119
Waxman Leavell Literary Agency, Inc. 256
Weiner Literary Agency, Cherry 257
Writers House 260

NEW ADULT
Axelrod Agency, The 116
Book Cents Literary Agency, LLC 120
Books & Such Literary Agency 121
CK Webber Associates Literary Management 257
Corvisiero Literary Agency 136
Dijkstra Literary Agency, Sandra 143
Marsal Lyon Literary Agency, LLC 207
McCarthy Agency, LLC, The 209
Morhaim Literary Agency, Howard 214
Mura Literary, Dee 215
New Leaf Literary & Media, Inc. 216
Perkins Agency, L. 219
Prospect Agency 221
P.S. Literary Agency 221
Rebecca Friedman Literary Agency 162
Rees Literary Agency, Helen 225
Rotrosen Agency LLC, Jane 231
Sanders & Associates, Victoria 234
Seymour Agency, The 238
The Knight Agency 190

Triada U.S. Literary Agency, Inc. 252
Vicky Bijur Literary Agency 119

PARANORMAL
Bradford Literary Agency 122
Corvisiero Literary Agency 136
DeFiore & Co. 142
Maass Literary Agency, Donald 203
Marsal Lyon Literary Agency, LLC 207
Mura Literary, Dee 215
New Leaf Literary & Media, Inc. 216
Perkins Agency, L. 219
Spencerhill Associates 244
Talcott Notch Literary 249
Trident Media Group 253
Waxman Leavell Literary Agency, Inc. 256

PICTURE BOOKS
Adams Literary 111
Agency Group LLC, The 111
Bent Agency, The 118
Bradford Literary Agency 122
Brown Literary Agency, Inc., Andrea 126
Connor Literary Agency 135
Corcoran Literary Agency, Jill 135
Corvisiero Literary Agency 136
Curtis Brown, Ltd. 138
D4EO Literary Agency 139
DeChiara Literary Agency, The Jennifer 141
Dunham Literary, Inc. 146
Dunow, Carlson, & Lerner Agency 146
Dupree/Miller and Associates Literary 147
Dystel & Goderich Literary Management 148
East/West Literary Agency, LLC 149
Eden Street Literary 150
Fielding Agency, LLC, The 155
Folio Literary Management, LLC 158
Full Circle Literary, LLC 163
Gallt Literary Agency, Nancy 165
Greenburger Associates, Inc., Sanford J. 171
Greenhouse Literary Agency, The 172
Harwood Limited, Antony 175
Heacock Hill Literary Agency, Inc. 177
HSG Agency 180
InkWell Management, LLC 182
LR Children's Literary 203
Marsal Lyon Literary Agency, LLC 207
Mendel Media Group, LLC 212
Miriam Altshuler Literary Agency 114
Murphy Literary Agency, Erin 215
Naggar Literary Agency, Inc. Jean V. 215
New Leaf Literary & Media, Inc. 216
Perkins Agency, L. 219
Pfeffer Content, Rubin 219
Pippin Properties, Inc. 220
Prospect Agency 221
P.S. Literary Agency 221
Regal Literary Agency 225
Rights Factory, The 227
RLR Associates, Ltd. 228
Rodeen Literary Management 229
Sadler Children's Literary 234
Sanders & Associates, Victoria 234
Sean McCarthy Literary Agency 210
Sherman & Associates, Ken 239
Spieler Agency, The 244
Sterling Lord Literistic, Inc. 246
Unter Agency, The 254
Upstart Crow Literary 254
Wells Arms Literary 258
Writers House 260

POLICE
Agency Group LLC, The 111
Alive Communications, Inc. 113
Diana Finch Literary Agency 156
Don Congdon Associates Inc. 134
Dupree/Miller and Associates Literary 147
Dystel & Goderich Literary Management 148
Fielding Agency, LLC, The 155
Green Literary Agency, LLC, Kathryn 173
Harwood Limited, Antony 175
Henshaw Group, Richard 177
International Transactions, Inc. 183
Jabberwocky Literary Agency 184

J de S Associates, Inc. 186
Klinger, Inc., Harvey 189
Lampack Agency, Inc., Peter 192
Langlie, Literary Agent, Laura 193
Larsen/Elizabeth Pomada, Literary Agents, Michael 193
Lecker Agency, Robert 196
Levine Literary Agency, Paul S. 198
Maass Literary Agency, Donald 203
MacGregor Literary Inc. 204
McBride Literary Agency, Margret 209
Mendel Media Group, LLC 212
Robbins Literary Agency, B.J. 228
Simmons Literary Agency, Jeffrey 241
Triada U.S. Literary Agency, Inc. 252
Venture Literary 254
Weiner Literary Agency, Cherry 257
Writers House 260

REGIONAL
Agency Group LLC, The 111
Barone Literary Agency 117
Curtis Brown, Ltd. 138
Harwood Limited, Antony 175
Jabberwocky Literary Agency 184
Jenks Agency, The Carolyn 186
Levine Literary Agency, Paul S. 198
Lippincott Massie McQuilkin 198
Literary Group International, The 199
McCarthy Creative Services 210
Sherman & Associates, Ken 239
Writers House 260

RELIGIOUS
Agency Group LLC, The 111
Alive Communications, Inc. 113
Barone Literary Agency 117
Books & Such Literary Agency 121
Crichton & Associates 137
Curtis Brown, Ltd. 138
Dupree/Miller and Associates Literary 147
Folio Literary Management, LLC 158
Harwood Limited, Antony 175
Jenks Agency, The Carolyn 186
Kern Literary Agency, The Natasha 188
Larsen/Elizabeth Pomada, Literary Agents, Michael 193
Laube Agency, The Steve 194
Levine Literary Agency, Paul S. 198
MacGregor Literary Inc. 204
Marshall Agency, The Evan 208
Mendel Media Group, LLC 212
Seymour Agency, The 238
Sherman & Associates, Ken 239

ROMANCE
Agency Group LLC, The 111
Ahearn Agency, Inc., The 112
Axelrod Agency, The 116
Barone Literary Agency 117
Bent Agency, The 118
Book Cents Literary Agency, LLC 120
BookEnds, LLC 120
Books & Such Literary Agency 121
Bradford Literary Agency 122
Cameron & Associates, Kimberley 129
Capital Talent Agency 129
Chalberg & Sussman 131
CK Webber Associates Literary Management 257
Crichton & Associates 137
Curtis Associates, Inc., Richard 137
Curtis Brown, Ltd. 138
D4EO Literary Agency 139
DeFiore & Co. 142
Dijkstra Literary Agency, Sandra 143
Donaghy Literary Group 144
Einstein Literary Management 151
Fielding Agency, LLC, The 155
FinePrint Literary Management 156
Folio Literary Management, LLC 158
Fox Literary 159
Goodman Literary Agency, Irene 169
Grayson Literary Agency, Ashley 171
Greenburger Associates, Inc., Sanford J. 171

Green Literary Agency, LLC, Kathryn 173
Greyhaus Literary 173
Grinberg Literary Agency, Jill 174
Harwood Limited, Antony 175
Hopkins Literary Associates 180
Hurst Literary Management, Andrea 181
InkWell Management, LLC 182
Kern Literary Agency, The Natasha 188
Larsen/Elizabeth Pomada, Literary Agents,
Michael 193
Levine Literary Agency, Paul S. 198
Literary Group International, The 199
Maass Literary Agency, Donald 203
MacGregor Literary Inc. 204
McCarthy Creative Services 210
McGill Agency, Inc., The 211
Mendel Media Group, LLC 212
Millard Literary Agency, Martha 213
Morhaim Literary Agency, Howard 214
Moveable Type Management 214
Mura Literary, Dee 215
Nelson Literary Agency 216
New Leaf Literary & Media, Inc. 216
Prospect Agency 221
P.S. Literary Agency 221
Rebecca Friedman Literary Agency 162
Red Sofa Literary 224
Rees Literary Agency, Helen 225
Rights Factory, The 227
RLR Associates, Ltd. 228
Rosenberg Group, The 230
Rotrosen Agency LLC, Jane 231
Schiavone Literary Agency, Inc. 234
Seligman, Literary Agent, Lynn 237
Serendipity Literary Agency, LLC 237
Seymour Agency, The 238
Sherman & Associates, Ken 239
Spencerhill Associates 244
Steele-Perkins Literary Agency 245
Stringer Literary Agency, LLC, The 247
Talcott Notch Literary 249
The Knight Agency 190
Three Seas Literary Agency 251
Triada U.S. Literary Agency, Inc. 252
Waxman Leavell Literary Agency, Inc. 256
Weiner Literary Agency, Cherry 257
Writers House 260

SATIRE
Agency Group LLC, The 111
Alive Communications, Inc. 113
Dupree/Miller and Associates Literary 147
Fielding Agency, LLC, The 155
Golomb Literary Agency, The Susan 168
Green Literary Agency, LLC, Kathryn 173
Harwood Limited, Antony 175
International Transactions, Inc. 183
Jabberwocky Literary Agency 184
Larsen/Elizabeth Pomada, Literary Agents,
Michael 193
Levine Literary Agency, Paul S. 198
Lippincott Massie McQuilkin 198
Marshall Agency, The Evan 208
McBride Literary Agency, Margret 209
Mendel Media Group, LLC 212
Mura Literary, Dee 215

SCIENCE FICTION
Barone Literary Agency 117
Cameron & Associates, Kimberley 129
Castiglia Literary Agency 131
Chalberg & Sussman 131
CK Webber Associates Literary Management
257
Corvisiero Literary Agency 136
Curtis Associates, Inc., Richard 137
Darhansoff & Verrill Literary Agents 140
Dijkstra Literary Agency, Sandra 143
Donaghy Literary Group 144
FinePrint Literary Management 156
Fletcher & Company 157
Fox Literary 159
Gelfman Schneider Literary Agents, Inc. 166
Gernert Company, The 167
Grad Literary Agency, Inc., Doug 170

Grayson Literary Agency, Ashley 171
Greenburger Associates, Inc., Sanford J. 171
Grinberg Literary Agency, Jill 174
Harwood Limited, Antony 175
Henshaw Group, Richard 177
Hurst Literary Management, Andrea 181
Jabberwocky Literary Agency 184
Jenks Agency, The Carolyn 186
Joelle Delbourgo Associates, Inc. 143
Kidd Agency, Inc., Virginia 188
Lowenstein Associates Inc. 201
Lownie Literary Agency, Ltd., Andrew 203
Maass Literary Agency, Donald 203
Marshall Agency, The Evan 208
McCarthy Agency, LLC, The 209
Millard Literary Agency, Martha 213
Morhaim Literary Agency, Howard 214
Mura Literary, Dee 215
Nelson Literary Agency 216
Perkins Agency, L. 219
Rebecca Friedman Literary Agency 162
Red Sofa Literary 224
Rees Literary Agency, Helen 225
Rights Factory, The 227
Schiavone Literary Agency, Inc. 234
Scribe Agency, LLC 236
Seligman, Literary Agent, Lynn 237
Seymour Agency, The 238
Spectrum Literary Agency 243
Speilburg Literary Agency 244
Sternig & Byrne Literary Agency 246
Talcott Notch Literary 249
The Knight Agency 190
Trident Media Group 253
Veritas Literary Agency 254
Weiner Literary Agency, Cherry 257
Zuckerbrot Literary Agency, Renèe 262

SHORT STORY COLLECTIONS
Agency Group LLC, The 111
Cheney Literary Associates, LLC, Elyse 132
DeFiore & Co. 142
Don Congdon Associates Inc. 134
InkWell Management, LLC 182
Lazin Books, Sarah 195
Watkins Loomis Agency, Inc. 256
Zuckerbrot Literary Agency, Renèe 262

SUPERNATURAL
Agency Group LLC, The 111
Dupree/Miller and Associates Literary 147
Henshaw Group, Richard 177
Jabberwocky Literary Agency 184
Jenks Agency, The Carolyn 186
Maass Literary Agency, Donald 203
Weiner Literary Agency, Cherry 257

SUSPENSE
Agency Group LLC, The 111
Ahearn Agency, Inc., The 112
Alive Communications, Inc. 113
Anderson Literary Management, LLC 116
Bent Agency, The 118
Brandt Agency, The Joan 123
Brandt & Hochman Literary Agents, Inc. 123
Chelius Literary Agency, Jane 132
Cheney Literary Associates, LLC, Elyse 132
Chudney Agency, The 132
CK Webber Associates Literary Management
257
Connor Literary Agency 135
Crichton & Associates 137
Darhansoff & Verrill Literary Agents 140
DeChiara Literary Agency, The Jennifer 141
DeFiore & Co. 142
Dijkstra Literary Agency, Sandra 143
Don Congdon Associates Inc. 134
Dupree/Miller and Associates Literary 147
Dystel & Goderich Literary Management 148
English Literary Agency, The Elaine P. 152
Fairbank Literary Representation 154
Fielding Agency, LLC, The 155
FinePrint Literary Management 156

Foundry Literary + Media 158
Gelfman Schneider Literary Agents, Inc. 166
Grayson Literary Agency, Ashley 171
Green Literary Agency, LLC, Kathryn 173
Harwood Limited, Antony 175
Hawkins & Associates, Inc., John 176
Henshaw Group, Richard 177
Hurst Literary Management, Andrea 181
InkWell Management, LLC 182
International Transactions, Inc. 183
J de S Associates, Inc. 186
Kern Literary Agency, The Natasha 188
Klinger, Inc., Harvey 189
Lampack Agency, Inc., Peter 192
Langlie, Literary Agent, Laura 193
Larsen/Elizabeth Pomada, Literary Agents,
Michael 193
Lecker Agency, Robert 196
Levine Literary Agency, Paul S. 198
Maass Literary Agency, Donald 203
MacGregor Literary Inc. 204
Marcil Literary Agency, Inc., The Denise 207
Maria Carvainis Agency, Inc. 130
Marsal Lyon Literary Agency, LLC 207
Marshall Agency, The Evan 208
McBride Literary Agency, Margret 209
Millard Literary Agency, Martha 213
Mura Literary, Dee 215
Park Literary Group, LLC 218
Rebecca Friedman Literary Agency 162
Rees Literary Agency, Helen 225
Rinaldi Literary Agency, Angela 227
Robbins Literary Agency, B.J. 228
Rotrosen Agency LLC, Jane 231
Schiavone Literary Agency, Inc. 234
Seymour Agency, The 238
Sheree Bykofsky Associates, Inc. 128
Simmons Literary Agency, Jeffrey 241
Slopen Literary Agency, Beverley 241
Spitzer Literary Agency, Inc., Philip G. 245
Sternig & Byrne Literary Agency 246
Talcott Notch Literary 249
Trident Media Group 253
Venture Literary 254

THRILLER
Agency Group LLC, The 111
Ahearn Agency, Inc., The 112
Aitken Alexander Associates 112
Alive Communications, Inc. 113
Anderson Literary Management, LLC 116
Barone Literary Agency 117
Bent Agency, The 118
Book Cents Literary Agency, LLC 120
Bradford Literary Agency 122
Brandt & Hochman Literary Agents, Inc. 123
Cameron & Associates, Kimberley 129
Capital Talent Agency 129
Castiglia Literary Agency 131
Chalberg & Sussman 131
Chase Literary Agency 131
CK Webber Associates Literary Management
257
Corvisiero Literary Agency 136
Curtis Associates, Inc., Richard 137
Curtis Brown, Ltd. 138
D4EO Literary Agency 139
Darhansoff & Verrill Literary Agents 140
David Black Literary Agency 119
DeChiara Literary Agency, The Jennifer 141
DeFiore & Co. 142
Diana Finch Literary Agency 156
Dijkstra Literary Agency, Sandra 143
Don Congdon Associates Inc. 134
Dreisbach Literary Management 146
Dunow, Carlson, & Lerner Agency 146
Dupree/Miller and Associates Literary 147
Dystel & Goderich Literary Management 148
English Literary Agency, The Elaine P. 152
Fairbank Literary Representation 154
Fielding Agency, LLC, The 155
FinePrint Literary Management 156
Folio Literary Management, LLC 158
Foundry Literary + Media 158
Fox Literary 159

Fresh Books Literary Agency 161
Gernert Company, The 167
Golomb Literary Agency, The Susan 168
Goodman Literary Agency, Irene 169
Grad Literary Agency, Inc., Doug 170
Greenburger Associates, Inc., Sanford J. 171
Green Literary Agency, LLC, Kathryn 173
Gregory & Co. Authors' Agents 173
Harwood Limited, Antony 175
Hawkins & Associates, Inc., John 176
Henshaw Group, Richard 177
Hill Bonnie Nadell, Inc., Frederick 179
HSG Agency 180
Hurst Literary Management, Andrea 181
InkWell Management, LLC 182
International Transactions, Inc. 183
Jabberwocky Literary Agency 184
Jenks Agency, The Carolyn 186
Joelle Delbourgo Associates, Inc. 143
Kern Literary Agency, The Natasha 188
Klinger, Inc., Harvey 189
Kraas Literary Agency 191
Lampack Agency, Inc., Peter 192
Langlie, Literary Agent, Laura 193
Lecker Agency, Robert 196
Levine Greenberg Literary Agency, Inc. 197
Levine Literary Agency, Paul S. 198
Literary Group International, The 199
Lownie Literary Agency, Ltd., Andrew 203
Maass Literary Agency, Donald 203
Maccoby Literary Agency, Gina 204
MacGregor Literary Inc. 204
Manus & Associates Literary Agency, Inc. 206
Marcil Literary Agency, Inc., The Denise 207
Maria Carvainis Agency, Inc. 130
Marsal Lyon Literary Agency, LLC 207
McBride Literary Agency, Margret 209
McCarthy Creative Services 210
McGill Agency, Inc., The 211
Mendel Media Group, LLC 212
Mura Literary, Dee 215
Naggar Literary Agency, Inc. Jean V. 215
New Leaf Literary & Media, Inc. 216
Park Literary Group, LLC 218
Pavilion Literary Management 218
Perkins Agency, L. 219
Prentis Literary, Linn 220
Prospect Agency 221
P.S. Literary Agency 221
Publication Riot Group 223
Queen Literary Agency 223
Rees Literary Agency, Helen 225
Regal Literary Agency 225
Robbins Literary Agency, B.J. 228
Rotrosen Agency LLC, Jane 231
Rudy Agency, The 232
Sanders & Associates, Victoria 234
Schiavone Literary Agency, Inc. 234
Scribe Agency, LLC 236
Serendipity Literary Agency, LLC 237
Seymour Agency, The 238
Sherman & Associates, Ken 239
Simmons Literary Agency, Jeffrey 241
Speilburg Literary Agency 244
Spencerhill Associates 244
Spieler Agency, The 244
Spitzer Literary Agency, Inc., Philip G. 245
Stringer Literary Agency, LLC, The 247
Talcott Notch Literary 249
The Knight Agency 190
Three Seas Literary Agency 251
Trident Media Group 253
Venture Literary 254
Vicky Bijur Literary Agency 119
Waxman Leavell Literary Agency, Inc. 256
Weiner Literary Agency, Cherry 257
Wordserve Literary Group 259
Writers House 260

URBAN FANTASY

Corvisiero Literary Agency 136
Perkins Agency, L. 219
Rees Literary Agency, Helen 225
Talcott Notch Literary 249

WESTERNS

Anderson Literary Management, LLC 116
Gelfman Schneider Literary Agents, Inc. 166
Harwood Limited, Antony 175
J de S Associates, Inc. 186
Jenks Agency, The Carolyn 186
Levine Literary Agency, Paul S. 198
Maass Literary Agency, Donald 203

WOMEN'S

Agency Group LLC, The 111
Ahearn Agency, Inc., The 112
Amster Literary Enterprises, Betsy 115
Anderson Literary Management, LLC 116
Axelrod Agency, The 116
Barone Literary Agency 117
Bent Agency, The 118
Book Cents Literary Agency, LLC 120
BookEnds, LLC 120
Bradford Literary Agency 122
Brandt Agency, The Joan 123
Brandt & Hochman Literary Agents, Inc. 123
Brown Literary Agency, Inc., Andrea 126
Cameron & Associates, Kimberley 129
Chalberg & Sussman 131
Chelius Literary Agency, Jane 132
Cheney Literary Associates, LLC, Elyse 132
CK Webber Associates Literary Management 257
Curtis Brown, Ltd. 138
DeChiara Literary Agency, The Jennifer 141
DeFiore & Co. 142
Dijkstra Literary Agency, Sandra 143
Don Congdon Associates Inc. 134
Dystel & Goderich Literary Management 148
Einstein Literary Management 151
Empire Literary 152
English Literary Agency, The Elaine P. 152
Fairbank Literary Representation 154
Fielding Agency, LLC, The 155
FinePrint Literary Management 156
Fletcher & Company 157
Folio Literary Management, LLC 158
Foundry Literary + Media 158
Full Circle Literary, LLC 163
Gelfman Schneider Literary Agents, Inc. 166
Gernert Company, The 167
Golomb Literary Agency, The Susan 168
Goodman Literary Agency, Irene 169
Grayson Literary Agency, Ashley 171
Greenburger Associates, Inc., Sanford J. 171
Green Literary Agency, LLC, Kathryn 173
Gregory & Co. Authors' Agents 173
Greyhaus Literary 173
Hill Bonnie Nadell, Inc., Frederick 179
Hopkins Literary Associates 180
HSG Agency 180
Hurst Literary Management, Andrea 181
InkWell Management, LLC 182
International Transactions, Inc. 183
Jenks Agency, The Carolyn 186
Joelle Delbourgo Associates, Inc. 143
Kern Literary Agency, The Natasha 188
Levine Greenberg Literary Agency, Inc. 197
Lowenstein Associates Inc. 201
Lownie Literary Agency, Ltd., Andrew 203
Maass Literary Agency, Donald 203
MacGregor Literary Inc. 204
Marcil Literary Agency, Inc., The Denise 207
Maria Carvainis Agency, Inc. 130
Marsal Lyon Literary Agency, LLC 207
McCarthy Agency, LLC, The 209
McCarthy Creative Services 210
Morhaim Literary Agency, Howard 214
Moveable Type Management 214
Mura Literary, Dee 215
Nelson Literary Agency 216
New Leaf Literary & Media, Inc. 216
Newman Literary, Dana 216
Park Literary Group, LLC 218
Prospect Agency 221
P.S. Literary Agency 221
Publication Riot Group 223
Rebecca Friedman Literary Agency 162
Rees Literary Agency, Helen 225
Regal Literary Agency 225
Rinaldi Literary Agency, Angela 227
RLR Associates, Ltd. 228
Rosenberg Group, The 230
Rotrosen Agency LLC, Jane 231
Schulman Literary Agency, Susan 235
Serendipity Literary Agency, LLC 237
Steele-Perkins Literary Agency 245
Straus Agency, Inc., Robin 247
Stringer Literary Agency, LLC, The 247
Talcott Notch Literary 249
Tessler Literary Agency, LLC 250
The Knight Agency 190
Three Seas Literary Agency 251
Triada U.S. Literary Agency, Inc. 252
Trident Media Group 253
Upstart Crow Literary 254
Venture Literary 254
Waxman Leavell Literary Agency, Inc. 256
Wolf Literary Services 259
Wordserve Literary Group 259
Writers House 260
Zuckerbrot Literary Agency, Renèe 262

YOUNG ADULT

Adams Literary 111
Agency Group LLC, The 111
Aitken Alexander Associates 112
Anderson Literary Management, LLC 116
Barone Literary Agency 117
Bent Agency, The 118
Book Cents Literary Agency, LLC 120
Books & Such Literary Agency 121
Bradford Literary Agency 122
Brown Literary Agency, Inc., Andrea 126
Cameron & Associates, Kimberley 129
Capital Talent Agency 129
Castiglia Literary Agency 131
Chalberg & Sussman 131
Chudney Agency, The 132
CK Webber Associates Literary Management 257
Connor Literary Agency 135
Corcoran Literary Agency, Jill 135
Corvisiero Literary Agency 136
Curtis Associates, Inc., Richard 137
Curtis Brown, Ltd. 138
David Black Literary Agency 119
DeChiara Literary Agency, The Jennifer 141
DeFiore & Co. 142
Diana Finch Literary Agency 156
Dijkstra Literary Agency, Sandra 143
Donadio & Olson, Inc. 144
Donaghy Literary Group 144
Don Congdon Associates Inc. 134
Dreisbach Literary Management 146
Dunham Literary, Inc. 146
Dunow, Carlson, & Lerner Agency 146
Dystel & Goderich Literary Management 148
East/West Literary Agency, LLC 149
Eden Street Literary 150
Einstein Literary Management 151
Fielding Agency, LLC, The 155
FinePrint Literary Management 156
Flannery Literary 157
Fletcher & Company 157
Folio Literary Management, LLC 158
Foundry Literary + Media 158
Fox Literary 159
Freymann Literary Agency, Sarah Jane 162
Full Circle Literary, LLC 163
Gallt Literary Agency, Nancy 165
Gelfman Schneider Literary Agents, Inc. 166
Gernert Company, The 167
Goldblatt Literary LLC, Barry 167
Golomb Literary Agency, The Susan 168
Goodman Literary Agency, Irene 169
Grad Literary Agency, Inc., Doug 170
Grayson Literary Agency, Ashley 171
Greenburger Associates, Inc., Sanford J. 171
Greenhouse Literary Agency, The 172
Green Literary Agency, LLC, Kathryn 173
Grinberg Literary Agency, Jill 174
Harwood Limited, Antony 175
Heacock Hill Literary Agency, Inc. 177

Heller Agency Inc., Helen 177
Henshaw Group, Richard 177
Hill Bonnie Nadell, Inc., Frederick 179
HSG Agency 180
Hurst Literary Management, Andrea 181
InkWell Management, LLC 182
International Transactions, Inc. 183
Jabberwocky Literary Agency 184
J de S Associates, Inc. 186
Jenks Agency, The Carolyn 186
Joelle Delbourgo Associates, Inc. 143
KT Literary, LLC 191
Langlie, Literary Agent, Laura 193
Laura Dail Literary Agency, Inc. 140
Leigh Feldman Literary 155
Leshne Agency, The 197
Levine Greenberg Literary Agency, Inc. 197
Literary Group International, The 199
LKG Agency 201
Lowenstein Associates Inc. 201
LR Children's Literary 203
Maass Literary Agency, Donald 203
Maccoby Literary Agency, Gina 204
Mann Agency, Carol 205
Mansion Street Literary Management 205
Maria Carvainis Agency, Inc. 130
Marsal Lyon Literary Agency, LLC 207
Martin Literary Management 208
McCarthy Agency, LLC, The 209
Mendel Media Group, LLC 212
Miriam Altshuler Literary Agency 114
Morhaim Literary Agency, Howard 214
Moveable Type Management 214
Mura Literary, Dee 215
Murphy Literary Agency, Erin 215
Naggar Literary Agency, Inc. Jean V. 215
Nelson Literary Agency 216
New Leaf Literary & Media, Inc. 216
Park Literary Group, LLC 218
Perkins Agency, L. 219
Pfeffer Content, Rubin 219
Pippin Properties, Inc. 220
Prospect Agency 221
P.S. Literary Agency 221
Rebecca Friedman Literary Agency 162
Red Sofa Literary 224
Red Tree Literary Agency 225
Rees Literary Agency, Helen 225
Regal Literary Agency 225
Rights Factory, The 227
RLR Associates, Ltd. 228
Rodeen Literary Management 229
Ross Literary Agency, Andy 231
Sadler Children's Literary 234
Sanders & Associates, Victoria 234
Schiavone Literary Agency, Inc. 234
Schmalz Agency, Wendy 235
Sean McCarthy Literary Agency 210
Serendipity Literary Agency, LLC 237
Seymour Agency, The 238
Sherman & Associates, Ken 239
Speilburg Literary Agency 244
Spieler Agency, The 244
Sterling Lord Literistic, Inc. 246
Stringer Literary Agency, LLC, The 247
Strothman Agency, LLC, The 248
Talcott Notch Literary 249
The Knight Agency 190
The Purcell Agency, LLC 223
Three Seas Literary Agency 251
Triada U.S. Literary Agency, Inc. 252
Trident Media Group 253
Unter Agency, The 254
Upstart Crow Literary 254
Veritas Literary Agency 254
Vicky Bijur Literary Agency 119
Waterside Productions, Inc. 256
Waxman Leavell Literary Agency, Inc. 256
Wells Arms Literary 258
Wolf Literary Services 259
Writers House 260

NONFICTION:

ANIMALS
Bent Agency, The 118
Curtis Brown, Ltd. 138
Doyen Literary Services, Inc. 145
Dreisbach Literary Management 146
Dupree/Miller and Associates Literary 147
Dystel & Goderich Literary Management 148
Ebeling Agency, The 150
Felicia Eth Literary Representation 153
Fielding Agency, LLC, The 155
Folio Literary Management, LLC 158
Fredericks Literary Agency, Inc., Jeanne 159
Freedson's Publishing Network, Grace 160
Fresh Books Literary Agency 161
Freymann Literary Agency, Sarah Jane 162
Gartenberg Literary Agency, Max 166
Golomb Literary Agency, The Susan 168
Harwood Limited, Antony 175
Henshaw Group, Richard 177
Kern Literary Agency, The Natasha 188
Levine Greenberg Literary Agency, Inc. 197
Lippincott Massie McQuilkin 198
Literary Group International, The 199
LKG Agency 201
Marsal Lyon Literary Agency, LLC 207
McCarthy Creative Services 210
Mendel Media Group, LLC 212
Mura Literary, Dee 215
Parks Agency, The Richard 218
Red Sofa Literary 224
Rosenkranz Literary Agency, Rita 230
Ryan Publishing Enterprises, Inc., Regina 233
Sheree Bykofsky Associates, Inc. 128
Sherman & Associates, Ken 239
Writers House 260

ANTHROPOLOGY
Agency Group LLC, The 111
Anderson Literary Management, LLC 116
Curtis Brown, Ltd. 138
Don Congdon Associates Inc. 134
Doyen Literary Services, Inc. 145
Dunham Literary, Inc. 146
Dupree/Miller and Associates Literary 147
Dystel & Goderich Literary Management 148
Felicia Eth Literary Representation 153
Fielding Agency, LLC, The 155
Fresh Books Literary Agency 161
Freymann Literary Agency, Sarah Jane 162
Golomb Literary Agency, The Susan 168
Harwood Limited, Antony 175
Hornfischer Literary Management 180
International Transactions, Inc. 183
James Peter Associates, Inc. 184
Larsen/Elizabeth Pomada, Literary Agents,
  Michael 193
Lippincott Massie McQuilkin 198
Literary Group International, The 199
Mann Agency, Carol 205
McCarthy Creative Services 210
Mendel Media Group, LLC 212
Mura Literary, Dee 215
Parks Agency, The Richard 218
Rabinoff Agency, Lynne 224
Red Sofa Literary 224
Rosenkranz Literary Agency, Rita 230
Ross Literary Agency, Andy 231
Rudy Agency, The 232
Seligman, Literary Agent, Lynn 237
Sherman & Associates, Ken 239
Slopen Literary Agency, Beverley 241
Venture Literary 254

ARCHEOLOGY
Agency Group LLC, The 111
Anderson Literary Management, LLC 116
Don Congdon Associates Inc. 134
Doyen Literary Services, Inc. 145
Dunham Literary, Inc. 146
Dupree/Miller and Associates Literary 147
Dystel & Goderich Literary Management 148
Fielding Agency, LLC, The 155
Fresh Books Literary Agency 161

Harwood Limited, Antony 175
Hornfischer Literary Management 180
International Transactions, Inc. 183
James Peter Associates, Inc. 184
Larsen/Elizabeth Pomada, Literary Agents,
  Michael 193
Lippincott Massie McQuilkin 198
Mann Agency, Carol 205
Mura Literary, Dee 215
Parks Agency, The Richard 218
Rabinoff Agency, Lynne 224
Red Sofa Literary 224
Rudy Agency, The 232
Slopen Literary Agency, Beverley 241

ARCHITECTURE
Agency Group LLC, The 111
Anderson Literary Management, LLC 116
Braun Associates, Inc., Barbara 124
Doyen Literary Services, Inc. 145
Dupree/Miller and Associates Literary 147
Fairbank Literary Representation 154
Fielding Agency, LLC, The 155
Fresh Books Literary Agency 161
Freymann Literary Agency, Sarah Jane 162
Harwood Limited, Antony 175
International Transactions, Inc. 183
James Peter Associates, Inc. 184
Jenks Agency, The Carolyn 186
Larsen/Elizabeth Pomada, Literary Agents,
  Michael 193
Levine Literary Agency, Paul S. 198
Lippincott Massie McQuilkin 198
Literary Services Inc. 200
Mann Agency, Carol 205
Mendel Media Group, LLC 212
Millard Literary Agency, Martha 213
Newman Literary, Dana 216
Ryan Publishing Enterprises, Inc., Regina 233
Sheree Bykofsky Associates, Inc. 128
Toby Eady Associates 149
Wm Clark Associates 133

ART
Agency Group LLC, The 111
Anderson Literary Management, LLC 116
Braun Associates, Inc., Barbara 124
Curtis Brown, Ltd. 138
D4EO Literary Agency 139
DeChiara Literary Agency, The Jennifer 141
Doyen Literary Services, Inc. 145
Dunow, Carlson, & Lerner Agency 146
Dupree/Miller and Associates Literary 147
Fairbank Literary Representation 154
Fielding Agency, LLC, The 155
Folio Literary Management, LLC 158
Fresh Books Literary Agency 161
Freymann Literary Agency, Sarah Jane 162
Friedman and Co., Inc., Frederica 163
Gartenberg Literary Agency, Max 166
Gernert Company, The 167
Greenburger Associates, Inc., Sanford J. 171
Harris Literary Agency, Inc., The Joy 174
Harwood Limited, Antony 175
Heacock Hill Literary Agency, Inc. 177
International Transactions, Inc. 183
James Peter Associates, Inc. 184
Jenks Agency, The Carolyn 186
Larsen/Elizabeth Pomada, Literary Agents,
  Michael 193
Levine Greenberg Literary Agency, Inc. 197
Levine Literary Agency, Paul S. 198
Lippincott Massie McQuilkin 198
Literary Services Inc. 200
Mann Agency, Carol 205
McCarthy Creative Services 210
Mendel Media Group, LLC 212
Millard Literary Agency, Martha 213
Mura Literary, Dee 215
Newman Literary, Dana 216
Park Literary Group, LLC 218
Parks Agency, The Richard 218
Rosenkranz Literary Agency, Rita 230
Seligman, Literary Agent, Lynn 237
Sheree Bykofsky Associates, Inc. 128

Sherman & Associates, Ken 239
Toby Eady Associates 149
Weingel-Fidel Agency, The 257
Whimsy Literary Agency, LLC 258
Wm Clark Associates 133
Wolf Literary Services 259
Writers House 260

AUTOBIOGRAPHY

Agency Group LLC, The 111
Alive Communications, Inc. 113
Anderson Literary Management, LLC 116
Daniel Literary Group 140
DeFiore & Co. 142
Diana Finch Literary Agency 156
Don Congdon Associates Inc. 134
Doyen Literary Services, Inc. 145
Dupree/Miller and Associates Literary 147
Dystel & Goderich Literary Management 148
Fairbank Literary Representation 154
Felicia Eth Literary Representation 153
Fielding Agency, LLC, The 155
Fredericks Literary Agency, Inc., Jeanne 159
Freymann Literary Agency, Sarah Jane 162
Graham Maw Christie Literary Agency 170
Green Literary Agency, LLC, Kathryn 173
Henshaw Group, Richard 177
Hornfischer Literary Management 180
International Transactions, Inc. 183
Jabberwocky Literary Agency 184
Jenks Agency, The Carolyn 186
Klinger, Inc., Harvey 189
Langlie, Literary Agent, Laura 193
Larsen/Elizabeth Pomada, Literary Agents, Michael 193
Lecker Agency, Robert 196
Levine Literary Agency, Paul S. 198
Lippincott Massie McQuilkin 198
Literary and Creative Artists, Inc. 199
Lownie Literary Agency, Ltd., Andrew 203
Maccoby Literary Agency, Gina 204
Mann Agency, Carol 205
March Tenth, Inc. 206
Martin Literary Management 208
McBride Literary Agency, Margret 209
Millard Literary Agency, Martha 213
Newman Literary, Dana 216
Parks Agency, The Richard 218
P.S. Literary Agency 221
Rabinoff Agency, Lynne 224
Robbins Literary Agency, B.J. 228
Rosenkranz Literary Agency, Rita 230
Ross Literary Agency, Andy 231
Rudy Agency, The 232
Sanders & Associates, Victoria 234
Sheree Bykofsky Associates, Inc. 128
Simmons Literary Agency, Jeffrey 241
Slopen Literary Agency, Beverley 241
Smith Literary Agency, Ltd., Robert 242
Watkins Loomis Agency, Inc. 256
Weingel-Fidel Agency, The 257
Wm Clark Associates 133
Writers House 260
Seventh Avenue Literary Agency 238
Yates & Yates 261

BIOGRAPHY

Agency Group LLC, The 111
Alive Communications, Inc. 113
Allen O'Shea Literary Agency 113
Ambassador Literary Agency 115
Amster Literary Enterprises, Betsy 115
Anderson Literary Management, LLC 116
Arcadia 116
Bradford Literary Agency 122
Brandt & Hochman Literary Agents, Inc. 123
Braun Associates, Inc., Barbara 124
Chase Literary Agency 131
Chelius Literary Agency, Jane 132
Cheney Literary Associates, LLC, Elyse 132
Curtis Brown, Ltd. 138
Cynthia Cannell Literary Agency 129
D4EO Literary Agency 139
Daniel Literary Group 140
David Black Literary Agency 119

DeFiore & Co. 142
Diana Finch Literary Agency 156
Dijkstra Literary Agency, Sandra 143
Don Congdon Associates Inc. 134
Donnaud & Associates, Inc., Janis A. 144
Doyen Literary Services, Inc. 145
Dreisbach Literary Management 146
Dunham Literary, Inc. 146
Dunow, Carlson, & Lerner Agency 146
Dupree/Miller and Associates Literary 147
Dystel & Goderich Literary Management 148
E.J. McCarthy Agency 209
Fairbank Literary Representation 154
Felicia Eth Literary Representation 153
Fielding Agency, LLC, The 155
FinePrint Literary Management 156
Fletcher & Company 157
Folio Literary Management, LLC 158
Fox Literary 159
Franklin Associates, Ltd., Lynn C. 159
Fredericks Literary Agency, Inc., Jeanne 159
Freymann Literary Agency, Sarah Jane 162
Friedman and Co., Inc., Frederica 163
G Agency, LLC, The 165
Gartenberg Literary Agency, Max 166
Golomb Literary Agency, The Susan 168
Graham Maw Christie Literary Agency 170
Greenburger Associates, Inc., Sanford J. 171
Green Literary Agency, LLC, Kathryn 173
Grinberg Literary Agency, Jill 174
Harwood Limited, Antony 175
Hawkins & Associates, Inc., John 176
Henshaw Group, Richard 177
Hill and Associates, Julie A. 179
Hill Bonnie Nadell, Inc., Frederick 179
Hornfischer Literary Management 180
InkWell Management, LLC 182
International Transactions, Inc. 183
Jabberwocky Literary Agency 184
James Peter Associates, Inc. 184
J de S Associates, Inc. 186
Jenks Agency, The Carolyn 186
Judith Ehrlich Literary Management, LLC 151
Klinger, Inc., Harvey 189
LA Literary Agency, The 192
Langlie, Literary Agent, Laura 193
Larsen/Elizabeth Pomada, Literary Agents, Michael 193
Lazin Books, Sarah 195
Lecker Agency, Robert 196
Levine Greenberg Literary Agency, Inc. 197
Levine Literary Agency, Paul S. 198
Lippincott Massie McQuilkin 198
Literary and Creative Artists, Inc. 199
Literary Group International, The 199
Literary Management Group, Inc. 200
Literary Services Inc. 200
Lownie Literary Agency, Ltd., Andrew 203
Maccoby Literary Agency, Gina 204
Mann Agency, Carol 205
March Tenth, Inc. 206
Maria Carvainis Agency, Inc. 130
Marsal Lyon Literary Agency, LLC 207
Martin Literary Management 208
McBride Literary Agency, Margret 209
McCarthy Creative Services 210
McGill Agency, Inc., The 211
Mendel Media Group, LLC 212
Millard Literary Agency, Martha 213
Mura Literary, Dee 215
Naggar Literary Agency, Inc. Jean V. 215
Newman Literary, Dana 216
Oscard Agency, Inc., Fifi 217
Parks Agency, The Richard 218
Paul Bresnick Literary Agency, LLC 124
Perkins Agency, L. 219
Prentis Literary, Linn 220
Prospect Agency 221
P.S. Literary Agency 221
Rabinoff Agency, Lynne 224
Rennert Agency, The Amy 226
Richards Agency, The Lisa 226
Rick Broadhead & Associates Literary 125
Rights Factory, The 227

Rinaldi Literary Agency, Angela 227
Robbins Literary Agency, B.J. 228
Rosenkranz Literary Agency, Rita 230
Ross Literary Agency, Andy 231
Rudy Agency, The 232
Sagalyn Agency, The 234
Sanders & Associates, Victoria 234
sazTracy Brown Literary Agency 126
Schiavone Literary Agency, Inc. 234
Schulman Literary Agency, Susan 235
Seligman, Literary Agent, Lynn 237
Shannon Literary Agency, Inc., Denise 239
Sheree Bykofsky Associates, Inc. 128
Sherman & Associates, Ken 239
Simmons Literary Agency, Jeffrey 241
Slopen Literary Agency, Beverley 241
Smith Literary Agency, Ltd., Robert 242
Speilburg Literary Agency 244
Spitzer Literary Agency, Inc., Philip G. 245
Sterling Lord Literistic, Inc. 246
Straus Agency, Inc., Robin 247
Sweeney Agency, LLC, Emma 249
Tessler Literary Agency, LLC 250
Triada U.S. Literary Agency, Inc. 252
Trident Media Group 253
Unter Agency, The 254
Venture Literary 254
Watkins Loomis Agency, Inc. 256
Waxman Leavell Literary Agency, Inc. 256
Weingel-Fidel Agency, The 257
Whimsy Literary Agency, LLC 258
Wm Clark Associates 133
Wordserve Literary Group 259
Writers House 260
Seventh Avenue Literary Agency 238
Yates & Yates 261

BUSINESS

Agency Group LLC, The 111
Alive Communications, Inc. 113
Allen O'Shea Literary Agency 113
Amster Literary Enterprises, Betsy 115
BookEnds, LLC 120
Bradford Literary Agency 122
Chase Literary Agency 131
Cheney Literary Associates, LLC, Elyse 132
Curtis Brown, Ltd. 138
D4EO Literary Agency 139
Daniel Literary Group 140
David Black Literary Agency 119
DeFiore & Co. 142
Diana Finch Literary Agency 156
Dijkstra Literary Agency, Sandra 143
Donnaud & Associates, Inc., Janis A. 144
Doyen Literary Services, Inc. 145
Dreisbach Literary Management 146
Dupree/Miller and Associates Literary 147
Dystel & Goderich Literary Management 148
Ebeling Agency, The 150
Felicia Eth Literary Representation 153
Fielding Agency, LLC, The 155
FinePrint Literary Management 156
Fletcher & Company 157
Folio Literary Management, LLC 158
Freedson's Publishing Network, Grace 160
Fresh Books Literary Agency 161
Freymann Literary Agency, Sarah Jane 162
Friedman and Co., Inc., Frederica 163
G Agency, LLC, The 165
Garamond Agency, Inc., The 165
Golomb Literary Agency, The Susan 168
Grad Literary Agency, Inc., Doug 170
Grayson Literary Agency, Ashley 171
Greenburger Associates, Inc., Sanford J. 171
Green Literary Agency, LLC, Kathryn 173
Harwood Limited, Antony 175
Hawkins & Associates, Inc., John 176
Heacock Hill Literary Agency, Inc. 177
Henshaw Group, Richard 177
Herman Agency, LLC, The Jeff 178
Holmes Agency, The 179
Hornfischer Literary Management 180
HSG Agency 180
Hurst Literary Management, Andrea 181
InkWell Management, LLC 182

Jabberwocky Literary Agency 184
James Peter Associates, Inc. 184
J de S Associates, Inc. 186
Jenks Agency, The Carolyn 186
Judith Ehrlich Literary Management, LLC 151
Keller Media Inc. 187
LA Literary Agency, The 192
Larsen/Elizabeth Pomada, Literary Agents, Michael 193
LaunchBooks Literary Agency 194
Leshne Agency, The 197
LevelFiveMedia, LLC 197
Levine Greenberg Literary Agency, Inc. 197
Levine Literary Agency, Paul S. 198
Lippincott Massie McQuilkin 198
Literary and Creative Artists, Inc. 199
Literary Group International, The 199
Literary Services Inc. 200
MacGregor Literary Inc. 204
Mann Agency, Carol 205
Marcil Literary Agency, Inc., The Denise 207
Maria Carvainis Agency, Inc. 130
Marsal Lyon Literary Agency, LLC 207
Martin Literary Management 208
McBride Literary Agency, Margret 209
McCarthy Creative Services 210
McGill Agency, Inc., The 211
Mendel Media Group, LLC 212
Millard Literary Agency, Martha 213
Morhaim Literary Agency, Howard 214
Moveable Type Management 214
Mura Literary, Dee 215
Newman Literary, Dana 216
Oscard Agency, Inc., Fifi 217
Parks Agency, The Richard 218
P.S. Literary Agency 221
Queen Literary Agency 223
Rabinoff Agency, Lynne 224
Rebecca Friedman Literary Agency 162
Rees Literary Agency, Helen 225
Rennert Agency, The Amy 226
Rick Broadhead & Associates Literary 125
Rights Factory, The 227
Rinaldi Literary Agency, Angela 227
Rosenkranz Literary Agency, Rita 230
Rudy Agency, The 232
Sagalyn Agency, The 234
Schiavone Literary Agency, Inc. 234
Schulman Literary Agency, Susan 235
Seligman, Literary Agent, Lynn 237
Seymour Agency, The 238
Shannon Literary Agency, Inc., Denise 239
Sheree Bykofsky Associates, Inc. 128
Sherman & Associates, Ken 239
Slopen Literary Agency, Beverley 241
Strothman Agency, LLC, The 248
Stuart Agency, The 248
Sweeney Agency, LLC, Emma 249
Talcott Notch Literary 249
Tessler Literary Agency, LLC 250
Triada U.S. Literary Agency, Inc. 252
Trident Media Group 253
Venture Literary 254
Waterside Productions, Inc. 256
Whimsy Literary Agency, LLC 258
Writers House 260
Seventh Avenue Literary Agency 238
Yates & Yates 261

CHILD GUIDANCE
Agency Group LLC, The 111
Alive Communications, Inc. 113
Amster Literary Enterprises, Betsy 115
Crichton & Associates 137
Daniel Literary Group 140
DeFiore & Co. 142
Diana Finch Literary Agency 156
Don Congdon Associates Inc. 134
Doyen Literary Services, Inc. 145
Dupree/Miller and Associates Literary 147
Dystel & Goderich Literary Management 148
Felicia Eth Literary Representation 153
Fielding Agency, LLC, The 155
Folio Literary Management, LLC 158

Fredericks Literary Agency, Inc., Jeanne 159
Fresh Books Literary Agency 161
Freymann Literary Agency, Sarah Jane 162
Graham Maw Christie Literary Agency 170
Green Literary Agency, LLC, Kathryn 173
Harwood Limited, Antony 175
Henshaw Group, Richard 177
Hornfischer Literary Management 180
Kern Literary Agency, The Natasha 188
Levine Literary Agency, Paul S. 198
Lippincott Massie McQuilkin 198
Literary Group International, The 199
Literary Services Inc. 200
Mann Agency, Carol 205
Martin Literary Management 208
McGill Agency, Inc., The 211
Mendel Media Group, LLC 212
Millard Literary Agency, Martha 213
Newman Literary, Dana 216
Parks Agency, The Richard 218
P.S. Literary Agency 221
Rosenkranz Literary Agency, Rita 230
Ross Literary Agency, Andy 231
Rudy Agency, The 232
Seligman, Literary Agent, Lynn 237
Sheree Bykofsky Associates, Inc. 128
Whimsy Literary Agency, LLC 258
Writers House 260

COMPUTERS
Curtis Brown, Ltd. 138
Diana Finch Literary Agency 156
Doyen Literary Services, Inc. 145
Fresh Books Literary Agency 161
G Agency, LLC, The 165
Grayson Literary Agency, Ashley 171
Harwood Limited, Antony 175
International Transactions, Inc. 183
Levine Greenberg Literary Agency, Inc. 197
Levine Literary Agency, Paul S. 198
Rosenkranz Literary Agency, Rita 230
Rudy Agency, The 232
Sherman & Associates, Ken 239
Waterside Productions, Inc. 256
Seventh Avenue Literary Agency 238

COOKING
Agency Group LLC, The 111
Allen O'Shea Literary Agency 113
Bent Agency, The 118
Bidnick & Company 119
Book Cents Literary Agency, LLC 120
Brandt & Hochman Literary Agents, Inc. 123
Compass Talent 134
Curtis Brown, Ltd. 138
DeChiara Literary Agency, The Jennifer 141
DeFiore & Co. 142
Don Congdon Associates Inc. 134
Doyen Literary Services, Inc. 145
Dupree/Miller and Associates Literary 147
Ebeling, The 150
Einstein Literary Management 151
Ekus Group, LLC, The Lisa 151
Empire Literary 152
Fairbank Literary Representation 154
Fielding Agency, LLC, The 155
Folio Literary Management, LLC 158
Fredericks Literary Agency, Inc., Jeanne 159
Freedson's Publishing Network, Grace 160
Fresh Books Literary Agency 161
Freymann Literary Agency, Sarah Jane 162
Friedman and Co., Inc., Frederica 163
Grad Literary Agency, Inc., Doug 170
Graham Maw Christie Literary Agency 170
Green Literary Agency, LLC, Kathryn 173
Grinberg Literary Agency, Jill 174
Harwood Limited, Antony 175
Henshaw Group, Richard 177
Hill and Associates, Julie A. 179
Holmes Agency, The 179
InkWell Management, LLC 182
International Transactions, Inc. 183
Jabberwocky Literary Agency 184
Klinger, Inc., Harvey 189
LA Literary Agency, The 192

Lecker Agency, Robert 196
LevelFiveMedia, LLC 197
Levine Greenberg Literary Agency, Inc. 197
Levine Literary Agency, Paul S. 198
Literary and Creative Artists, Inc. 199
Literary Services Inc. 200
Mansion Street Literary Management 205
Manus & Associates Literary Agency, Inc. 206
Marsal Lyon Literary Agency, LLC 207
McBride Literary Agency, Margret 209
Mendel Media Group, LLC 212
Millard Literary Agency, Martha 213
Morhaim Literary Agency, Howard 214
Mura Literary, Dee 215
Newman Literary, Dana 216
Oscard Agency, Inc., Fifi 217
Parks Agency, The Richard 218
P.S. Literary Agency 221
Rinaldi Literary Agency, Angela 227
Rosenkranz Literary Agency, Rita 230
Schiavone Literary Agency, Inc. 234
Schulman Literary Agency, Susan 235
Seligman, Literary Agent, Lynn 237
Sheree Bykofsky Associates, Inc. 128
Sherman & Associates, Ken 239
Smith Literary Agency, Ltd., Robert 242
Spieler Agency, The 244
Sterling Lord Literistic, Inc. 246
Straus Agency, Inc., Robin 247
Talcott Notch Literary 249
Toby Eady Associates 149
Triada U.S. Literary Agency, Inc. 252
Upstart Crow Literary 254
Vicky Bijur Literary Agency 119
Whimsy Literary Agency, LLC 258
Writers House 260

CRAFTS
Allen O'Shea Literary Agency 113
Curtis Brown, Ltd. 138
Doyen Literary Services, Inc. 145
Dupree/Miller and Associates Literary 147
Fairbank Literary Representation 154
Fielding Agency, LLC, The 155
Freedson's Publishing Network, Grace 160
Fresh Books Literary Agency 161
Gernert Company, The 167
Hurst Literary Management, Andrea 181
Levine Literary Agency, Paul S. 198
Literary Group International, The 199
Literary Services Inc. 200
Morhaim Literary Agency, Howard 214
Parks Agency, The Richard 218
Red Sofa Literary 224
Rosenkranz Literary Agency, Rita 230
Sheree Bykofsky Associates, Inc. 128
Sherman & Associates, Ken 239
Talcott Notch Literary 249
Wolf Literary Services 259

CREATIVE NONFICTION
Aitken Alexander Associates 112
Bent Agency, The 118
Bidnick & Company 119
Bradford Literary Agency 122
Brandt & Hochman Literary Agents, Inc. 123
Cameron & Associates, Kimberley 129
Castiglia Literary Agency 131
Cheney Literary Associates, LLC, Elyse 132
Compass Talent 134
Cornerstone Literary, Inc. 136
Curtis Brown, Ltd. 138
Darhansoff & Verrill Literary Agents 140
David Black Literary Agency 119
DeChiara Literary Agency, The Jennifer 141
Dijkstra Literary Agency, Sandra 143
Don Congdon Associates Inc. 134
Donnaud & Associates, Inc., Janis A. 144
Dunow, Carlson, & Lerner Agency 146
Einstein Literary Management 151
Empire Literary 152
FinePrint Literary Management 156
Fletcher & Company 157
Folio Literary Management, LLC 158

Foundry Literary + Media 158
Fox Literary 159
Friedrich Agency, The 163
Full Circle Literary, LLC 163
Gelfman Schneider Literary Agents, Inc. 166
Gernert Company, The 167
Ghosh Literary 167
Goldin Literary Agency, Inc., Frances 168
Grad Literary Agency, Inc., Doug 170
Greenburger Associates, Inc., Sanford J. 171
Harris Literary Agency, Inc., The Joy 174
HSG Agency 180
InkWell Management, LLC 182
Joelle Delbourgo Associates, Inc. 143
Judith Ehrlich Literary Management, LLC 151
Krichevsky Literary Agency, Inc., Stuart 191
LA Literary Agency, The 192
LaunchBooks Literary Agency 194
Leigh Feldman Literary 155
Leshne Agency, The 197
Levine Greenberg Literary Agency, Inc. 197
Literary Group International, The 199
LKG Agency 201
Lowenstein Associates Inc. 201
Maass Literary Agency, Donald 203
Marsal Lyon Literary Agency, LLC 207
McMillan & Associates, Inc., Sally Hill 211
Miriam Altshuler Literary Agency 114
Morhaim Literary Agency, Howard 214
Moveable Type Management 214
Mura Literary, Dee 215
Naggar Literary Agency, Inc. Jean V. 215
Pavilion Literary Management 218
Perkins, L. 219
Rees Literary Agency, Helen 225
Regal Literary Agency 225
Rennert Agency, The Amy 226
Rittenberg Literary Agency, Inc., Ann 227
RLR Associates, Ltd. 228
Ross Literary Agency, Andy 231
Sagalyn Agency, The 234
Serendipity Literary Agency, LLC 237
Sheree Bykofsky Associates, Inc. 128
Sherman Associates, Inc., Wendy 240
Slopen Literary Agency, Beverley 241
Snell Literary Agency, Michael 243
Sterling Lord Literistic, Inc. 246
Straus Agency, Inc., Robin 247
Stuart Agency, The 248
Tessler Literary Agency, LLC 250
Trident Media Group 253
Upstart Crow Literary 254
Wolf Literary Services 259

CULTURAL INTERESTS
Agency Group LLC, The 111
Anderson Literary Management, LLC 116
Crichton & Associates 137
Diana Finch Literary Agency 156
Doyen Literary Services, Inc. 145
Dunham Literary, Inc. 146
Dunow, Carlson, & Lerner Agency 146
Dystel & Goderich Literary Management 148
Fairbank Literary Representation 154
Felicia Eth Literary Representation 153
Fielding Agency, LLC, The 155
Fresh Books Literary Agency 161
Goldin Literary Agency, Inc., Frances 168
International Transactions, Inc. 183
J de S Associates, Inc. 186
Jenks Agency, The Carolyn 186
Judith Ehrlich Literary Management, LLC 151
Kern Literary Agency, The Natasha 188
Langlie, Literary Agent, Laura 193
Lecker Agency, Robert 196
Levine Literary Agency, Paul S. 198
Lippincott Massie McQuilkin 198
Maccoby Literary Agency, Gina 204
Mann Agency, Carol 205
McBride Literary Agency, Margret 209
Millard Literary Agency, Martha 213
Newman Literary, Dana 216
Parks Agency, The Richard 218

Rabinoff Agency, Lynne 224
Red Sofa Literary 224
Robbins Literary Agency, B.J. 228
Rosenkranz Literary Agency, Rita 230
Ross Literary Agency, Andy 231
Rudy Agency, The 232
Sanders & Associates, Victoria 234
Sheree Bykofsky Associates, Inc. 128
Toby Eady Associates 149
Venture Literary 254
Watkins Loomis Agency, Inc. 256
Wm Clark Associates 133

CURRENT AFFAIRS
Allen O'Shea Literary Agency 113
Ambassador Literary Agency 115
Amster Literary Enterprises, Betsy 115
Anderson Literary Management, LLC 116
Arcadia 116
Castiglia Literary Agency 131
Chase Literary Agency 131
Cheney Literary Associates, LLC, Elyse 132
Curtis Brown, Ltd. 138
D4EO Literary Agency 139
Daniel Literary Group 140
David Black Literary Agency 119
Diana Finch Literary Agency 156
Don Congdon Associates Inc. 134
Doyen Literary Services, Inc. 145
Dunow, Carlson, & Lerner Agency 146
Dupree/Miller and Associates Literary 147
Dystel & Goderich Literary Management 148
Fairbank Literary Representation 154
Felicia Eth Literary Representation 153
Fielding Agency, LLC, The 155
Foundry Literary + Media 158
Franklin Associates, Ltd., Lynn C. 159
Freedson's Publishing Network, Grace 160
Fresh Books Literary Agency 161
Freymann Literary Agency, Sarah Jane 162
Friedman and Co., Inc., Frederica 163
Garamond Agency, Inc., The 165
Gartenberg Literary Agency, Max 166
Golomb Literary Agency, The Susan 168
Greenburger Associates, Inc., Sanford J. 171
Green Literary Agency, LLC, Kathryn 173
Harwood Limited, Antony 175
Henshaw Group, Richard 177
Hill Bonnie Nadell, Inc., Frederick 179
Hornfischer Literary Management 180
HSG Agency 180
InkWell Management, LLC 182
International Transactions, Inc. 183
Jabberwocky Literary Agency 184
James Peter Associates, Inc. 184
J de S Associates, Inc. 186
Jenks Agency, The Carolyn 186
Joelle Delbourgo Associates, Inc. 143
Judith Ehrlich Literary Management, LLC 151
Keller Media Inc. 187
Kern Literary Agency, The Natasha 188
Langlie, Literary Agent, Laura 193
Larsen/Elizabeth Pomada, Literary Agents, Michael 193
LaunchBooks Literary Agency 194
Levine Literary Agency, Paul S. 198
Lippincott Massie McQuilkin 198
Literary Group International, The 199
Lownie Literary Agency, Ltd., Andrew 203
Maccoby Literary Agency, Gina 204
MacGregor Literary Inc. 204
Mann Agency, Carol 205
March Tenth, Inc. 206
Marsal Lyon Literary Agency, LLC 207
Martin Literary Management 208
McBride Literary Agency, Margret 209
McCarthy Creative Services 210
McGill Agency, Inc., The 211
Mendel Media Group, LLC 212
Millard Literary Agency, Martha 213
Mura Literary, Dee 215
Naggar Literary Agency, Inc. Jean V. 215
Newman Literary, Dana 216
Park Literary Group, LLC 218

Parks Agency, The Richard 218
Prentis Literary, Linn 220
P.S. Literary Agency 221
Rabinoff Agency, Lynne 224
Red Sofa Literary 224
Richards Agency, The Lisa 226
Rick Broadhead & Associates Literary 125
Rinaldi Literary Agency, Angela 227
Robbins Literary Agency, B.J. 228
Rosenberg Group, The 230
Rosenkranz Literary Agency, Rita 230
Ross Literary Agency, Andy 231
Rudy Agency, The 232
Sanders & Associates, Victoria 234
sazTracy Brown Literary Agency 126
Seligman, Literary Agent, Lynn 237
Serendipity Literary Agency, LLC 237
Sheree Bykofsky Associates, Inc. 128
Sherman & Associates, Ken 239
Simmons Literary Agency, Jeffrey 241
Slopen Literary Agency, Beverley 241
Spitzer Literary Agency, Inc., Philip G. 245
Sterling Lord Literistic, Inc. 246
Straus Agency, Inc., Robin 247
Strothman Agency, LLC, The 248
Stuart Agency, The 248
Toby Eady Associates 149
Trident Media Group 253
Venture Literary 254
Veritas Literary Agency 254
Watkins Loomis Agency, Inc. 256
Wm Clark Associates 133
Yates & Yates 261

DANCE
Agency Group LLC, The 111
Anderson Literary Management, LLC 116
Diana Finch Literary Agency 156
Don Congdon Associates Inc. 134
Dupree/Miller and Associates Literary 147
Fresh Books Literary Agency 161
Henshaw Group, Richard 177
James Peter Associates, Inc. 184
Lecker Agency, Robert 196
Mendel Media Group, LLC 212
Parks Agency, The Richard 218
Robbins Literary Agency, B.J. 228
Rosenkranz Literary Agency, Rita 230
Sheree Bykofsky Associates, Inc. 128
Venture Literary 254
Weingel-Fidel Agency, The 257
Wm Clark Associates 133

DESIGN
Agency Group LLC, The 111
Anderson Literary Management, LLC 116
Braun Associates, Inc., Barbara 124
Dijkstra Literary Agency, Sandra 143
Doyen Literary Services, Inc. 145
Dupree/Miller and Associates Literary 147
Fairbank Literary Representation 154
Fielding Agency, LLC, The 155
Fresh Books Literary Agency 161
Freymann Literary Agency, Sarah Jane 162
Full Circle Literary, LLC 163
Harwood Limited, Antony 175
International Transactions, Inc. 183
James Peter Associates, Inc. 184
Jenks Agency, The Carolyn 186
Larsen/Elizabeth Pomada, Literary Agents, Michael 193
Levine Literary Agency, Paul S. 198
Lippincott Massie McQuilkin 198
Literary Services Inc. 200
Mann Agency, Carol 205
Mansion Street Literary Management 205
Millard Literary Agency, Martha 213
Morhaim Literary Agency, Howard 214
Newman Literary, Dana 216
Sheree Bykofsky Associates, Inc. 128
Toby Eady Associates 149
Wm Clark Associates 133

DIET/NUTRITION
Doyen Literary Services, Inc. 145

Dupree/Miller and Associates Literary 147
Ebeling Agency, The 150
Ekus Group, LLC, The Lisa 151
Empire Literary 152
Fairbank Literary Representation 154
Fielding Agency, LLC, The 155
Foundry Literary + Media 158
Freedson's Publishing Network, Grace 160
Freymann Literary Agency, Sarah 162
International Transactions, Inc. 183
Lecker Agency, Robert 196
Marsal Lyon Literary Agency, LLC 207
Parks Agency, The Richard 218
P.S. Literary Agency 221
Rebecca Friedman Literary Agency 162
Smith Literary Agency, Ltd., Robert 242
Toby Eady Associates 149
Triada U.S. Literary Agency, Inc. 252
Waterside Productions, Inc. 256
Writers House 260
Zimmermann Literary Agency, Helen 262

ECONOMICS

Agency Group LLC, The 111
Alive Communications, Inc. 113
Cheney Literary Associates, LLC, Elyse 132
Daniel Literary Group 140
DeFiore & Co. 142
Diana Finch Literary Agency 156
Doyen Literary Services, Inc. 145
Dupree/Miller and Associates Literary 147
Dystel & Goderich Literary Management 148
Felicia Eth Literary Representation 153
Fielding Agency, LLC, The 155
Folio Literary Management, LLC 158
Freedson's Publishing Network, Grace 160
Fresh Books Literary Agency 161
Freymann Literary Agency, Sarah Jane 162
Garamond Agency, Inc., The 165
Golomb Literary Agency, The Susan 168
Grayson Literary Agency, Ashley 171
Green Literary Agency, LLC, Kathryn 173
Harwood Limited, Antony 175
Henshaw Group, Richard 177
Herman Agency, LLC, The Jeff 178
Hornfischer Literary Management 180
Jabberwocky Literary Agency 184
J de S Associates, Inc. 186
Larsen/Elizabeth Pomada, Literary Agents, Michael 193
LevelFiveMedia, LLC 197
Levine Literary Agency, Paul S. 198
Lippincott Massie McQuilkin 198
Literary and Creative Artists, Inc. 199
Literary Services Inc. 200
MacGregor Literary Inc. 204
Martin Literary Management 208
McBride Literary Agency, Margret 209
Millard Literary Agency, Martha 213
Oscard Agency, Inc., Fifi 217
Parks Agency, The Richard 218
P.S. Literary Agency 221
Rabinoff Agency, Lynne 224
Rosenkranz Literary Agency, Rita 230
Rudy Agency, The 232
Sagalyn Agency, The 234
Sheree Bykofsky Associates, Inc. 128
Slopen Literary Agency, Beverley 241
Triada U.S. Literary Agency, Inc. 252
Trident Media Group 253
Venture Literary 254
Writers House 260
Seventh Avenue Literary Agency 238

EDUCATION

Anderson Literary Management, LLC 116
Curtis Brown, Ltd. 138
Doyen Literary Services, Inc. 145
Dupree/Miller and Associates Literary 147
Fielding Agency, LLC, The 155
Freedson's Publishing Network, Grace 160
Fresh Books Literary Agency 161
Friedman and Co., Inc., Frederica 163
Green Literary Agency, LLC, Kathryn 173
Harwood Limited, Antony 175

HSG Agency 180
Jenks Agency, The Carolyn 186
Levine Literary Agency, Paul S. 198
Literary Group International, The 199
McCarthy Creative Services 210
McGill Agency, Inc., The 211
Mendel Media Group, LLC 212
Millard Literary Agency, Martha 213
Newman Literary, Dana 216
Ross Literary Agency, Andy 231
Rudy Agency, The 232
Seligman, Literary Agent, Lynn 237
Sheree Bykofsky Associates, Inc. 128
Sherman & Associates, Ken 239
Sterling Lord Literistic, Inc. 246
Triada U.S. Literary Agency, Inc. 252
Whimsy Literary Agency, LLC 258

ENVIRONMENT

Agency Group LLC, The 111
Anderson Literary Management, LLC 116
Daniel Literary Group 140
Diana Finch Literary Agency 156
Don Congdon Associates Inc. 134
Doyen Literary Services, Inc. 145
Dunham Literary, Inc. 146
Dupree/Miller and Associates Literary 147
Ebeling Agency, The 150
Fairbank Literary Representation 154
Fielding Agency, LLC, The 155
Folio Literary Management, LLC 158
Freedson's Publishing Network, Grace 160
Fresh Books Literary Agency 161
Golomb Literary Agency, The Susan 168
Harwood Limited, Antony 175
Henshaw Group, Richard 177
Hill Bonnie Nadell, Inc., Frederick 179
Holmes Agency, The 179
Hornfischer Literary Management 180
Kern Literary Agency, The Natasha 188
Langlie, Literary Agent, Laura 193
Larsen/Elizabeth Pomada, Literary Agents, Michael 193
LaunchBooks Literary Agency 194
Mendel Media Group, LLC 212
Mura Literary, Dee 215
Parks Agency, The Richard 218
P.S. Literary Agency 221
Rick Broadhead & Associates Literary 125
Ross Literary Agency, Andy 231
Sheree Bykofsky Associates, Inc. 128
Spieler Agency, The 244
Strothman Agency, LLC, The 248
Unter Agency, The 254
Venture Literary 254
Watkins Loomis Agency, Inc. 256

ETHNIC

Agency Group LLC, The 111
Ambassador Literary Agency 115
Amster Literary Enterprises, Betsy 115
Anderson Literary Management, LLC 116
BookEnds, LLC 120
Crichton & Associates 137
Curtis Brown, Ltd. 138
Diana Finch Literary Agency 156
Doyen Literary Services, Inc. 145
Dunham Literary, Inc. 146
Dupree/Miller and Associates Literary 147
Dystel & Goderich Literary Management 148
Fairbank Literary Representation 154
Fielding Agency, LLC, The 155
Fresh Books Literary Agency 161
Freymann Literary Agency, Sarah Jane 162
Friedman and Co., Inc., Frederica 163
Greenburger Associates, Inc., Sanford J. 171
Grinberg Literary Agency, Jill 174
Harwood Limited, Antony 175
Hill and Associates, Julie A. 179
International Transactions, Inc. 183
James Peter Associates, Inc. 184
J de S Associates, Inc. 186
Jenks Agency, The Carolyn 186
Kern Literary Agency, The Natasha 188
Larsen/Elizabeth Pomada, Literary Agents,

Michael 193
Lecker Agency, Robert 196
Levine Literary Agency, Paul S. 198
Lippincott Massie McQuilkin 198
Literary Group International, The 199
Maccoby Literary Agency, Gina 204
Mann Agency, Carol 205
McBride Literary Agency, Margret 209
McCarthy Creative Services 210
McGill Agency, Inc., The 211
Mendel Media Group, LLC 212
Millard Literary Agency, Martha 213
Mura Literary, Dee 215
Newman Literary, Dana 216
Parks Agency, The Richard 218
Prentis Literary, Linn 220
Rabinoff Agency, Lynne 224
Robbins Literary Agency, B.J. 228
Rosenkranz Literary Agency, Rita 230
Ross Literary Agency, Andy 231
Rudy Agency, The 232
Sanders & Associates, Victoria 234
Schulman Literary Agency, Susan 235
Seligman, Literary Agent, Lynn 237
Sheree Bykofsky Associates, Inc. 128
Sherman & Associates, Ken 239
Toby Eady Associates 149
Venture Literary 254
Watkins Loomis Agency, Inc. 256
Wm Clark Associates 133

FILM

Braun Associates, Inc., Barbara 124
Curtis Brown, Ltd. 138
Daniel Literary Group 140
DeChiara Literary Agency, The Jennifer 141
Diana Finch Literary Agency 156
Don Congdon Associates Inc. 134
Doyen Literary Services, Inc. 145
Dupree/Miller and Associates Literary 147
Friedman and Co., Inc., Frederica 163
Gartenberg Literary Agency, Max 166
Harwood Limited, Antony 175
Jabberwocky Literary Agency 184
James Peter Associates, Inc. 184
Langlie, Literary Agent, Laura 193
Larsen/Elizabeth Pomada, Literary Agents, Michael 193
Lecker Agency, Robert 196
Levine Literary Agency, Paul S. 198
Lippincott Massie McQuilkin 198
Literary Group International, The 199
March Tenth, Inc. 206
Millard Literary Agency, Martha 213
Newman Literary, Dana 216
Parks Agency, The Richard 218
Perkins Agency, L. 219
Robbins Literary Agency, B.J. 228
Rosenkranz Literary Agency, Rita 230
Sanders & Associates, Victoria 234
Seligman, Literary Agent, Lynn 237
Sheree Bykofsky Associates, Inc. 128
Sherman & Associates, Ken 239
Simmons Literary Agency, Jeffrey 241
Smith Literary Agency, Ltd., Robert 242
Spieler Agency, The 244
Wm Clark Associates 133
Writers House 260

FOODS

Agency Group LLC, The 111
Brandt & Hochman Literary Agents, Inc. 123
Chase Literary Agency 131
Compass Talent 134
DeChiara Literary Agency, The Jennifer 141
DeFiore & Co. 142
Don Congdon Associates Inc. 134
Doyen Literary Services, Inc. 145
Dunow, Carlson, & Lerner Agency 146
Dupree/Miller and Associates Literary 147
Ebeling Agency, The 150
Ekus Group, LLC, The Lisa 151
Fairbank Literary Representation 154
Fielding Agency, LLC, The 155
FinePrint Literary Management 156

Fletcher & Company 157
Folio Literary Management, LLC 158
Fredericks Literary Agency, Inc., Jeanne 159
Freedson's Publishing Network, Grace 160
Freymann Literary Agency, Sarah Jane 162
Gernert Company, The 167
Graham Maw Christie Literary Agency 170
Green Literary Agency, LLC, Kathryn 173
Henshaw Group, Richard 177
Holmes Agency, The 179
HSG Agency 180
InkWell Management, LLC 182
International Transactions, Inc. 183
Jabberwocky Literary Agency 184
Klinger, Inc., Harvey 189
Larsen/Elizabeth Pomada, Literary Agents, Michael 193
Lecker Agency, Robert 196
LevelFiveMedia, LLC 197
Levine Literary Agency, Paul S. 198
Literary and Creative Artists, Inc. 199
McBride Literary Agency, Margret 209
Mendel Media Group, LLC 212
Newman Literary, Dana 216
Parks Agency, The Richard 218
Perkins Agency, L. 219
P.S. Literary Agency 221
Queen Literary Agency 223
Rosenberg Group, The 230
Sheree Bykofsky Associates, Inc. 128
Sherman Associates, Inc., Wendy 240
Smith Literary Agency, Ltd., Robert 242
Speilburg Literary Agency 244
Spieler Agency, The 244
Tessler Literary Agency, LLC 250
Toby Eady Associates 149
Triada U.S. Literary Agency, Inc. 252
Unter Agency, The 254
Upstart Crow Literary 254
Writers House 260

GARDENING

Amster Literary Enterprises, Betsy 115
Book Cents Literary Agency, LLC 120
Curtis Brown, Ltd. 138
Doyen Literary Services, Inc. 145
Dupree/Miller and Associates Literary 147
Fredericks Literary Agency, Inc., Jeanne 159
Harwood Limited, Antony 175
Heacock Hill Literary Agency, Inc. 177
Kern Literary Agency, The Natasha 188
Levine Greenberg Literary Agency, Inc. 197
Mendel Media Group, LLC 212
Mura Literary, Dee 215
Parks Agency, The Richard 218
Ryan Publishing Enterprises, Inc., Regina 233
Sheree Bykofsky Associates, Inc. 128
Sherman & Associates, Ken 239
Talcott Notch Literary 249

GAY/LESBIAN

David Black Literary Agency 119
DeChiara Literary Agency, The Jennifer 141
Dystel & Goderich Literary Management 148
Fairbank Literary Representation 154
Fielding Agency, LLC, The 155
Fresh Books Literary Agency 161
Harwood Limited, Antony 175
Henshaw Group, Richard 177
International Transactions, Inc. 183
Jabberwocky Literary Agency 184
James Peter Associates, Inc. 184
Jenks Agency, The Carolyn 186
Konner Literary Agency, Linda 190
Larsen/Elizabeth Pomada, Literary Agents, Michael 193
Levine Literary Agency, Paul S. 198
Lippincott Massie McQuilkin 198
Mendel Media Group, LLC 212
Newman Literary, Dana 216
Parks Agency, The Richard 218
Red Sofa Literary 224
Rudy Agency, The 232
Sanders & Associates, Victoria 234

GOVERNMENT

Agency Group LLC, The 111
Ambassador Literary Agency 115
Anderson Literary Management, LLC 116
Crichton & Associates 137
Curtis Brown, Ltd. 138
Diana Finch Literary Agency 156
Don Congdon Associates Inc. 134
Doyen Literary Services, Inc. 145
Dupree/Miller and Associates Literary 147
Fairbank Literary Representation 154
Fielding Agency, LLC, The 155
Fresh Books Literary Agency 161
Friedman and Co., Inc., Frederica 163
Harwood Limited, Antony 175
Herman Agency, LLC, The Jeff 178
Hill Bonnie Nadell, Inc., Frederick 179
Hornfischer Literary Management 180
International Transactions, Inc. 183
Jabberwocky Literary Agency 184
James Peter Associates, Inc. 184
J de S Associates, Inc. 186
Jenks Agency, The Carolyn 186
Levine Literary Agency, Paul S. 198
Lippincott Massie McQuilkin 198
Literary and Creative Artists, Inc. 199
Literary Group International, The 199
Lownie Literary Agency, Ltd., Andrew 203
Mann Agency, Carol 205
McBride Literary Agency, Margret 209
McCarthy Creative Services 210
Mendel Media Group, LLC 212
Newman Literary, Dana 216
Parks Agency, The Richard 218
P.S. Literary Agency 221
Rabinoff Agency, Lynne 224
Red Sofa Literary 224
Rosenkranz Literary Agency, Rita 230
Ross Literary Agency, Andy 231
Rudy Agency, The 232
Ryan Publishing Enterprises, Inc., Regina 233
Sanders & Associates, Victoria 234
Seligman, Literary Agent, Lynn 237
Sheree Bykofsky Associates, Inc. 128
Sherman & Associates, Ken 239
Simmons Literary Agency, Jeffrey 241
Strothman Agency, LLC, The 248
Toby Eady Associates 149
Venture Literary 254
Vicky Bijur Literary Agency 119

HEALTH

Agency Group LLC, The 111
Allen O'Shea Literary Agency 113
Arcadia 116
Curtis Brown, Ltd. 138
D4EO Literary Agency 139
Daniel Literary Group 140
David Black Literary Agency 119
DeChiara Literary Agency, The Jennifer 141
Diana Finch Literary Agency 156
Don Congdon Associates Inc. 134
Donnaud & Associates, Inc., Janis A. 144
Doyen Literary Services, Inc. 145
Dreisbach Literary Management 146
Dunham Literary, Inc. 146
Dunow, Carlson, & Lerner Agency 146
Dupree/Miller and Associates Literary 147
Dystel & Goderich Literary Management 148
Empire Literary 152
Felicia Eth Literary Representation 153
Fielding Agency, LLC, The 155
FinePrint Literary Management 156
Folio Literary Management, LLC 158
Foundry Literary + Media 158
Fredericks Literary Agency, Inc., Jeanne 159
Freedson's Publishing Network, Grace 160
Fresh Books Literary Agency 161
Freymann Literary Agency, Sarah Jane 162
Friedman and Co., Inc., Frederica 163
Gartenberg Literary Agency, Max 166
Golomb Literary Agency, The Susan 168
Graham Maw Christie Literary Agency 170
Harwood Limited, Antony 175
Henshaw Group, Richard 177

Herman Agency, LLC, The Jeff 178
Hill and Associates, Julie A. 179
Hill Bonnie Nadell, Inc., Frederick 179
Holmes Agency, The 179
Hornfischer Literary Management 180
Hurst Literary Management, Andrea 181
InkWell Management, LLC 182
International Transactions, Inc. 183
Jabberwocky Literary Agency 184
James Peter Associates, Inc. 184
J de S Associates, Inc. 186
Judith Ehrlich Literary Management, LLC 151
Keller Media Inc. 187
Kern Literary Agency, The Natasha 188
Klinger, Inc., Harvey 189
Konner Literary Agency, Linda 190
LA Literary Agency, The 192
Larsen/Elizabeth Pomada, Literary Agents, Michael 193
Leshne Agency, The 197
LevelFiveMedia, LLC 197
Levine Greenberg Literary Agency, Inc. 197
Levine Literary Agency, Paul S. 198
Lippincott Massie McQuilkin 198
Literary and Creative Artists, Inc. 199
Literary Group International, The 199
Literary Services Inc. 200
Living Word Literary Agency 201
LKG Agency 201
Lowenstein Associates Inc. 201
Mann Agency, Carol 205
March Tenth, Inc. 206
Marcil Literary Agency, Inc., The Denise 207
Martin Literary Management 208
McBride Literary Agency, Margret 209
McCarthy Creative Services 210
McGill Agency, Inc., The 211
McMillan & Associates, Inc., Sally Hill 211
Mendel Media Group, LLC 212
Millard Literary Agency, Martha 213
Morhaim Literary Agency, Howard 214
Mura Literary, Dee 215
Naggar Literary Agency, Inc. Jean V. 215
Newman Literary, Dana 216
Oscard Agency, Inc., Fifi 217
Parks Agency, The Richard 218
Paul Bresnick Literary Agency, LLC 124
P.S. Literary Agency 221
Red Sofa Literary 224
Rees Literary Agency, Helen 225
Rennert Agency, The Amy 226
Rick Broadhead & Associates Literary 125
Rinaldi Literary Agency, Angela 227
Robbins Literary Agency, B.J. 228
Rosenkranz Literary Agency, Rita 230
Rudy Agency, The 232
sazTracy Brown Literary Agency 126
Schiavone Literary Agency, Inc. 234
Schulman Literary Agency, Susan 235
Seligman, Literary Agent, Lynn 237
Seymour Agency, The 238
Shannon Literary Agency, Inc., Denise 239
Sheree Bykofsky Associates, Inc. 128
Sherman & Associates, Ken 239
Smith Literary Agency, Ltd., Robert 242
Snell Literary Agency, Michael 243
Speilburg Literary Agency 244
Talcott Notch Literary 249
Toby Eady Associates 149
Triada U.S. Literary Agency, Inc. 252
Trident Media Group 253
Unter Agency, The 254
Vicky Bijur Literary Agency 119
Waterside Productions, Inc. 256
Whimsy Literary Agency, LLC 258
Writers House 260
Seventh Avenue Literary Agency 238
Zimmermann Literary Agency, Helen 262

HISTORY

Agency Group LLC, The 111
Allen O'Shea Literary Agency 113
Ambassador Literary Agency 115
Amster Literary Enterprises, Betsy 115

Anderson Literary Management, LLC 116
Arcadia 116
Brandt & Hochman Literary Agents, Inc. 123
Brattle Agency, The 124
Braun Associates, Inc., Barbara 124
Chalberg & Sussman 131
Chase Literary Agency 131
Compass Talent 134
Curtis Brown, Ltd. 138
Cynthia Cannell Literary Agency 129
D4EO Literary Agency 139
Daniel Literary Group 140
David Black Literary Agency 119
DeChiara Literary Agency, The Jennifer 141
Diana Finch Literary Agency 156
Dijkstra Literary Agency, Sandra 143
Don Congdon Associates Inc. 134
Donnaud & Associates, Inc., Janis A. 144
Doyen Literary Services, Inc. 145
Dunham Literary, Inc. 146
Dunow, Carlson, & Lerner Agency 146
Dupree/Miller and Associates Literary 147
Dystel & Goderich Literary Management 148
Ebeling Agency, The 150
E.J. McCarthy Agency 209
Felicia Eth Literary Representation 153
Fielding Agency, LLC, The 155
FinePrint Literary Management 156
Fletcher & Company 157
Folio Literary Management, LLC 158
Foundry Literary + Media 158
Fox Literary 159
Fredericks Literary Agency, Inc., Jeanne 159
Freedson's Publishing Network, Grace 160
Fresh Books Literary Agency 161
Freymann Literary Agency, Sarah Jane 162
Friedman and Co., Inc., Frederica 163
G Agency, LLC, The 165
Garamond Agency, Inc., The 165
Gartenberg Literary Agency, Max 166
Gernert Company, The 167
Golomb Literary Agency, The Susan 168
Grayson Literary Agency, Ashley 171
Greenburger Associates, Inc., Sanford J. 171
Green Literary Agency, LLC, Kathryn 173
Grinberg Literary Agency, Jill 174
Harwood Limited, Antony 175
Hawkins & Associates, Inc., John 176
Herman Agency, LLC, The Jeff 178
Hill and Associates, Julie A. 179
Hill Bonnie Nadell, Inc., Frederick 179
Hornfischer Literary Management 180
InkWell Management, LLC 182
International Transactions, Inc. 183
Jabberwocky Literary Agency 184
James Peter Associates, Inc. 184
J de S Associates, Inc. 186
Jenks Agency, The Carolyn 186
Joelle Delbourgo Associates, Inc. 143
Judith Ehrlich Literary Management, LLC 151
Keller Media Inc. 187
LA Literary Agency, The 192
Langlie, Laura Agent, Laura 193
Larsen/Elizabeth Pomada, Literary Agents, Michael 193
LaunchBooks Literary Agency 194
Lazin Books, Sarah 195
LevelFiveMedia, LLC 197
Levine Literary Agency, Paul S. 198
Lippincott Massie McQuilkin 198
Literary Group International, The 199
Literary Services Inc. 200
Lownie Literary Agency, Ltd., Andrew 203
Maccoby Literary Agency, Gina 204
MacGregor Literary Inc. 204
Mann Agency, Carol 205
Manus & Associates Literary Agency, Inc. 206
March Tenth, Inc. 206
Maria Carvainis Agency, Inc. 130
Marsal Lyon Literary Agency, LLC 207
Martin Literary Management 208
McBride Literary Agency, Margret 209
McCarthy Creative Services 210

McGill Agency, Inc., The 211
McMillan & Associates, Inc., Sally Hill 211
Mendel Media Group, LLC 212
Millard Literary Agency, Martha 213
Moveable Type Management 214
Mura Literary, Dee 215
Naggar Literary Agency, Inc. Jean V. 215
Newman Literary, Dana 216
Oscard Agency, Inc., Fifi 217
Park Literary Group, LLC 218
Parks Agency, The Richard 218
Paul Bresnick Literary Agency, LLC 124
Perkins Agency, L. 219
P.S. Literary Agency 221
Rabinoff Agency, Lynne 224
Red Sofa Literary 224
Rees Literary Agency, Helen 225
Rennert Agency, The Amy 226
Richards Agency, The Lisa 226
Rick Broadhead & Associates Literary 125
Rights Factory, The 227
Robbins Office, Inc., The 229
Rosenkranz Literary Agency, Rita 230
Ross Literary Agency, Andy 231
Rudy Agency, The 232
Ryan Publishing Enterprises, Inc., Regina 233
Sanders & Associates, Victoria 234
sazTracy Brown Literary Agency 126
Schiavone Literary Agency, Inc. 234
Schulman Literary Agency, Susan 235
Seligman, Literary Agent, Lynn 237
Sheree Bykofsky Associates, Inc. 128
Sherman & Associates, Ken 239
Simmons Literary Agency, Jeffrey 241
Speilburg Literary Agency 244
Spieler Agency, The 244
Spitzer Literary Agency, Inc., Philip G. 245
Sterling Lord Literistic, Inc. 246
Straus Agency, Inc., Robin 247
Strothman Agency, LLC, The 248
Stuart Agency, The 248
Sweeney Agency, LLC, Emma 249
Talcott Notch Literary 249
Toby Eady Associates 251
Trident Media Group 253
Venture Literary 254
Vicky Bijur Literary Agency 119
Watkins Loomis Agency, Inc. 256
Whimsy Literary Agency, LLC 258
Wm Clark Associates 133
Wolf Literary Services 259
Writers House 260
Seventh Avenue Literary Agency 238

HOBBIES

Doyen Literary Services, Inc. 145
Fairbank Literary Representation 154
Fielding Agency, LLC, The 155
Freedson's Publishing Network, Grace 160
Fresh Books Literary Agency 161
Levine Literary Agency, Paul S. 198
Parks Agency, The Richard 218
Red Sofa Literary 224
Rosenkranz Literary Agency, Rita 230
Sheree Bykofsky Associates, Inc. 128

HOW-TO

Agency Group LLC, The 111
Alive Communications, Inc. 113
Allen O'Shea Literary Agency 113
BookEnds, LLC 120
Brandt Agency, The Joan 123
Chalberg & Sussman 131
Curtis Brown, Ltd. 138
D4EO Literary Agency 139
Daniel Literary Group 140
DeFiore & Co. 142
Diana Finch Literary Agency 156
Dupree/Miller and Associates Literary 147
Ebeling Agency, The 150
Empire Literary 152
Fairbank Literary Representation 154
Fielding Agency, LLC, The 155
Folio Literary Management, LLC 158
Foundry Literary + Media 158

Fredericks Literary Agency, Inc., Jeanne 159
Freedson's Publishing Network, Grace 160
Full Circle Literary, LLC 163
Graham Maw Christie Literary Agency 170
Green Literary Agency, LLC, Kathryn 173
Harwood Limited, Antony 175
Herman Agency, LLC, The Jeff 178
Hill and Associates, Julie A. 179
Hornfischer Literary Management 180
Hurst Literary Management, Andrea 181
Larsen/Elizabeth Pomada, Literary Agents, Michael 193
Lecker Agency, Robert 196
LevelFiveMedia, LLC 197
Levine Literary Agency, Paul S. 198
Literary and Creative Artists, Inc. 199
MacGregor Literary Inc. 204
Martin Literary Management 208
McBride Literary Agency, Margret 209
McGill Agency, Inc., The 211
Mendel Media Group, LLC 212
Millard Literary Agency, Martha 213
Miriam Altshuler Literary Agency 114
Moveable Type Management 214
Newman Literary, Dana 216
Parks Agency, The Richard 218
P.S. Literary Agency 221
Rosenkranz Literary Agency, Rita 230
Rudy Agency, The 232
Seligman, Literary Agent, Lynn 237
Seymour Agency, The 238
Snell Literary Agency, Michael 243
Triada U.S. Literary Agency, Inc. 252
Whimsy Literary Agency, LLC 258

HUMOR

Agency Group LLC, The 111
Allen O'Shea Literary Agency 113
Books & Such Literary Agency 121
Bradford Literary Agency 122
Chalberg & Sussman 131
Chelius Literary Agency, Jane 132
Curtis Brown, Ltd. 138
D4EO Literary Agency 139
Daniel Literary Group 140
David Black Literary Agency 119
DeChiara Literary Agency, The Jennifer 141
Diana Finch Literary Agency 156
Don Congdon Associates Inc. 134
Dupree/Miller and Associates Literary 147
Dystel & Goderich Literary Management 148
Ebeling Agency, The 150
Fielding Agency, LLC, The 155
FinePrint Literary Management 156
Fletcher & Company 157
Folio Literary Management, LLC 158
Foundry Literary + Media 158
Freedson's Publishing Network, Grace 160
Fresh Books Literary Agency 161
Friedman and Co., Inc., Frederica 163
Greenburger Associates, Inc., Sanford J. 171
Green Literary Agency, LLC, Kathryn 173
Harwood Limited, Antony 175
Henshaw Group, Richard 177
Hornfischer Literary Management 180
Hurst Literary Management, Andrea 181
InkWell Management, LLC 182
International Transactions, Inc. 183
Jabberwocky Literary Agency 184
Krichevsky Literary Agency, Inc., Stuart 191
Larsen/Elizabeth Pomada, Literary Agents, Michael 193
LaunchBooks Literary Agency 194
Laura Dail Literary Agency, Inc. 140
Levine Greenberg Literary Agency, Inc. 197
Levine Literary Agency, Paul S. 198
Literary Group International, The 199
Literary Services Inc. 200
MacGregor Literary Inc. 204
March Tenth, Inc. 206
Martin Literary Management 208
McCarthy Creative Services 210
Mendel Media Group, LLC 212
Morhaim Literary Agency, Howard 214
Moveable Type Management 214

Mura Literary, Dee 215
Naggar Literary Agency, Inc. Jean V. 215
Parks Agency, The Richard 218
Paul Bresnick Literary Agency, LLC 124
Perkins Agency, L. 219
Prentis Literary, Linn 220
P.S. Literary Agency 221
Red Sofa Literary 224
Rick Broadhead & Associates Literary 125
Robbins Literary Agency, B.J. 228
Rosenkranz Literary Agency, Rita 230
Sanders & Associates, Victoria 234
Seligman, Literary Agent, Lynn 237
Serendipity Literary Agency, LLC 237
Sheree Bykofsky Associates, Inc. 128
Sherman Associates, Inc., Wendy 240
Sherman & Associates, Ken 239
Talcott Notch Literary 249
Upstart Crow Literary 254
Waxman Leavell Literary Agency, Inc. 256
Whimsy Literary Agency, LLC 258
Writers House 260

INSPIRATIONAL
Alive Communications, Inc. 113
Ambassador Literary Agency 115
Daniel Literary Group 140
DeFiore & Co. 142
Dystel & Goderich Literary Management 148
Ebeling Agency, The 150
Folio Literary Management, LLC 158
Hornfischer Literary Management 180
Hurst Literary Management, Andrea 181
Kern Literary Agency, The Natasha 188
Larsen/Elizabeth Pomada, Literary Agents,
Michael 193
LevelFiveMedia, LLC 197
Lippincott Massie McQuilkin 198
MacGregor Literary Inc. 204
Manus & Associates Literary Agency, Inc.
206
Martin Literary Management 208
Mura Literary, Dee 215
Oscard Agency, Inc., Fifi 217
Rabinoff Agency, Lynne 224
Rosenkranz Literary Agency, Rita 230
Serendipity Literary Agency, LLC 237
Talcott Notch Literary 249
Waterside Productions, Inc. 256
Wm Clark Associates 133
Wordserve Literary Group 259

INVESTIGATIVE
Agency Group LLC, The 111
Castiglia Literary Agency 131
Crichton & Associates 137
Diana Finch Literary Agency 156
Dystel & Goderich Literary Management 148
Fairbank Literary Representation 154
Felicia Eth Literary Representation 153
Fielding Agency, LLC, The 155
Fletcher & Company 157
Goldin Literary Agency, Inc., Frances 168
Grayson Literary Agency, Ashley 171
Green Literary Agency, LLC, Kathryn 173
Henshaw Group, Richard 177
Hornfischer Literary Management 180
International Transactions, Inc. 183
Klinger, Inc., Harvey 189
Larsen/Elizabeth Pomada, Literary Agents,
Michael 193
Lazin Books, Sarah 195
Levine Literary Agency, Paul S. 198
Lownie Literary Agency, Ltd., Andrew 203
Marsal Lyon Literary Agency, LLC 207
Martin Literary Management 208
Mendel Media Group, LLC 212
Red Sofa Literary 224
Robbins Literary Agency, B.J. 228
Serendipity Literary Agency, LLC 237
Slopen Literary Agency, Beverley 241
Smith Literary Agency, Ltd., Robert 242
Speilburg Literary Agency 244
Venture Literary 254

JUVENILE NONFICTION
Brown Literary Agency, Inc., Andrea 126
Diana Finch Literary Agency 156
Fielding Agency, LLC, The 155
Green Literary Agency, LLC, Kathryn 173
Jenks Agency, The Carolyn 186
Literary Group International, The 199
Maccoby Literary Agency, Gina 204
The Purcell Agency, LLC 223
Writers House 260

LANGUAGE
Curtis Brown, Ltd. 138
Don Congdon Associates Inc. 134
Doyen Literary Services, Inc. 145
Dunham Literary, Inc. 146
Dupree/Miller and Associates Literary 147
Fielding Agency, LLC, The 155
Friedman and Co., Inc., Frederica 163
Harwood Limited, Antony 175
Hill and Associates, Julie A. 179
Hill Bonnie Nadell, Inc., Frederick 179
International Transactions, Inc. 183
Jabberwocky Literary Agency 184
James Peter Associates, Inc. 184
Jenks Agency, The Carolyn 186
Langlie, Literary Agent, Laura 193
Lecker Agency, Robert 196
Levine Literary Agency, Paul S. 198
Lippincott Massie McQuilkin 198
Literary Group International, The 199
Literary Services Inc. 200
March Tenth, Inc. 206
McCarthy Creative Services 210
Mendel Media Group, LLC 212
Newman Literary, Dana 216
Parks Agency, The Richard 218
Rosenkranz Literary Agency, Rita 230
Ross Literary Agency, Andy 231
Rudy Agency, The 232
Seligman, Literary Agent, Lynn 237
Sheree Bykofsky Associates, Inc. 128
Sherman & Associates, Ken 239
Simmons Literary Agency, Jeffrey 241
Strothman Agency, LLC, The 248

LAW
Agency Group LLC, The 111
Anderson Literary Management, LLC 116
Crichton & Associates 137
Diana Finch Literary Agency 156
Don Congdon Associates Inc. 134
Doyen Literary Services, Inc. 145
Fairbank Literary Representation 154
Felicia Eth Literary Representation 153
Fielding Agency, LLC, The 155
FinePrint Literary Management 156
Fresh Books Literary Agency 161
Garamond Agency, Inc., The 165
Golomb Literary Agency, The Susan 168
Herman Agency, LLC, The Jeff 178
Hornfischer Literary Management 180
International Transactions, Inc. 183
Jabberwocky Literary Agency 184
J de S Associates, Inc. 186
Jenks Agency, The Carolyn 186
Langlie, Literary Agent, Laura 193
Larsen/Elizabeth Pomada, Literary Agents,
Michael 193
Levine Literary Agency, Paul S. 198
Lippincott Massie McQuilkin 198
Literary and Creative Artists, Inc. 199
Lownie Literary Agency, Ltd., Andrew 203
Mann Agency, Carol 205
McBride Literary Agency, Margret 209
Newman Literary, Dana 216
Parks Agency, The Richard 218
P.S. Literary Agency 221
Rabinoff Agency, Lynne 224
Rosenkranz Literary Agency, Rita 230
Ross Literary Agency, Andy 231
Rudy Agency, The 232
Ryan Publishing Enterprises, Inc., Regina 233
Sanders & Associates, Victoria 234
Sheree Bykofsky Associates, Inc. 128

Strothman Agency, LLC, The 248
Toby Eady Associates 149
Venture Literary 254

LITERATURE
DeChiara Literary Agency, The Jennifer 141
Don Congdon Associates Inc. 134
Dunham Literary, Inc. 146
Dupree/Miller and Associates Literary 147
Fielding Agency, LLC, The 155
Hill Bonnie Nadell, Inc., Frederick 179
International Transactions, Inc. 183
Jabberwocky Literary Agency 184
James Peter Associates, Inc. 184
Jenks Agency, The Carolyn 186
Langlie, Literary Agent, Laura 193
Lecker Agency, Robert 196
Lippincott Massie McQuilkin 198
Literary Services Inc. 200
March Tenth, Inc. 206
Newman Literary, Dana 216
Rosenkranz Literary Agency, Rita 230
Ross Literary Agency, Andy 231
Rudy Agency, The 232
Sanders & Associates, Victoria 234
Strothman Agency, LLC, The 248

MEDICINE
Agency Group LLC, The 111
Chelius Literary Agency, Jane 132
Daniel Literary Group 140
Diana Finch Literary Agency 156
Don Congdon Associates Inc. 134
Doyen Literary Services, Inc. 145
Dunham Literary, Inc. 146
Dupree/Miller and Associates Literary 147
Dystel & Goderich Literary Management 148
Ebeling Agency, The 150
Felicia Eth Literary Representation 153
Fielding Agency, LLC, The 155
Foundry Literary + Media 158
Fredericks Literary Agency, Inc., Jeanne 159
Freedson's Publishing Network, Grace 160
Fresh Books Literary Agency 161
Freymann Literary Agency, Sarah Jane 162
Graham Maw Christie Literary Agency 170
Hawkins & Associates, Inc., John 176
Herman Agency, LLC, The Jeff 178
Hill Bonnie Nadell, Inc., Frederick 179
Hornfischer Literary Management 180
International Transactions, Inc. 183
Jabberwocky Literary Agency 184
James Peter Associates, Inc. 184
J de S Associates, Inc. 186
Kern Literary Agency, The Natasha 188
Klinger, Inc., Harvey 189
Konner Literary Agency, Linda 190
Larsen/Elizabeth Pomada, Literary Agents,
Michael 193
LevelFiveMedia, LLC 197
Levine Literary Agency, Paul S. 198
Lippincott Massie McQuilkin 198
Literary and Creative Artists, Inc. 199
Mann Agency, Carol 205
March Tenth, Inc. 206
Martin Literary Management 208
McBride Literary Agency, Margret 209
Mendel Media Group, LLC 212
Mura Literary, Dee 215
Newman Literary, Dana 216
Rick Broadhead & Associates Literary 125
Robbins Literary Agency, B.J. 228
Rosenkranz Literary Agency, Rita 230
Rudy Agency, The 232
Smith Literary Agency, Ltd., Robert 242
Toby Eady Associates 149
Writers House 260
Seventh Avenue Literary Agency 238

MEMOIRS
Agency Group LLC, The 111
Aitken Alexander Associates 112
Ambassador Literary Agency 115
Amster Literary Enterprises, Betsy 115
Anderson Literary Management, LLC 116

Barone Literary Agency 117
Bradford Literary Agency 122
Brandt & Hochman Literary Agents, Inc. 123
Brown Literary Agency, Inc., Andrea 126
Capital Talent Agency 129
Chalberg & Sussman 131
Chase Literary Agency 131
Cheney Literary Associates, LLC, Elyse 132
CK Webber Associates Literary Management 257
Compass Talent 134
Curtis Brown, Ltd. 138
Cynthia Cannell Literary Agency 129
D4EO Literary Agency 139
Daniel Literary Group 140
Darhansoff & Verrill Literary Agents 140
David Black Literary Agency 119
DeChiara Literary Agency, The Jennifer 141
Diana Finch Literary Agency 156
Dijkstra Literary Agency, Sandra 143
Don Congdon Associates Inc. 134
Donnaud & Associates, Inc., Janis A. 144
Doyen Literary Services, Inc. 145
Dreisbach Literary Management 146
Dunow, Carlson, & Lerner Agency 146
Dupree/Miller and Associates Literary 147
Einstein Literary Management 151
E.J. McCarthy Agency 209
Empire Literary 152
Fairbank Literary Representation 154
Fielding Agency, LLC, The 155
FinePrint Literary Management 156
Fletcher & Company 157
Folio Literary Management, LLC 158
Foundry Literary + Media 158
Fox Literary 159
Franklin Associates, Ltd., Lynn C. 159
Freymann Literary Agency, Sarah Jane 162
Friedman and Co., Inc., Frederica 163
Friedrich Agency, The 163
Gernert Company, The 167
Goldin Literary Agency, Inc., Frances 168
Golomb Literary Agency, The Susan 168
Graham Maw Christie Literary Agency 170
Greenburger Associates, Inc., Sanford J. 171
Green Literary Agency, LLC, Kathryn 173
Harwood Limited, Antony 175
Hill and Associates, Julie A. 179
Holmes Agency, The 179
Hornfischer Literary Management 180
HSG Agency 180
Hurst Literary Management, Andrea 181
InkWell Management, LLC 182
International Transactions, Inc. 183
Jenks Agency, The Carolyn 186
Joelle Delbourgo Associates, Inc. 143
Judith Ehrlich Literary Management, LLC 151
Krichevsky Literary Agency, Inc., Stuart 191
LA Literary Agency, The 192
Langlie, Literary Agent, Laura 193
Larsen/Elizabeth Pomada, Literary Agents, Michael 193
Lazin Books, Sarah 195
Leigh Feldman Literary 155
Leshne Agency, The 197
Levine Greenberg Literary Agency, Inc. 197
Levine Literary Agency, Paul S. 198
Lippincott Massie McQuilkin 198
Literary and Creative Artists, Inc. 199
Literary Group International, The 199
LKG Agency 201
Lowenstein Associates Inc. 201
Lownie Literary Agency, Ltd., Andrew 203
Maass Literary Agency, Donald 203
Manus & Associates Literary Agency, Inc. 206
Maria Carvainis Agency, Inc. 130
Marsal Lyon Literary Agency, LLC 207
Martin Literary Management 208
McCarthy Creative Services 210
McGill Agency, Inc., The 211
Mendel Media Group, LLC 212
Millard Literary Agency, Martha 213
Miriam Altshuler Literary Agency 114

Morhaim Literary Agency, Howard 214
Moveable Type Management 214
Mura Literary, Dee 215
Naggar Literary Agency, Inc. Jean V. 215
Newman Literary, Dana 216
Parks Agency, The Richard 218
Paul Bresnick Literary Agency, LLC 124
Pavilion Literary Management 218
Prentis Literary, Linn 220
Prospect Agency 221
P.S. Literary Agency 221
Publication Riot Group 223
Rabinoff Agency, Lynne 224
Rebecca Friedman Literary Agency 162
Rees Literary Agency, Helen 225
Regal Literary Agency 225
Richards Agency, The Lisa 226
Rights Factory, The 227
Robbins Literary Agency, B.J. 228
Robbins Office, Inc., The 229
Rudy Agency, The 232
Ryan Publishing Enterprises, Inc., Regina 233
Serendipity Literary Agency, LLC 237
Sheree Bykofsky Associates, Inc. 128
Sherman Associates, Inc., Wendy 240
Sherman & Associates, Ken 239
Simmons Literary Agency, Jeffrey 241
Smith Literary Agency, Ltd., Robert 242
Spieler Agency, The 244
Sterling Lord Literistic, Inc. 246
Straus Agency, Inc., Robin 247
Stuart Agency, The 248
Talcott Notch Literary 249
Tessler Literary Agency, LLC 250
Toby Eady Associates 149
Triada U.S. Literary Agency, Inc. 252
Trident Media Group 253
Unter Agency, The 254
Upstart Crow Literary 254
Venture Literary 254
Veritas Literary Agency 254
Vicky Bijur Literary Agency 119
Weingel-Fidel Agency, The 257
Whimsy Literary Agency, LLC 258
Wm Clark Associates 133
Wolf Literary Services 259
Wordserve Literary Group 259
Yates & Yates 261
Zimmermann Literary Agency, Helen 262

MILITARY

Allen O'Shea Literary Agency 113
Chase Literary Agency 131
Curtis Brown, Ltd. 138
D4EO Literary Agency 139
Diana Finch Literary Agency 156
Don Congdon Associates Inc. 134
Doyen Literary Services, Inc. 145
Dystel & Goderich Literary Management 148
E.J. McCarthy Agency 209
Fielding Agency, LLC, The 155
Folio Literary Management, LLC 158
Fresh Books Literary Agency 161
G Agency, LLC, The 165
Golomb Literary Agency, The Susan 168
Grad Literary Agency, Inc., Doug 170
Harwood Limited, Antony 175
Hornfischer Literary Management 180
International Transactions, Inc. 183
James Peter Associates, Inc. 184
J de S Associates, Inc. 186
Jenks Agency, The Carolyn 186
Levine Literary Agency, Paul S. 198
Lippincott Massie McQuilkin 198
Literary Group International, The 199
Lownie Literary Agency, Ltd., Andrew 203
McCarthy Creative Services 210
McGill Agency, Inc., The 211
Mendel Media Group, LLC 212
Parks Agency, The Richard 218
P.S. Literary Agency 221
Rabinoff Agency, Lynne 224
Rees Literary Agency, Helen 225
Rick Broadhead & Associates Literary 125
Rosenkranz Literary Agency, Rita 230

Ross Literary Agency, Andy 231
Rudy Agency, The 232
Sheree Bykofsky Associates, Inc. 128
Sherman & Associates, Ken 239
Trident Media Group 253
Venture Literary 254
Writers House 260

MONEY

Agency Group LLC, The 111
Allen O'Shea Literary Agency 113
Amster Literary Enterprises, Betsy 115
BookEnds, LLC 120
Curtis Brown, Ltd. 138
D4EO Literary Agency 139
David Black Literary Agency 119
DeFiore & Co. 142
Diana Finch Literary Agency 156
Donnaud & Associates, Inc., Janis A. 144
Doyen Literary Services, Inc. 145
Dupree/Miller and Associates Literary 147
Ebeling Agency, The 150
Fielding Agency, LLC, The 155
Freedson's Publishing Network, Grace 160
Fresh Books Literary Agency 161
Friedman and Co., Inc., Frederica 163
G Agency, LLC, The 165
Gartenberg Literary Agency, Max 166
Golomb Literary Agency, The Susan 168
Harwood Limited, Antony 175
Henshaw Group, Richard 177
Hornfischer Literary Management 180
Jabberwocky Literary Agency 184
James Peter Associates, Inc. 184
Jenks Agency, The Carolyn 186
Konner Literary Agency, Linda 190
Larsen/Elizabeth Pomada, Literary Agents, Michael 193
LevelFiveMedia, LLC 197
Levine Greenberg Literary Agency, Inc. 197
Levine Literary Agency, Paul S. 198
Lippincott Massie McQuilkin 198
Literary Services Inc. 200
Lowenstein Associates Inc. 201
Mann Agency, Carol 205
McBride Literary Agency, Margret 209
McCarthy Creative Services 210
Mendel Media Group, LLC 212
Millard Literary Agency, Martha 213
Moveable Type Management 214
Parks Agency, The Richard 218
P.S. Literary Agency 221
Rennert Agency, The Amy 226
Rosenkranz Literary Agency, Rita 230
Rudy Agency, The 232
Schulman Literary Agency, Susan 235
Seligman, Literary Agent, Lynn 237
Sheree Bykofsky Associates, Inc. 128
Sherman & Associates, Ken 239
Venture Literary 254
Waterside Productions, Inc. 256
Whimsy Literary Agency, LLC 258
Writers House 260

MULTICULTURAL

Curtis Brown, Ltd. 138
DeFiore & Co. 142
Doyen Literary Services, Inc. 145
Dreisbach Literary Management 146
Dupree/Miller and Associates Literary 147
Harwood Limited, Antony 175
Hornfischer Literary Management 180
Literary Group International, The 199
Lowenstein Associates Inc. 201
Mendel Media Group, LLC 212
Paul Bresnick Literary Agency, LLC 124
Sheree Bykofsky Associates, Inc. 128
Sherman & Associates, Ken 239
Sterling Lord Literistic, Inc. 246
Venture Literary 254

MUSIC

Aitken Alexander Associates 112
Anderson Literary Management, LLC 116
Brandt & Hochman Literary Agents, Inc. 123

Curtis Brown, Ltd. 138
Diana Finch Literary Agency 156
Don Congdon Associates Inc. 134
Doyen Literary Services, Inc. 145
Dunow, Carlson, & Lerner Agency 146
Dupree/Miller and Associates Literary 147
Ebeling Agency, The 150
FinePrint Literary Management 156
Foundry Literary + Media 158
Fresh Books Literary Agency 161
Friedman and Co., Inc., Frederica 163
Gartenberg Literary Agency, Max 166
Grad Literary Agency, Inc., Doug 170
Greenburger Associates, Inc., Sanford J. 171
Harwood Limited, Antony 175
Henshaw Group, Richard 177
Hill and Associates, Julie A. 179
International Transactions, Inc. 183
James Peter Associates, Inc. 184
Jenks Agency, The Carolyn 186
Larsen/Elizabeth Pomada, Literary Agents,
    Michael 193
Lecker Agency, Robert 196
Levine Literary Agency, Paul S. 198
Lippincott Massie McQuilkin 198
Literary Group International, The 199
Mann Agency, Carol 205
March Tenth, Inc. 206
McCarthy Creative Services 210
Mendel Media Group, LLC 212
Millard Literary Agency, Martha 213
Naggar Literary Agency, Inc. Jean V. 215
Newman Literary, Dana 216
Parks Agency, The Richard 218
Perkins Agency, L. 219
Robbins Literary Agency, B.J. 228
Rosenkranz Literary Agency, Rita 230
Rudy Agency, The 232
Sanders & Associates, Victoria 234
Seligman, Literary Agent, Lynn 237
Serendipity Literary Agency, LLC 237
Sheree Bykofsky Associates, Inc. 128
Sherman & Associates, Ken 239
Simmons Literary Agency, Jeffrey 241
Smith Literary Agency, Ltd., Robert 242
Speilburg Literary Agency 244
Venture Literary 254
Weingel-Fidel Agency, The 257
Wm Clark Associates 133
Writers House 260
Zimmermann Literary Agency, Helen 262

NARRATIVE NONFICTION
See "Creative Nonfiction"

NATURE
Agency Group LLC, The 111
Anderson Literary Management, LLC 116
Daniel Literary Group 140
Gartenberg Literary Agency, Max 166
Literary Group International, The 199
McCarthy Creative Services 210
Rosenkranz Literary Agency, Rita 230
Seligman, Literary Agent, Lynn 237
Sheree Bykofsky Associates, Inc. 128
Sherman & Associates, Ken 239

NEW AGE
Curtis Brown, Ltd. 138
Dystel & Goderich Literary Management 148
Henshaw Group, Richard 177
Hill and Associates, Julie A. 179
J de S Associates, Inc. 186
Jenks Agency, The Carolyn 186
Kern Literary Agency, The Natasha 188
Larsen/Elizabeth Pomada, Literary Agents,
    Michael 193
Levine Greenberg Literary Agency, Inc. 197
Levine Literary Agency, Paul S. 198
Millard Literary Agency, Martha 213
Mura Literary, Dee 215
Sheree Bykofsky Associates, Inc. 128
Whimsy Literary Agency, LLC 258

PARENTING

Agency Group LLC, The 111
Alive Communications, Inc. 113
Amster Literary Enterprises, Betsy 115
Bradford Literary Agency 122
Chelius Literary Agency, Jane 132
Crichton & Associates 137
Daniel Literary Group 140
David Black Literary Agency 119
DeChiara Literary Agency, The Jennifer 141
DeFiore & Co. 142
Diana Finch Literary Agency 156
Don Congdon Associates Inc. 134
Doyen Literary Services, Inc. 145
Dreisbach Literary Management 146
Dupree/Miller and Associates Literary 147
Dystel & Goderich Literary Management 148
Ebeling Agency, The 150
Empire Literary 152
Felicia Eth Literary Representation 153
Fielding Agency, LLC, The 155
FinePrint Literary Management 156
Folio Literary Management, LLC 158
Foundry Literary + Media 158
Fredericks Literary Agency, Inc., Jeanne 159
Fresh Books Literary Agency 161
Freymann Literary Agency, Sarah Jane 162
Graham Maw Christie Literary Agency 170
Green Literary Agency, LLC, Kathryn 173
Harwood Limited, Antony 175
Henshaw Group, Richard 177
Hornfischer Literary Management 180
Hurst Literary Management, Andrea 181
Judith Ehrlich Literary Management, LLC
    151
Kern Literary Agency, The Natasha 188
Konner Literary Agency, Linda 190
LA Literary Agency, The 192
Lazin Books, Sarah 195
Leshne Agency, The 197
LevelFiveMedia, LLC 197
Levine Literary Agency, Paul S. 198
Lippincott Massie McQuilkin 198
Living Word Literary Agency 201
LKG Agency 201
MacGregor Literary Inc. 204
Mann Agency, Carol 205
Marcil Literary Agency, Inc., The Denise 207
Marsal Lyon Literary Agency, LLC 207
Martin Literary Management 208
Mendel Media Group, LLC 212
Millard Literary Agency, Martha 213
Morhaim Literary Agency, Howard 214
Mura Literary, Dee 215
Parks Agency, The Richard 218
P.S. Literary Agency 221
Rosenkranz Literary Agency, Rita 230
Ross Literary Agency, Andy 231
Rudy Agency, The 232
Ryan Publishing Enterprises, Inc., Regina 233
Serendipity Literary Agency, LLC 237
Sheree Bykofsky Associates, Inc. 128
Sherman Associates, Inc., Wendy 240
Sterling Lord Literistic, Inc. 246
Straus Agency, Inc., Robin 247
Talcott Notch Literary 249
Waterside Productions, Inc. 256
Wordserve Literary Group 259
Writers House 260

PHILOSOPHY
Curtis Brown, Ltd. 138
Dupree/Miller and Associates Literary 147
Goldin Literary Agency, Inc., Frances 168
Harwood Limited, Antony 175
Literary and Creative Artists, Inc. 199
Mendel Media Group, LLC 212
Sheree Bykofsky Associates, Inc. 128
Sherman & Associates, Ken 239

PHOTOGRAPHY
Braun Associates, Inc., Barbara 124
Curtis Brown, Ltd. 138
Diana Finch Literary Agency 156
Doyen Literary Services, Inc. 145
Dupree/Miller and Associates Literary 147

Fairbank Literary Representation 154
Fredericks Literary Agency, Inc., Jeanne 159
Fresh Books Literary Agency 161
Friedman and Co., Inc., Frederica 163
Harwood Limited, Antony 175
HSG Agency 180
International Transactions, Inc. 183
Levine Literary Agency, Paul S. 198
Millard Literary Agency, Martha 213
Mura Literary, Dee 215
Rosenkranz Literary Agency, Rita 230
Seligman, Literary Agent, Lynn 237
Sheree Bykofsky Associates, Inc. 128
Sherman & Associates, Ken 239
Spieler Agency, The 244

POLITICS
Agency Group LLC, The 111
Aitken Alexander Associates 112
Anderson Literary Management, LLC 116
Brattle Agency, The 124
Cheney Literary Associates, LLC, Elyse 132
Crichton & Associates 137
David Black Literary Agency 119
DeFiore & Co. 142
Diana Finch Literary Agency 156
Don Congdon Associates Inc. 134
Doyen Literary Services, Inc. 145
Dunham Literary, Inc. 146
Fairbank Literary Representation 154
Felicia Eth Literary Representation 153
Fielding Agency, LLC, The 155
Fletcher & Company 157
Folio Literary Management, LLC 158
Fresh Books Literary Agency 161
Garamond Agency, Inc., The 165
Gernert Company, The 167
Golomb Literary Agency, The Susan 168
Greenburger Associates, Inc., Sanford J. 171
Hawkins & Associates, Inc., John 176
Heacock Hill Literary Agency, Inc. 177
Henshaw Group, Richard 177
Herman Agency, LLC, The Jeff 178
Hill Bonnie Nadell, Inc., Frederick 179
Hornfischer Literary Management 180
HSG Agency 180
International Transactions, Inc. 183
Jabberwocky Literary Agency 184
J de S Associates, Inc. 186
Joelle Delbourgo Associates, Inc. 143
Keller Media Inc. 187
Langlie, Literary Agent, Laura 193
Larsen/Elizabeth Pomada, Literary Agents,
    Michael 193
LaunchBooks Literary Agency 194
Leshne Agency, The 197
Levine Literary Agency, Paul S. 198
Lippincott Massie McQuilkin 198
Literary and Creative Artists, Inc. 199
Literary Group International, The 199
Lownie Literary Agency, Ltd., Andrew 203
Mann Agency, Carol 205
Manus & Associates Literary Agency, Inc.
    206
Marsal Lyon Literary Agency, LLC 207
McBride Literary Agency, Margret 209
Newman Literary, Dana 216
Park Literary Group, LLC 218
Parks Agency, The Richard 218
P.S. Literary Agency 221
Publication Riot Group 223
Rabinoff Agency, Lynne 224
Red Sofa Literary 224
Rick Broadhead & Associates Literary 125
Robbins Office, Inc., The 229
Rosenkranz Literary Agency, Rita 230
Ross Literary Agency, Andy 231
Rudy Agency, The 232
Ryan Publishing Enterprises, Inc., Regina 233
Sanders & Associates, Victoria 234
Schiavone Literary Agency, Inc. 234
Sheree Bykofsky Associates, Inc. 128
Spitzer Literary Agency, Inc., Philip G. 245
Sterling Lord Literistic, Inc. 246
Strothman Agency, LLC, The 248

Toby Eady Associates 149
Trident Media Group 253
Unter Agency, The 254
Venture Literary 254
Veritas Literary Agency 254
Yates & Yates 261

POPULAR CULTURE

Agency Group LLC, The 111
Allen O'Shea Literary Agency 113
Ambassador Literary Agency 115
Amster Literary Enterprises, Betsy 115
Bent Agency, The 118
Chalberg & Sussman 131
Chelius Literary Agency, Jane 132
Curtis Brown, Ltd. 138
Daniel Literary Group 140
DeChiara Literary Agency, The Jennifer 141
DeFiore & Co. 142
Diana Finch Literary Agency 156
Don Congdon Associates Inc. 134
Doyen Literary Services, Inc. 145
Dunham Literary, Inc. 146
Dunow, Carlson, & Lerner Agency 146
Dupree/Miller and Associates Literary 147
Dystel & Goderich Literary Management 148
Fairbank Literary Representation 154
Felicia Eth Literary Representation 153
Fielding Agency, LLC, The 155
FinePrint Literary Management 156
Fletcher & Company 157
Folio Literary Management, LLC 158
Foundry Literary + Media 158
Fox Literary 159
Freedson's Publishing Network, Grace 160
Fresh Books Literary Agency 161
Friedman and Co., Inc., Frederica 163
Full Circle Literary, LLC 163
G Agency, LLC, The 165
Gelfman Schneider Literary Agents, Inc. 166
Golomb Literary Agency, The Susan 168
Grad Literary Agency, Inc., Doug 170
Graham Maw Christie Literary Agency 170
Grayson Literary Agency, Ashley 171
Greenburger Associates, Inc., Sanford J. 171
Green Literary Agency, LLC, Kathryn 173
Harris Literary Agency, Inc., The Joy 174
Harwood Limited, Antony 175
Henshaw Group, Richard 177
Hill and Associates, Julie A. 179
Hill Bonnie Nadell, Inc., Frederick 179
Hornfischer Literary Management 180
Hurst Literary Management, Andrea 181
InkWell Management, LLC 182
Jabberwocky Literary Agency 184
James Peter Associates, Inc. 184
Kern Literary Agency, The Natasha 188
Konner Literary Agency, Linda 190
Krichevsky Literary Agency, Inc., Stuart 191
Langlie, Literary Agent, Laura 193
Larsen/Elizabeth Pomada, Literary Agents, Michael 193
LaunchBooks Literary Agency 194
Lazin Books, Sarah 195
Lecker Agency, Robert 196
Levine Literary Agency, Paul S. 198
Lippincott Massie McQuilkin 198
Literary Group International, The 199
Literary Services Inc. 200
Lowenstein Associates Inc. 201
Lownie Literary Agency, Ltd., Andrew 203
Maass Literary Agency, Donald 203
Maccoby Literary Agency, Gina 204
MacGregor Literary Inc. 204
Mann Agency, Carol 205
Mansion Street Literary Management 205
March Tenth, Inc. 206
Maria Carvainis Agency, Inc. 130
Marsal Lyon Literary Agency, LLC 207
Martin Literary Management 208
McBride Literary Agency, Margret 209
McCarthy Creative Services 210
Mendel Media Group, LLC 212
Millard Literary Agency, Martha 213
Moveable Type Management 214

Mura Literary, Dee 215
Naggar Literary Agency, Inc. Jean V. 215
Newman Literary, Dana 216
Parks Agency, The Richard 218
Paul Bresnick Literary Agency, LLC 124
Perkins Agency, L. 219
Prentis Literary, Linn 220
P.S. Literary Agency 221
Publication Riot Group 223
Rabinoff Agency, Lynne 224
Red Sofa Literary 224
Richards Agency, The Lisa 226
Rick Broadhead & Associates Literary 125
Robbins Literary Agency, B.J. 228
Rosenberg Group, The 230
Rosenkranz Literary Agency, Rita 230
Ross Literary Agency, Andy 231
Rudy Agency, The 232
Sagalyn Agency, The 234
Sanders & Associates, Victoria 234
Seligman, Literary Agent, Lynn 237
Serendipity Literary Agency, LLC 237
Sheree Bykofsky Associates, Inc. 128
Sherman Associates, Inc., Wendy 240
Sherman & Associates, Ken 239
Simmons Literary Agency, Jeffrey 241
Smith Literary Agency, Ltd., Robert 242
Speilburg Literary Agency 244
Spieler Agency, The 244
Sterling Lord Literistic, Inc. 246
Straus Agency, Inc., Robin 247
Talcott Notch Literary 249
Toby Eady Associates 149
Triada U.S. Literary Agency, Inc. 252
Trident Media Group 253
Unter Agency, The 254
Venture Literary 254
Veritas Literary Agency 254
Watkins Loomis Agency, Inc. 256
Whimsy Literary Agency, LLC 258
Wm Clark Associates 133
Zimmermann Literary Agency, Helen 262

PSYCHOLOGY

Agency Group LLC, The 111
Allen O'Shea Literary Agency 113
Amster Literary Enterprises, Betsy 115
Anderson Literary Management, LLC 116
Arcadia 116
Braun Associates, Inc., Barbara 124
Cameron & Associates, Kimberley 129
Chalberg & Sussman 131
Curtis Brown, Ltd. 138
D4EO Literary Agency 139
DeFiore & Co. 142
Diana Finch Literary Agency 156
Dijkstra Literary Agency, Sandra 143
Don Congdon Associates Inc. 134
Donnaud & Associates, Inc., Janis A. 144
Doyen Literary Services, Inc. 145
Dunham Literary, Inc. 146
Dunow, Carlson, & Lerner Agency 146
Dupree/Miller and Associates Literary 147
Dystel & Goderich Literary Management 148
Ebeling Agency, The 150
Felicia Eth Literary Representation 153
Fielding Agency, LLC, The 155
Folio Literary Management, LLC 158
Foundry Literary + Media 158
Franklin Associates, Ltd., Lynn C. 159
Fredericks Literary Agency, Inc., Jeanne 159
Freedson's Publishing Network, Grace 160
Fresh Books Literary Agency 161
Freymann Literary Agency, Sarah Jane 162
Friedman and Co., Inc., Frederica 163
Garamond Agency, Inc., The 165
Gartenberg Literary Agency, Max 166
Golomb Literary Agency, The Susan 168
Graham Maw Christie Literary Agency 170
Green Literary Agency, LLC, Kathryn 173
Harwood Limited, Antony 175
Henshaw Group, Richard 177
Herman Agency, LLC, The Jeff 178
Hill and Associates, Julie A. 179
Holmes Agency, The 179

Hornfischer Literary Management 180
HSG Agency 180
Hurst Literary Management, Andrea 181
James Peter Associates, Inc. 184
Joelle Delbourgo Associates, Inc. 143
Judith Ehrlich Literary Management, LLC 151
Keller Media Inc. 187
Kern Literary Agency, The Natasha 188
Klinger, Inc., Harvey 189
Konner Literary Agency, Linda 190
LA Literary Agency, The 192
Langlie, Literary Agent, Laura 193
Larsen/Elizabeth Pomada, Literary Agents, Michael 193
LevelFiveMedia, LLC 197
Levine Literary Agency, Paul S. 198
Lippincott Massie McQuilkin 198
Literary Group International, The 199
Literary Services Inc. 200
LKG Agency 201
Mann Agency, Carol 205
Manus & Associates Literary Agency, Inc. 206
Maria Carvainis Agency, Inc. 130
Marsal Lyon Literary Agency, LLC 207
Martin Literary Management 208
McBride Literary Agency, Margret 209
McCarthy Creative Services 210
McGill Agency, Inc., The 211
Mendel Media Group, LLC 212
Millard Literary Agency, Martha 213
Mura Literary, Dee 215
Naggar Literary Agency, Inc. Jean V. 215
Parks Agency, The Richard 218
Perkins Agency, L. 219
Queen Literary Agency 223
Rabinoff Agency, Lynne 224
Rees Literary Agency, Helen 225
Regal Literary Agency 225
Rinaldi Literary Agency, Angela 227
Robbins Literary Agency, B.J. 228
Rosenberg Group, The 230
Rosenkranz Literary Agency, Rita 230
Ross Literary Agency, Andy 231
Rudy Agency, The 232
Ryan Publishing Enterprises, Inc., Regina 233
Sanders & Associates, Victoria 234
sazTracy Brown Literary Agency 126
Seligman, Literary Agent, Lynn 237
Sheree Bykofsky Associates, Inc. 128
Sherman Associates, Inc., Wendy 240
Sherman & Associates, Ken 239
Slopen Literary Agency, Beverley 241
Straus Agency, Inc., Robin 247
Stuart Agency, The 248
Talcott Notch Literary 249
Venture Literary 254
Vicky Bijur Literary Agency 119
Waterside Productions, Inc. 256
Weingel-Fidel Agency, The 257
Whimsy Literary Agency, LLC 258
Writers House 260

RELIGIOUS

Alive Communications, Inc. 113
Daniel Literary Group 140
DeChiara Literary Agency, The Jennifer 141
DeFiore & Co. 142
Dystel & Goderich Literary Management 148
Ebeling Agency, The 150
Folio Literary Management, LLC 158
Hill and Associates, Julie A. 179
Hornfischer Literary Management 180
InkWell Management, LLC 182
Jenks Agency, The Carolyn 186
Kern Literary Agency, The Natasha 188
Larsen/Elizabeth Pomada, Literary Agents, Michael 193
Laube Agency, The Steve 194
Lippincott Massie McQuilkin 198
Literary Group International, The 199
Manus & Associates Literary Agency, Inc. 206
Mendel Media Group, LLC 212

Mura Literary, Dee 215
Oscard Agency, Inc., Fifi 217
Rabinoff Agency, Lynne 224
Rosenkranz Literary Agency, Rita 230
Schulman Literary Agency, Susan 235
Serendipity Literary Agency, LLC 237
Sheree Bykofsky Associates, Inc. 128
Sweeney Agency, LLC, Emma 249
Wm Clark Associates 133
Yates & Yates 261

SCIENCE

Allen O'Shea Literary Agency 113
Arcadia 116
Castiglia Literary Agency 131
Chase Literary Agency 131
Cheney Literary Associates, LLC, Elyse 132
Compass Talent 134
Curtis Brown, Ltd. 138
Cynthia Cannell Literary Agency 129
D4EO Literary Agency 139
DeChiara Literary Agency, The Jennifer 141
DeFiore & Co. 142
Diana Finch Literary Agency 156
Dijkstra Literary Agency, Sandra 143
Don Congdon Associates Inc. 134
Doyen Literary Services, Inc. 145
Dunham Literary, Inc. 146
Dunow, Carlson, & Lerner Agency 146
Dupree/Miller and Associates Literary 147
Dystel & Goderich Literary Management 148
Fairbank Literary Representation 154
Felicia Eth Literary Representation 153
Fielding Agency, LLC, The 155
FinePrint Literary Management 156
Fletcher & Company 157
Folio Literary Management, LLC 158
Foundry Literary + Media 158
Freedson's Publishing Network, Grace 160
Fresh Books Literary Agency 161
Garamond Agency, Inc., The 165
Gartenberg Literary Agency, Max 166
Golomb Literary Agency, The Susan 168
Grad Literary Agency, Inc., Doug 170
Grayson Literary Agency, Ashley 171
Grinberg Literary Agency, Jill 174
Harris Literary Agency, Inc., The Joy 174
Harwood Limited, Antony 175
Hawkins & Associates, Inc., John 176
Henshaw Group, Richard 177
Hill Bonnie Nadell, Inc., Frederick 179
Holmes Agency, The 179
Hornfischer Literary Management 180
HSG Agency 180
Hurst Literary Management, Andrea 181
InkWell Management, LLC 182
International Transactions, Inc. 183
Jabberwocky Literary Agency 184
Jenks Agency, The Carolyn 186
Joelle Delbourgo Associates, Inc. 143
Judith Ehrlich Literary Management, LLC 151
Keller Media Inc. 187
Klinger, Inc., Harvey 189
Konner Literary Agency, Linda 190
LA Literary Agency, The 192
Larsen/Elizabeth Pomada, Literary Agents, Michael 193
LaunchBooks Literary Agency 194
Lecker Agency, Robert 196
Levine Greenberg Literary Agency, Inc. 197
Levine Literary Agency, Paul S. 198
Lippincott Massie McQuilkin 198
Literary Group International, The 199
Literary Services Inc. 200
Maria Carvainis Agency, Inc. 130
Marsal Lyon Literary Agency, LLC 207
McBride Literary Agency, Margret 209
McCarthy Creative Services 210
Mendel Media Group, LLC 212
Mura Literary, Dee 215
Naggar Literary Agency, Inc. Jean V. 215
Newman Literary, Dana 216
Oscard Agency, Inc., Fifi 217
Park Literary Group, LLC 218

Parks Agency, The Richard 218
Pavilion Literary Management 218
Perkins Agency, L. 219
P.S. Literary Agency 221
Publication Riot Group 223
Queen Literary Agency 223
Rabinoff Agency, Lynne 224
Rees Literary Agency, Helen 225
Regal Literary Agency 225
Rick Broadhead & Associates Literary 125
Rights Factory, The 227
Rosenkranz Literary Agency, Rita 230
Ross Literary Agency, Andy 231
Rudy Agency, The 232
Sagalyn Agency, The 234
Schiavone Literary Agency, Inc. 234
Schulman Literary Agency, Susan 235
Seligman, Literary Agent, Lynn 237
Sheree Bykofsky Associates, Inc. 128
Sherman & Associates, Ken 239
Speilburg Literary Agency 244
Sterling Lord Literistic, Inc. 246
Stuart Agency, The 248
Talcott Notch Literary 249
Tessler Literary Agency, LLC 250
Triada U.S. Literary Agency, Inc. 252
Trident Media Group 253
Venture Literary 254
Vicky Bijur Literary Agency 119
Weingel-Fidel Agency, The 257
Wm Clark Associates 133
Wolf Literary Services 259
Writers House 260
Seventh Avenue Literary Agency 238

SELF-HELP

Agency Group LLC, The 111
Alive Communications, Inc. 113
Amster Literary Enterprises, Betsy 115
Bradford Literary Agency 122
Cameron & Associates, Kimberley 129
Chalberg & Sussman 131
Curtis Brown, Ltd. 138
Cynthia Cannell Literary Agency 129
Daniel Literary Group 140
David Black Literary Agency 119
DeFiore & Co. 142
Diana Finch Literary Agency 156
Dijkstra Literary Agency, Sandra 143
Doyen Literary Services, Inc. 145
Dupree/Miller and Associates Literary 147
Ebeling Agency, The 150
Fielding Agency, LLC, The 155
FinePrint Literary Management 156
Fletcher & Company 157
Folio Literary Management, LLC 158
Franklin Associates, Ltd., Lynn C. 159
Fredericks Literary Agency, Inc., Jeanne 159
Freedson's Publishing Network, Grace 160
Freymann Literary Agency, Sarah Jane 162
Grad Literary Agency, Inc., Doug 170
Grayson Literary Agency, Ashley 171
Green Literary Agency, LLC, Kathryn 173
Harwood Limited, Antony 175
Henshaw Group, Richard 177
Herman Agency, LLC, The Jeff 178
Hill and Associates, Julie A. 179
Hornfischer Literary Management 180
Hurst Literary Management, Andrea 181
James Peter Associates, Inc. 184
J de S Associates, Inc. 186
Joelle Delbourgo Associates, Inc. 143
Keller Media Inc. 187
Kern Literary Agency, The Natasha 188
Klinger, Inc., Harvey 189
Konner Literary Agency, Linda 190
Larsen/Elizabeth Pomada, Literary Agents, Michael 193
LevelFiveMedia, LLC 197
Levine Literary Agency, Paul S. 198
Lippincott Massie McQuilkin 198
Literary Group International, The 199
Literary Services Inc. 200
Living Word Literary Agency 201
MacGregor Literary Inc. 204

Mann Agency, Carol 205
Manus & Associates Literary Agency, Inc. 206
Marcil Literary Agency, Inc., The Denise 207
Marsal Lyon Literary Agency, LLC 207
Martin Literary Management 208
McBride Literary Agency, Margret 209
McGill Agency, Inc., The 211
Mendel Media Group, LLC 212
Millard Literary Agency, Martha 213
Miriam Altshuler Literary Agency 114
Morhaim Literary Agency, Howard 214
Mura Literary, Dee 215
Newman Literary, Dana 216
Parks Agency, The Richard 218
P.S. Literary Agency 221
Rees Literary Agency, Helen 225
Rick Broadhead & Associates Literary 125
Rinaldi Literary Agency, Angela 227
Robbins Literary Agency, B.J. 228
Rosenkranz Literary Agency, Rita 230
Seligman, Literary Agent, Lynn 237
Serendipity Literary Agency, LLC 237
Sherman Associates, Inc., Wendy 240
Smith Literary Agency, Ltd., Robert 242
Snell Literary Agency, Michael 243
Talcott Notch Literary 249
Waterside Productions, Inc. 256
Whimsy Literary Agency, LLC 258
Wordserve Literary Group 259
Writers House 260

SEX

BookEnds, LLC 120
Curtis Brown, Ltd. 138
Doyen Literary Services, Inc. 145
Dupree/Miller and Associates Literary 147
Harwood Limited, Antony 175
Holmes Agency, The 179
Mendel Media Group, LLC 212
Sheree Bykofsky Associates, Inc. 128
Sherman & Associates, Ken 239

SOCIOLOGY

Amster Literary Enterprises, Betsy 115
Curtis Brown, Ltd. 138
Doyen Literary Services, Inc. 145
Dunow, Carlson, & Lerner Agency 146
Dupree/Miller and Associates Literary 147
Fairbank Literary Representation 154
Felicia Eth Literary Representation 153
Fielding Agency, LLC, The 155
Friedman and Co., Inc., Frederica 163
Gernert Company, The 167
Goldin Literary Agency, Inc., Frances 168
Golomb Literary Agency, The Susan 168
Harwood Limited, Antony 175
Henshaw Group, Richard 177
Hornfischer Literary Management 180
Jabberwocky Literary Agency 184
J de S Associates, Inc. 186
Keller Media Inc. 187
Larsen/Elizabeth Pomada, Literary Agents, Michael 193
LaunchBooks Literary Agency 194
Levine Greenberg Literary Agency, Inc. 197
Levine Literary Agency, Paul S. 198
Lippincott Massie McQuilkin 198
Literary Group International, The 199
Mann Agency, Carol 205
McBride Literary Agency, Margret 209
McCarthy Creative Services 210
Mendel Media Group, LLC 212
Newman Literary, Dana 216
Parks Agency, The Richard 218
Publication Riot Group 223
Red Sofa Literary 224
Robbins Literary Agency, B.J. 228
Ross Literary Agency, Andy 231
Rudy Agency, The 232
Seligman, Literary Agent, Lynn 237
Sheree Bykofsky Associates, Inc. 128
Sherman & Associates, Ken 239
Simmons Literary Agency, Jeffrey 241
Slopen Literary Agency, Beverley 241

Vicky Bijur Literary Agency 119
Waterside Productions, Inc. 256
Weingel-Fidel Agency, The 257
Wm Clark Associates 133

SPIRITUALITY

Curtis Brown, Ltd. 138
Cynthia Cannell Literary Agency 129
Ebeling Agency, The 150
FinePrint Literary Management 156
Franklin Associates, Ltd., Lynn C. 159
Harwood Limited, Antony 175
Herman Agency, LLC, The Jeff 178
Holmes Agency, The 179
Kern Literary Agency, The Natasha 188
Klinger, Inc., Harvey 189
Levine Greenberg Literary Agency, Inc. 197
Mendel Media Group, LLC 212
Miriam Altshuler Literary Agency 114
Mura Literary, Dee 215
Serendipity Literary Agency, LLC 237
Sheree Bykofsky Associates, Inc. 128
Sherman & Associates, Ken 239

SPORTS

Agency Group LLC, The 111
Aitken Alexander Associates 112
Brandt & Hochman Literary Agents, Inc. 123
Chase Literary Agency 131
Curtis Brown, Ltd. 138
D4EO Literary Agency 139
Daniel Literary Group 140
DeFiore & Co. 142
Diana Finch Literary Agency 156
Dunow, Carlson, & Lerner Agency 146
Dupree/Miller and Associates Literary 147
Ebeling Agency, The 150
E.J. McCarthy Agency 209
Fairbank Literary Representation 154
Fielding Agency, LLC, The 155
Fletcher & Company 157
Foundry Literary + Media 158
Freedson's Publishing Network, Grace 160
Fresh Books Literary Agency 161
Gartenberg Literary Agency, Max 166
Grad Literary Agency, Inc., Doug 170
Grayson Literary Agency, Ashley 171
Greenburger Associates, Inc., Sanford J. 171
Green Literary Agency, LLC, Kathryn 173
Harwood Limited, Antony 175
Henshaw Group, Richard 177
Hornfischer Literary Management 180
International Transactions, Inc. 183
Jabberwocky Literary Agency 184
J de S Associates, Inc. 186
Klinger, Inc., Harvey 189
LA Literary Agency, The 192
Larsen/Elizabeth Pomada, Literary Agents,
Michael 193
LaunchBooks Literary Agency 194
Leshne Agency, The 197
Levine Greenberg Literary Agency, Inc. 197
Levine Literary Agency, Paul S. 198
Literary Group International, The 199
Literary Services Inc. 200
MacGregor Literary Inc. 204
Mann Agency, Carol 205
Manus & Associates Literary Agency, Inc.
206
Marsal Lyon Literary Agency, LLC 207
McCarthy Creative Services 210
Mendel Media Group, LLC 212
Morhaim Literary Agency, Howard 214
Mura Literary, Dee 215
Newman Literary, Dana 216
Oscard Agency, Inc., Fifi 217
Paul Bresnick Literary Agency, LLC 124
P.S. Literary Agency 221
Queen Literary Agency 223
Rennert Agency, The Amy 226
Robbins Literary Agency, B.J. 228
Rosenberg Group, The 230
Rosenkranz Literary Agency, Rita 230
Rudy Agency, The 232
Schiavone Literary Agency, Inc. 234

Serendipity Literary Agency, LLC 237
Sheree Bykofsky Associates, Inc. 128
Sherman & Associates, Ken 239
Simmons Literary Agency, Jeffrey 241
SLW Literary Agency 242
Smith Literary Agency, Ltd., Robert 242
Spitzer Literary Agency, Inc., Philip G. 245
Stuart Agency, The 248
Triada U.S. Literary Agency, Inc. 252
Trident Media Group 253
Venture Literary 254
Waxman Leavell Literary Agency, Inc. 256
Seventh Avenue Literary Agency 238
Yates & Yates 261
Zimmermann Literary Agency, Helen 262

TECHNOLOGY

Diana Finch Literary Agency 156
Don Congdon Associates Inc. 134
Doyen Literary Services, Inc. 145
Dunham Literary, Inc. 146
Dupree/Miller and Associates Literary 147
Dystel & Goderich Literary Management 148
Fairbank Literary Representation 154
Felicia Eth Literary Representation 153
Fielding Agency, LLC, The 155
FinePrint Literary Management 156
Folio Literary Management, LLC 158
Freedson's Publishing Network, Grace 160
Fresh Books Literary Agency 161
G Agency, LLC, The 165
Garamond Agency, Inc., The 165
Golomb Literary Agency, The Susan 168
Grayson Literary Agency, Ashley 171
Harris Literary Agency, Inc., The Joy 174
Harwood Limited, Antony 175
Hawkins & Associates, Inc., John 176
Henshaw Group, Richard 177
Herman Agency, LLC, The Jeff 178
Hill Bonnie Nadell, Inc., Frederick 179
Hornfischer Literary Management 180
Jenks Agency, The Carolyn 186
Klinger, Inc., Harvey 189
LaunchBooks Literary Agency 194
Lecker Agency, Robert 196
Lippincott Massie McQuilkin 198
Literary Services Inc. 200
McBride Literary Agency, Margret 209
Mura Literary, Dee 215
Newman Literary, Dana 216
Oscard Agency, Inc., Fifi 217
Parks Agency, The Richard 218
P.S. Literary Agency 221
Rabinoff Agency, Lynne 224
Rosenkranz Literary Agency, Rita 230
Ross Literary Agency, Andy 231
Rudy Agency, The 232
Sagalyn Agency, The 234
Talcott Notch Literary 249
Trident Media Group 253
Venture Literary 254
Waterside Productions, Inc. 256
Watkins Loomis Agency, Inc. 256
Weingel-Fidel Agency, The 257
Wm Clark Associates 133
Writers House 260
Seventh Avenue Literary Agency 238

THEATER

Daniel Literary Group 140
DeChiara Literary Agency, The Jennifer 141
Diana Finch Literary Agency 156
Don Congdon Associates Inc. 134
Doyen Literary Services, Inc. 145
Dupree/Miller and Associates Literary 147
Grad Literary Agency, Inc., Doug 170
Jabberwocky Literary Agency 184
James Peter Associates, Inc. 184
Langlie, Laura 193
Lecker Agency, Robert 196
Levine Literary Agency, Paul S. 198
March Tenth, Inc. 206
Millard Literary Agency, Martha 213
Newman Literary, Dana 216
Parks Agency, The Richard 218

Perkins Agency, L. 219
Robbins Literary Agency, B.J. 228
Rosenkranz Literary Agency, Rita 230
Sanders & Associates, Victoria 234
Smith Literary Agency, Ltd., Robert 242
Wm Clark Associates 133
Writers House 260

TRANSLATION

Curtis Brown, Ltd. 138
Diana Finch Literary Agency 156
Dupree/Miller and Associates Literary 147
Fielding Agency, LLC, The 155
Harwood Limited, Antony 175
International Transactions, Inc. 183
J de S Associates, Inc. 186
Jenks Agency, The Carolyn 186
McCarthy Creative Services 210
Sanders & Associates, Victoria 234
Sheree Bykofsky Associates, Inc. 128
Sherman & Associates, Ken 239
Simmons Literary Agency, Jeffrey 241
Wm Clark Associates 133

TRAVEL

Book Cents Literary Agency, LLC 120
Cameron & Associates, Kimberley 129
Curtis Brown, Ltd. 138
DeChiara Literary Agency, The Jennifer 141
Don Congdon Associates Inc. 134
Dreisbach Literary Management 146
Foundry Literary + Media 158
Gernert Company, The 167
Grad Literary Agency, Inc., Doug 170
Grinberg Literary Agency, Jill 174
Harwood Limited, Antony 175
Hill and Associates, Julie A. 179
Hurst Literary Management, Andrea 181
James Peter Associates, Inc. 184
Larsen/Elizabeth Pomada, Literary Agents,
Michael 193
Literary Group International, The 199
Lowenstein Associates Inc. 201
Mura Literary, Dee 215
Parks Agency, The Richard 218
Paul Bresnick Literary Agency, LLC 124
Richards Agency, The Lisa 226
Robbins Literary Agency, B.J. 228
Ryan Publishing Enterprises, Inc., Regina 233
sazTracy Brown Literary Agency 126
Schulman Literary Agency, Susan 235
Sheree Bykofsky Associates, Inc. 128
Sherman & Associates, Ken 239
Speilburg Literary Agency 244
Spitzer Literary Agency, Inc., Philip G. 245
Strothman Agency, LLC, The 248
Talcott Notch Literary 249
Tessler Literary Agency, LLC 250
Trident Media Group 253
Unter Agency, The 254
Seventh Avenue Literary Agency 238

TRUE CRIME

Agency Group LLC, The 111
Crichton & Associates 137
Curtis Brown, Ltd. 138
D4EO Literary Agency 139
Diana Finch Literary Agency 156
Don Congdon Associates Inc. 134
Doyen Literary Services, Inc. 145
Dreisbach Literary Management 146
Dupree/Miller and Associates Literary 147
Dystel & Goderich Literary Management 148
Fairbank Literary Representation 154
Fielding Agency, LLC, The 155
Friedman and Co., Inc., Frederica 163
Gartenberg Literary Agency, Max 166
Grayson Literary Agency, Ashley 171
Green Literary Agency, LLC, Kathryn 173
Harwood Limited, Antony 175
Henshaw Group, Richard 177
Hornfischer Literary Management 180
Hurst Literary Management, Andrea 181
International Transactions, Inc. 183
Jenks Agency, The Carolyn 186

Klinger, Inc., Harvey 189
Levine Literary Agency, Paul S. 198
Lippincott Massie McQuilkin 198
Literary Group International, The 199
Literary Services Inc. 200
Lownie Literary Agency, Ltd., Andrew 203
Martin Literary Management 208
McCarthy Creative Services 210
McGill Agency, Inc., The 211
Mendel Media Group, LLC 212
Millard Literary Agency, Martha 213
Paul Bresnick Literary Agency, LLC 124
P.S. Literary Agency 221
Red Sofa Literary 224
Rees Literary Agency, Helen 225
Robbins Literary Agency, B.J. 228
Rudy Agency, The 232
Schiavone Literary Agency, Inc. 234
Seligman, Literary Agent, Lynn 237
Sheree Bykofsky Associates, Inc. 128
Sherman & Associates, Ken 239
Simmons Literary Agency, Jeffrey 241
Slopen Literary Agency, Beverley 241
Smith Literary Agency, Ltd., Robert 242
Talcott Notch Literary 249
Unter Agency, The 254
Venture Literary 254
Veritas Literary Agency 254
Whimsy Literary Agency, LLC 258
Writers House 260

WAR

Diana Finch Literary Agency 156
Don Congdon Associates Inc. 134
Fielding Agency, LLC, The 155
Folio Literary Management, LLC 158
Harwood Limited, Antony 175
Hornfischer Literary Management 180
International Transactions, Inc. 183
Jabberwocky Literary Agency 184
James Peter Associates, Inc. 184
Lownie Literary Agency, Ltd., Andrew 203
Mendel Media Group, LLC 212
P.S. Literary Agency 221
Rees Literary Agency, Helen 225
Rosenkranz Literary Agency, Rita 230
Ross Literary Agency, Andy 231
Rudy Agency, The 232
Sheree Bykofsky Associates, Inc. 128

WOMEN'S ISSUES

Alive Communications, Inc. 113
Anderson Literary Management, LLC 116
Book Cents Literary Agency, LLC 120
Braun Associates, Inc., Barbara 124
Chelius Literary Agency, Jane 132
Crichton & Associates 137
Daniel Literary Group 140
David Black Literary Agency 119
Diana Finch Literary Agency 156
Don Congdon Associates Inc. 134
Doyen Literary Services, Inc. 145
Dreisbach Literary Management 146
Dunham Literary, Inc. 146
Dupree/Miller and Associates Literary 147
Dystel & Goderich Literary Management 148
Fairbank Literary Representation 154
Felicia Eth Literary Representation 153
Fielding Agency, LLC, The 155
Fletcher & Company 157
Folio Literary Management, LLC 158
Fredericks Literary Agency, Inc., Jeanne 159
Freymann Literary Agency, Sarah Jane 162
Full Circle Literary, LLC 163
Golomb Literary Agency, The Susan 168
Green Literary Agency, LLC, Kathryn 173
Harwood Limited, Antony 175
Hawkins & Associates, Inc., John 176
Henshaw Group, Richard 177
Hill and Associates, Julie A. 179
Holmes Agency, The 179
Hurst Literary Management, Andrea 181
International Transactions, Inc. 183
Jabberwocky Literary Agency 184
James Peter Associates, Inc. 184

Jenks Agency, The Carolyn 186
Judith Ehrlich Literary Management, LLC 151
Keller Media Inc. 187
Kern Literary Agency, The Natasha 188
Klinger, Inc., Harvey 189
Konner Literary Agency, Linda 190
Larsen/Elizabeth Pomada, Literary Agents, Michael 193
Levine Literary Agency, Paul S. 198
Lippincott Massie McQuilkin 198
Literary Group International, The 199
LKG Agency 201
Maccoby Literary Agency, Gina 204
Mann Agency, Carol 205
Manus & Associates Literary Agency, Inc. 206
Marcil Literary Agency, Inc., The Denise 207
Marsal Lyon Literary Agency, LLC 207
Martin Literary Management 208
McBride Literary Agency, Margret 209
McMillan & Associates, Inc., Sally Hill 211
Mendel Media Group, LLC 212
Millard Literary Agency, Martha 213
Miriam Altshuler Literary Agency 114
Newman Literary, Dana 216
Oscard Agency, Inc., Fifi 217
Parks Agency, The Richard 218
Prentis Literary, Linn 220
P.S. Literary Agency 221
Rabinoff Agency, Lynne 224
Red Sofa Literary 224
Rinaldi Literary Agency, Angela 227
Rittenberg Literary Agency, Inc., Ann 227
Robbins Literary Agency, B.J. 228
Rosenberg Group, The 230
Rosenkranz Literary Agency, Rita 230
Rudy Agency, The 232
Ryan Publishing Enterprises, Inc., Regina 233
Sanders & Associates, Victoria 234
sazTracy Brown Literary Agency 126
Schulman Literary Agency, Susan 235
Snell Literary Agency, Michael 243
Sterling Lord Literistic, Inc. 246
Venture Literary 254
Veritas Literary Agency 254
Weingel-Fidel Agency, The 257
Whimsy Literary Agency, LLC 258
Wolf Literary Services 259
Writers House 260
Zimmermann Literary Agency, Helen 262

WOMEN'S STUDIES

Alive Communications, Inc. 113
Anderson Literary Management, LLC 116
Chelius Literary Agency, Jane 132
Crichton & Associates 137
Daniel Literary Group 140
Diana Finch Literary Agency 156
Don Congdon Associates Inc. 134
Doyen Literary Services, Inc. 145
Dunham Literary, Inc. 146
Dupree/Miller and Associates Literary 147
Dystel & Goderich Literary Management 148
Fairbank Literary Representation 154
Felicia Eth Literary Representation 153
Fielding Agency, LLC, The 155
Fletcher & Company 157
Folio Literary Management, LLC 158
Freymann Literary Agency, Sarah Jane 162
Golomb Literary Agency, The Susan 168
Green Literary Agency, LLC, Kathryn 173
Harwood Limited, Antony 175
Henshaw Group, Richard 177
International Transactions, Inc. 183
Jabberwocky Literary Agency 184
James Peter Associates, Inc. 184
Jenks Agency, The Carolyn 186
Kern Literary Agency, The Natasha 188
Klinger, Inc., Harvey 189
Langlie, Literary Agent, Laura 193
Larsen/Elizabeth Pomada, Literary Agents, Michael 193
Levine Literary Agency, Paul S. 198
Lippincott Massie McQuilkin 198

Literary Group International, The 199
Maccoby Literary Agency, Gina 204
Mann Agency, Carol 205
Marsal Lyon Literary Agency, LLC 207
Martin Literary Management 208
McMillan & Associates, Inc., Sally Hill 211
Mendel Media Group, LLC 212
Millard Literary Agency, Martha 213
Newman Literary, Dana 216
Oscard Agency, Inc., Fifi 217
Parks Agency, The Richard 218
P.S. Literary Agency 221
Rabinoff Agency, Lynne 224
Red Sofa Literary 224
Robbins Literary Agency, B.J. 228
Rosenberg Group, The 230
Rosenkranz Literary Agency, Rita 230
Rudy Agency, The 232
Ryan Publishing Enterprises, Inc., Regina 233
Sanders & Associates, Victoria 234
Schulman Literary Agency, Susan 235
Venture Literary 254
Weingel-Fidel Agency, The 257
Whimsy Literary Agency, LLC 258
Writers House 260

YOUNG ADULT

Brandt & Hochman Literary Agents, Inc. 123
Briggs, M. Courtney 124
Brown Literary Agency, Inc., Andrea 126
DeFiore & Co. 142
Jabberwocky Literary Agency 184
Lippincott Massie McQuilkin 198

AGENT NAME INDEX

Abel, Dominick (Dominick Abel Literary Agency, Inc.) 111
Abell, Whitley (Inklings Literary Agency) 182
Abkemeier, Laurie (DeFiore & Co.) 142
Abou, Stephanie (Lippincott Massie McQuilkin) 198
Abramo, Lauren E. (Dystel & Goderich Literary Management) 148
Adams, Josh (Adams Literary) 111
Adams, Lisa (The Garamond Agency, Inc.) 165
Adams, Tracey (Adams Literary) 111
Agyeman, Janell Walden (Marie Brown Associates, Inc.) 125
Ahearn, Pamela G. (The Ahearn Agency, Inc) 112
Aitken, Gillon (Aitken Alexander Associates) 112
Akolekar, Nalini (Spencerhill Associates) 244
Alexander, Britta (The Ned Leavitt Agency) 196
Alexander, Clare (Aitken Alexander Associates) 112
Alexander, Heather (Pippin Properties, Inc.) 220
Allen, Marilyn (Allen O'Shea Literary Agency) 113
Altman, Elias (Zachary Shuster Harmsworth) 261
Altshuler, Miriam (Miriam Altshuler Literary Agency) 114
Alvarez, Jessica (Bookends, LLC) 120
Amster, Betsy (Betsy Amster Literary Enterprises) 115
Andelman, Michelle (Regal Literary Agency) 225
Anderson, Kathleen (Anderson Literary Management, LLC) 116
Anderson-Wheeler, Claire (Regal Literary Agency) 225
Anthony, Jason (Lippincott Massie McQuilkin) 198
Aponte, Natalia (Aponte Literary Agency) 116
Armada, Kurestin (P.S. Literary Agency) 221
Arms, Victoria Wells (Wells Arms Literary) 258
Axelrod, Steven (The Axelrod Agency) 116
Azantian, Jennifer (Azantian Literary Agency) 117

Bagdasarian, Donna (Publication Riot Group) 223
Bagood, Samantha (Adams Literary) 111
Bail, Margaret (Inklings Literary Agency) 182
Baker-Baughman, Bernadette (Victoria Sanders & Associates) 234

Baker, John F. (Barbara Braun Associates, Inc.) 124
Baker, Lucy Childs (Aaron M. Priest Literary Agency) 220
Ball, Karen (The Steve Laube Agency) 194
Ballard, Noah (Curtis Brown, Ltd.) 138
Balow, Dan (The Steve Laube Agency) 194
Barba, Alex (Inklings Literary Agency) 182
Barbara, Stephen (Inkwell Management, LLC) 182
Barbour, Bruce (Literary Management Group, Inc.) 200
Barer, Julie (The Book Group) 121
Barone, Denise (Barone Literary Agency) 117
Baror, Danny (Baror International, Inc.) 117
Baror, Heather (Baror International, Inc.) 117
Barr, Stephen (Writers House) 260
Bassoff, Ethan (Lippincott Massie McQuilkin) 198
Beaty, Tish (L. Perkins Agency) 219
Becker, Laney Katz (Lippincott Massie McQuilkin) 198
Behar, Ann (Scovil Galen Ghosh Literary Agency, Inc.) 236
Bell, Folade (Serendipity Literary Agency, LLC) 237
Bell, Justin (Spectrum Literary Agency) 243
Belli, Lorella (Lorella Belli Literary Agency [LBLA]) 118
Bender, Faye (The Book Group) 121
Bendimerad, Soumeya (The Susan Golomb Literary Agency) 168
Bennett, David (Transatlantic Literary Agency) 251
Bennett, Lynn (Transatlantic Literary Agency) 251
Bent, Jenny (The Bent Agency) 118
Berkey, Jane Rotrosen (Jane Rotrosen Agency LLC) 231
Berkower, Amy (Writers House) 260
Biagi, Laura (Jean V. Naggar Literary Agency, Inc.) 215
Bialer, Matt (Sanford J. Greenburger Associates, Inc.) 171
Bidnick, Carole (Bidnick & Company) 119
Bijur, Vicky (Vicky Bijur Literary Agency) 119
Bilmes, Joshua (Jabberwocky Literary Agency) 184
Bishop, Sandra (Transatlantic Literary Agency) 251
Black, David (David Black Literary Agency) 119
Blaise, Lizz (Inkwell Management, LLC) 182
Blasdell, Caitlin (Liza Dawson Associates) 141
Bloom, Brettne (The Book Group) 121
Boals, Judy (Judy Boals, Inc.) 120

Boates, Reid (Reid Boates Literary Agency) 226
Bodnar, Jamie, Dr. (Inklings Literary Agency) 182
Boggs, Amy (Donald Maass Literary Agency) 203
Bollinger, Jack (The McGill Agency, Inc.) 211
Bond, Sandra (Bond Literary Agency) 120
Borchardt, Anne (Georges Borchardt, Inc.) 122
Borchardt, Georges (Georges Borchardt, Inc.) 122
Borchardt, Valerie (Georges Borchardt, Inc.) 122
Bourret, Michael (Dystel & Goderich Literary Management) 148
Boutillier, Katie Shea (Donald Maass Literary Agency) 203
Bowen, Brenda (Sanford J. Greenburger Associates, Inc.) 171
Bowles, Brandi (Foundry Literary + Media) 158
Bowman, Hannah (Liza Dawson Associates) 141
Boyle, Katherine (Veritas Literary Agency) 254
Brabec, Kimberly (Waterside Productions, Inc.) 256
Bradford, Laura (Bradford Literary Agency) 122
Bradley, Shaun (Transatlantic Literary Agency) 251
Brady, Mackenzie (New Leaf Literary & Media, Inc.) 216
Brandt, Joan (The Joan Brandt Agency) 123
Braun, Barbara (Barbara Braun Associates, Inc.) 124
Breitwieser, Helen (Cornerstone Literary, Inc.) 136
Bremekamp, Samantha (Corvisiero Literary Agency) 136
Bresnick, Paul (Bresnick Weil Literary Agency) 124
Bresnick, Polly (Bresnick Weil Literary Agency) 124
Bridgins, Sarah (Frances Goldin Literary Agency, Inc.) 168
Briggs, Courtney (M. Courtney Briggs) 124
Brissie, Gene (James Peter Associates, Inc.) 184
Broadhead, Rick (Rick Broadhead & Associates Literary Agency) 125
Brooks, Adele (Barron's Literary Management) 117
Brooks, Rachel (L. Perkins Agency) 219
Brooks, Regina (Serendipity Literary Agency,

LLC) 237
Brophy, Philippa (Sterling Lord Literistic, Inc.) 246
Brower, Kimberly (Rebecca Friedman Literary Agency) 162
Brower, Michelle (Folio Literary Management, LLC) 158
Brower, Sue (Natasha Kern Literary Agency) 188
Brown, Andrea (Andrea Brown Literary Agency) 126
Brown, Marie (Marie Brown Associates, Inc.) 125
Brown, Tracy (Tracy Brown Literary Agency) 126
Bucci, Chris (Anne McDermid & Associates) 211
Bukowski, Denise (The Bukowski Agency) 127
Burby, Danielle (HSG Agency) 180
Burnes, Sarah (The Gernert Company) 167
Burns, Terry (Hartline Literary Agency) 175
Burson, Jana (The Burson Agency) 128
Buterbaugh, Erin (MacGregor Literary Inc.) 204
Byfield, Lydia (Carol Mann Agency) 205
Bykofsky, Sheree (Sheree Bykofsky Associates, Inc.) 128
Byrne, Jack (Sternig & Byrne Literary Agency) 246

Cabot, Stephanie (The Gernert Company) 167
Cahoon, Nancy Stauffer (Nancy Stauffer Associates) 245
Callahan, William (Inkwell Management, LLC) 182
Camacho, Linda (Prospect Agency) 221
Cameron, Kimberley (Kimberley Cameron & Associates) 129
Campbell, Beth (Bookends, LLC) 120
Campbell, Marie (Transatlantic Literary Agency) 251
Cannell, Cynthia (Cynthia Cannell Literary Agency) 129
Cantor, Carrie (Joelle Delbourgo Associates, Inc.) 143
Capron, Elise (Sandra Dijkstra Literary Agency) 143
Caravette, Loretta (LR Children's Literary) 203
Cardona, Moses (John Hawkins & Associates, Inc.) 176
Carleton, Kirsten (Waxman Leavell Literary Agency, Inc.) 255
Carlisle, Michael V (Inkwell Management, LLC) 182
Carlson, Jennifer (Dunow, Carlson, & Lerner Agency) 146
Carr, Michael (Veritas Literary Agency) 254
Carson, Lucy (The Friedrich Agency) 163
Carvainis, Maria (Maria Carvainis Agency, Inc.) 130
Casella, Maura Kye (Don Congdon Associates Inc.) 134
Cashman, Ann (The LA Literary Agency) 192
Castiglia, Julie (Castiglia Literary Agency) 131
Chalberg, Terra (Chalberg & Sussman) 131
Chalfant, Sarah (The Wylie Agency) 261
Chase, Farley (Chase Literary Agency) 131
Chelius, Jane (Jane Chelius Literary Agency) 132
Chelius, Mark (Jane Chelius Literary Agency) 132
Cheney, Elyse (Elyse Cheney Literary Agency Associates, LLC) 132
Chilton, Jamie Weiss (Andrea Brown Literary Agency) 126
Chinchillo, Melissa (Fletcher & Company) 157
Chiotti, Danielle (Upstart Crow Literary) 254
Choron, Harry (March Tenth, Inc.) 206
Christian, Rick (Alive Communications, Inc.) 113
Christie, Jennifer (Graham Maw Christie Literary Agency) 170

Chromy, Adam (Moveable Type Management) 214
Chu, Lynn (Writers' Representatives, LLC) 260
Chudney, Steven (The Chudney Agency) 132
Cirillo, Andrea (Jane Rotrosen Agency LLC) 231
Clark, Ginger (Curtis Brown, Ltd.) 138
Clark, June (Fineprint Literary Management) 156
Clark, Madeleine (Sterling Lord Literistic, Inc.) 246
Clark, William (WM Clark Associates) 133
Close, Megan (Keller Media Inc.) 187
Cloughley, Amy (Kimberley Cameron & Associates) 129
Cohane, Drea (The Rights Factory) 227
Cohen, Shana (Stuart Krichevsky Literary Agency) 191
Cohen, Susan (Writers House) 260
Cohen, Susan Lee (Riverside Literary Agency) 228
Cohn, Amy (The McGill Agency, Inc.) 211
Coker, Deborah (Connor Literary Agency) 135
Colchie, Elaine (Colchie Agency, GP) 134
Colchie, Thomas (Colchie Agency, GP) 134
Coleridge, Gill (Rogers, Coleridge & White) 229
Collette, Ann (Rees Literary Agency) 225
Collin, Frances (Frances Collin, Literary Agent) 134
Collins, JoAnn (International Transactions, Inc.) 183
Concepcion, Christina (Don Congdon Associates Inc.) 134
Congdon, Michael (Don Congdon Associates Inc.) 134
Contardi, Bill (Brandt & Hochman Literary Agents, Inc.) 123
Conway, Dan (Writers House) 260
Cooper, Gemma (The Bent Agency) 118
Coover, Doe (The Doe Coover Agency) 135
Copeland, Sam (Rogers, Coleridge & White) 229
Corcoran, Jill (Jill Corcoran Literary Agency) 135
Corvisiero, Marisa A. (Corvisiero Literary Agency) 136
Cottle, Anna (Cine/Lit Representation) 133
Crawford, Rachel (Fletcher & Company) 157
Crichton, Sha-Shana (Crichton & Associates) 137
Crider, Alice (Wordserve Literary Group) 259
Crockett, Laura (Triada U.S. Literary Agency, Inc.) 252
Cross, Claudia (Folio Literary Management, LLC) 158
Crowe, Sara (Harvey Klinger, Inc.) 189
Cummings, Mary (Betsy Amster Literary Enterprises) 115
Curtis, Richard (Richar Curtis Associates, Inc.) 137
Cusick, John M. (The Greenhouse Literary Agency) 172

D'Agostino, Kerry (Curtis Brown, Ltd.) 138
Dail, Laura (Laura Dail Literary Agency, Inc) 140
Daley, Michael (Margret McBride Literary Agency) 209
Daniel, Greg (Daniel Literary Group) 140
Darhansoff, Liz (Darhansoff & Verrill Literary Agents) 140
Dark, Tom (Heacock Hill Literary Agency, Inc.) 177
Davidson, Caroline (Caroline Davidson Literary Agency) 141
Davies, Sarah (The Greenhouse Literary Agency) 172
Davis, Jamie (Evatopia, Inc.) 153
Davis, Kaylee (Dee Mura Literary) 215
Davis, Naomi (Inklings Literary Agency) 182
Davis, Reiko (Miriam Altshuler Literary Agency) 114

Dawson, Liza (Liza Dawson Associates) 141
Debi Shruti (Aitken Alexander Associates) 112
DeChiara, Jennifer (The Jennifer DeChiara Literary Agency) 141
Decker, Stacia (Donald Maass Literary Agency) 203
DeFiore, Brian (DeFiore & Co.) 142
Delbourgo, Joelle (Joelle Delbourgo Associates, Inc.) 143
De Spoelberch, Jacques (J Des Associates) 186
Detweiler, Katelyn (Jill Grinberg Literary Agency) 174
Devereux, Allison (Wolf Literary Services, LLC) 259
Devlin, Anne G. (Max Gartenberg Literary Agency) 166
Devlin, Dirk (Max Gartenberg Literary Agency) 166
Deyoe, Cori (Three Seas Literary Agency) 251
Diforio, Bob (D4eo Literary Agency) 139
Dijkstra, Sandra (Sandra Dijkstra Literary Agency) 143
DiMona, Lisa (Writers House) 260
Diver, Lucienne (The Knight Agency) 190
Dolan, Shaun (Union Literary) 253
Dominguez, Adriana (Full Circle Literary, LLC) 163
Donaghy, Stacey (Donaghy Literary Group) 144
Donnaud, Janis A. (Janis A. Donnaud & Associates, Inc.) 144
Donovan, Jim (Jim Donovan Literary) 145
Doyen, B.J. (Doyen Literary Services, Inc.) 145
Drayton, Catherine (Inkwell Management, LLC) 182
Dreisbach, Verna (Dreisbach Literary Management) 146
Duff, Susan (Bresnick Weil Literary Agency) 124
Dugas, Rachael (Talcott Notch Literary) 249
Dunham, Jennie (Dunham Literary, Inc.) 146
Dunow, Henry (Dunow, Carlson, & Lerner Agency) 146
Dunton, David (Harvey Klinger, Inc.) 189
DuVall, Jennifer (Schiavone Literary Agency, Inc.) 234
Dystel, Jane (Dystel & Goderich Literary Management) 148

Eady, Toby (Toby Eady Associates) 149
Eagan, Scott (Greyhaus Literary) 173
Eaglin, Adam (Elyse Cheney Literary Agency Associates, LLC) 132
Ebeling, Michael (Ebeling & Associates) 150
Eckstut, Arielle (Levine Greenberg Rostan Literary Agency, Inc.) 197
Edelman, Francine (Schiavone Literary Agency, Inc.) 234
Edgecombe, Lindsay (Levine Greenberg Rostan Literary Agency, Inc.) 197
Edwards, Melissa (Aaron M. Priest Literary Agency) 220
Edwards, Stephen (Rogers, Coleridge & White) 229
Egan-Miller, Danielle (Browne & Miller Literary Associates, LLC) 127
Ehrlich, Judith (Judith Ehrlich Literary Management, LLC) 151
Einstein, Susanna (Einstein Literary Management) 151
Ekstrom, Rachel (Irene Goodman Literary Agency) 169
Ekus-Saffer, Lisa (The Lisa Ekus Group, LLC) 151
Ekus, Sally (The Lisa Ekus Group, LLC) 151
Elblonk, Matthew (DeFiore & Co.) 142
Ellenberg, Ethan (Ethan Ellenberg Literary Agency) 152
Ellison, Nicholas (Sanford J. Greenburger Associates, Inc.) 171
Else, Barbara (The TFS Literary Agency) 250
Else, Chris (The TFS Literary Agency) 250
Elwell, Jake (Harold Ober Associates) 217

English, Elaine (The Elaine P. English Literary Agency) 152
Epstein, Linda (The Jennifer DeChiara Literary Agency) 141
Esersky, Gareth (Carol Mann Agency) 205
Eth, Felicia (Felicia Eth Literary Representation) 153
Evans, Elizabeth (Jean V. Naggar Literary Agency, Inc.) 215
Evans, Mary (Mary Evans, Inc.) 153
Evans, Stephany (Fineprint Literary Management) 156

Fairbank, Sorche (Fairbank Literary Representation) 154
Fargis, Alison (Stonesong) 247
Fausset, Katherine (Curtis Brown, Ltd.) 138
Faust, Jessica (Bookends, LLC) 120
Fehr, Don (Trident Media Group) 253
Feldman, Leigh (Leigh Feldman Literary) 155
Ferrara, Moe (Bookends, LLC) 120
Ferrari-Adler, Jenni (Union Literary) 253
Finkelstein, Jesse (Transatlantic Literary Agency) 251
Filina, Olga (The Rights Factory) 227
Finarelli, Amberly (Andrea Hurst & Associates) 181
Finch, Diana (Diana Finch Literary Agency) 156
Fine, Celeste (Sterling Lord Literistic, Inc.) 246
Fisher, Elizabeth (Levine Greenberg Rostan Literary Agency, Inc.) 197
Fishman, Seth (The Gernert Company) 167
Fitzgerald, James (James Fitzgerald Agency) 157
Flaherty, Heather (The Bent Agency) 118
Flannery, Jennifer (Flannery Literary) 157
Flashman, Melissa (Trident Media Group) 253
Flegal, Diana (Hartline Literary Agency) 175
Fletcher, Christy (Fletcher & Company) 157
Flum, Caitie (Liza Dawson Associates) 141
Flynn, Jacqueline (Joelle Delbourgo Associates, Inc.) 143
Flynn, Katherine (Kneerim & Williams) 189
Forland, Emily (Brandt & Hochman Literary Agents, Inc.) 123
Forrer, David (Inkwell Management, LLC) 182
Forster, Clare (Curtis Brown [AUST] Pty Ltd) 138
Foster, Roz (Sandra Dijkstra Literary Agency) 143
Fox, Gráinne (Fletcher & Company) 157
Franco, Carol (Kneerim & Williams) 189
Franklin, Lynn (Lynn C. Franklin Associates, Ltd.) 159
Frantz, Aislinn (Bret Adams Ltd. Agency) 111
Fraser-Bub, MacKenzie (Trident Media Group) 253
Fraser, Stephen (The Jennifer DeChiara Literary Agency) 141
Frazier, Warren (John Hawkins & Associates, Inc.) 176
Frederick, Dawn (Red Sofa Literary) 224
Frederick, Holly (Curtis Brown, Ltd.) 138
Frederick, Matthew (Fairbank Literary Representation) 154
Fredericks, Jeanne (Jeanne Fredericks Literary Agency, Inc.) 159
Freedson, Grace (Grace Freedson's Publishing Network) 160
Free, Liz (John Hawkins & Associates, Inc.) 176
Freese, Sarah (Wordserve Literary Group) 259
Freet, Roger (Foundry Literary + Media) 158
Freilich, Sam (Elyse Cheney Literary Agency Associates, LLC) 132
Freymann, Sarah Jane (Sarah Jane Freymann Literary Agency) 162
Fried, Rachael Dillon (Sanford J. Greenburger Associates, Inc.) 171
Friedman, Rebecca (Rebecca Friedman Literary Agency) 162

Friedrich, Molly (The Friedrich Agency) 163
Fugate, David (Launchbooks Literary Agency) 194
Fury, Louise (The Bent Agency) 118

Galen, Russell (Scovil Galen Ghosh Literary Agency, Inc.) 236
Galit, Lauren (LKG Agency) 201
Gallagher, Lisa (Sanford J. Greenburger Associates, Inc.) 171
Gallt, Nancy (Nancy Gallt Literary Agency) 165
Gardner, Rebecca (The Gernert Company) 167
Gardner, Rachelle (Books & Such Literary Agency) 121
Garrick, Kate (DeFiore & Co.) 142
Garrison, Logan (The Gernert Company) 167
Gates, Jennifer (Zachary Shuster Harmsworth) 261
Gatewood, Courtney (The Gernert Company) 167
Gaule, Mary (Mary Evans, Inc.) 153
Gayle, Nadeen (Serendipity Literary Agency, LLC) 237
Geiger, Ellen (Frances Goldin Literary Agency, Inc.) 168
Gelfman, Jane (Gelfman Schneider/ICM Partners) 166
Gendell, Yfat Reiss (Foundry Literary + Media) 158
Gerald, Marc (The Agency Group, LLC) 111
Gerecke, Jeff (The G Agency, LLC) 165
Getzler, Josh (HSG Agency) 180
Ghahremani, Lilly (Full Circle Literary, LLC) 163
Ginsberg, Peter (Curtis Brown, Ltd.) 138
Ginsburg, Susan (Writers House) 260
Giovinazzo, Elena (Pippin Properties, Inc.) 220
Gladstone, Bill (Waterside Productions, Inc.) 256
Glaz, Linda (Hartline Literary Agency) 175
Glencross, Stephanie (Gregory & Company Authors' Agents) 173
Glick, Mollie (Foundry Literary + Media) 158
Glick, Stacey Kendall (Dystel & Goderich Literary Management) 148
Goderich, Miriam (Dystel & Goderich Literary Management) 148
Goldblatt, Barry (Barry Goldblatt Literary LLC) 167
Golden, Win (Castiglia Literary Agency) 131
Goldin, Frances (Frances Goldin Literary Agency, Inc.) 168
Goldsmith, Connor (Fuse Literary) 164
Goldstein, Debra (DeFiore & Co.) 142
Goloboy, Jennie (Red Sofa Literary) 224
Golomb, Susan (The Susan Golomb Literary Agency) 168
Goodman, Arnold P. (Goodman Associates) 169
Goodman, Irene (Irene Goodman Literary Agency) 169
Goodson, Ellen (The Gernert Company) 167
Gordon, Hannah Brown (Foundry Literary + Media) 158
Gore, Clelia (Martin Literary Management) 208
Gottlieb, Mark (Trident Media Group) 253
Gould, Scott (RLR Associates, Ltd.) 228
Grad, Doug (Doug Grad Literary Agency, Inc.) 170
Gradinger, Rebecca (Fletcher & Company) 157
Grajkowski, Michelle (Three Seas Literary Agency) 251
Grant, Janet Kobobel (Books & Such Literary Agency) 121
Grayson, Ashley (Ashley Grayson Literary Agency) 171
Grayson, Carolyn (Ashley Grayson Literary Agency) 171
Green, Kathy (Kathryn Green Literary Agency, LLC) 173

Greenberg, Daniel (Levine Greenberg Rostan Literary Agency, Inc.) 197
Greenberg, Sylvie (Fletcher & Company) 157
Gregory, Evan (Ethan Ellenberg Literary Agency) 152
Gregory, Jane (Gregory & Company Authors' Agents) 173
Grimm, Katie (Don Congdon Associates Inc.) 134
Grinberg, Jill (Jill Grinberg Literary Agency) 174
Grosjean, Jill (Jill Grosjean Literary Agency) 174
Gross, Gerald (Kneerim & Williams) 189
Gross, Laura (Laura Gross Literary Agency) 174
Grossman, Loren R. (Paul S. Levine Literary Agency) 198
Grubka, Lisa (Fletcher & Company) 157
Gudovitz, Neil (Waterside Productions, Inc.) 256
Guinsler, Robert (Sterling Lord Literistic, Inc.) 246
Gwinn, Julie (The Seymour Agency) 238

Habib, Alia Hanna (McCormick Literary) 211
Hackett, Flora (The Gernert Company) 167
Haggerty, Taylor (Waxman Leavell Literary Agency, Inc.) 255
Halpern, David (The Robbins Office, Inc.) 229
Hamilton, Matthew (Aitken Alexander Associates) 112
Hamlin, Faith (Sanford J. Greenburger Associates, Inc.) 171
Hanjian, Cassie (Waxman Leavell Literary Agency, Inc.) 255
Hannigan, Carrie (HSG Agency) 180
Hanselman, Stephen (LevelFiveMedia, LLC) 197
Harding, Elizabeth (Curtis Brown, Ltd.) 138
Hardy, Dawn Michelle (Serendipity Literary Agency, LLC) 237
Harmsworth, Esmond (Zachary Shuster Harmsworth) 261
Harriot, Michael (Folio Literary Management, LLC) 158
Harris, Erin (Folio Literary Management, LLC) 158
Harris, Joy (The Joy Harris Literary Agency, Inc.) 174
Harris, Ross (Stuart Krichevsky Literary Agency) 191
Hart, Cate (Corvisiero Literary Agency) 136
Hart, Jim (Hartline Literary Agency) 175
Hart, Joyce A. (Hartline Literary Agency) 175
Hartley, Glen (Writers' Representatives, LLC) 260
Hartman, Amanda (Sarah Lazin Books) 195
Hartmann, Thomas V. (Sheree Bykofsky Associates, Inc.) 128
Harty, Pamela (The Knight Agency) 190
Harwood, Antony (Antony Harwood Limited) 175
Hassan, Shannon (Marsal Lyon Literary Agency, LLC) 207
Haviland, David (Andrew Lownie Literary Agency, Ltd.) 203
Hawk, Susan (The Bent Agency) 118
Hawkins, Anne (John Hawkins & Associates, Inc.) 176
Hawn, Molly Ker (The Bent Agency) 118
Hayden, Amy (Linn Prentis Literary) 220
Haywood, Samantha (Transatlantic Literary Agency) 251
Heiblum, Judy (Sterling Lord Literistic, Inc.) 246
Heifetz, Grace (Curtis Brown [AUST] Pty Ltd) 138
Heifetz, Merrilee (Writers House) 260
Heinecke, Andrea (Alive Communications, Inc.) 113
Heller, Chelsey (Zachary Shuster Harmsworth) 261
Heller, Helen (Helen Heller Agency Inc.) 177
Heller, Sarah (Helen Heller Agency Inc.) 177

Henkin, Alyssa Eisner (Trident Media Group) 253
Henshaw, Rich (Richard Henshaw Group) 177
Herman, Jeffery H. (The Jeff Herman Agency, LLC) 178
Herman, Ronnie Ann (Herman Agency) 178
Hernandez, Saritza (Corvisiero Literary Agency) 136
Hewson, Jenny (Rogers, Coleridge & White) 229
Heymont, Lane (The Seymour Agency) 238
Hibbert, Edward (Donadio & Olson, Inc.) 144
Hill, Julie (Julie A. Hill And Associates, LLC) 179
Hiyate, Sam (The Rights Factory) 227
Hochman, Gail (Brandt & Hochman Literary Agents, Inc.) 123
Hodgman, Sandy (The Leshne Agency) 197
Hoffmann, Markus (Regal Literary Agency) 225
Hoffman, Scott (Folio Literary Management, LLC) 158
Hogrebe, Christina (Jane Rotrosen Agency LLC) 231
Holland, Joyce (D4eo Literary Agency) 139
Holmes, Kristina A. (The Holmes Agency) 179
Hopkins, Pam (Hopkins Literary Associates) 180
Hornfischer, James D. (Hornfischer Literary Management) 180
Hosier, Erin (Dunow, Carlson, & Lerner Agency) 146
Hough, Lee (Alive Communications, Inc.) 113
Howard, Elise (Keller Media Inc.) 187
Howland, Carrie (Donadio & Olson, Inc.) 144
Hubbard, Mandy (D4eo Literary Agency) 139
Hughes, Amy (Dunow, Carlson, & Lerner Agency) 146
Hunt, Luc (Philip G. Spitzer Literary Agency, Inc.) 245
Hunter, Allison (Stuart Krichevsky Literary Agency) 191
Hurley, Alexis (Inkwell Management, LLC) 182
Hurst, Andrea (Andrea Hurst & Associates) 181
Husock, Leon (L. Perkins Agency) 219
Hutchinson, Margot Maley (Waterside Productions, Inc.) 256
Hyde, Dara (Hill Nadell Literary Agency) 179

Iannarino, Antonella (David Black Literary Agency) 119
Ingebretson, Krista (The Susan Golomb Literary Agency) 168
Inglis, Fiona (Curtis Brown [AUST] Pty Ltd) 138

Jacks, Nathaniel (Inkwell Management, LLC) 182
Jackson, Eleanor (Dunow, Carlson, & Lerner Agency) 146
Jackson, Jennifer (Donald Maass Literary Agency) 203
Jacobs, Alexander (Elyse Cheney Literary Agency Associates, LLC) 132
Jaffa, Molly (Folio Literary Management, LLC) 158
Janklow, Luke (Janklow & Nesbit Associates) 185
Janklow, Morton L. (Janklow & Nesbit Associates) 185
Jeglinski, Melissa (The Knight Agency) 190
Jelen, Carole (Waterside Productions, Inc.) 256
Jenks, Carolyn (The Carolyn Jenks Agency) 18
Jernigan, Jeff (Hidden Value Group) 178
Jernigan, Nancy (Hidden Value Group) 178
Johnson, Greg (Wordserve Literary Group) 259
Johnson, Kate (Wolf Literary Services, LLC)

259
Johnson, Michelle (Inklings Literary Agency) 182
Jones, Cara (Rogers, Coleridge & White) 229
Jones, Jill (Evatopia, Inc.) 153
Jones, Rebecca (Rogers, Coleridge & White) 229
Julien, Ria (Frances Goldin Literary Agency, Inc.) 168

Kaffel, Meredith (DeFiore & Co.) 142
Kahn, Jody (Brandt & Hochman Literary Agents, Inc.) 123
Kane, Cynthia (Capital Talent Agency) 129
Kardon, Julia (Mary Evans, Inc.) 153
Karinch, Maryann (The Rudy Agency) 232
Karmatz-Rudy, Caryn (DeFiore & Co.) 142
Karsbeak, Jen (Fuse Literary) 164
Kasdin, Steve (Curtis Brown, Ltd.) 138
Kay, Mary (Evatopia, Inc.) 153
Keating, Trena (Union Literary) 253
Keeley, Mary (Books & Such Literary Agency) 121
Keller, Wendy (Keller Media Inc.) 187
Kellogg, Jeff (Pavilion Literary Management) 218
Kennedy, Frances (The Doe Coover Agency) 135
Kennen, Ella (Corvisiero Literary Agency) 136
Kenny, Julia (Dunow, Carlson, & Lerner Agency) 146
Kenshole, Fiona (Transatlantic Literary Agency) 251
Kent, Rachel (Books & Such Literary Agency) 121
Kepner, Chris (Victoria Sanders & Associates) 234
Kern, Natasha (Natasha Kern Literary Agency) 188
Keyes, Emily S. (Fuse Literary) 164
Kier, Mary Alice (Cine/Lit Representation) 133
Kietlinski, Teresa (Prospect Agency) 221
Kifer, Andy (The Gernert Company) 167
Kim, Emily Sylvan (Prospect Agency) 221
Kirby, Kim (Janklow & Nesbit Associates) 185
Kirschbaum, Larry (Waxman Leavell Literary Agency, Inc.) 255
Klebanoff, Arthur (Scott Meredith Literary Agency) 212
Kleinman, Jeff (Folio Literary Management, LLC) 158
Klinger, Harvey (Harvey Klinger, Inc.) 189
Knapp, Peter (Park Literary Group, LLC) 218
Kneerim, Jill (Kneerim & Williams) 189
Knight, Deidre (The Knight Agency) 190
Knight, Judson (The Knight Agency) 190
Knowlton, Ginger (Curtis Brown, Ltd.) 138
Knowlton, Timothy (Curtis Brown, Ltd.) 138
Konner, Linda (Linda Konner Literary Agency) 190
Koons, Abigail (Park Literary Group, LLC) 218
Kopel, Lisa (Bresnick Weil Literary Agency) 124
Kotchman, Katie (Don Congdon Associates Inc.) 134
Kouts, Barbara S. (Barbara S. Kouts, Literary Agency) 190
Kraas, Irene (Kraas Literary Agency) 191
Kracht, Elizabeth (Kimberley Cameron & Associates) 129
Kramer, Jill (Waterside Productions, Inc.) 256
Krichevsky, Stuart (Stuart Krichevsky Literary Agency) 191
Kriss, Miriam (Irene Goodman Literary Agency) 169
Kroll, Edite (Edite Kroll Literary Agency, Inc.) 191

Lakosil, Natalie (Bradford Literary Agency) 122
Laluyaux, Laurence (Rogers, Coleridge & White) 229

Lamba, Marie (The Jennifer DeChiara Literary Agency) 141
Lamb, Paul (Howard Morhaim Literary Agency) 214
Lamm, Donald (Fletcher & Company) 157
Lampack, Andrew (Peter Lampack Agency, Inc.) 192
Lange, Heide (Sanford J. Greenburger Associates, Inc.) 171
Langlie, Laura (Laura Langlie, Literary Agency) 193
LaPolla, Sarah (Bradford Literary Agency) 122
Larsen, Mike (Michael Larsen/Elizabeth Pomada, Literary Agents) 193
Lasher, Eric (The LA Literary Agency) 192
Lasher, Maureen (The LA Literary Agency) 192
Latshaw, Katherine (Folio Literary Management, LLC) 158
Laube, Steve (The Steve Laube Agency) 194
Laughran, Jennifer (Andrea Brown Literary Agency) 126
La Via, Carmen (Fifi Oscard Agency, Inc.) 217
Lawrence, Tricia (Erin Murphy Literary Agency) 215
Lawton, Wendy (Books & Such Literary Agency) 121
Lazar, Daniel (Writers House) 260
Lazin, Sarah (Sarah Lazin Books) 195
Le, Thao (Sandra Dijkstra Literary Agency) 143
Lea, Victoria (Aponte Literary Agency) 116
Leavell, Byrd (Waxman Leavell Literary Agency, Inc.) 255
Leavitt, Ned (The Ned Leavitt Agency) 196
LeBaigue, Catt (Heacock Hill Literary Agency, Inc.) 177
Lecker, Robert (Robert Lecker Agency) 196
Lee, Whitney (The Fielding Agency, LLC) 155
LeFebvre, Nichole (The Friedrich Agency) 163
Lerner, Betsy (Dunow, Carlson, & Lerner Agency) 146
Lerner, Molly Reese (Einstein Literary Management) 151
Leshne, Lisa (The Leshne Agency) 197
Leuck, Amanda (Spencerhill Associates) 244
Levine, Deborah (The Jeff Herman Agency, LLC) 178
Levine, Ellen (Trident Media Group) 253
Levine, Jim (Levine Greenberg Rostan Literary Agency, Inc.) 197
Levine, Paul S. (Paul S. Levine Literary Agency) 198
Lewis, Bibi (Ethan Ellenberg Literary Agency) 152
Linden, Judy (Stonesong) 247
Linder, B. (Educational Design Services LLC) 150
Lindman, Chelsea (Sanford J. Greenburger Associates, Inc.) 171
Lionetti, Kim (Bookends, LLC) 120
Lippincott, Will (Lippincott Massie McQuilkin) 198
Lipskar, Simon (Writers House) 260
Liss, Laurie (Sterling Lord Literistic, Inc.) 246
Lockhart, James Macdonald (Antony Harwood Limited) 175
Loewenthal, Linda (David Black Literary Agency) 119
Loomis, Gloria (Watkins Loomis Agency, Inc.) 256
Lord, Sterling (Sterling Lord Literistic, Inc.) 246
Lorincz, Holly (MacGregor Literary Inc.) 204
Lowenstein, Barbara (Lowenstein Associates Inc.) 201
Lowes, Victoria (The Bent Agency) 118
Lownie, Andrew (Andrew Lownie Literary Agency, Ltd.) 203
Lu, Sandy (L. Perkins Agency) 219
Lucas, Paul (Janklow & Nesbit Associates) 185
Luck, Lucy (Aitken Alexander Associates) 112
Luttinger, Catherine (Darhansoff & Verrill Literary Agents) 140
Lynch, Lacy (Dupree/Miller and Associates

Inc. Literary) 147

Lynch, Marlene Connor (Connor Literary Agency) 135

Lyon, Kevan (Marsal Lyon Literary Agency, LLC) 207

Lyons, Jonathan (Curtis Brown, Ltd.) 138

Maass, Donald (Donald Maass Literary Agency) 203

Maccoby, Gina (Gina Maccoby Literary Agency) 204

MacGregor, Chip (MacGregor Literary Inc.) 204

Machinist, Alexandra (Janklow & Nesbit Associates) 185

MacKenzie, Joanna (Browne & Miller Literary Associates, LLC) 127

Mackwood, Robert (Seventh Avenue Literary Agency) 238

MacLeod, Lauren (The Strothman Agency, LLC) 248

Madan, Neeti (Sterling Lord Literistic, Inc.) 246

Madonia, Nena (Dupree/Miller and Associates Inc. Literary) 147

Malawer, Ted (Upstart Crow Literary) 254

Maldonado, Amy (B.J. Robbins Literary Agency) 228

Malk, Steven (Writers House) 260

Malpas, Pamela (Harold Ober Associates) 217

Mandel, Daniel (Sanford J. Greenburger Associates, Inc.) 171

Manges, Kirsten (Kirsten Manges Literary Agency) 205

Manguera, Jennifer (Ross Yoon Agency) 231

Mann, Carol (Carol Mann Agency) 205

Manus, Jillian (Manus & Associates Literary Agency, Inc.) 206

Marcil, Denise (The Denise Marcil Literary Agency, LLC) 207

Marini, Victoria (Gelfman Schneider/ICM Partners) 166

Mark, PJ (Janklow & Nesbit Associates) 185

Marks, Rachel (Rebecca Friedman Literary Agency) 162

Marr, Jill (Sandra Dijkstra Literary Agency) 143

Marsal, Jill (Marsal Lyon Literary Agency, LLC) 207

Marshall, Evan (The Evan Marshall Agency) 208

Martell, Alice (The Martell Agency) 208

Martin, Sharlene (Martin Literary Management) 208

Martindale, Taylor (Full Circle Literary, LLC) 163

Masnik, Julia (Watkins Loomis Agency, Inc.) 256

Massie, Maria (Lippincott Massie McQuilkin) 198

Masson, Pippa (Curtis Brown [AUST] Pty Ltd) 138

Matson, Peter (Sterling Lord Literistic, Inc.) 246

Mattero, Anthony (Foundry Literary + Media) 158

Mattson, Jennifer (Andrea Brown Literary Agency) 126

Matzie, Bridget Wagner (Zachary Shuster Harmsworth) 261

Maw, Jane Graham (Graham Maw Christie Literary Agency) 170

McAdams, Kevin (Schiavone Literary Agency, Inc.) 234

McBride, Margret (Margret McBride Literary Agency) 209

McCarthy, Bridget (McCormick Literary) 211

McCarthy, E.J. (E.J. McCarthy Agency) 209

McCarthy, Jim (Dystel & Goderich Literary Management) 148

McCarthy, Paul D. (McCarthy Creative Services) 210

McCarthy, Sean (Sean McCarthy Literary Agency) 210

McCarthy, Shawna (The McCarthy Agency, LLC) 209

McClure, Cameron (Donald Maass Literary Agency) 203

McCormick, David (McCormick Literary) 211

McDermid, Anne (Anne McDermid & Associates) 211

McDonald, Ali (The Rights Factory) 227

McDonald, Caitlin (Sterling Lord Literistic, Inc.) 246

McDonald, Doreen (Corvisiero Literary Agency) 136

McGhee, Holly (Pippin Properties, Inc.) 220

McGowan, Matt (Frances Goldin Literary Agency, Inc.) 168

McGuigan, Peter (Foundry Literary + Media) 158

McKean, Kate (Howard Morhaim Literary Agency) 214

McLean, Laurie (Fuse Literary) 164

McMillian, Sally Hill (Sally Hill McMillian & Associates, Inc.) 211

McQuilkin, Rob (Lippincott Massie McQuilkin) 198

Mecoy, Bob (Bob Mecoy Literary Agency) 211

Megibow, Sara (KT Literary, LLC) 191

Menon, Pooja (Kimberley Cameron & Associates) 129

Merola, Marianne (Brandt & Hochman Literary Agents, Inc.) 123

Meyer, Jackie (Whimsy Literary Agency, LLC) 258

Michaels, Doris S. (Doris S. Michaels Literary Agency Inc.) 213

Millard (Martha Millard Literary Agency) 213

Miller-Callihan, Courtney (Sanford J. Greenburger Associates, Inc.) 171

Miller, Barb (Transatlantic Literary Agency) 251

Miller, David (The Garamond Agency, Inc.) 165

Miller, David (Rogers, Coleridge & White) 229

Miller, Jan (Dupree/Miller and Associates Inc. Literary) 147

Miller, Kristin (D4eo Literary Agency) 139

Miller, Peter (Global Lion Intellectual Property Management) 167

Miller, Scott (Trident Media Group) 253

Miller, Thomas (Sanford J. Greenburger Associates, Inc.) 171

Miser-Marvin, Shannon (Dupree/Miller and Associates Inc. Literary) 147

Mitchell, Emily (Wernick & Pratt Agency) 258

Mitchell, Heather (Gelfman Schneider/ICM Partners) 166

Moed, Lydia (The Rights Factory) 227

Mohyde, Colleen (The Doe Coover Agency) 135

Moore, Fran (Curtis Brown [AUST] Pty Ltd) 138

Moore, Mary C. (Kimberley Cameron & Associates) 129

Morgan, Sam (Jabberwocky Literary Agency) 184

Morgen, Emmanuelle (Stonesong) 247

Morhaim, Howard (Howard Morhaim Literary Agency) 214

Morris, Gary (David Black Literary Agency) 119

Morris, Richard (Janklow & Nesbit Associates) 185

Mortenson, Scott (Secret Agent Man) 237

Mortimer, Michele (Darhansoff & Verrill Literary Agents) 140

Mozdzen, Alyssa (Inkwell Management, LLC) 182

Munier, Paula (Talcott Notch Literary) 249

Mura, Dee (Dee Mura Literary) 215

Murphy, Erin (Erin Murphy Literary Agency) 215

Myers, Eric (The Spieler Agency) 244

Murphy, Jacqueline (Inkwell Management, LLC) 182

Murray, Tamela Hancock (The Steve Laube Agency) 194

Mushens, Juliet (The Agency Group, LLC) 111

Nadell, Bonnie (Hill Nadell Literary Agency) 179

Nagel, Sarah (Writers House) 260

Naggar, Jean (Jean V. Naggar Literary Agency, Inc.) 215

Nakamura, Kimiko (Dee Mura Literary) 215

Necarsulmer, Edward IV (Dunow, Carlson, & Lerner Agency) 146

Negovetich, Sarah (Corvisiero Literary Agency) 136

Negron, Jessica (Talcott Notch Literary) 249

Nelson, David (Waterside Productions, Inc.) 256

Nelson, Jandy (Manus & Associates Literary Agency, Inc) 206

Nelson, Kristin (Nelson Literary Agency) 216

Nelson, Patricia (Marsal Lyon Literary Agency, LLC) 207

Nelson, Penny (Manus & Associates Literary Agency, Inc) 206

Nellis, Muriel (Literary And Creative Artists, Inc.) 199

Nesbit, Lynn (Janklow & Nesbit Associates) 185

Neuhaus, Kirsten (Foundry Literary + Media) 158

Newman, Dana (Dana Newman Literary) 216

Nine, Genevieve (Andrea Hurst & Associates) 181

Niumata, Erin (Folio Literary Management, LLC) 158

Noble, Valerie (Donaghy Literary Group) 144

Nolan, Polly (The Greenhouse Literary Agency) 172

Norman, Bryan (Alive Communications, Inc.) 113

Nussbaum, Haskell (The Rights Factory) 227

Nyen, Renee (KT Literary, LLC) 191

Nys, Claudia (Lynn C. Franklin Associates, Ltd.) 159

Odgen, Bree (D4eo Literary Agency) 139

Odom, Monica (Bradford Literary Agency) 122

O'Farrell, Anne Marie (The Denise Marcil Literary Agency, LLC) 207

O'Grady, Faith (The Lisa Richards Agency) 226

O'Higgins, Kristopher (Scribe Agency, LLC) 236

Olson, Neil (Donadio & Olson, Inc.) 144

Orloff, Edward (McCormick Literary) 211

Orr, Rachel (Prospect Agency) 221

Orsini, Mark (Bret Adams Ltd. Agency) 111

Ortiz, Kathleen (New Leaf Literary & Media, Inc.) 216

Ortiz, Lukas (Philip G. Spitzer Literary Agency, Inc.) 245

O'Shea, Coleen (Allen O'Shea Literary Agency) 113

Ostler, Bruce (Bret Adams Ltd. Agency) 111

O'Sullivan, Anna Stein (Aitken Alexander Associates) 112

Pacheco, Monica (Anne McDermid & Associates) 211

Pachnos, Mary (Aitken Alexander Associates) 112

Panettieri, Gina (Talcott Notch Literary) 249

Panitch, Amanda (Lippincott Massie McQuilkin) 198

Papin, Jessica (Dystel & Goderich Literary Management) 148

Paquette, Joan (Erin Murphy Literary Agency) 215

Park, Chris (Foundry Literary + Media) 158

Park, Theresa (Park Literary Group, LLC) 218

Parks, Richard (The Richard Parks Agency) 218

Parris-Lamb, Chris (The Gernert Company) 167

Parry, Emma (Janklow & Nesbit Associates) 185

Patterson, David (Stuart Krichevsky Literary

Agency) 191

Patterson, Emma (Brandt & Hochman Literary Agents, Inc.) 123

Pelham, Imogen (Aitken Alexander Associates) 112

Pelletier, Sharon (Dystel & Goderich Literary Management) 148

Penfold, Alexandra (Upstart Crow Literary) 254

Pennington, Travis (The Knight Agency) 190

Perel, Kim (Wendy Sherman Associates, Inc.) 240

Perkins, Lara (Andrea Brown Literary Agency) 126

Perkins, Lori (L. Perkins Agency) 219

Pestritto, Carrie (Prospect Agency) 221

Peterson, Laura Blake (Curtis Brown, Ltd.) 138

Pfeffer, Rubin (L. Perkins Agency) 219

Phelan, Beth (The Bent Agency) 118

Pientka, Cheryl (Jill Grinberg Literary Agency) 174

Pine, Richard (Inkwell Management, LLC) 182

Podos, Rebecca (Rees Literary Agency) 225

Poelle, Barbara (Irene Goodman Literary Agency) 169

Pomada, Elizabeth (Michael Larsen/Elizabeth Pomada, Literary Agents) 193

Pomerance, Ruth (Folio Literary Management, LLC) 158

Popovic, Lana (Chalberg & Sussman) 131

Porinchak, Eve (Jill Corcoran Literary Agency) 135

Portillo, Matias Lopez (Aitken Alexander Associates) 112

Posner, Marcy (Folio Literary Management, LLC) 158

Posternak, Jeff (The Wylie Agency) 261

Pratt, Linda (Wernick & Pratt Agency) 258

Prentis, Linn (Linn Prentis Literary) 220

Priest, Aaron (Aaron M. Priest Literary Agency) 220

Pulcini, Joanna (Joanna Pulcini Literary Management) 223

Pryor, Victoria Gould (Arcadia) 116

Queen, Lisa (Queen Literary Agency) 223

Queen, Pilar (McCormick Literary) 211

Rabinoff, Lynne (Lynne Rabinoff Agency) 224

Raihofer, Susan (David Black Literary Agency) 119

Ramer, Susan (Don Congdon Associates Inc.) 134

Ranta, Adriann (Wolf Literary Services, LLC) 259

Raskin, Sasha (The Agency Group, LLC) 111

Reamer, Jodi, Esq. (Writers House) 260

Reed, Katie (Andrea Hurst & Associates) 181

Rees, Lorin (Rees Literary Agency) 225

Regal, Joseph (Regal Literary Agency) 225

Regal, Jessica (Foundry Literary + Media) 158

Reid, Janet (Fineprint Literary Management) 156

Rennert, Amy (The Amy Rennert Agency) 226

Rennert, Laura (Andrea Brown Literary Agency) 126

Resciniti, Nicole (The Seymour Agency) 238

Reuben, Alyssa (Paradigm Talent and Literary Agency) 217

Rhodes, Christopher (James Fitzgerald Agency) 157

Ribar, Lindsay (Sanford J. Greenburger Associates, Inc.) 171

Ribas, Maria (Howard Morhaim Literary Agency) 214

Ribas, Maria (Stonesong) 247

Rice, Dabney (Dupree/Miller and Associates Inc. Literary) 147

Richter, Michelle (Fuse Literary) 164

Richter, Rick (Zachary Shuster Harmsworth) 261

Riva, Peter (International Transactions, Inc.) 183

Rinaldi, Angela (Angela Rinaldi Literary Agency) 227

Ritchkin, Deborah (Marsal Lyon Literary Agency, LLC) 207

Rittenberg, Ann (Ann Rittenberg Literary Agency) 227

Riva, Sandra (International Transactions, Inc.) 183

Robbins, B.J. (B.J. Robbins Literary Agency) 228

Robbins, Kathy P. (The Robbins Office, Inc.) 229

Robey, Annelise (Jane Rotrosen Agency LLC) 231

Roberts, Will (The Gernert Company) 167

Robinson, Peter (Rogers, Coleridge & White) 229

Rodeen, Paul (Rodeen Literary Management) 229

Rodgers, Lisa (Jabberwocky Literary Agency) 184

Roers, Deborah (Rogers, Coleridge & White) 229

Rofé, Jennifer (Andrea Brown Literary Agency) 126

Roghaar, Linda L. (Linda Roghaar Literary Agency, LLC) 230

Rosen, Janet (Sheree Bykofsky Associates, Inc.) 128

Rosenberg, Barbara Collins (The Rosenberg Group) 230

Rosenkranz, Rita (Rita Rosenkranz Literary Agency) 230

Ross, Andy (Andy Ross Literary Agency) 231

Ross, Gail (Ross Yoon Agency) 231

Rostan, Stephanie (Levine Greenberg Rostan Literary Agency, Inc.) 197

Roth, Elana (Red Tree Literary Agency) 225

Rothstein, Eliza (Inkwell Management, LLC) 182

Rowland, Damaris (The Damaris Rowland Agency) 232

Rowland, Melissa (Levine Greenberg Rostan Literary Agency, Inc.) 197

Rubie, Peter (Fineprint Literary Management) 156

Rubino-Bradway, Caitlen (LKG Agency) 201

Rudolph, John (Dystel & Goderich Literary Management) 148

Rue, Robin (Writers House) 260

Ruley, Meg (Jane Rotrosen Agency LLC) 231

Rushall, Kathleen (Marsal Lyon Literary Agency, LLC) 207

Russell, Curtis (P.S. Literary Agency) 221

Russell, Gillie (Aitken Alexander Associates) 112

Rutherford, Laetitia (Toby Eady Associates) 149

Rutman, Jim (Sterling Lord Literistic, Inc.) 246

Rutter, Amanda (Red Sofa Literary) 224

Ryan, Regina (Regina Ryan Publishing Enterprises, Inc.) 233

Rydzinski, Tamar (Laura Dail Literary Agency, Inc) 140

Sadler, Jodell (Sadler Children's Literary) 234

Sagalyn, Raphael (The Sagalyn Agency/ ICM Partners) 234

Sagendorph, Jean (Mansion Street Literary Management) 205

Salky, Jesseca (HSG Agency) 180

Sampsel, Shelby (Vicky Bijur Literary Agency) 119

Sanders, Rayhane (Lippincott Massie McQuilkin) 198

Sanders, Victoria (Victoria Sanders & Associates) 234

Sands, Katharine (Sarah Jane Freymann Literary Agency) 162

Sattersten, Todd (Fletcher & Company) 157

Saul, Abby (Browne & Miller Literary Associates, LLC) 127

Sawyer, Peter (Fifi Oscard Agency, Inc.) 217

Scalissi, Linda (Three Seas Literary Agency) 251

Scatoni, Frank R. (Venture Literary) 254

Schear, Adam (DeFiore & Co.) 142

Scheer, Andy (Hartline Literary Agency) 175

Schepp, Brad (Waterside Productions, Inc.) 256

Scherer, Rebecca (Jane Rotrosen Agency LLC) 231

Schiavone, James, Dr. (Schiavone Literary Agency, Inc.) 234

Schlee, Emma (Inkwell Management, LLC) 182

Schmalz, Wendy (Wendy Schmalz Agency) 235

Schmidt, Harold (Harold Schmidt Literary Agency) 235

Schneider, Deborah (Gelfman Schneider/ICM Partners) 166

Schneider, Eddie (Jabberwocky Literary Agency) 184

Schroder, Heather (Compass Talent) 134

Schulman, Susan (Susan Schulman Literary Agency) 235

Schwartz, Hannah (Inkwell Management, LLC) 182

Schwartz, Steven (Sarah Jane Freymann Literary Agency) 162

Schwartz, Tina P. (The Purcell Agency) 223

Sciuto, Sara (Fuse Literary) 164

Scordato, Ellen (Stonesong) 247

Seidner, Sophia (Judith Ehrlich Literary Management, LLC) 151

Seidman, Yishai (Dunow, Carlson, & Lerner Agency) 146

Seligman, Lynn (Lynn Seligman, Literary Agent) 237

Selvaggio, Victoria (The Jennifer DeChiara Literary Agency) 141

Seymour, Mary Sue (The Seymour Agency) 238

Shahbazian, Pouya (New Leaf Literary & Media, Inc.) 216

Shane, Alec (Writers House) 260

Shannon, Denise (Denise Shannon Literary Agency, Inc.) 239

Shea, Samantha (Georges Borchardt, Inc.) 122

Sheil, Anthony (Aitken Alexander Associates) 112

Sherman, Brooks (The Bent Agency) 118

Sherman, Ken (Ken Sherman & Associates) 239

Sherman, Rebecca (Writers House) 260

Sherman, Wendy (Wendy Sherman Associates, Inc.) 240

Shoemaker, Victoria (The Spieler Agency) 244

Shultz, Melissa (Jim Donovan Literary) 145

Shumate, Kimberly (Living Word Literary Agency) 201

Shuster, Todd (Zachary Shuster Harmsworth) 261

Sibbald, Anne (Janklow & Nesbit Associates) 185

Siegel, Rosalie (Rosalie Siegel, International Literary Agency, Inc.) 240

Silberman (Folio Literary Management, LLC) 158

Silbersack, John (Trident Media Group) 253

Silver, Janet (Zachary Shuster Harmsworth) 261

Silverman, Erica Rand (Sterling Lord Literistic, Inc.) 246

Simmons, Jeffrey (Jeffrey Simmons Literary Agency) 241

Sinclair, Stephanie (Transatlantic Literary Agency) 251

Sinsheimer, Jessica (Sarah Jane Freymann Literary Agency) 162

Skomal, Lenore (Whimsy Literary Agency, LLC) 258

Skurnick, Victoria (Levine Greenberg Rostan Literary Agency, Inc.) 197

Slater, Alexander (Trident Media Group) 253

Slopen, Beverly (Beverly Slopen Literary Agency) 241

Smith, Chandler (Fredrica S. Friedman and Co., Inc.) 136

Smith, David Hale (Inkwell Management,

LLC) 182

Smith, Robert (Robert Smith Literary Agency, Ltd.) 242

Smith, Sarah (David Black Literary Agency) 119

Smythe, Lauren (Inkwell Management, LLC) 182

Snell, Michael (Michael Snell Literary Agency) 243

Snell, Patricia (Michael Snell Literary Agency) 243

Solem, Karen (Spencerhill Associates) 244

Somberg, Andrea (Harvey Klinger, Inc.) 189

Sonnack, Kelly (Andrea Brown Literary Agency) 126

Sparks, Kerry (Levine Greenberg Rostan Literary Agency, Inc.) 197

Speilburg, Alice (Speilburg Literary Agency) 244

Spellman-Silverman, Erica (Trident Media Group) 253

Spencer, Elaine (The Knight Agency) 190

Spieler, Joe (The Spieler Agency) 244

Spitzer, Philip G. (Philip G. Spitzer Literary Agency, Inc.) 245

Sproul-Latimer, Anna (Ross Yoon Agency) 231

Stanley, Cullen (Janklow & Nesbit Associates) 185

Stead, Rebecca (The Book Group) 121

Stearns, Michael (Upstart Crow Literary) 254

Steele-Perkins, Pattie (Steele-Perkins Literary Agency) 245

Steinberg, Peter (Foundry Literary + Media) 158

Stender, Uwe (Triada U.S. Literary Agency, Inc.) 252

Stephanides, Myrsini (Carol Mann Agency) 205

Stephens, Jenny (Sterling Lord Literistic, Inc.) 246

Sterling, Michael (Folio Literary Management, LLC) 158

Stevenson, Julie (Waxman Leavell Literary Agency, Inc.) 255

Stimola, Rosemary B. (Stimola Literary Studio) 247

Stoloff, Sam (Frances Goldin Literary Agency, Inc.) 168

Storella, Erika (The Gernert Company) 167

Stout, Rachel (Dystel & Goderich Literary Management) 148

Straus, Robin (Robin Straus Agency, Inc.) 247

Straus, Peter (Rogers, Coleridge & White) 229

Strauss, Rebecca (DeFiore & Co.) 142

Stringer, Marlene (The Stringer Literary Agency, LLC) 247

Strothman, Wendy (The Strothman Agency, LLC) 248

Stuart, Andrew (The Stuart Agency) 248

Stumpf, Becca (Prospect Agency) 221

Sulaiman, Suba (Talcott Notch Literary) 249

Svetcov, Danielle (Levine Greenberg Rostan Literary Agency, Inc.) 197

Swain, Neal (Wales Literary Agency, Inc.) 255

Sweeney, Jillian (The Ned Leavitt Agency) 196

Sweeney, Emma (Emma Sweeney Agency, LLC) 249

Swetky, Faye M. (The Swetky Agency) 249

Tade, Stephanie (Stephanie Tade Literary Agency) 249

Tallack, Peter (The Science Factory) 236

Tannenbaum, Amy (Jane Rotrosen Agency LLC) 231

Tasman, Alice (Jean V. Naggar Literary Agency, Inc.) 215

Taylor, Brent (Triada U.S. Literary Agency, Inc.) 252

Taylor, Susannah (Richard Henshaw Group) 177

Tempest, Nephele (The Knight Agency) 190

Tenney, Craig (Harold Ober Associates) 217

Tessler, Michelle (Tessler Literary Agency, LLC) 250

Testa, Stacy (Writers House) 260

Testerman, Kate Shafer (KT Literary, LLC) 191

Thayer, Henry (Brandt & Hochman Literary Agents, Inc.) 123

Thoma, Geri (Writers House) 260

Thomas, Karen (Serendipity Literary Agency, LLC) 237

Thompson, Meg (Thompson Literary Agency) 251

Thorne, Lesley (Aitken Alexander Associates) 112

Thornton, John (The Spieler Agency) 244

Thonrton, Nan (Zachary Shuster Harmsworth) 261

Tompkins, Amy (Transatlantic Literary Agency) 251

Townsend, Suzie (New Leaf Literary & Media, Inc.) 216

Tran, Jennifer Chen (Fuse Literary) 164

Treimel, Scott (Scott Treimel NY) 252

Tribuzzo, Fred (The Rudy Agency) 232

Troha, Steve (Folio Literary Management, LLC) 158

Trupin, Jim (JET Literary Associates) 187

Trupin-Pulli, Liz (JET Literary Associates) 187

Tutela, Joy E. (David Black Literary Agency) 119

Udden, Jennifer (Donald Maass Literary Agency) 203

Unter, Jennifer (The Unter Agency) 254

Unwin, Jo (Rogers, Coleridge & White) 229

Van Beek, Emily (Folio Literary Management, LLC) 158

Vance, Lisa Erbach (Aaron M. Priest Literary Agency) 220

Verma, Monika (Levine Greenberg Rostan Literary Agency, Inc.) 197

Verrill, Chuck (Darhansoff & Verrill Literary Agents) 140

Vesel, Beth (Irene Goodman Literary Agency) 169

Vicente, Maria (P.S. Literary Agency) 221

Vlieg, Pam van Hycklama (D4eo Literary Agency) 139

Vogel, Rachel (Waxman Leavell Literary Agency, Inc.) 255

Voges, Liza (Eden Street Literary) 150

Volpe, Joanna (New Leaf Literary & Media, Inc.) 216

Von Borstel, Stephanie (Full Circle Literary, LLC) 163

Von Mehren, Jane (Zachary Shuster Harmsworth) 261

Vyce, Christopher (The Brattle Agency) 124

Wade, Robin (Wade & Co. Literary Agency, Ltd.) 255

Wagoner, Matt (Fresh Books Literary Agency) 161

Waldie, Zoe (Rogers, Coleridge & White) 229

Wales, Elizabeth (Wales Literary Agency, Inc.) 255

Walters, Maureen (Curtis Brown, Ltd.) 138

Warnock, Gordon (Fuse Literary) 164

Warren, Deborah (East/West Literary Agency, LLC) 149

Watters, Carly (P.S. Literary Agency) 221

Waters, Mitchell (Curtis Brown, Ltd.) 138

Watterson, Jessica (Sandra Dijkstra Literary Agency) 143

Waxman, Scott (Waxman Leavell Literary Agency, Inc.) 255

Webb, Martha (Anne McDermid & Associates) 211

Webber, Carlie (CK Webber Associates, Literary Management) 257

Weber, John (Serendipity Literary Agency, LLC) 237

Weed, Elisabeth (The Book Group) 121

Weimann, Frank (The Literary Group International) 199

Weiner, Cherry (Cherry Weiner Literary Agency) 257

Weingel-Fidel, Loretta (The Weingel-Fidel Agency) 257

Weinmann, Frank (Folio Literary Management, LLC) 158

Weissman, Larry (Larry Weissman Literary, LLC) 258

Wells, Roseanne (The Jennifer DeChiara Literary Agency) 141

Weltz, Jennifer (Jean V. Naggar Literary Agency, Inc.) 215

Wenk, Shari (SLW Literary Agency) 242

Wernick, Marcia (Wernick & Pratt Agency) 258

Westberg, Phyllis (Harold Ober Associates) 217

Whalen, Kimberly (Trident Media Group) 253

Wheeler, Claire (Anderson Literary Management, LLC) 116

Wheeler, Paige (Creative Media Agency, Inc.) 136

Witte, Michelle (Mansion Street Literary Management) 205

White, Pat (Rogers, Coleridge & White) 229

White, Sarver Melissa (Folio Literary Management, LLC) 158

White, Trena (Transatlantic Literary Agency) 251

Williams, Alexis (Bret Adams Ltd. Agency) 111

Williams, Ike (Kneerim & Williams) 189

Williams, Mary (Robert Lecker Agency) 196

Williamson, Jo (Antony Harwood Limited) 175

Willig, John (Literary Services, Inc.) 200

Wing, Eric (The Carolyn Jenks Agency) 186

Winston, Lois (Ashley Grayson Literary Agency) 171

Wise, Matt (Foundry Literary + Media) 158

Wiseman, Caryn (Andrea Brown Literary Agency) 126

Witherspoon, Kimberly (Inkwell Management, LLC) 182

Witthohn, Christine (Book Cents Literary Agency, LLC) 120

Wofford-Girand, Sally (Union Literary) 253

Wojcik, Tom (Levine Greenberg Rostan Literary Agency, Inc.) 197

Wolf, Kent (Lippincott Massie McQuilkin) 198

Wolfson, Michelle (Wolfson Literary Agency) 259

Wood, Eleanor (Spectrum Literary Agency) 243

Wood, Laura (Fineprint Literary Management) 156

Woods, Monika (Inkwell Management, LLC) 182

Wyckoff, Joanne (Carol Mann Agency) 205

Wylie, Andrew (The Wylie Agency) 261

Wynne, Tara (Curtis Brown [AUST] Pty Ltd) 138

Yarbrough, Lena (Inkwell Management, LLC) 182

Yarn, Jason (Jason Yarn Literary Agency) 261

Yoder, Wes (Ambassador Literary Agency & Speakers Bureau) 115

Yoon, Howard (Ross Yoon Agency) 231

Zachary, Lane (Zachary Shuster Harmsworth) 261

Zacker, Marietta (Nancy Gallt Literary Agency) 165

Zahler, Karen Gantz (Karen Gantz Zahler Literary Management and Attorney at Law) 262

Zats, Laura (Red Sofa Literary) 224

Zimmermann, Helen (Helen Zimmermann Literary Agency) 262

Zuckerbrot, Renèe (Renèe Zuckerbrot Literary Agency) 262

Zuckerman, Albert (Writers House) 260